BOOK COLLECTING
A COMPREHENSIVE GUIDE
1995 EDITION

ALSO BY ALLEN AND PATRICIA AHEARN

Book Collecting: A Comprehensive Guide (1989 Edition)
Collected Books: The Guide to Values

BOOK
COLLECTING
A COMPREHENSIVE GUIDE

1995 EDITION

ALLEN AND PATRICIA AHEARN

G. P. PUTNAM'S SONS

New York

G. P. PUTNAM'S SONS

Publishers Since 1838
200 Madison Avenue
New York, NY 10016

Published simultaneously in Canada
The text of this book is set in Bembo
Book design by Marysarah Quinn
Library of Congress Cataloging in Publication Data
Ahearn, Allen.
Book collecting : a comprehensive guide /
Allen and Patricia Ahearn
p.   cm.
Includes bibliographical references and index.
ISBN 0-399-14049-2
1. Book collecting—United States.   2. English
imprints—Collectors and collecting—United States.   3. First
editions—United States.   4. Books—Prices—United States.
I. Ahearn, Patricia.
II.   Title.
Z987.5.U6A35   1995   94-43100 CIP
002'.075—dc20

Printed in the United States of America

3   5   7   9   10   8   6   4   2

This book is printed on acid-free paper. ∞

This title is available on CD-ROM from the authors at
P.O. Box 5365, Rockville, MD 20848

For our prized first editions:
BETH, SUE, ALLEN AND DYANNE

ACKNOWLEDGMENTS

We want especially to thank the following persons for providing corrections, suggesting authors for inclusion, and/or providing their opinion on prices for particular titles in this edition: Terry Halladay, James Jaffe, and Richard Shuh; as well as Alan Abrams, Bart Auerbach, John Ballinger, Steve Bernard, George Bixby, Lew Buckingham, Nigel Burwood, Andy Cahan, Henry Campbell, Pat Cather, Clark Chambers, Tom Congalton, Allan Covici, Lloyd Currey, Joseph Dermont, Steve Deutsch, Larry Dingman, Bob Fleck, Nelson Freck, Beth and Paul Garon, Chan Gordon, Josh Heller, John Hildebrand, David Holloway, David Holmes, Peter Howard, Priscilla Juvelis, John Knott, Ralph Kristiansen, Mark Samuels Lasner, Bill Loesser, Ken Lopez, Edmund Miller, George Robert Minkoff, Edward Moore, Larry Moskowitz, Rusty Mott, Maurice Neville, Al Newgarden, Doug O'Dell, Gary Oleson, Jim Pepper, Otto Penzler, John Ptak, Jo Ann Reisler, Hank Salerno, John Sanderson, Joel Sattler, Ralph Sipper, Dan Smith, Charles Stecy, Peter Stern, Henry Turlington, Stephen Weissman, Dick Wilson, Robert Wilson, Clarence Wolf, Howard Woolmer, and John Wronowski. These people were not asked their opinions on values on all of the books (no friend is that good a friend) but, if the values are right on target we're sure it must have been an entry they were asked about. On the other hand, if the price estimate is way off chances are we did it. Many of the titles included have not appeared in catalogs or at auction in recent years.

In addition, we want to acknowledge all of the dealers listed in Appendix B herein, who have kept Quill & Brush on their mailing lists.

Their catalogs have all provided first-book entries and price estimates; and this book is very much dependent on those reference works.

A special thanks to Elizabeth Jones, Suzanne Kalk, and Carl Hahn for all the help they have given us; and to Joe Coughlan and Mike Hayes, two old friends who helped tighten up our rambling prose one beautiful September weekend.

CONTENTS

CONTENTS

CONTENTS

INTRODUCTION

This book has been prepared to provide information for book collectors as well as librarians and book dealers.

It attempts to show that book collecting is enjoyable and a reasonably good investment over the long run. It explains some of the terms used in the trade and how to identify, purchase, care for, and sell first editions. Also included is an interpretation of the rationale that drives collecting interests, which admittedly may be an attempt to explain the unexplainable.

For those actively involved in the trade, the book includes opinions of the current retail value of first editions of about 5,500 books. These price estimates are not intended to be projections but to be representative of what are, one hopes, realistic current retail values based on the catalogs received, our own experiences in selling first editions, and discussions with collectors and dealers more knowledgeable on values for books that have not appeared in catalogs or at auction in recent years.

This is the first edition of this book to include both our names as authors. We have been working together for many years and our various book projects have become too much for either of us to handle alone.

The values listed are an estimate of retail prices for very good to fine copies of the books, with a dustwrapper if published in 1920 or later, and in original bindings if published between 1840 and 1920 (unless otherwise indicated).

The premise of this book is that the price of the first edition of the first book often sets an upper limit on an author's first editions, and therefore the estimated prices in this book for first books can assist in determining prices for later books by the authors listed.

Any of the general comments on book collecting are, of course, our own current perceptions.

The prices in this book are intended only as guides. Most dealers in collectible books do not handle rare books *per se*; they handle scarce books. However, very fine copies of scarce books are rare. These fine copies command high prices from knowledgeable collectors and libraries because these buyers realize the true relative scarcity of such material. We are certainly not particularly knowledgeable about other collecting fields such as coins or stamps, but our impression is that if an individual wanted five very fine examples of a certain rare coin or stamp and was willing to pay the going price, they could be found within a few weeks. On the other hand, if an individual wanted to buy five very fine copies of a certain edition of a particular title, it might take a few years. And this is not just for books costing thousands of dollars; it is equally true of books that sell for only a few hundred dollars (or less). The point is that many collectors, librarians, and dealers are very aware of how scarce certain items are, and feel a price in a guide such as this one is useful for getting in the ballpark as to whether a title is in the $50 or $500 range, but not as to whether a particular copy is worth $500 or $700.

We have attempted to make the contents as complete and accurate as possible; errors and omissions, however, are normal in projects such as this and correspondence thereon will be appreciated.

BOOK COLLECTING
A COMPREHENSIVE GUIDE
1995 EDITION

BOOK COLLECTING

ook collectors start as readers. This may seem obvious but is important to keep in mind, for the majority of book collectors collect authors or subjects that they are currently reading or have read and enjoyed. In fact, perhaps "enjoyed" is really not descriptive enough. Collectors do not just enjoy these books; they feel an affinity with the author and admire the author as one of the best in the field. The author expresses the collector's thoughts and inchoate insights and expresses them in ways the collector would if he or she had the talent, or takes him or her to a time and place the collector is interested in or to a setting that removes the collector from his or her current world and cares.

Book readers become book collectors when they find that books have become important as objects that they wish to own, admire, and enjoy at their leisure. This is an important point, for most readers are content with reading a library copy or a paperback reprint and have no desire to go beyond this point. In order to understand the drive of a book collector, one must understand that most are attracted to book collecting for three reasons: the true enjoyment or fun of the search, the love of the book as an object, and the economics or investment potential. From our experience with collectors—and most dealers for that matter—all three motivations exist in varying degrees.

FOR THE FUN OF IT

To us, book collecting seems to be more enjoyable than other collecting hobbies because the scope is broad and the availability of material is large.

One can find bookstores in just about every town, and reasonably priced books and even bargains can be found in most of them. But that's just the beginning, for there are also book fairs; garage sales; school, church, and charity book sales; friends' attics and basements; antique shops; and remainder sales (new books marked down to sell).

We haven't done any research, but we suspect that the quantity, variety, and availability far exceeds any other collecting field, such as stamps, coins, glassware, or furniture. And there is another plus for hardback books: there are fewer price guides in this field than in any other, which means it is not as regimented as coins, stamps, comic books, or even paperback books, all of which have price guides covering the majority of the material. We are publishing price guides (these will be discussed later), this book is a price guide, and there are others, but cumulatively all these guides cover only a very small portion of the out-of-print book market and most of their prices require a fair amount of interpretation in order to arrive at a reasonable conclusion on a particular copy in hand. This absence of consistency and regimentation is an attractive feature for book collectors.

There is a vast array of personalities in the book field, including dealers, bookscouts, other collectors, librarians, and the authors themselves, and you will meet many of them and the experience will, we hope, add to your enjoyment. Certainly, there will be few towns you visit in the future where you won't find a bookstore to spend a few hours in and learn something about the owner, prices, editions, and so on.

In his book *The Book-Collecting Game*, A. Edward Newton puts it as well as anyone has:

> Book-collecting. It's a great game. Anybody with ordinary intelligence can play it: there are, indeed, people who think that it takes no brains at all; their opinion may be ignored. No great amount of money is required, unless one becomes very ambitious. It can be played at home or abroad, alone or in company. It can even be played by correspondence. Everyone playing it can make his own rules—and change them during the progress of the game. It is not considered cricket to do this in other games.

In his *Modern Book Collecting for the Impecunious Amateur*, Herbert Faulkner West describes collectors in general thus:

> Some collectors desire beetles, while others have divergent and decided propensities for empty bottles, full bottles . . . silhouettes, tea caddies . . . horseshoes, guns, stuffed owls, stuffed animals,

stuffed shirts, candlesticks, trademarks, first editions. . . . Although it is quite evident that collectors are not entirely "all there," I have always found them to be nice, harmless people, whom any of my readers could invite home without danger of being disinherited.

And from *Book-Collecting As a Hobby*, by P. H. Muir:

Book-collecting is not exclusively a hobby for rich and leisured people. It is less a matter of money than of method. I know many people of quite modest means who have gathered valuable and important collections with no greater expenditure than casual book buying might entail.

The point is that the greatest pleasure for the collector is in the chase, and if you can afford to buy an occasional new book, you can also afford to buy an occasional old book.

BOOKS AS OBJECTS

It would seem that the transition from reader to collector occurs when the book itself is perceived as an object, akin to art perhaps. Certainly, if you are going to pay $25 or $50 for a first edition when you could borrow a copy from the library or purchase a paperback reprint for $5.95 (and up), you have bought an object that you want to own and actually look at occasionally, just as you want to own an original painting or a signed limited print when there are copies available at significantly lower prices.

ECONOMICS

When we started buying first editions years ago, the decision was based (rationalized) on a simple fact. If we bought a reprint or book club edition of a book by an author whose work we believed would stand the test of time, we knew that the most we would ever get for it when we sold it was a dollar or perhaps even less, if it was wanted at all. Whereas if we bought a first edition, we believed we would always be able to get back one half of the cost, and there was a good chance that we might eventually get all of our cost back and even more. Therefore, if we were going to buy a copy of Salinger's *Franny and Zooey* at $4, and we had a choice between a first and second printing, obviously we would buy a first. The economics of buying the second printing made absolutely no sense to us. But admittedly, we enjoyed owning a first edition of the book as an object on our shelves, because we had made the transition from readers to collectors. Today a first edition of *Franny and Zooey* is selling for $150.

Now the second step was a bit harder. We'd enjoyed Salinger's *Catcher in the Rye* and wanted a hardbound copy, but a first edition in the early 1960s was selling for $15 or $20, four to ten times what a hardback reprint would cost. A lot of money at the time, at least in our circumstances, but there still seemed little choice, given our feelings about the importance of the book, so we sprang for it. It turned out to be a good investment relative to the purchase of a reprint. Today a nice copy of *Catcher* is selling for $2,500. Whether it was a good investment relative to other investments, such as stock or real estate, is certainly questionable, but we wouldn't have made those investments anyway, so it's a moot point for us.

Three things seem clear to us:

1. Two people can buy the same titles over a ten-year period and each accumulate a library of 500 volumes, fifty a year, a book a week on average, and the person who was selective as to edition and condition will have a collection that is worth considerably more than the other, probably at no greater overall cost. It is no secret that very good to fine copies of recent books turn up on antiquarian bookstore shelves, as remainders in new bookstores, or at book sales for a fraction of their published price.

2. We are talking about a relatively long period of time, probably five years at a minimum and more likely ten to twenty years, for real growth in value.

3. Collectors can set their own financial limits. They can spend $100 or $100,000 a year or anything in between. They can collect books that few people are currently collecting and are low priced, or go for the big-name authors and "high spots," where the competition is the keenest and the prices reflect it.

In summary, if you are looking for a good investment for the short term, don't buy books, but if you want to spend a certain amount of money for books, or already spend a certain amount for books every year, we believe that a collection of good books will not only give you pleasure over the years but will also not disappoint you or your heirs when the time comes to sell them.

INVESTMENT

Ever since we started collecting first editions we have been asked how many collected authors lose popularity over the years and have been told that first edition collecting is a fad that will fade; that the market is false, the price inflated, and the bubble will burst any day. We've always wondered about these questions and comments ourselves, and so we've tried to find an answer.

From 1938 to 1941 the R. R. Bowker Company of New York published *Trade Prices Current of American First Editions*, which was subtitled "An indexing service for the American rare book trade." The authors included were all those listed in Merle Johnson's *American First Editions*, fourth edition, edited by Jacob Blanck. There were 209 authors included, and to see how many of these authors are still collected, we checked to see how many were still included in this book. The fact is that all but eight of these authors are still collected. The authors not included were:

Ray Stannard Baker (David Grayson)
Charles Egbert Craddock (M. N. Murfree)
Mazo de la Roche
Edgar Fawcett
Morgan Robertson
Susan Rowson
Harriet Prescott Spofford
Henry Van Dyke

At the time, the average price for these eight authors' first books was $4. Some of these authors may not belong on this list, as there may still be interest in their work, but we have not included them to date. Eight out of 209 is less than 4 percent, leaving more than 96 percent of the authors still being collected after more than fifty years.

The next question is whether the market prices for these 201 authors have held up over the years. *Trade Prices Current* indexed dealer catalog prices of the authors' books from 1937 to 1941. Given that the prices in this book represent estimates of dealer retail prices, it seemed reasonable to compare the prices for the first books in *Trade Prices Current* to the prices in this book. A complete comparison could not be made because

Trade Prices Current did not record any first books for sale during this period for 28 of the authors on the list, but that still left 166 authors, which we believe is a representative sample. The comparison was actually made on 180 books by the 166 authors, because there were sixteen cases where either separate editions of the first book or first and second books were covered by both reference works. The results are as follows:

Adams, Andy. THE LOG OF A COWBOY	$4	250
Ade, George. ARTIE, A STORY . . .	5	75
Aiken, Conrad. EARTH TRIUMPHANT	5	250
Alcott, Louisa May. FLOWER FABLES	10	600
Aldrich, T. B. THE BELLS	5	250
Allen, Hervey. WAMPUM . . .	5	175
Allen, James Lane. FLUTE & VIOLIN . . .	6	100
Anderson, Sherwood. WINDY MCPHERSON'S SON	15	500
Atherton, Gertrude. WHAT DREAMS . . . (Cloth)	57	350
(Wraps)	44	750
Audubon, John J. BIRDS OF NORTH AMERICA (1840-1844)	500	30,000
Austin, Jane G. FAIRY DREAMS . . .	4	75
Austin, Mary. LAND OF LITTLE RAIN	8	350
Bacheller, Irving. MASTER OF SILENCE	5	100
Bancroft, George. POEMS	10	200
Bangs, J. K. THE LORGNETTE	5	450
Beebe, William. TWO BIRD-LOVERS . . .	15	1,750
Bellamy, Edward. SIX TO ONE	7	400
Benét, Stephen V. FIVE MEN AND POMPEY	40	250
Benét, William Rose. MERCHANTS FROM CATHAY	10	75
Bierce, Ambrose. FIEND'S DELIGHT (New York)	5	750
Bird, Robt. Montgomery. CALAVAR	35	500
Boyd, James. DRUMS	2	350
Bradford, G. TYPES OF AMERICAN CHARACTER	14	150
Bradford, Roark. OL' MAN ADAM . . .	7	125

Bromfield, Louis. GREEN BAY TREE	13	300
Buck, Pearl. EAST WIND, WEST WIND	8	400
Bunner, H. C. A WOMAN OF HONOR	5	100
Burgess, Gelett. THE PURPLE COW	38	400
Burroughs, John. NOTES ON WALT WHITMAN ...	60	1,250
Bynner, Witter. AN ODE TO HARVARD	6	75
Byrne, Donn. STORIES WITHOUT WOMEN	55	125
Cabell, J. B. EAGLE'S SHADOW	16	150
Cable, George W. OLD CREOLE DAYS	30	300
Caldwell, Erskine. THE BASTARD	6	750
Carman, Bliss. LOW TIDE ... (Toronto)	88	4,500
(New York)	16	500
Cather, Willa. APRIL TWILIGHTS	160	1,500
Chambers, Robert W. IN THE QUARTER	2	600
Churchill, Winston (U.S.). THE CELEBRITY	7	75
Clemens, Samuel L. CELEBRATED JUMPING FROG	230	17,500
Cobb, Irwin. BACK HOME	3	75
Cooke, John Esten. LEATHERSTOCKING & SILK	35	300
Cooper, James F. PRECAUTION	210	4,500
Crane, Stephen. MAGGIE	225	750
Crapsey, Adelaide. VERSE	6	125
Cummings, E. E. THE ENORMOUS ROOM	8	1,000
Curtis, George Wm. NILE NOTES OF A HOWADJI	3	200
Dana, Richard H. TWO YEARS BEFORE THE MAST	83	5,000
Davis, Richard Harding. GALLEGHER	15	300
Day, Clarence. DECENNIAL RECORD ...	8	75
Deland, Margaret. THE OLD GARDEN	15	150
Dickinson, Emily. POEMS	92	4,500
Dodge, Mary Mapes. IRVINGTON STORIES	13	125
Dos Passos, John. ONE MAN'S INITIATION (London)	7	750

Drake, Joseph Rodman. THE CULPRIT FAY	18	125
Dreiser, Theodore. SISTER CARRIE	150	3,500
Dunbar, Paul L. OAK AND IVY	25	6,000
Dunne, Finley Peter. MR. DOOLEY . . .	3	75
Farrell, James T. YOUNG LONIGAN	10	750
Faulkner, William. MARBLE FAUN	43	20,000
SOLDIER'S PAY	9	15,000
Ferber, Edna. DAWN O'HARA	9	125
Ficke, Arthur. THEIR BOOK	20	1,000
FROM THE ISLES	4	400
Field, Eugene. TRIBUNE PRIMER (Brooklyn)	26	7,500
Fisher, Vardis. SONNETS TO . . .	6	300
Fox, John. A CUMBERLAND VENDETTA	5	200
Frederick, Harold. SETH'S BROTHER'S WIFE	16	300
Frost, Robert. A BOY'S WILL	10	5,000
Gale, Zona. ROMANCE ISLAND	6	100
Garland, Hamlin. MAIN-TRAVELLED ROADS	12	250
Glasgow, Ellen. THE DESCENDANT	6	300
Guiney, Louise I. SONGS AT THE START	12	125
Halleck, Fitz-Greene. FANNY	65	400
Harris, Joel Chandler. UNCLE REMUS	50	1,500
Harte, Bret. OUTCROPPINGS	5	150
Hawthorne, Nathaniel. FANSHAWE	850	30,000
Hay, John. JIM BLUDSO	18	150
Hearn, Lafcadio. STRAY LEAVES	70	650
Hecht, Ben. HERO OF SANTA MARIA	3	200
Hemingway, Ernest. THREE STORIES . . .	100	25,000
IN OUR TIME	75	22,500
Herbert, Henry W. THE BROTHERS	70	450
Herford, Oliver. ARTFUL ANTICS	25	150

Hergesheimer, Joseph. THE LAY ANTHONY	7	100
Heyward, DuBose. CAROLINA CHANSONS	6	175
SKYLINE AND HORIZONS	2	150
Holmes, Oliver Wendell. POEMS	19	400
Hough, Emerson. THE SINGING MOUSE STORIES	20	200
Hovey, Richard. POEMS	75	1,000
Howells, William Dean. POEMS OF TWO FRIENDS	10	750
LIVES AND SPEECHES OF ABRAHAM LINCOLN . . .	9	400
VENETIAN LIFE . . . (New York)	3	500
Huneker, James. MEZZOTINTS . . .	5	150
Irving, Washington. HISTORY OF NEW YORK	100	1,250
Jackson, H. H. VERSES	4	300
James, Henry. A PASSIONATE PILGRIM	10	2,000
James, Will. COWBOYS NORTH AND SOUTH	4	600
James, William. PRINCIPLES OF PSYCHOLOGY	20	750
Janvier, Thomas. COLOR STUDIES	5	150
Jeffers, Robertson. FLAGONS AND APPLES	33	1,500
Jewett, Sarah Orne. DEEPHAVEN	9	500
Johnston, Mary. PRISONER OF HOPE	4	75
Kennedy, John P. SWALLOW BARN	63	600
Kent, Rockwell. WILDERNESS	20	400
Kilmer, Joyce. SUMMER OF LOVE	10	350
Lanier, Sidney. TIGER-LILIES	45	500
Lardner, Ring. BIB BALLADS	45	350
Lewis, Sinclair. HIKE AND THE AEROPLANE	95	5,000
Lindsay, Vachel. THE TRAMP'S EXCUSE	100	1,500
London, Jack. SON OF THE WOLF	22	1,500
Longfellow, Henry W. OUTRE-MER	17	1,500
Lowell, Amy. DREAM DROPS (Cloth)	200	3,000
(Wraps)	135	2,250

Lowell, James R. CLASS POEM	63	1,250
McCutcheon, George Barr. GRAUSTARK	30	100
McFee, William. LETTERS FROM AN OCEAN TRAMP	38	200
MacLeish, Archibald. TOWER OF IVORY	10	150
Markham, Edwin. THE MAN WITH THE HOE (San Francisco)	67	350
(New York)	9	75
Marquis, Don. DANNY'S OWN STORY	5	75
Masters, Edgar Lee. A BOOK OF VERSES	12	750
Melville, Herman. TYPEE . . .	200	8,500
Mencken, H. L. VENTURES INTO VERSE	150	7,500
Millay, Edna St. V. RENASCENSE (Vellum)	1,150	7,500
Mitchell, S. Weir. WONDERFUL STORY (Large paper copy)	35	1,000
(Trade)	10	300
Moody, Wm. Vaughn. THE MASQUE OF JUDGEMENT		
(Limited edition)	6	100
(Trade)	2	50
Nathan, Robert. PETER KINDRED	8	150
Neihardt, John G. DIVINE ENCHANTMENT	18	750
Newton, A. Edward. AMENITIES OF BOOK COLLECTING	17	125
Norris, Frank. YVERNELLE	70	2,000
O'Neill, Eugene. THIRST	40	400
Page, Thomas Nelson. IN OLE VIRGINIA	18	150
Parker, Dorothy. MEN I'M NOT MARRIED TO	10	450
Parkman, Francis. THE CALIFORNIA AND OREGON TRAIL	85	8,500
Paulding, James K. THE DIVERTING HISTORY OF . . .	15	600
Porter, Wm. S. (O. Henry). CABBAGES AND KINGS	32	350
Pound, Ezra. A LUME SPENTO	125	40,000
Pyle, Howard. THE MERRY ADVENTURES OF ROBIN HOOD . . . (Leather)	15	1,000
Remington, Frederic. PONY TRACKS	30	1,000
Repplier, Agnes. BOOKS AND MEN	3	75

Riley, James W. THE OLD SWIMMIN' HOLE	175	600
Roberts, Eliz. Madox. UNDER THE TREE	4	350
Robinson, Edw. A. THE TORRENT AND THE NIGHT . . .	227	2,500
CHILDREN OF THE . . . (Vellum)	275	2,000
(Trade)	50	750
Robinson, Rowland E. UNCLE 'LISHA'S SHOP	18	125
Roosevelt, Theodore. NAVAL WAR OF 1812	7	750
Saltus, Edgar. BALZAC	4	100
Sandburg, Carl. IN RECKLESS ECSTASY	150	7,500
CHICAGO POEMS	8	250
Santayana, George. SONNETS . . .	11	750
Smith, Thorne. BILTMORE OSWALD	3	75
Steinbeck, John. CUP OF GOLD	30	7,500
Stockton, Frank B. TING-A-LING	26	750
Stribling, T. S. CRUISE OF THE DRY DOCK	15	150
Tabb, John B. POEMS	135	400
Tarkington, Booth. GENTLEMAN FROM INDIANA	27	150
Teasdale, Sara. SONNETS TO DUSE . . .	25	1,000
Thompson, David P. ADVENTURES OF TIMOTHY PEACOCK	7	750
Thompson, Maurice. HOOSIER MOSAICS	9	125
Thoreau, H. D. A WEEK ON THE CONCORD AND MERRIMACK RIVERS	40	6,000
Van Loon, H. THE FALL OF THE DUTCH REPUBLIC	3	150
Van Vechten, Carl. MUSIC AFTER THE GREAT WAR	6	100
Wallace, Lew. THE FAIR GOD	6	125
Wescott, Glenway. THE BITTERNS	16	750
Westcott, Edw. Noyes. DAVID HARUM	18	100
Wharton, Edith. THE DECORATION OF HOUSES	3	600
Whistler, James. WHISTLER VS. RUSKIN	15	600
White, Stewart Edw. THE CLAIM JUMPERS (Wraps)	16	150
(Cloth)	20	200

White, Wm. Allen. RHYMES . . .	12	150
Whitman, Walt. FRANKLIN EVANS	50	5,000
Whittier, John A. LEGENDS OF NEW ENGLAND	67	750
Wilder, Thornton. THE CABALA	6	350
Wilson, Harry Leon. ZIG ZAG TALES	27	200
Wilson, Woodrow. CONGRESSIONAL GOVERNMENT	17	250
Wolfe, Thomas. LOOK HOMEWARD ANGEL	25	2,500
Wylie, Elinor. NETS TO CATCH THE WIND	14	300
	$8,953	$383,600

This seems to us to be a fair representation of the average increase in value for these titles and, by extension, for first editions generally over a 50-year period. The above comparisons show that few authors go completely out of favor and that the prices of first editions have shown steady increases over the years.

We have been asked to compare the increase to normal inflation. We took the Cost of Living Index (all items, 1982-84 = 100) prepared by the U.S. Bureau of Labor Statistics for 1940 = 13.2, and for 1993 = 144.5, or an increase of 1,100%. This would have meant the $8,953 in 1940 would have increased to $98,483 with normal inflation (for what it's worth).

If your only concern is making sure the books you buy go up in value, you probably shouldn't collect books. But if you decide to collect anyway, you should stick with proven winners that have withstood the test of time. There are still no guarantees, but it is doubtful that the major masterpieces in fine condition will fall in value. None of them will be cheap, either. You can make your own list, but books such as Crane's *Red Badge of Courage*, London's *Call of the Wild*, Fitzgerald's *The Great Gatsby*, Faulkner's *The Sound and the Fury*, Steinbeck's *Grapes of Wrath*, Mitchell's *Gone with the Wind*, Huxley's *Brave New World*, Graves's *Goodbye to All That*, Orwell's *1984*, Salinger's *Catcher in the Rye*, Merton's *Seven Storey Mountain*, or Bradbury's *Martian Chronicles* will more than likely hold a continuing interest for collectors in the foreseeable future; if you have a hundred or more of these classics in fine condition in dust-wrappers and are tired of them, please call us immediately.

If you don't have much money, you might consider collecting some of the authors first published in the 1970s or early 1980s that you like. If ten years ago you had bought books by the authors whose first books were listed in the first edition of this book and were published in the 1950s or early 1960s, you would find that most have increased in value.

It makes sense that it would take ten to twenty-five years for the collectors and critics to agree on the important authors, and that some more recent authors tend to become overvalued because of the success of their first books, but then go down in value when they publish a few bombs.

Who knows whether the trend will continue. In this edition of *Book Collecting* we decided to include the values as they appeared in the 1978 and 1986 editions as well as the new estimated values so that a comparison could be readily made.

The biggest risk would seem to be paying a good deal of money ($200 and up) for relatively recent trade editions. There are some that will be worth it, and more, but many of the recent first books may fade in popularity as later works fail to live up to the author's initial performance.

WHAT TO COLLECT

B ook collecting allows you a wide choice. Most subjects have been covered by a number of authors. If you are interested in the labor movement, farming, espionage, chess, Americana, law, medicine, a foreign country, a state, a county, a city, railroads, wars, the military, artists, westerns, philosophy, sociology, grammar, writing, cooking, animals, cars, general or specific histories, the future, science fiction, utopias, detectives, or slavery, you will find that hundreds if not thousands of novels, poetry, and nonfiction books have been written about the subject. And if you are interested in a nonfiction area don't overlook the fiction that has been written using the subject as a vehicle, because you will find interesting additions to your knowledge and library. If there is only one book in your life that you really enjoyed, don't overlook the possibility of collecting all the different editions of that book. There are really interesting collections of *The Rubaiyat, The Compleat Angler,* and other classics.

If you've found a subject or author that interests you, the next decision is which edition to collect. You could decide to collect paperback editions because you have little money and the cover art interests you, or

- hardback editions with dustwrappers, but not necessarily first editions;
- first editions without dustwrappers;
- first editions with dustwrappers;
- hardback editions signed by the author;
- all first editions in English, including American, British, Canadian, Australian, etc.;

- All editions of an author's work including reprints, foreign editions, and specially illustrated editions.

As you can see, there are many avenues, and you should give some consideration to choices before starting; although it is likely, however, that you will modify your initial decision as your collection grows.

FIRST EDITIONS

A first edition is the first printing of a book. It's true that a first edition may have one or more printings and that a second edition will normally be noted only if there are actual changes, usually major, in the text. But for a collector, a first printing is the only true first edition.

Within the first printing there can be differences that make the earlier books in the printing more valuable than the later books in the same printing. These differences are identified by "points," which are discussed elsewhere.

If it's difficult to explain book collecting in general, the reason for collecting first editions is even more difficult to explain to those who are not afflicted with the mania. Bob Wilson, in his book *Modern Book Collecting*, deals with the question when he comments on book collecting in general:

A great many people over a great number of decades, have written pamphlets, whole books even, to justify the collecting of books. This seems to me to be an unnecessary exercise. If you are predisposed to collect books, you don't need any *ex post facto* justification for having done so. And on the other hand, if you are not convinced before you start, the chances are that no argument is going to win you over.

Now, we believe there is a little more logic and reason in book collecting than this, but Wilson's argument is not without merit. At any rate, for a collector, the first edition/first printing is the most desirable. It's the edition the author actually saw through production, the closest in time to the writing, and the edition most likely to represent the author's intent. This may seem a minor point, but one only has to read Ray Bradbury's Afterword to a later edition of his book *Fahrenheit 451* to become aware of what can happen to later printings or editions.

Some five years back, the editors of yet another anthology for school readers put together a volume with 400 (count 'em) short stories in it. How do you cram 400 short stories by Twain, Irving, Poe . . . into one book?

Simplicity itself. Skin, debone, demarrow, scarify, melt, render down and destroy . . .

Every story, slenderized, starved, blue-penciled, leeched and bled white, resembled every other story . . .

Only six weeks ago, I discovered that, over the years, some cubby-hole editors at Ballantine Books, fearful of contaminating the young, had, bit by bit, censored some 75 separate sections from the novel. . . .

All you umpires, back to the bleachers. Referees, hit the showers It's my game, I pitch, I hit, I catch, I run the bases . . .

And no one can help me. Not even you.

I can only assume that many first edition collectors do not want to take a chance with their favorite authors.

First editions are normally identified by publishers. Each publisher has its own method of identification. Many publishers have changed their method of identification over the years; a few have been so inconsistent that one has to resort to individual author bibliographies to be sure one has the true first.

For information on how to identify first editions by publisher, turn to page 116. At present we are aware of only two books on the market (other than this one) that include a list of publishers and how each identifies first editions. They are *First Editions: A Guide to Identification*, edited by Edward N. Zempel and Linda A. Verkley (The Spoon River Press, 2319C West Rohmann Avenue, Peoria, IL 61604); and *A Pocket Guide to the Identification of First Editions*, by Bill McBride (585 Prospect Avenue, West Hartford, CT 06105).

PROOFS AND ADVANCE REVIEW COPIES

The publication date of a book is normally set sufficiently far after the printing to allow the publisher to distribute copies of the book to reviewers, bookstore owners, store managers, and others, and actually ship an initial order to bookstores so that the book will be available to customers when the reviews appear.

Prior to the trade edition and the limited edition, if one is published, a book will take different forms. The most common forms that become available on the first edition market are galley proofs, uncorrected proofs, advance reading copies, and the normal trade edition with evidence that the particular book has been sent out in advance. The latter would usually contain a slip of paper or letter from the publisher stating that the copy is sent for advance review, or perhaps a publication date stamped on one of the preliminary pages.

As discussed previously, a first edition collector is always anxious to obtain the first issue within the first printing; therefore, it should come as no surprise that proofs or advance review copies of the first printing are also collected and bring a premium.

It is difficult to place a value on these "prepublication" copies because there does not seem to be any consistent formula, but generally we find that trade editions containing advance review slips or other advance publication evidence will sell for perhaps 50 percent more than the regular trade edition; the advance review/reading copies in paperwraps will sell for twice the trade value; the uncorrected proofs (also in paperwraps but with uncorrected indicated) for somewhat more than the advance review copies; and the galley proofs (normally on long sheets either bound or unbound) will bring the most of all.

The recent "galleys," run off on copiers, are so easily duplicated that we don't feel they have much monetary value above duplication cost, but this is a personal view; and we must admit that they will prove very valuable to researchers, as they do contain numerous corrections. This is an important consideration in forming a collection. If you are interested in the evolution of a writer's thoughts, the page proofs and uncorrected proofs could prove very useful. If the collection is being formed with the thought in mind of eventual donation to a library, we believe the proofs should be included if at all possible. The number of proof copies actually produced is normally relatively low, 50 to 500 copies, and if eventual scarcity is a determinant of future value, a proof that was printed in an edition of 200 copies (and is very fragile by nature) will certainly have more value than the first trade printing, which for popular authors can run from 75,000 to 800,000 copies (recent examples: Tom Clancy's *Debt of Honor*—2,000,000 copies; James Clavell's *Whirlwind*—850,000 copies; Norman Mailer's *Harlot's Ghost*—186,000 copies; and Tim O'Brien's *In the Lake of the Woods*—75,000 copies).

It should be noted that many publishers do not bother with paperbound proofs and only send out copies of the trade edition with review slips.

One example of a limited proof is James Clavell's *Noble House*. We understand the publisher photocopied four copies on one side of the page only, and then sixteen copies on both sides of the page. These copies were put in large three-ring binders, but after assembling twenty copies the publisher stopped. We assume they changed to sending out copies of the regular trade edition with review slips. We believe we know why they changed, as we handled one of the sixteen copies. It was about three inches thick and very unwieldy.

Shown below are two prepublication copies. On the left is a proof of James Baldwin's first book, which is of special interest as the cover differs from the one finally selected for the book; and an uncorrected proof of the first American edition of Adams's *Watership Down* (the true first edition is the English edition).

LIMITED EDITIONS

The limited edition comes in varying forms as discussed below. A limited edition of a new book is usually signed, numbered, and in a slipcase and costs three to five times the cost of the regular first edition, which is referred to as the trade, or first trade, edition. The first printing of the trade edition is still considered the first edition, so the collector must decide if both the limited signed and the first trade are required or if only one is necessary for the collection.

Limited editions of 200 copies are usually still available when one has a hard time finding fine copies of first trade editions from the same period

which were published in an edition of 5,000 copies. This is because there is an aversion to throwing away a book signed and numbered by an author, even if one has never heard of the author, but no aversion at all to throwing away novels, poetry, drama, detective stories, medical and scientific books by an author one has never heard of.

Limited Editions Club (LEC). George Macy started the LEC in 1929. The books were printed on good paper and bound in various interesting and attractive covers, illustrated and signed by famous artists of the period, numbered and limited to 1,500 copies (later 2,000). The books were issued in boxes or slipcases. They're very attractive and actually easy to read. The LEC issued one book a month until recent years, when it changed hands a number of times (it is currently issuing books at a cost of $400 and up per volume). If we look at the total output, we find that one or two titles a year have gone up significantly in price and the balance can be purchased at reasonable prices, particularly at auction.

If you are interested in well-bound and -illustrated books, you should not overlook the LEC.

Heritage Press editions are not limited, but are mentioned because the Heritage Press was an offshoot of the LEC. It produced the trade edition, so to speak. The Heritage editions were printed on good paper, nicely bound, and issued in slipcases. They contained the same illustrations as the comparable LEC editions, but were not signed or limited. You can still subscribe to the Heritage Press (for under $25 a volume) and buy most of the earlier editions in the series in used bookstores in the $5 to $25 range. If you like the classics in a very readable form, attractively bound, and at a reasonable price, it would be hard to go wrong collecting these editions although it must be remembered they are reprints.

Franklin Press. The Franklin Mint is a truly interesting phenomenon. Franklin publishes leather-bound "limited editions." What we find interesting is that they publish literary titles and seem to have a bigger clientele than all the specialist literary bookdealers in the country combined. The publishers do not usually disclose the quantities printed, but a John Updike bibliography included a quantity of 12,600 for a reprint of *Rabbit Run* in 1977, and Ray Bradbury informed a collector that he had signed about 13,000 sheets for *Death Is a Lonely Business* in 1985.

When the Franklin Press started advertising its Pulitzer Prize editions of fiction, a friend asked for advice on whether to purchase them. We told him that for less money he could probably buy first editions in very good condition of not only the fiction but also the poetry and drama winners. He bought around 150 titles and it probably didn't cost him $4,000. A nice copy of only one of the books he bought (*Gone with the Wind*) is selling for $4,000.

Trade Book Publishers. When an author becomes popular the publisher may decide to issue a signed, numbered limited edition. This edition is usually 300 copies, plus or minus 50, but can be as few as 100 copies or as many as 1,000 copies. These books are normally composed of the first trade edition sheets bound up in a binding different from the trade edition binding and in a slipcase. Most people are very happy with the trade edition. But if you think that James Michener is an important writer, and you could buy one of 1,000 signed and numbered copies of *Texas* for $150–200, versus one of 750,000 copies of the trade edition at $40, we'd advise you to buy the signed limited. Of course, if the choice is between a first edition and a second printing for the same price, always buy the first edition.

Private Press Publishers. When an author becomes popular with book collectors, there are a number of small presses that will publish signed limited editions of his or her work. Sometimes it is new material that has not been published before, or it may be a short story, novella, or poetry which appeared previously in magazine or short-story anthologies, and its publication by the press is considered the first separate edition or publication. These present real problems for the collector because these books may come out in different states, for example:

10 signed and numbered copies for presentation
26 signed and lettered copies
300 signed and numbered copies
700 hardbound (not signed) copies
1,000 paperbound copies

All of the above are legitimate first editions, usually printed on the same paper at the same time, only bound differently; and in the case of the first three, with an extra leaf with the limitation and signature. If you must have one of each, you can see the problem and expense involved. If the author continues to remain popular, the prices would probably rise proportionally; thus, if one of the twenty-six copies sold at $100 and one of the three hundred copies at $50, their respective values in the future might be $200 and $100.

Fine Press Books. These are also private presses, similar to the last category, but concentrating more on the classics, the quality of paper, binding, and illustrations. Their books often contain the signed work of an artist of note. We have made them a separate group because there is significant difference in the published prices of these books, usually ranging from $200 to $2,000, but sometimes significantly higher.

THIS
SPECIAL
EDITION
IS LIMITED TO 310 COPIES
OF WHICH 300 ARE FOR SALE
EACH COPY
NUMBERED
& SIGNED
BY THE
AUTHOR
THIS IS
COPY
NUMBER
163

William Faulkner

THIS AUTOGRAPHED FIRST EDITION

OF *EAST OF EDEN* IS LIMITED

TO FIFTEEN HUNDRED COPIES,

OF WHICH SEVEN HUNDRED AND FIFTY

ARE FOR PRIVATE DISTRIBUTION.

John Steinbeck

PAPERBACKS OR PAPERWRAPS

The bindings of most books published in this century vary from paper covers weighing only slightly more than the pages of the book (paperwraps) to stiffer, heavier paper covers that are flexible (stiff paperwraps) to completely stiff paper covers (boards) and finally to cloth and/or leather-bound covers. Recent books in paperwraps are normally published after the original edition and are not particularly valuable in the first edition market; however, if the paper edition contains a new introduction, or some major changes in the text, the value could approach that of the regular first edition.

It should be noted that the first printings of these paper reprint editions have found a market of their own, which operates separately from the hardback market. This market is very interested in the cover art as well as the content.

In some cases the paper edition is the true first edition because no hardback edition was published; this may become more common in the future as publishing costs continue to increase. Recently there has been a move to print the same sheets and bind some in hard cover and some in paperwraps. Over the next ten to twenty years there may be a reversal of the ratio of original hardback to original paperback editions, with the paperback books becoming the normal medium and the hardback first editions the exception.

LITERARY PRIZE WINNERS

Some collectors center their collecting around categories of major prize winners: the Booker, Caldecott, Edgar (Edgar Allan Poe), Hugo, National, Nebula, Newbery, PEN/Faulkner, Pulitzer, or lists of highspots compiled by knowledgeable authors, such as the Connolly 100, Queen's Quorum, and on and on. The following are some of these award winners, the years the awards were won and the books for which they won.

Note that we have listed the books in the year of publication, although in most cases the prizes were awarded the next year (i.e. the 1992 Hugo Award is for the Best Novel Published in 1991).

The Booker Prize

The Booker Prize is awarded annually for the best literature in the British Commonwealth of Nations.

1969: P. H. Newby. SOMETHING TO ANSWER FOR

1970: Bernice Rubens. THE ELECTED MEMBER

1971: V. S. Naipaul. IN A FREE STATE

1972: John Berger. G

1973:   J. G. Farrell. SIEGE OF KRISHNAPUR

1974:   Stanley Middleton. HOLIDAY

1975:   Nadine Gordimer. THE CONSERVATIONIST

1975:   Ruth Prawer Jhabvala. HEAT AND DUST

1976:   David Storey. SAVILLE

1977:   Paul Scott. STAYING ON

1978:   Iris Murdoch. THE SEA, THE SEA

1979:   Penelope Fitzgerald. OFFSHORE

1980:   William Golding. RITES OF PASSAGE

1981:   Salman Rushdie. MIDNIGHT'S CHILDREN

1982:   Thomas Keneally. SCHINDLER'S ARK

1983:   J. M. Coetzee. LIFE AND TIMES OF MICHAEL K

1984:   Anita Brookner. HOTEL DU LAC

1985:   Keri Hulme. THE BONE PEOPLE

1986:   Kingsley Amis. THE OLD DEVILS

1987:   Penelope Lively. MOON TIGER

1988:   Peter Carey. OSCAR AND LUCINDA

1989:   Kazuo Ishiguro. THE REMAINS OF THE DAY

1990:   A. S. Byatt. POSSESSION

1991:   Ben Okri. THE FAMISHED ROAD

1992:   Michael Ondaatje. THE ENGLISH PATIENT

1993:   Barry Unsworth. SACRED HUNGER

1994:   Roddy Doyle. PADDY CLARKE HA HA HA

1995:   James Kelman. HOW LITTLE IT WAS, HOW LATE

1996: _____

1997: _____

1998: _____

1999: _____

2000: _____

The Caldecott Medal

The Caldecott Medal is awarded annually by the American Library Association's Children's Services Division for the most distinguished picture book for children. The award was named in honor of Randolph Caldecott, a 19th century illustrator whose work is still delighting children.

1938:   Helen Dean Fish. ANIMALS OF THE BIBLE

Illustrated by Dorothy P. Lathrop

1939:   Thomas Handforth. MEI LI

1940:   Ingri and Edgar Parin. ABRAHAM LINCOLN

1941:   Robert Lawson. THEY WERE STRONG AND GOOD

1942:   Robert McCloskey. MAKE WAY FOR DUCKLINGS

1943:   Virginia Lee Burton. THE LITTLE HOUSE

1944:   James Thurber. MANY MOONS

Illustrated by Louis Slobodkin

1945:   Rachel Field. PRAYER FOR A CHILD

Illustrated by Elizabeth Orton Jones

1946:   THE ROOSTER CROWS . . . (Traditional Mother Goose)

Illustrated by Maud and Miska Petersham

1947:   Golden MacDonald. THE LITTLE ISLAND

Illustrated by Leonard Weisgard

1948:   Alvin Tresselt. WHITE SNOW, BRIGHT SNOW

Illustrated by Roger Duvoisin

1949:   Berta and Elmer Hader. THE BIG SNOW

1950:   Leo Politi. SONG OF THE SWALLOWS

1951:   Katherine Milhous. THE EGG TREE

1952:   Will Lipkind and Nicolas Mordvinoff. FINDERS KEEPERS

Illustrated by Nicolas Mordvinoff

1953:   Lynd Ward. THE BIGGEST BEAR

1954:   Ludwig Bemelmans. MADELINE'S RESCUE

1955:   Charles Perrault. CINDERELLA, OR THE LITTLE GLASS SLIPPER.

Illustrated by Marcia Brown

1956:   John Langstaff. FROG WENT A-COURTIN'

Illustrated by Feodor Rojankovsky

1957:   Janice May Udry. A TREE IS NICE

Illustrated by Marc Simont

1958:   Robert McCloskey. TIME OF WONDER

1959:   CHANTICLEER AND THE FOX. Adapted from Chaucer

and illustrated by Barbara Cooney

1960:   Marie Hall Ets and Aurora Labastida. NINE DAYS TO CHRISTMAS

Illustrated by Marie Hall Ets

1961:   Ruth Robbins. BABOUSHKA AND THE THREE KINGS

Illustrated by Nicolas Sidjakov

1962:   Marcia Brown. ONCE A MOUSE . . .

1963:   Ezra Jack Keats. THE SNOWY DAY

1964:   Maurice Sendak. WHERE THE WILD THINGS ARE

1965:   Beatrice Schenk de Regniers. MAY I BRING A FRIEND?

Illustrated by Beni Montresor

1966:   Sorche Nic Leodhas. ALWAYS ROOM FOR ONE MORE

Illustrated by Nonny Hogrogian

1967:   Evaline Ness. SAM, BANGS & MOONSHINE

1968:   Barbara Emberley. DRUMMER HOFF

Illustrated by Ed Emberley

1969:   Arthur Ransome. THE FOOL OF THE WORLD AND THE FLYING SHIP.
Illustrated by Uri Shulevitz

1970:   William Steig. SYLVESTER AND THE MAGIC PEBBLE

1971:   Gail E. Haley. A STORY, A STORY

1972:   Nonny Hogrogian. ONE FINE DAY

1973:   Arlene Mosel. THE FUNNY LITTLE WOMAN

Illustrated by Blair Lent

1974:   Harve Zemach. DUFFY & THE DEVIL

Illustrated by Margot Zemach

1975:   Gerald McDermott. ARROW TO THE SUN

1976:   Verna Aardema. WHY MOSQUITOES BUZZ IN PEOPLE'S EARS

Illustrated by Leo and Diane Dillon

1977:   Margaret Musgrove. ASHANTI TO ZULU

Illustrated by Leo and Diane Dillon

1978:   Peter Spier. NOAH'S ARK

1979:   Paul Goble. THE GIRL WHO LOVED HORSES

1980:   Donald Hall. OX-CART MAN

1981:   Arnold Lobel. FABLES

1982:   Chris Van Allsburg. JUMANJI

1983:   Blaise Cendrar. SHADOW

Illustrated by Marcia Brown

1984:   Alice & Martin Provenson. THE GLORIOUS FLIGHT ACROSS THE CHAN-
NEL WITH LOUIS BLERIOT

1985:   Margaret Hodges. SAINT GEORGE & THE DRAGON

Illustrated by Trina Schart Hyman

1986:   Chris Van Allsburg. THE POLAR EXPRESS

1987:   Arthur Yorinks. HEY, AL

Illustrated by Richard Egielski

1988:   Jane Yolen. OWL MOON

Illustrated by John Schoenherr

1989:   Stephen Gammell. SONG AND DANCE MAN

1990:   Ed Young. LON PO PO . . .

1991:   David Macaulay. BLACK & WHITE

1992:   David Weisner. TUESDAY

1993:   Emily Arnold McCully. MIRETTE ON THE HIGH WIRE

1994:   Allen Say. GRANDFATHER'S JOURNEY

1995:   Eve Bunting. SMOKY NIGHT

Illustrated by David Diaz

1996: _____

1997: _____

1998: _____

1999: _____

2000: _____

The Edgar

The Edgar is an annual award and was named in honor of Edgar Allan Poe.

THE EDGAR FOR BEST (MYSTERY) NOVEL

1953:   Charlotte Jay. BEAT NOT THE BONES

1954:   Raymond Chandler. THE LONG GOODBYE

1955:   Margaret Millar. BEAST IN VIEW

1956:   Charlotte Armstrong. A DRAM OF POISON

1957:   Ed Lacy. ROOM TO SWING

1958:   Stanley Ellin. THE EIGHTH CIRCLE

1959:   Celia Fremlin. THE HOUSE BEFORE DAWN

1960:   Julian Symons. THE PROGRESS OF A CRIME

1961:   J. J. Marric. GIDEON'S FIRE

1962:   Ellis Peters. DEATH AND THE JOYFUL WOMAN

1963:   Eric Ambler. THE LIGHT OF DAY

1964:   John Le Carré. THE SPY WHO CAME IN FROM THE COLD

1965:   Adam Hall. THE QUILLER MEMORANDUM

1966:   Nicholas Freeling. KING OF THE RAINY COUNTRY

1967:   Donald E. Westlake. GOD SAVE THE MARK

1968:   Jeffrey Hudson. A CASE OF NEED

1969:   Dick Francis. FORFEIT

1970:   Maj Sjöwall and Per Wahlöö. THE LAUGHING POLICEMAN

1971:   Frederick Forsyth. THE DAY OF THE JACKAL

1972:   Warren Kiefer. THE LINGALA CODE

1973:   Tony Hillerman. DANCE HALL OF THE DEAD

1974:   Jon Cleary. PETER'S PENCE

1975:   Brian Garfield. HOPSCOTCH

1976:   Robert B. Parker. PROMISED LAND

1977:   William Hallahan. CATCH ME: KILL ME

1978:   Ken Follett. THE EYE OF THE NEEDLE

1979:   Arthur Maling. THE RHEINGOLD ROUTE

1980:   Dick Francis. WHIP HAND

1981:   William Bayer. PEREGRINE

1982:   Rick Boyer. BILLINGSGATE SHOAL

1983:   Elmore Leonard. LA BRAVA

1984:   Ross Thomas. BRIARPATCH

1985:   L. R. Wright. THE SUSPECT

1986:   Barbara Vine. DARK-ADAPTED EYE

1987:   Aaron Elkins. OLD BONES

1988:   Stuart M. Kaminsky. A COLD RED SUNRISE

1989:   James Lee Burke. BLACK CHERRY BLUES

1990:   Julie Smith. NEW ORLEANS MOURNING

1991:   Lawrence Block. A DANCE AT THE SLAUGHTER HOUSE

1992:   Margaret Maron. BOOTLEGGER'S DAUGHTER

1993:   Minette Walters. THE SCULPTRESS

1994: ————————————————————————————

1995: ————————————————————————————

1996: ————————————————————————————

1997: ————————————————————————————

1998: ————————————————————————————

1999: ————————————————————————————

2000: ————————————————————————————

THE EDGAR FOR BEST FIRST (MYSTERY) NOVEL

1945:   Julius Fast. WATCHFUL AT NIGHT

1946:   Helen Eustis. THE HORIZONTAL MAN

1947:   Fredric Brown. THE FABULOUS CLIPJOINT

1948:   Mildred Davis. THE ROOM UPSTAIRS

1949:   Alan Green. WHAT A BODY!

1950:   Thomas Walsh. NIGHTMARE IN MANHATTAN

1951:   Mary McMullen. STRANGLE HOLD

1952:   William Campbell Gault. DON'T CRY FOR ME

1953:   Ira Levin. A KISS BEFORE DYING

1954:   Jean Potts. GO, LOVELY ROSE

1955:   Lane Kauffman. THE PERFECTIONIST

1956:   Donald McNutt Douglas. REBECCA'S PRIDE

1957:   William Rawle Weeks. KNOCK AND WAIT A WHILE

1958:   Richard Martin Stern. THE BRIGHT ROAD TO FEAR

1959:   Henry Sleasar. THE GREY FLANNEL SHROUD

1960:   John Holbrook Vance. THE MAN IN THE CAGE

1961:   Suzanne Blanc. THE GREEN STONE

1962:   Robert L. Fish. THE FUGITIVE

1963:   Cornelius Hirschberg. THE FLORENTINE FINISH

1964:   Harry Kemelman. FRIDAY THE RABBI SLEPT LATE

1965:   John Ball. IN THE HEAT OF THE NIGHT

1966:   Ross Thomas. THE COLD WAR SWAP

1967:   Michael Collins. ACT OF FEAR

1968:   E. Richard Johnson. SILVER STREET

1969:   Joe Gores. A TIME OF PREDATORS

1970:   Lawrence Sanders. THE ANDERSON TAPES

1971:   A. H. Z. Carr. FINDING MAUBEE

1972:   R. H. Shimer. SQUAW POINT

1973:   Paul E. Erdman. THE BILLION DOLLAR SURE THING

1974:   Gregory Mcdonald. FLETCH

1975:   Rex Burns. THE ALVAREZ JOURNAL

1976:   James Patterson. THE THOMAS BERRYMAN NUMBER

1977:   Robert Ross. A FRENCH FINISH

1978:   William L. DeAndrea. KILLED IN THE RATINGS

1979:   Richard North Patterson. THE LASKO TANGENT

1980:   Kay Nolte Smith. THE WATCHER

1981:   Stuart Woods. CHIEFS

1982:   Thomas Perry. THE BUTCHER'S BOY

1983:   Will Harriss. THE BAY PSALM BOOK MURDER

1984:   R. D. Rosen. STRIKE THREE, YOU'RE DEAD

1985:   Jonathan Kellerman. WHEN THE BOUGH BREAKS

1986:   Larry Beinhart. NO ONE RIDES FOR FREE

1987:   Deirdre Laiken. DEATH AMONG STRANGERS

1988:   David Stout. CAROLINA SKELETONS

1989:   Susan Wolfe. THE LAST BILLABLE HOUR

1990:   Patricia Daniels Cornwell. POSTMORTEM

1991:   Peter Blauner. SLOW MOTION RIOT

1992:   Michael Connelly. THE BLACK ECHO

1993:   Laurie King. A GRAVE TALENT

1994: _____

1995: _____

1996: _____

1997: _____

1998: _____

1999: _____

2000: _____

The Hugo Award for
Best Science Fiction Achievement

The Hugo was named in honor of Hugo Gernsback, the founder of the first professional science fiction magazine. The winner is chosen by a mail vote by the attending and supporting members of each World Science Fiction Convention.

1952:   Alfred Bester. THE DEMOLISHED MAN

1953:   No award

1954:   Frank Riley and Mark Clifton. THEY'D RATHER BE RIGHT

1955:   Robert A. Heinlein. DOUBLE STAR

1956:   No award

1957:   Fritz Leiber. THE BIG TIME

1958:   James Blish. A CASE OF CONSCIENCE

1959:   Robert A. Heinlein. STARSHIP TROOPERS

1960:   Walter M. Miller, Jr. A CANTICLE FOR LEIBOWITZ

1961:   Robert A. Heinlein. STRANGER IN A STRANGE LAND

1962:   Philip K. Dick. THE MAN IN THE HIGH CASTLE

1963:   Clifford D. Simak. WAY STATION

1964:   Fritz Leiber. THE WANDERER

1965:   (tie) Roger Zelazny. THE DREAM MASTER

Frank Herbert. DUNE

1966:   Robert A. Heinlein. THE MOON IS A HARSH MISTRESS

1967:   Roger Zelazny. LORD OF LIGHT

1968:   John Brunner. STAND ON ZANZIBAR

1969:   Ursula K. Le Guin. THE LEFT HAND OF DARKNESS

1970:   Larry Niven. RINGWORLD

1971:   Philip José Farmer. TO YOUR SCATTERED BODIES GO

1972:   Isaac Asimov. THE GODS THEMSELVES

1973:   Arthur C. Clarke. RENDEZVOUS WITH RAMA

1974:   Ursula K. Le Guin. THE DISPOSSESSED

1975:   Joe Haldeman. THE FOREVER WAR

1976:   Kate Wilhelm. WHERE THE SWEET BIRDS SANG

1977:   Frederik Pohl. GATEWAY

1978:   Vonda N. McIntyre. DREAMSNAKE

1979:   Arthur C. Clarke. THE FOUNTAINS OF PARADISE

1980:   Joan D. Vinge. THE SNOW QUEEN

1981:   C. J. Cherryh. DOWNBELOW STATION

1982:   Isaac Asimov. FOUNDATION'S EDGE

1983:   David Brin. STARTIDE RISING

1984:   William Gibson. NEUROMANCER

1985:   Orson Scott Card. ENDER'S GAME

1986:   Orson Scott Card. SPEAKER FOR THE DEAD

1987:   David Brin. THE UPLIFT WAR

1988:   C. J. Cherryh. CYTEEN

1989:   Dan Simmons. HYPERION

1990:   Lois McMaster Bujold. THE VOR GAME

1991:   Lois McMaster Bujold. BARRAYAR

1992:   (tie) Vernor Vinge. A FIRE UPON THE DEEP

Connie Willis. THE DOOMSDAY BOOK

1993:   Kim S. Robinson. GREEN MARS

1994: _____

1995: _____

1996: _____

1997: _____

1998: _____

1999: _____

2000: _____

National Book Award

An annual award ($10,000) given by the National Book Foundation for best fiction.

1950: Nelson Algren. THE MAN WITH THE GOLDEN ARM

1951: William Faulkner. THE COLLECTED STORIES . . .
Brenda Gill. THE TROUBLE OF ONE HOUSE

1952: James Jones. FROM HERE TO ETERNITY

1953: Ralph Ellison. INVISIBLE MAN

1954: Saul Bellow. THE ADVENTURES OF AUGIE MARCH

1955: William Faulkner. A FABLE

1956: John O'Hara. TEN NORTH FREDERICK

1957: Wright Morris. THE FIELD OF VISION

1958: John Cheever. THE WAPSHOT CHRONICLE

1959: Bernard Malamud. THE MAGIC BARREL

1960: Philip Roth. GOODBYE, COLUMBUS

1961: Conrad Richter. THE WATERS OF KRONOS

1962: Walker Percy. THE MOVIEGOER

1963: J. F. Powers. MORTE D'URBAN

1964: John Updike. THE CENTAUR

1965: Saul Bellow. HERZOG

1966: Katherine Anne Porter. THE COLLECTED STORIES

1967: Bernard Malamud. THE FIXER

1968: Thornton Wilder. THE EIGHTH DAY

1969: Jerzy Kosinski. STEPS

1970: Joyce Carol Oates. THEM

1971: Saul Bellow. MR. SAMMLER'S PLANET

1972: Flannery O'Connor. THE COMPLETE STORIES

1973: John Barth. CHIMERA
John Williams. AUGUSTUS

1974:   Isaac Bashevis Singer. A CROWN OF FEATHERS . . .
Thomas Pynchon. GRAVITY'S RAINBOW

1975:   Robert Stone. DOG SOLDIERS
Thomas Williams. THE HAIR OF HAROLD ROUX

1976:   William Gaddis. JR

1977:   Wallace Stegner. THE SPECTATOR BIRD

1978:   Mary Lee Settle. BLOOD TIE

1979:   Tim O'Brien. GOING AFTER CACCIATO

1980:   John Irving. THE WORLD ACCORDING TO GARP
William Styron. SOPHIE'S CHOICE

1981:   Wright Morris. PLAIN SONG

1982:   William Maxwell. SO LONG, SEE YOU TOMORROW

1983:   Alice Walker. THE COLOR PURPLE
Eudora Welty. THE COLLECTED STORIES

1984:   Ellen Gilchrist. VICTORY OVER JAPAN

1985:   Don DeLillo. WHITE NOISE

1986:   E. L. Doctorow. WORLD'S FAIR
Barry Lopez. ARCTIC DREAMS

1987:   Larry Heinemann. PACO'S STORY

1988:   Pete Dexter. PARIS TROUT

1989:   John Casey. SPARTINA

1990:   Charles Johnson. MIDDLE PASSAGE

1991:   Norman Rush. MATING

1992:   Cormac McCarthy. ALL THE PRETTY HORSES

1993:   E. Annie Proulx. THE SHIPPING NEWS

1994:   William Gaddis. A FROLIC OF HIS OWN

1995: _____

1996: _____

1997: _____

1998: _____

1999: _____

2000: _____

The Nebula Award

The Nebula is awarded annually by the Science Fiction Writers of America (SFWA).

1965:   Frank Herbert. DUNE

1966:   (tie) Samuel R. Delany. BABEL-17
Daniel Keyes. FLOWERS FOR ALGERNON

1967:   Samuel R. Delany. THE EINSTEIN INTERSECTION

1968:   Alexei Panshin. RITE OF PASSAGE

1969:   Ursula K. Le Guin. THE LEFT HAND OF DARKNESS

1970:   Larry Niven. RINGWORLD

1971:   Robert Silverberg. A TIME OF CHANGE

1972:   Isaac Asimov. THE GODS THEMSELVES

1973:   Arthur C. Clarke. RENDEZVOUS WITH RAMA

1974:   Ursula K. Le Guin. THE DISPOSSESSED

1975:   Joe Haldeman. THE FOREVER WAR

1976:   Frederik Pohl. MAN PLUS

1977:   Frederik Pohl. GATEWAY

1978:   Vonda N. McIntyre. DREAMSNAKE

1979:   Arthur C. Clarke. THE FOUNTAINS OF PARADISE

1980:   Gregory Benford. TIMESCAPE

1981:   Gene Wolfe. THE CLAW OF THE CONCILIATOR

1982:   Michael Bishop. NO ENEMY BUT TIME

1983:   David Brin. STARTIDE RISING

1984:   William Gibson. NEUROMANCER

1985:   Orson Scott Card. ENDER'S GAME

1986:   Orson Scott Card. SPEAKER FOR THE DEAD

1987:   Pat Murphy. THE FALLING WOMAN

1988:   Lois McMaster Bujold. FALLING FREE

1989:   Elizabeth Ann Scarborough. THE HEALER'S WAR

1990: Ursula K. Le Guin. THE LAST BOOK OF EARTHSEA

1991: Michael Swanwick. STATIONS OF THE TIDE

1992: Connie Willis. THE DOOMSDAY BOOK

1993: Kim S. Robinson. RED MARS

1994: _____

1995: _____

1996: _____

1997: _____

1998: _____

1999: _____

2000: _____

The Newbery Medal

The Newbery is awarded annually by the Association for Library Service to Children (a division of the American Library Association) to the author of the most distinguished contribution to American literature for children.

1922: Hendrik Willem Van Loon. THE STORY OF MANKIND

1923: Hugh Lofting. THE VOYAGES OF DOCTOR DOLITTLE

1924: Charles Boardman Hawes. THE DARK FRIGATE

1925: Charles J. Finger. TALES FROM SILVER LANDS

1926: Arthur Bowie Chrisman. SHEN OF THE SEA

1927: Will James. SMOKY, THE COWHORSE

1928: Dhan Gopal Mukerji. GAYNECK, THE STORY OF A PIGEON

1929: Eric P. Kelley. THE TRUMPETER . . .

1930: Rachel Field. HITTY, HER FIRST HUNDRED YEARS

1931: Elizabeth Coatsworth. THE CAT WHO WENT TO HEAVEN

1932: Laura Adams Armer. WATERLESS MOUNTAIN

1933: Elizabeth Foreman Lewis. YOUNG FU OF THE UPPER YANGTZE

1934: Cornelia Meigs. INVINCIBLE LOUISA

1935: Monica Shannon. DOBRY

1936: Carol Brink. CADDIE WOODLAWN

1937: Ruth Sawyer. ROLLER SKATES

1938: Kate Seredy. THE WHITE STAG

1939: Elizabeth Enright. THIMBLE SUMMER

1940: James Daugherty. DANIEL BOONE

1941: Armstrong Sperry. CALL IT COURAGE

1942: Walter D. Edmonds. THE MATCHLOCK GUN

1943: Elizabeth Janet Gray. ADAM OF THE ROAD

1944: Esther Forbes. JOHNNY TREMAIN

1945: Robert Lawson. RABBIT HILL

1946: Lois Lenski. STRAWBERRY GIRL

1947: Carolyn Sherwin Bailey. MISS HICKORY

1948: William Pène du Bois. TWENTY-ONE BALLOONS

1949: Marguerite Henry. KING OF THE WIND

1950: Marguerite de Angeli. THE DOOR IN THE WALL

1951: Elizabeth Yates. AMOS FORTUNE . . .

1952: Eleanor Estes. GINGER PYE

1953: Ann Nolan Clark. SECRET OF THE ANDES

1954: Joseph Krumgold. . . . AND NOW MIGUEL

1955: Meindert DeJong. THE WHEEL ON THE SCHOOL

1956: Jean Lee Latham. CARRY ON, MR. BOWDITCH

1957: Virginia Sorensen. MIRACLES ON MAPLE HILL

1958: Harold Keith. RIFLES FOR WATIE

1959: Elizabeth George Speare. THE WITCH OF BLACKBIRD POND

1960: Joseph Krumgold. ONION JOHN

1961: Scott O'Dell. ISLAND OF THE BLUE DOLPHINS

1962: Elizabeth George Speare. THE BRONZE BOW

1963: Madeleine L'Engle. A WRINKLE IN TIME

1964: Emily Cheney Neville. IT'S LIKE THIS, CAT

1965:   Maia Wojciechowska. SHADOW OF A BULL

1966:   Elizabeth Borten de Treviño. I, JUAN DE PAREJA

1967:   Irene Hunt. UP A ROAD SLOWLY

1968:   E. L. Konigsburg. FROM THE MIXED-UP FILES OF MRS. BASIL E. FRANKWEILER

1969:   Lloyd Alexander. THE HIGH KING

1970:   William H. Armstrong. SOUNDER

1971:   Betsy Byars. SUMMER OF THE SWANS

1972:   Robert C. O'Brien. MRS. FRISBY AND THE RATS OF NIMH

1973:   Jean Craighead George. JULIE OF THE WOLVES

1974:   Paula Fox. THE SLAVE DANCER

1975:   Virginia Hamilton. M. C. HIGGINS THE GREAT

1976:   Susan Cooper. GREY KING

1977:   Mildred D. Taylor. ROLL OF THUNDER, HEAR MY CRY

1978:   Katherine Paterson. BRIDGE TO TERABITHIA

1979:   Ellen Raskin. THE WESTING GAME

1980:   Joan Blos. A GATHERING OF DAYS

1981:   Katherine Paterson. JACOB HAVE I LOVED

1982:   Nancy Willard. A VISIT TO WILLIAM BLAKE'S INN: POEMS FOR INNOCENT AND EXPERIENCED TRAVELERS

1983:   Cynthia Voigt. DICEY'S SONG

1984:   Beverly Cleary. DEAR MR. HENSHAW

1985:   Robin McKinley. THE HERO AND THE CROWN

1986:   Patricia MacLachlan. SARAH, PLAIN AND TALL

1987:   Sid Fleischman. THE WHIPPING BOY

1988:   Russell Freedman. LINCOLN: A PHOTOBIOGRAPHY

1989:   Paul Fleischman. JOYFUL NOISE: POEMS FOR TWO VOICES

1990:   Lois Lowry. NUMBER THE STARS

1991:   Jerry Spinelli. MANIAC MAGEE

1992:   Phyllis Reynolds Naylor. SHILOH

1993:   Cynthia Rylant. MISSING MAY

1994:   Lois Lowry. THE GIVER

1995:   Sharon Creech. WALK TWO MOONS

1996: —————————————————————

1997: —————————————————————

1998: —————————————————————

1999: —————————————————————

2000: —————————————————————

PEN/Faulkner Awards

PEN/Faulkner was founded in 1980 by writers to honor their peers, and is now the largest juried award for fiction in the U.S. It is named in honor of William Faulkner, who used his Nobel Prize funds to create an award for young writers.

1981:   Walter Abish. HOW GERMAN IS IT?

1982:   David Bradley. THE CHANEYSVILLE INCIDENT

1983:   Toby Olson. SEAVIEW

1984:   John Edgar Wideman. SENT FOR YOU YESTERDAY

1985:   Tobias Wolff. THE BARRACKS THIEF

1986:   Peter Taylor. THE OLD FOREST . . .

1987:   Richard Wiley. SOLDIERS IN HIDING

1988:   T. Coraghessan Boyle. WORLD'S END

1989:   James Salter. DUSK . . .

1990:   E. L. Doctorow. BILLY BATHGATE

1991:   John Edgar Wideman. PHILADELPHIA FIRE

1992:   Don DeLillo. MAO II

1993:   E. Annie Proulx. POSTCARDS

1994:   Philip Roth. OPERATION SHYLOCK

1995: —————————————————————

1996: —————————————————————

1997: —————————————————————

1998: _____

1999: _____

2000: _____

Pulitzer Prize Winners for Literature

Joseph Pulitzer, a publisher of the *New York Globe*, established the Pulitzer Prize through an endowment to Columbia University. The prizes are awarded annually. The Literature Award is given for fiction in book form by an American author, preferably dealing with American life.

1918: Ernest Poole. HIS FAMILY

1919: Booth Tarkington. THE MAGNIFICENT AMBERSONS

1920: No award

1921: Edith Wharton. THE AGE OF INNOCENCE

1922: Booth Tarkington. ALICE ADAMS

1923: Willa Cather. ONE OF OURS

1924: Margaret Wilson. THE ABLE MCLAUGHLINS

1925: Edna Ferber. SO BIG

1926: Sinclair Lewis. ARROWSMITH

1927: Louis Bromfield. EARLY AUTUMN

1928: Thornton Wilder. THE BRIDGE OF SAN LUIS REY

1929: Julia Peterkin. SCARLET SISTER MARY

1930: Oliver La Farge. LAUGHING BOY

1931: Margaret Ayer Barnes. YEARS OF GRACE

1932: Pearl S. Buck. THE GOOD EARTH

1933: T. S. Stribling. THE STORE

1934: Caroline Miller. LAMB IN HIS BOSOM

1935: Josephine Winslow Johnson. NOW IN NOVEMBER

1936: Harold Davis. HONEY IN THE HORN

1937: Margaret Mitchell. GONE WITH THE WIND

1938: John Phillips Marquand. THE LATE GEORGE APLEY

1939:   Marjorie Kinnan Rawlings. THE YEARLING

1940:   John Steinbeck. THE GRAPES OF WRATH

1941:   No award

1942:   Ellen Glasgow. IN THIS OUR LIFE

1943:   Upton Sinclair. DRAGON'S TEETH

1944:   Martin Flavin. JOURNEY IN THE DARK

1945:   John Hersey. A BELL FOR ADANO

1946:   No award

1947:   Robert Penn Warren. ALL THE KING'S MEN

1948:   James A. Michener. TALES OF THE SOUTH PACIFIC

1949:   James Gould Cozzens. GUARD OF HONOR

1950:   A. B. Guthrie. THE WAY WEST

1951:   Conrad Richter. THE TOWN

1952:   Herman Wouk. THE CAINE MUTINY

1953:   Ernest Hemingway. THE OLD MAN AND THE SEA

1954:   No award

1955:   William Faulkner. A FABLE

1956:   Mackinlay Kantor. ANDERSONVILLE

1957: No award

1958:   James Agee. A DEATH IN THE FAMILY

1959:   Robert Lewis Taylor. THE TRAVELS OF JAIMIE MCPHEETERS

1960:   Allen Drury. ADVISE AND CONSENT

1961:   Harper Lee. TO KILL A MOCKINGBIRD

1962:   Edwin O'Connor. THE EDGE OF SADNESS

1963:   William Faulkner. THE REIVERS

1964:   No award

1965:   Shirley Anne Grau. THE KEEPERS OF THE HOUSE

1966:   Katherine Anne Porter. COLLECTED STORIES OF KATHERINE ANNE PORTER

1967:   Bernard Malamud. THE FIXER

1968:   William Styron. THE CONFESSIONS OF NAT TURNER

1969:   N. Scott Momaday. HOUSE MADE OF DAWN

1970:   Jean Stafford. COLLECTED STORIES

1971:   No award

1972:   Wallace Stegner. THE ANGLE OF REPOSE

1973:   Eudora Welty. THE OPTIMIST'S DAUGHTER

1974:   No award

1975:   Michael Shaara. THE KILLER ANGELS

1976:   Saul Bellow: HUMBOLDT'S GIFT

1977:   No award

1978:   James Alan McPherson. ELBOW ROOM

1979:   John Cheever. THE STORIES OF JOHN CHEEVER

1980:   Norman Mailer. THE EXECUTIONER'S SONG

1981:   John Kennedy Toole. A CONFEDERACY OF DUNCES

1982:   John Updike. RABBIT IS RICH

1983:   Alice Walker. THE COLOR PURPLE

1984:   William Kennedy. IRONWEED

1985:   Alison Lurie. FOREIGN AFFAIRS

1986:   Larry McMurtry. LONESOME DOVE

1987:   Peter Taylor. A SUMMONS TO MEMPHIS

1988:   Toni Morrison. BELOVED

1989:   Anne Tyler. BREATHING LESSONS

1990:   Oscar Hijuelos. THE MAMBO KINGS PLAY SONGS OF LOVE

1991:   John Updike. RABBIT AT REST

1992:   Jane Smiley. THOUSAND ACRES

1993:   Robert Olen Butler. A GOOD SCENT FROM A STRANGE MOUNTAIN

1994: _____

1995: _____

1996: _____

1997: _____

1998: _____

1999: _____

2000: _____

Pulitzer Prize Winners for Drama

The Pulitzer Prize for Drama is for an American play, preferably original and dealing with American life.

1917:   No award

1918:   Jesse Lynch Williams. WHY MARRY?

1919:   No award

1920:   Eugene O'Neill. BEYOND THE HORIZON

1921:   Zona Gale. MISS LULU BETT

1922:   Eugene O'Neill. ANNA CHRISTIE

1923:   Owen Davis. ICEBOUND

1924:   Hatcher Hughes. HELL-BENT FOR HEAVEN

1925:   Sidney Howard. THEY KNEW WHAT THEY WANTED

1926:   George Kelly. CRAIG'S WIFE

1927:   Paul Green. IN ABRAHAM'S BOSOM

1928:   Eugene O'Neill. STRANGE INTERLUDE

1929:   Elmer L. Rice. STREET SCENE

1930:   Marc Connelly. THE GREEN PASTURES

1931:   Susan Glaspell. ALISON'S HOUSE

1932:   George S. Kaufman, Morrie Ryskind, and Ira Gershwin. OF THEE I SING

1933:   Maxwell Anderson. BOTH YOUR HOUSES

1934:   Sidney Kingsley. MEN IN WHITE

1935:   Zoë Akins. THE OLD MAID

1936:   Robert E. Sherwood. IDIOT'S DELIGHT

1937:   George S. Kaufman and Moss Hart. YOU CAN'T TAKE IT WITH YOU

1938:   Thornton Wilder. OUR TOWN

1939:   Robert E. Sherwood. ABE LINCOLN IN ILLINOIS

1940:   William Saroyan. THE TIME OF YOUR LIFE

1941:   Robert E. Sherwood. THERE SHALL BE NO NIGHT

1942:   No award

1943:   Thornton Wilder. THE SKIN OF OUR TEETH

1944:   No award

1945:   Mary Chase. HARVEY

1946:   Russel Crouse and Howard Lindsay. STATE OF THE UNION

1947:   No award

1948:   Tennessee Williams. A STREETCAR NAMED DESIRE

1949:   Arthur Miller. DEATH OF A SALESMAN

1950:   Richard Rodgers, Oscar Hammerstein, and Joshua Logan.
SOUTH PACIFIC

1951:   No award

1952:   Joseph Kramm. THE SHRIKE

1953:   William Inge. PICNIC

1954:   John Patrick. TEAHOUSE OF THE AUGUST MOON

1955:   Tennessee Williams. CAT ON A HOT TIN ROOF

1956:   Frances Goodrich and Albert Hackett. THE DIARY OF ANNE FRANK

1957:   Eugene O'Neill. LONG DAY'S JOURNEY INTO NIGHT

1958:   Ketti Frings. LOOK HOMEWARD, ANGEL

1959:   Archibald MacLeish. J. B.

1960:   George Abbott, Jerome Weidman, Sheldon Harnick, and Jerry Bock.
FIORELLO!

1961:   Tad Mosel. ALL THE WAY HOME

1962:   Frank Loesser and Abe Burrows. HOW TO SUCCEED IN BUSINESS
WITHOUT REALLY TRYING

1963:   No award

1964:   No award

1965:   Frank D. Gilroy. THE SUBJECT WAS ROSES

1966:   No award

1967:   Edward Albee. A DELICATE BALANCE

1968:   No award

1969:   Howard Sackler. THE GREAT WHITE HOPE

1970:   Charles Gordone. NO PLACE TO BE SOMEBODY

1971:   Paul Zindel. THE EFFECT OF GAMMA RAYS ON MAN-IN-THE-MOON
MARIGOLDS

1972:   No award

1973:   Jason Miller. THAT CHAMPIONSHIP SEASON

1974:   No award

1975:   Edward Albee. SEASCAPE

1976:   Michael Bennett, James Kirkwood, Nicholas Dante, Marvin Hamlisch, and
Edward Kleban. A CHORUS LINE

1977:   Michael Cristofer. THE SHADOW BOX

1978:   Donald Coburn. THE GIN GAME

1979:   Sam Shepard. BURIED CHILD

1980:   Lanford Wilson. TALLEY'S FOLLY

1981:   Beth Henley. CRIMES OF THE HEART

1982:   Charles Fuller. A SOLDIER'S PLAY

1983:   Marsha Norman. 'NIGHT, MOTHER

1984:   David Mamet. GLENGARRY GLEN ROSS

1985:   Stephen Sondheim and James Lapine. SUNDAY IN THE
PARK WITH GEORGE

1986:   No award

1987:   August Wilson. FENCES

1988:   Alfred Uhry. DRIVING MISS DAISY

1989:   Wendy Wasserstein. THE HEIDI CHRONICLES

1990:   August Wilson. THE PIANO LESSON

1991:   Neil Simon. LOST IN YONKERS

1992:   Robert Schenkkan. THE KENTUCKY CYCLE

1993:   Tony Kushner. ANGELS IN AMERICA: MILLENNIUM APPROACHES

1994: _____

1995: _____

1996: _____

1997: _____

1998: _____

1999: _____

2000: _____

Pulitzer Prize Winners for American Poetry

1922: Edwin Arlington Robinson. COLLECTED POEMS

1923: Edna St. Vincent Millay. THE BALLAD OF THE HARP-WEAVER; A FEW FIGS
FROM THISTLES; EIGHT SONNETS IN AMERICAN POETRY, 1922; and
A MISCELLANY

1924: Robert Frost: NEW HAMPSHIRE: A POEM WITH NOTES AND GRACE
NOTES

1925: Edwin Arlington Robinson. THE MAN WHO DIED TWICE

1926: Amy Lowell. WHAT'S O'CLOCK

1927: Leonora Speyer. FIDDLER'S FAREWELL

1928: Edwin Arlington Robinson. TRISTRAM

1929: Stephen Vincent Benét. JOHN BROWN'S BODY

1930: Conrad Aiken. SELECTED POEMS

1931: Robert Frost. COLLECTED POEMS

1932: George Dillon. THE FLOWERING STONE

1933: Archibald MacLeish. CONQUISTADOR

1934: Richard Hillyer. COLLECTED VERSE

1935: Audrey Wurdemann. BRIGHT AMBUSH

1936: Robert P. Tristram Coffin. STRANGE HOLINESS

1937: Robert Frost. A FURTHER RANGE

1938: Marya Zaturenska. COLD MORNING SKY

1939: John Gould Fletcher. SELECTED POEMS

1940: Mark Van Doren. COLLECTED POEMS

1941: Leonard Bacon. SUNDERLAND CAPTURE

1942: William Rose Benét. THE DUST WHICH IS GOD

1943: Robert Frost. A WITNESS TREE

1944: Stephen Vincent Benét. WESTERN STAR

1945: Karl Shapiro. V-LETTER AND OTHER POEMS

1946:   No award

1947:   Robert Lowell. LORD WEARY'S CASTLE

1948:   W. H. Auden. THE AGE OF ANXIETY

1949:   Peter Viereck. TERROR AND DECORUM

1950:   Gwendolyn Brooks. ANNIE ALLEN

1951:   Carl Sandburg. COMPLETE POEMS

1952:   Marianne Moore. COLLECTED POEMS

1953:   Archibald MacLeish. COLLECTED POEMS

1954:   Theodore Roethke. THE WAKING: POEMS, 1933–1953

1955:   Wallace Stevens. COLLECTED POEMS

1956:   Elizabeth Bishop. POEMS, NORTH AND SOUTH

1957:   Richard Wilbur. THINGS OF THIS WORLD

1958:   Robert Penn Warren. PROMISES: POEMS 1954–1956

1959:   Stanley Kunitz. SELECTED POEMS 1928–1958

1960:   W. D. Snodgrass. HEART'S NEEDLE

1961:   Phyllis McGinley. TIMES THREE: SELECTED VERSE FROM THREE DECADES

1962:   Alan Dugan. POEMS

1963:   William Carlos Williams. PICTURES FROM BRUEGHEL

1964:   Louis Simpson. AT THE END OF THE OPEN ROAD

1965:   John Berryman. 77 DREAM SONGS

1966:   Richard Eberhart. SELECTED POEMS 1930–1965

1967:   Anne Sexton. LIVE OR DIE

1968:   Anthony Hecht. THE HARD HOURS

1969:   George Oppen. OF BEING NUMEROUS

1970:   Richard Howard. UNTITLED SUBJECTS

1971:   William S. Merwin. THE CARRIER OF LADDERS

1972:   James Wright. COLLECTED POEMS

1973:   Maxine Winokur Kumin. UP COUNTRY

1974:   Robert Lowell. THE DOLPHIN

1975:   Gary Snyder. TURTLE ISLAND

1976:   John Ashbery. SELF-PORTRAIT IN A CONVEX MIRROR

1977:   James Merrill. THE DIVINE COMEDIES

1978:   Howard Nemerov. COLLECTED POEMS

1979:   Robert Penn Warren. NOW AND THEN: POEMS 1976–1978

1980:   Donald Justice. SELECTED POEMS

1981:   James Schuyler. THE MORNING OF THE POEM

1982:   Sylvia Plath. THE COLLECTED POEMS

1983:   Galway Kinnell. SELECTED POEMS

1984:   Mary Oliver. AMERICAN PRIMITIVE

1985:   Carolyn Kizer. YIN

1986:   Henry Taylor. THE FLYING CHANGE

1987:   Rita Dove. THOMAS AND BEULAH

1988:   William Meredith. PARTIAL ACCOUNTS: NEW AND SELECTED POEMS

1989:   Richard Wilbur. NEW AND COLLECTED POEMS

1990:   Charles Simic. THE WORLD DOESN'T END

1991:   Mona Van Duyn. NEAR CHANGES

1992:   James Tate. SELECTED POEMS

1993:   Louise Glück. THE WILD IRIS

1994: ——

1995: ——

1996: ——

1997: ——

1998: ——

1999: ——

2000: ——

HIGH SPOTS IN LITERATURE

Some collectors center their collecting around titles that have been selected by a notable writer or bibliographer who has chosen what he or
she thinks are the best books ever published in a particular genre. The

dates on the following lists are the year the particular book was first published.

Anthony Burgess's *Ninety-nine Novels*

Author Anthony Burgess lists his choices of the best ninety-nine novels published in English from 1939-1984. He opens his introduction with "1984 has arrived, but Orwell's glum prophecy has not been fulfilled. Some of us half-feared that, on the morning of January 1, we would wake with our seasonal hangovers to see Ingsoc posters on the walls, the helicopters of the Thought Police hovering, and our television sets looking at us."

1939:   Henry Green. PARTY GOING

1939:   Aldous Huxley. AFTER MANY A SUMMER

1939:   James Joyce. FINNEGANS WAKE

1939:   Flann O'Brian. AT SWIM-TWO-BIRDS

1940:   Graham Greene. THE POWER AND THE GLORY

1940:   Ernest Hemingway. FOR WHOM THE BELL TOLLS

1940–70:   C. P. Snow. STRANGERS AND BROTHERS

1941:   Rex Warner. THE AERODROME

1944:   Joyce Cary. THE HORSE'S MOUTH

1944:   Somerset Maugham. THE RAZOR'S EDGE

1945:   Evelyn Waugh. BRIDESHEAD REVISITED

1946:   Mervyn Peake. TITUS GROAN

1947:   Saul Bellow. THE VICTIM

1947:   Malcolm Lowry. UNDER THE VOLCANO

1948:   Graham Greene. THE HEART OF THE MATTER

1948:   Aldous Huxley. APE AND ESSENCE

1948:   Norman Mailer. THE NAKED AND THE DEAD

1948:   Nevil Shute. NO HIGHWAY

1949:   Elizabeth Bowen. THE HEAT OF THE DAY

1949:   George Orwell. NINETEEN EIGHTY-FOUR

1949:   William Sansom. THE BODY

1950:   William Cooper. SCENES FROM PROVINCIAL LIFE

1950:   Budd Schulberg. THE DISENCHANTED

1951:   Anthony Powell. A DANCE TO THE MUSIC OF TIME

1951:   J. D. Salinger. THE CATCHER IN THE RYE

1951–69: Henry Williamson. A CHRONICLE OF ANCIENT SUNLIGHT

1951:   Herman Wouk. THE CAINE MUTINY

1952:   Ralph Ellison. INVISIBLE MAN

1952:   Ernest Hemingway. THE OLD MAN AND THE SEA

1952:   Mary McCarthy. THE GROVES OF ACADEME

1952:   Flannery O'Connor. WISE BLOOD

1952–61:   Evelyn Waugh. SWORD OF HONOUR

1953:   Raymond Chandler. THE LONG GOODBYE

1954:   Kingsley Amis. LUCKY JIM

1957:   John Braine. ROOM AT THE TOP

1957–60:   Lawrence Durrell. THE ALEXANDRIA QUARTET

1957–60:   Colin MacInnes. THE LONDON NOVELS

1957:   Bernard Malamud. THE ASSISTANT

1958:   Iris Murdoch. THE BELL

1958:   Alan Sillitoe. SATURDAY NIGHT AND SUNDAY MORNING

1958:   T. H. White. THE ONCE AND FUTURE KING

1959:   William Faulkner. THE MANSION

1959:   Ian Fleming. GOLDFINGER

1960:   L. P. Hartley. FACIAL JUSTICE

1960–65:   Olivia Manning. THE BALKAN TRILOGY

1961:   Ivy Compton-Burnett. THE MIGHTY AND THEIR FALL

1961:   Joseph Heller. CATCH-22

1961:   Richard Hughes. THE FOX IN THE ATTIC

1961:   Patrick White. RIDERS IN THE CHARIOT

1961:   Angus Wilson. THE OLD MEN AT THE ZOO

1962:   James Baldwin. ANOTHER COUNTRY

1962:   Pamela Hansford Johnson. AN ERROR OF JUDGEMENT

1962:   Aldous Huxley. ISLAND

1962:   Doris Lessing. THE GOLDEN NOTEBOOK

1962:   Vladimir Nabokov. PALE FIRE

1963:   Muriel Spark. GIRLS OF SLENDER MEANS

1964:   William Golding. THE SPIRE

1964:   Wilson Harris. HEARTLAND

1964:   Christopher Isherwood. A SINGLE MAN

1964:   Vladimir Nabokov. THE DEFENCE

1964:   Angus Wilson. LATE CALL

1965:   John O'Hara. THE LOCKWOOD CONCERN

1965:   Muriel Spark. THE MANDELBAUM GATE

1966:   Chinua Achebe. A MAN OF THE PEOPLE

1966:   Kingsley Amis. THE ANTI-DEATH LEAGUE

1966:   John Barth. GILES GOAT-BOY

1966:   Nadine Gordimer. THE LATE BOURGEOIS WORLD

1966:   Walker Percy. THE LAST GENTLEMAN

1967:   R. K. Narayan. THE VENDOR OF SWEETS

1968:   J. B. Priestley. THE IMAGE MEN

1968:   Mordecai Richler. COCKSURE

1968:   Keith Roberts. PAVANE

1969:   John Fowles. THE FRENCH LIEUTENANT'S WOMAN

1969:   Philip Roth. PORTNOY'S COMPLAINT

1970:   Len Deighton. BOMBER

1973:   Michael Frayn. SWEET DREAMS

1973:   Thomas Pynchon. GRAVITY'S RAINBOW

1975:   Saul Bellow. HUMBOLDT'S GIFT

1975:   Malcolm Bradbury. THE HISTORY MAN

1976:   Brian Moore. THE DOCTOR'S WIFE

1976:   Robert Nye. FALSTAFF

1977:   Erica Jong. HOW TO SAVE YOUR OWN LIFE

1977:   James Plunkett. FAREWELL COMPANIONS

1977:   Paul Scott. STAYING ON

1978:   John Updike. THE COUP

1979:   J. G. Ballard. THE UNLIMITED DREAM COMPANY

1979:   Bernard Malamud. DUBIN'S LIVES

1979:   V. S. Naipaul. A BEND IN THE RIVER

1979:   William Styron. SOPHIE'S CHOICE

1980:   Brian Aldiss. LIFE IN THE WEST

1980:   Russell Hoban. RIDDLEY WALKER

1980:   David Lodge. HOW FAR CAN YOU GO?

1980:   John Kennedy Toole. A CONFEDERACY OF DUNCES

1981:   Alasdair Gray. LANARK

1981:   Paul Theroux. THE MOSQUITO COAST

1981:   Gore Vidal. CREATION

1982:   Robertson Davies. THE REBEL ANGELS

1983:   Norman Mailer. ANCIENT EVENINGS

Cyril Connolly's *The Modern Movement*

Cyril Connolly defined the Modern Movement as a revolt against the bourgeois in France, the Victorians in England, the puritanism and materialism of America and has chosen as his "Key" books those that reflected this spirit.

1881:   Henry James. THE PORTRAIT OF A LADY

1881:   Gustave Flaubert. BOUVARD ET PÉCUCHET

1883:   Villiers de L'Isle-Adam. CONTES CRUELS

1884:   Joris Karl Huysmans. À REBOURS

1887:   Charles Baudelaire. OEUVRES POSTHUMES

1886:   Arthur Rimbaud. LES ILLUMINATIONS

1887: Stéphane Mallarmé. LES POÉSIES

1885: Guy de Maupassant. BEL AMI

1887–96: Edmond and Jules de Goncourt. JOURNAL DE CONCOURT

1891: Joris Karl Huysmans. LÀ-BAS

1896: Alfred Jarry. UBU ROI

1899: Henry James. THE AWKWARD AGE

1902: André Gide. L'IMMORALISTE

1902: Joseph Conrad. YOUTH: A NARRATIVE, AND TWO OTHER STORIES

1907: Joseph Conrad. THE SECRET AGENT

1903: Henry James. THE AMBASSADORS

1906: George Moore. MEMOIRS OF MY DEAD LIFE

1907: J. M. Synge. THE PLAYBOY OF THE WESTERN WORLD

1907: E. M. Forster. THE LONGEST JOURNEY

1911: Norman Douglas. SIREN LAND

1913: D. H. Lawrence. SONS AND LOVERS

1913: Guillaume Apollinaire. ALCOOLS; POÈMES, 1898–1913

1913: Marcel Proust. DU CÔTÉ DE CHEZ SWANN

1914: William Butler Yeats. RESPONSIBILITIES

1914: Thomas Hardy. SATIRES OF CIRCUMSTANCE

1917: James Joyce. A PORTRAIT OF THE ARTIST AS A YOUNG MAN

1915: Ford Madox Ford. THE GOOD SOLDIER

1916: Ezra Pound. LUSTRA

1917: Norman Douglas. SOUTH WIND

1917: T. S. Eliot. PRUFROCK AND OTHER OBSERVATIONS

1917: Paul Valéry. LA JEUNE PARQUE

1918: Percy Wyndham Lewis. TARR

1918: Guillaume Apollinaire. CALLIGRAMMES

1918: Gerard Manley Hopkins. POEMS

1918: Arthur Waley. A HUNDRED AND SEVENTY CHINESE POEMS

1918: Lytton Strachey. EMINENT VICTORIANS

1920: Wilfred Owen. POEMS

1921: D. H. Lawrence. SEA AND SARDINIA

1921:   Aldous Huxley. CROME YELLOW

1922:   Katherine Mansfield. THE GARDEN PARTY AND OTHER STORIES

1922:   William Butler Yeats. LATER POEMS

1922:   James Joyce. ULYSSES

1923:   Raymond Radiguet. LE DIABLE AU CORPS

1923:   Ronald Firbank. THE FLOWER BENEATH THE FOOT

1923:   Wallace Stevens. HARMONIUM

1923:   e. e. Cummings. TULIPS AND CHIMNEYS

1924:   E. M. Forster. A PASSAGE TO INDIA

1925:   F. Scott Fitzgerald. THE GREAT GATSBY

1924:   Ernest Hemingway. IN OUR TIME

1925:   Ezra Pound. A DRAFT OF XVI CANTOS

1926:   Ernest Hemingway. THE SUN ALSO RISES

1926:   André Gide. SI LE GRAIN NE MEURT

1926:   William Somerset Maugham. THE CASUARINA TREE

1927:   Virginia Woolf. TO THE LIGHTHOUSE

1928:   André Breton. NADJA

1928:   William Butler Yeats. THE TOWER

1928:   D. H. Lawrence. LADY CHATTERLEY'S LOVER

1928:   Evelyn Waugh. DECLINE AND FALL

1929:   Henry Green. LIVING

1929:   Ernest Hemingway. A FAREWELL TO ARMS

1929:   Robert Graves. GOODBYE TO ALL THAT

1929:   Jean Cocteau. LES ENFANTS TERRIBLES

1929:   Ivy Compton-Burnett. BROTHERS AND SISTERS

1930:   Hart Crane. THE BRIDGE

1930:   T. S. Eliot. ASH WEDNESDAY

1928:   Edith Sitwell. COLLECTED POEMS

1931:   Antoine de Saint-Éxupery. VOL DE NUIT

1931:   William Faulkner. SANCTUARY

1931:   Virginia Woolf. THE WAVES

1931:   Edmund Wilson. AXEL'S CASTLE . . .

1932:   T. S. Eliot. SELECTED ESSAYS

1932:   W. H. Auden. THE ORATORS

1932:   Louis-Ferdinand Céline. VOYAGE AU BOUT DE LA NUIT

1932:   Aldous Huxley. BRAVE NEW WORLD

1933:   Nathanael West. MISS LONELYHEARTS

1933:   André Malraux. LA CONDITION HUMAINE

1934:   Dylan Thomas. EIGHTEEN POEMS

1934:   F. Scott Fitzgerald. TENDER IS THE NIGHT

1934:   Henry James. THE ART OF THE NOVEL

1935:   Marianne Moore. SELECTED POEMS

1936–39:   Henry de Montherlant. LES JEUNES FILLES

1936:   Henri Michaux. VOYAGE EN GRANDE GARABAGNE

1938:   Jean-Paul Sartre. LA NAUSÉE

1939:   Louis MacNeice. AUTUMN JOURNAL

1939:   Christopher Isherwood. GOODBYE TO BERLIN

1939:   James Joyce. FINNEGANS WAKE

1940:   Graham Greene. THE POWER AND THE GLORY

1940:   Arthur Koestler. DARKNESS AT NOON

1940:   W. H. Auden. ANOTHER TIME

1942:   Stephen Spender. RUINS AND VISIONS

1942:   Albert Camus. L'ÉTRANGER

1944:   T. S. Eliot. FOUR QUARTETS

1945:   George Orwell. ANIMAL FARM

1946:   Dylan Thomas. DEATHS AND ENTRANCES

1946–51:   William Carlos Williams. PATERSON 1, 2, 3, 4

1947:   Albert Camus. LA PESTE

1948:   John Betjeman. SELECTED POEMS

1948:   Ezra Pound. THE PISAN CANTOS

1949:   George Orwell. NINETEEN EIGHTY-FOUR

Haycraft-Queen Cornerstones, 1748–1948

Howard Haycraft was an historian of the detective story and chose the books he believed formed cornerstones in detective fiction. Mystery writer Ellery Queen then added those titles that he believed should also be included. We have put the year in **bold** type if the title was placed on the list originally by Mr. Haycraft.

1748:   Voltaire. ZADIG

1828–29:   François Eugène Vidocq. MÉMOIRES DE VIDOCQ

1845:   Edgar Allan Poe. TALES

1852–53:   Charles Dickens. BLEAK HOUSE

1856:   "Waters" (William Russell). RECOLLECTIONS OF A DETECTIVE POLICE-OFFICER

1860:   Wilkie Collins. THE WOMAN IN WHITE

1862:   Victor Hugo. LES MISÉRABLES

1866:   Feodor Dostoevsky. CRIME AND PUNISHMENT

1866:   Émile Gaboriau. L'AFFAIRE LEROUGE

1867:   Émile Gaboriau. LE DOSSIER NO. 113

1868:   Émile Gaboriau. LE CRIME D'ORCIVAL

1868:   Wilkie Collins. THE MOONSTONE

1869:   Émile Gaboriau. MONSIEUR LECOQ

1870:   Charles Dickens. THE MYSTERY OF EDWIN DROOD

1872:   (Harlan Page Halsey). OLD SLEUTH, THE DETECTIVE

1874:   Allan Pinkerton. THE EXPRESSMAN AND THE DETECTIVE

1878:   Anna Katharine Green. THE LEAVENWORTH CASE

1882:   Robert Louis Stevenson. NEW ARABIAN NIGHTS

1886:   Robert Louis Stevenson. STRANGE CASE OF DR JEKYLL AND MR HYDE

1887:   Fergus W. Hume. THE MYSTERY OF A HANSOM CAB

1887:   A. Conan Doyle. A STUDY IN SCARLET

1890:   A. Conan Doyle. THE SIGN OF FOUR

1892:   A. Conan Doyle. THE ADVENTURES OF SHERLOCK HOLMES

1892:   Israel Zangwill. THE BIG BOW MYSTERY

1894:   Mark Twain. THE TRAGEDY OF PUDD'NHEAD WILSON . . .

1894:   Arthur Morrison. MARTIN HEWITT, INVESTIGATOR

1894:   A. Conan Doyle. THE MEMOIRS OF SHERLOCK HOLMES

1895:   M. P. Shiel. PRINCE ZALESKI

1897:   Bram Stoker. DRACULA

1899:   E. W. Hornung. THE AMATEUR CRACKSMAN

1902:   A. Conan Doyle. THE HOUND OF THE BASKERVILLES

1903:   (Erskine Childers). THE RIDDLE OF THE SANDS

1905:   A. Conan Doyle. THE RETURN OF SHERLOCK HOLMES

1906:   Godfrey R. Benson. TRACKS IN THE SNOW

1906:   Robert Barr. THE TRIUMPHS OF EUGÈNE VALMONT

1905:   Jacques Futrelle. THE THINKING MACHINE

1907:   Maurice Leblanc. ARSÈNE LUPIN, GENTLEMAN-CAMBRIOLEUR

1907:   Gaston Leroux. LE MYSTÈRE DE LA CHAMBRE JAUNE

1907:   R. Austin Freeman. THE RED THUMB MARK

1908:   Mary Roberts Rinehart. THE CIRCULAR STAIRCASE

1908:   O. Henry. THE GENTLE GRAFTER

1908:   G. K. Chesterton. THE MAN WHO WAS THURSDAY

1908-9:   Gaston Leroux. LE PARFUM DE LA DAME EN NOIR

1909:   R. Austin Freeman. JOHN THORNDYKE'S CASES

1909:   Cleveland Moffett: THROUGH THE WALL

1909:   Baroness Orczy. THE OLD MAN IN THE CORNER

1909:   Carolyn Wells. THE CLUE

1910:   Maurice Leblanc. "813"

1910:   A. E. W. Mason. AT THE VILLA ROSE

1910:   William MacHarg and Edwin Balmer. THE ACHIEVEMENTS OF LUTHER
TRANT

1911:   R. Austin Freeman. THE EYE OF OSIRIS

1911:   G. K. Chesterton. THE INNOCENCE OF FATHER BROWN

1912:   R. Austin Freeman. THE SINGING BONE

1912:   Arthur B. Reeve. THE SILENT BULLET

1913:   Mrs. Belloc Lowndes. THE LODGER

1913:   Sax Rohmer. THE MYSTERY OF DR FU-MANCHU

1913:   E. C. Bentley. TRENT'S LAST CASE

1914:   Ernest Bramah. MAX CARRADOS

1914:   Louis Joseph Vance. THE LONE WOLF

1915:   A. Conan Doyle. THE VALLEY OF FEAR

1915:   John Buchan. THE THIRTY-NINE STEPS

1916:   Thomas Burke. LIMEHOUSE NIGHTS

1917:   A. Conan Doyle. HIS LAST BOW

1918:   Melville Davisson Post. UNCLE ABNER

1918:   J. S. Fletcher. THE MIDDLE TEMPLE MURDER

1920:   Agatha Christie. THE MYSTERIOUS AFFAIR AT STYLES

1920:   Freeman Wills Crofts. THE CASK

1920:   H. C. Bailey. CALL MR FORTUNE

1920:   "Sapper" (Cyril McNeile). BULL-DOG DRUMMOND

1920:   Arthur Train. TUTT AND MR. TUTT

1921:   Eden Phillpotts. THE GREY ROOM

1922:   Maurice Leblanc. LES HUITS COUPS DE L'HORLOGE

1922:   A. A. Milne. THE RED HOUSE MYSTERY

1923:   G. D. H. Cole. THE BROOKLYN MURDERS

1923:   Dorothy Sayers. WHOSE BODY?

1924:   A. E. W. Mason. THE HOUSE OF THE ARROW

1924:   Freeman Wills Crofts. INSPECTOR FRENCH'S GREATEST CASE

1924:   Philip MacDonald. THE RASP

1925:   Edgar Wallace. THE MIND OF MR. J. G. REEDER

1925:   John Rhode. THE PADDINGTON MYSTERY

1925:   Earl Derr Biggers. THE HOUSE WITHOUT A KEY

1925:   Theodore Dreiser. AN AMERICAN TRAGEDY

1925:   Liam O'Flaherty. THE INFORMER

1925:   Ronald A. Knox. THE VIADUCT MURDER

1926:   Agatha Christie. THE MURDER OF ROGER ACKROYD

1926: S. S. Van Dine. THE BENSON MURDER CASE

(Or alternate: THE CANARY MURDER CASE. 1927)

1926: C. S. Forester. PAYMENT DEFERRED

1927: A. Conan Doyle. THE CASE-BOOK OF SHERLOCK HOLMES

1927: S. S. Van Dine. (See 1926)

1927: Frances Noyes Hart. THE BELLAMY TRIAL

1928: John Rhode. THE MURDERS IN PRAED STREET

1928: W. Somerset Maugham. ASHENDEN

1929: Anthony Berkeley. THE POISONED CHOCOLATES CASE

1929: Ellery Queen. THE ROMAN HAT MYSTERY

1929: Rufus King. MURDER BY THE CLOCK

1929: W. R. Burnett. LITTLE CAESAR

1929: T. S. Stribling. CLUES OF THE CARIBBEES

1929: Harvey J. O'Higgins. DETECTIVE DUFF UNRAVELS IT

1929: Migeon G. Eberhart. THE PATIENT IN ROOM 18

1930: Dorothy Sayers and Robert Eustace. THE DOCUMENTS IN THE CASE

1930: Frederick Irving Anders. BOOK OF MURDER

1930: Dashiell Hammett. THE MALTESE FALCON

1930: David Frome. THE HAMMERSMITH MURDERS

1931: Dashiell Hammett. THE GLASS KEY

1931: Stuart Palmer. THE PENGUIN POOL MURDER

1931: Francis Beeding. DEATH WALKS IN EASTREPPS

1931: Glen Trevor (James Hilton). MURDER AT SCHOOL

1931: Damon Runyon. GUYS AND DOLLS

1931: Phoebe Atwood Taylor. THE CAPE COD MYSTERY

1932: H. C. Bailey. THE RED CASTLE

1932: Francis Iles. BEFORE THE FACT

1932: Barnaby Ross. THE TRAGEDY OF X

1932: Barnaby Ross. THE TRAGEDY OF Y

1932: R. A. J. Walling. THE FATAL FIVE MINUTES

1932: Clemence Dane and Helen Sipson. RE-ENTER SIR JOHN

1933:   Erle Stanley Gardner. THE CASE OF THE VELVET CLAWS

1933:   Erle Stanley Gardner. THE CASE OF THE SULKY GIRL

1934:   Dorothy Sayers. THE NINE TAILORS

1934:   Margery Allingham. DEATH OF A GHOST

1934:   James M. Cain. THE POSTMAN ALWAYS RINGS TWICE

1934:   Rex Stout. FER-DE-LANCE

1935:   Rex Stout. THE LEAGUE OF FRIGHTENED MEN

1935:   Richard Hull. THE MURDER OF MY AUNT

1935:   John P. Marquand. NO HERO

1937:   Anthony Berkeley. TRIAL AND ERROR

1938:   Philip MacDonald. THE NURSEMAID WHO DISAPPEARED

1938:   John Dickson Carr. THE CROOKED HINGE

1938:   John Dickson Carr. THE JUDAS WINDOW

1938:   Nicholas Blake. THE BEAST MUST DIE

1938:   Michael Innes. LAMENT FOR A MAKER

1938:   Clayton Rawson. DEATH FROM A TOP HAT

1938:   Graham Greene. BRIGHTON ROCK

1938:   Daphne Du Maurier. REBECCA

1938:   Mabel Seeley. THE LISTENING HOUSE

1939:   Ngaio Marsh. OVERTURE TO DEATH

1939:   Eric Ambler. A COFFIN FOR DIMITRIOS

1939:   Raymond Chandler. THE BIG SLEEP

1939:   Georges Simenon. THE PATIENCE OF MAIGRET

1940:   Raymond Chandler. FAREWELL, MY LOVELY

1940:   Raymond Postgate. VERDICT OF TWELVE

1940:   Frances and Richard Lockridge. THE NORTHS MEET MURDER

1940:   Dorothy B. Hughes. THE SO BLUE MARBLE

(Or alternate: IN A LONELY PLACE. 1947)

1940:   Cornell Woolrich. THE BRIDE WORE BLACK

1940:   Manning Coles. DRINK TO YESTERDAY

1941:   Manning Coles. A TOAST TO TOMORROW

1941:   H. F. Heard. A TASTE FOR HONEY

1941:   Craig Rice. TRIAL BY FURY

(Or alternate: HOME SWEET HOMICIDE. 1944)

1942:   Ellery Queen. CALAMITY TOWN

1942:   William Irish. PHANTOM LADY

1942:   H. H. Holmes. ROCKET TO THE MORGUE

1942:   James Gould Cozzens. THE JUST AND THE UNJUST

1944:   Dashiell Hammett. THE ADVENTURES OF SAM SPADE

1944:   Hilda Lawrence. BLOOD UPON THE SNOW

1944:   Craig Rice. (Alternate. See 1941)

1946:   Helen Eustis. THE HORIZONTAL MAN

1946:   Charlotte Armstrong. THE UNSUSPECTED

1946:   Lillian de la Torre. DR. SAM JOHNSON, DETECTOR

1946:   Edmund Crispin. THE MOVING TOYSHOP

(Or alternate: LOVE LIES BLEEDING. 1948)

1947:   Dorothy B. Hughes. (See 1940)

1947:   Edgar Lustgarten. ONE MORE UNFORTUNATE

1947:   Roy Vickers. THE DEPARTMENT OF DEAD ENDS

1948:   Edmund Crispin. (Alternate. See 1946)

1948:   Josephine Tey. THE FRANCHISE AFFAIR

1948:   William Faulkner. INTRUDER IN THE DUST

Merle Johnson's *High Spots* *of American Literature*

In 1929 Merle Johnson defined "high spots" as being "those literary land-marks that rise above mediocrity."

1819:   Washington Irving. THE SKETCH BOOK OF GEOFFREY CRAYON, GENT.
(Seven volumes)

1821:   William Cullen Bryant. POEMS

1826:   James Fenimore Cooper. THE LAST OF THE MOHICANS

1837:   Nathaniel Hawthorne. TWICE-TOLD TALES

1840:   Richard Henry Dana, Jr. TWO YEARS BEFORE THE MAST

1841:   Ralph Waldo Emerson. ESSAYS

1844:   Clement C. Moore. POEMS

1845:   Edgar A. Poe. TALES

1845:   Edgar A. Poe. THE RAVEN AND OTHER POEMS

1847:   Henry Wadsworth Longfellow. EVANGELINE: A TALE OF ACADIE

1848:   James Russell Lowell. THE BIGLOW PAPERS

1849:   Henry D. Thoreau. A WEEK ON THE CONCORD
AND MERRIMACK RIVERS

1850:   Nathaniel Hawthorne. THE SCARLET LETTER

1850:   Ik Marvel. REVERIES OF A BACHELOR: OR A BOOK OF THE HEART

1851:   Herman Melville. MOBY-DICK; OR, THE WHALE

1852:   Harriet Beecher Stowe. UNCLE TOM'S CABIN

1854:   Henry D. Thoreau. WALDEN; OR, LIFE IN THE WOODS

1855:   Henry Wadsworth Longfellow. THE SONG OF HIAWATHA

1855:   Walt Whitman. LEAVES OF GRASS

1856:   George William Curtis. PRUE AND I

1857:   William Allen Butler. NOTHING TO WEAR: AN EPISODE OF CITY LIFE

1858:   Oliver Wendell Holmes. THE AUTOCRAT OF THE BREAKFAST-TABLE

1861:   Oliver Wendell Holmes. ELSIE VENNER: A ROMANCE OF DESTINY

1865:   Edward Everett Hale. THE MAN WITHOUT A COUNTRY

1866:   John Greenleaf Whittier. SNOW-BOUND

1868–69:   Louisa May Alcott. LITTLE WOMEN (two volumes)

1868:   Charles Godfrey Leland. HANS BREITMANN'S PARTY

1870:   Thomas Bailey Aldrich. THE STORY OF A BAD BOY

1870:   Bret Harte. THE LUCK OF ROARING CAMP

1871:   Louisa May Alcott. LITTLE MEN

1871:   John Burroughs. WAKE-ROBIN

1871:   Edward Eggleston. THE HOOSIER SCHOOL-MASTER

1871: Bret Harte. POEMS

1871: John Hay. JIM BLUDSO OF THE PRAIRIE BELL, AND LITTLE BREECHES

1871: Joaquin Miller. SONGS OF THE SIERRAS

1873: Will Carleton. FARM BALLADS

1873: Lew Wallace. THE FAIR GOD; OR, THE LAST OF THE 'TZINS

1876: Mark Twain. THE ADVENTURES OF TOM SAWYER

1879: George W. Cable. OLD CREOLE DAYS

1879: Henry James. DAISY MILLER

1880: Lew Wallace. BEN-HUR: A TALE OF THE CHRIST

1881: Joel Chandler Harris. UNCLE REMUS, HIS SONGS AND HIS SAYINGS

1883: Edward Eggleston. THE HOOSIER SCHOOL-BOY

1883: James Whitcomb Riley. THE OLD SWIMMIN'-HOLE

1884: Helen Hunt Jackson. RAMONA. A STORY

1884: Frank R. Stockton. THE LADY, OR THE TIGER?

1885: Mark Twain. ADVENTURES OF HUCKLEBERRY FINN

1885: William Dean Howells. THE RISE OF SILAS LAPHAM

1886: Frances Hodgson Burnett. LITTLE LORD FAUNTLEROY

1886: Frank R. Stockton. THE CASTING AWAY OF MRS. LECKS
AND MRS. ALESHINE

1887: Lafcadio Hearn. SOME CHINESE GHOSTS

1887: Thomas Nelson Page. IN OLE VIRGINIA

1888: Edward Bellamy. LOOKING BACKWARD 2000-1887

1888: Frank R. Stockton. THE DUSANTES

1889: Eugene Field. A LITTLE BOOK OF WESTERN VERSE

1889: Eugene Field. A LITTLE BOOK OF PROFITABLE TALES

1890: Harold Frederic. IN THE VALLEY

1890: Lafcadio Hearn. TWO YEARS IN THE FRENCH WEST INDIES

1890: William Dean Howells. A BOY'S TOWN

1890: Thomas A. Janvier. THE AZTEC TREASURE-HOUSE

1891: James Lane Allen. FLUTE AND VIOLIN AND OTHER KENTUCKY TALES

1891: Ambrose Bierce. TALES OF SOLDIERS AND CIVILIANS

1891:   Henry Cuyler Bunner. "SHORT SIXES"

1891:   Hamlin Garland. MAIN-TRAVELLED ROADS

1891:   F. Hopkinson Smith. COLONEL CARTER OF CARTERSVILLE

1892:   Howard Pyle. MEN OF IRON

1893:   Edwin Markham. THE MAN WITH THE HOE

1894:   Paul Leicester Ford. THE HONORABLE PETER STIRLING AND WHAT PEOPLE THOUGHT OF HIM

1894:   Mark Twain. THE TRAGEDY OF PUDD'NHEAD WILSON . . .

1895:   James Lane Allen. A KENTUCKY CARDINAL

1895:   Gelett Burgess. THE PURPLE COW

1895:   Stephen Crane. THE RED BADGE OF COURAGE

1896:   James Lane Allen. AFTERMATH

1896:   Mary Mapes Dodge. HANS BRINKER; OR, THE SILVER SKATES

1896:   Harold Frederic. THE DAMNATION OF THERON WARE

1897:   Alfred Henry Lewis. WOLFVILLE

1897:   S. Weir Mitchell, M.D. HUGH WYNNE, FREE QUAKER . . .

1897:   Henry Van Dyke. THE FIRST CHRISTMAS-TREE

1898:   Finley Peter Dunn. MR. DOOLEY IN PEACE AND WAR

1898:   Ernest Seton Thompson. WILD ANIMALS I HAVE KNOWN

1898:   Edward Noyes Westcott. DAVID HARUM: A STORY OF AMERICAN LIFE

1899:   Stephen Crane. WAR IS KIND

1899:   Margaret Deland. OLD CHESTER TALES

1899:   Elbert Hubbard. A MESSAGE TO GARCIA

1899:   Frank Norris. MCTEAGUE: A STORY OF SAN FRANCISCO

1899:   Morgan Robertson. WHERE ANGELS FEAR TO TREAD

1899:   Booth Tarkington. THE GENTLEMAN FROM INDIANA

1899:   William Allen White. THE COURT OF BOYVILLE

1900:   George Ade. FABLES IN SLANG

1900:   Theodore Dreiser. SISTER CARRIE

1900:   Mary Johnston. TO HAVE AND TO HOLD

1900:   Booth Tarkington. MONSIEUR BEAUCAIRE

1901:   Henry Van Dyke. THE RULING PASSION

1902:   Owen Wister. THE VIRGINIAN

1903:   Jack London. THE CALL OF THE WILD

1903:   Frank Norris. THE EPIC OF THE WHEAT / THE PIT / A STORY OF CHICAGO

1904:   Henry James. THE GOLDEN BOWL

1904:   Charles G. D. Roberts. THE WATCHERS OF THE TRAILS

1906:   Gelett Burgess. ARE YOU A BROMIDE?

1906:   Ellis Parker Butler. PIGS IS PIGS

1906:   O. Henry. THE FOUR MILLION

1906:   Frederic Remington. THE WAY OF AN INDIAN

1906:   Upton Sinclair. THE JUNGLE

1906:   William Allen White. IN OUR TOWN

1907:   Jack London. BEFORE ADAM

1908:   John Fox, Jr. THE TRAIL OF THE LONESOME PINE

1911:   Theodore Dreiser. JENNIE GERHARDT

1911:   Edith Wharton. ETHAN FROME

1913:   Jack London. JOHN BARLEYCORN

1913:   Stewart Edward White. GOLD

1913:   Harry Leon Wilson. BUNKER BEAN

1914:   Emily Dickinson. THE SINGLE HOUND POEMS FOR A LIFETIME

1914:   Robert Frost. NORTH OF BOSTON

1914:   Joyce Kilmer. TREES AND OTHER POEMS

1914:   Booth Tarkington. PENROD

1915:   Edgar Lee Masters. SPOON RIVER ANTHOLOGY

1915:   Stewart Edward White. THE GRAY DAWN

1915:   Woodrow Wilson. WHEN A MAN COMES TO HIMSELF

1916:   Amy Lowell. MEN, WOMEN AND GHOSTS

1916:   William McFee. CASUALS OF THE SEA: THE VOYAGE OF A SOUL

1916:   Alan Seeger. POEMS

1916: Booth Tarkington. SEVENTEEN

1917: Joseph Hergesheimer. THE THREE BLACK PENNYS

1917: Edna St. Vincent Millay. RENASCENCE AND OTHER POEMS

1917: David Graham Phillips. SUSAN LENOX: HER FALL AND RISE

1918: William Beebe. JUNGLE PEACE

1918: Willa Cather. MY ÁNTONIA

1919: Sherwood Anderson. WINESBURG, OHIO

1919: James Branch Cabell. JURGEN: A COMEDY OF JUSTICE

1920: Sinclair Lewis. MAIN STREET

1920: Carl Sandburg. SMOKE AND STEEL

1920: Stewart Edward White. THE ROSE DAWN

1921: Sherwood Anderson. THE TRIUMPH OF THE EGG

1921: John Dos Passos. THREE SOLDIERS

1921: Hendrik Van Loon. THE STORY OF MANKIND

1922: Hamlin Garland. A PIONEER MOTHER

1922: Emerson Hough. THE COVERED WAGON

1922: Sinclair Lewis. BABBITT

1923: Joseph Hergesheimer. THE PRESBYTERIAN CHILD

1924: Sherwood Anderson. A STORY TELLER'S STORY

1925: Theodore Dreiser. AN AMERICAN TRAGEDY

Jacob Blanck's *Peter Parley to Penrod*

Noted bibliographer Jacob Blanck's selection of the best-loved American juvenile books. He asks in the preface of *Peter Parley to Penrod* "since bookcollecting is a sentimental manifestion what truer type of bookcollecting than the gathering together of the books read as a child and affectionately recalled? Certainly there is no period of man's reading life more often remembered than the first wondering years and the discovery of the strange new worlds that are the printed page."

1827: Peter Parley. THE TALES OF PETER PARLEY

1834?: (Jacob Abbott). ROLLO: LEARNING TO TALK

1851:   Elizabeth Wetherell. THE WIDE, WIDE WORLD

1852:   Nathaniel Hawthorne. A WONDER-BOOK FOR GIRLS AND BOYS

1852:   Elizabeth Wetherwell. QUEECHY

1852:   F. R. Goulding. YOUNG MAROONERS

1853:   Nathaniel Hawthorne. TANGLEWOOD TALES, FOR GIRLS AND BOYS

1854:   (Maria Susanna Cummins). THE LAMPLIGHTER

1855:   Oliver Optic. THE BOAT CLUB

1855:   Thomas Bulfinch. THE AGE OF FABLE

1859:   Thomas Bulfinch. THE AGE OF CHIVALRY

1860:   Edward S. Ellis. SETH JONES

1861:   (Jane Andrews). THE SEVEN LITTLE SISTERS WHO LIVE ON THE ROUND
BALL THAT FLOATS IN THE AIR

1863:   (Adeline D. T. Whitney). FAITH GARTNEY'S GIRLHOOD

1864:   J. T. Trowbridge. CUDJO'S CAVE

1864:   Sophie Mae. LITTLE PRUDY

1865:   Pansy. HELEN LESTER

1865:   Sophie May. DOTTY DIMPLE

1865:   (Edward Everett Hale). THE MAN WITHOUT A COUNTRY

1866:   M. E. Dodge. HANS BRINKER

1867:   Martha Farquharson. ELSIE DINSMORE

1867:   Harry Castlemon. FRANK ON THE LOWER MISSISSIPPI

1868:   Paul Du Chaillu. STORIES OF THE GORILLA COUNTRY

1868:   Horatio Alger, Jr. RAGGED DICK

1868:   Louisa M. Alcott. LITTLE WOMEN

1869:   Rev. Elijah Kellogg. LION BEN OF ELM ISLAND

1870:   Frank R. Stockton. TING A LING

1870:   Louisa M. Alcott. AN OLD FASHIONED GIRL

1870:   Thomas Bailey Aldrich. THE STORY OF A BAD BOY

1871:   Louisa M. Alcott. LITTLE MEN

1871:   Horatio Alger, Jr. TATTERED TOM

1871:   J. T. Trowbridge. JACK HAZARD AND HIS FORTUNES

1873:   Susan Collidge. WHAT KATY DID

1874:   C. A. Stephens. THE YOUNG MOOSE HUNTERS

1875:   (Horace E. Scudder). DOINGS OF THE BODLEY FAMILY IN TOWN
AND COUNTRY

1876:   Mark Twain. THE ADVENTURES OF TOM SAWYER

1876:   (John Habberton). HELEN'S BABIES

1877:   Charles Carleton Coffin. THE BOYS OF '76

1877:   Noah Brooks. THE BOY EMIGRANTS

1880:   Hezekiah Butterworth. ZIGZAG JOURNEYS IN EUROPE

1880:   Lucretia P. Hale. THE PETERKIN PAPERS

1880:   Thomas W. Knox. THE BOY TRAVELLERS IN THE FAR EAST

1880:   Margaret Sidney. FIVE LITTLE PEPPERS AND HOW THEY GREW

1881:   Joel Chandler Harris. UNCLE REMUS

1881:   Rev. E. E. Hale and Miss Susan Hale. A FAMILY FLIGHT THROUGH
FRANCE, GERMANY, NORWAY AND SWITZERLAND

1881:   James Otis. TOBY TYLER

1881:   Rossiter Johnson. PHAETON ROGERS

1881:   Frank R. Stockton. THE FLOATING PRINCE

1882:   D. C. Beard. THE AMERICAN BOYS HANDY BOOK

1882:   James Baldwin. THE STORY OF SIEGFRIED

1882:   Louise-Clarke Pyrnelle. DIDDIE, DUMPS, AND TOT

1882:   Mark Twain. THE PRINCE AND THE PAUPER

1883:   Geo. W. Peck. PECK'S BAD BOY AND HIS PA

1883:   Lizzie W. Champney. THREE VASSAR GIRLS ABROAD

1883:   Edward Eggleston. THE HOOSIER SCHOOL-BOY

1883:   Howard Pyle. THE MERRY ADVENTURES OF ROBIN HOOD OF GREAT
RENOWN, IN NOTTINGHAMSHIRE

1885:   Mark Twain. ADVENTURES OF HUCKLEBERRY FINN

1886:   Charles E. Carryl. DAVY AND THE GOBLIN

1886:   Jane Andrews. TEN BOYS WHO LIVED ON THE ROAD FROM LONG AGO
TO NOW

1886:   Frances Hodgson Burnett. LITTLE LORD FAUNTLEROY

1886: Amelia E. Barr. THE BOW OF ORANGE RIBBON

1887: Kirk Munroe. THE FLAMINGO FEATHER

1886: Palmer Cox. THE BROWNIES

1887: James Baldwin. A STORY OF THE GOLDEN AGE

1887: Kate Douglas Wiggin. THE BIRDS' CHRISTMAS CAROL

1888: Robert Grant. JACK HALL

1888: Frances Hodgson Burnett. EDITHA'S BURGLAR

1888: Thomas Nelson Page. TWO LITTLE CONFEDERATES

1888: Frances Courtenay Baylor. JUAN AND JUANITA

1888: Howard Pyle. OTTO OF THE SILVER HAND

1890: W. D. Howells. A BOY'S TOWN

1890: Sarah Orne Jewett. BETTY LEICESTER

1891: Laura E. Richards. CAPTAIN JANUARY

1891: William O. Stoddard. LITTLE SMOKE

1892: Charles E. Carryl. THE ADMIRAL'S CARAVAN

1893: James Otis. JENNY WREN'S BOARDING-HOUSE

1894: Captain Charles King. CADET DAYS

1894: Everett T. Tomlinson. SEARCH FOR ANDREW FIELD

1894: Marshall Saunders. BEAUTIFUL JOE

1894: Kirk Munroe. THE FUR-SEAL'S TOOTH

1896: Annie Fellows-Johnson. THE LITTLE COLONEL

1897: John Bennett. MASTER SKYLARK

1898: Albert Bigelow Paine. THE HOLLOW TREE

1898: Ernest Seton Thompson. WILD ANIMALS I HAVE KNOWN

1899: Ralph Henry Barbour. THE HALF-BACK

1899: William Allen White. THE COURT OF BOYVILLE

1900: Gelett Burgess. GOOPS AND HOW TO BE THEM

1900: L. Frank Baum. THE WONDERFUL WIZARD OF OZ

1901: Alice Caldwell Hegan. MRS. WIGGS OF THE CABBAGE PATCH

1901: Josephine Diebitsch Peary. THE SNOW BABY

1902: John Bennett. BARNABY LEE

1902: W. D. Howells. THE FLIGHT OF PONY BAKER

1902: Henry A. Shute. THE REAL DIARY OF A REAL BOY

1903: Jack London. THE CALL OF THE WILD

1903: Kate Douglas Wiggin. REBECCA OF SUNNYBROOK FARM

1906: Jack London. WHITE FANG

1908: L. M. Montgomery. ANNE OF GREEN GABLES

1908: Peter Newell. THE HOLE BOOK

1908: Emerson Hough. THE YOUNG ALASKANS

1909: Frances Boyd Calhoun. MISS MINERVA AND WILLIAM GREEN HILL

1910: Owen Johnson. THE VARMINT

1911: Owen Johnson. THE TENNESSEE SHAD

1912: Jean Webster. DADDY-LONG-LEGS

1913: Eleanor H. Porter. POLLYANNA

1914: Booth Tarkington. PENROD

1914: Edgar Rice Burroughs. TARZAN OF THE APES

1916: Booth Tarkington. PENROD AND SAM

1917: Dorothy Canfield. UNDERSTOOD BETSY

1920: Hugh Lofting. THE STORY OF DOCTOR DOLITTLE

1922: Carl Sandburg. ROOTABAGA STORIES

1922: Stewart Edward White. DANIEL BOONE, WILDERNESS SCOUT

1923: Charles Boardman Hawes. THE DARK FRIGATE

1926: Will James. SMOKY THE COWHORSE

Queen's Quorum

Mystery writer Ellery Queen (a collaboration of Frederic Dannay and Manfred B. Lee) won five annual Edgars, including the Grand Master award in 1960. Queen originally selected 106 most important books published in the Detective-Crime field in 1948 and later added 19 additional titles.

1845: Edgar Allan Poe. TALES

1856: "Waters." RECOLLECTIONS OF A DETECTIVE POLICE-OFFICER

1859: Wilkie Collins. THE QUEEN OF HEARTS

1860: Charles Dickens. HUNTED DOWN

1861: "Anonyma's." THE EXPERIENCES OF A LADY DETECTIVE

1862: Thomas Bailey. OUT OF HIS HEAD

1867: Mark Twain. THE CELEBRATED JUMPING FROG OF
CALAVERAS COUNTY

1876: Emile Gaboriau. THE LITTLE OLD MAN OF BATIGNOLLES

1878: James M'Govan. BROUGHT TO BAY

1881: "A New York Detective." DETECTIVE SKETCHES

1882: Robert Louis Stevenson. NEW ARABIAN NIGHTS

1884: Frank R. Stockton. THE LADY, OR THE TIGER?

1888: Eden Phillpotts. MY ADVENTURE IN FLYING SCOTSMAN

1888: Dick Donovan. THE MAN-HUNTER

1892: Israel Zangwill. THE BIG BOW MYSTERY

1892: A. Conan Doyle. THE ADVENTURES OF SHERLOCK HOLMES

1894: L. T. Meade and Dr. Clifford Halifax. STORIES FROM THE
DIARY OF A DOCTOR

1894: Arthur Morrison. MARTIN HEWITT, INVESTIGATOR

1895: M. P. Shiel. PRINCE ZALESKI

1896: Melville Davisson Post. THE STRANGE SCHEMES OF
RANDOLPH MASON

1897: Grant Allen. AN AFRICAN MILLIONAIRE

1897: George R. Sims. DORCAS DENE, DETECTIVE

1898: M. McDonnell Bodkin. PAUL BECK, THE RULE OF THUMB
DETECTIVE

1898: Rodriquest Ottolengui. FINAL PROOF

1899: Nicholas Carter. THE DETECTIVE'S PRETTY NEIGHBOR

1899: L. T. Meade and Robert Eustace. THE BROTHERHOOD OF KINGS

1900: Herbert Cadett. THE ADVENTURES OF A JOURNALIST

1901:   Richard Harding Davis. IN THE FOG

1902:   Clifford Ashdown. THE ADVENTURES OF ROMNEY PRINGLE

1902:   Bret Harte. CONDENSED NOVELS

1903:   Percival Pollard. LINGO DAN

1905:   B. Fletcher Robinson. THE CHRONICLES OF ADDINGTON PEACE

1905:   Arnold Bennett. THE LOOT OF CITIES

1906:   Robert Barr. THE TRIUMPHS OF EUGENE VALMONT

1906:   Alfred Henry Lewis. CONFESSIONS OF A DETECTIVE

1907:   Maurice Leblanc. THE EXPLOITS OF ARSENE LUPIN

1907:   Jacques Futrelle. THE THINKING MACHINE

1908:   George Randolph Chester. GET-RICH-QUICK WALLINGFORD

1908:   O. Henry. THE GENTLE GRAFTER

1909:   Baroness Orczy. THE OLD MAN IN THE CORNER

1909:   R. Austin Freeman. JOHN THORNDYKE'S CASES

1909:   J. S. Fletcher. THE ADVENTURES OF ARCHER DAWE (SLEUTH-HOUND)

1910:   Balduin Groller. DETECTIVE DAGOBERT'S DEEDS AND ADVENTURES

1910:   T. W. Hanshew. THE MAN OF THE FORTY FACES

1910:   William MacHarg and Edwin Balmer. THE ACHIEVEMENTS OF LUTHER TRANT

1911:   G. K. Chesterton. THE INNOCENCE OF FATHER BROWN

1911:   Samuel Hopkins Adams. AVERAGE JONES

1912:   Arthur B. Reeve. THE SILENT BULLET

1912:   [Gelett Burgess]. THE MASTER OF MYSTERIES

1912:   Victor L. Whitechurch. THRILLING STORIES OF THE RAILWAY

1912:   R. Austin Freeman. THE SINGING BONE

1913:   William Hope Hodgson. CARNACKI THE GHOST-FINDER

1913:   Anna Katharine Green. MASTERPIECES OF MYSTERY

1913:   Hesketh Prichard. NOVEMBER JOE

1914:   Ernest Bramah. MAX CARRODOS

1914:   Arthur Sherburne Hardy. DIANE AND HER FRIENDS

1916:   Thomas Burke. LIMEHOUSE NIGHTS

1917: A. E. W. Mason. THE FOUR CORNERS OF THE WORLD

1918: Melville Davisson Post. UNCLE ABNER

1918: Ellis Parker Butler. PHILO GUBB

1919: John Russell. THE RED MARK

1920: William Le Queux. MYSTERIES OF A GREAT CITY

1920: Sax Rohmer. THE DREAM-DETECTIVE

1920: J. Storer Clouston. CARRINGTON'S CASES

1920: Vincent Starrett. THE UNIQUE HAMLET

1920: Arthur Train. TUTT AND MR. TUTT

1920: H. C. Bailey. CALL MR. FORTUNE

1922: Maurice Leblanc. THE EIGHT STROKES OF THE CLOCK

1923: Octavus Roy Cohen. JIM HANVEY, DETECTIVE

1924: Agatha Christie. POIROT INVESTIGATES

1925: Edgar Wallace. THE MIND OF MR. J. G. REEDER

1926: Louis Golding. LUIGI OF CATANZARO

(or see alternate 1936 listing)

1927: Anthony Wynne. SINNERS GO SECRETLY

1927: Susan Glaspell. A JURY OF HER PEERS

1928: Dorothy L. Sayers. LORD PETER VIEWS THE BODY

1928: G. D. H. and M. I. Cole. SUPERINTENDENT WILSON'S HOLIDAY

1928: W. Somerset Maugham. ASHENDEN

1929: Percival Wilde. ROGUES IN CLOVER

1929: T. S. Stribling. CLUES OF THE CARIBBEES

1929: Harvey J. O'Higgins. DETECTIVE DUFF UNRAVELS IT

1930: Frederick Irving Anderson. BOOK OF MURDER

1931: F. Tennyson Jesse. THE SOLANGE STORIES

1931: Damon Runyon. GUYS AND DOLLS

1932: Georges Simenon. THE THIRTEEN CULPRITS

1933: Leslie Charteris. THE BRIGHTER BUCCANEER

1933: Henry Wade. POLICEMAN'S LOT

1934:   Mignon G. Eberhart. THE CASES OF SUSAN DARE

1934:   Irvin S. Cobb. FAITH, HOPE AND CHARITY

1934:   Ellery Queen. THE ADVENTURES OF ELLERY QUEEN

1936:   C. Daly King. THE CURIOUS MR. TARRANT

1936:   Louis Golding. PALE BLUE NIGHTGOWN

(Alternate, see 1926 listing)

1938:   E. C. Bentley. TRENT INTERVENES

1939:   Margery Allingham. MR. CAMPION AND OTHERS

1940:   Carter Dickson. THE DEPARTMENT OF QUEER COMPLAINTS

1940:   William MacHarg. THE AFFAIRS OF O'MALLEY

1942:   H. Bustos Domecq. SIX PROBLEMS FOR DON ISIDRO PARODI

1944:   William Irish. AFTER-DINNER STORY

1944:   Dashiell Hammett. THE ADVENTURES OF SAM SPADE

1944:   Raymond Chandler. FIVE MURDERERS

1946:   Lillian de la Torre. DR. SAM: JOHNSON, DETECTOR

1946:   Rafael Sabatini. TURBULENT TALES

1946:   Antonio Helú. THE COMPULSION TO MURDER

1947:   Stuart Palmer. THE RIDDLES OF HILDEGARDE WITHERS

1947:   Roy Vicker. THE DEPARTMENT OF DEAD ENDS

1949:   William Faulkner. KNIGHT'S GAMBIT

1950:   Lawrence G. Blochman. DIAGNOSIS: HOMICIDE

1951:   John Collier. FANCIES AND GOODNIGHTS

1952:   Philip MacDonald. SOMETHING TO HIDE

1952:   Lord Dunsany. THE LITTLE TALES OF SMETHERS

1953:   Edmund Crispin. BEWARE OF THE TRAINS

1953:   Roald Dahl. SOMEONE LIKE YOU

1954:   Michael Innes. APPLEBY TALKING

1956:   Stanley Ellin. MYSTERY STORIES

1956:   Evan Hunter. THE JUNGLE KIDS

1957:   Charlotte Armstrong. THE ALBATROSS

1958:   Craig Rice. THE NAME IS MALONE

1958:   Rufus King. MALICE IN WONDERLAND

1959:   Georges Simenon. THE SHORT CASES OF INSPECTOR MAIGRET

1961:   Patrick Quentin. THE ORDEAL OF MRS. SNOW

1963:   Stuart Palmer and Craig Rice. PEOPLE VS. WITHERS & MALONE

1965:   Helen McCloy. SURPRISE, SURPRISE!

1966:   Robert L. Fish. THE INCREDIBLE SCHLOCK HOMES

1967:   Miriam Allen De Ford. THE THEME IS MURDER

1967:   Michael Gilbert. GAME WITHOUT RULES

1967:   Harry Kemelman. THE NINE MILE WALK

SOURCES FOR BOOKS

Book collecting requires on-the-job training, particularly in the pricing area. As mentioned previously, the price guides in the field are not extensive, and the best way to get a feel for prices is to visit a number of shops and obtain as many catalogs as possible. The first alternative may not be practical if you don't travel much, although you will find that book collecting and travel go very well together, providing a good excuse to take short trips to towns within a few hundred miles or so. In addition to the tourist attractions, hotels, and restaurants, you will now have the pleasure of looking over the stock of the bookstores in town.

Once you have decided what to collect and have a feel for prices, you need to spend some money. There is nothing like spending money to sharpen your wits and force you to take the whole business a little more seriously.

CATALOGS

Catalogs can be obtained for the asking, at least initially. There is a list of dealers who issue catalogs in Appendix B. A complete list of all of the members of the Antiquarian Booksellers Association of America (ABAA) can be obtained free by requesting a copy of the ABAA Membership Directory from ABAA, 50 Rockefeller Plaza, New York, NY 10020. ABAA members offer a broad choice of antiquarian material in all areas of the printed and written word.

The vast majority of dealers do not charge for their catalogs and will usually send you the current catalog and perhaps one or two more. There are many standard abbreviations and terms used in these catalogs, and we have tried to cover many of them in the Glossary. If you don't purchase anything from their catalogs, the dealers will drop you from their mailing lists on the assumption that you just wanted the catalogs for pricing information or that you are not really interested in the type of books they stock. If you are interested in their books but just do not find anything in the first two catalogs, you should ask if you can send them a list of exactly what you are looking for so they may quote you specific titles as they arrive. Keeping your name on mailing lists is very simple—just buy books. We have people who have asked for our catalogs every two years since we started in business and have never bought a book from us. The cost of preparing, printing, and mailing catalogs is such that few dealers can afford to keep someone on their mailing list that doesn't buy from them. After all, that is the reason the catalogs were prepared—to sell books.

GENERAL USED-BOOK STORES AND SALES

There are a great number of sources for books. There are garage sales; school, charity, library, and church book sales; antique stores; and general used-book stores. Most of these are not particularly interested in either keeping up with current prices or trying to sell for the going market price. But you should keep in mind that these are also the places where you can occasionally get stung the worst as a beginner, because there are always a few books that the owners or operators have heard are worth $100 and so they have priced their copy at $100 even though the condition is such that a specialist in the field might be embarrassed to ask more than $25.

There are many dealers in Canada, England, and the U.S., and with pricing being somewhat subjective and collecting interests varying from one geographical location to another, there are always certain authors or subjects that bring premium prices in one region while attracting little interest elsewhere. If you are in a store that doesn't catalog, there is a good chance that the books that don't sell well in that area will be priced much lower than the market price.

SPECIALIST DEALERS

The next group is the specialist dealers. These dealers may specialize in just one field or a number of collecting interests, but don't consider themselves general book dealers, and except for the occasional volume, they will not stock books in other fields. Many have favorite authors or books that they may price above the market, and authors and books they dislike and price below the market. Then there are the books a dealer has never seen before and therefore assumes are extremely scarce and worth more than the market would indicate, and the books everyone else seems to believe are scarce but that they know are not scarce because they have had five copies in the last two years, and thus they price the book lower than the market would indicate. But on 95 to 99 percent of the stock, they're all pricing in the same range, plus or minus 20 percent.

There are a few dealers who claim (and fewer still who are right) that the condition of any book they carry is so superior to any other available copy that the collector should not mind paying two or three times the going market price for their copy. In these cases the collector should be very satisfied that the book received is in fact in very fine condition and worth the price; otherwise, if the collector finds another copy in similar or better condition at a significantly lower price in the future, she or he will be disappointed not only in the copy but also in the dealer from whom it was purchased.

AUCTIONS

For the book collector there are a number of auction houses which handle books. Swann Galleries in New York City is probably the most active auction house as far as number of books is concerned, because Swann has weekly sales. There are other houses such as Christie's and Sotheby's that have important (read expensive) book sales during the year. Christie's is also auctioning less "pricey" books at their Christie's East location. There are a number of other houses that have monthly or quarterly sales. A few of these houses are listed in Appendix C.

Auction prices tend to vary widely. Many of the books at auction will sell for half the market price, particularly the cheaper books, while sales of books from a major collection will often garner prices for many lots far in excess of the market prices.

There are auction houses in most cities and occasionally those auctions which handle estate sales contain books. These auctions are advertised in the local paper and it's possible to find some real bargains.

KNOWLEDGEABLE BUYING

In order to become a knowledgeable buyer you should be aware of issue points, bibliographies in your field, and available pricing information.

We believe strongly that one of the major drawbacks for a beginning book collector is the difficulty of finding out what is available by an author, how to identify the editions, and what is a reasonable price range for individual books. The following will provide some information on these subjects.

FIRST ISSUE OR STATE AND "POINTS"

In the case of a number of books, particularly those published before the turn of the twentieth century, one can differentiate between the first and later printings only by being aware of the changes made between printings. These changes can be in the text, the type used, the number of pages, the dates in the ads, or the type of binding (cloth, leather, boards, wrappers). In some cases the authors may have wished to make changes in the text themselves, or the publishers may have run out of a certain color cloth for the covers and switched to another color. These differences are known as the "points." The most common points are typographical errors that are discovered and corrected between printings or even midway through the first printing.

When these changes occur, the points indicate the first issue or first state of the printing. The Glossary (at the end of this section) includes a discussion of these terms, but it is worthwhile to quote P. H. Muir's *Book-Collecting as a Hobby*, where the difference between issues and states is summarized as follows:

> An 'issue' is caused by some change . . . after some copies have already been circulated, [while] a 'state' is caused by a . . . change before any copies of the book have been circulated.

In the following list of first books any points associated with a book will be mentioned. The difference in value between issues or states can be great. For instance, the first issue of Dylan Thomas's *18 Poems* (1934) has a flat spine, a leaf between the half-title and title pages, and front edge roughly trimmed; the second issue (1936) has a rounded spine, leaf (ads) added and front edge cut evenly. The difference in value between the first and second issue of that book is $2,000 ($3,000 for the first issue and $1,000 for the second).

BIBLIOGRAPHIES

The first-edition collector and dealer must know the points connected with the books that they collect or deal in. These points are contained in reference books known as bibliographies. General bibliographies cover many authors or a wide field such as Americana or Black Literature. One of the most famous is Jacob Blanck's *Bibliography of American Literature* (BAL), which was finally completed with Volume 9 in 1991. BAL is the best single source for bibliographic information on authors who published before 1920. In addition to these general bibliographies, there are specific bibliographies on individual authors. These include books written by or about the author, and, in many cases, also list the author's appearances in magazines and anthologies, or as contributor of an introduction or preface. The Selected Bibliography at the end of this book is our start on compiling a bibliography of bibliographies.

We would caution the buyer of a bibliography to attempt to examine a copy of the book before purchasing it. As dealers, we maintain a large reference library of individual-author bibliographies, and we must say that we're surprised at the number of bibliographies that, although extensive and expensive, do not assist one in identifying first editions.

The standard-setter in modern bibliography, in our opinion, is Donald Gallup. In his book *On Contemporary Bibliography*, Mr. Gallup states:

It is the bibliographer's first duty to make his bibliography useful . . . .

And what exactly should be his job: His function as I see it may be summarized under three principal headings:

First, to establish the canon of the author's printed work;

Second, to identify and describe first and important later editions of the books, in their variants, states, and issues, with their various bindings and dust jackets, explaining their significance where it is not readily apparent, and accounting, if possible, for any unusual aspects; and

Third, to establish for at least each major book the exact date of publication, date of composition (where this differs substantially), number of copies printed, and price at which the book sold when it was first published. He may, and doubtless will, do other things, but these seem to me to be the essentials.

There are books that are entitled "Checklists" which do not include precise information on how to identify the first printing, but these are not misleading, for they are billed as "Checklists" and not as "Bibliographies." But what do you do when you've bought a "Bibliography" and find that the bibliographer has not bothered to mention the existence of limited editions or how to identify the first editions?

The foregoing complaint has been made so often that we decided that rather than complain (or in addition to complaining) we would do something positive, so we started to publish a series of *Author Price Guides* (APGs) which we try to make as bibliographically correct as possible.

The APGs include:

- A facsimile of the author's signature.
- A brief biographical sketch.
- A separate listing for each issue of each book or pamphlet [by the author]. In other words, for each title there are separate listings for a limited lettered edition, a numbered edition, first American and first British editions, if applicable.
- Each individual listing includes the title, publisher, place of publication, date of publication, number of copies (if known), exact information for identifying the first printing, retail price estimates for the book with and without a dustwrapper, and a reference to the source of the bibliographical information.

An author's "A" items, that is, the books, pamphlets, and broadsides attributed to the author (147 titles and almost 300 items in the case of

Robert Graves) will be expanded over the years to include important "B" items. Proof copies will be included as seen or reported, but only if color or some other means of differentiating them is known, for we assume almost all books are preceded by proofs.

Given the nature of bibliographic research and volatility of prices, each APG is updated as necessary, and as it does not seem reasonable to require the purchaser to pay full price for updates, the original purchasers of an individual APG are charged full price only the first time they purchase that APG; extra copies and subsequent updates are made available at half price.

The APGs have proved useful as accurate, current, and reasonably priced bibliographical checklists, which include relatively accurate retail price estimates. The APGs will, of course, be improved over the years as collectors, librarians, and dealers contribute new or revised information, which will be incorporated in updates.

A list of the APGs is available from *Author Price Guides*, Box 5365, Rockville, MD 20848.

General sources for bibliographic information include:

First Printings of American Authors (FPAA) edited by Matthew G. Bruccoli, C. E. Frazer Clark, Jr., et al., Gale Research, Detroit (1977–79). These five volumes cover about 360 authors, both U.S. and English editions, with title page and first edition identification for all U.S. editions, and fifty of the authors' English editions (title, publisher, and dates for English editions of the other 310 authors). In print for $100 a volume, it should be in most libraries.

A Bibliographical Introduction to Seventy-five Modern American Authors by Gary M. Lepper, Serendipity Books, Berkeley (1976). Includes first edition identification for the U.S. editions of the 75 novelists and poets (unless a title was first published elsewhere, in which case the foreign edition is included). Out of print.

Science Fiction and Fantasy Authors, A Bibliography of First Printings of Their Fiction, edited by L. W. Currey, G. K. Hall & Co., Boston (1979). Covers 216 authors' works, including first edition identification. The book is excellent for all science fiction and fantasy titles (further checking will be required to obtain titles outside these fields).

Bibliography of American Literature (BAL), compiled by Jacob Blanck (Volumes 1–6) and edited and completed by Virginia L. Smyers and Michael Winship (Volume 7), and by Michael Winship alone (Volumes 8 and 9), Yale University Press, New Haven and London (1955–91), nine volumes. From Henry Adams through Elinor Wylie, 281 authors with full bibliographical details, covering up to the early part of this century. In print and at most libraries.

A general source for title, publisher, and date, by author, would be the series *Contemporary Authors* (over one hundred volumes; in most public libraries).

PRICING

The following is paraphrased from an article we did for *Rare Books & Manuscripts Librarianship*, Volume 9, Number 1, which is a publication of the Association of College and Research Libraries.

How are rare or scarce items priced? Not easily.

There was a comedian named Brother Dave Gardner. You'd have had to have been around in the 1950s to remember him. When someone would say, "Let's do that again," Brother Dave would say, "You can't do anything again. You can do something similar." Well, if a book or manuscript is truly rare or unique, you won't be able to find anything exactly comparable to base your price on, so you have to find something similar.

In order to provide a complete picture of the process of pricing, we must consult all the sources, though some of these may not be helpful in many cases. It is relatively easy to arrive at a price or, at least, a price range for most collected books because copies are bought and sold fairly regularly throughout the year. It does, however, become much more difficult to arrive at a price as one explores the pricing of a unique item, such as a great association copy of a book; a unique manuscript; or even a perfect copy of a relatively common book.

The prices paid by dealers and, in turn, the prices they set on the books or manuscripts they sell are a factor of the individual dealer's sense of the real market price based on their own knowledge and readings of the auction records, other dealers' catalogs and price guides.

To show how a price is set for a modern first edition, let's look, for example, at Larry McMurtry's *Lonesome Dove* (New York: Simon and Schuster, 1985), a title published in a relatively large first printing of 42,000 copies at the publication price of $18.95. A nice copy started out on the market, in 1985, at $25. It sold easily. The price moved to $40, then $50, $75, $100, $125, $150 and finally, to $175. We had continued to sell the book at $150, but at $175 we had no orders. Now this is a snapshot of a period of a few years. We eventually sold the $175 copy and now the book may sell for more if in mint condition, but the point is that the marketplace set the price. The dealers, of course, couldn't continue buying *Lonesome Dove* at $10 or $15, but paid more for each successive copy as the scouts or other sellers demanded a higher price at the whole-sale level which, of course, dictated a higher price at the retail level.

The foregoing is a relatively common process in the marketplace and is easy to understand; however, there is a tendency in some cases in recent years to jump straight to the higher value. In other words, a book which was in high demand, such as Tom Clancy's *The Hunt for Red October,* moved from $50 to $100 to $650 to $750, almost overnight. A dealer (or dealers) decided the book was truly scarce and would sell at the higher level. In this case they appear to have been right, even though the first printing was 30,000 copies, of which 15,000 went to libraries. The book continues to sell at the higher level. Whether it will continue to sell at this level in future years is anyone's guess. But now let's consider the uncor-rected proof of *The Hunt for Red October.* The proof in paper wrappers had a proof dust jacket which was different from the dust jacket used on the first edition. A copy in dust jacket was offered for $3,500. A Clancy col-lector who wanted the proof, but was not willing to pay more than $2,000, had asked us to find him one. Eventually, we purchased the copy that had been priced at $3,500 at a lower price and sold it to our collector for $1,850. This is not to say that the $3,500 price was too high. We have heard of only three copies being offered on the market, so it is a rare item. We don't know what the others sold for, but we believe the price we sold our copy for influenced the asking price of the other two copies.

So it is clear the buyers—the market—really set the prices in these three examples. In the last example, the seller could have held out for the $3,500, and perhaps our customer would have eventually paid it; or someone else might have bought it for $3,500. We'll never know.

There are three types of published value guides that are used to deter-mine prices.

1. PRICE GUIDES BASED ON DEALER CATALOG ENTRIES

The most common price guides are those that report the prices asked for books in dealer catalogs. The oldest and largest of these is the *Bookman's Price Index,* which is published twice a year and is up to 46 vol-umes (and does include a section on association copies). There are others, including Zempel and Verkler's *Book Prices Used and Rare*; the series edited by Michael Cole under the title *International Rare Book Prices*; and many others that are general or specific, such as Shelly and Richard Morrison's annual price guides to *Western Americana* and *Texiana.*

These are the most useful sources for finding relatively common col-lected books. Occasionally, one may be lucky and find an item very close to the one being priced; or being offered. Although it is not certain if an item actually sold for the price asked (more on that below), if one finds multiple entries by different dealers year after year it can be assumed the prices are in the ballpark.

The problems with these guides are that:

a) It is not at all certain that a book sold for the price asked, and it may not always be possible to verify a sale with the dealer.

b) The price may be so out of date that a sale isn't relevant to today's market, plus the market for certain types of books and manuscripts changes very rapidly.

c) These guides report only on books that have appeared on the market; rare books either do not show up often, or, more realistically, are sold without ever being cataloged.

So it is recommended that you start with one of these guides because it is possible something similar has been cataloged recently; but keep in mind that they may not prove useful in every case.

2. AUCTION RECORDS

In the United States, the *American Book Prices Current* is published annually (with index volumes published every four years). There are comparable publications in Europe and elsewhere. The chances of finding a price for a comparable rare book, association copy, or manuscript in the auction records would be greater than in the dealer catalog price guides, but the prices for the same title in the auction records will vary greatly, which may reflect the condition of each book, or, more likely, who bid that day. It should be understood that many dealers buy books for stock at auctions; therefore, many auction prices may represent wholesale rather than retail prices. In some cases, auction prices may represent forced sales and low prices, while in other cases, when the auction has received high visibility, prices paid may be significantly higher than retail. A recent example of a highly inflated auction price was that of Henry James's *The Ambassadors,* which sold for $5,000, yet at the same time, a buyer could have found five or more copies in comparable condition on dealers' shelves for $500 to $750.

Auction prices, therefore, require the knowledge of a dealer, rare book librarian, or collector of the particular author to be interpreted properly.

Another point worth mentioning is that since index volumes and annual volumes provide little or no description of condition, when using the auction records, it is best to check the index first, then go back to the annual volumes, and then to the actual auction catalog (if it is available) for a complete description.

The problems with auction records are similar to price guide problems, in that they can report only what is put at auction; the prices, therefore, may be out of date. Their advantage over price guides based on dealer catalog entries is that you know the auction prices were actually paid. Remember, auction houses charge a premium to the buyer and seller, so find out if the price included the premium(s).

3. Price guides prepared by individuals

These are price guides that express the opinions (informed, we hope) of the compilers of the guides. The prices are based on their experience buying and selling books, as well as their interpretation of auction prices and other dealer catalog prices.

The most commonly used guide at present is (and, obviously, we are not at all biased) our *Collected Books: The Guide to Values* (Putnam, 1991), which lists estimated prices for about 15,000 books.

The *Author Price Guides*, which we also compile, include all the American and English first editions by a particular author, with points for identification of the first edition and values. One of the reasons for the popularity of these guides is that they contain bibliographical information useful in determining if a particular book in hand is a first edition (or a first state or issue within the first edition).

There are similar works such as Joseph Connolly's *Modern First Editions* and Tom Broadfoot's *Civil War Books: A Priced Checklist with Advice*. These books represent the authors' opinions of what they would price a copy of the individual book at if they were cataloging it the day the guide was prepared.

The problem with these guides is that the prices are only as good as the knowledge of the authors. The tendency is to price relatively common books high and scarce or rare books low. This is reasonable: common books are cataloged often and the expense of cataloging makes it difficult to price a book at under $25. Also, if the book was published at $25, it is hard to value it at, say $5, which, in fact, is the price you might find it at your local used book store. On the other hand, if one is attempting to price a fine copy of Faulkner's *Soldier's Pay* in a dust jacket, and no copy in this condition has been on the market for ten years—at least none that the author is aware of—what price do you put in the guide? You list a price based on the last price you can find, perhaps ten years old, tempered by the prices that you know a few inferior copies have brought on the market in recent years. This may or may not be a reasonable estimate, but the odds are that it will be low, particularly if there is a pent-up demand for the book.

A standard comment on price guides is that they are out-of-date as soon as they are published; actually, we don't find this to be true. Most collected books tend to stay at a certain level for a year or two, and most prices do not become really out of date for three or four years. The comment relates mostly to the current "hot" authors or books that many have heard so much about and for which they find the price guides very low compared to current prices. Did anyone foresee Cormac McCarthy's *The Orchard Keeper* as a $2,000 book before *All the Pretty Horses* was published? Was it obvious in 1990 that Hemingway's *For Whom the Bell Tolls* and *The Old Man and the Sea* would be selling for $500 to $600 in 1994?

No one could have known *The Orchard Keeper* would reach such price heights. Of course, $2,000 was a catalog price and will eventually appear in a price guide; we will have to ask if it actually sold at that figure (although it probably did). As to Hemingway, if one had been astute enough in 1990 to realize that after the October 1987 stock market crash the prices of "high spots" of collected books would rise faster than those of other collected books, you might have foreseen that *For Whom the Bell Tolls* and *The Old Man and the Sea* would go up from about $100 to $150 in 1990 to $500 to $600 in 1994, while *Across the River and into the Trees* would only go up from $100 to $150. Incidentally, the prices of other post-1930 Hemingway titles have followed the latter trend, and the price guide prices in our 1991 book, although a little low, are not bad.

"High spots" are hot and if you are trying to price a beautiful copy of one that hasn't appeared in dealer catalogs or at auction in years, you will not find any help anywhere, because there are new price records set whenever one appears, and most of these sales are not recorded.

As a final note on price guides and auction records, it should be said that users of these reference works have their own ways of interpreting the prices. A number of people have told us that they always use our guides: some use half our values; some use three-quarters of them; some double our prices; and some believe that our prices are for very good copies and that prices for fine copies would be double and mint copies would be triple.

A local bookstore owner who buys our guides told us he got a copy of a certain book and, if it hadn't been for our guides, would have priced it $10. As it was, he found the book listed in our guide for $150 and priced it at $60. We bought it.

For auction records, one can usually assume that the retail price for a comparable copy of a book would be 50 to 100 percent above the auction price; as mentioned above, however, there are many instances where this rule of thumb is way off the mark.

OTHER CONSIDERATIONS

1. COST

Obviously, the seller's cost for a book will influence the price that he or she asks for it. This is often a factor when dealers handle unusual if not unique books; and can cause concern on the part of a buyer when a book priced at $x appears in another dealer's catalog or is offered to the buyer at $2x or $3x. In this case, the buyer knows the dealer's cost and may believe the "profit" is too high, but it must be realized that the dealer bought the book because he or she believed the first dealer underpriced it. The price may be "high" but time will tell if it is too high. One of our esteemed colleagues, whenever asked if a book is really worth the price he has placed on it, always responds "Not yet." This means a sale must legitimize the price. If no sale occurs, the dealer normally has two choices: maintaining the price or lowering it, although the dealer may decide to withdraw the book from the market for a period; or, the dealer may raise the price which occasionally results in a sale. The antiquarian book field is a marketplace, and the law of supply and demand applies.

2. CONSIGNOR'S DESIRED PRICE

It is not uncommon for an unusual or unique book to be on consignment with a dealer. In this case, the price asked may simply be the price the consignor has set plus a nominal profit for the dealer. The dealer may believe the price is high but knows that the consignor will not sell the book for less; therefore, the price is firm.

We recall a case in which a library that had a comprehensive collection of an author's works, including manuscripts and letters, was offered an important collection of the author's letters for a high five-figure amount. The librarian believed that the price was too high. The dealer had the letters on consignment. Eventually the letters were purchased by another university at the same price. Again, if there were no other buyer for the letters, the price might have been lowered or the letters taken off the market.

3. INDIVIDUAL DEALER "EXPERIENCE"

Often a book becomes more attractive and thus more valuable following a change of ownership. If dealer A has a book that dealer B is interested in, dealer B will often exclaim about the high price, how common the book is, the obvious defects that make it only a marginally collectable book, and so on. But having gotten dealer A's price as low as he can and having purchased the book, dealer B becomes transfixed with the beauty and rarity of the volume. A price is not set immediately as time is needed for dealer B to absorb the aura of the volume and determine a "fair" price for this now "priceless" tome.

We remember a very knowledgeable dealer seeing a second edition, albeit the first illustrated edition, of a very famous book. He told the dealer who owned it that it was nicely bound but only a second edition, after all, and perhaps worth no more than $300. The other dealer, who had not priced the book yet, listened to the sage advice of the first dealer and priced it at $750. The first dealer bought the book immediately and returned to his shop. After some deliberation, he priced it at $1,250. A third dealer came in and asked how anyone could price a second edition of this book at over $1,000! After much discussion, the third dealer bought the book. This dealer went to some lengths to check on previous prices and found nothing useful in any of the price guides available. He then checked all the major libraries in the United States, England and France, and he discovered that none of them had a copy of the book. He then priced the book at $10,000, and ultimately sold it at a figure approaching this amount. As a footnote, the second dealer proclaimed that the third dealer and his customer were both fools.

Another story about how dealers' prices are set might also prove educational. A dealer on a trip spied a book he believed was truly rare. The book was priced at $17,500 and was included in a catalog just mailed by the shop. The dealer asked for and received a dealer discount and left the shop with the book. He was aware that the local university did not have a copy of the book and decided to offer the book to the librarian at $24,000. The librarian, however, had just received the catalog from the shop where the book had been purchased, realized that this was the same copy offered in the catalog at $17,500, and mentioned that she had seen this book for $17,500. The dealer responded that he had bought the book and believed it was much scarcer than the catalog price would indicate and had therefore repriced it $24,000, which he believed was a much more realistic price. The librarian told him that she thought $17,500 was a fair price and that she would be willing to pay that amount. The dealer replied that he owned the book now and believed his price was fair, and left. He then went home and did more research. He learned that the Library of Congress did not have a copy and decided that the book was even scarcer than he had originally thought. He made an appointment with the rare book librarian at the Library of Congress and at their meeting offered him the book for $28,000. The LC librarian had also seen the catalog and stated that the price was much too high, implying that the dealer was price gouging. No sale was made. Although the dealer was upset that the librarian believed the book was overpriced, he was becoming more convinced that it was indeed scarcer than he had thought. He offered it to a midwestern university en route to California the following week for $34,000, and promptly sold it at that price.

We must admit we're not sure that all the details of these stories are accurate, but we know that similar scenarios have played out before and will play out again.

Most dealers do not want to sell a customer a book at a high price when another copy may turn up on the market at a much lower price within a few years. However, when a dealer is pricing a unique book, there is no possibility that another copy will come on the market. The problem then is, what is comparable? If it is a great association copy inscribed by Ernest Hemingway, what prices have other Hemingway association copies brought? If it is a manuscript by a prominent author, what prices have other manuscripts by that author brought? If none has been sold, what prices have the manuscripts of authors with comparable reputations sold for? There is usually some comparison that can be made, but many times these comparisons may be tenuous.

Another approach is to have an independent appraisal of the book, but this may present a problem if the appraisal is either very high or very low. We were once asked to reappraise a collection because the owners of the collection refused to sell the material at the original appraised value. We made our own appraisal of the material and honestly thought the original appraisal had been ludicrously low. The owner and the university were able to agree on a price, probably somewhere between the two appraisals, although we were never told the final result. It must be added, though, that there are different kinds of, and reasons for, appraisals—for tax or estate purposes, to help the owner know what to ask for the collection if she or he were to sell or otherwise dispose of it, to inform a potential buyer of the value of an item or a collection, and so on. It would seem reasonable when contemplating the purchase of an expensive collection or item to have one, or perhaps even two, independent appraisals of the value to assure the prospective buyer that the price is within reason.

The truly rare or unique item, if demand is high, can be priced as high as the seller wants, but the seller must find a buyer in order to legitimize the price. Even the fact that a book sells for a certain amount does not necessarily mean another copy will also sell for the same amount. The first book may have found the only buyer in the marketplace willing to pay that much. Also, a high price on one copy may bring other copies into the market thus increasing the supply and lowering the price. The market is constantly changing with new hyper-modern authors coming into fashion and record prices being set every week, or so it seems. All the materials and expertise available should be used in making a purchasing decision.

CONDITION ISN'T EVERYTHING— IT'S THE ONLY THING

Vince Lombardi was talking about winning, but book collectors could well rephrase his famous quote. The condition of a first edition or any collectible book is the major determinant of its value. The retail prices estimated herein for an author's first book are for very good to fine copies (in dustwrappers after 1920). There is no doubt that certain collectors might pay two or perhaps even three times this amount for an absolutely mint copy of a book.

First edition collectors are by nature very hard to please. They would like each of their first editions to look new, and they will pay for such copies. The reverse is also true—a book in poor condition is very difficult to sell. Books valued at $100 in fine condition are practically valueless in very poor condition. If the book is rare it will of course have some value whatever its condition, but only a fraction of what it would be worth if it were a fine to mint copy.

One thing that should be remembered, in spite of the Lombardi restatement, is that lesser copies (unless they are really dogs) will probably increase in value at the same rate as fine copies, only the starting base is significantly lower.

Unless one is a book collector, dealer, or bookscout, it is difficult to understand how to describe the condition of a book. Even within this group there can be wide differences of opinion, which only confirms the fact that condition descriptions are somewhat subjective.

Many people believe that if a book is twenty or thirty years old, it is in very good condition if the covers are still attached, and if the book is one hundred years old, one should not downgrade it just because the covers are no longer attached. ("What do you expect, it's one hundred years old!") We're sympathetic with their confusion, but we're not interested in buying their books.

The following general gradings are used by book dealers:

MINT—As new, unread.

FINE—Close to new, showing slight signs of age but without any defects.

VERY GOOD—A used book that shows some sign of wear but still has
no defects

GOOD—A book that shows normal wear and aging, still complete and
with no major defects.

FAIR—A worn and used copy, probably with cover tears and other
defects.

READING COPY—A poor copy with text complete but not much else.

We were called by a family who had been left a copy of Thomas
Paine's famous pamphlet published in January of 1776, in which he ap-
pealed to the common man to declare his independence. This is a rare
and fragile item, having been handed out in the streets during winter, and
few have survived intact. Needless to say, we were very excited about the
possibility of acquiring this pamphlet. Sad to say, the copy was missing
the very last page on which there was a half-page of text. We advised the
family to consign it to an auction house. It fetched $8,500. Had it been
complete, we would have paid the family $50,000.

DUSTWRAPPERS OR DUST JACKETS

The dust jacket or dustwrapper that covers a book is a valuable part of a
first edition. On recently published books, it is difficult to sell a first edition without a dustwrapper to a collector. On books twenty years old or
older, the average increase in value added by the dustwrapper would be
close to 400 percent, providing the dustwrapper is in fine condition. This
rule would not apply to inexpensive books in the $5 to $20 range, where
the dustwrapper value would be in the 50 to 100 percent range, but is
fairly consistent on books valued above $25 without a dustwrapper.
There are, of course, exceptions to this rule, the most obvious being the
value added by the presence of a dustwrapper on the books of
Hemingway, Faulkner, or Fitzgerald. It is not unusual for these authors'
books to sell for five to ten times more with a fine dustwrapper than
without one; in fact, a very good copy of Faulkner's *Soldier's Pay* has been
sold at twenty to twenty-five times the unjacketed price ($600 vs.
$17,000) and a fine copy might bring $25,000 to $30,000.

The condition of the dustwrapper is just as important, and perhaps as
difficult to describe, as the condition of the book. If a catalog entry does not
specifically state that a book is in a dustwrapper, one must assume it is not.

A few examples of dustwrappers illustrating reasonably good condition:

AUTOGRAPHED BOOKS

Author autographs in a book may be considered in various categories, including signed limited editions, signed trade editions, and association copies.

Signed trade editions are copies of the regular trade first edition signed by the author, with or without an inscription. If the original recipient of the book is not well known or of general interest, some collectors prefer the author's signature without the inscription. These signed books will usually sell for at least twice as much as an unsigned copy, but the real determinant of price will be the value of the author's signature. Some authors are very generous in signing their books; as a result, their signatures may be worth only $10 or $15, representing the price difference between a signed and an unsigned copy of a first edition, or the price of a signed later printing. On the other hand, some authors very rarely sign a book and their signatures alone may be worth $50 or more; again, this would establish a price. Further, some authors are very free with their signatures but very rarely inscribe copies of their books, and therefore inscribed copies, even if the recipient is unknown, will command a premium.

Association copies are books that include a signed inscription from the author to another famous personality or someone important within the framework of the particular author's life and work. These will be valued more highly than the normal signed first edition, depending on the importance of the recipient involved.

Association copy of a first book. Sylvia Beach, owner of Shakespeare and Company, Paris, from Malcolm Lowry (reduced).

GLOSSARY

The following is a partial list of terms used in book collecting. The most complete list is contained in John Carter's *ABC for Book Collectors* (see "Selected Bibliography").

A.B.A.   Antiquarian Booksellers' Association (English); also the American Booksellers' Association, primarily publishers and sellers of new books.

A.B.A.A.   Antiquarian Booksellers' Association of America.

A.B.P.C.   *American Book Prices Current* (see "Price Guides").

Advance copy   A copy for booksellers and reviewers, either bound in paperwraps or a copy of the trade edition with a review slip laid in.

A.L.S.   Autographed Letter Signed, all in the author's hand.

A.M.S.   Autographed Manuscript Signed, all in the author's hand.

Antiquarian Books A loose term implying collectible books rather than used books. Refers to old, rare, and out-of-print, which covers the waterfront.

As issued   Used to emphasize original condition or to highlight something unusual, such as recent books without dustwrappers.

Association Copy	A book that belonged to the author, or that the author gave to another person with whom he or she was associated. The book contains some tangible identifying evidence, such as inscriptions, signatures, bookplates, letters or photographs laid in or tipped in.
As usual	A favorite term to describe defects which probably occur only on copies of the book the particular dealer handles, such as "lacks endpapers, as usual," or "lacks title page, as usual."
Backstrip	The spine of the book.
B.A.L.	*Bibliography of American Literature* (see "Knowledgeable Buying: Bibliographies").
Bastard title	See *Front Matter* and *Half-Title*.
Biblio	From the Greek: signifying or pertaining to books.
Biblioclast	A destroyer of books.
Bibliognost	Having a deep knowledge of books.
Biblioklept	A stealer of books.
Bibliomaniac	Many bookdealers and certain collectors.
Bibliophile	A lover of books.
Bibliophobe	A fear of books (sometimes extended to hate).
Bibliopole	The people behind the booths at the book fairs.
Binding	The cover of the book.
Blind stamped	Impressions in the bindings of books which are not colored, as in the Book-of-the-Month Club blind stamp on the back cover.
Blurb	A comment from a review (often by another author praising the particular book) printed on the dustwrapper or covers of a proof copy, or on a wrap-around band.
Boards	The front and back covers of the book are the boards. This term is also used to describe books that have boards covered in paper rather than cloth or leather.

Book sizes	The following are approximate heights, in inches: Double Elephant folio–50 Atlas folio–25 Elephant folio–23 F = Folio–15 Q = Quarto, 4to–12 O = Octavo, 8vo–9 $\frac{3}{4}$ D = Duodecimo, 12mo–7 $\frac{3}{4}$ S = Sixteenmo, 16mo–6 $\frac{3}{4}$ T = Twenty-fourmo, 24mo–5 $\frac{3}{4}$ 　　Thirty-twomo, 32mo–5 　　Forty-eightmo, 48mo–4 　　Sixty-fourmo, 64mo–3
Breaker	A person who breaks up books to sell the plates individually, or the book itself when the covers are so bad that it either has to be rebound or broken up.
Broadside	A single sheet printed on one side only.
Buckram	A coarse linen binding cloth.
Cancel	A cancel is literally any printed matter change to any part of a book, but most commonly it refers to one or more pages which are substituted for existing pages in a book that has already been bound. In other words, an error is found, a new, corrected page is printed (cancel, or cancel leaf), and the original page is cut out of the book, leaving a stub upon which the cancel page is glued.
Chipped	Usually used to describe the fact that small pieces on the edge of the paper dustwrapper have been torn off (chipped away).
Cloth	Refers to the binding of the book, when the boards are covered in cloth.
Collate	At one time it really meant to compare one copy of a book with another to see if it was the same. Even without another copy, one can determine if the book was complete by knowing how books are made. In modern times many bibliographies furnish enough physical information to determine if the book is complete and the correct edition. *Collate* also means to

check each page and plate to assure that the book is complete, which is not a bad idea even on modern books.

Colophon

Derived from the Greek, it means "finishing touch." It was on the last page and provided facts about the production, author, title, date, etc. The title page has superseded the colophon as an information source. In modern books, *colophon page* is used to refer to the page in limited editions that lists the type of paper, printer, number of copies, and author's signature.

Contemporary

Refers to bindings and hand-colored plates (generally of the period when the book was published) and author inscription (dated the year of publication, preferably near the publication date).

Covers

The binding of the book, most particularly the front and back panels of the book.

Covers bound-in

The original cloth covers, usually including the spine, bound into the book when a new binding is made. Normally they are mounted as pages at the end of the book. Also refers to the covers of books originally issued in boards or paperwraps, but in these cases the covers are usually bound in their proper positions.

Cut edges

Edges trimmed by machine, which applies to most modern books, as opposed to leaving the page edges roughly cut (see *Uncut*).

C.W.O.

Check or cash with order.

Deckled edge

Rough, irregular edges usually found on handmade paper, but which can be produced in machine-made paper.

Dedication copy

A copy of a book with the author's presentation inscription to the person or persons to whom the book was dedicated.

Dos-a-dos

Two separate books bound together so that each cover represents the cover for a different title. The Ace paperbacks of many science fiction books were issued this way, as was William Burroughs's first book, *Junkie*, written under the pseudonym "William Lee."

Dummy	A mock-up of the book, used by salesmen in the late 19th and early 20th century to show prospective buyers what the book would look like. It usually had a title page, 10 or 20 pages of text, and then blank pages to fill out the rest of the binding.
Dustwrapper	The paper cover, either printed or pictorial, which is issued with the book. Also referred to as a dust jacket or dust cover. Abbreviated *dw*.
Edition	Actually, an edition will stand until changed. There may be 20 printings of an edition before a change in the text is made that is significant enough to require a notation that it is a second edition. For the collector, though, the *first edition* is the first printing—or first impression—which means the whole number of books ordered by the publisher to be printed from the same set of type and issued at the same time.
Else fine	Usually follows a long list of defects. One of our local bookscouts, Ralph Hirschtritt, usually refers to his copies as *ex-mint*, which is certainly descriptive.
Endpapers	When a book is bound, the binder adds a double leaf, half of which is pasted down to the inside covers, leaving the other half to form the endpapers or first and last leaves of the book.
Ephemera	Perishable productions never meant to last. Pamphlets, broadsides, photographs, advertisements, in fact almost anything not classified elsewhere.
Errata	A printed page or slip of paper tipped or laid in, which lists all the mistakes and misprints found after binding.
First and second printing before publication	This indicates the publisher was successful in promoting the book and had more orders before the actual publication date than the first printing quantity would cover, therefore, a second printing was ordered. *Not* a first edition.
First edition	The total number of copies produced in the first impression or printing of a book. Abbreviated *1st eds*. In reality the first edition may have many printings, but

only the first printing is considered the first edition as far as collectors are concerned.

First separate edition　First printing in book form of something previously published with other matter. Usually stories or poems which appeared in magazines, anthologies or collections of the same author's works. For first separate appearance see *Offprint*.

First thus　Means not a first edition, but something is new. It may be revised, have a new introduction by the author or someone else, be the first publication in paperback form, or first by another publisher.

Fly leaf　The blank page following the endpaper, but often used to describe the endpaper itself.

Fly title　See *Half-title*.

Folio　Has several meanings: (a) a leaf numbered on the front; (b) the numeral itself; and (c) a folio-sized book. See *Book Sizes*.

Follow the flag　A term which means that if one collects American authors, precedence would be given to American editions, even if the chronological first edition was published in England. The practice today seems to be to either collect both editions of all titles or, if a few titles were printed on the "wrong" side of the Atlantic, to collect the true first of that title or both editions of that title.

Fore-edge painting　The front page edges of the book are bent back to expose a greater area and a watercolor painting is applied to this surface. After completion the book is closed and the painting cannot be seen.

Foxing　Discoloration spots on the pages or page edges, usually brown or yellow, resulting from chemical reaction of certain properties in the paper to the atmosphere.

F.P.A.A.　*First Printings of American Authors* (see "Knowledgeable Buying: Bibliographies").

Frontispiece　An illustration at the front of the book, normally across from the title page. Also referred to as the *frontis*.

Front matter	The pages preceding the text of a book. *The Bookman's Glossary* gives the following order: bastard title or fly title frontispiece title page copyright page dedication preface or foreword table of contents list of illustrations introduction acknowledgments half title Usually each of these are on a right-hand page except the frontispiece, which faces the title page, and copyright page, which is on the reverse or verso of the title page.
Galley proofs	Early proof copies of a book on long strips of paper usually containing two or three pages of text per strip. Normally only a few copies are pulled in order for the author and/or editor(s) to make changes and catch typographical errors. They are also referred to as galleys or loose galleys. They precede the perfect bound uncorrected proofs and advance reading copies. Recently many publishers have changed to galley proofs of the sheets made on copiers, which presents a problem to bookdealers and collectors because these sheets are so easily duplicated.
Gathering	A group of leaves formed after the printed sheet has been folded to the size of the book for sewing or gluing into the binding. Also called a *signature*, *section*, or *quire*.
Gilt edges	The page edges have been trimmed smooth and gilt, or gold, has been applied. The abbreviation *g.e.* means gilt edges; *a.e.g.* means all edges gilt; *g.t.* means gilt top; *t.e.g.* means top edge gilt.
Glassine	A transparent paper dustwrapper which some people put a high value on, but which is certainly unattractive and ill-fitting with age.

Half cloth	Paper-covered boards with the spine bound in cloth.
Half leather	The spine is bound in leather and the balance in cloth or paper. Also referred to as *three-quarter leather* when the corners are also bound, but the latter designation was supposed to imply that a good portion of the covers were bound in leather, not just the corners. Also called *half-bound, half binding*.
Half title	A page preceding the text containing only the title of the book. There are usually two of these, one before the title page and one after the title page. The former was called a *bastard* or *fly title*, but in recent years booksellers do not seem to differentiate.
Hinge	The junctions where the front and back covers meet the spine. John Carter differentiated the inner and outer junctions as *hinges* and *joints*, respectively. Bookdealers refer to hinges as being weak or starting, which can mean anything from the paper making up the pastedown and the endpaper is starting to split at the hinge to the cover actually starting to come off. If the copy is also described as *tight* or *still tight*, it could be assumed the break in the paper hasn't yet weakened the binding.
Holograph	Means entirely in the handwriting of the author. Usually used for notes, marginal comments and particularly manuscripts, as the term *autograph* is used for letters entirely in the author's hand (see A.L.S.).
Hypermodern	Collected first editions published within last ten years or so. Most were published so recently that there is no track record on author or book.
Impression	The copies of an edition printed at one time. The first impression is the first edition in collector's parlance.
Imprint	Originally it meant the person or firm responsible for the actual production of the book. More recently it is used to refer to the publisher (and place and date) as it appears at the foot of the title page, but can also be used to refer to the printer's name or the publisher's name on the spine.

Incunabula

A Latin word for "things in the cradle." It is used to refer to books printed from movable type before 1501. *Incunable* is used as the singular, with *incunables* as an alternative plural.

Inscribed copy

A copy inscribed by the author, for a particular person; not merely autographed by the author. It is often difficult to differentiate between inscribed copies and presentation copies, and for the most part the terms seem to be used interchangeably.

Integral

Refers to a leaf when it is part of a gathering or signature, rather than a cancel or tipped-in leaf.

Interleaved

When blank leaves alternate with the printed leaves a book is said to be interleaved.

Issue

Issues and *states* of the first impression seem to be used interchangeably, and the differences are at times confusing. An issue occurs when alterations, additions, or excisions are made after all the copies are printed and the book has been published or gone on sale. The most obvious examples would be books where a number of sets of sheets are run off, but the sheets are bound at different times and in many cases by different publishers. Books such as John Steinbeck's *Cup of God* and Dylan Thomas's *18 Poems* (see entries in "First Book List") exist in more than one issue.

States, on the other hand, occur when changes are made during printing or, at least, before publication or sale, so that variant copies go on sale at the same time.

So, if the publisher finds an error and inserts a cancel page before the first impression is distributed (of course, some copies have gone out to reviewers) we have two states. But some people will call them issues and in the overall scheme of things this mistake will not be fatal.

Jacket

The printed or unprinted cover, usually paper, placed around the bound book. Sometimes called *dust jacket* (dj), *dustwrapper* (dw), *dust cover,* or *book jacket.*

Jap(anese) vellum	A rather stiff paper with a very smooth glossy surface not unlike vellum. *Japon* is used to refer to French- and British-made imitations, and American imitations are sometimes called *Japon vellum*.
Joints	The exterior hinges of books, which are rarely referred to these days because if they're bad you can just say that the covers are off and you'll be close enough.
Juveniles	Children's books.
Juvenilia	Works written when the author was a child.
Label	Printed paper, cloth, or leather slips glued to the spine or front cover of a book.
Laid in	A photo, errata, autograph, letter, or review slip laid in the book, not attached to it.
Laid paper	Paper that, when held up to the light, shows fine parallel lines (wiremarks) and crosslines (chainmarks), produced naturally by the wires of the mold in hand-made papers. It can also be simulated by a pattern on the first roller in machine-made paper.
Large-paper edition	Produced using the same type as the regular edition but printed on larger paper, resulting in larger margins.
Leaf	A piece of paper comprising one page on the front (recto, obverse) and another on the back (verso, reverse).
Limited edition	An edition that is limited to a stated number of copies and is usually numbered (or lettered) and signed by the author and/or illustrator. It is not necessarily a first edition. Limited editions are normally issued in a different binding than the trade edition and in a slipcase, sometimes referred to as a box (although it really isn't).
	Limited editions should be produced in small numbers to be meaningful. Five hundred copies or less is usually more than enough for all but the most popular of authors. One hundred to 200 copies is more re-

alistic for many collected authors, as many collectors are satisfied with trade editions or simply do not have the money for the higher-priced editions.

To have much meaning, the edition must have the total limitation noted in the book; otherwise, one must assume the limitation is very large, particularly if the publisher will not reveal the total on the request of a collector. There have been a number of "Limited Editions" of over 100,000 copies.

Marbling

The process of decorating sheets of paper or cloth or the edges of books with a variety of colors in a pattern that has the appearance of marble.

Modern firsts

A category which seems to include all authors whose first editions were published in this century. The term has been used since the 1920s. At present it is not very descriptive. "Twentieth-century first editions" is a much better term to define the stock of most "modern" first edition dealers.

No date

A catalog entry stating "no date" (abbreviated *n-d*) has two meanings as we understand it. In British catalogs, if the date is included in the book on the title page, copyright page, introduction, or cover, the dealer will state "1960." If the date does not appear in the book but the dealer knows the date, the entry will state "n-d (1960)." American catalogs will list the date only if it appears elsewhere in the book or on its cover; the American catalog entry will read "(1960)." If the date does not appear in the book at all, the American dealer, if the date is known, will follow the English lead and state "n-d (1960)" or "n-d [1960]."

No place

Similar treatment as in no date. Abbreviated as *n-p* or *n-pl*.

No publisher

Similar treatment as in no date. Abbreviated as *n-publ*.

Obverse

The front of a leaf; the right-hand page of an open book. More commonly called the *recto*.

Offprint

A separate printing of a section of a larger publication, generally of composite authorship, in periodicals or books. Offprints are made from the same typesetting and occasionally are given their own pagination. They normally have a separate paper cover and sometimes a special title page. They are of interest because they represent the first separate appearance of the work, although they are not really a first separate edition.

Offset	Normally describes the transfer of ink from a printed page or an engraving to the opposite page. Also used as an abbreviation for photo-offset lithography.
Out of print	Means the publisher no longer has copies that may be ordered. If the publisher plans on reprinting the book it will merely be out of stock.
Out of series	Refers to overruns or extra copies of limited editions. This is normal as a hedge against defective copies, and in order to have a few copies for the author's and publisher's use and to send out for review. These copies are not numbered, but occasionally state "out of series." They are normally not signed by the author and even if signed are not usually as attractive to the collector as the numbered copies.
Page	One side of a leaf.
Pamphlet	A small separate work issued in paperwraps.
Paperback	Refers primarily to books in paperwraps published since the 1930s, although it can describe any book with a paper cover.
Paper boards	As used today, this means stiff cardboard covered in paper; otherwise, there should be a fuller description in the catalog.
Parts	Refers to part issues or the practice of publishing novels in separate monthly installments in magazine format, particularly in the nineteenth century. Most avidly sought are the Dickens novels in parts with all the advertisements in the "proper" order.
Pastedown	That half of the paper that lines the inner side of the cover.
Perfect binding	Used in most mass-market paperback books and magazines that have too many pages to be stapled. The

leaves are glued together on one side rather than stitched and covered. Many hardbound books are actually perfect bound these days.

Pictorial

Describes a book with a picture on the cover; a *printed cover* implies lettering only.

Pirated edition

An edition published without the consent of the author or copyright owner. The ones we most often see are the Taiwan piracies.

Plates

Whole-page illustrations printed separately from the text. Illustrations printed in the text pages are called *cuts*.

Points

Misprints, corrections, advertisements, cloth color, etc., used to distinguish states, issues, impressions/printings, or editions of one book. Catalogers seem to fall into various categories: those that assume the reader doesn't know anything; those that assume the reader knows everything; and those that assume the reader knows what the cataloger knew before that particular catalog was prepared (why repeat something in catalog 59 that you already covered in detail in catalog 23?).

Presentation copy

Assumes the author meant to inscribe the copy for the recipient and actually gave or sent the copy to the recipient, as opposed to inscribing the book for someone the author didn't know, at his or her request. Obviously a difficult call to make in many instances.

Price clipped

Refers to the fact that the price has been clipped from the corner of the dustwrapper flap.

Printed cover

Used to describe a dustwrapper or paper cover that is only lettered (without any picture). Most commonly used currently to describe the covers of uncorrected proof copies, e.g., "white printed wraps" (white cover printed in black).

Printing

An alternative word for *impression*.

Privately printed

Refers to a book that is not published for sale and is distributed by other than the normal commercial channels.

Private press	One whose owners or operators print what they like, rather than what a publisher pays them to print. The interest is in fine books. The print runs are small, and although the books are sold to the public directly through subscription, or occasionally through a publisher's organization, the motivation is more to make a fine book than to make a profit. Some examples would include the Baskerville, Daniel, Kelmscott, Ashendene, Cuala, and Golden Cockerel presses.
Proofs	Precede the published book. The normal sequence would be galley proof (described above), uncorrected bound (in paperwraps) proof, and advance reading copy bound in paperwraps. The latter is not as common a form as the first two because publishers prefer to send out early copies of clothbound trade editions for review.
Provenance	A record of the previous ownership of a particular copy of a book.
Publication date	The date the book is to be put on sale, allowing time for distribution to stores and reviewers after the actual printing is complete.
Rare	Implies the book is extremely scarce, perhaps only turning up once every ten years or so.
Rebacked	Means the binding has been given a new spine or backstrip.
Recased	Means the book was loose or out of its covers and it has been resewn or glued back in, usually with new endpapers.
Recto	The front of a leaf, the right-hand page of an open book. Also called the *obverse*.
Rejointed	Means the book has been repaired preserving the original covers, including the spine. The repair is always either "almost imperceptible" or "skillfully accomplished."
Remainder marks	In many cases the publisher will mark the bottom edges of books sold as remainders with a stamp, a black marker, or spray paint, which speckles the bottom.

Remainders	Books that publishers have decided not to stock any longer. The remainder of the stock is sold to a wholesaler, who resells the books to bookstores to sell to the public significantly below the original price. You can find these books for $.99 to $4.98 at most new bookstores. Some very expensive first editions were on remainder shelves at one time. The definition has to be qualified somewhat, however, because occasionally a publisher will remainder a part of his stock, while retaining the title on his list at full retail price.
Reverse	The back of a leaf or the page on the left of an open book. More commonly called the *verso*.
Signatures	The letters or numerals printed in the margin of the first leaf of each gathering. The term is also used to refer to the gathering or section itself.
Slipcase	A cardboard case usually covered in paper, cloth, or leather which holds a book with only the spine exposed.
State	See *Issue.*
Stub	A narrow strip of paper left after the majority of a leaf has been cut away.
Sunned	Means the covers have been bleached or faded by sunlight.
Thousands	A few publishers in the nineteenth century added a notice on the title page stating, for instance, "Eighth Thousand," to indicate a later printing, although they did not state second printing, third printing, etc. These are not first editions.
Three-decker	A book in three volumes, almost exclusively used to describe Victorian novels of the late nineteenth century.
Tipped-in	Means the plate, autograph, letter, photo, etc., is actually attached to the book.
Top edge gilt	See *Gilt edges.*

Trade edition	The regularly published edition. The term is used to differentiate it from a limited signed edition of the same book.
Uncut	Means the edges have not been trimmed smooth by a machine. The edges are rough. It is not the same as *unopened*.
Unopened	The leaves of the book are still joined at the folds, not slit apart.
Unsophisticated	Pure, genuine, unrestored, and if a book is so described, it can mean trouble as far as condition is concerned.
Variant	A book that differs in one or more features from others of the same impression, but a positive sequence has not been established. If the sequence were known it would be a particular state or issue.
Vellum	A thin sheet of specially prepared skin of calf, lamb, or kid used for writing or printing, or for the cover.
Verso	The left page of an open book. The back of a leaf. Also called the *reverse*.
Waterstained	Discoloration and perhaps actual shrinking of the leaves or binding.
Working copy	You should receive most of the leaves.
Wrap-around band	The band of printed paper the length of the dust-wrapper of a book. Wrap-around bands contain favorable reviews and are put around some copies of books. Obviously fragile, they are of interest to collectors.
Wrappers	The printed or unprinted cover of a pamphlet or book bound in paper.
Yapped	Refers to the edges of the cover of a book bound in paper or another soft material. These yapped edges are not flush with the pages but extend beyond the edges of the book and are fragile by nature.

SOME SUGGESTIONS

The following comments may be of some help. They are basically our own feelings and may not be shared by others, but here they are for what they are worth.

BUILDING A COLLECTION

If you have decided to collect a number of currently popular authors whose books are not particularly scarce, and you want to do it quickly, the best method would be to send a want list of the books (including the minimum condition you will accept) to a limited number of specialist dealers. You will receive a variety of quotes and can choose among them. If you do buy books on the first round, you should send a revised list, perhaps every month, to the dealers who responded so they will not waste their time searching for books you have already bought, and to remind them that you are still actively searching for certain titles.

If your budget only allows for a few books a month, it would probably be wise to limit the want lists to a few dealers, explain your budget limitations, and limit the number of books on the list. In other words, if you have decided to spend $100 a month on your collection and most of the books you want are in the $25-to-$50 range, you will only be buying two to four books a month and there is no sense in obtaining quotes from dealers on hundreds of books. Also, it will be hard to convince a dealer who quoted you once to do it again if you didn't buy anything from the initial quotes. Alternatively, if you have found a dealer you believe has been fair with you and whom you trust, give him your complete want list, explain your budget limitation, and ask him to buy for you. The dealer will see most of the catalogs that are issued every year and can work with you to build your collection. Make it clear that either the dealer will be the only one buying for you, or that you will also be buying at other local stores and from catalogs and you will keep your want list updated regularly so that dealer can also keep current with your collection.

If you are interested in only a few authors who have produced a large body of work and have a number of scarce and expensive books in their canon, it seems to us advisable to limit the number of dealers searching for the books. If your job is such that you are tied up most of the day and evening, the correspondence and telephone calls from twenty dealers can get on your nerves and spoil some of your enjoyment in building your collection. Also there is always the possibility that, if an expensive item comes up at auction, the dealers might bid against each other to buy it for eventual sale to you at a higher price than you might otherwise have paid.

CARING FOR BOOKS

Most dealers in scarce or rare books have taken up the practice of protecting the covers of books without dustwrappers by making a cover for the book out of a sheet of acetate and protecting books with dust jackets by covering them with plain acetate or an acetate cover that is backed with acid-free paper. The latter are made by Bro-Dart and other companies and your dealer should be able to order some for you or tell you where you can buy them in your area.

From the viewpoint of the dealer, acetate covers improve the appearance of books, but more important, they protect the books and dustwrappers while they are on the dealer's shelves. The original dustwrappers are an expensive part of the book and it is easy to tear their edges just by taking the book off the shelf; therefore, it is only reasonable to go to the expense of putting on covers. There are dealers who do not like the idea or looks of the covers, a view I respect; but it is depressing to see a $200 copy of a book turn into a $50 copy after it has been handled by fifty or a hundred people over a few months.

The collector who takes books home may not feel the need to keep the covers on the books, and if the books are not handled much and you don't like their appearance, then we do not see any reason to keep them on. The covers do provide a measure of protection, but they do age over time and probably should be changed after a number of years.

The best protection for a book is a specially made box, but these are labor-intensive and expensive, in the $75 to $150 range, and are hardly worth the cost to protect a $50 book.

If boxes are not within your budget or cost effective, I would recommend glass-front bookcases as a good investment for your more valuable books.

The most important thing is to keep the books in a relatively clean environment at consistent temperature and humidity levels. This can be accomplished with air conditioning, a humidifier, and perhaps an air cleaner.

It is also important to watch the little things, like leaving a book out on a table, where a visitor might set a glass on it or something could be spilled nearby and spread to the cover before the book could be picked up; shelving books too tightly so that the top edges are torn when a book is removed; leaving acid-content paper such as newsprint stored in the books, which will darken the pages; or putting thick sheaves of paper in the book, which can loosen the bindings.

Books are fragile, but the worst made of them have resided in attics for decades without serious damage. So worry more about dampness than dryness; avoid direct sunlight, which can fade the covers badly; and don't put stickers or gummed labels directly on the covers, as they will discolor. The latter is mentioned because we've seen a number of book collections marked with different-colored labels. Try to resist the urge to write your name in your books and only lay in acid-free bookplates instead of gluing them in if you are planning to one day sell your books. We had a gentleman call and ask if he could bring in for an offer some signed copies of an author that is quite collectible and when he arrived we were stunned to see that not only had he written his name (in a large bold signature) above the author's signature but had written that the book was a first edition in ball-point pen and then *stapled* the dustwrapper (all the way through the boards) to keep anyone from removing it!

INSURANCE AND APPRAISALS

As far as insurance is concerned, we understand that most homeowner policies have a limit on collectibles and you may have to purchase a special rider to the policy to cover your books. If the books are covered under your basic insurance policy or a rider is required, your company will normally require an appraisal for its files. The easiest and least expensive way to obtain an appraisal is to type an itemized list of your books or at least the ones that have a value over $25. Include the author, title, publisher, place, date, edition, and very brief description, and leave room on the right margin for the dealer to add the appraisal prices. After you have this list, visit a bookdealer and ask the dealer what the charge would be to appraise the books on the list. The dealer will have to visit your home to actually look at the books, but the cost will be significantly lower if the dealer does not have to take the time to make up a list in order to do the appraisal. The dealer can type in the values on your list and provide a cover sheet with the appraisal total. If you have a thousand books and only a hundred of them have a value over $25, just list the hundred books and then add a miscellaneous category for hardbacks and paperbacks, so that these can be included. Many people do not feel the lesser books are worth the trouble, but if you have eight hundred hardback books with an average value of $10 each, it would be nice to get the $8,000 if there were ever a fire in your house.

CREDIT

Most specialist dealers accept Visa, MasterCard, and/or American Express. If they do not take credit cards and the amount of the purchase is relatively large, dealers will usually allow you thirty days to pay and may arrange longer time payments if necessary. If this is the first time you have dealt with the dealer, he or she will probably want to hold the book until the balance is paid.

Terms may be preferable to charging even if the dealer does accept credit cards as the dealer is charged anywhere from 3 to 5 percent by the card company and many times an expensive book will not have a large margin and 5 percent could equal 25 to 50 percent of the profit.

BARGAINING

Bargaining with a dealer is not unheard of, and if a book has been on the shelf for a year or so, the dealer might be willing to accept an offer of something less than the marked price. But the collector should be careful, because dealers have different attitudes about this and some will never discount. You should ask the dealer very straightforwardly and politely if an offer on a specific title would be acceptable. One must understand that most banks have little confidence in books as collateral and so all the books on the dealers' shelves have probably been paid for. The nature of the business is to wait for the right buyer to come along, even if this takes over a year in some cases.

One must be aware that some dealers seem to price many of their books much higher than other dealers in the same field and, of course, because of this they can offer significant discounts. This is confusing to the beginning collector who may become used to a dealer automatically giving discounts of 10, 20, 30 percent or more, and then assume another dealer will do the same, but instead finds the other dealer is absolutely incensed when asked for a discount.

There is also a danger in continual bargaining if you are a serious collector, because if a scarce book you have wanted for years comes into the store and the dealer has other customers for the book, you can rest assured that you will not be offered the book first if you have established a pattern of bargaining in the past.

We have cataloged for thirty years, had an open shop for ten years, and visited hundreds of other shops, and it is our feeling that an antiquarian bookstore is a great negative-cash-flow business. Many, but by no means all, of the owners are getting along on a relatively low income, particularly if you compute it on an hourly basis. This is not a complaint, as the vast majority of the owners are perfectly aware that they could be doing something else, but do not have any desire to work in another field.

There are reciprocal discounts within the trade because dealers purchase much of their inventory from other dealers. There are no warehouses stocking inscribed copies of Fitzgerald's books, and if you have a customer for one, your best chance of finding it is on the shelves of another dealer. You, as a collector, do not offer the dealer the long-range opportunities to buy salable inventory, and therefore there is no compelling reason to give you a discount, which seems to come as a shock to certain collectors, fortunately a minority.

SELLING YOUR BOOKS

The antiquarian book field represents a true marketplace. A book is worth what someone will pay for it. Prices can vary widely for the same book during the same year. When you sell a book to a dealer, the value of the book will depend on what the dealer believes to be a reasonable resale value in his particular market. If the book is scarce or rare and the dealer has a ready market for it, the dealer may be willing to pay close to the retail value of the book. If the dealer has no immediate market for the book, but is confident that it will sell within a few months, he will probably offer about 30 to 50 percent of the retail value. If he is uncertain of selling the book within the year he may only be willing to pay 10 to 20 percent of the value or not be interested at all.

The best market for a collector is another collector. If another collector is not available, one might investigate the possibility of advertising the book(s) for sale in the "Books for Sale" section of the *Antiquarian Bookman*, P.O. Box AB, Clifton, NJ 07105, or putting the books at auction.

FIRST EDITION
IDENTIFICATION BY PUBLISHER

It is obvious, in looking over the entries, that the first key in starting to determine whether or not a particular book is a first edition is the date on the title page. This seems particularly true in the case of titles before 1900: whether the titles be fiction or nonfiction, it would appear that the vast majority of the first editions listed herein before 1900 had the date on the title page. After 1900, there are a number of publishers that did or currently do not put the date on the title page, but you can determine first editions of these titles by using the identification by publisher below.

The following publishers in the last few decades may have used a series of numbers including a "1" on the copyright page of the first edition. Prior to this they stated "First Edition," "First Printing," "First Impression," "First published" (month and year, or just year), "Published" (month and year, or just year), or put their logo or colophon on the copyright page of the first edition. Later printings would normally be noted on the copyright page. Exceptions will be noted in the entry:

Atheneum
Ballantine Books
Bobbs-Merrill (Since 1920. Prior to that, they used a
    bow-and-arrow design in some cases)
Bodley Head
Book Supply Co.
Brentano's (1928–33)

E. R. Burroughs, Inc.

Jonathan Cape

Cassell & Co.

Crime Club (U.S.)

Delacorte Press

George H. Doran (GHD logo on copyright page), but no indication
on later printings (1927 statement), but Doran started in 1909 or
1910 and we don't think they started consistently using the logo
until 1922 or so

Doubleday and Co. (but no statement on later printings)

Doubleday, Doran (but no statement on later printings)

Duell, Sloan (used "1" on copyright page)

E. P. Dutton

Editions Poetry

Eyre & Spottiswoode (since late 1940s)

Faber & Faber

Fantasy Press

Farrar, Rinehart (FR logo on copyright page but no statement on
later printings)

Farrar, Straus (FS initials on copyright page but no statement on later
printings)

Farrar, Straus & Cudahy

Farrar, Straus & Giroux

Fawcett

Funk & Wagnalls (used "1")

Gambit

Bernard Geis

Gnome Press

Grove Press

Robert Hale

Hamish Hamilton

Harcourt, Brace (& World) (since 1930 but no indication on later
printings. More recently used "First Edition/BCDE" and in the
last few years "First Edition/ABCDE")

Harper Bros. (Harper & Row) (since 1922, except for a period in
the late 1960s and early 1970s when they put the series of
numbers on the last blank leaf of the book on the first printing
and failed to remove "First edition" from the copyright page on
later printings but did adjust the numbers on the last blank leaf)
In addition they have used the following codes on the copyright
page to identify the month and year of publication:

Months

A = January	**E** = May	**I** = September
B = February	**F** = June	**K** = October
C = March	**G** = July	**L** = November
D = April	**H** = August	**M** = December

Years

M = 1912	**Z** = 1925	**N** = 1938
N = 1913	**A** = 1926	**O** = 1939
O = 1914	**B** = 1927	**P** = 1940
P = 1915	**C** = 1928	**Q** = 1941
Q = 1916	**D** = 1929	**R** = 1942
R = 1917	**E** = 1930	**S** = 1943
S = 1918	**F** = 1931	**T** = 1944
T = 1919	**G** = 1932	**U** = 1945
U = 1920	**H** = 1933	**V** = 1946
V = 1921	**I** = 1934	**W** = 1947
W = 1922	**K** = 1935	**X** = 1948
X = 1923	**L** = 1936	**Y** = 1949
Y = 1924	**M** = 1937	

Rupert Hart-Davis

Hart-Davis MacGibbon

Heinemann (since the 1920s)

Hodder & Stoughton Ltd. (up to the 1940s stated that "our methods [of identifying first editions] vary with every book." In 1947 they stated that "First Printed" are usually included on all first editions)

Henry Holt (since 1945)

Houghton, Mifflin (did not state "First Printing" until recently but always put date on title page and deleted the date in all later printings, but did not include a statement on later printings)

Michael Joseph (since mid 1930s)

Alfred A. Knopf (since 1933–34) have stated "First Edition"

John Lane (since 1925)

Little, Brown (since 1940)

Longmans

Robert M. McBride

A. C. McClurg ("Published in [year]")

McGraw-Hill (since 1956)

Macmillan

Methuen & Co.

William Morrow (since 1973)

New English Library
Norton
Pantheon (since 1964)
Random House (until changing to "First Edition/23456789." On
    the second printing the "First Edition" was deleted. The only
    publisher that does not use a "1" on its first editions)
Rinehart & Co. ("R" in a circle on copyright page, but no
    indication on later printings)
Scribners (since 1930 have put an "A" on copyright page on first
    printings, but no indication on later printings)
Martin Secker, Ltd.
Secker & Warburg
Simon & Schuster (since 1952)
William Sloane Associates
Viking Press ("First Published by Viking in [year]" or "Published by
    Viking in [year]")
Walker ("First Published By Walker in [year]")
Weidenfeld & Nicolson
Wesleyan University
John C. Winston (until the 1940s had no consistent practice but
    usually did not put any statements on any printing. Sometime in
    the 1940s started stating the printing on the copyrignt page)

In the last few decades the following publishers may have used a series of
numbers including a "1" on their first editions, but prior to this did not
include any indication of the printings on the copyright page of the first
edition/first printing. Most university presses follow this method.
Normally, later printings were indicated on the copyright page, although
very occasionally they did put "First . . ." on the copyright page—and
these would be first editions.

Appleton-Century (used a numerical identification: "(1)" = first
    printing, "(2)" = second printing, etc., at the foot of the last page
    of the book)
Arkham House (very rarely reprinted titles. There is a colophon at
    the back of each book)
Avalon Books
Robert A. Ballou
A. S. Barnes
Ernest Benn
William Blackwood

Bobbs-Merrill (until 1920)
A. & C. Boni
Boni & Liveright
Brentano's (until 1928)
Calder & Boyars
Jonathan Cape & Harrison Smith
Cassell & Windus
Caxton Printers
Chapman & Hall
Chatto & Windus (sometimes "Published by . . ." but did not
    include date)
Clarke, Irwin
Collier
Contact Editions
Pascal Covici
Covici-Friede
Covici McGee
Coward-McCann
Creative Age
Crime Club (U.K.)
Crowell
John Day (established 1928 and stated "First" the first few years)
Devin-Adair
Dial Press
Dillingham
Dodd Mead
Doubleday, Page
Egoist Press
Eyre & Spottiswoode (until late 1940s)
Four Seas
Lee Furman
Gollancz
Harcourt, Brace (until 1930)
Harper Brothers (until 1922)
Harvard University Press
William Heinemann (until the 1920s)
Hodder & Stoughton Ltd. (up to the 1940s stated that "our methods
    [of identifying first editions] vary with every book." In 1947 they
    stated that "First Printed is usually included on all first editions")
Hogarth Press
Henry Holt (prior to 1945)
B. W. Huebsch

Hutchinson & Co.

Alfred A. Knopf (until 1933–34 either stated "Published [month or year]" or did not have any indication on copyright page but noted later printings)

J. B. Lippincott

Little, Brown (prior to 1940 either did not state or showed month and year of publication on copyright page. Later printings were normally indicated)

Liveright

John Long

John Lovell

Lovell, Crowell

Macaulay

McClure, Phillips

McDowell, Obolensky

McGraw-Hill (until 1956)

Metropolitan Books

William Morrow (until 1973)

Museum of Modern Art

George Newnes

Peter Owen

Oxford University Press

Pantheon (until 1964)

Payson & Clarke

G. P. Putnam's Sons

Rapp & Whiting

Reynal & Hitchcock

Grant Richards

Scribners (until 1930)

Simon & Schuster (until 1952)

Small, Maynard

Harrison Smith & Robert Haas

Smith, Elder

Stokes

Alan Swallow

Trident Press

United Book

T. Fisher Unwin

Vanguard

Ward, Lock (normally dropped date from title page on later printings but did not indicate later printings in any other way)

John C. Winston (until the 1940s had no consistent practice but usually did not put any statements on any printing. Sometime in the 1940s started stating the printing on the copyright page)

REPRINT PUBLISHERS AND BOOK CLUBS

There are certain publishers that normally only reprint books originally published by others. The most common are Grosset & Dunlap, A. L. Burt, Blakison, Hurst, Modern Library, Sun Dial, Triangle, and World's Tower Books (although the latter did publish two of Raymond Chandler's first editions). These reprints are not particularly valuable unless a new introduction is included in the edition, although some of the very early scarce titles by very popular authors are sought by collectors if they are in fine condition in dustwrappers, principally because the dustwrappers on these reprints duplicated the front cover and spine of the original trade first editions.

We understand there have been over eight hundred book clubs in the United States during this century. Many of these, we assume, sent their members regular trade editions of a book. In the case of book clubs which printed their own editions, there is normally no problem identifying them if the book has a dustwrapper, as the front flap of the dustwrapper will state that it is a book club edition and will not have a price on the flap.

If the book is by a publisher that states "First Edition" or "First Printing" on the verso of the title page, the lack of this statement will make it easily identifiable as other than a first edition. Book-of-the-Month Club (BOMC) editions, since 1948 or 1949, although they look exactly like the publisher's edition and frequently state "First Edition/Printing," are also easy to identify without the dustwrapper, as they contain a small mark on the lower right corner of the rear cover. (Prior to 1949 it is difficult to differentiate the BOMC edition from the true first edition.) The mark can be a small black circle in earlier books, or, in more recent years, merely a circular or square depression (blind stamp) in the lower right-hand corner of the back cover. At some point in the last few years the BOMC stopped putting their mark on the back cover and now has a short series of letters and numbers printed so that it runs along the hinge or gutter on the last page (or one of the last pages) of the book. You may have to open the book almost flat to see it.

The Literary Guild book club editions also state "First Edition," but they are easy to identify as the spine and title page indicate "Literary Guild."

If a book club edition does not have a dustwrapper and is not a Book-of-the-Month Club edition, it may still be identified by the binding and paper, which will be of poorer quality than a normal publisher's edition. The most difficult book club editions to identify are, in our opinion, those originally published by New Directions and Viking.

USING THIS GUIDE

In most cases, in our opinion, an author's first book puts an upper limit on the value of his or her books. This is why the value of the first book can often be used as a rough guide to estimating the prices of later books. If a current catalog price or auction record is available it would, of course, be more reliable. But if such records are not available and you find two books by the same author, one published in 1930 and one in 1940, the one published in 1930 will normally be valued higher, and it will be important to know if the author's first book was published in 1900 or 1929. This rule applies to unsigned trade editions only (often a signed and limited edition of a later book will be valued more highly than the first or earlier book). There are exceptions, e.g., when a first or early book had a large printing or when a later book is much scarcer and/or acclaimed as an "important" book with lasting literary value.

The entries consist of:

Author, title, place of publication, date of publication, and only that additional information needed to identify the issue, state or edition, and the value.

All entries are first editions (first printings) unless otherwise stated. "Trade" is used to indicate the first general edition available for public sale after a limited edition has been issued; usually the same sheets are used for both the limited and trade editions.

If the author's name does not appear on the title page, the entry will start with the title. If the author used a pseudonym, the pseudonym will appear first and the entry will include the author's name in parentheses.

If the place of publication or date does not appear on the title page but does appear somewhere in the book, this infor-

mation will be in parentheses ( ). This is *particularly significant* because the presence of a date on the title page may be the only way to differentiate between first and later printings. If information is known but does not appear in the book, it will be in brackets [ ].

A FIRST BOOK

Our definition of a first book is any single-title publication containing more than one page regardless of size or format, that is bound, stapled, or laid in covers. We do not consider broadsides to be books, and thus have not included James Joyce's first publication, *Et Tu, Kelley*, published in 1891 or 1892, as his first book.

We do consider as first books those that represent a collaboration with one other author, although in the first-book list we also include the author's first separate book, as we suspect many collectors may not consider collaborations as valid first books.

Also included are books edited and translated by an author if they preceded the first book written by the author. We do not consider these to be first books but assume some collectors may consider them as the first, as these books are the first to include the author's name on the title page.

In many cases we have included the author's second book. Normally in these cases the first was written anonymously, written under a pseudonym, is so rare as to be unobtainable, or we just felt like it.

It should be understood that in many cases we have never seen these books and have merely listed first books and values as we have come upon them in dealer or auction catalogs. This means that there are many authors not covered because we have not encountered listings of their first books and do not feel comfortable listing a price.

Our definition of a first book is necessary in order to understand our selection in the first-book list. There is no real agreement among collectors on what constitutes a first book and this is probably just as well, as it means the collector must buy three or four titles by certain authors to cover all bets.

Note:
Persons interested in offering books listed within this book for sale to bookdealers must understand that the prices included here represent the estimated retail price one might expect to pay to a bookdealer to purchase a particular book when the book is in the condition noted below.

Lesser copies are worth less. Exceptional copies of notable rarities are worth more. Bookdealers are classic examples of small independent businesses, and they cannot be expected to pay the estimated value for copies of books listed here. The percentage of value one can expect in sale to a dealer will vary, but one should not anticipate more than 40 to 50 percent of estimated value for other than prime items from a dealer. One alternative to consider is acceptance in trade of books the dealer owns; the percentage of return most likely will come closer to 60 percent or more, depending on what you are offering and what you wish to swap for. Most dealers are also not interested in accepting several lower-value books in exchange for higher-value books. Understand further that even though you may own books listed in this volume, that is no guarantee that a dealer will automatically be interested in buying or trading for them. Most dealers specialize in particular areas and are not interested in less than prime titles outside their fields. On the other hand, most responsible dealers would be glad to suggest dealers in other fields for books that he or she has no interest in purchasing; this is usually done as a courtesy and not as a payable service.

ESTIMATED VALUES

The dollar values shown are our estimates of the retail value of the book in very good to fine condition, with a dustwrapper for those published in 1920 and after. Estimated values of books published between 1840 and 1920 are for very good to fine copies without dustwrappers but in original bindings. Therefore, if you have a book published prior to 1920 with a complete dustwrapper, the value would be higher than the value shown. Estimates for books before 1840 are for rebound copies unless otherwise stated. The estimated values are believed to be accurate, plus or minus 20 percent. This may seem to be a very wide range, but it is not unusual to see the same book in different dealer catalogs or at auction with that wide a range (or even wider) within the same year. If you prefer, you can consider the range to represent the difference in condition between a very good copy and a fine copy of the individual book. It is also not unusual for an absolutely mint copy of a book to bring twice the price of a very good to fine copy. On the other hand, copies with even minor defects might sell for as little as 50 percent of the values shown, worn and chipped copies (books and/or dustwrappers) might only be worth 25 to 30 percent of the values shown, and books without dustwrappers (after 1920) would normally sell for 15 to 25 percent of the values shown.

The value listed for any particular title should be considered only as a guide. In some cases the books are truly rare, and the fact that we have estimated a price based on a catalog or auction entry that may have been a few years old does not mean this price is accurate. As many dealers will tell you, when you have found a book on their shelves for $100 that is listed in a pricing guide for $50, "*go buy it from them.*"

CONDITION

1975 to 1995: These are really "modern" first editions. Ninety-nine percent of these books are fiction or poetry. Because they have been published so recently, the prices listed herein would be for very fine copies in **DUSTWRAPPERS** (unless in wraps or a limited edition in slipcase) with *NO DEFECTS,* including such minor things as price-clipped dustwrappers, former owners' names written in, bookplates, remainder marks on bottom page edges, or closed tears (no tape repairs) in the dustwrappers—even though there may be no actual loss of paper on the dustwrappers.

1945 to 1974: These books are a little older, but still copies must be in **ORIGINAL DUSTWRAPPERS** (unless in wraps or a limited edition in slipcase) with no major defects. These books do not have to look as new as the foregoing (1975–95). Also, the price-clipped dustwrapper and closed tears would be more acceptable, but the book has to be fine with the dustwrapper showing only minor wear, fading, or soiling. The absence of the dustwrapper decreases the estimated price of fiction or poetry titles by about 75 percent of the value shown. For nonfiction titles, the absence of the dustwrapper probably decreases the estimated price shown by 20 percent.

1920 to 1944: The book must be very good to fine with only minimal (if any) soiling, **IN A DUSTWRAPPER** (unless in wraps or a limited edition in slipcase) that is clean with only minimal soiling or fading and only a few small chips (1/8 inch or less) and closed tears. Again, as in the above grouping, the absence of a dustwrapper on fiction or poetry titles would greatly reduce the value of the first edition (75 percent on fiction and 20 percent on nonfiction).

1880 to 1919: The book must be clean and bright with no loss or tears on the edges. The estimated prices are for copies without dustwrappers.

It should be noted that books published in multiple volumes (usually three volumes, but also two- and four-volume editions), are rare and prices here are for very good copies in matching condition. Fine to very fine copies would probably bring much more.

1840 to 1879:   The book is good to very good with minor edge wear or loss but still tight and clean. If the title is nonfiction, particularly with maps or plates, the condition of the maps or plates is more important than the condition of the binding. The comment above on multiple-volume editions also applies here.

1839 and prior: The book would be re-bound (probably within 20 or 30 years of publication) unless otherwise stated, in a clean binding. Copies in early or "contemporary" bindings usually command more than books newly re-bound. If the book in question is fiction, poetry, or an extremely important nonfiction work, the original binding would greatly increase the value above the estimated prices shown herein. However, if the title is a nonfiction work, especially with maps and plates, the original or contemporary binding increases the value—but only by a small percentage, perhaps 10 to 20 percent. It is the condition and color (if applicable) of the plates and maps that would determine the value.

THE FIRST BOOK LIST

All books listed herein are
**FIRST EDITIONS/FIRST PRINTINGS
OF THE INDIVIDUAL TITLES.**

The three columns of prices represent retail estimates
for the titles in 1978, 1986, and 1995 respectively.
The section *First Edition Identification by
Publisher* on pages 116 to 123 is applicable
to each entry unless otherwise stated.

	1978	1986	1995

A

A., T. B. (Thomas Bailey Aldrich). THE BELLS . . .
  Boston/New York, 1855 — 150 250

A. E. (George Russell). *See* E., A.

Abbe, George. VOICES IN THE SQUARE. New York, 1938. — — 75

  (Edited his brother's work in 1936)

Abbey, Edward. JONATHAN TROY. New York (1954) 25 175 1,250

Abbott, Anthony (Charles Fulton Oursler). ABOUT THE
  MURDER OF GERALDINE FOSTER. New York (1930).
  (First mystery) — 75 250

Abbott, Berenice. CHANGING NEW YORK. New York, 1939.
  Two states of blue cloth, priority unknown — — 400

Abbott, Edward Abbott. *See* A. SQUARE

Abdullah, Achmed. THE RED STAIN. New York, 1915 — — 60

Abe, Kobo. WOMAN IN THE DUNES. New York, 1964.
  (First U.S. edition) — — 100

Abel, Lionel. SOME POEMS OF RIMBAUD. New York (1939).
  Wraps. (Translated by L. Abel) — 60 75

Abercrombie, Lascelles. INTERLUDES AND POEMS. 1908   25   75   75

Abish, Walter. DUEL SITE. New York, 1970.
    Wraps. (300 copies)   —   75   175

Ableman, Paul. I HEAR VOICES. Paris, 1957   15   40   60

Abrahams, Peter. A BLACKMAN SPEAKS OF FREEDOM.
    Durban, 1938   —   150   250

    DARK TESTAMENT. London, 1942   —   125   200

Abrahams, William. INTERVAL IN CAROLINA.
    New York, 1945   15   30   40

Abse, Dannie. AFTER EVERY GREEN THING. London, 1949   —   60   75

Achebe, Chinua. THINGS FALL APART. London, 1958   —   75   200
New York, 1958   —   35   125

Ackerly, J. R. THE PRISONERS OF WAR. London, 1925.
    Wraps   35   125   200

    (Preceded by *Poems by Four Authors*. London, 1923)

Ackroyd, Peter. OUCH. London, 1971. Wraps. Entire issue
    of *The Curiously Strong*   —   —   250

    LONDON LICKPENNY. London, 1973.
    Wraps. (26 signed/lettered copies)   —   50   250
    Wraps. (474 copies)   —   —   60

Acorn, Milton. IN LOVE AND ANGER. Montreal, 1956   —   — 1,250

Acton, Harold. AQUARIUM. London, 1923.
    (Plain dustwrapper)   50   200   400

Adair, Gilbert. HOLLYWOOD'S VIETNAM. London, 1981   —   —   60

Adam, Helen (Douglas). THE ELFIN PEDLAR 7 TALES TOLD
    BY PIXIE POOL. London, 1923   75   100   175

Adamic, Louis. ROBINSON JEFFERS: A PORTRAIT.
    Seattle, 1929. Wraps   40   75   75

Adams, Alice. CARELESS LOVE. (New York, 1966)   —   350   350

    THE FALL OF DAISY DUKE. London, 1967. (New title)   —   —   250

Adams, Andy. THE LOG OF A COWBOY. Boston, 1903. First
    issue has map at page 28 not in list of illustrations 75   125   250

Adams, Ansel. TAOS PUEBLO. Grabhorn Press. San Francisco,
    1930. Written with Mary Austin. (108 copies)   — 12,000 20,000
    Boston, 1977. 950 signed (Adams) and numbered copies —   —   750

Adams, Charles Francis. RAILROAD LEGISLATION.
Boston, 1868. Wraps — 75 150

Adams, Douglas. THE HITCHHIKER'S GUIDE TO THE
GALAXY. London, 1979 — 30 100
New York (1980) — 25 60

Adams, Edward C. L. CONGAREE SKETCHES . . .
Chapel Hill, 1927. 200 signed and numbered copies — 75 225
Trade edition — — 100

Adams, Franklin P. IN CUPID'S COURT. Evanston, 1902 — — 100

TOBOGGANING ON PARNASSUS. Garden City, 1911 — — 75

Adams, Frederick Upham. PRESIDENT JOHN SMITH.
Chicago, 1897 20 50 75

Adams, Hannah. AN ALPHABETICAL COMPENDIUM . . .
Boston, 1784 — — 2,500

Adams, Henry (Brooks). CIVIL SERVICE REFORM.
Boston, 1869. Wraps 300 1,000 1,500

CHAPTERS OF ERIE . . . Boston, 1871. Written with
Charles F. Adams — — 200

Adams, Herbert. THE SECRET OF BOGEY HOUSE.
London, 1924 — 50 200

Adams, James Truslow. MEMORIALS OF BRIDGEHAMPTON.
1916 — 75 150

Adams, John Quincy. LETTERS OF SILESIA. London, 1804 — — 250

Adams, Leonie. THOSE NOT ELECT. New York, 1925.
10 signed copies on Ingres paper. In plain gray boards — — 750
Trade edition 65 200 250

Adams, Ramon F. COWBOY LINGO. Boston, 1936 — 150 200

Adams, Richard. WATERSHIP DOWN. London, 1972 — 600 1,000
New York, 1972 15 40 75
London, 1976. 250 signed and numbered copies bound
in morocco. In slipcase. Illustrated by John Lawrence — — 1,000

Adams, William Taylor. See Warren T. Ashton

Addams, Charles. DRAWN AND QUARTERED.
New York (1942) — 75 275

Ade, George. CIRCUS DAY. Chicago (1896). (5 previous
anonymous offprints from Chicago Quarterly) — 300 600

ARTIE, A STORY OF . . . Chicago, 1896   20   60   75

Adeler, Max (Charles Heber Clark). OUT OF THE HURLEY-
  BURLY. Phildelphia, 1874. (Also first book illustrated by
  A. B. Frost)   50   75   200

Adler, Edward. NOTES FROM A DARK STREET.
  New York, 1962   —   20   30

ADVENTURES OF A YOUNGER SON. (Edward John
  Trelawny). London, 1831. 3 volumes   250   350   350

ADVENTURES OF HARRY FRANCO (THE). (Charles
  Frederick Briggs). New York, 1839. 2 volumes   200   150   300

ADVENTURES OF RODERICK RANDOM (THE). (Written
  by Tobias Smollett). London, 1748. 2 volumes   300   750   1,000

ADVENTURES OF TIMOTHY PEACOCK . . . (THE). (Daniel
  Pierce Thompson). Middlebury, 1835   —   400   750

Agate, James. L. OF C. (Lines of Communication).
  London, 1917   —   100   100

Agee, James. PERMIT ME VOYAGE. New Hampshire, 1934   200   600   600

AGNES DE CASTRO. (by Catherine Trotter Cockburn).
  London, 1696   —   —   750

Ai (Florence Ogawa). CRUELTY. Boston, 1973   —   35   75

Aiken, Conrad (Potter). EARTH TRIUMPHANT.
  New York, 1914   200   200   250

Aiken, Joan (Delano). ALL YOU'VE EVER WANTED.
  London, 1953   —   —   75

Ainsworth, William Harrison. *See* SIR JOHN CHIVERTON

Akins, Zoe. INTERPRETATIONS. London, 1912   35   50   125

ALARIC AT ROME. (Matthew Arnold). A Prize Poem
  Recited at Rugby School. 12 pages in wraps.
  Rugby, England, 1840   600   5,000   7,500

Albee, Edward. THE ZOO STORY AND THE SANDBOX.
  (New York, 1960). Wraps   —   150   150

  THE ZOO STORY, THE DEATH OF BESSIE SMITH, THE
  SANDBOX. New York, 1960. Dustwrapper price: $2.75   75   125   175
  London (1962)   —   100   100

Albert, Marvin. *See* Albert Conroy

Albert, Neil. JANUARY CORPSE. New York, 1991   —   —   75

ALCEDAMA. (Aleister Crowley). London, 1898. Wraps	300	500	750
Alcott, Amos Bronson. OBSERVATIONS ON THE PRINCIPLES AND METHODS OF INFANT INSTRUCTION. Boston, 1830. Wraps	400	850	1,000
Alcott, Louisa May. FLOWER FABLES. Boston, 1855.			
Gift binding	—	250	600
Regular binding	—	125	250
ALCUIN: A DIALOGUE. (Charles B. Brown). New York, 1798	—	300	2,500
Aldington, Richard. IMAGES. (London, 1915). Wraps	150	250	450
Boston, 1916. Wraps	75	75	150
Aldiss, Brian W(ilson). THE BRIGHTFOUNT DIARIES. London (1955)	—	75	150
SPACE, TIME AND NATHANIEL . . . London (1957). First science fiction	—	—	350
Aldrich, Thomas Bailey. See A., T. B.			
Aldridge, James. SIGNED WITH THEIR HONOUR.			
London, 1942	—	30	50
Boston, 1942	—	25	30
Aldridge, John W. AFTER THE LOST GENERATION. New York (1951)	—	30	40
Alegria, Ciro. BROAD AND ALIEN IS THE WORLD. New York, 1940	—	—	100
Alger, Horatio, Jr. BERTHA'S CHRISTMAS VISION. Boston, 1856	100	850	2,000
Algren, Nelson. SOMEBODY IN BOOTS. New York (1935).			
Issued in rust cloth	250	1,000	1,500
Smooth tan cloth, remainder binding	—	—	1,250
Ali, Ahmed. TWILIGHT IN DELHI. London, 1940	—	60	75
(Previous privately printed books in Urdu)			
Alkin, Anna Laetitia. See POEMS			
Allbeury, Ted. A CHOICE OF ENEMIES. New York, 1972	—	—	125
London (1973)	—	40	125
Allegrotto, Michael. DEATH ON THE ROCKS. New York, 1987	—	—	50

Allen, Gracie. HOW TO BECOME PRESIDENT.
New York (1940)   —   75   150

Allen, (Charles) Grant. PHYSIOLOGICAL AESTHETICS.
London, 1877   —   —   250

   BABYLON. London, 1885   —   50   100

Allen, James Lane. FLUTE AND VIOLIN AND OTHER
KENTUCKY TALES. New York, 1891. First issue: sheets
bulk 1 1/6"   30   40   100
Second issue: sheets bulk 15/16"   —   —   75
Also variant 11/16"   —   —   75

Allen, Phoebe. GILMORY. London, 1876. 3 volumes   —   —   250

Allen, William Hervey. BALLADS OF THE BORDER. (El Paso)
1916. Wraps. (Name misspelled "Hervy" on
copyright page)   300   600   750

   WAMPUM AND OLD GOLD. New Hampshire, 1921.
Stiff wraps   30   75   175

Allen, Woody (Allen Stewart Konigsberg). DON'T DRINK
THE WATER. French. New York, 1967. Wraps   —   40   100
Random House. New York (1967)   —   60   300

Allende, Isabel. THE HOUSE OF THE SPIRITS.
New York, 1985   —   —   125

Alling, Kenneth Slade. CORE OF FIRE.
New York (1939). Wraps   —   75   75
New York, 1940. Cloth   —   40   40

Allingham, Margery (Louise). BLACK'ER CHIEF DICK.
London (1923)   —   250   850
Garden City, 1923   60   200   750

Allingham, William. POEMS. London, 1850   —   —   300

Allison, Dorothy. WOMEN WHO HATE ME.
Brooklyn, 1983. Wraps   —   —   100

Allott, Kenneth. POEMS. Hogarth Press. London, 1938 —   60   125

Allsop, Kenneth. ADVENTURES LIT THEIR STAR.
London, 1949   —   —   40

Allston, Washington, THE SYLPHS OF THE SEASONS . . .
Boston, 1813   —   —   300

Alpert, Hollis. THE SUMMER LOVERS. New York, 1958 —   25   40

Alpha and Omega (Oliver St. John Gogarty). BLIGHT, THE			
TRAGEDY OF DUBLIN. Dublin, 1917	—	200	300
Alta. FREEDOM'S IN SIGHT. (Berkeley) 1969. Wraps	—	—	50
Revised, 1970. Wraps	—	—	25
Alther, Lisa. KINFLICKS. New York, 1976	—	20	35
Altsheler, Joseph Alexander. THE HIDDEN MINE.			
New York, 1896	—	—	250
Alvarez, A. (POEMS) FANTASY POETS #15. Oxford, 1952.			
Wraps	—	75	125
Alvarez, Julia. HOMECOMING. New York, 1984	—	—	125
Amadi, Elechi. THE CONCUBINE. London (1966)	—	—	100
Amado, Jorge. THE VIOLENT LAND. New York, 1945.			
(First English translation)	—	40	125
Ambler, Eric. THE DARK FRONTIER. London, 1936	50	1,500	4,500
Amis, Kingsley (William). BRIGHT NOVEMBER.			
London (1947)	50	300	600
LUCKY JIM. London, 1953	—	—	1,500
Garden City, 1954	—	—	300
Amis, Martin. THE RACHEL PAPERS. London, 1973	—	40	450
New York, 1974	—	—	150
Ammons, A(rchie) R(andolph). OMMATEUM, WITH			
DOXOLOGY. Philadelphia (1955). 300 copies,			
200 destroyed	300	800	1,250
Anaya, Rudolfo A. BLESS ME, ULTIMA (Berkeley) 1972.			
Wraps	—	—	60
Anderson, Alston. LOVER MAN. London (1959).			
(Graves introduction)	—	30	75
Garden City, 1959. (Graves introduction)	—	—	60
Anderson, Forrest. SEA PIECES . . . New York, 1935.			
(155 copies)	—	125	150
Anderson, Frederick Irving. ADVENTURES OF THE			
INFALLIBLE GODAHL. New York (1914)	—	200	250
Anderson, J(ohn) Redwood. THE MUSIC OF DEATH.			
Clifton, England, 1904. Wraps	—	75	125
Anderson, Kent. SYMPATHY FOR THE DEVIL.			
Garden City, 1987	—	—	50

Anderson, Lindsay. MAKING A FILM. London, 1952   —   —   75

Anderson, Maxwell. YOU WHO HAVE DREAMS. New York,
    1925. (1,000 copies printed). 25 signed and numbered
    copies. Issued without dustwrapper   75   300   300
    975 numbered copies   35   60   75

    (Four collaborations in 1924/25)

Anderson, Patrick. A TENT FOR APRIL. Montreal, 1945. Stiff
    wraps and dustwrapper. First regularly published
    book, preceded by two published items in his teens   —   100   350

Anderson, Poul. VAULT OF THE AGES. Philadelphia (1952).
    Blue binding with black lettering   —   50   200

Anderson, Sherwood. WINDY MCPHERSON'S SON. New
    York, 1916. First issue: Blue binding with black letters —   250   500

Anderson, Thomas. YOUR OWN BELOVED SONS.
    New York, 1956   —   —   35

Andrews, Jane. THE SEVEN LITTLE SISTERS . . . Boston, 1861   90   100   125

Andrews, Raymond. APPALACHEE RED. New York, 1978   —   40   100

Andrews, William Loring. A CHOICE COLLECTION OF
    BOOKS FROM THE ALDINE PRESSES. New York, 1885.
    Wraps. (50 copies)   40   400   500

Angell, Roger. THE STONE ARBOR . . . Boston (1960).
    (Edward Gorey dustwrapper)   40   40   50

Angelo, Valenti. NINO. New York, 1938   —   75   125

Angelou, Maya. I KNOW WHY THE CAGED BIRD SINGS.
    New York (1969). First issue: text bulks 5/16", top
    stained magenta   —   35   200

ANONYMOUS. (Michael Fraenkel). Paris (1930). Wraps.
    (First Carrefour Editions book. Written with
    Walter Lowenfels)   75   150   300

Ansen, Alan. THE OLD RELIGION. New York, 1959.
    (300 copies). Wraps   —   —   75

Anstey, Christopher. See THE NEW BATH GUIDE

Anstey, F. (Thomas Anstey Guthrie). VICE VERSA . . .
    London, 1882   40   75   100

Anthony, Peter (Peter and Anthony Shaffer). THE WOMEN IN
    THE WARDROBE. London (1951)   —   100   175

Anthony, Piers (P. A. Dillingham Jacob). CHTHON.
    New York (1967). Wraps — — 25
    London, 1970 — — 125

Antin, David. MARTIN BUBER'S TALES OF ANGELS, SPIRITS
    AND DEMONS. New York, 1958. Translated by Antin
    and Jerome Rothenberg. Wraps 25 60 125

    DEFINITIONS. (New York, 1967). Spiral bound stiff
    wraps. (300 copies) 25 60 75

Antin, Mary. FROM PLOTZK TO BOSTON. Boston, 1899.
    Cloth — 250 300
    Wraps — 150 250

Antoninus, Brother. *See* William Everson

Apes, William. THE EXPERIENCE OF WILLIAM APES . . .
    New York, 1829 — — 1,500

Appel, Benjamin. BRAIN GUY. New York, 1934 — — 200

Apple, Max. INTRODUCING THE ORANGING OF AMERICA.
    (New York, 1973). Wraps — 75 75

    THE ORANGING OF AMERICA . . . New York, 1976 — 30 50

Appleton (Publisher). CRUMBS FROM THE MASTER'S TABLE.
    New York, 1831. By W. Mason. (First book of press) — 100 200

Archer, Jeffrey. NOT A PENNY MORE, NOT A PENNY LESS.
    London, 1976 — — 150
    New York, 1976 — — 75

ARCHITEC-TONICS . . . New York, 1914. (Includes first
    book illustrations by Rockwell Kent) — 75 250

Ard, William (Thomas). THE PERFECT FRAME.
    New York (1951). Wraps — — 75

    BABE IN THE WOODS. (Completed by Lawrence Block.
    His first book). New York, 1960 — — 100

Arden, John Serjeant. MUSGRAVE DANCE. London, 1960 15 35 35

Ardizzone, Edward (Jeffrey Irving). IN A GLASS DARKLY. By
    J. Sheridan Le Fanu. London, 1929. (First book
    illustrated by Ardizzone) 35 125 250

    LITTLE TIM AND THE BRAVE SEA CAPTAIN.
    London, 1936 — — 300

Arenas, Reinaldo. HALLUCINATIONS. New York, 1971.
    (First English translation) — — 125

Arensberg, Ann. SISTER WOLF. New York, 1980   —   20   40

Arensberg, Walter Conrad. POEMS. Boston/New York, 1914   20   60   75

Arion Press. PICTURE/POEMS . . . San Francisco, 1975.
By Andrew Hoyem. (First book of press)   —   75   125

Arkham House. THE OUTSIDER . . . By H. P. Lovecraft.
Sauk City, 1939. (Note: there is a reprint dustwrapper
not as clear as original)   500   900   2,500

Arlen, Michael. THE LONDON VENTURE. London (1920).
(Copies with "1919" reportedly printed later)   75   125   250
New York (1920)   —   50   150

Armitage, Merle. THE ARISTOCRACY OF ART. Los Angeles,
1929. Wraps. 500 copies   —   75   125

Armour, Richard. YOURS FOR THE ASKING. Boston (1942)   —   35   40

Armstrong, Martin. EXODUS . . . London, 1912   25   50   100

Arno, Peter. WHOOPS, DEARIE! (New York, 1927)   40   75   125

Arnold, Matthew. CROMWELL . . . Oxford, 1843. Wraps   —   1,000   1,500

Also see ALARIC AT ROME

Arnow, Harriette (Louisa Simpson). *See* Harriette Simpson

HUNTER'S HORN. New York (1949). Second book—
first under real name. (Note: states first edition)   —   50   125

Arthur, T(imothy) S(hay). *See* INSUBORDINATION

Asbury, Herbert. UP FROM METHODISM. New York, 1926   30   90   125

Ashbery, John (Lawrence). TURANDOT . . . New York,
1953. Wraps. (300 copies)   125   750   1,000

SOME TREES. New Hampshire, 1956   —   150   250

[Preceded by *The Heros*. (Living Theatre. New
York, 1952). Mimeographed legal sheets in folder]

Ashdown, Clifford (R. Austin Freeman). THE ADVENTURES
OF ROMNEY PRINGLE. London, 1902. Written with
J. J. Pitcairn   —   1,000   1,250

Asher, Don. THE PIANO SPORT. New York, 1966   —   25   35

Ashton, Warren T. (William Taylor Adams). HATCHIE, THE
GUARDIAN SLAVE. Boston, 1853   75   75   650

Asimov, Isaac. PEBBLE IN THE SKY. New York, 1950   35   150   750

I ROBOT. New York, 1950	—	350	1,000
Asprin, Robert Lynn. THE COLD CASH WAR. New York (1977)	—	—	60
Asquith, Cynthia. THE GHOST BOOK . . . London (1926). (Edited by Asquith)	—	350	600
Astrachan, Sam. AN END TO DYING. New York (1956)	20	35	40
London (1958)	—	35	35
Athas, Daphne. THE WEATHER OF THE HEART. New York (1947)	—	40	60
Atherton, Gertrude. *See* Frank Lin			
HERMIA SUYDAM. New York (1889). Wraps. Second book, first under own name	40	100	250
Atkinson, Justin Brooks. SKYLINE PROMENADES. New York, 1925. 50 numbered copies in bluish-gray cloth	—	100	175
1,950 numbered copies in blue cloth and patterned boards	15	75	125
Atlee, Philip. THE INHERITORS. New York, 1940	—	125	125
Attansio, A. A. RADIX. New York, 1981. Hardback	—	—	200
Wraps	—	—	30
Attaway, William. LET ME BREATHE THUNDER. New York, 1939	35	150	300

HOMEWARD ❧
SONGS BY ❧❧❧
THE WAY. A.E.

DUBLIN. WHALEY ❧❧❧
46 DAWSON CHAMBERS 46
MDCCCXCIV. PRICE 1/6 ❧❧❧

POEMS

BY

W. H. AUDEN

LONDON
FABER & FABER
24 RUSSELL SQUARE

Atterley, Joseph (George Tucket). A VOYAGE TO THE
   MOON. New York, 1827 — 350   500   750

Attoe, David. LION AT THE DOOR. Boston (1989) — — — 50

Atwood, Margaret (Eleanor). DOUBLE PERSEPHONE.
   Toronto, 1961. Wraps — —   1,200   2,500

   THE EDIBLE WOMAN. London (1969) — — — 400
   Toronto (1969). U.K. sheets — —   200   500
   Boston (1969) — —   60   300

Aubrey-Fletcher, Henry Lancelot. *See* Henry Wade

Auchincloss, Louis (Stanton). *See* Andrew Lee

   THE INJUSTICE COLLECTORS. Boston, 1950.
   Second book, first under own name — 35   75   175

Auden, W(ystan) H(ugh). POEMS. (Hampstead, England,
   1928). Wraps. 12 copies recorded — 1,000   10,000   25,000

   POEMS. London (1930). Stiff wraps in dustwrapper — 200   350   750

   POEMS. New York (1934) — 50   125   300

Audubon, John James. THE BIRDS OF AMERICA FROM
   ORIGINAL DRAWINGS. London, 1827–1838. 87 parts or
   4 double elephant folios containing 435 plates (no text) — —750,000   3mil
   First octavo edition. New York/Philadelphia, 1840–1844.
   7 volumes — — —30,000
   New York, 1870. 8 volumes — — —17,500

Auel, Jean M. THE CLAN OF THE CAVE BEAR.
   New York (1980) — —   50   100

Auslander, Joseph. SUNRISE TRUMPETS. New York, 1924 — 15   35   40

Austen, Jane. *See* SENSE AND SENSIBILITY

Auster, Paul. *See* Paul Benjamin

   UNEARTH LIVING HAND. 1974. Wraps — — — 250

   (Previous translation)

Austin, Jane Goodwin. FAIRY DREAMS . . . Boston (1859) — —   60   75

Austin, Mary (Hunter). THE LAND OF LITTLE RAIN.
   Boston, 1903 — 100   200   350
   Boston, 1950. (Photographs by Ansel Adams) — — — 150

AUTHORSHIP OF THE IMPRECATORY PSALMS. (Thomas
   Bulfinch). Boston (1852). Wraps — —   300   450

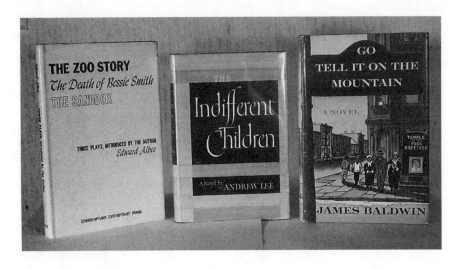

AUTOBIOGRAPHY OF AN EX-COLOURED MAN. (James W.
    Johnson). Boston, 1912   —   350   1,500

Avedon, Richard. OBSERVATIONS. New York, 1959.
    Glassine dustwrapper. Issued in slipcase. Text by
    James Baldwin   —   —   400

Awahsoose the Bear (Rowland Evans Robinson). FOREST
    AND STREAM FABLES. New York (1886). Wraps   150   200   750

Axelrod, George. BEGGAR'S CHOICE. New York, 1947   —   75   150

Aydy, Catherine (Emma Tennant). THE COLOUR OF RAIN.
    London, 1964   —   —   250

Ayrton, Michael. GILLES DE RAIS. By Cecil Gray. London
    (1945). First book illustrated by Ayrton. Stiff wraps and
    dustwrapper. (200 signed and numbered copies)   —   250   350

B

B., H. M. (Max Beerbohm). CARMEN BECCERIENSE . . .
    (Surrey) 1890. 4 pages Latin with notes in English. 2
    known copies   —   5,000   5,000

B., J. K. (John Kendrick Bangs). THE LORGNETTE.
    New York (1886)   50   300   450

B., M. (Maurice Baring). DAMOZEL BLANCHE.
    (Eton, 1891). Wraps   —   —   150

Babel, Isaac. RED CAVALRY. New York, 1929   —   —   750

Babitz, Eve. EVE'S HOLLYWOOD. New York, 1974	—	—	40
Bach, Richard. STRANGER TO THE GROUND. New York (1963)	—	35	75
Bacheller, Irving. THE MASTER OF SILENCE. New York, 1892	30	75	100
Bacon, Delia S(alter). TALES OF THE PURITANS. New Hampshire, 1831	—	—	200
Bacon, Josephine Dodge. SMITH COLLEGE STORIES. New York, 1900	—	40	60
Bacon, Leonard. THE BALLAD OF BLONAY . . . Vevy, 1906. Wraps	—	250	300
Bacon, Peggy. THE TRUE PHILOSOPHER . . . Boston, 1919	—	60	175
Bagnold, Enid. A DIARY WITHOUT DATES. London, 1918	—	35	75
Bahr, Jerome. ALL GOOD AMERICANS. New York, 1937. (Hemingway introduction). Blue cloth (yellow cloth, also with Scribner's "A" on copyright page, published in 1939)	—	150	200
Bailey, H(enry) C(hristopher). MY LADY OF ORANGE. London, 1901	—	35	60
Bailey, Paul. AT THE JERUSALEM. London, 1967	—	—	50
Bainbridge, Beryl. A WEEKEND WITH CLAUDE. (London) 1967	—	40	125
Baird, Thomas. TRIUMPHAL ENTRY. New York (1962)	—	40	40
Baker, Asa (Davis Dresser). MUM'S THE WORD FOR MURDER. New York, 1938	—	75	300
Baker, Carlos H. SHADOWS IN THE STONE. Hanover, 1930. 125 signed and numbered copies. Wraps	—	125	200
Baker, Dorothy. YOUNG MAN WITH A HORN. (Boston) 1938	20	50	150
Baker, Elliott. A FINE MADNESS. New York (1964) London (1964)	— —	50 30	75 50
Baker, Nicholson. THE MEZZANINE. New York (1988) London (1988)	— —	— —	125 35
Baker, Russell. AN AMERICAN IN WASHINGTON. New York, 1961	—	—	35

Balchin, Nigel. *See* Mark Spade

Baldwin, James (Arthur). GO TELL IT ON THE MOUNTAIN.
New York (1953)	150	400	2,000
London, 1954	50	100	300

Baldwin, Joseph G. REMARKS OF MR. BALDWIN . . .
(No-place, no-date [House of Representatives,
Montgomery, Alabama 1843–44]). 16-page pamphlet
(speech favoring resolution to rescind . . .) — — 350

   THE FLUSH TIMES OF ALABAMA AND MISSISSIPPI.
New York, 1853	100	200	300

Baldwin, Michael. THE SILENT MIRROR. London (1951) — 40 75

Ball, John. IN THE HEAT OF THE NIGHT. New York, 1965 — — 150

Ballantine, Sheila. NORMA JEAN THE TERMITE QUEEN.
New York, 1975 — 30 40

Ballantyne, Robert Michael. HUDSON'S BAY . . . Privately
printed, Edinburgh, 1848	—	1,000	2,500
Edinburgh/London, 1848	—	350	400

Ballard, J(ames) G(raham). THE WIND FROM NOWHERE.
New York, 1962. Wraps — — 100

   THE DROWNED WORLD. London, 1962 — — 1,500
   New York (1962) — — 50

Ballau, Jenny. SPANISH PRELUDE. Boston, 1937 — 30 40

Balliett, Whitney. THE SOUND OF SURPRISE.
New York, 1959	—	125	125
London, 1960	—	75	75

Ballinger, John. THE WILLIAMSBURG FORGERIES.
New York, 1989 — — 40

Bambara, Toni Cade. GORILLA, MY LOVE. New York (1972) — 40 125

(Edited two books previously)

Bancroft, George. PROSPECTUS OF A SCHOOL . . .
(Cambridge, 1823). Written with J. C. Coggswell. Wraps — 350 200

   POEMS. Cambridge (Mass.), 1823 — 100 200

Bancroft, Irving. THE MASTER OF SILENCE. New York, 1892 100 125 125

Bangs, John Kendrick. *See* J. K. B.

   ROGER CAMERDEN. New York, 1887. Wraps 50 125 250

Banks, Iain. THE WASP FACTORY. London (1984)   —   —   75
    Boston, 1984   —   —   50

Banks, Lynne Reid. THE L-SHAPED ROOM. London, 1960   —   —   60

Banks, Russell. WAITING TO FREEZE. Northwood Narrows,
    1969. Wraps   —   —   125

Bannerman, Helen. THE STORY OF LITTLE BLACK SAMBO.
    London, 1899   —   — 6,000
    New York, 1900   —   — 2,500

Bannister, Don. SAM CHARD. London, 1979   —   —   35

Bantock, Nick. GRIFFIN & SABINE. San Francisco (1991)   —   —   200

Banville, John. LONG LANKIN. London, 1970   —   —   250

Banyan Press. *See* Gil Orlovitz

Barbellion, W. N. P. (Bruce Frederick Cummings). THE
    JOURNAL OF A DISAPPOINTED MAN. London, 1919   25   100   100
    New York, 1919   —   75   75

Barfield, Owen. DANCER, UGLINESS AND WASTE. (London,
    circa 1922–24). Wraps   —   —   200

    HISTORY IN ENGLISH WORDS. London, 1926. (8 pages
    of advertisements)   25   75   125

Barich, Bill. LAUGHING IN THE HILLS. New York, 1980   —   —   35

Baring, Maurice. *See* M. B.

Barker, A(udrey) L(illian). INNOCENTS. London, 1947   —   60   75

Barker, Clive. THE BOOKS OF BLOOD. London, 1984/1985.
    Wraps. Volumes I through VI   —   —   200
    London (1985/1986). Cloth. 6 volumes. 200 signed and
    numbered copies   —   —   750
    London (1985/1986) Cloth. 6 volumes   —   —   250

Barker, Eric (Wilson). THE PLANETARY HEART.
    Mill Valley, 1942   60   90   100

Barker, George (Granville). CATALOG OF EMOTIONS.
    (London) 1932. Wraps   —   —   300

    ALANNA AUTUMNAL. London, 1933   —   125   250

Barker, Shirley. THE DARK HILLS UNDER. New Haven, 1933   —   50   50

Barlow, William. THE NAVIGATORS SUPPLY. London, 1597   —   — 9,000

Barnard, Robert. DEATH OF AN OLD GOAT. London, 1974	—	—	125
New York (1977)	—	—	75
Barnes, Arthur K. INTERPLANETARY HUNTER.			
New York (1956)	—	20	40
Barnes, Djuna. THE BOOK OF REPULSIVE WOMEN. (New			
York, 1915). Wraps	200	400	750
New York (1948). 1,000 copies. Wraps	—	—	100
Barnes, Julian. METROLAND. London (1980)	—	50	300
New York, 1981	—	—	150
Also see Dan Kavanagh			
Barney, Natalie C(lifford). QUELQUES PORTRAITS.			
Paris, 1900	—	300	450
Barnsley, Alan. THE FROG PRINCE . . . Aldington, 1952.			
Wraps	—	60	75
Barnum, Phineas Taylor. THE LIFE OF P. T. BARNUM.			
New York, 1855	—	150	150
Baron, Alexander. FROM THE CITY FROM THE PLOUGH.			
London, 1948	—	60	60
Barr, Nevada. BITTERSWEET. New York (1984)	—	—	175
Barr, Robert. *See* Luke Sharp			
Barrett, Clifton Waller. BLUEPRINT FOR A BASIC . . .			
(New York) 1944. Mimeographed sheets	30	60	75
Barrett, E. B. (Elizabeth Barrett Browning). THE BATTLE OF			
MARATHON. London, 1820	—	12,000	40,000
Barrie, James M. BETTER DEAD. London, 1888. Wraps	—	400	1,000
Barstow, Stan(ley). A KIND OF LOVING. London (1960)	—	40	40
Barth, John (Simmons). THE FLOATING OPERA.			
New York (1956)	150	300	450
London (1968). Revised edition	—	40	75
Barthelme, Donald. TWO STORIES FROM DR. CALIGARI.			
(Boston) 1964. Unbound sheets in box.			
(Promotional item)	—	—	500
COME BACK DR. CALIGARI. Boston (1964)	40	150	200
London (1966)	—	75	75
Barthelme, Fredrick. RANGOON. New York, 1970. Cloth	—	60	150
Wraps	—	25	50

Barthes, Roland. WRITING DEGREE ZERO. London, 1967	—	—	100
New York, 1968	—	—	75
Bartlett, John. A BOOK OF HYMNS FOR YOUNG PERSONS. Cambridge (Eng.), 1854	—	100	150
Also see A COLLECTION OF FAMILIAR QUOTATIONS			
Barton, Bruce. MORE POWER TO YOU. New York, 1917	15	25	35
Bartram, William. TRAVELS THROUGH NORTH & SOUTH CAROLINA. Philadelphia, 1791	—	8,000	7,500
London, 1792	—	4,500	3,000
Barzun, Jacques Martin. SAMPLINGS AND CHRONICLES. (Edited by JMB). New York, 1927. (500 copies)	—	100	125
Bass, Rick. THE DEER PASTURE. College Station, Texas (1985)	—	—	100
Basso, Hamilton. RELICS AND ANGELS. New York, 1929	35	75	125
Batchelor, John Calvin. THE FURTHUR ADVENTURES OF HALEY'S COMET. New York, 1980. Cloth	—	—	175
Wraps	—	—	35
Bates, H. E. THE LAST BREAD. London (1926). Wraps	40	150	350
Bates, Ralph. SIERRA. London, 1933	—	60	125
Baum, L(yman) Frank. THE BOOK OF HAMBURGS. Hartford, 1886	200	1,500	2,500
MOTHER GOOSE IN PROSE. Chicago (1897). (First Maxfield Parrish illustrations). First issue: gatherings of 8 and 4 leaves at end concluding on p. (268)	300	1,200	3,500
Bausch, Richard. REAL PRESENCE. New York (1980)	—	—	50
Bausch, Robert. ON THE WAY HOME. New York (1982)	—	—	40
Bawden, Nina. WHO CALLS THE TUNE. London, 1953	—	—	75
Bax, Clifford. TWENTY CHINESE POEMS. Hampstead, 1910	—	75	125
Baxter, Glen. DRAWINGS. New York, 1974. Wraps	—	—	75
Baxter, Richard. POETICAL FRAGMENTS. London, 1821	—	150	150
Bayley, Nicola. NICOLA BAYLEY'S BOOK OF NURSERY RHYMES. London, 1975	—	—	100
Bayliss, John. THE WHITE KNIGHT . . . London, 1944	—	40	40
Beach, Abel. *See* AN EARLY PIONEER			

Beach, Joseph Warren. SONNETS OF THE HEAD AND HEART.			
Boston, 1903	40	50	75
Beach, Rex (Ellingwood). PARDNERS. New York, 1905	25	60	75
Beagle, Peter S. A FINE AND PRIVATE PLACE.			
New York, 1960	35	75	200
(London, 1960)	—	—	75
Bear, Greg. HEGIRA. New York (1975). Wraps	—	—	50
New York (1968). Cloth. Revised	—	—	40
Beard, Charles Austin. THE OFFICE OF THE JUSTICE . . .			
New York, 1904. Wraps	—	75	200
Beard, James. HORS D'OEUVRES AND CANAPES.			
New York (1940)	125	125	200
Beasley, Gertrude. MY FIRST THIRTY YEARS . . .			
(Paris, 1925). Wraps	—	400	600
Beaton, Cecil. THE TWILIGHT OF THE NYMPHS. London,			
1928. 1,200 copies. Book by Pierre Louys, Illustrations			
by Beaton	—	100	125
THE BOOK OF BEAUTY. London (1930)	—	250	300
Beaton, George (Gerald Brenan). JACK ROBINSON.			
London (1933)	—	75	400
New York, 1934	—	—	300
Beattie, Ann. CHILLY SCENES OF WINTER.			
Garden City, 1976	—	75	100
DISTORTIONS. Garden City, 1976. (Published			
simultaneously)	—	75	125
Beaumont, Charles (Charles Nutt). THE HUNGER . . .			
New York (1957)	—	75	150
Beaumont Press. TIDES. Written by John Drinkwater.			
(London) 1917. 20 signed copies on vellum	—	—	1,500
250 copies	50	75	200
Beauvoir, Simone de. THE BLOOD OF OTHERS.			
London, 1948. (First English translation)	—	75	100
New York, 1948	—	35	50
Bechko, P. A. NIGHT OF THE FLAMING GUNS.			
New York, 1974	—	—	35
Becke, Louis. BY REEF AND PALM. London, 1894. Cloth	—	—	100
Wraps	40	75	75

Becker, Stephen. THE SEASON OF THE STRANGER.
New York (1951)   —   50   75

Beckett, Samuel (Barclay). WHOROSCOPE. Hours Press.
Paris, 1930. Stapled wraps. 100 signed copies   1,500   2,250   3,000
200 unsigned copies   500   1,000   1,500

PROUST. London, 1931   300   300   350
Paris, 1931. Wraps   —   300   400
New York (1957). 250 signed and numbered copies.
Issued without dustwrapper   —   200   500

Beckford, William. *See* BIOGRAPHICAL MEMOIRS . . .

Beckham, Barry. MY MAIN MOTHER. New York (1969)   —   —   75

Bedford, Sybille. THE SUDDEN VIEW. London, 1953   —   —   100
New York, 1953   —   —   75

Bedichek, Roy. ADVENTURES WITH A TEXAS NATURALIST.
Garden City, 1947   —   100   1500

Beebe, Lucius. FALLEN STARS. Cambridge (Mass.), 1921.
Wraps. 50 copies   —   —   150
Boston, 1921   —   100   100

Beebe, (Charles) William. TWO BIRD-LOVERS IN MEXICO.
Boston, 1905. First issue: Charles M. Beebe on cover   100   1,500   1,750
Second issue: C. William Beebe on cover   50   250   350
Third issue: gold sky background lacking   30   125   150
Fourth issue: lacks pictorial design, just lettered   20   60   75

Beecher, Harriet Elizabeth. PRIMARY GEOGRAPHY FOR
CHILDREN . . . Cincinnati, 1833. (Written with
Catherine Beecher)   —   —   2,500

PRIZE TALE: A NEW ENGLAND SKETCH. Lowell,
Massachusetts, 1834   1,000   500   1,000

Beecher, John. AND I WILL BE HEARD. New York (1940).
Wraps   50   75   25

Beechwood, Mary. MEMPHIS JACKSON'S SON. Boston, 1956   —   —   125

Beeding, Francis (John Leslie Palmer and Hilary Saunders).
THE SEVEN SLEEPERS. London, 1925   —   60   100

Beer, Patricia. LOSS OF THE MAGYAR. London, 1959. Issued
in glassine dustwrapper   —   50   75

Beer, Thomas. THE FAIR REWARDS. New York, 1922   25   150   150

*with sincere regards to
Mr. and Mrs. Bull from*

TWO BIRD-LOVERS IN MEXICO

BY

C. WILLIAM BEEBE

*Curator of Ornithology of the New York Zoölogical Park and Life
Member of the New York Zoölogical Society; Member
of the American Ornithologists' Union*

C. William Beebe.

ILLUSTRATED WITH PHOTOGRAPHS
FROM LIFE TAKEN BY THE AUTHOR

Mary Blair Beebe

BOSTON AND NEW YORK
HOUGHTON, MIFFLIN AND COMPANY
The Riverside Press, Cambridge
1905

Beerbohm, Max. THE WORKS OF MAX BEERBOHM. New
  York, 1896. 1,000 copies—400 pulped   300   225   350
  London, 1896   150   150   250

Beeton, Isabella. THE BOOK OF HOUSEHOLD MANAGEMENT.
  London, 1861. 2 volumes. First issue: "18 Bouverie St."
  on woodcut title page   —   500 1,000

Begley, Louis. WARTIME LIES. New York, 1991   —   —   75

Behan, Brendan. THE QUARE FELLOW. London, 1956   50   150   200
  New York (1956). Boards. 100 numbered copies. Issued
  without dustwrapper   35   100   150
  Wraps   20   25   35

Behm, Marc. THE QUEEN OF THE NIGHT. Boston, 1977   —   —   60

Behn, Noel. THE KREMLIN LETTER. New York (1966)   —   35   100

Behrman, Samuel Nathaniel. BEDSIDE MANNER. New York,
  1924. Written with J. K. Nicholson. Wraps   —   50   250

  THE SECOND MAN. New York, 1927. Stiff wraps in
  dustwrapper   25   100   200
  London, 1928   —   75   125

  (Another collaboration 1926)

Beinhart, Larry. NO ONE RIDES FOR FREE. New York, 1986   —   —   50

Belitt, Ben. THE FIVE FOLD MESH. New York, 1938   —   60   60

Belknap, Jeremy. See THE FORESTERS . . .

Bell, Acton (Ann Brontë). See Ellis Bell

Bell, Clive. ART. London, 1914   —   75   200
  New York (1914). English sheets   —   —   150

Bell, Currer (Charlotte Brontë). JANE EYRE. London, 1847.
  3 volumes. First issue: Bell as editor. 36 page catalog in
  volume one dated June and October   —   6,000 15,000
  New York, 1848   —   —   3,000

Bell, Currer, Ellis, and Acton (Charlotte, Emily, and Ann
  Brontë). POEMS. London, 1846. (Published by
  Aylott and Jones)   —   7,500 25,000
  Philadelphia, 1848   —   —   2,000
  London, 1846. (Published by Smith, Elder in 1848)   —   750 2,000

Bell, DeWitt. RAVENSWOOD . . . Hanover, 1963.
  (250 copies)   —   50   75

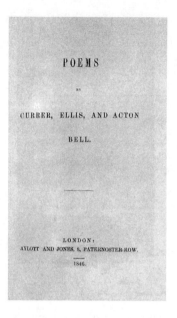

Bell, Ellis (Emily Brontë). WUTHERING HEIGHTS. London, 1847. 2 volumes. (1,000 copies); and AGNES GREY by Acton Bell (Ann Bronte). (1,000 copies). 3 volumes in total   —   8,000   50,000

Bell, Josephine (Doris Bell and Collier Ball). MURDER IN HOSPITAL. London, 1937   —   50   100

Bell, Julian. CHAFFINCHES. Cambridge (Eng.), 1929. Wraps   —   75   150

Bell, Madison Smartt. THE WASHINGTON SQUARE ENSEMBLE. New York, 1983   —   35   125
(London, 1983)   —   —   75

Bell, Marvin. TWO POEMS. Iowa City, 1965. Issued without dustwrapper   —   —   350

Bell, Quentin. ON HUMAN FINERY. Hogarth Press. London, 1947   —   40   100

Bell, Robert. THE BUTTERFLY TREE. Philadelphia (1959)   —   35   40

Bellah, James Warner. SKETCH BOOK OF A CADET FROM GASCONY. New York, 1923   —   75   125

Bellamy, Edward. *See* SIX TO ONE

Belli, Melvin M. BELLI LOOKS AT LIFE AND LAW IN JAPAN. Indianapolis (1960)   —   30   75

Belloc, Hilaire. VERSES AND SONNETS. London, 1896	75	400	600
Bellow, Saul. DANGLING MAN. New York (1944)	200	600	1,500
London, 1946	75	250	300
Bemelmans, Ludwig. HANSI. New York, 1934	35	250	400
Benchley, Nathaniel. SIDE STREET. New York, 1950	—	35	60
Benchley, Robert C. OF ALL THINGS. New York, 1921. With and without advertisements at end, priority unknown	50	300	750
London, 1922	35	150	350
Benedict, Pinckney. TOWN SMOKES. Princeton (1987). Wraps	—	—	75
Benet, Laura. FAIRY BREAD. New York, 1921	—	50	150
Benét, Stephen Vincent. FIVE MEN AND POMPEY. Boston, 1915. First issue in purple wraps (trial)	150	350	250
Second issue: brown wraps. (Also noted in a white dustwrapper)	50	75	125
Benét, William Rose. MERCHANTS FROM CATHAY. New York, 1913	40	35	75
Benford, Gregory. DEEPER THAN THE DARKNESS. New York (1970). Wraps	—	—	30
THE STARS IN SHROUD. New York, 1978. New title, revised, of first book	—	—	40
Benjamin, Paul. SQUEEZE PLAY. London, 1982. Wraps	—	—	200
Bennett, E. A(rnold). A MAN FROM THE NORTH. London, 1898	50	250	400
Bennett, Emerson. THE BRIGAND . . . New York, 1842. Wraps	—	400	400
Bennett, Hal. A WILDERNESS OF VINES. Garden City, 1966	—	40	150
Bensko, John. GREEN SOLDIERS. New Hampshire (1981)	—	—	25
Benson, Arthur Christopher. *See* Christopher Carr			
WILLIAM LAUD, ARCHBISHOP OF CANTERBURY. London, 1887. (Second book, first under own name)	75	100	250
Benson, E(dward) F(redric). DODO. London, 1893. 2 volumes	—	100	350
Benson, R. H. THE LIGHT INVISIBLE. London, 1903	—	60	60
Benson, Sally. PEOPLE ARE FASCINATING. New York (1936)	—	—	60

Benson, Stella. I POSE. London, 1915	—	—	75
New York, 1916	—	—	50
Bentley, E(dmund) C(lerihew). *See* E. Clerihew			
TRENT'S LAST CASE. London (1913)	—	125	250
THE WOMAN IN BLACK. New York, 1913. (New title)	—	75	200
Bentley, Eric Russell. A CENTURY OF HERO WORSHIP. Philadelphia/New York (1944)	—	40	40
Benton, Thomas Hart. EUROPE AFTER 8:15. New York, 1914. (First illustrated. Written by Mencken, Nathan, and W. H. Wright). First issue: cloth stamped in blue	—	100	200
Second issue: cloth stamped in gold	—	75	150
Berendt, John. MIDNIGHT IN THE GARDEN OF GOOD AND EVIL. New York (1994)	—	—	40
Beresford, J(ohn) D(avys). THE HAMPDENSHIRE WONDER. London, 1911	—	—	350
Beresford-Howe, Constance. THE UNREASONING HEART. New York, 1946	—	—	50
Bereton, Ford (Samuel Rutherford Crockett). DOLCE COR . . . London, 1886	—	—	250
Berge, Carol. THE VULNERABLE ISLAND. Cleveland, 1964. Wraps. (105 copies)	25	50	100
Berger, John. A PAINTER OF OUR TIME. London, 1958	—	75	125
New York, 1959	—	—	75
Berger, Thomas (Louis). CRAZY IN BERLIN. New York (1958)	30	175	250
Bergman, Andrew. WE'RE IN THE MONEY. New York (1971)	—	—	75
THE BIG KISS-OFF OF 1944. New York (1974)	—	35	60
Berkeley, Anthony. *See* THE LAYTON COURT MYSTERY			
Berkman, Alexander. PRISON MEMOIRS OF AN ANARCHIST. New York, 1912	—	75	100
Berkson, Bill. SATURDAY NIGHT POEMS. New York, 1961. Wraps. (300 copies)	15	60	125
Berlin, Lucia. A MANUAL FOR CLEANING LADIES. (No-place, 1977). Wraps in envelope	—	—	75
Berne, Eric. THE MIND IN ACTION. New York, 1947	—	50	75

Bernhard, Thomas. GARGOYLES. New York, 1970. (First
  U.S. publication) — — 125

Bernstein, Aline. THREE BLUE SUITS. New York, 1933.
  (600 signed copies. Issued in slipcase) 60 100 125

Bernstein, Jane. DEPARTURES. New York (1979) — — 35

Berriault, Gina. THE DESCENT. New York, 1960 — 30 50

Berrigan, Daniel. TIME WITHOUT NUMBERS.
  New York, 1957 20 50 50

Berrigan, Ted (Edmund J.). THE SONNETS. (New York)
  1964. (300 copies). Stapled mimeographed sheets 25 60 100
  Grove Press. New York (1964). Wraps — 25 35

  (Preceded by at least 2 privately printed pamphlets)

Berry, Don. TRASK. New York, 1960 — 30 40

Berry, Francis. GOSPEL OF FIRE. London, 1933 15 60 60

Berry, Wendell (Erdman). NATHAN COLTER.
  Boston, 1960 40 200 300
  San Francisco, 1985. Revised. 26 signed and lettered
  copies — — 200

Berryman, John. *See* FIVE YOUNG AMERICAN POETS

POEMS. Norfolk (1942). Boards. (500 copies).	125	250	400
Wraps. (1,500 copies)	75	75	125

Berton, Pierre. THE GOLDEN TRAIL. Toronto, 1954	—	—	150

Bessie, Alvah Cecil. DWELL IN THE WILDERNESS.

New York (1935)	50	100	250
London, 1936	—	—	150

(Previous translations)

Bester, Alfred. THE DEMOLISHED MAN. Chicago (1953).

200 signed copies	—	250	400
Unsigned	—	150	300
London (1953)	—	60	100

Betjeman, John. MOUNT ZION, OR IN TOUCH WITH . . .
London (1931). Issued without dustwrapper. First issue:

blue and gold pattern cover	200	450	750
Second issue: striped paper cover	—	350	500

Betts, Doris. THE GENTLE INSURRECTION . . .

New York, 1954	—	100	175

Beveridge, Albert Jeremiah. THE RUSSIAN ADVANCE.

New York, 1903	—	50	125

Beynon, John (John Beynon Harris). THE SECRET PEOPLE.

London (1935)	50	400	600
Second issue: in green binding with black lettering; dustwrapper priced "2/6" (probably published in 1936)	—	—	250

Bezzerides, A. I. LONG HAUL. New York (1938)	—	40	75

Bianco, Margery (Williams). THE LITTLE WOODEN DOLL.

New York, 1925. (First under this name)	—	—	75

Also see Margery Williams

Bierce, Ambrose (Gwinnett). *See* Dod Grile

Biggers, Earl Derr. IF YOU'RE ONLY HUMAN. 1912	100	100	350
SEVEN KEYS TO BALDPATE. Indianapolis (1913)	50	75	200

Bingham, Sallie. AFTER SUCH KNOWLEDGE. Boston, 1960	—	40	60

Binns, Archie. LIGHTSHIP. New York (1934)	—	60	75

Binyon, Laurence. PERSEPHONE. London, 1890. Wraps.

(Newdigate Prize–winner)	—	300	400

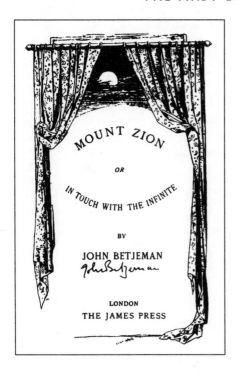

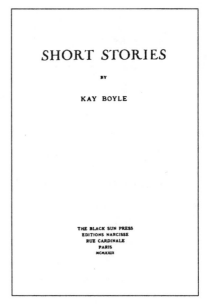

LYRIC POEMS. London, 1894	100	150	250
POEMS. Oxford, 1895. (200 copies). Wraps	—	125	200
BIOGRAPHICAL MEMOIRS OF EXTRAORDINARY PAINTERS. (By William Beckford). London, 1780	—	—	1,000
Bion and Moschos (Robert Lovell and Robert Southey). POEMS. Bristol, 1794	—	400	1,500
Bird, Bessie Calhoun. AIRS FROM THE WOOD WINDS. Philadelphia (1935). (Only book). 25 signed and numbered copies	50	150	750
300 signed and numbered copies	—	50	300
Bird, Robert Montgomery. See CALAVAR			
Bird, William. A PRACTICAL GUIDE TO FRENCH WINE. Paris (no-date: 1922?). Wraps	—	150	200
Bird & Bull Press. A COLLECTION OF RECEIPTS . . . Philadelphia, 1958. (First book of press of Henry Morris). Wraps. 100 numbered copies	—	1,250	2,000
Birdsell, Sandra. NIGHT TRAVELLERS. Winnipeg, 1982	—	—	50

Birmingham, Stephen. YOUNG MR. KEEFE. Boston, 1958	—	35	40
Birney, (Alfred) Earle. *See* E. Robertson			
DAVID . . . Toronto, 1942. (500 copies)	—	200	350
Biro, Val. BUMBY'S HOLIDAY. London, 1943	—	—	150
Birrell, Augustine. *See* OBITER DICTA			
Bishop, Elizabeth. NORTH AND SOUTH. Boston, 1946. (1,000 copies)	50	350	600
Bishop, John Peale. GREEN FRUIT. Boston, 1917	50	150	300
Bishop, Zealia. THE CURSE OF YIG. South Carolina, 1953	—	75	175
Bissell, Richard. A STRETCH ON THE RIVER. Boston, 1950	—	40	50
Bissoondath, Neil. DIGGING UP THE MOUNTAINS . . . Toronto, 1985	—	—	100
London, 1986	—	—	50
Black, E. L. (Sir John Ellerman). WHY DO THEY LIKE IT . . . (Dijon, 1927). Wraps	—	200	300
Black, (Harvey) MacKnight. MACHINERY. New York, 1929	—	75	75
Black, Mansell (Elleston Trevor). SINISTER CARGO. London, 1951	—	100	150
Black Manikin Press. *See* Ralph Cheever Dunning			
Black Sparrow Press. NOT MEANING NOT TO *SEE*. By Bernard A. Forrest. (Los Angeles, 1967). (75 signed copies)	—	150	250
Blackburn, Paul. PROENSA . . . (Majorca) 1953. (Translation). Wraps	100	225	225
THE DISSOLVING FABRIC. (Majorca) 1955. Wraps	50	175	300
Blackmore, Richard Doddridge. *See* Melanter			
Blackmur, R(ichard) P(almer). T. S. ELIOT. (Cambridge, Mass.) 1929. Wraps		100	200
DIRTYHANDS OR THE TRUE BORN CENSOR. Cambridge (Mass.), 1932. (Offprint from *Hound and Horn*). Wraps	50	150	150
Blackwood, Algernon. THE EMPTY HOUSE . . . London, 1906	75	200	250
New York, 1917	—	75	100

Blackwood, Caroline. FOR ALL THAT I FOUND THERE.
London, 1973 — 35 40

Blaikie, John Arthur. *See* Edmund Gosse

Blaise, Clark. A NORTH AMERICAN EDUCATION.
Garden City, 1973 — — 50

Blake, Nicholas (C. Day-Lewis pseudonym). A QUESTION
OF PROOF. London, 1935. (First under this name) — 300 500

Blanding, Don. LEAVES FROM A GRASS-HOUSE. (Honolulu,
1923). Wraps — 50 100

Blatty, William. ULYSSES AND THE CYCLOPS. Los Angeles (1956).
Pictorial boards issued w/o dustwrapper. Written with
James J. Cullen — — 150

WHICH WAY TO MECCA, JACK? New York, 1960 — 35 40

Blaylock, James P. THE ELFIN SHIP. New York (1982).
Wraps — — 25

Blechman, Burt. HOW MUCH? New York (1961) — 40 40

Blesh, Rudi. THIS IS JAZZ. San Francisco (1943). Wraps — 150 100
London, 1943. Wraps — — 75

Blish, James (Benjamin). JACK OF EAGLES. New York (1952) — 100 150

Bloch, Robert. SEA KISSED. (London, 1945). Wraps. First
issue: 39 pages. "Printed in Great Britain" on p. 39 — 250 750
Second issue: 36 pages. "Printed in Eire" on p. 36 — 200 600

THE OPENER OF THE WAY. Sauk City, 1945.
(2,000 copies) 75 150 500

Block, Herbert. THE HERBLOCK BOOK. Boston, 1952 75 35 30

Block, Lawrence. *See* William Ard

DEATH PULLS A DOUBLE CROSS. New York (1961).
Wraps — 100 100

Blondal, Patricia. A CANDLE TO LIGHT THE SUN.
(Toronto, 1960) — — 60

Blum, Etta. POEMS. New York, 1937 — 40 50

Blunden, E(dmund) C(harles). POEMS 1913 AND 1914.
(Horsham, 1914). Wraps. (100 copies) 100 300 850

Blunt, Wilfred Scawen. *See* PROTEUS SONNETS AND SONGS

Bly, Robert (Elwood). *See* Hans Hvass

THE LION'S TAIL AND EYES. Madison, 1962. (Written with J. Wright and W. Duffy).	30	100	175

SILENCE IN THE SNOWY FIELDS. Middleton (1962).

Cloth	—	125	150
Wraps	40	50	50

(Previous broadside in 1961)

Blyton, Enid (Mary). CHILD WHISPERS. London, 1922	—	—	100
Bodenheim, Maxwell. MINNA AND MYSELF. New York, 1918. First issue: "Master-Posner" for "Master-Poisoner" p. (67). (Written with Ben Hecht. This was also his first book)	50	75	75
Bodine, A. Aubrey. MY MARYLAND. Baltimore, 1952	—	—	50
Bodkin, M(atthais) McDonald. WHITE MAGIC. London, 1897	—	150	150
PAUL BECK: THE RULE OF THUMB DETECTIVE. London, 1898	—	500	500
Bodley Booklets #1. THE HAPPY HYPOCRITE: A FAIRY TALE. By Max Beerbohm. New York/London, 1897. First issue: period on cover, colophon dated December 1896	—	200	200
Bogan, Louise. BODY OF THIS DEATH. New York, 1923	60	250	600
Bogner, Norman. IN SPELLS NO LONGER BOUND. London (1961)	—	40	40
Bogosian, Eric. DRINKING IN AMERICA. New York, 1987. Wraps	—	—	35
Bok, Edward W(illiam). THE YOUNG MAN IN BUSINESS. Philadelphia, 1894. Wraps	—	100	100
Boles, Robert. THE PEOPLE ONE KNOWS. Boston, 1964	—	30	60
Bolitho, William. LEVIATHAN. London, 1923	—	30	75
Bolt, Robert (Oxton). FLOWERING CHERRY. London, 1958	—	50	100

(First play, *A Man for All Seasons,* not published until 1961)

Bolton, George G. A SPECIALIST IN CRIME. London, 1904. (Only book)	—	150	150
Bombal, Maria-Luisa. HOUSE OF MIST. New York (1947). First English translation	—	—	60

Bond, (Thomas) Michael. BEAR CALLED PADDINGTON.
London, 1958   —   —   250
Boston, 1960   —   —   175

Bond, Nelson (Slade). MR. MERGENTHWIRKER'S
LOBBLIES . . . New York, 1946   40   60   75

Bontemps, Arna (Wendall). GOD SENDS SUNDAY.
New York, 1931   —   175   950

Booth, Evangeline Cory. LOVE IS ALL. New York (1908)   35   50   75

Booth, Philip. LETTER FROM A DISTANT LAND: POEMS.
New York, 1957   15   35   75

Booth, General William. IN DARKEST ENGLAND AND THE
WAY OUT. London (1880). First issue: last line of
dedication in small type than preceding line   —   —   250

Borges, Jorge Luis. FICCIONES. London (1962)   —   —   250
New York (1962)   —   —   125

Borrow, George (Henry). *See* CELEBRATED TRIALS

Boswell, Robert. DANCING AT THE MOVIES. Iowa City,
1986. (1,500 copies)   —   —   125

Boswell, Thomas. HOW LIFE IMITATES THE WORLD SERIES.
Garden City, 1972   —   —   40

Bottoms, David. JAMMING WITH THE BAND AT THE VFW.
(Austell, Georgia, 1978). Wraps   —   —   60

     SHOOTING RATS AT THE BIBB COUNTY DUMP.
(New York, 1980)   —   —   50

Bottrall, Ronald. THE LOOSENING . . . Cambridge (Eng.), 1931.
Issued in tissue dustwrapper   25   50   75

Boucher, Anthony (William Anthony Parker White). THE
CASE OF THE SEVEN OF CALVARY. New York, 1937   —   150   450

Boulle, Pierre. THE BRIDGE OVER THE RIVER KWAI. (First
translation in English). London, 1954   —   100   175
New York, 1954   —   50   100

Bourdillon, Francis W. AMONG THE FLOWERS . . .
London, 1878   50   75   125

Bourjaily, Vance (Nye). THE END OF MY LIFE.
New York, 1947   30   75   100

Bourke-White, Margaret. EYES ON RUSSIA.
New York, 1931   75   300   400

Bourne, Randolph S(illiman). YOUTH AND LIFE.
  Boston, 1913   125   125   200

Bova, Ben. STAR CONQUERORS. Philadelphia (1959)   —   150   200

Bowen, Catherine Drinker. A HISTORY OF LEHIGH
  UNIVERSITY. (Bethlehem, Pennsylvania) 1924   —   —   200

Bowen, Elizabeth. ENCOUNTERS. London, 1923   50   750 1,000

Bowen, Marjorie (Gabrielle M. V. Long). THE VIPER OF
  MILAN. London, 1906   —   100   125

Bowers, Edgar. THE FORM OF LOSS. Denver, 1956   —   —   150

Bowles, Jane. TWO SERIOUS LADIES. New York (1943)   100   400   750
  London, 1965   —   75   100

Bowles, Paul (Frederick). TWO POEMS. (New York, 1934).
  Wraps   200   600 4,000

  THE SHELTERING SKY. London (1949)   40   250 1,000
  (New York, 1949)   30   150   750

Bowman, David. LET THE DOG DRIVE. New York (1992)   —   —   175

Boyd, Blanche. NERVES. Plainfield, Vermont (1973). Wraps —   —   35

Boyd, James. DRUMS. New York, 1925	25	200	350
New York (1928). Illustrated by N. C. Wyeth.			
525 signed and numbered copies	—	125	750
Trade edition	—	—	75
Boyd, Thomas. THROUGH THE WHEAT. New York, 1923	35	125	150
Boyd, William. A GOOD MAN IN AFRICA. London, 1981	—	75	750
New York (1982)	—	30	75
Boyer, Richard L. THE GIANT RAT OF SUMATRA. New York, 1976. Wraps	—	—	60
Boyle, Jack. BOSTON BLACKIE. New York (1919)	—	100	450
Boyle, Kay. SHORT STORIES. Paris, 1929. Wraps in tied folder. 15 signed and numbered copies	600	1,000	1,250
150 numbered copies	150	350	600
WEDDING DAY . . . New York (1930). (New title). (Two spine variants noted: "KAY | BOYLE | WEDDING | DAY | & | OTHER | STORIES" and "SHORT | STORIES |KAY | BOYLE" otherwise the same—priority unknown)	50	75	300
London, 1932	—	—	200
Also see Gladys Palmer Brook			
Boyle, Patrick. LIKE ANY OTHER MAN. London, 1966	—	40	60
Boyle, T. Coraghessan. DESCENT OF MAN. Boston (1979). 2,500 copies	—	40	350
London, 1980	—	—	150

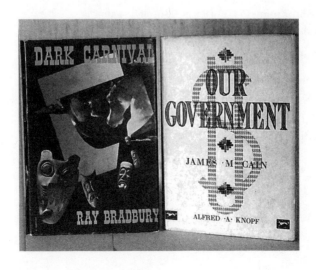

Boyle, Thomas. THE COLD STOVE LEAGUE. Chicago, 1983   —   —   50

BOZ. (Charles Dickens). *See* SKETCHES BY "BOZ"

Brackenridge, H(ugh) H(enry). *See* A POEM ON THE RISING
    GLORY . . .

Bradbury, Malcolm (Stanley). EATING PEOPLE IS WRONG.
    London, 1959   —   50   125
    New York, 1960   —   —   60

Bradbury, Ray (Douglas). DARK CARNIVAL. Sauk City, 1947   200   500   850
    London (1948)   150   250   350

Bradby, Anne (Anne Ridler). SHAKESPEARE CRITICISM
    1919–1935. London, 1936   —   100   125

Braddon, Mary Elizabeth. GARIBALDI . . . London, 1861   75   400   750

    LADY AUDLEY'S SECRET. London, 1862. (3 volumes)   —   400   1,000

Bradford, Gamaliel. TYPES OF AMERICAN CHARACTER.
    New York, 1895   20   50   150

Bradford, Richard. RED SKY AT MORNING.
    Philadelphia, (1968)   —   35   40

Bradford, Roark. OL' MAN ADAM AND HIS CHILLUN.
    New York, 1928   20   75   125

Bradford, Scott. THE SECRET OF HOUSES. London, 1988   —   —   60

Bradley, David. SOUTH STREET. New York, 1975   —   75   200

Bradley, Edward. COLLEGE LIFE. Oxford, 1849/1850.
    (6 parts in 5)   —   600   750

Bradley, Marion Zimmer. THE DOOR THROUGH SPACE.
    New York (1961). Wraps   —   —   25

Bradstreet, Anne. *See* THE TENTH MUSE . . .

Bragdon, Claude F. THE GOLDEN PERSON IN THE HEART.
    Gouverner, New York, 1898. 350 numbered copies   —   75   75

Braine, John (Gerard). ROOM AT THE TOP. London, 1957   40   100   200
    Boston, 1957   20   25   60

Braithwaite, E. R. TO SIR, WITH LOVE.
    Englewood Cliffs (1959)   —   35   100
    London, 1959   —   —   75

Braithwaite, William Stanley. LYRICS OF LIFE AND LOVE.
    Boston, 1904. (500 copies)   15   150   300

Bramah, Ernest (Ernest Bramah Smith). ENGLISH
    FARMING . . . London, 1894. Stiff wraps   70   150   200

Brammer, William. THE GAY PLACE. Boston, 1961. First
    issue: rear dustwrapper flap has name of designer   —   100   250
    Second issue: rear dustwrapper flap has name of designer
    covered by design   —   60   150
    Third issue: rear dustwrapper flap has name of designer
    removed   —   40   100

Branch, Anna Hempstead. THE HEART OF THE ROAD . . .
    Boston, 1901   —   40   40

Brand, Christianna (Mary Christianna Lewis). DEATH IN
    HIGH HEELS. London, 1941   —   60   150

Brand, Max (Frederick Schiller Faust). THE UNTAMED.
    New York, 1919   50   75   175

Brand, Millen. THE OUTWARD ROOM. New York, 1937.
    First issue: pictorial dustwrapper, Sinclair Lewis blurb   15   30   30
    Second issue: printed dustwrapper, Lewis, Dreiser, and
    Hurst blurbs   —   15   15

Brandeis, Louis D. OTHER PEOPLE'S MONEY.
    New York (1914)   —   —   300

Brandt, Bill. THE ENGLISH AT HOME. London (1936). Issued
    in glassine dustwrapper   —   —   450
    New York, 1936. Issued in tissue dustwrapper   —   —   350

Brashler, William. THE BINGO LONG TRAVELING . . .
    New York (1973)   —   30   100

Brasil, Angela. A TERRIBLE TOMBOY. London, 1904   —   —   300

Brassai. PARIS DE NUIT. Paris, 1933. Text by Paul Morand.
    Spiral bound stiff wraps   —   —   850

Bratby, John. BREAKDOWN. Cleveland (1960)   —   —   60

Braun, Lilian Jackson. THE CAT WHO COULD READ
    BACKWARDS. New York, 1966   —   —   150

Brautigan, Richard. THE RETURN OF THE RIVERS.
    (San Francisco, 1958). Wraps   50   1,000   1,500

Braverman, Katherine. DROPPING IN. Los Angeles, 1973   —   50   75

Brecht, Bertolt. A PENNY FOR THE POOR. New York, 1938.
    First English translation (partially by Christopher
    Isherwood)   —   —   200

Bremser, Ray. POEMS OF MADNESS. (New York) 1965.
Wraps. (Ginsberg introduction) — 30 50

Brenan, Gerald. *See* George Beaton

Brennan, Joseph Payne. HEART OF EARTH.
Prairie City (1949) — 125 200

   NINE HORRORS AND A DREAM. Sauk City, 1958 — 90 200

Brenton, Howard. REVENGE. London, 1970. Wraps.
(Previous private printing) — — 75

Breslin, Jimmy. *See* Jimmy Demaret

   SUNNY JIM . . . FITZSIMMONS. Garden City, 1962 — 40 60

Breton, André. YOUNG CHERRY TREES SECURED AGAINST
HARES. New York, 1946 — — 150

Brett, Simon (Anthony Lee). CAST, IN ORDER OF
DISAPPEARANCE. London, 1975 — 40 75
New York (1976) — 25 35

Brewster, Ralph H. THE GOOD BEARDS OF ATHOS.
Hogarth. London, 1935 — 100 150

Breytenbach, Breyten. SINKING SHIP BLUES. Toronto, 1977.
Wraps — — 100

Bridges, Robert. POEMS. London, 1873. (Suppressed by
author in 1878) 75 400 400

Bridie, James. SOME TALK OF ALEXANDER. London, 1926.
Purple cloth with gilt lettering — 100 100

Briggs, Charles Frederick. *See* THE ADVENTURES OF
HARRY FRANCO

Briggs, K(atherine) M(ary). THE LEGEND OF MAIDEN-HAIR.
London, 1915 — — 200

Brilliant, Ashley. I MAY NOT BE TOTALLY PERFECT,
BUT . . . Santa Barbara (1979). Cloth. Issued without
dustwrapper. (1,000 copies) — — 150
Wraps — — 30

Brink, Andre (Philippus). THE AMBASSADOR. (Cape Town)
1964. First English translation — — 60

   FILE ON A DIPLOMAT. London, 1967. (New title) — — 40

Brinnin, John Malcolm. THE GARDEN IS POLITICAL.
New York, 1942 — 20 50 50

Brisbane, Albert. SOCIAL DESTINY OF
MAN . . . Philadelphia, 1840 — 300 500

Brissman, Barry. SWING LOW. New York (1972) — 25 35

Bristow, Gwen. THE INVISIBLE HOST. New York, 1930.
With Bruce Manning — 50 75

Brittain, Vera M. VERSES OF A V. A. D. . . . London, 1918 — 75 150

Brodeur, Paul (Adrian). THE SICK FOX. Boston (1963) — 25 35 35

Brodkey, Harold. FIRST LOVE & OTHER SORROWS.
New York (1957) — 100 200
London, 1958 — — 100

Bromell, Henry. THE SLIGHTEST DISTANCE. Boston, 1974 — 25 25

Bromfield, Louis. THE GREEN BAY TREE. New York, 1924 — 40 250 300

Bromige, David (Mansfield). THE GATHERING BUFFALO.
(New York) 1965. Wraps. (350 copies) — 20 50 75

Bronk, William. LIGHT AND DARK. (Ashland) 1956. Wraps — 30 150 150

Bronowski, Jacob. THE POET'S DEFENCE. Cambridge (Mass.),
1919. First issue: red cloth lettered in gilt — 50 100

Brontë, Anne, Charlotte, and Emily. *See* Acton, Currer, and
Ellis Bell.

Brook, Gladys Palmer. RELATIONS & COMPLICATIONS . . .
London (1929). Ghost written by Kay Boyle — — 350

Brooke, Jocelyn. SIX POEMS. Oxford, 1928. Wraps — 300 300

DECEMBER SPRING. London, 1946 — 25 75 100

Brooke, Rupert. THE PYRAMIDS. Rugby, 1904. Wraps — 6,000 10,000

THE BASTILLE. A. J. Lawrence. Rugby, 1905. Wraps — 500 4,000 6,000
George E. Over. Rugby, 1905 (1920). Wraps — 200 250

POEMS. London, 1911. (First commercial publication).
Issued without dustwrapper. (500 copies) — 150 200 600

Brookner, Anita. WATTEAU. London, 1968 — — 150

THE DEBUT. New York, 1981. (New title) — 25 75

A START IN LIFE. London (1981). (First novel) — — 150

(Three translations 1960–63)

Brooks, Cleanth. THE RELATIONS OF THE ALABAMA-
GEORGIA DIALECT . . . Baton Rouge, 1935. Issued
without dustwrapper   —   200   125

Brooks, Gwendolyn. SONG AFTER SUNSET. 1936. (One
known copy)   —   3,000   5,000

A STREET IN BRONZEVILLE. New York, 1945   75   250   400

Brooks, Jeremy. THE WATER CARNIVAL. London, 1957   —   50   50

Brooks, Richard. THE BRICK FOXHOLE. New York (1945)   —   50   75

Brooks, Van Wyck. *See* VERSES BY TWO UNDERGRADUATES

THE WINE OF PURITANS. Boston, 1908   40   75   100

Brophy, Brigid. THE CROWN PRINCESS . . . London, 1953   25   50   60

Brossard, Chandler. WHO WALK IN DARKNESS.
(New York, 1952). Cloth   25   75   125
Wraps   —   —   40
London (1952)   —   60   75

BROTHERS (THE): A TALE OF THE FRONDE. (Henry William
Herbert). New York, 1835. 2 volumes. First issue:
brown cloth. In original cloth   250   150   450

Broughton, James (Richard). SONGS FOR CERTAIN
CHILDREN. San Francisco, 1947   —   350   350

THE PLAYGROUND . . . (San Francisco) 1949	30	60	60
Broumas, Olga. BEGINNING WITH O. New Haven, 1977	—	—	75
Broun, Heywood. A. E. F.: WITH GENERAL PERSHING . . . New York, 1918	—	—	150
Brown, Alice. *See* STRATFORD-BY-THE-SEA			
Brown, Cecil. THE LIFE & LOVES OF MR. JIVEASS NIGGER. New York, 1969	—	30	75
Brown, Charles Brockton. *See* ALCUIN . . . *and* WIELAND . . .			
Brown, Christy. MY LEFT FOOT. London, 1954	—	—	200
Brown, Claude. MANCHILD IN THE PROMISED LAND. New York (1965)	15	30	100
London (1966)	—	50	60
Brown, Frank Landon. TRUMBULL PARK. Chicago (1959)	—	40	60
Brown, Fredric. THE FABULOUS CLIPJOINT. New York, 1947	50	200	500
Brown, George Douglas. *See* Kennedy King THE HOUSE WITH THE GREEN SHUTTERS. London, 1901	—	50	75
Brown, George MacKay. LET'S SEE THE ORKNEY ISLAND. Port William [1948]. Wraps	—	—	125
Brown, H. Rap. DIE, NIGGER, DIE! New York, 1969	—	40	100
Brown, Harry. THE END OF A DECADE. Norfolk (1940). Boards in dustwrapper	—	35	35
Wraps	—	15	15
Brown, Larry. FACING THE MUSIC. Chapel Hill, 1988	—	—	100
Brown, Lloyd (Lewis). IRON CITY. New York, 1951. Cloth	—	75	75
Wraps	—	40	40
Brown, Norman O. HERMES THE THIEF. (Madison, Wisconsin) 1947	—	—	100
Brown, Oliver Madox. GABRIEL DENVER. London, 1873	—	—	1,200
Brown, Rita Mae. THE HAND THAT CRADLES THE ROCK. New York, 1971	—	40	100
Brown, Robert Carlton (Bob). THE REMARKABLE ADVENTURES OF CHRISTOPHER POE. Chicago, 1913	—	—	100

Brown, Rosellen. SOME DEATHS IN THE DELTA. University of Massachusetts Press (1970). Cloth	—	30	75
Wraps	—	15	25
Brown, Sterling A. SOUTHERN ROAD. New York (1932)	—	750	1,000
Brown, Wesley. TRAGIC MAGIC. New York (1978)	—	20	40
Brown, William W. THE NARRATIVE OF WILLIAM W. BROWN, FUGITIVE SLAVE. Boston, 1847	—	—	1,250
Brown, Zenith Jones. *See* David Frome			
Browne, Howard. WARRIOR OF THE DAWN. Chicago (1943)	—	75	100
Browning, E(lizabeth) B(arrett). *See* E. B. Barrett			
Browning, Robert. *See* PAULINE: A FRAGMENT OF A CONFESSION			
PARACELSUS. London, 1835	—	1,000	1,000
Brownjohn, Alan (Charles). TRAVELERS ALONE. Liverpool, 1954. Wraps	20	75	75
Brownmiller, Susan. SHIRLEY CHISHOLM. Garden City (1970)	—	—	50
Brownson, Orestes Augustus. AN ADDRESS, ON THE FIFTY-FIFTH . . . Ithaca, 1831. Wraps	—	300	300
Brownstein, Michael. BEHIND THE WHEEL. C Press. (1967). (200 copies). Wraps. 6 signed and lettered copies	—	150	200
10 signed and numbered copies	—	125	150
184 unsigned copies	—	50	50
Bruce, Lenny. HOW TO TALK DIRTY . . . (Chicago, 1965)	—	—	100
Bruce, Leo (Rupert Croft-Cooke). RELEASE THE LIONS. London, 1933. (First mystery)	—	75	450
Brunner, John. *See* Gill Hunt			
Brunton, Mary. *See* SELF-CONTROL			
Bryan, C. D. P. S. WILKINSON. New York (1965)	—	—	40
Bryant, Arthur. RUPERT BUXTON. Cambridge (Eng.), 1926	—	—	100
Bryant, Edward. AMONG THE DEAD. New York (1973)	—	15	75
Bryant, William Cullen. *See* EMBARGO			
THE EMBARGO . . . Boston, 1809. (Second edition) First issue: wraps	500	750	1,000
Second issue: wraps stitched	300	500	750

Bryher. *See* Annie Winfred Ellerman

Buchan, John. ESSAYS AND APOTHEGMS OF FRANCIS BACON. London (1894). Edited by Buchan	50	175	400
SIR QUIXOTE OF THE MOORS. London, 1895. First issue: title running down spine	75	250	600
New York, 1895. First issue: full title on spine	50	125	300
Second issue: just "Sir Quixote" on spine	—	—	200
Third issue: just "Sir Quixote" on spine; 188 pages, 4 pages of advertisements	—	—	150
Buck, Howard. THE TEMPERING. New Hampshire, 1919. Wraps. (First title in Yale series of Younger Poets)	—	40	75
Buck, Pearl. EAST WIND, WEST WIND. New York (1930)	75	300	400
Buckler, Ernest. THE MOUNTAIN & THE VALLEY. New York, 1952	—	75	200
Buckley, Christopher. 6 POEMS. (Fresno) 1975	—	—	60
Buckley, William F. GOD AND MAN AT YALE. Chicago, 1951	—	75	125
Budrys, Algis. FALSE NIGHT. New York (1954). Wraps	—	—	50
Buechner, (Carl) Frederick. THIS IS A CHAPTER FROM A LONG DAY'S DYING . . . New York (1949). Wraps	—	175	175
A LONG DAY'S DYING. New York, 1950	15	50	75
Bukowski, Charles. FLOWER, FIST AND BESTIAL WAIL. (Eureka, California, 1959). Wraps			
(Two previous broadsides 1956 and 1950)	—	350	1,000
Bulfinch, Thomas. *See* AUTHORSHIP . . .			
Bullen, Frank T. THE CRUISE OF THE "CACHALOT." London, 1898	50	200	300
New York, 1899	—	75	150
Bullett, Gerald (William). DREAMS O' MINE. London, 1915	—	—	100
THE PROGRESS OF KAY. London, 1916	—	60	75
Bullins, Ed. HOW DO YOU DO . . . Mill Valley (1967). Wraps	15	30	60
Bull-us, Hector (James K. Paulding). THE DIVERTING HISTORY OF JOHN BULL . . . New York, 1812	—	600	600
Bulwer-Lytton, Edward George. ISMAEL: AN ORIENTAL TALE. London, 1820	125	350	450
FALKLAND. London, 1827	—	—	850

Bulwer Lytton, Edward Robert. *See* CLYTEMNESTRA

Bumpus, Jerry. ANACONDA. Western Springs (1967). Issued
    without dustwrapper   —   30   40

Bunin, Ivan. THE GENTLEMAN FROM SAN FRANCISCO.
    Boston, 1918. (Published with Andreyev's *Lazarus*)   —   75   100
    Hogarth Press. Richmond, 1922   —   175   175

Bunner, H(enry) C(uyler). A WOMAN OF HONOR.
    Boston, 1883   —   60   100

    (Previous pamphlets and collaborations)

Bunting, Basil. REDIMICULUM MATELLARUM. Milan, 1930   —   2,000   3,500

Burdette, Robert J(ones). THE RISE AND FALL OF THE
    MUSTACHE . . . Burlington, Iowa, 1877   20   50   75

Burford, William. MAN NOW. Dallas, 1954   —   75   75

Burgess, Anthony (John Anthony Burgess Wilson). TIME
    FOR A TIGER. London, 1956   —   350   750

Burgess, (Frank) Gelett. THE PURPLE COW. (San Francisco,
    1895). First issue: printed on both sides of paper   200   200   400
    Second issue: printed on one side only   100   75   125

Burke, James. FLEE SEVEN WAYS. London, 1963   —   30   40

Burke, James Lee. HALF OF PARADISE. Boston, 1965   —   —   1,250

Burke, Kenneth (Duva). THE WHITE OXEN . . .
    New York, 1924   40   200   350

Burke, Leda (David Garnett). DOPE-DARLING. London,
    1919. (Second book)   40   125   200

Burke, Thomas. VERSES. (Guilford, 1906). Wraps.
    (25 copies)   —   1,000   1,000

    NIGHTS IN TOWN. London, 1915   —   100   125

Burland, Brian. ST. NICHOLAS & THE TUB.
    New York (1964)   —   —   75

Burnett, Frances Hodgson. THAT LASS O' LOWRIE'S. New
    York, 1877. First issue: illustrator's name on title page   125   100   150
    Second issue: illustrator's name not on title page   —   —   75

Burnett, W(illiam) R(iley). LITTLE CAESAR.
    New York, 1929   30   500   750

Burnett, Whit. THE MAKER OF SIGNS. New York, 1934   20   60   75

Burnham, David. THIS OUR EXILE. New York, 1931   —   40   50

Burns, John Horne. THE GALLERY. New York (1947)   25   75   100

Burns, Olive Ann. COLD SASSY TREE. New York (1984)   —   —   75

Burns, Rex. THE ALVAREZ JOURNAL. New York (1975)   —   —   75

Burns, Robert. POEMS, CHIEFLY IN THE SCOTTISH DIALECT.
   Kilmarnock, 1786   — 6,000 15,000
   Edinburgh, 1787. First issue: "Skinking" p. 263   —   500   1,250
   Second issue: "stinking" p. 263   —   250   600
   London, 1787   —   —   400
   Philadelphia, 1788   —   —   750

Burnshaw, Stanley. POEMS. Pittsburgh, 1927   —   200   200

Burroughs, Edgar Rice. TARZAN OF THE APES. McClurg.
   Chicago, 1914. First issue: printer's name on copyright
   page in Old English letters   — 1,000 2,000
   A. L. Burt. New York (1914)   —   —   150
   London (1917). Advertisements dated "Autumn"   —   300   750

Burroughs, John. NOTES ON WALT WHITMAN AS POET AND
   PERSON . . . New York, 1867. First issue: leaves
   trimmed to 6-9/16"; cloth and wraps   125   200 1,250
   Second issue: leaves trimmed to 7-1/4"   40   75   750

   WAKE-ROBIN. New York, 1871   —   —   300

Burroughs, William (Seward). *See* William Lee

   NAKED LUNCH. Paris, 1959. Wraps and dustwrapper.
   (Green border on title page. "Francs : 1500" on back
   cover of book)   20   250 1,000
   New York (1962). (3,500 copies)   —   50   300
   London (1964)   —   —   125

Burroughs, William, Jr. SPEED. New York, 1970. Wraps   —   —   75

Burroway, Janet. DESCENT AGAIN. London, 1960   —   30   35

Burt, (Maxwell) Struthers. THE MAN FROM WHERE.
   Philadelphia, 1904. Pictorial wraps   —   —   150

   IN THE HIGH HILLS. Boston, 1914   25   50   60

Burton, Sir Richard F(rancis). GOA, AND THE BLUE
   MOUNTAINS . . . London, 1851. First issue: light fawn
   cloth, 5 x 8-1/8"   —   750 3,500
   Second issue: light blue cloth, 4-3/4 × 8"   —   400 2,000

Burton, Robert. THE ANATOMY OF MELANCHOLY. Oxford,
   1621. With conclusion (omitted in later editions)   —   — 25,000

Busch, Frederick. I WANTED A YEAR WITHOUT FALL. London (1971)	—	60	100
Buss, Kate. JEVONS BLOCK. Boston, 1917	40	50	60
Butler, Ellis Parker. *See* PIGS IS PIGS			
PIGS IS PIGS. New York, 1906. (Second edition)	—	30	60
Butler, Frances Anne (Kemble). POEMS. Philadelphia, 1844	—	150	150
Butler, Jack. WEST OF HOLLYWOOD. Little Rock (1980).			
Cloth	—	—	175
Wraps	—	—	35
Butler, Octavia E. PATTERNMASTER. Garden City, 1976	—	—	150
Butler, Robert Olen. THE ALLEYS OF EDEN. New York (1981)	—	—	200
Butler, Samuel. A FIRST YEAR IN CANTERBURY SETTLEMENT. London, 1863. First issue: 32 pages of advertisements; light brown end papers	200	400	400
Butler, William. THE EXPERIMENT. London (1961)	—	75	75
Butor, Michael. A CHANGE OF HEART. New York (1958). First English translation	—	—	60
Butts, Mary (Francis). SPEED THE PLOW . . . London (1923)	100	500	500
Byatt, A. S. SHADOW OF A SUN. London, 1964	—	60	200
Byles, Mather. A POEM ON THE DEATH OF HIS LATE MAJESTY KING GEORGE. (Boston, 1727)	750	1,000	1,000
Bynner, Edwin Lasseter. *See* NIMPORT			
Bynner, (Harold) Witter. AN ODE TO HARVARD . . . Boston, 1907. (Issued in three different bindings)	50	50	75
Byrd, Richard. SKYWARD. New York, 1928. (500 signed copies, boxed)	—	150	350
First trade edition	—	35	75
Byrne, (Brian Oswald) Donn. STORIES WITHOUT WOMEN. New York, 1915	75	75	125
Byron, George Gordon, Lord. FUGITIVE PIECES. London, 1806. 3 known copies	—	—	75,000?
London, 1886. (100 copies)	—	—	750
Byron, Robert. EUROPE IN THE LOOKING GLASS . . . London, 1926	—	300	650

C

Cabell, James Branch. THE EAGLE'S SHADOW. New York,

1904. First issue: dedication to "M.L.P.B."	60	100	150
Second issue: dedication to "Martha Louise Branch"	20	50	75
New York, 1923. Revised edition	—	30	75

Cable, George Washington. OLD CREOLE DAYS. New York,

1879. First issue: no advertisements in back	100	150	300
Second issue: advertisements in back	50	75	150

Cabrera Infante, Guillermo. THREE TRAPPED TIGERS. New

York (1971)	—	—	150

Cadigan, Pat. MIND PLAYERS. London, 1988.

First hardback	—	—	40

Cahan, Abraham. YEKL . . .

New York, 1896	—	150	250

Cain, George. BLUESCHILD BABY.

New York (1970)	—	50	50

Cain, James M(allahan). 79TH DIVISION HEADQUARTERS
TROOP: A RECORD. Written with Gilbert Malcolm.

(No-place, circa 1919)	—	—	750
OUR GOVERNMENT. New York, 1930	100	250	500

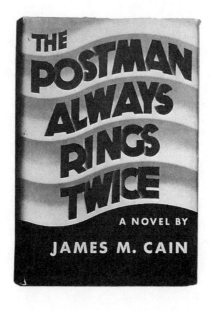

THE POSTMAN ALWAYS RINGS TWICE.
New York, 1934   —   750 1,250
London, 1934   —   —   600

Cain, Paul (George Sims). FAST ONE.
Garden City, 1933   40   400   750

CALAVAR . . . (Robert Montgomery Bird).
Philadelphia, 1834. 2 volumes   250   400   500

Calder, Alexander. ANIMAL SKETCHING.
New York (1926)   —   350   450

Caldwell, Erskine. THE BASTARD. New York (1929).
(1,100 copies in total edition). 200 signed copies.   125   400   750
(6-page prospectus preceded)
900 unsigned copies   50   175   250

Caldwell, James. PRINGLE . . . Denver
(1948). Wraps. (400 copies)   —   40   75

Caldwell, Taylor. DYNASTY OF DEATH.
New York, 1938   15   50   75

Calisher, Hortense. IN THE ABSENCE OF ANGELS . . .
Boston, 1951   40   75   100
London, 1953   —   60   75

Calkins, Clinch. POEMS. New York, 1928   20   40   50

Callaghan, Morley (Edward). STRANGE FUGITIVE.
New York, 1928   75   200   500

Calvert, George Henry. ILLUSTRATIONS OF PHRENOLOGY.
Baltimore, 1832. (Edited by Calvert)   —   100   175

Calvin, Ross. SKY DETERMINES . . . New York, 1934   —   100   150

Calvino, Italo. THE PATH TO THE NEST OF SPIDERS.
Boston (1957)   —   75   125

Camberg, Muriel (Muriel Spark). OUT OF A BOOK.
Leith (1933?)   —   300 1,250

Cameron, Norman. THE WINTER HOUSE . . .
London, 1935   25   60   75

Campbell, Alice. JUGGERNAUT. London
(no-date [1928])   —   —   125

Campbell, Bebe Moore. SUCCESSFUL WOMEN, ANGRY MEN.
New York (1986)   —   —   75

Campbell, J. Ramsey. THE INHABITANT OF THE LAKE . . .
   Sauk City, 1964. (2,000 copies)   —   75   150

Campbell, John W., Jr. THE ATOMIC STORY.
   New York (1947)   30   75   150

   THE MIGHTIEST MACHINE.
   Providence (1947)   40   75   200

Campbell, Roy. THE FLAMING TERRAPIN. London (1924)   60   150   200
   New York, 1924   35   75   100

Campbell, Walter S. *See* Stanley Vestal

Campbell, Will. BROTHER TO A DRAGONFLY.
   New York, 1977   —   25   35

Camus, Albert. THE OUTSIDER. London (1946).
   (Cyril Connolly introduction)   —   125   350

   THE STRANGER. (New title). New York, 1946. (Does
   not include Connolly introduction)   —   75   250

Cane, Melville. JANUARY GARDEN. New York (1926)   25   35   35

Canetti, Elias. THE TOWER OF BABEL. New York, 1946   —   —   125

Canin, Ethan. EMPEROR OF THE AIR. Boston, 1988   —   —   75

Canning, Victor. MR. FINCHLEY DISCOVERS HIS ENGLAND.
   London, 1934   —   —   60

   THE CHASM. London, 1947. (First mystery)   —   35   75

Cantor, Jay. THE SPACE BETWEEN. Baltimore (1981)   —   —   75

Cantwell, Robert. LAUGH AND LIE DOWN. New York, 1931.
   First issue: in pictorial dustwrapper   —   —   500
   Second issue: in printed dustwrapper with reviews   25   75   250

Capa, Robert. DEATH IN THE MAKING. New York (1938)   —   150   350

Čapek, Karel. THE MAKROPOULOS AFFAIR. London, 1922.
   (First English translation)   —   200   300
   Boston, 1925   —   125   200

Capote, Truman. OTHER VOICES, OTHER ROOMS.
   New York (1948)   50   150   300
   London, 1948   —   100   200

Caputo, Philip. A RUMOR OF WAR. New York (1977)   —   —   100

   THE FAT MAN IN HISTORY. St. Lucia, 1974   —   —   200
   London & New York, 1980   —   —   50

Carleton, William M. FAX: A CAMPAIGN POEM.
Chicago, 1868. Wraps ... 500 750 750

Carlile, Clancy. AS I WAS YOUNG AND EASY.
New York, 1958 ... — 25 30

Carlyle, Thomas. *See* LIFE OF SCHILLER

Carmen, Bliss (Bliss Carman). LOW TIDE ON GRAND PREÉ.
Toronto (1889/1890?). 13 pages. (Name misspelled).
Wraps ... 100 2,500 4,500
New York, 1893. Cloth ... 30 400 500
London, 1893 ... — 200 250

Carmer, Carl. FRENCH TOWN. New Orleans (1928).
(500 copies). Stiff wraps ... 40 100 150

(Previous textbook collaboration and edited books)

Carnevali, Emanuel. A HURRIED MAN. (Paris, 1925). Wraps.
(300 copies) ... — 150 300

Carpenter, Don. HARD RAIN FALLING. New York (1966) ... 20 35 50
London (1966) ... — 30 35

Carpenter, Edward. NARCISSUS . . . London, 1873 ... — 200 250

Carpentier, Alejo. THE LOST STEPS. London, 1956 ... — — 125
New York, 1956. First book in English ... — — 100

Carr, Christopher (A. C. Benson). MEMOIRS OF ARTHUR
HAMILTON. London, 1886 ... — 100 200

Carr, John Dickson. IT WALKS BY NIGHT. New York, 1930 ... 75 750 1,750

Carrefour Press. *See* ANONYMOUS

Carrier, Constance. THE MIDDLE VOICE. Denver (1955) ... 15 40 75

Carroll, James. MADONNA RED. Boston (1976) ... — 20 40

Carroll, Jim. ORGANIC TRAINS. (New York, 1968). Wraps ... — 125 175

Carroll, Jonathan. THE LAND OF LAUGHS. New York (1980) ... — — 175

Carroll, Paul. THE POEM IN ITS SKIN. Chicago (1968). ... — 30 50

(Carroll edited the *Dahlberg Reader* in 1966)

Carruth, Hayden. THE CROW AND THE HEART. New York,
1959. Wraps ... — 40 75

Carryl, Charles E. THE RIVER SYNDICATE. New York, 1899 ... — 40 75

Carryl, Guy Wetmore. FABLES FOR THE FRIVOLOUS. New
York, 1898 ... 25 50 75

(Previous pamphlets)

Carson, Rachel. UNDER THE SEA WIND. New York, 1941	40	150	350
Carter, Angela. UNICORN. Leeds, 1966	—	150	400
SHADOW DANCE. London, 1966	—	60	250
HONEYBUZZARD. New York (1966). (New title)	—	40	75
Carter (Asa). *See* GEORGE & LURLEEN WALLACE			
Carter, Forrest. THE REBEL OUTLAW: JOSEY WALES. (Gannt, Alabama, 1973)	—	—	450
GONE TO TEXAS. (New York, 1975). (New title)	—	—	150
Carter, Hodding. CIVILIAN DEFENSE . . . New York (1942). (Written with Col Dupuy)	—	50	100
LOWER MISSISSIPPI. New York (1942)	—	50	75
Carter, Lin. SANDALWOOD AND JADE. St. Petersburg, 1951. Wraps	—	—	35
Carter, Ross S. THOSE DEVILS IN BAGGY PANTS. New York (1951)	—	40	60
Cartier-Bresson, Henri. THE DECISIVE MOMENT. New York (1952)	175	450	650
Cartland, Barbara. JIG-SAW. London (1925)	—	300	400
Caruso, Enrico. CARICATURES. New York, 1922	—	—	250
Caruthers, William Alexander. *See* VIRGINIAN, A			
Carver, Raymond. NEAR KLAMATH. Sacramento, 1968. Wraps. (3 offprints precede)	—	500	2,000
WINTER INSOMNIA. (Santa Cruz, 1970). (1,000 copies). Wraps. Noted in green and yellow and also green and white (but less often)	—	125	175
Cary, Arthur (Joyce). VERSE. Edinburgh, 1908	—	2,500	3,500
Also see (Arthur) Joyce Cary			
Cary, (Arthur) Joyce. AISSA SAVED. London, 1932	75	400	600
Case, David. THE CELL . . . New York (1969)	—	—	75
Casey, John. AN AMERICAN ROMANCE. New York, 1977	—	20	100
Casey, Michael. OBSCENITIES. New Hampshire, 1972. Cloth in dustwrapper	—	75	100
Wraps	—	—	35

Caskoden, Edwin (Charles Major). WHEN KNIGHTHOOD WAS IN FLOWER . . . Indianapolis, 1898	—	—	100
Cassady, Neal. THE FIRST THIRD. San Francisco, 1971. Wraps	—	—	50
Cassidy, Carolyn. HEART BEAT. Berkeley, 1976. 150 signed and numbered copies	—	75	200
Cassidy, John. A STATION IN THE DELTA. New York (1979)	—	25	40
Cassill, R(onald) V(erlin). THE EAGLE ON THE COIN. New York (1950)	—	30	60
Castaneda, Carlos. THE TEACHINGS OF DON JUAN. Berkeley, 1968	—	90	250
Castle, John (Arthur Hailey and John Castle). FLIGHT INTO DANGER. London, 1958	—	100	150
Castlemon, H(arry) C. (Charles Austin Fosdick). FRANK, THE YOUNG NATURALIST. Cincinnati, 1865	—	150	350
Cather, Willa Sibert. APRIL TWILIGHTS. Boston, 1903. Issued without dustwrapper	500	850	2,000
Cato, Nancy. THE DARKENED WINDOW. Sydney, 1950	—	—	75
Caudwell, Sarah. THUS WAS ADONIS MURDERED. London (1981)	—	—	250
New York, 1981	—	—	50
Caunitz, William J. ONE POLICE PLAZA. New York, 1984	—	30	40
Causley, Charles. FAREWELL AGGIE WESTON. Aldington, 1951. Wraps	—	—	75
Caute, David. AT FEVER PITCH. London, 1959	—	40	60
Cawein, Madison Julius. BLOOMS OF THE BERRY. Louisville, 1887. (500 copies)	35	75	125
Cecil, Henry. FULL CIRCLE. London, 1948	—	—	125
CELEBRATED TRIALS AND REMARKABLE CASES. (Written by Geo. Barrow). London, 1825. 6 volumes	—	500	500
Céline, Louis-Ferdinand. JOURNEY TO THE END OF THE NIGHT. London, 1934	—	—	300
Boston, 1934	25	50	100
Centaur Press. SONG OF THE BROAD AX. By Walt Whitman. Philadelphia, 1924	—	100	200

APRIL
TWILIGHTS

POEMS BY

Willa   Sibert   Cather

ARTI   ET   VERI   TATI

Boston: Richard G. Badger

The Gorham Press: 1903

Chabon, Michael. THE MYSTERIES OF PITTSBURGH.
New York (1988)   —   —   40

Chambers, Robert W(illiam). IN THE QUARTER.
Chicago, 1893   —   150   600

Chandler, Raymond. THE BIG SLEEP. New York, 1939   150 1,750 9,500
London, 1939   —   —   2,500
San Francisco, 1986. (425 copies).
Issued without dustwrapper   —   —   450

Channing, William Ellery. THE DUTIES OF CHILDREN.
Boston, 1807. Wraps   —   250   500

Channing, William Ellery (1818–1901). POEMS.
Boston, 1843   —   75   125

Chant, Joy. RED MOON AND BLACK MOUNTAIN.
London, 1970   —   —   150

Chaplin, Sid. THE LEAPING LAD . . . London, 1946   —   60   60

Chapman, Arthur. OUT WHERE THE WEST BEGINS.
Boston, 1917   —   25   75

Chapman, John Jay. See THE TWO PHILOSOPHERS

EMERSON AND OTHER ESSAYS. New York, 1898   25   50   75

Chappell, Fred. RENAISSANCE PAPERS 1962: SHAKESPEARE'S
CORIOLANUS . . . (no-place, no-date [1962]). Wraps —   —   100

IT IS TIME, LORD. New York, 1963   —   100   175
London, 1965   —   —   125

Chappell, George S. COLONIAL ARCHITECTURE IN
VERMONT. New York, 1918. Wraps   —   50   175

Char, Rene. HYPNOS WALKING. New York (1956). First
English translation   —   —   75

Charles, Kate. A DRINK OF DEADLY WINE. London (1991) —   —   75

CHARLES AUCHESTER. (Elizabeth Sara Sheppard). London,
1853. 3 volumes   60   300   500

Charteris, Hugo. A SHARE OF THE WORLD. London, 1953 —   50   60

Charteris, Leslie (Charles Bowyer Lin). X ESQUIRE.
London, 1927   40   300 1,500

Charyn, Jerome. ONCE UPON A DROSHKY.
New York (1964)   25   40   40

Chase, Joan. DURING THE REIGN OF THE QUEEN OF PERSIA.
New York (1983)   —   —   35

Chatwin, Bruce. IN PATAGONIA. London, 1977	—	125	600
New York (1978)	—	—	150
Chavez, Fray Angelico. CLOTHED WITH THE SUN.			
Santa Fe, 1939	—	—	75
Chayefsky, Paddy. TELEVISION PLAYS. New York, 1955	—	35	60
Cheever, John. THE WAY SOME PEOPLE LIVE.			
New York (1943)	75	500	1,250
Cheever, Susan. LOOKING FOR WORK. New York (1979)	—	15	30
London, 1979	—	15	20
Cheney, Brainard. LIGHTWOOD. Boston, 1939	—	—	60
Chesbro, George. SHADOW OF A BROKEN MAN.			
New York, 1977	—	—	75
Chesnutt, Charles W(addell). THE CONJURE WOMAN.			
Boston, 1899. 150 Large paper copies	100	1,000	1,250
Trade edition	40	250	500
Chester, Alfred. HERE BE DRAGONS. Paris, 1955. Wraps. 125			
deluxe copies. (25 for presentation)	—	125	300
1,000 regular copies	35	75	150
Chester, George Randolph. GET-RICH-QUICK-			
WALLINGFORD. New York, 1908	—	75	100
Chesterton, Cecil. GLADSTONIAN GHOSTS. London (1905)	15	60	100
Chesterton, G(ilbert) K(eith). GREYBEARDS AT PLAY . . .			
London, 1900	100	250	500
Chestnut, Robert (Clarence L. Cooper, Jr.). THE SYNDICATE.			
Chicago (1960). Wraps	—	75	125
Child, Lydia Marie. HOBOMOK . . . Boston, 1824	125	400	1,500
Childress, Alice. LIKE ONE OF THE FAMILY. Brooklyn (1956).			
100 numbered copies. Issued without			
dustwrapper in slipcase	—	—	200
Trade edition	—	100	125
Childress, Mark. A WORLD MADE OF FIRE. New York, 1984	—	—	60
CHINESE POEMS. (Arthur Waley). London, 1916. Wraps.			
(About 50 copies)	—	1,500	4,500
Chivers, Thomas Holley. THE PATH OF SORROW. Franklin			
(Tennessee), 1832	400	850	1,000
NACOOCHEE . . . New York, 1837	—	—	450

Chomsky, Noam. SYNTACTIC STRUCTURES. (The Hague) 1957. Wraps	—	—	300
Chopin, Kate. AT FAULT. St. Louis, 1890. Wraps	—	—	3,000
Chopping, Richard. THE FLY. New York, 1965	—	—	75
Christie, Agatha (Mary Clarissa). MYSTERIOUS AFFAIR AT STYLES (THE). New York, 1920	—	2,000	15,000
London, 1921	200	2,000	12,500
Chubb, Ralph. MANHOOD. Curridge, 1924. (200 copies). 45 copies on handmade paper	—	—	500
Regular edition. (200 copies?). Wraps	—	125	250
Chubb, Thomas Caldecott. THE WHITE GOD . . . New Hampshire, 1920. Stiff wraps	—	35	60
Churchill, Caryl. OWNERS. London, 1973. Cloth	—	—	75
Wraps	—	—	15
Churchill, Winston. (American author). THE CELEBRITY. New York, 1898	20	35	75
Churchill, Sir Winston S. THE STORY OF MALAKAND FIELD FORCE. London, 1898. Errata slip preceding first map	500	1,000	4,000
Churton, Henry (Albion W. Tourgee). TOINETTE. New York, 1874. (First novel)	—	100	200
Chute, Carolyn. THE BEANS OF EGYPT, MAINE. New York, 1985	—	60	300
THE BEANS. London, 1985. Dustwrapper back panel blank.	—	—	100
Ciardi, John (Anthony). HOMEWARD TO AMERICA. New York, 1940	20	75	125
Cicellis, Kay. THE EASY WAY. London, 1950. (Sackville-West introduction)	—	35	60
New York (1950)	—	35	40
Cioran, E. M. THE TEMPTATION TO EXIST. Chicago, 1968	—	—	150
City Lights. *See* L. Ferlinghetti			
Clampitt, Amy. MULTITUDES, MULTITUDES. New York (1973). Wraps	—	90	250
Clancy, Tom. THE HUNT FOR RED OCTOBER. Annapolis (1984)	—	150	650

Clark, Charles E. PRINCE AND BOATSWAIN. Greenfield,
  Massachusetts (1915). (Edited and three chapters by
  Marquand and J. M. Morgan). Issued without
  dustwrapper   75   175   200

Clark, Dick. YOUR HAPPIEST YEARS. (New York, 1959)   —   —   30

Clark, Eleanor. THE BITTER BOX. Garden City, 1946   —   75   100

Clark, Emily. INNOCENCE ABROAD. New York, 1931   —   —   60

Clark, John(son). PEPPER SONG OF A GOAT. Ibadan (1961) —   —   50

Clark, Larry. (PHOTOGRAPHS). New York, 1971.
  Stiff wraps   —   —   300

Clark, Mary Higgins. ASPIRE TO HEAVEN . . .
  New York, 1969   —   —   125

  WHERE ARE THE CHILDREN? New York, 1975.
  (First mystery)   —   —   100

Clark, Tom. TO GIVE A PAINLESS LIGHT. 1963. Typescript
  carbon. (3 copies)   —   500 1,000

  THE SAND BURG. London (1966). Wraps. 60 signed and
  numbered copies   —   75   250
  Trade edition. (440 copies)   —   35   100

  AIRPLANES. (Essex, England) 1966. Wraps. 4 signed and
  numbered copies   50   150   500
  Trade   20   40   100

  (Priority in 1966 uncertain)

Clark, Walter Van Tilburg. CHRISTMAS COMES TO HJALSEN.
  (Reno, 1930). Wraps   200   350   750

  TEN WOMEN IN GALE'S HOUSE. Boston (1932)   —   —   600

Clarke, Arthur C(harles). INTERPLANETARY FLIGHT.
  London, 1950   30   100   450
  New York (1951)   —   60   250

Clarke, Austin. THE VENGEANCE OF FIONN. Dublin, 1917   75   100   150

Clarke, Austin C. THE SURVIVORS OF THE CROSSING.
  Toronto, 1964   —   60   125

CLASS POEM. (James Russell Lowell). (Cambridge, Mass.) 1838.
  In original wraps   300   600 1,500

Claude (Claude Durrell). MRS. O'. London (1957).
  (Lawrence Durrell's third wife)   —   40   75

Clavell, James. KING RAT. Boston (1962)	—	150	450
London (1963)	—	100	125
Cleaver, Eldridge. SOUL ON ICE. New York (1968).			
(2,500 copies)	—	25	75
London, 1969	—	25	50
Cleeves, Ann. A BIRD IN THE HAND. London, 1986	—	—	60
Clemens, Samuel Langhorne. *See* Mark Twain			
Clement, Hal (Harry C. Stubbs). NEEDLE. Garden City, 1950	15	75	250
Clemons, Walter. THE POISON TREE . . . Boston, 1959	20	60	60
London, 1959	—	—	50
Clerihew, E. (E. C. Bentley). BIOGRAPHY FOR BEGINNERS. London (1905). Illustrated by G. K. Chesterton. Wraps (Also issued in cloth?)	—	250	500
Clifton, Lucille. GOOD TIMES. New York (1969)	—	—	100
Clifton, Mark. THEY'D RATHER BE RIGHT. New York (1957). (Written with Frank Riley)	—	60	60
CLOCKMAKER (THE). (Thomas Chandler Haliburton). Halifax, 1836	700	750	750
Clough, A(rthur) H(ugh). A CONSIDERATION OF OBJECTS Oxford, 1847	—	500	500
(2 previous pamphlets at Rugby)			
Clouston, J(oseph) Storer. THE LUNATIC AT LARGE. London, 1899	—	50	75
CLYTEMNESTRA . . . (Edw. Robert Bulwer-Lytton). London, 1855	—	350	500
Coates, Robert M(yron). THE EATER OF DARKNESS. (Paris, 1926). Wraps	200	450	500
New York, 1929	75	350	350
Cobb, Humphrey. PATHS OF GLORY. New York, 1935. (Only book)	30	50	125
London (1935)	—	50	75
Cobb, Irvin Shrewsbury. BACK HOME. New York (1912). First issue: "Plimpton Press" on copyright page and publisher's name in 3 lines	25	60	75
Coblentz, Stanton A(rthur). THE THINKER . . . New York, 1923	—	—	125

THE WONDER STICK. New York, 1929 — 75 75

Cockburn, Catherine Trotter. *See* AGNES DE CASTRO

Cockton, Henry. THE LIFE AND ADVENTURES OF
VALENTINE VOX . . . London (1840) — — 300

Codrescu, Andrei. LICENSE TO CARRY A GUN.
Chicago (1970) — 25 50

Coester, A. (Arthur Koestler). *See* Dr. A. Costler

Coetzee, J(ohn) M(ichael). DUSKLANDS.
Johannesburg, 1974 — 125 500
New York (1985). Wraps — — 75

Coffey, Brian. POEMS. Dublin, 1930. (Written with
Dennis Devlin). Wraps — 200 200

THREE POEMS. Paris, 1933. (250 copies). Wraps — 175 175

Coffin, Robert Peter Tristram. CHRISTCHURCH.
New York, 1924 35 75 125

Cohen, Arthur A. MARTIN BUBER. London (1957) — — 125

THE CARPENTER YEARS. (New York, 1967) — 35 60

Cohen, Leonard (Norman). LET US COMPARE
MYTHOLOGIES. Montreal (1956) — 450 2,000

Cohen, Lester. SWEEPINGS. New York, 1926 — — 75

Cohen, Marvin. THE SELF-DEVOTED FRIEND.
New York, 1967 — 25 40

Cohen, Octavus Roy. THE OTHER WOMAN. New York,
1917. (Written with J. U. Giesy) — 60 100

THE CRIMSON ALIBI. New York, 1919 25 60 100

Coker, Elizabeth Boatwright. DAUGHTER OF STRANGERS.
New York, 1950 — — 75

Cole, G(eorge) D(ouglas) H(oward). THE BROOKLYN
MURDERS. London, 1923 — 350 350

Cole, Tom. AN END TO CHIVALRY. Boston (1965) — 25 35

Coleman, Wanda. ART IN THE COURT OF THE BLUE FAG.
Santa Barbara, 1977. Wraps — 15 25

MAD DOG BLACK LADY. Santa Barbara, 1979. 26 signed
and lettered copies — 60 125
200 signed and numbered copies — 25 60

Coleridge, Hartley. POEMS. (Volume 1, all published).
Leeds, 1833 75 250 350

Coleridge, Samuel Taylor. THE FALL OF ROBESPIERRE.
London, 1794 — 500 1,750

Coles, Manning (Cyril Henry Coles and Adelaide Manning).
DRINK TO YESTERDAY. London (1940) — 600 750
New York, 1941 — — 200

Colette (Sidonie Gabrielle). THE VAGRANT. London, 1912 — 60 350

COLLECTION OF FAMILIAR QUOTATIONS (A). (John Bartlett).
Cambridge (Eng.), 1855. First issue: brown cloth — 250 650
Second issue: blue cloth — — 350

Collier, John. HIS MONKEY WIFE. London, 1930 50 350 450
New York, 1931 35 200 300

Collins, Michael (Dennis Lynds). ACT OF FEAR.
New York (1967) — 30 75

Collins, Wilkie. MEMOIRS OF THE LIFE OF WILLIAM COLLINS.
London, 1848. 2 volumes 150 450 1,250

Colony, Horatio. A BROOK OF LEAVES. Boston, 1955 — 35 40

Colter, Cyrus. THE BEACH UMBRELLA. Iowa City (1970) — 25 75

Colton, James (Joseph Hansen). LOST ON TWILIGHT ROAD.
Fresno (1964). Wraps — 50 200

Colum, Mary. FROM THESE ROOTS. London, 1935	— 50	75
Colum, Padriac. THE LAND. Dublin, 1905	— 75	100
Colwin, Laurie. PASSION AND AFFECT. New York, 1974. (14 stories)	— 40	75
DANGEROUS FRENCH MISTRESS. London (1975). New title. (10 stories)	— 30	50
Combs, Tram. PILGRIM TERRACE . . . San German, Puerto Rico, 1957. Wraps	15 40	50
Comfort, Alex(ander). THE SILVER RIVER. London, 1937	25 75	100
Comfort, Will Levington. TROOPER TALES. New York (1899)	— —	75
Compton-Burnett, Ivy. DOLORES. London, 1911. (Written with her brother). (1,055 copies)	100 400	750
PASTORS AND MASTERS. London, 1925	50 250	350
Conaway, James. THE BIG EASY. Boston, 1970	— —	50
Condon, Richard (Thomas). THE OLDEST CONFESSION. New York (1958)	— 30	60
CONFESSIONS OF AN ENGLISH OPIUM-EATER. (Thomas De Quincey). London, 1822. (Advertisement leaf at end) (Without advertisement leaf)	— 750 — 500	1,250 1,000
CONFESSIONS OF HARRY LORREQUER (THE). (Charles Lever). Dublin (1839)	50 250	400
Congdon, A. Kirby. IRON ARK. (New York, 1962). Wraps. (500 copies)	— 30	50
Conley, Robert J. BACK TO MALACHI. Garden City, 1986	— —	60
Connell, Evan S(helby). THE ANATOMY LESSON . . . New York, 1957 London (1958)	25 60 — 40	125 75
Connelly, Marc(us). DULCY. New York, 1921. (Written with George S. Kaufman)	— 125	500
Connett, Eugene V. *See* Derrydale Press		
Connolly, Cyril. THE ROCK POOL. Paris, 1936. Wraps New York, 1936 London, 1947. (New postscript)	200 350 — 150 — 50	500 250 75
Connolly, James B(rendan). JEB HUTTON. New York, 1902	50 100	150

Connolly, Michael. THE BLACK ECHO. Boston, 1992	—	—	40
Conquest, (George) Robert (Acworth). POEMS. London, 1955	—	50	75
CONQUEST (THE) . . . By A Negro Pioneer (Oscar Micheaux). Lincoln, Nebraska, 1913	—	125	750
Conrad, Barnaby. THE INNOCENT VILLA. New York (1948)	—	40	50
Conrad, Joseph (Józef Teodor Konrad Korzeniowski). ALMAYER'S FOLLY. London, 1895. First issue: "e" missing in "generosity" and "of" omitted in penultimate line p. 110	400	1,000	2,000
New York, 1895. (650 copies)	300	600	750
Conroy, Albert (Marvin Albert). THE ROAD'S END. New York, 1952. Wraps	—	—	100
Conroy, Frank. STOP-TIME. New York (1967)	—	40	75
London (1968)	—	30	40
Conroy, Jack (John Weley). THE DISINHERITED. (New York, 1933). First issue: pictorial dustwrapper	60	150	250
Second issue: printed dustwrapper	—	—	125
(Previously co-edited three books)			
Conroy, Pat. THE BOO. Verona (1970). (2,000 copies)	—	150	2,500
Atlanta, 1988. 20 signed and lettered copies	—	—	600
250 signed and numbered copies	—	—	300
THE WATER IS WIDE. Boston, 1972	—	75	500
CONSIDERATIONS ON SOME RECENT SOCIAL THEORIES. (Charles Eliot Norton). Boston, 1853	—	125	175
Constantine, K. C. (pseudonym). THE ROCKSBURG RAILROAD MURDERS. New York, 1972. First issue: no reviews on back of dustwrapper	—	150	300
Second issue: reviews on back of dustwrapper	—	100	200
Cook, Kenneth. WAKE IN FRIGHT. London, 1961	—	—	50
Cook, Robin. THE CRUST AND ITS UPPERS. London, 1962	—	—	50
Cook, Thomas H. BLOOD INNOCENTS. New York, 1980. Wraps	—	—	60
Cooke, John Esten. See LEATHER STOCKING AND SILK			
Cooke, Rose. TERRY POEMS. Boston, 1861	—	—	125

Coolbrith, Ina Donna. A PERFECT DAY . . . San Francisco,
  1881. Folio issue   75   150   250
  Regular issue   25   60   100

Coolidge, Calvin. ADDRESS DELIVERED BY . . . JULY 4, 1916.
  Boston, 1916. Wraps   —   —   350

Coolidge, Dane. HIDDEN WATER . . . Chicago, 1910   —   75   75

Coonts, Stephen. FLIGHT OF THE INTRUDER.
  Annapolis, 1986   —   —   60

Cooper, Clarence. See Robert Chestnut

  THE SCENE. New York (1960)   —   25   50

Cooper, J(oan) California. A PIECE OF MINE. Navarro (1984).
  Wraps   —   —   75

Cooper, James Fenimore. See PRECAUTION

Cooper, Madison. SIRONIA, TEXAS. Boston, 1952. 2 volumes.
  (350 copies with signed page—only seen with second
  printing of first volume)   —   200   200
  Regular edition   —   60   75

Cooper, Susan Rogers. THE MAN IN THE GREEN CHEVY.
  New York, 1988   —   —   350

Cooper, William. See H(arry) S(ummerfield) Hoff

Coover, Robert. THE ORIGIN OF THE BRUNISTS.
  New York (1966)   50   125   200
  London (1967)   —   75   100

  (Previous translation published in Guatemala in 1965)

Cope, Wendy. ACROSS THE CITY. London, 1980. Wraps.
  30 signed and numbered copies   —   —   200
  150 copies. Wraps   100

Coppard, A(lfred) E(dgar). ADAM & EVE & PINCH ME.
  Waltham, 1921. (Also first Golden Cockerel Press). First
  issue: white buckram. (160 copies)   50   300   400
  Second issue: salmon boards. (340 copies)   —   150   200
  New York (1922). (350 copies)   —   100   125

Corby, Herbert. HAMPDENS GOING OVER. London, 1945   25   30   75

Corle, Edwin. MOJAVE. New York, 1934   20   100   200

Corley, Edwin. FIVE PLAYS FOR TWO MEN. (No-place) 1951.
  Wraps. (Written with Claude Hubbard)   —   75   100

Corman, Avery. OH, GOD! New York (1971)	—	—	50
Corman, Cid (Sidney). SUBLUNA. (Dorchester, Mass., 1944). Wraps. (400 copies)	25	75	150
Corn, Alfred. ALL ROADS AT ONCE. New York (1976)	—	—	35
Cornford, Frances. *See* F. C. D.			
POEMS. Hampstead (1910)	75	150	300
Cornford, John. A MEMOIR. London, 1938. Posthumously published. Edited by Pat Sloan	—	75	75
Cornwell, Bernard. SHARPE'S EAGLE. London, 1981 New York, 1981	— —	— —	250 75
Cornwell, Patricia. A TIME FOR REMEMBERING . . . San Francisco (1983)	—	—	250
POSTMORTEM. New York, 1990 (London, 1990)	— —	— —	500 200
Correll & Gosden. SAM 'N' HENRY. Chicago (1926). Cloth Wraps	— —	— —	350 150
Corrington, John William. WHERE WE ARE. Washington, D.C., 1962. Wraps. (225 copies)	—	—	100
Corso, (Nunzio) Gregory. THE VESTAL LADY ON BRATTLE . . . Cambridge (Mass.), 1955. Wraps. (500 copies)	125	200	200
Cortazar, Julio. THE WINNERS. New York (1965) London, 1965	— —	35 —	75 60
Corvo, Baron (Frederick William Rolfe). *See* TARCISSUS . . .			
STORIES TOTO TOLD ME. London, 1898. Wraps	300	400	850
Corwin, Norman. THEY FLY THROUGH THE AIR WITH THE GREATEST OF EASE. Weston, Vermont (1939)	—	—	100
Cossery, Albert. MEN GOD FORGOT. Cairo (1944). Wraps. First English translation (Berkeley) 1946	— —	125 50	125 50
Costler, Dr. A. (Arthur Koestler). ENCYCLOPEDIA OF SEXUAL KNOWLEDGE. London (1934)	—	250	450
THE PRACTICE OF SEX. London (1936). "Coester" on title page	—	200	350
Cotton, John. GOD'S PROMISE . . . London, 1630	—	750	750

Coulette, Henri. THE WAR OF THE SECRET AGENTS . . .
New York (1966) — 20 30

Coupland, Douglas. GENERATION "X." Toronto, 1991.
(Canadian edition of *The Term*) — — 150

Cournos, John. A DILEMMA . . . Philadelphia, 1910.
Translation of Leonid Andrei Yeff's book by Cournos — 75 100

THE MASK. London, 1919 — 100 150

Coward, (Sir) Noel (Pierce). I'LL LEAVE IT TO YOU.
London, 1920. Wraps. (French Acting Edition
No. 2496) 75 300 450

Cowen, William Joyce. MAN WITH FOUR LIVES.
New York (1934) 15 50 50

Cowley, Malcolm. RACINE. Paris, 1923. (150 to 200 copies
but most burned per author). Wraps 200 3,500 3,500

ON BOARD THE MORNING STAR. Written by P.
MacOrlan, translated by Cowley. New York, 1924 — 200 250

BLUE JUNIATA. New York (1929) 75 300 400

Cox, A(nthony) B(erkeley). *See* THE LAYTON COURT MYSTERY

Cox, Palmer. SQUIBS OF CALILFORNIA. Hartford, 1874 — 75 300

Coxe, George Harman. MURDER WITH PICTURES.
New York, 1935 — 250 300

Coxe, Louis O(sbourne). UNIFORM OF FLESH.
Princeton, 1947. Mimeographed sheets in stiff
wraps. (With R. H. Chapman) — 100 150

THE SEA FARING . . . New York (1947) 25 50 50

Coyle, Kathleen. PICADILLY. London, 1923 — 200 300
New York (1923) — — 100

Cozzens, Frederick Swarthout. *See* Richard Haywarde

Cozzens, James Gould. CONFUSION. Boston, 1924.
(2,000 copies). First issue: gray-green cloth,
top edge red 75 500 750

Crace, Jim. CONTINENT. London (1986) — — 60
New York (1987) — — 30

Crackanthorpe, Hubert. WRECKAGE. London, 1893.
16 pages of advertisements dated Oct 1892 60 75 200

Cradock, Mrs. Henry. JOSEPHINE AND HER DOLLS.
London, 1916 — — 250

Craik, Dinah Marie Mulock. *See* THE OGILVIES

Crais, Robert. THE MONKEY'S RAINCOAT.
New York (1987). Wraps — — 75
London, 1989 — — 60

Cranch, Christopher Pearse. A POEM DELIVERED IN THE
FIRST CONGREGATION CHURCH . . . Boston, 1840.
Wraps 40 200 350

Crane, Hart. WHITE BUILDINGS. (New York) 1926. (500
copies in total). First issue: Allen Tate's name incorrectly
spelled on title page as "Allan" 1,500 2,500 3,500
Second issue: tipped in title page with corrected spelling 600 1,250 1,750
Paris, 1930. Wraps and dustwrapper. (200 copies) 400 600 750

Crane, Nathalia. THE JANITOR'S BOY . . . New York, 1924.
(500 signed copies) — 75 100

Crane, Stephen. *See* Johnston Smith

BLACK RIDERS . . . Boston, 1895. 50 copies
on Japan vellum in white vellum or full green levant — 1,000 2,000
Trade edition. (500 copies) — 300 750
(No-place) 1905 — — 150

MAGGIE . . . New York, 1896. First issue: title page in old
English type 40 200 750
Second issue: title page in Roman type — 125 350
London, 1896 — 200 500

Cranston, Alan. THE KILLING OF PEACE.
New York, 1945. — 30 60

(Preceded by a translation of *Mein Kampf*)

Crapsey, Adelaide. VERSE. Rochester, New York, 1915 50 75 125

Crawford, F(rancis) Marion. OUR SILVER . . . New York,
1881. Wraps — 300 350

MR. ISAACS. New York, 1882 — 40 75

Crawford, Lucy. THE HISTORY OF THE WHITE
MOUNTAINS . . . White Hills, 1846 — 125 250

Crawford, Max. WALTZ ACROSS TEXAS. New York (1975) — 25 50

Crawford, Stanley. GASCOYNE. New York (1966) — 40 75
London, 1966 — — 50

White Buildings:
Poems by Hart Crane

With a Foreword by
ALLEN   TATE

BONI & LIVERIGHT, 1926

Creasey, John. SEVEN TIMES SEVEN. London, 1932	—	250	450
Creekmore, Hubert. PERSONAL SUN. Prairie City, 1940. Wraps	—	50	50
Creeley, Robert (White). LEFOU, POEMS. Columbus, 1952. Wraps. (500 copies)	150	500	750
Crévecoeur, Michel Guillaume Jean de. *See* LETTERS			
Crews, Harry. THE GOSPEL SINGER. New York, 1968	—	200	750
Creyton, Paul (John Townsend Trowbridge). PAUL CREYTON'S GREAT ROMANCE! KATE THE ACCOMPLICE . . . Boston (1849). Wraps	—	1,500	2,000
Crichton, (John) Michael. *See* John Lange			
Cripps, Arthur Shearly. LYRE EVANGELISTICA. Oxford/London, 1909	20	60	150
Crisp, Quentin. COLOUR IN DISPLAY. London, 1938	—	100	200
Crispin, Edmund (Robert Bruce Montgomery). THE CASE OF THE GILDED FLY. London, 1944	—	150	200
OBSEQUIES AT OXFORD. Philadelphia (1945). (New title)	—	75	125
Croaker, Croaker & Co. & Croaker, Jr. (Joseph Rodman Drake and Fitz-Green Halleck). POEMS. New York, 1819	1,250	750	750
Crockett, S(amuel) R(utherford). *See* Ford Bereton			
THE STICKIT MINISTER . . . London, 1893	20	50	100
Croft-Cooke, Rupert. SONGS OF A SUSSEX TRAMP. Steyning, 1922. 600 numbered copies	—	100	175
Also see Leo Bruce			
Crofts, Freeman Wills. THE CASK. London (1920). 2 pages of advertisements at back and "Spring List, 1920"	200	1,500	3,000
Crompton, Richmal. JUST WILLIAM. London, 1922	—	—	450
Cronin, A(rchibald) J(ospeh). DUST INHALATION BY HEMATITE MINERS. (London) 1926. Wraps. Offprint	—	300	300
INVESTIGATIONS IN FIRST-AID ORGANIZATION. London, 1927. Wraps	—	250	250
HATTER'S CASTLE. London, 1931	—	125	150
Crosby, Caresse. CROSSES OF GOLD. Paris, 1925. (100 copies)	150	750	1,500
Exeter (Engand), 1925. Wraps	60	150	300

Crosby, Henry Grew (Harry). ANTHOLOGY. (Paris, 1924).
    Wraps (or perhaps bound in half leather, seems most are)   —   750   2,250

Cross, Amanda (Carolyn G. Heilbrun). THE GARNETT
    FAMILY. New York, 1961   —   —   125

    IN THE LAST ANALYSIS. New York (1964)   —   75   150

Crothers, Rachel. CRISS CROSS. New York, 1904. Wraps   —   —   150

Crothers, Samuel McChord. MISS MUFFET'S CHRISTMAS
    PARTY . . . St. Paul, 1891. Wraps   100   250   250

Crowder, Henry. HENRY MUSIC. Paris, 1930. 100 signed and
    numbered copies. Issued in tissue dustwrapper   —   2,500   5,000

Crowley, (Edward Alexander) Aliester. See ALCEDAMA

Crowley, John. THE DEEP. New York (1975)   —   100   200
    (London, 1977)   —   —   125

Crowley, Mart. THE BOYS IN THE BAND. New York (1968)   —   40   60

Crumley, James. ONE TO COUNT CADENCE.
    New York, 1969   —   150   350

    THE WRONG CASE. New York, 1975   —   400

Crump, Paul. BURN, KILLER, BURN. Chicago (1962)   —   25   35

Cruz, Victor Hernandez. PAPO GOT HIS GUN! New York,
    1966. Wraps. (260 copies)   —   —   100

Cullen, Countee. COLOR. New York, 1925   50   250   300

Cummings, Bruce Frederick. See W. N. P. Barbellion

Cummings, E(dward) E(stlin). THE ENORMOUS ROOM.
    New York (1922). First issue: word not blacked out
    p. 219 last line   350   600   1,000
    Second issue: word blacked out p. 219   250   400   750
    London (1928)   75   200   350

Cummings, Ray(mond King). THE GIRL IN THE GOLDEN
    ATOM. London (1922)   —   350   750

Cummington Press. FIVE CUMMINGTON POETS.
    Cummington, Massachusetts, 1939. 300 copies. Wraps   —   250   250

Cummins, Maria S. See THE LAMPLIGHTER

Cunard, Nancy. OUTLAWS. London, 1921. (Assume issued
    without dustwrapper)   300   600   300

Cuney, Waring. PUZZLES. Utrecht, 1960.
    (175 copies in slipcase)   —   250   250

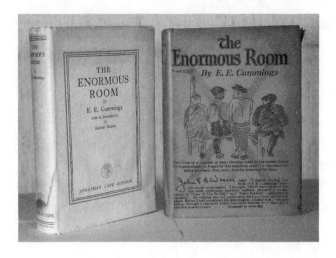

Cunningham, A(lbert) B(enjamin). SINGING MOUNTAINS.
New York (1919)   —   —   300

MURDER AT DEER LICK. New York, 1939   —   200   300

Cunningham, J(ames) V(incent). THE HELMSMAN.
San Francisco, 1942. (300 copies in total). Cloth —   600   750
Wraps. First issue: beige wallpaper (floral design) 35   250   400
Second issue: plain green   —   —   300

Cunningham, Michael. A HOME AT THE END OF THE
WORLD. New York, 1990   —   —   35

Cunninghame Graham, R. B. ECONOMIC EVOLUTION.
Leatham, 1891   —   —   125

NOTES ON THE DISTRICT OF MENTEITH. London, 1895.
Wraps   50   150   150

Cuppy, William J(acob). MAROON TALES. Chicago, 1910 25   35   35

Curley, Thomas. IT'S A WISE CHILD. New York (1960) —   40   40

Curly, Daniel. THAT MARRIAGE BED . . . Boston (1957) —   25   25

Curran, Dale. A HOUSE ON A STREET. New York (1934) 25   40   40

Curtis, George William. *See* NILES NOTE OF A HOWADJI

Curtis, Jack. GREEN AGAIN. (Mexico City, 1951). Wraps.
500 numbered copies   —   40   75

Curwood, James Oliver. THE COURAGE OF CAPTAIN PLUM.
Indianapolis (1908)   15   50   150

OUTLAWS

BY
NANCY CUNARD

LONDON
ELKIN MATHEWS, CORK STREET
MCMXXI

EDWARD DAHLBERG

BOTTOM
DOGS

WITH AN INTRODUCTION BY
D. H. LAWRENCE

LONDON
G P PUTNAM'S SONS

Cushing, Harvey. THE PITUITARY BODY AND ITS
DISORDERS. Philadelphia (1912) — — 750

Cushman, Dan. STAY AWAY, JOE. New York, 1953 — 40 40

Cussler, Clive. ICEBERG. New York (1975) — — 125

Custance, Olive. OPALS. London, 1897 — 150 150

D
D., F. C. (Frances Crofts Darwin Cornford).
THE HOLTBURY IDYLL. [No-place, no-date (circa 1908)] — 1,500 1,750

D., H. (Hilda Doolittle). CHORUSES FROM IPHIGENEIA IN
AULIS. London, 1916 — 250 350
Cleveland, 1916. Wraps. 40 numbered copies 600 1,250 1,500

SEA GARDEN. London, 1916. Stiff wraps 150 350 500
Boston, 1916. (U.K. sheets) 75 200 300

Dabbs, James McBride. THERE IS A LAD HERE.
(Louisville, 1943?) — 50 75

WHEN JUSTICE AND EXPEDIENCY MEET (Columbia, 1947).
Wraps — 25 40

Dabydeen, David. SLAVE SONG. London, 1984 — — 75

Dahl, Roald. THE GREMLINS. New York (1943)	40	300	500
London (1944)	—	250	450
OVER TO YOU . . . New York (1946)	—	100	300
London, 1946	—	100	300
Dahlberg, Edward. BOTTOM DOGS.			
London (1929). (520 copies)	125	250	250
New York (1930)	—	150	150
Daiches, David. THE PLACE OF MEANING IN			
POETRY. London, 1935	—	50	75
Dalton, John. METEOROLOGICAL OBSERVATIONS			
AND ESSAYS. London, 1793	—	—	3,500
Daly Elizabeth. UNEXPECTED NIGHT. New York, 1940	—	60	75
Daly, Thomas Augustine. CANZONI. Philadelphia, 1906.			
First issue: "feety" on p. 17	30	50	50
Dana, Richard H(enry), Sr. POEMS. Boston, 1827.	—	175	200
(Several pamphlets preceded)			
Dana, Richard Henry. *See* TWO YEARS BEFORE THE MAST			
TWO YEARS BEFORE THE MAST. Boston, 1869.			
With new preface and added chapter	—	—	250
Dane, Clemence (Winifred Ashton). REGIMENT OF			
WOMEN. London, 1917	—	35	75
Daniels, Jonathan. DEVIL TRENDS. Chapel Hill, 1922	—	—	100
CLASH OF ANGELS. New York, 1930	—	60	60
Dannay, Frederic. *See* Ellery Queen			
Darrow, Clarence (Seward). REALISM IN LITERATURE			
AND ART. Chicago (1899). Wraps	—	—	300
A PERSIAN PEARL . . . Erie County, New York, 1899	—	—	600
Darwin, Charles. EXTRACTS FROM LETTERS ADDRESSED			
TO PROF HENSLOW . . . Cambridge (1835?). Wraps	—	—	10,000
JOURNAL OF RESEARCHES . . . London, 1839.			
With two folding maps	—	1,250	4,500
Davenport, Guy (Mattison). THE INTELLIGENCE OF LOUIS			
AGASSIZ. Boston (1963). Edited and introduction			
by Davenport	—	125	150

CARMINA ARCHILOCHI. Berkeley/Los Angeles, 1964.

Cloth	—	—	250
Wraps	—	—	75

Davidman, Joy. LETTER TO A COMRADE.
New Hampshire, 1938 — 75 100

Davidson, Donald. AN OUTLAND PIPER. Boston, 1924   125   200   300

Davidson, John. DIABOLUS AMANS. Glasgow, 1885   —   500   750

Davidson, Lionel. NIGHT OF WENCESLAS. London, 1960   —   100   100

Davie, Donald (Alfred). PURITY OF DICTION IN ENGLISH
VERSE. London, 1952   —   75   125

(POEMS) FANTASY POETS. Oxford, 1954. Cloth	—	150	450
Wraps	—	50	250

Davies, Hugh Sykes. PETRON. London, 1935   —   75   100

Davies, Rhys. THE SONG OF SONGS . . . London (1927).

Wraps. (1,000 copies in total). 100 signed copies	75	150	200
900 unsigned copies	35	40	40

Davies, W(illiam) H. THE SOUL'S DESTROYER . . .
(London, 1905). Wraps   150   600   600

Davies, W. Robertson. SHAKESPEARE'S BOY ACTOR.
London (1939)   —   500   1,500

Davies, William. SONGS OF A WAYFARER. London, 1869   —   50   75

Daviot, Gordon (Elizabeth MacKintosh). THE MAN IN THE

QUEUE. London, 1929	40	200	300
New York, 1929	—	125	200

Davis, Angela. IF THEY COME IN THE MORNING.
New York, 1971   —   40   60

Davis, Burke. WHISPER MY NAME. New York, 1949   —   60   125

Davis, Deborah. KATHERINE THE GREAT . . .
New York (1979)   —   —   125

Davis, Dorothy Salisbury. THE JUDAS CAT. New York, 1949   —   25   75

Davis, H(arold) L(enoir). HONEY IN THE HORN.
New York, 1935   —   50   175

Davis, Lindsey. SILVER PIGS. New York, 1989   —   —   75

Davis, Rebecca Harding. MARGRET HOWTH. Boston, 1862   75   50   75

Davis, Richard Harding. ADVENTURES OF MY FRESHMAN.
　　Bethlehem (Pennsylvania) (1883). Wraps 　　　　　150　　600　1,500

　　GALLEGHER . . . New York, 1891. First issue: no
　　advertisement for "Famous Women . . . " in back.
　　Wraps 　　　　　　　　　　　　　　　　　50　　200　　300
　　Cloth 　　　　　　　　　　　　　　　　　—　　　75　　150
　　London, 1891 　　　　　　　　　　　　　—　　　75　　125

Davis, Tech. TERROR AT COMPASS LAKE.
　　Garden City, 1935 　　　　　　　　　　—　　　—　　　75

Davis, Terry. VISION QUEST. New York, 1979 　　—　　　—　　　50

Davison, Peter. THE BREAKING OF DAY. New Haven, 1964 　—　　—　　45

Davy, Sir Humphry. RESEARCHES, CHEMICAL AND
　　PHILOSOPHICAL . . . London, 1800 　　　—　　　— 6,000

Dawkins, Cecil. THE QUIET ENEMY. London, 1963 　—　　—　　75
　　New York, 1963 　　　　　　　　　　　—　　　—　　　50

Dawson, Fielding. A SIMPLE WISH FOR A SINCERE . . .
　　Black Mountain (1949).
　　Wraps 　　　　　　　　　　　　　　　—　　　250　　350

　　6 STORIES OF THE LOVE OF LIFE. Black Mountain (1949).
　　Wraps 　　　　　　　　　　　　　　　—　　　225　　250

Day, Clarence (Shepard). DECENNIAL RECORD OF THE
　　CLASS OF 1896. New York, 1907 　　　　—　　　75　　75

　　THE '96 HALF-WAY BOOK. New York, 1915 　　25　　35　　50

　　THIS SIMIAN WORLD. New York, 1920 　　40　　150　　200
　　London (1921) 　　　　　　　　　　　25　　125　　150

Day, John (publisher). THE MUSIC FROM BEHIND THE
　　MOON. New York, 1926. By James Branch Cabell.
　　(Boxed) 　　　　　　　　　　　　　　15　　30　　75

Dayan, Yael. NEW FACE IN THE MIRROR. London (1959) 　—　　—　　40

Day-Lewis, C(ecil). BEECHEN VIGIL . . . London (1925).
　　Wraps. (At least one copy in cloth) 　　200　　350　　450

　　Also see Nicholas Blake

Dean, Capt. Harry. *See* Sterling North

DeAssis, Machado. EPITAPH OF A SMALL WINNER.
　　London, 1953. First English translation 　—　　—　　75

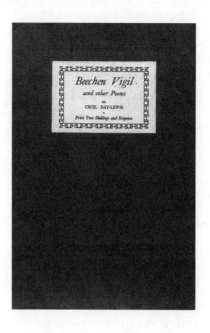

De Bernières, Louis. THE WAR OF DON EMMANUEL'S
   NETHER PARTS. London, 1990   —   —   100

De Casseres, Benjamin. THE SHADOW EATER.
   New York, 1915. (Boni). 150 signed copies   50   75   75
   650 unsigned copies   20   50   50
   New York, 1917. (Wilmarth)   —   25   25

DeCasseres, Walter. THE SUBLIME BOY. New York, 1926.
   Deluxe. (100 copies)   —   75   75
   Trade edition   25   40   40

Deck, John. ONE MORNING FOR PLEASURE.
   New York (1968)   —   30   40

Deeping, (George) Warwick. UTHER AND IGRAINE.
   London, 1903   25   75   100
   New York, 1903   —   50   75

De Forest, John W(illiam). HISTORY OF THE INDIANS OF
   CONNECTICUT . . . Hartford, 1851. First issue:
   p. vii misnumbered "iiv"   —   150   250

Dehn, Paul. THE DAY'S ALARM. London (1949)   —   35   50

Deighton, Len. THE IPCRESS FILE. London (1962). First issue:
no reviews on front dustwrapper flap .... 15　150　600
New York, 1963 ....　—　　75　250

DeJong, David Cornel. BELLY FULLA STRAW.
New York, 1936 ....　—　　35　　35

De La Mare, Walter. *See* Walter Ramal

HENRY BROCKEN. London, 1904. First issue: without
top edges gilt ....　30　　75　150

De Land, Margaret. THE OLD GARDEN . . . Boston, 1886　35　100　150

Delaney, Shelagh. A TASTE OF HONEY. New York (1959).
50 numbered copies. Issued in wraps
without dustwrapper ....　—　100　150

Delany, Samuel R(ay). THE JEWELS OF APTOR. New York
(1962). Wraps. Bound dos-a-dos with a James
White novel ....　15　　40　　40
London, 1968. (First hardcover) ....　—　　—　　75

De La Roche, Mazo. EXPLORERS OF THE DAWN.
New York, 1922 ....　—　　—　125

Delbanco, Nicholas. THE MARTLET'S TALE.
Philadelphia (1966) ....　—　　50　　75
London, 1966 ....　—　　—　　60

DeLillo, Don. AMERICANA. Boston, 1971 ....　15　　60　300

Dell, Floyd. WOMEN AS WORLD BUILDERS. Chicago, 1913.
(A few hundred copies according to author) ....　50　150　150

Del Rey, Lester. " . . . AND SOME WERE HUMAN."
Philadelphia, 1948. (Hand-lettered title page) ....　—　　75　150
Philadelphia, 1949 ....　—　　50　　60

Del Vecchio, John M. THE 13TH VALLEY (CHAPTER 26).
New York (1981). Wraps ....　—　　60　　75

THE 13TH VALLEY. New York, 1982 ....　—　　25　　50

Delving, Michael (Jay Williams). THE STOLEN ORACLE.
New York, 1943 ....　—　　—　　75

SMILING THE BOY FELL DEAD. New York, 1967.
(First mystery) ....　—　　30　　50

Demaret, Jimmy. MY PARTNER BEN HOGAN. New York
(1954). (Ghost written by Jimmy Breslin) ....　—　　50　　60

DeMarinis, Rich. A LOVELY MONSTER. New York, 1975 — — 60

Demby, William. BEETLECREEK. New York, 1950.
(Preceded by publication of this book in Italian
in Milan) 40 60 150

DeMorgan, William Frend. JOSEPH VANCE . . .
London, 1906 30 75 75

Denby, Edwin. SECOND HURRICANE. Boston (1938).
Wraps. (Lyrics from play) — — 300

IN PUBLIC, IN PRIVATE. Prairie City (1948). First issue:
blue cloth 150 300 450
Second issue: gray cloth — 175 350

Dennie, Joseph. THE LAY PREACHER . . . Walpole,
New Hampshire, 1796 — — 600
Philadelphia, 1817. (Different content) — — 450

Dennis, Patrick. AUNTIE MAME. New York (1955) — — 125

Dentinger, Jane. MURDER ON CUE. Garden City, 1983 — — 50

Depons, F. TRAVELS IN SOUTH AMERICA . . . London,
1807. 2 volumes — — 350

De Quincey, Thomas. *See* CONFESSIONS OF AN ENGLISH
OPIUM-EATER

Derleth, August. TO REMEMBER. Vermont, 1931. Wraps.
(129-page pamphlet) 100 300 600

MURDER STALKS THE WAKELY FAMILY. New
York, 1934 100 200 600

DEATH STALKS THE WAKELY FAMILY. London, 1937 75 125 350

Derrydale Press. MAGIC HOURS. By Eugene V. Connett.
New York, 1927. (100 copies). (First book of press) — 7,500 9,000

DERRY, DERRY DOWN. (Edward Lear). London (1846).
Wraps. (175 copies). (First book for children) 400 2,000 5,000

Desani, G(ovindas) V(ishnoodes). ALL ABOUT H. HATTERR.
London (1948) — 40 75

DESCENDANT, THE. (Ellen Glasgow). New York, 1897.
First issue: author's name not on spine. New York
imprint only. Last advertisement is *Tom Sawyer Abroad.* 75 100 300

DESPERATE REMEDIES. (Thomas Hardy). London, 1871.
3 volumes. (500 copies) 1,000 3,000 12,500
New York, 1874. ("author's edition"). Yellow cloth 100 250 500

DeTeran, Lisa St. Aubin. KEEPERS OF THE HOUSE. London (1982)	—	60	150
Deutsch, Babette. BANNERS. New York (1919)	75	50	75
Devlin, Denis. INTERCESSIONS: POEMS. London (1937). (300 copies)	—	40	75
(Previous collaboration)			
De Voto, Bernard. THE CROOKED MILE. New York, 1924	35	75	125
De Vries, Peter. BUT WHO WAKES THE BUGLER? Boston, 1940	30	200	450
Dew, Robb Foreman. DALE LOVES SOPHIE TO DEATH. New York, 1981	—	25	40
Dewdney, Christopher. GOLDER'S GREEN. (Toronto) 1971	—	—	650
Dewey, John. PSYCHOLOGY. New York, 1887	—	350	500
Dewey, Thomas B. HUE AND CRY. New York, 1944	—	—	75
LIBERAL STUDIES. Oxford, 1964. 2 volumes	—	—	150
Dexter, Colin. LAST BUS TO WOODSTOCK. London (1975) (New York, 1975)	— —	— —	750 350
Dexter, Pete. GOD'S POCKET. New York (1983)	—	—	100
DIARY OF SECTION VIII AMERICAN AMBULANCE FIELD SERVICE. (William Seabrook). (Boston) 1917	—	75	75
Dibdin, Michael. THE LAST SHERLOCK HOLMES STORY. London, 1978	—	—	125
Dibdin, T(homas) F(rognall). POEMS. London, 1797. (500 copies)	450	500	500
Dick, Philip K(indred). SOLAR LOTTERY. New York (1955). Wraps. (Ace Double novel D-103)	—	—	100
A HANDFUL OF DARKNESS. London, 1955. First issue: blue boards lettered in silver Second issue: orange boards lettered in black	— —	600 400	750 500
Dick, R. A. (Josephine A. Lincoln). THE GHOST AND MRS. MUIR. Chicago/New York (1945)	—	50	200
Dickens, Charles. See SKETCHES BY "BOZ"			
Dickens, Monica. ONE PAIR OF HANDS. New York, 1939	—	60	100

Dickey, James (Lafayette). DROWNING WITH OTHERS.
Middleton, Connecticut, 1962. Cloth — 30 — 150 — 250

Dickey, James (Lafayette). DROWNING WITH OTHERS. Middleton, Connecticut, 1962. Cloth	30	150	250
Wraps	—	100	125
Dickey, William. OF THE FESTIVITY. New York, 1959	—	40	40
Dickinson, Charles. WALTZ IN MARATHON. New York, 1983	—	—	35
Dickinson, Emily. POEMS. Boston, 1890. (500 copies)	600	1,000	4,500
London, 1891. (480 copies)	100	500	2,000
Dickinson, G. Lowes. FROM KING TO KING. London, 1891	40	—	75
Dickinson, Patric. THE SEVEN DAYS OF JERICHO. London (1944). Wraps	—	30	40
Dickinson, Peter. THE WEATHERMONGER. London, 1968. (Children's book)	—	75	100
SKIN DEEP. London (1968). (First mystery)	—	75	200
Didion, Joan. RUN RIVER. New York (1963)	60	75	125
Cape: London (1964)	—	—	75
Di Donato, Pietra. CHRIST IN CONCRETE. Esquire Publ. Chicago (1937). Pictorial boards in glassine dustwrapper	25	60	75
Indianapolis (1939). (Expanded). Signed tipped-in leaf	—	40	50
Trade edition	—	20	25
Dillard, Annie. TICKETS FOR A PRAYER WHEEL. Columbia (Missouri, 1974)	—	60	400
Dillon, George. BOY IN THE WIND. New York, 1927	30	50	60
Diment, Adam. THE DOLLY DOLLY SPY. London, 1967	—	50	75
Dinesen, Isak (Karen Blixen). SEVEN GOTHIC TALES. New York, 1934. 1,010 numbered copies in slipcase. Leather	35	250	400
Black cloth	—	150	250
Trade edition	—	100	150
London, 1934. Rex Whistler dustwrapper	—	150	400
DiPalma, Ray. MAX. (Iowa City) 1969. Wraps	—	—	150
Di Prima, Diane. THIS KIND OF BIRD FLIES BACKWARD. (New York, 1958). Wraps	35	40	60
Disch, Thomas M. THE GENOCIDES. New York (1965). Wraps	—	—	50
London, 1967	—	—	750

Disney, Doris Miles. A COMPOUND FOR DEATH. Garden
    City, 1943   —   30   40

Disney, Walter E. MICKEY MOUSE BOOK. New York, 1930.
    Wraps with green background (or white background)
    without illustrated strip on back cover. (Priority uncertain
    although white is less common)   —   — 7,500

DISSERTATION ON THE HISTORY . . . OF THE BIBLE . . ., A.
    (Timothy Dwight). New Hampshire, 1772   — 250 250

Dixon, Stephen. NO RELIEF. Ann Arbor (1976). Stiff wraps   — 25 30

Dixon, Thomas, Jr. THE LEOPARD'S SPOT'S . . . New York,
    1902. Presentation issue signed   — 90 125
    Regular   — 30 50

Dobie, James Frank. A VAQUERO OF THE BRUSH
    COUNTRY. Dallas, 1929. First issue: "Rio Grande
    River" on map   100 300 500
    Second issue: "Rio Grande"   —   — 300

Dobree, Bonamy. RESTORATION COMEDY 1660–1720.
    Oxford, 1924   — 125 125

Dobson, Austin. VIGNETTES IN RHYME . . . London, 1873   25 125 200

Dobyns, Stephen. CONCURRING BEASTS. New York, 1972   — — 50

Doctorow, E(dgar) L(awrence). WELCOME TO HARD TIMES.
    New York, 1960   75 150 450

    BAD MAN FROM BODIE. London, 1961. (New title)   — 125 300

Dodd, E. R. THIRTY-TWO POEMS. London, 1929. Wraps   — — 60

Dodd, Susan. NO EARTHLY NOTION. New York, 1986   — — 40

Dodge, David. DEATH AND TAXES. New York, 1941   — 75 75

Dodge, Jim. FUP. Berkeley (1983). Wraps   — — 75

Dodge, M. E. (Mary Mapes Dodge). THE IRVINGTON
    STORIES. New York, 1865   75 125 125

Dodge, Mary Abigail. *See* Gail Hamilton

Dodson, Owen. POWERFUL LONG LADDER.
    New York, 1946   25 75 300

Doerr, Harriet. STONES FOR IBARRA. New York, 1984   — — 100

Doig, Ivan. THIS HOUSE IN THE SKY. New York, 1978   — — 100

Donaldson, D. J. CAJUN NIGHTS. New York, 1988   — — 40

Donaldson, Stephen R. LORD FOUL'S BANE.
New York, 1977   —   40   60

Donleavy, J. P. THE GINGER MAN. Paris (1955). Wraps   75   350   600
London, 1956   —   100   175
Paris, 1958. Cloth. First issue: original dustwrapper flaps — 100   500
Second issue: dustwrapper flaps glued on   —   50   125
New York (1958)   —   50   100

Donne, John. PSEUDO-MARTYR . . . London, 1610   — 5,000   6,000

Donnelly, I(gnatius). THE MOURNER'S VISION. Philadelphia,
1850. Gray boards   —   —   250

ATLANTIS . . . New York, 1882   —   150   150

(Pamphlets preceded)

Donoso, Jose. CORONATION. London, 1965   —   —   150
New York, 1965. (First publication in English)   —   —   100

Donovan, Dick (Joyce E. Muddock). THE MAN HUNTER.
London, 1888   —   250   350

Dooley, Roger B. LESS THAN THE ANGELS.
Milwaukee (1946)   —   —   75

Dooley, Thomas A. DELIVER US FROM EVIL.
New York, 1956   —   —   75

Doolittle, Hilda. See H. D.

Doolittle, Jerome. THE BOMBING OFFICER.
New York (1982)   —   —   50

Dorfman, Ariel. MISSING. London, 1974. Wraps. First book
in English   —   —   75

Dorn, Edward (Merton). WHAT I SEE IN THE MAXIMUS
POEMS. (Ventura, California) 1960. Wraps   75   150   175

Dorr, Nell. IN A BLUE MOON. New York, 1939. Issued
without dustwrapper in slipcase   —   —   125

Dorris, Michael. A YELLOW RAFT IN BLUE WATER.
New York, 1987   —   —   40

Dos Passos, John (Roderigo). ONE MAN'S INITIATION—1917.
London (1920). (750 copies bound for English edition)   150   600   750
New York, 1922. (500 copies from English sheets). First
issue: both have the word "flat" obliterated p. 35:32   100   500   600

Dostoevsky, F. POOR FOLK. London, 1894. Beardsley cover.
(First English publication)   —   150   500

Douglas, Lord Alfred. POEMS. Paris, 1896. Wraps.

20 on Hollande paper	—	450	450
Trade edition	60	150	150

(Previous translation)

Douglas, Ellen (Josephine Haxton). A FAMILY'S AFFAIRS.

Boston, 1962	—	100	200
London (1963)	—	50	100

Douglas, Keith. ALAMEIN TO ZEM ZEM. London, 1946	—	100	250

Douglas, Norman. *See* Normyx

Douglass, Frederick. NARRATIVE OF THE LIFE OF FREDERICK DOUGLASS AN AMERICAN SLAVE. Written By Himself. Boston, 1845	—	—	1,250

Douskey, Franz. INDECENT EXPOSURE. New Hampshire, 1976. Wraps	—	30	30

Dove, Rita. TEN POEMS. Lisbon, 1977	—	—	250

Doves Press. DE VITA ET MORIBUS . . . By C. Tacitus.

London, 1900. 5 vellum copies	—	3,000	4,500
regular edition. (225 copies)	—	850	850

Dowden, Edward. A WOMAN'S RELIQUARY. Churchtown, Dumdrum (Ireland), 1913. (300 copies)	—	150	150
MR. TENNYSON AND MR. BROWNING. (London) 1863	—	—	250

Dowdy, Andrew. NEVER TAKE A SHORT PRICE. New York (1972)	—	25	35

Dowell, Coleman. THE GRASS DIES. London (1968)	—	75	125
ONE OF THE CHILDREN IS CRYING. New York, 1968. (New title)	—	40	100

Dowson, Ernest. VERSES. London, 1896. (30 large paper

copies in imitation vellum)	—	1,500	3,500
Trade edition. (300 copies)	—	200	600

Doyle, Arthur Conan. A STUDY IN SCARLET. London, 1888.

Wraps. First issue: "younger" spelled correctly in Preface	4,000	15,000	100,000
Second issue: "youuger" for "younger" in Preface	2,000	10,000	15,000
Philadelphia, 1890. Wraps	—	2,500	3,000
Cloth	—	1,500	2,000

Doyle, Roddy. THE COMMITMENTS. Dublin, 1987. Wraps	—	—	250

Drabble, Margaret. A SUMMER BIRD-CAGE. London, 1963	—	150	150
New York, 1964	—	75	75

Drake, Joseph Rodman. *See* Croaker . . .

THE CULPRIT FAY . . .
New York, 1835. Bound in leather — 125 125
Various cloths — 60 60

Drake, Leah Bodine. A HORNBOOK FOR WITCHES.
Sauk City, 1950 — 750 1,500

Drant, R. Palasco (Art Young). HELL UP TO DATE. Chicago
(1982). Pictorial boards without dustwrapper — — 200

DREAM DROPS . . . BY A DREAMER. (Amy Lowell). Boston
(1887). Cloth with white linen spine. (99 copies) 900 2,500 3,000
Wrappers. (151 copies) 500 1,500 2,250

Dreiser, Theodore. SISTER CARRIE. New York, 1900.
(About 1,000 copies) 800 800 3,500
London, 1901 250 350 1,000
New York, 1907 — — 250

Drexler, Rosalyn. I AM THE BEAUTIFUL STRANGER.
New York (1965) — 35 40

Drinkwater, John. POEMS. Birmingham, England, 1903 50 150 300

Dr. Seuss (Theodor Seuss Geisel). AND TO THINK THAT I
SAW IT ON MULBERRY STREET. New York, 1937.
Pictorial boards in dustwrapper — 250 1,000

Du Bois, W(illiam) E(dward) B(urghardt). SUPPRESSION OF
THE AMERICAN SLAVE TRADE. New York, 1896 100 750 1,000

Dubus, Andre. THE LIEUTENANT. New York, 1967 — 50 250

Duer, Alice (Later Miller). POEMS. New York, 1896.
(Written with Caroline Duer) — 30 60

Duffy, Bruce. THE WORLD AS I FOUND IT. New York, 1897 — — 40

Dugan, Alan. GENERAL PROTHALAMION IN POPULOUS
TIMES. (New York, 1961). Broadside. (100 copies) 50 90 150

POEMS. New York, 1961. Cloth 30 50 75
Wraps — 20 20

Duggan, Alfred. KNIGHT WITHOUT ARMOUR.
London, 1950 — 60 75

Dujardin, Edouard. WE'LL TO THE WOODS MORE.
New York, 1938. (First English translation) — 75 100

Duke, Osbourne. SIDEMAN. New York (1956) — 40 60

Sister Carrie

By
Theodore Dreiser

NEW YORK
Doubleday, Page & Co.
1900

Dulles, Allen (Welsh). GERMANY'S UNDERGROUND.
New York, 1947   50   40   60

Du Maurier, Daphne. THE LOVING SPIRIT. London, 1931   50   100   300

Du Maurier, George. SIR GAWAINE HYS PENANCE: A
LEGEND OF CAMELOT. (London) 1866. Wraps   —   —   1,000

PETER IBBETSON. New York, 1892   —   100   100
London, 1892. 2 volumes   —   150   150

Dunbar, Paul (Laurence). OAK AND IVY. Dayton, Ohio,
1893. (500 copies)   125   350   6,000

Duncan, Robert (Edward). HEAVENLY CITY, EARTHLY CITY.
(Berkeley) 1947. Green cloth. (100 signed copies)   300   750   1,500
White pictorial boards in dustwrapper. (250 copies)   100   500   1,000

Duncan, Ronald (Frederick). THE COMPLETE PACIFIST.
London (1937). Wraps   50   75   100

Duncan, Sara Jeanette. A SOCIAL DEPARTURE.
New York, 1890   —   50   75

Dunn, Douglas. TERRY STREET. London, 1969   —   —   50

Dunn, Katherine. ATTIC. New York, 1970   —   —   250

Dunn, Nell. UP THE JUNCTION. London, 1963   —   40   40
Philadelphia, 1966   —   30   30

Dunne, Finley Peter. *See* MR. DOOLEY IN PEACE AND WAR

Dunne, John Gregory. DELANO . . . New York (1967)   —   25   75

Dunnett, Dorothy. THE GAME OF KINGS. London (1961)   —   —   250

Dunning, John. THE HOLLAND SUGGESTIONS.
Indianapolis, 1975   —   —   200

Dunning, Ralph Cheever. ROCOCO. Black Manikin Press.
Paris, 1926. (First book of this press)   —   200   200

Dunphy, Jack. JOHN FURY. New York (1946)   —   40   60

Dunsany, Lord (Edward J. M. D. P.). THE GODS OF PEGANA.
London, 1905. First issue: drummer blind-stamped on
front cover   150   150   300
Second issue: without blindstamp   100   100   200

Durant, Will (William James). PHILOSOPHY AND THE
SOCIAL PROBLEM. New York, 1917   —   50   75

Durham, Marilyn. THE MAN WHO LOVED CAT DANCING.
New York (1972)   —   25   40

Durrell, Claude. *See* Claude

Durrell, Gerald. THE OVERLOADED ARK. London (1953) — 75 125
　　New York, 1953 — 30 75

Durrell, Lawrence (George). QUAINT FRAGMENT . . . (London)
　　1931. Blue wraps or red boards. (Fewer than 10 copies) 3,500 12,000 35,000

　　TEN POEMS. London, 1932. (12 signed copies) — 4,000 15,000
　　Wraps — 2,000 5,000

　　PIED PIPER OF LOVERS. London, 1935. (First novel) — 2,000 3,500

　　(Four other items from 1932–35)

Dutton, Geoffrey. NIGHT FLIGHT AND SUNRISE.
　　Adelaide, 1944 — — 75

Dwight, Theodore. AN ORATION, SPOKEN BEFORE THE
　　SOCIETY OF THE CINCINNATI. New Haven, 1792 — 125 200

Dwight, Timothy. *See* A DISSERTATION . . .

Dwyer, K. R. (Dean R. Koontz). CHASE. New York, 1972.
　　(First hardback) — — 250

Dwyer-Jones, Alice. PRICE OF INHERITANCE.
　　London (1963) — 50 50

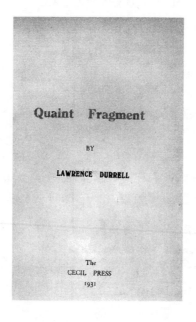

Dykeman, Wilma. THE FRENCH BROAD. New York (1955)   —   50   50

Dylan, Bob. TARANTULA. New York, 1966   —   —   75

Dyment, Clifford. FIRST DAY. London, 1935   —   40   75

E

E., A. (George W. Russell). HOMEWARD: SONGS BY THE
     WAY. Oxford, 1894. Wraps   100   250   450

EARLY PIONEER, AN. (Abel Beach). Buffalo, 1895.
     600 numbered copies   —   40   75

Eastlake, William (Derry). GO IN BEAUTY. New York (1956)   100   125   300
     London, 1957   —   75   100

Eastman, Max. ENJOYMENT OF POETRY.
     New York, 1913   —   —   150
     London, 1913   —   —   100

Eaton, Charles Edward. THE BRIGHT PLAIN.
     Chapel Hill, 1942   —   —   60

Eberhart, Mignon G(ood). THE PATIENT IN ROOM 18.
     Garden City, 1929   —   150   250

Eberhart, Richard. A BRAVERY OF EARTH. London (1930)   125   250   300
     New York (1930). (U.K. sheets)   100   150   200

Eckert, Allan W. THE GREAT AUK. Boston/Toronto (1963)   —   50   50

Eco, Umberto. THE PICTURE HISTORY OF INVENTIONS.
     New York, 1962   —   —   150

Economou, George. THE GEORGIC. London, 1968. Wraps.
     50 signed and numbered copies   —   75   75
     250 signed and numbered copies   —   35   35

Eddings, David. HIGH HUNT. New York, 1973   —   —   50

Eddington, Arthur Stanley. STELLAR MOVEMENTS . . .
     London, 1914   —   125   150

Eddison, E(ric) R(ucker). POEMS, LETTERS AND MEMORIES
     OF PHILIP SIDNEY NAIRN. London, 1916. (109 pages.
     Introduction by Eddison). Issued without dustwrapper   —   150   250

     THE WORM OUROBOROS. London (1922). First issue:
     no blindstamped windmill on rear cover   150   250   450
     Second issue: with windmill   125   200   350
     New York, 1926   75   150   150

Eddy, Mary (Morse) Baker. *See* Mary Baker Glover

Edel, Leon. HENRY JAMES: LES ANNÉE DRAMATIQUES. Paris, 1931. Wraps. (300 copies)	—	—	100
Edgar, Patrick Nisbett. THE AMERICAN RACE-TURF REGISTER . . . New York, 1833. Volume 1 (all published)	—	750	750
Edgerton, Clyde. RANEY. Chapel Hill (1985)	—	—	350
Edman, Irwin. HUMAN TRAITS . . . New York, 1919. Wraps	—	100	125
New York, 1920. Cloth	—	50	75
Edmonds, Walter D(umaux). ROME HAUL. Boston, 1929	25	200	300
Edson, Russell. APPEARANCES. Stamford, 1961. Wraps	—	50	60
Edwards, Dorothy. RHAPSODY. Wishart. London, 1927	—	60	60
Edwards, Junius. IF WE MUST DIE. Garden City, 1963	—	—	100
Edwards, Page. THE MULES THAT ANGELS RIDE. Chicago, 1972	—	35	50
Edwards, S. W. GO NOW IN DARKNESS. Chicago, 1964. Wraps in dustwrapper	—	35	35
Egerton, George [Mary Chavelita Dunne (later Bright)]. KEYNOTES. London, 1893. Green cloth	—	100	100
Eggleston, Edward. NORTHWESTERN SANITARY FAIR . . . (No-place, no-date [1865?]). (4-page appeal for funds)	—	—	750
THE MANUAL: A PRACTICAL GUIDE TO SUNDAY-SCHOOLWORK. Chicago, 1869. First issue: with "A. Zeese" imprint on copyright page	75	150	300
MR. BLAKE'S WALKINGSTICK. Chicago, 1870. Wraps	300	200	200
(One previous anonymous pamphlet)			
Ehle, John. MOVE OVER, MOUNTAIN. New York, 1957	—	—	175
Ehrlich, Max. THE BIG EYE. Garden City, 1949	—	60	75
Eigner, Larry (Lawrence Joel). POEMS. Canton, MA. 1941. Wraps. (25 copies)	200	2,000	2,000
FROM THE SUSTAINING AIR. Mallorca, 1953. (250 copies). Wraps	75	300	400
Eiseley, Loren. THE IMMENSE JOURNEY. New York (1957)	—	75	150
Eliot, George (Mary Ann Evans). *See* David Friedrich Strauss			
SCENES OF CLERICAL LIFE. London, 1858. 2 volumes	350	750	7,500
Also see Mary Ann Evans			

Eliot, Henry Ward, Jr. HARVARD CELEBRITIES.
    Cambridge (Mass., 1901). (T. S.'s father) — — 75

Eliot, T(homas) S(tearns). PRUFROCK . . . London, 1917.
    (500 copies). Wraps 2,000 2,000 6,000

Elkin Mathews, Publisher. *See* Richard Le Gallienne

Elkin, Stanley (Lawrence). BOSWELL. New York (1964) — 100 100

Elkins, Aaron. FELLOWSHIP OF FEAR. New York, 1982 — — 350

Ellenbogen, George. WINDS OF UNREASON.
    Montreal (1957) — 50 50

Ellerman, Annie Winifred. REGION OF LUTANY . . .
    London, 1914. Wraps — 750 750

Ellerman, Sir John. *See* E. L. Black

Ellet, Mrs. E(lizabeth). POEMS. Philadelphia, 1835 — 125 175

    (Previous translation)

Ellin, Stanley. DREADFUL SUMMIT. New York, 1948 — 75 125

Elliott, Bob, and Ray Goulding. BOB AND RAY'S STORY OF
    LINDA LOVELY AND THE FLEEBUS. New York, 1960 — — 75

Elliott, George P(aul). PARKTILDEN VILLAGE. Boston (1958) 20 50 50

Elliott, Janice. CAVE WITH ECHOES. London, 1967 — 35 35

Elliott, Sumner Locke. CAREFUL, HE MIGHT HEAR YOU.
    New York, 1963. Author's name on spine of
    dustwrapper in red or black (variant) — 30 75

Elliott, William. ADDRESS TO THE PEOPLE OF ST. HELENA
    PARISH. Charleston, 1832. Wraps — 150 350

Ellis, A. E. THE RACK. London, 1958 — 50 40

Ellis, Alice Thomas. THE SIN EATER. London, 1977 — — 60

Ellis, Bret Easton. LESS THAN ZERO. New York (1985) — — 50

Ellis, Havelock. THE NEW SPIRIT. London, 1890 — 100 200

Ellison, Harlan (Jay). THE DEADLY STREETS. New York
    (1958). Wraps — 60 125

    RUMBLE. New York, 1958. (Note: priority uncertain) — — 150

Ellison, James Whitfield. I'M OWEN HARRISON HARDING.
    New York, 1955 — 20 25

Ellison, Ralph. INVISIBLE MAN. New York (1952)	50	200	1,000
London, 1953	—	100	250
Ellroy, James. BROWN'S REQUIEM. (New York, 1981).			
Wraps	—	—	100
London (1984)	—	—	75
Ellson, Hal. DUKE. New York, 1949	—	40	75
Ellsworth, Robert. CHINESE FURNITURE. New York, 1971	—	—	400
Elmslie, Kenward. PAVILIONS. New York, 1961. Wraps.			
(300 copies)	—	—	100
Ely, David (David Ely Lilienthal). TROT. New York (1963)	—	25	25
EMBARGO (THE), OR SKETCHES OF THE TIMES . . .			
(William Cullen Bryant). Boston, 1808. 12 pages in			
self-wraps with cover title	1,000	4,000	8,500
Emerson, Ralph Waldo. *See* NATURE			
LETTER FROM THE REV R. W. EMERSON TO . . .			
Boston (1832). Wraps	—	—	20,000
A HISTORICAL DISCOURSE . . . Concord, 1835	—	250	400
Emmons, Richard. THE FREDONIAD. Boston, 1827.			
4 volumes	—	200	200

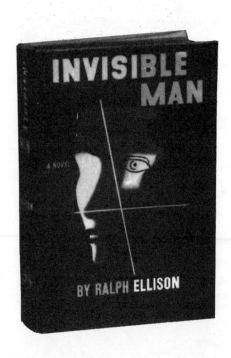

Empson, William. LETTER IV. London, 1929 — — 250

    POEMS. London, 1935 — 125 175

Emshwiller, Carol. JOY IN OUR CAUSE. New York (1974) — — 40

Endore, S. Guy. CASANOVA: HIS KNOWN AND UNKNOWN
LIFE. New York (1929) 15 40 50
London (1930) — 40 50

England, George Allan. UNDERNEATH THE BOUGH.
New York (1903) — — 200

Engle, Howard. THE SUICIDE MURDERS. Toronto, 1980 — — 100

Engle, Marian. NO CLOUDS OF GLORY. Toronto, 1968 — — 100

Engle, Paul (Hamilton). WORN EARTH. New Haven, 1932 35 125 125

    (Co-edited anthology in 1931)

ENQUIRY INTO THE PRESENT STATE OF POLITE LEARNING
IN EUROPE, AN. (Oliver Goldsmith's first original work).
London, 1759 — — 1,000

Enright, D. J. SEASON TICKET. Alexandria, Egypt, 1948.
Wraps — — 250

Enslin, Theodore (Vernon). THE WORK PROPOSED.
(Ashland, Massachusetts) 1958. Limited to 250 copies.
Stiff wraps 35 175 175

Ephron, Nora. WALLFLOWER AT THE ORGY. New York,
1970 — — 35

Epstein, Seymour. PILLAR OF SALT. New York (1960) — 60 75

Erdman, Paul E. THE BILLION DOLLAR SURE THING.
New York, 1974 — — 40

Erdrich, Louise. JACKLIGHT. New York (1984). Wraps — 100 200
London, 1984 — — 100

    LOVE MEDICINE. New York (1984) — — 175

Erickson, Steve. DAYS BETWEEN STATIONS. New York
(1985) — — 50

Ertz, Susan. MADAME CLAIRE. London, 1923 — 75 125

Eshleman, Clayton. MEXICO & NORTH. (New York/San
Francisco, 1961). Wraps. 26 lettered copies — 75 250
Trade edition 35 40 75

EUPHRANOR, A DIALOGUE ON YOUTH. (Edward Fitzgerald).
London, 1851 60 300 750

Evans, Donald. DISCORDS. Philadelphia, 1912	20	100	100
Evans, E. Everett. MAN OF MANY MINDS. Reading (1953).			
300 signed and numbered copies	—	60	100
Trade edition. First issue: blue cloth	—	25	40
Second issue: boards	—	15	25
Evans, John. ANDREWS' HARVEST. New York, 1933	25	75	75
Evans, John (Howard Browne). HALO IN BLOOD. Indianapolis (1946). (First under this name)	—	—	100
Evans, Margiad. COUNTRY DANCE. London, 1932	30	75	100
Evans, Mary Ann (George Eliot). THE ESSENCE OF CHRISTIANITY. London, 1854. First issue: black cloth with "Marian Evans" on spine	—	1,000	2,000
Second issue: purple cloth with "George Eliot" on spine (Evans's translation of Ludwig Feuerbach's book. Her second "book" [translation] The only use of her real name)	—	750	1,500
Evans, Max. SOUTHWEST WIND. San Antonio, 1958	—	—	50
Evans, Walker. THE CRIME OF CUBA. Philadelphia (1933). Book by Carlton Beals. First book appearance of Evans's photos	—	150	400
AMERICAN PHOTOGRAPHS. New York (1939)	—	—	400
Everett, Edward. A DEFENCE OF CHRISTIANITY. Boston, 1814	40	100	200
Everson, William (Oliver). (Brother Antoninus). THESE ARE THE RAVENS. San Leandro, California, 1935. Wraps	200	400	500
Ewart, Gavin. POEMS AND SONGS. London (1939)	—	150	250
Ewing, Max. TWENTY-SIX SONNETS FROM THE PARONOMASIAN . . . (New York, 1924). Wraps	—	50	50
Exley, Frederick. A FAN'S NOTES. New York (1968)	25	50	150
London (1970)	—	50	75

F

F., M. T. (Katherine Anne Porter). MY CHINESE MARRIAGE. New York, 1921	100	400	1,250
Fabes, Gilbert. THE AUTOBIOGRAPHY OF A BOOK. London (1926)	—	75	150
Fainlight, Harry. SUSSICRAN. (London, 1965). Wraps.			
50 signed copies	—	75	100
100 unsigned copies	—	35	50

YOUNG
LONIGAN

A Boyhood in Chicago Streets

by

JAMES T. FARRELL

Introduction by
FREDERIC M. THRASHER
Associate Professor of Education, New York University
Author of "The Gang"

NEW YORK
THE VANGUARD PRESS
1932

Odette D'Antrevernes

AND

A Study in Temperament

BY

ARTHUR FIRBANK

LONDON
ELKIN MATHEWS, VIGO STREET, W.
1905

SONNETS
TO AN
IMAGINARY
MADONNA

BY VARDIS FISHER

NEW YORK · HAROLD VINAL
MCMXXVII

WEBSTER GENEALOGY.

COMPILED AND PRINTED
FOR
PRESENTATION ONLY
BY
NOAH WEBSTER
NEW HAVEN
1836.

WITH
NOTES AND CORRECTIONS
BY
HIS GREAT-GRANDSON,
PAUL LEICESTER FORD.

BROOKLYN, N.Y.
PRIVATELY PRINTED.
1876.

Fair, Ronald L. MANY THOUSANDS GONE.
New York (1965)   — 60 125

FAIR DEATH, A. (Sir Henry Newbolt). London (1881).
Wraps   40 100 125

Fairless, Michael (Margaret Fairless Barber). THE
GATHERING OF BROTHER HILARIUS. London, 1901   — 50 125

Fairman, Henry Clay. THE THIRD WORLD . . . Atlanta, 1895   — 200 350
New York, 1896   — 100 125

Falkner, J. Meade. THE LOST STRADIVARIUS. London, 1895   75 75 75

Falkner, W(illiam) C(lark). THE WHITE ROSE OF MEMPHIS.
New York, 1881   — — 125

Fallaci, Oriana. THE USELESS SEX. New York, 1964   — — 75

FANNY. (Fitz-Greene Halleck). New York, 1819. Gray wraps   150 300 400

FANSHAWE: A TALE. (Nathaniel Hawthorne). Boston, 1828   3,000 12,000 30,000

Fante, John. WAIT UNTIL SPRING, BANDINI.
New York (1938)   — 125 300

Farina, Richard. BEEN DOWN SO LONG IT LOOKS LIKE UP
TO ME. New York (1966)   20 50 200

Farjeon, Eleanor. PAN-WORSHIP . . . London, 1908   30 60 100

Farmer, Philip Jose. THE GREEN ODYSSEY. New York
(1957). Cloth   — 850 1,250
Wraps   — 30 60

Farnol, (John) Jeffery. MY LADY CAPRICE. London, 1907   40 35 35

Farrar, John Chapman. DREAMS OF BOYHOOD . . .
(No-place) 1914. Wraps   — — 75

Farrell, Henry. WHAT EVER HAPPENED TO BABY JANE?
New York (1960)   — 35 100

Farrell, J. G. A MAN FROM ELSEWHERE. London, 1963   — 125 175

Farrell, James T(homas). YOUNG LONIGAN . . .   125 250 750
New York, 1932 [Reissued in 1935 with new
introduction (dated 1935)
by F. Thrasher inserted, title page still dated 1932]   50 100 350

Farren, Julian. THE TRAIN FROM PITTSBURGH.
New York, 1948   — 25 25

Fast, Howard (Melvin). TWO VALLEYS. New York, 1933   60 250 600

Fats, Minnesota. THE BANKSHOT . . . Cleveland (1966).
Written with Tom Fox   — — 75

Faulkner, Fritz. WINDLESS SKY. London, 1936	—	—	125
Faulkner, John. MEN WORKING. New York (1941)	—	60	75
Faulkner, William. THE MARBLE FAUN. Boston (1924)	4,000	15,000	20,000
SOLDIER'S PAY. New York, 1926	750	6,000	15,000
London, 1930	150	750	1,250
Fauset, Jessie Redmond. THERE IS CONFUSION. New York, 1924	—	100	150
Faust, Frederick. *See* Max Brand			
Faust, Irvin. ENTERING ANGEL'S WORLD . . . New York, 1963	25	50	60
ROAR LION ROAR . . . New York (1964)	—	40	50
Faust, Seymour. THE LOVELY QUARRY. New York, 1958. Wraps	—	20	25
Favil Press. GLEANINGS. By Clifford Bax. Kensington, 1921. (40 copies)	—	100	200
FAVORITE OF NATURE, THE. (Mary Ann Kelty). London, 1821. 3 volumes	—	—	400
Fay, Theodore Sedgwick. *See* DREAMS AND REVERIES . . .			
Fearing, Kenneth. ANGEL ARMS. New York, 1929	50	200	250
Feather, Leonard. INSIDE JAZZ (INSIDE BE-BOP). New York (1949). Wraps	—	125	125
Feibleman, James. DEATH OF THE GOD IN MEXICO. New York (1931)	—	150	200
Feibleman, Peter S. A PLACE WITHOUT TWILIGHT. Cleveland (1958)	—	50	60
Feiffer, Jules. SICK, SICK, SICK. New York, 1958	—	40	50
Feikema, Feike (Frederick Manfred). THE GOLDEN BOWL. St. Paul, 1944	20	100	125
Feinstein, Elaine. IN A GREEN EYE. London, 1966. 30 signed and numbered copies	—	60	100
Feinstein, Isidor. *See* I. F. Stone			
Feldman, Irving (Mordecai). WORKS AND DAYS . . .			
London (1961)	—	75	75
Boston (1961)	—	60	60
Fenollosa, Ernest Francisco. EAST AND WEST. New York, 1893	—	—	250

Fenton, James. OUR WESTERN FURNITURE. Oxford (1968).			
Wraps. 200 copies	—	125	300
12 signed and numbered copies	—	—	850
Ferber, Edna. DAWN O'HARA. New York (1911)	30	50	125
Ferguson, Helen (Helen Woods). A CHARMED CIRCLE.			
London (1929)	—	350	350
Ferlinghetti, Lawrence. PICTURES OF THE GONE WORLD.			
San Francisco (1955). 25 signed hardbound copies.	150	500	750
Wraps. (500 copies). (Price: 65¢). (First City Lights book)	75	200	350
Fermor, Patrick Leigh. THE TRAVELLER'S TREE.			
London, 1950	—	60	200
(Preceded by a 1938 translation)			
Ferrell, Anderson. WHERE SHE WAS. New York, 1985	—	25	25
Ferrier, Susan E. MARRIAGE, A NOVEL. Edinburgh/London,			
1818. 3 volumes	—	300	400
Ferril, Thomas Hornsby. HIGH PASSAGE. New York, 1926	20	75	75
Ferrini, Vincent. NO SMOKE. Portland, 1941	25	50	100
Fessier, Michael. FULLY DRESSED AND IN HIS RIGHT MIND.			
New York, 1935	—	50	50
Fetherston, Patrick. DAY OFF. (London, 1955). Wraps	—	—	40
Ficke, Arthur Davidson (and Thomas Newell Metcalf).			
THEIR BOOK. (Chicago, 1901). 50 numbered copies	100	150	1,000
FROM THE ISLES. (Surrey) 1907. Wraps	—	100	400
Fiedler, Leslie (Aaron). AN END TO INNOCENCE.			
Boston (1955)	—	25	40
Field, Ben. THE COCK'S FUNERAL. New York (1937)	25	40	40
Field, Edward. STAND UP, FRIEND. New York (1963)	—	20	25
Field, Eugene. TRIBUNE PRIMER. (Denver, 1881). Wraps	2,000	5,000	7,500
Brooklyn, 1882	100	300	400
THE MODEL PRIMER. Brooklyn (1882)	—	—	350
Field, Peter (Francis Hobson). OUTLAWS THREE.			
New York, 1934	—	250	350
DRY GULCH ADAMS. New York, 1934	—	250	300
Field, Rachel Lyman. RISE UP, JENNIE SMITH. New York			
(1918). Wraps	25	125	250

Fielding, Gabriel. *See* Alan Barnsley

Fielding, Sarah. THE ADVENTURES OF DAVID SIMPLE.
    London, 1744. 2 volumes   —   — 1,000

Fields, James T(homas). ANNIVERSARY POEM . . . Boston,
    1838. In original wraps   —   50   125

    POEMS. Boston, 1849   25   50   75

Fields, W. C. FIELDS FOR PRESIDENT. New York, 1940   —   —   600

FIGHT AT DAME EUROPA'S SCHOOL. [H. W. Pullen,
    anonymously]. New York, 1871. (First book illustrated
    by Thomas Nast).   — 100 200

Finch, Amanda. BACK TRAIL . . . New York, 1951. Wraps   — 50 50

Findley, Timothy. THE LAST OF THE CRAZY PEOPLE.
    London, 1967   —   —   60

Finkel, Donald. SIMEON. New York, 1964   —   —   75

Finlay, Ian H(amilton). THE SEA-BED . . . Edinburgh (1958).
    Wraps in dustwrapper   — 200 250

Finley, Karen. SHOCK TREATMENT. San Francisco (1990).
    Wraps   —   —   35

Finley, Timothy. THE LAST OF THE CRAZY PEOPLE.
    Toronto, 1967   —   — 250

Finney, Charles G. THE CIRCUS OF DR. LAO.
    New York, 1935   75 175 300

Finney, Jack (Walter Braden Finney). 5 AGAINST THE
    HOUSE. Garden City, 1954   25 75 150

Finney, Sterling (E. B. White). LESS THAN NOTHING . . .
    New York (1927). Issued without dustwrapper   — 250 350

Firbank, (Arthur Annesly) Ronald. ODETTE
    D'ANTREVERNES and A STUDY IN TEMPERAMENT.
    London, 1905. 10 large paper copies on vellum. Signed   650 1,000 2,500
    Wraps. (500 copies)   175 250 500

FIRE OVER LONDON . . . (William Sansom). London, 1941.
    Wraps   —   — 175

FIRST LESSONS IN GRAMMAR . . . (Elizabeth Peabody).
    Boston, 1830   — 150 250

Fish, Donald. AIRLINE DETECTIVE. London, 1962. (Ian
    Fleming introduction)   — 75 100

Fish, Robert L(loyd). THE FUGITIVE. New York, 1962	—	50	60
Fisher, Alfred Young. THE GHOST IN THE UNDERBLOWS. Los Angeles, 1940. (300 copies)	—	125	125
Fisher, Bud (Harry Conway). THE MUTT AND JEFF CARTOONS. Boston, 1910	25	100	250
Fisher, M(ary) F(rances) K(ennedy). SERVE IT FORTH New York, 1937	—	150	500
Fisher, Roy. CITY. Worcester, 1961. Wraps	—	75	100
Fisher, Vardis. SONNETS TO AN IMAGINARY MADONNA. New York, 1927	50	150	300
Fisher, William. THE WAITERS. Cleveland (1953)	—	35	100
Fiske, John. TOBACCO AND ALCOHOL. New York, 1869	—	50	300
Fitch, Ensign Clarke (Upton Sinclair). SAVED BY THE ENEMY. New York, 1898	—	200	600
Fitch, (Wm.) Clyde. THE KNIGHTING OF THE TWINS . . . Boston (1891)	—	150	150
Fitch, George. THE BIG STRIKE AT SIWASH. New York, 1909	25	60	60
Fitts, Dudley. TWO POEMS. (No-place, 1932). Wraps. (100 signed copies)	35	125	150
Fitzgerald, Edward. See EUPHRANOR . . .			
Fitzgerald, F(rancis) Scott (Key). THIS SIDE OF PARADISE. New York, 1920. (Published April 1920 and Scribner seal)	400	3,000	7,500
(Four previous musical scores)			
Fitzgerald, Robert (Stuart). POEMS. New York (1935)	—	75	125
Fitzgerald, Zelda. SAVE ME THE WALTZ. New York, 1932. (3,010 copies)	75	600	1,250
London (1953)	—	60	125
Fitzgibbon, Constantine. THE ARIAN BIRD. London, 1949	—	50	75
FIVE YOUNG AMERICAN POETS. Norfolk (1940). (John Berryman, et al.). (800 copies). Considered Berryman's first book as the five "books" were combined by publisher	—	200	300
Flaccus, Kimball. IN PRAISE OF MARA. Hanover, 1932. Wraps. (100 copies in total). 25 Signed and numbered			

copies	—	—	200
75 unsigned copies	50	100	100
AVALANCHE OF APRIL. New York, 1934	—	50	50
Flagg, Fannie. COMING ATTRACTIONS. New York (1981)	—	—	60
Flaherty, Robert. MY ESKIMO FRIENDS. New York, 1924	150	300	450
Flanagan, Mary. BAD GIRLS. London, 1984	—	—	40
Flanner, Hildegarde. THIS MORNING. New York, 1921. Wraps	—	—	200
Flanner, Janet. THE CUBICAL CITY. New York, 1926	100	350	1,000
Flecker, James (Elroy). THE BEST MAN EIGHT'S WEEK. London, 1906. Wraps	—	300	300
THE BRIDGE OF FIRE: POEMS. London, 1907. Wraps. First issue: no quote from *Sunday Times*	60	125	125
Fleetwood, Hugh. A PAINTER OF FLOWERS. London, 1972	—	40	40
Fleming, Ian (Lancaster). CASINO ROYALE. London, 1953	40	1,250	4,500
New York, 1954	25	300	1,000
Fleming, Oliver (Philip and Ronald MacDonald). AMBROTOX AND LIMPING DICK. London, 1920	—	150	300
Fleming, Peter. BRAZILIAN ADVENTURE. London (1933)	—	75	125
New York, 1934	—	—	75
Flender, Harold. PARIS BLUES. New York (1957)	—	30	50
Fletcher, J(oseph) S(mith). ANDREWLINA. London, 1889	—	50	75
Fletcher, John Gould. FIRE AND WINE. London (1913). (First or second book—there were five published in 1913)	—	100	125
THE DOMINANT CITY. London, 1913	—	—	175
Flexner, Hortense. CLOUDS AND COBBLESTONES. Boston, 1920	—	—	60
Flint, F. S. IN THE NET OF THE STARS. London, 1909	50	125	125
Flint, Timothy. A SERMON, PREACHED . . . Newburyport, 1808. Wraps	—	150	300
Flower, Robin. ERIE . . . London (1910). Wraps	—	60	75
Flynn, Errol. SHOWDOWN. New York, 1946	—	—	75
Flynn, Robert. NORTH TO YESTERDAY. New York, 1967	—	40	40
Follett, Ken(eth Martin). *See* Symon Myles			

Foote, Horton. HARRISON, TEXAS: EIGHT TELEVISION
    PLAYS. New York (1956) — 60 75

    THE CHASE. New York (1956). Issued the same day as
    the foregoing book — 40 75

Foote, John Tintor. BLISTER JONES. Indianapolis (1913) 20 50 60

Foote, Shelby. THE MERCHANT OF BRISTOL. (Greenville,
    1947). Wraps. 260 signed and numbered copies — 350 600

    TOURNAMENT. New York, 1949 — 75 175

Forbes, Bryan. TRUTH LIES SLEEPING. London (1950) — 75 75

Forché, Carloyn. GATHERING THE TRIBES. New Hampshire,
    1976. Cloth — — 125
    Wraps — — 35

Ford, Charles Henry. THE YOUNG AND THE EVIL. (Written
    with Parker Tyler). Paris (1933). (First book for both).
    Wraps. 50 numbered copies 150 400 600
    Trade edition — 250 300

    A PAMPHLET OF SONNETS. Majorca, 1936. (50 copies
    signed by Ford and Pavel Tchelitchew, the illustrator) — 250 450
    Unsigned — — 250

    THE GARDEN OF DISORDER . . . London (1938). 30
    signed copies. Issued without dustwrapper 175 250 300
    460 unsigned copies 75 100 150
    Norfolk (1938). English edition in New Directions
    dustwrapper — 100 150

Ford, Ford Madox. *See* Ford Madox Hueffer

Ford, Jesse Hill. MOUNTAINS OF GILEAD. Boston, 1961 — 40 75

Ford, Leslie (Mrs. Zenith Jones Brown). *See* David Frome

Ford, Paul Leicester. WEBSTER GENEALOGY . . . NEW
    HAVEN 1836. Brooklyn, 1876. Notes by Ford.
    (250 copies). Wraps 100 150 200

    THE BEST LAID PLANS. Brooklyn, 1889 35 50 75

Ford, Richard. A PIECE OF MY HEART. New York, 1976 — 35 200
    London, 1987 — — 75

Fordham, Mary Weston. MAGNOLIA LEAVES. Tuskegee
    (1897). Introduction by Booker T. Washington — 100 300

Foreman, Michael. THE PERFECT PRESENT. London, 1967 — — 125

Forester, C. S. A PAWN AMONG KINGS. London, 1924 — 150 750 1,500

FORESTERS, AN AMERICAN TALE, THE. (Jeremy Belknap).
Boston, 1792. 3 variants, no priority — — 600

(Preceded by *The History of New Hampshire* . . .
and a number of broadsides)

Forrest, Felix C. (Paul Linebarger). RIA. New York (1947) — 75 100

Forrest, Leon. THERE IS A TREE MORE ANCIENT THAN
EDEN. New York (1973) — — 50

Forster, E(dward) M(organ). WHERE ANGELS FEAR TO
TREAD. Edinburgh, 1905. First issue: title not stated in
ads. (1,050 copies) 150 500 1,750
Second issue: title in ads — 150 1,250

Forsyth, Frederick. THE BIAFRA STORY. (Middlesex, 1969).
Wraps — 75 125

THE DAY OF THE JACKAL. London (1971) — 75 150
New York, 1971 15 35 75

Fort, Charles. THE OUTCAST MANUFACTURERS. New York,
1909. First issue: blue ribbed cloth lettered in gold 60 150 200
Second issue: blue mesh cloth lettered in red — 125 150

FORTRESS OF SORRENTO, THE. (Mordecai M. Noah). New
York, 1808. Wraps — 300 750
Re-bound — — 250

Foster, Michael. FORGIVE ADAM . . . New York, 1935 — 60 60

FOUR ELEGIES . . . (John Scott). London, 1760 — — 500

Fowler, Gene. TRUMPET IN THE DUST. New York (1930) — — 125

Fowles, John. THE COLLECTOR. London, 1963. First issue:
dustwrapper flap without reviews 35 650 750
Boston (1963) 20 100 125

Fox, John (William). A CUMBERLAND VENDETTA. New
York, 1896. First issue: final entry in contents is "Hell
Fer Sartain" 25 50 200
Second issue: final entry is "Hell-Fer-Sartain Creeek" — — 125

Fox, Len. GUM LEAVES AND BAMBOO. (New South
Wales, 1959) — — 100

Fox, Paula. POOR GEORGE. New York (1967) — 50 125

Fox, William Price. SOUTHERN FRIED. Greenwich (1962).
Wraps 20 35 50

Fraenkel, Michael. *See* ANONYMOUS *and* WERTHER'S . . .

Frame, Janet. THE LAGOON. Christchurch, 1951	15	300	450
OWLS DO CRY. London, 1961	—	—	100
Francis, Dick (Richard Stanley). SPORT OF QUEENS. London, 1957	—	200	950
DEAD CERT. London, 1962	—	450	3,000
New York, 1962	—	150	1,000
New York, 1989. 26 signed and lettered copies in slipcase	—	—	250
100 signed and numbered copies	—	—	100
Francis, Robert. STAND WITH ME HERE. New York, 1936	—	60	175
Frank, Pat. MR. ADAM. New York, 1946	—	—	50
Frank, Robert. (Photographs). FROM INCAS TO INDIOS. New York, 1956	—	—	125
London, 1956	—	—	125
Frank, Waldo. THE UNWELCOME MAN. Boston, 1917	50	125	125
Frankau, Gilbert. ETON ECHOES. Eton, 1901. Wraps	—	100	125
Frankenberg, Lloyd. THE RED KITE. New York (1939). (500 copies)	—	40	60
FRANKENSTEIN. (Mary Wollstonecraft Shelley). London, 1818. 3 volumes	—	15,000	35,000
Fraser, Antonia. *See* Antonia Pakenham			
Fraser, G. S. THE FATAL LANDSCAPE . . . London (1943)	—	—	125
Fraser, George MacDonald. FLASHMAN. London (1969)	—	60	200
New York, 1969	—	—	125
Frayn, Michael. THE DAY OF THE DOG. London, 1962	—	—	75
Frazer, Sir James George. TOTEMISM. Edinburgh, 1887	60	125	350
Frazier, Ian. DATING YOUR MOM. New York (1986)	—	—	30
Frederic, Harold. SETH'S BROTHER'S WIFE. New York, 1887. First issue: copyright 1886 and no advertisements	100	150	300
Frederick, John T. GREEN BUSH. New York, 1925	—	—	60
Freeling, Nicolas. LOVE IN AMSTERDAM. London, 1962	—	60	100
Freeman, Arthur. IZMIR. (Cambridge, Eng., 1959). Wraps	—	—	75
Freeman, Gillian. THE LIBERTY MAN. London, 1955	—	40	40

Freeman, John. TWENTY POEMS. London, 1909. Wraps   —   60   60

Freeman, Mary E. Wilkins. *See* Mary Wilkins

Freeman, R(ichard) Austin. TRAVELS AND LIFE IN ASHANTI
AND JAPAN. London, 1898   —   750   1,250

     TRAVELS AND LIFE IN ASHANTI AND JAPAN.
London, 1898   —   —   1,000

     Also see Clifford Ashdown

Freneau, Philip (Morin). *See* A POEM, ON THE
RISING GLORY . . .

     THE AMERICAN VILLAGE. New York, 1772   —   —   2,000

Freud, Sigmund. THE INTERPRETATION OF DREAMS.
New York, 1913   —   150   1,000

Fried, Erich. THEY FIGHT IN THE DARK. (London, 1944).
Wraps   —   75   100

Friedan, Betty. THE FEMININE MYSTIQUE. New York (1963)   —   40   125

Friedman, Bruce Jay. THE RASCAL'S GUIDE. New York
(1958). Wraps. Edited by JBS   —   —   35

     STERN. New York, 1962   35   50   75

     (Previous edited anthology)

Friedman, I. K. THE LUCKY NUMBER. Chicago, 1896   —   75   100

Friedman, Kinky. GREENWICH KILLING TIME.
New York, 1986   —   —   30

Friedman, Mickey. HURRICANE SEASON. New York, 1983   —   —   50

Frome, David (Zenith Jones Brown). THE MURDER OF AN
OLD MAN. London, 1929   —   75   200

Frost, A(rthur) B(urdette). STUFF AND NONSENSE. New
York (1884). Boards   50   100   175

     Also see Max Adeler

Frost, Robert (Lee). TWILIGHT. (Lawrence, Massachusetts,
1894). 2 known copies   5,000   40,000   50,000
Charlottesville, 1966. Facsimile wraps. 20 copies on
handmade paper   —   —   350
150 copies   —   —   150

     A BOY'S WILL. London, 1913. First issue: brown or
bronze cloth with lettering in gilt, edges rough cut   1,000   1,250   5,000
Vellum-paper boards stamped in red   —   350   2,500

Cream linen-paper wraps, stamped in black without border rule; 8-petaled flower ornament	—	—	1,500
With 4-petaled flower ornament	—	—	1,250
135 signed and numbered copies of above	—	—	1,750
New York, 1915. "aind" for "and" in last line on p. 14	200	350	600
"and" corrected on p. 14	—	—	250
Fruchter, Norman. COAT UPON A STICK. (London, 1962)	15	50	50
Fry, Christopher. THE BOY WITH A CART . . . London, 1939. Wraps	—	75	250
Fry, Roger E. GIOVANNI BELLINI. London, 1899	—	75	150
Frye, Northrop. FEARFUL SYMMETRY: A STUDY OF WILLIAM BLAKE. Princeton, New Jersey, 1947	—	—	125
Fuchs, Daniel. SUMMER IN WILLIAMSBURG.			
New York (1934)	—	200	1,250
London (1935)	—	125	350
FUCK THE SYSTEM. (Abbie Hoffman). (New York, 1967). (Privately published). Stapled wraps	—	75	150
Fuentes, Carlos. WHERE THE AIR IS CLEAR.			
New York (1960)	—	30	75
Fugard, Athol. THE BLOOD KNOT. Johannesburg, 1963. (Issued without dustwrapper)	—	200	300
New York, 1964	—	—	75
Fugard, Sheila. THE CASTAWAYS. Johannesburg, 1972	—	—	125
FULL VINDICATION OF THE MEASURES OF THE CONGRESS . . . , A. (Alexander Hamilton). New York, 1774. Wraps	—	—	4,000
Fuller, Henry Black. See Stanton Page			
Fuller, John. FAIRGROUND MUSIC. London, 1961	15	25	25
Fuller, R(ichard) Buckminster. NINE CHAINS TO THE MOON. Philadelphia (1938)	—	150	200
Fuller, Roy (Broadbent). POEMS. London (1939)	—	150	150
Fuller, S(arah) M(argaret). CONVERSATIONS WITH GOETHE. Boston, 1839. (Translated by Fuller). In original cloth	—	500	500
SUMMER ON THE LAKES . . . Boston/New York, 1844	—	300	300
Boston/New York, 1845. Wraps	—	75	100
Furman, Garrit. RURAL HOURS. (No-place) 1824. Boards	125	125	150

Fussell, Paul. THEORY OF PROSODY IN EIGHTEENTH-
CENTURY ENGLAND. New London, Connecticut, 1954.
Wraps   —   40   75

Futrelle, Jacques. THE CHASE OF THE GOLDEN PLATE.
New York, 1906   —   200   200

Fyfield, Frances (Frances Hegarty). A QUESTION OF GUILT.
London, 1988   —   —   60
New York, 1989   —   —   25

G

Gaddis, Thomas E. BIRDMAN OF ALCATRAZ.
New York (1955)   —   35   75
London (1962)   —   —   50

Gaddis, William. THE RECOGNITIONS. New York (1955)   75   200   500
London (1962)   —   —   150

Gág, Wanda. MILLIONS OF CATS. New York, 1928.
250 signed and numbered copies with original
engraving. Issued in slipcase   —   350   1,000
Trade edition in dustwrapper   —   125   350

Gaines, Charles. STAY HUNGRY. New York, 1972   —   20   25

Gaines, Ernest J. CATHERINE CARMIER. New York, 1964   60   125   350

Gaitskill, Mary. BAD BEHAVIOR. New York, 1988   —   —   40

Gale, Zona. ROMANCE ISLAND. Indianapolis (1906)   25   50   100

Gallagher, Tess. STEPPING OUTSIDE. Lisbon, Iowa (1974).
Cloth   —   250   750
Wraps   —   —   300

Gallant, Mavis. THE OTHER PARIS. Boston, 1956   —   75   125
London (1957). (Len Deighton dustwrapper)   —   —   75

Gallico, Paul (William). FAREWELL TO SPORT.
New York, 1938   —   150   200

THE ADVENTURES OF HIRAM HOLIDAY.
New York, 1939   —   150   250

Gallup, George. A GUIDE TO PUBLIC OPINION POLLS.
Puerto Rico, 1944   —   75   75

Galsworthy, John. *See* John Sinjohn

Gann, Ernest. ISLAND IN THE SKY. New York, 1944   —   —   100

García Lorca, Federico. BITTER OLEANDER. London, 1935 —   150   200

García-Marquez, Gabriel. NO ONE WRITES TO
  THE COLONEL. New York (1968) — 125 600
  (London, 1971) — — 350

Gardiner, John Rolf. GREAT DREAM OF HEAVEN.
  New York, 1974 — — 60

Gardner, Erle Stanley. THE CASE OF THE VELVET CLAWS.
  New York, 1932 50 1,000 3,500

Gardner, Isabella (Stewart). BIRTHDAYS FROM THE OCEAN.
  Cambridge, 1955 25 35 50

  THE LIQUIDATOR. London, 1964 — 50 75

Gardner, John (Champlin). THE FORMS OF FICTION. New
  York, 1962. (Written with Lennis Dunlap). Issued
  without dustwrapper 75 125 150

  DRAGON, DRAGON . . . (No-place, Christmas, 1962).
  Mimeographed pages in stiff boards — 1,500 1,500

  THE MILLER'S MULE . . . (No-place) 1965.
  Mimeographed pages in stiff boards — 1,000 1,000

  THE COMPLETE WORKS OF THE GAWAIN POET.
  Chicago (1965). Translated by Gardner 75 200 300

  THE RESURRECTION. (New York, 1966) 200 450 500

  (Ph.D. dissertation prior to 1962)

Gardner, John (Edmund). SPIN THE BOTTLE. London (1964) — 75 125

Gardner, Leonard. FAT CITY. New York (1969) 15 25 50

Garfield, Brian. RANGE JUSTICE. New York, 1960 — — 75

Garland, (Hannibal) Hamlin. UNDER THE WHEEL. Boston,
  1890. Wraps 250 250 500

  MAIN TRAVELED ROADS. Boston, 1891 60 100 250
  Chicago, 1893. 110 large paper copies — 75 250

Garner, Alan. THE WEIRDSTONE OF BRISINGAMEN.
  London, 1960 — — 450

Garnett, David. THE KITCHEN GARDEN . . . London (1909).
  Wraps. (Translated and adapted by DG from French
  work of Prof. Gressent) 60 150 300

  Also see Leda Burke

Garnett, Edward. THE PARADOX CLUB. London, 1888 — 40 150

Garnett, Richard. *See* PRIMULA

Garrett, George (Palmer). KING OF THE MOUNTAIN.
New York (1957)   25   50   75

Garrett, (Gordon) Randall. *See* Robert Randall

Garrigue, Jean. THE EGO AND THE CENTAUR.
(Norfolk, 1947)   15   35   50

Garson, Barbara. MACBIRD: *Independent Socialist Club.*
(Berkeley, 1966). Legal sheets mimeographed and stapled   —   35   125
(Berkeley, 1966). Wraps   —   —   25

Garth, Will. LAWLESS GUNS. New York, 1937   —   —   250

Garve, Andrew (Paul Winterton). NO TEARS FOR HILDA.
London, 1950   —   50   75
New York, 1950   —   —   40

Gary, Romain. THE COMPANY OF MEN. New York, 1950   —   50   60

Gascoyne, David. ROMAN BALCONY. London, 1932   200   750   1,500

Gash, Jonathan. THE JUDAS PAIR. London, 1977.
(First mystery)   —   —   200
New York, 1977   —   —   75

Gaskell, Elizabeth C. *See* MARY BARTON . . .

Gaskell, Jane. STRANGE EVIL. London, 1957   —   50   60

Gass, William H(oward). OMENSETTER'S LUCK.
(New York, 1966)   60   125   200
London, 1967   —   75   100

Gathorne-Hardy, Robert. LACEBURY MANOR.
London, 1930   —   100   100

Gault, William Campbell. DON'T CRY FOR ME.
New York, 1952   —   35   100

Gavin, Ewart. POEMS AND SONGS. New York, 1939   —   —   100

Gavin, Thomas. KING-KILL. New York, 1977   —   20   25

Geddes, Virgil. FORTY POEMS. Paris (1926). Wraps   —   75   125

Gee, Maurice. THE BIG SEASON. London, 1962   —   60   60

Geertz, Clifford. THE RELIGION OF JAVA. Glencoe, 1960   —   —   75

Geismar, Maxwell. WRITERS IN CRISIS. Boston, 1942 —   35   35

Gelber, Jack. THE CONNECTION. New York (1960). Wraps	30	35	40
London (1961). Cloth	—	30	40
Geller, Stephen. SHE LET HIM CONTINUE. New York, 1960	—	—	40
Gellhorn, Martha (Ellis). WHAT MAD PURSUIT. New York, 1934	—	125	200
Genet, Jean. OUR LADY OF THE FLOWERS. Paris (1949). (475 copies). Imitation red or blue morocco, without dustwrapper	—	150	250
GENIUS OF OBLIVION. By a Lady of New Hampshire (Sarah Josepha Hale). Concord, 1823	40	125	400
Gent, Peter. NORTH DALLAS FORTY. New York, 1973	—	25	40
Genthe, Arnold. PICTURES OF OLD CHINATOWN. New York, 1908. (Text by Will Irwin)	—	125	200
New York, 1913. Issued in slipcase	—	—	350
George, Elizabeth. A GREAT DELIVERANCE. New York, 1988	—	—	60
George, Henry. OUR LAND AND LAND POLICY . . . San Francisco, 1871. (Map in black and red)	—	600	1,000
GEORGE AND LURLEEN WALLACE. (Asa Forest Carter). (Centre, Alabama, 1967)	—	—	450
GEORGE BALCOMBE. (Nathaniel Beverly Tucker). New York, 1836. 2 volumes	—	100	100
GEORGIA SCENES, CHARACTERS, INCIDENTS, ETC . . . (Augustine Baldwin Longstreet). Augusta, 1835	—	1,500	3,000
Second edition: New York, 1840. Illustrated	—	200	350
Gerhardi, William (Alexander). FUTILITY. London (1922)	—	175	200
New York (1922)	—	125	150
Gernsback, Hugo. RADIO FOR ALL. Philadelphia, 1922	—	—	150
RALPH 124C41 . . . Boston, 1925	—	600	1,500
Ghiselin, Brewster. AGAINST THE CIRCLE. New York, 1946. (1,250 copies)	—	50	75
GHOST IN THE BANK OF ENGLAND, THE. (Eden Phillpotts). London, 1888	125	500	1,500
GIANNI JUNE 23RD– APRIL 30TH, 1933. (Iris Origo). (London) 1933	—	—	250
Gibbings, Robert. IORANA! A TAHITIAN JOURNAL. Boston, 1932. 385 signed and numbered copies	—	250	350

Trade edition in slipcase	— 125	175
London, 1932	— 100	150

Gibbons, Euell. STALKING THE WILD ASPARAGUS.
New York (1962)   — 35 40

Gibbons, Kaye. ELLEN FOSTER. Chapel Hill, 1987 — — 125
London (1988)   — — 60

Gibbons, Stella. THE MOUNTAIN BEAST . . . London, 1930.
Wraps   — 60 75

Gibbs, Barbara. THE WELL. Albuquerque (1941). Wraps — 150 250

Gibbs, Wolcott. BIRD LIFE AT THE POLE. New York, 1931 — 75 175

Gibran, Kahlil. THE MADMAN: HIS PARABLES AND POEMS.
New York, 1918   — 75 125

Gibson, Charles Dana. DRAWINGS. New York, 1897 — 200 250

Gibson, Richard. MIRROR FOR MAGISTRATES.
London (1968)   — — 60

Gibson, W(ilfrid) W(ilson). URLYN THE HARPER . . .
London, 1902. Wraps   — 150 200

Gibson, Walter B. AFTER DINNER TRICKS. Columbus,
Ohio, 1921   — — 100

Also see Maxwell Grant

Gibson, William. I LAY IN ZION. New York, 1947. Wraps — 35 75

A WINTER CROOK. New York, 1948   — 50 50

Gibson, William. NEUROMANCER. New York (1984).
Wraps. (Ace paperback)   — — 100
London, 1984   — — 500
West Bloomfield, 1986. 375 signed and numbered copies.
(Origin of Cyber-Punk)   — — 350

Gidlow, Elsa. ON A GREY THREAD. Chicago, 1923 — 50 50

Gilbert, Michael (Francis). CLOSE QUARTERS. London, 1947 — 150 250

Gilbert, Ruth. LAZARUS . . . Wellington, 1949. 65 signed
and numbered copies   — 100 150

Gilbert, W(illiam) S(chwenk). A NEW AND ORIGINAL
EXTRAVAGANZA ENTITLED DULCAMARA . . .
London, 1866. Wraps   500 750 1,000

Gilbreth, Frank B(unker). CHEAPER BY THE DOZEN. New
York, 1948. (Written with Ernestine Carey)   — 25 50

Gilchrist, Ellen. THE LAND SURVEYOR'S DAUGHTER.
(Fayetteville) 1979. Wraps — 75 500

IN THE LAND OF DREAMY DREAMS. Fayetteville, 1981.
Cloth — 200 850
Wraps. (1,000 copies) — 75 150
(London, 1982) — — 75

Gilder, Richard Watson. THE NEW DAY . . .
New York, 1876 — 50 60

Gill, Brendan. DEATH IN APRIL . . . Windham, Connecticut,
1935. (160 copies) 35 150 200

Gill, Eric. SERVING AT MASS. Sussex, 1916. Wraps — 1,200 1,500

Gilliatt, Penelope. ONE BY ONE. London, 1965 — — 75
New York, 1965 — — 40

Gillilan, Strickland W. INCLUDING FINNIGIN.
(Philadelphia, 1908) — 100 100

Gilman, Charlotte Perkins. *See* Charlotte Perkins

Gilmore, Millen. SWEET MAN. New York (1930) — 75 150

Gilpin, Laura. THE PUEBLOS: A CAMERA CHRONICLE.
New York, 1941 — — 175

Gingrich, Arnold. CAST DOWN THE LAUREL.
(New York, 1935) — 25 50

Ginsberg, Allen. HOWL: FOR CARL SOLOMON. San
Francisco, 1955. Wraps. (50 mineographed copies) 1,500 5,000 7,500

SIESTA IN BALBA AND RETURN. Icy Cape, Alaska, 1956.
Wraps. (56 copies) 500 3,000 5,000

HOWL . . . San Francisco (1956). Wraps. (Cover
price: 75¢) 125 300 450

HOWL. San Francisco, 1971. 275 signed copies issued
without dustwrapper 50 150 400

GINX'S BABY: HIS BIRTH AND OTHER MISFORTUNES.
(John Edward Jenkins). London, 1870 — 250 250

Giono, Jean. HILL OF DESTINY. New York, 1929. First
English translation — — 60

Giorno, John. POEMS. New York, 1967. 50 signed and
numbered copies. Wraps — 75 200

Giovanni, Nikki. BLACK JUDGEMENT. (Detroit) 1968. Wraps   25   75   100

Gissing, George. WORKERS IN THE DAWN. London, 1880.
3 volumes. (Black end papers)   1,000   1,000   7,500

Givens, John. SONS OF THE PIONEERS.   New York (1977)   —   —   35

Gladstone, William (Ewart). THE STATE IN ITS RELATIONS
WITH THE CHURCH. London, 1838   —   300   500

Glasgow, Ellen. *See* THE DESCENDENT

PHASES OF AN INFERIOR PLANET. New York, 1898.
With erratum slip   40   75   175

Glaspell, Susan. THE GLORY OF THE CONQUERED.
New York (1909)   —   60   75

Glass, Montague (Marsden). POTASH & PERLMUTTER.
Boston (1910)   15   40   60

Glasser, Ronald J. 365 DAYS. New York (1971)   —   —   60

GLENARVON. (Lady Caroline Lamb). London, 1816.
3 volumes   —   —   500

Glover, Mary Baker (Eddy). SCIENCE AND HEALTH . . .
Boston, 1875. (1,000 copies). First issue: errata slip
without index. Seen in black, red or purple cloth   300   1,500   3,000

Glück, Louise. FIRSTBORN: POEMS.
(New York, 1968). Cloth   —   75   175
Wraps   —   30   40
London, 1969. 50 signed copies   25   125   200
Trade edition. Wraps   —   20   35

Godden, Rumer. CHINESE PUZZLE. London (1936)   35   150   250

Godey, John (Morton Freedgood). THE GUN & MRS.
SMITH. Garden City (1947)   —   50   125

Godfrey, Dave. DEATH GOES BETTER WITH COCA-COLA.
Toronto, 1967   —   —   100

Godoy, Jose F. WHO DID IT? San Francisco, 1883. Wraps   —   150   150

Godwin, Gail. THE PERFECTIONISTS. New York (1970)   —   75   200

Gogarty, Oliver St. John. *See* Alpha and Omega

Gogol, Nikolai. *See* HOME LIFE IN RUSSIA

Gold, H. L. THE OLD DIE RICH . . . New York (1955)   —   30   30

"A book all dog-lovers will delight in"

CHINESE PUZZLE

by

RUMER GODDEN

Gold, Herbert. BIRTH OF A HERO. New York, 1951	35	50	60
Gold, Ivan. NICKEL MISERIES. New York (1963)	—	25	30
London, 1964	—	25	30
Gold, Michael (Irving Granich). JOHN BROWN. New York, 1923	—	150	150
Goldberg, Gerald Jay. THE NATIONAL STANDARD. New York (1968)	—	30	30
Goldberg, R(ube). FOOLISH QUESTIONS. Boston (1909)	—	100	150
Golden Cockerel Press. *See* A. E. Coppard			
GOLD-HUNTER'S ADVENTURE . . . , THE. (William Henry Thomes). Boston, 1864	—	250	250
Golding, Louis. SORROW OF WAR. London (1919)	25	25	35
Golding, W(illiam) G(erald). POEMS. London, 1934. Wraps	—	3,500	4,000
LORD OF THE FLIES. London (1954). Red cloth	125	1,000	2,000
Trial binding in blue cloth	—	—	2,000
New York (1955)	75	175	750
Goldman, Emma. ANARCHISM . . . New York, 1910	—	125	200
Goldman, William. TEMPLE OF GOLD. New York, 1957	25	100	150
Goldring, Douglas. A COUNTRY BOY . . . London, 1910. Wraps	—	50	50
Goldsmith, Oliver. *See* James Willington			
Gombrowicz, Witold. PORNOGRAFIA. New York (1966). (First English translation)	—	—	50
Gooch, Mrs. (Elizabeth Sara Villa-Real). AN APPEAL TO THE PUBLIC . . . London, 1788	—	—	500
Goodis, David. RETREAT FROM OBLIVION. New York, 1939	—	—	2,000
Goodman, Paul. TEN LYRIC POEMS. (New York, 1934). Wraps	50	200	400
Goodrich, Marcus. DELILAH. New York (1941). Only book	—	25	35
Goodrich, Samuel Griswold. *See* Peter Parley			
Goodwin, Stephen. KIN. New York (1975)	—	25	40
Goodwyn, Frank. THE DEVIL IN TEXAS. Dallas, 1936	—	—	75
Goran, Lester. THE PARATROOPER OF MECHANIC AVENUE. Boston, 1960	—	30	30

Gordimer, Nadine. FACE TO FACE. Johannesburg (1949)	75	400	1,250
THE SOFT VOICE OF THE SERPENT. New York, 1952	35	75	300
London (1953)	—	100	150
Gordon, Caroline. PENHALLY. New York, 1931	100	600	1,500
Gordon, Giles. PICTURES FROM AN EXHIBITION. London, 1970	—	—	40
Gordon, Mary. FINAL PAYMENTS. New York (1978)	—	25	40
London (1978)	—	—	35
Gordon, Mildred. THE LITTLE MAN WHO WASN'T THERE. Garden City, 1946	—	35	60
Gordon, Taylor. BORN TO BE. New York, 1929. (Covarrubias illustrations)	—	75	150
Gore–Booth, Eva. POEMS. London, 1898	25	35	35
Gores, Joe (Joseph N.). A TIME OF PREDATORS. New York, 1969	—	100	125
Gorey, Edward. THE UNSTRUNG HARP. New York (1953)	50	125	200
GORGEOUS POETRY. (J. B. [Beachcomber] Morton). London, 1920	30	60	100
Gorman, Herbert S. THE FOOL OF LOVE. New York (1920). Wraps	—	—	125
Gosling, Paula. A RUNNING DUCK. London, 1978	—	—	60
Gosse, Edmund. MADRIGALS, SONGS AND SONNETS. London, 1870. (Written with John A. Blaikie)	40	150	600
Gottschalk, Laura Riding. THE CLOSE CHAPLET. London, 1926. Issued without dustwrapper	125	600	750
New York (1926). Tissue dustwrapper	—	450	500
ANATOLE FRANCE AT HOME. By Marcel Le Guff. New York, 1926. (Translated by Gottschalk)	—	200	250
Gough, Laurence. GOLDFISH BOWL. Toronto, 1987	—	—	125
Gould, Gerald. LYRICS. London, 1906. Wraps	—	35	75
Gould, John. A CENTURY OF BIRDS FROM THE HIMALAYA MOUNTAINS. London, 1832 (actually 1831). 80 plates. First issue: backgrounds uncolored	—	—	12,000
Second issue: backgrounds colored	—	—	15,000
Gould, Wallace. CHILDREN OF THE SUN . . . Boston (1917)	—	35	50

Gover, (John) Robert. THE ONE HUNDRED DOLLAR
    MISUNDERSTANDING. London, 1961   25   50   75
    New York, 1962   15   35   50

Gowen, Emmett. MOUNTAIN BORN. Indianapolis (1932)   —   75   75

Goyen, (Charles) William. THE HOUSE OF BREATH.
    New York (1950)   30   75   125
    London, 1951   20   50   75

Goytisolo, Juan. THE YOUNG ASSASSINS. New York, 1958   —   25   40

Grady, James. SIX DAYS OF THE CONDOR. New York, 1974   —   25   75

Grafton, C. W. THE RAT BEGAN TO GNAW THE ROPE.
    New York, 1943   —   —   60

Grafton, Sue. KEZIAH DANE. New York (1967)   —   —   500
    London (1968)   —   —   200

    "A" IS FOR ALIBI. New York (1982)   —   —   950
    (London, 1986)   —   —   300

Graham, Caroline. THE KILLINGS AT BADGER'S DRIFT.
    Bethesda, 1987   —   —   50

Graham, John (David Graham Phillips). THE GREAT GOD
    SUCCESS. New York (1901)   35   60   100

Graham, Jorie. HYBRIDS OF PLANTS AND OF GHOSTS.
    Princeton (1980)   —   —   60

Graham, R. B. Cunninghame. NOTES ON THE DISTRICT OF
    MENTIETH. London, 1895. Wraps   50   150   300

Graham, Sheilah. GENTLEMAN-CROOK. London, 1933   —   75   75

Graham, Tom (Sinclair Lewis). HIKE AND THE AEROPLANE.
    New York (1912). First issue: August 1912 on copyright
    page. (Auctioned in 1994 in chipped dustwrapper
    for $11,500)   500   200   5,000

Graham, W(illiam) S(ydney). CAGE WITHOUT GRIEVANCE.
    Glasgow (1942)   30   75   300

Grahame, Kenneth. PAGAN PAPERS. London, 1894. (Title
    page designed by Aubrey Beardsley)   90   150   350

Grainger, Francis Edward. *See* Headon Hill

Granger, Bill. THE NOVEMBER MAN. New York (1979).
    Wraps   —   —   60

Grant, Anne. POEMS OF VARIOUS SUBJECTS.
    Edinburgh, 1803   —   50   100

NOTES ON THE DISTRICT

OF MENTEITH

FOR TOURISTS AND OTHERS

BY

R. B. CUNNINGHAME GRAHAM

LONDON
ADAM & CHARLES BLACK
1895

Grant, George P. PHILOSOPHY IN THE MASSAGE.
Toronto (1959)   —   —   50

Grant, J. C. THE ROCK SHOOT. Edinburgh, 1928   —   35   75

Grant, Marie M. ARTISTE. London, 1871. 3 volumes   —   —   300

Grant, Maxwell (Walter B. Gibson). THE LIVING SHADOW.
New York (1931). (First hardbound of *Shadow*). Issued
without dustwrapper. (First mystery)   —   100   250

Grass, Günter. THE TIN DRUM. New York (1962)   —   40   75
London, 1962   —   40   60

Grau, Shirley Ann. THE BLACK PRINCE. New York, 1955.
Dustwrapper without reviews   30   60   100
With reviews   —   —   75

Graves, Alfred Percival. SONGS OF KILLARNEY.
London, 1873   —   —   125

Graves, John. HOME PLACE. Fort Worth, 1958. Wraps.
(200 copies)   —   400   500

GOODBYE TO A RIVER. New York, 1960   —   75   125
(Austin) 1989. 500 signed copies. Issued without
dustwrapper   —   —   150

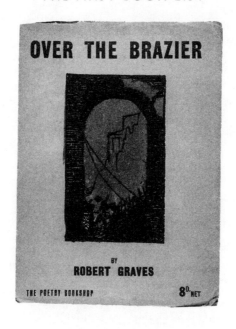

Graves, Robert (Ranke). OVER THE BRAZIER. London,

1916. Wraps	600	1,000	1,250
London (1920). Second edition	200	400	400

Gray, Alasdair. LANARK. Edinburgh, 1981 — — 200
    Edinburgh, 1985. 1,000 signed and numbered copies — — 150

Gray, Francine du Plessix. DIVINE DISOBEDIENCE.
    New York, 1970 — 30 50
    London (1970) — — 40

Gray, John Henry. SILVER POINTS. London, 1893. (250 numbered
    copies). Original cloth designed by Charles Ricketts — 450 2,000

Gray, Simon. COLMAIN. London, 1963 — 50 75

Graywolf Press. THE EARTH. Port Townsend, 1974. Wraps.
    5 signed copies. (First book of press. A single poem by
    William Stafford. Sewn into wraps. Only 4 copies exist) — 300 1,250

Greacen, Robert. THE BIRD. Dublin, 1941. (250 copies).
    Stiff wraps — 150 200

Green, Anna K(atherine Rohles). THE LEAVENWORTH CASE.
    New York, 1878. First issue: "f" missing from "fresh"
    last line p. 215 250 1,500 1,500

Green, Annie. THE SELBYS. New York, 1930 20 40 50

Green, Ben K. HORSE CONFORMATION . . .
   (Ft. Worth, 1963) — 125 125

Green, Hannah. I NEVER PROMISED YOU A ROSE GARDEN.
   New York (1964) — — 75

Green, Henry (Henry Vincent Yorke). BLINDNESS.
   London, 1926 75 1,500 3,000
   New York (1926) 50 250 1,250

Green, Julian. AVARICE HOUSE. New York, 1917 — 30 50

Green, Leonard. DREAM COMRADES . . . Oxford, 1916 — — 125

Green, Paul. TRIFLES OF THOUGHT. New York, 1917 25 50 75

Greenan, Russell H. IT HAPPENED IN BOSTON?
   New York (1968) — 30 35

Greenaway, Kate. THE QUIVER OF LOVE. (Written with
   Walter Crane). (London, 1876) — 250 750

   UNDER THE WINDOW. London (1878). With printer's
   imprint on back of title page and "End of
   Contents" p. 14 — 150 500

Greenberg, Joanne. THE KING'S PERSONS. New York (1963) — 40 100
   London (1963) — 35 75

Greene, A. C. A PERSONAL COUNTRY. New York, 1969 — 50 50

Greene, Barbara. LAND BENIGHTED. London, 1938 — — 175

Greene, Bob. WE DIDN'T HAVE NONE OF THEM FAT FUNKY
   ANGELS. California (1971) — — 50

Greene, Graham. BABBLING APRIL. London, 1925 600 2,500 5,000

   THE MAN WITHIN. London (1929) 150 1,000 2,500
   Garden City, 1929 — 300 1,000

Greenleaf, Stephen. GRAVE ERROR. New York (1979) — 30 50

Greer, Ben. SLAMMER. New York, 1975 — 35 50

Gregor, Arthur. OCTAVIAN SHOOTING TARGETS.
   New York (1954) 20 40 75

Gregory, Dick. FROM THE BACK OF THE BUS. New York,
   1962. Wraps — — 40

Gregory, Horace. CHELSEA ROOMING HOUSE: POEMS.
   New York, 1930 40 100 125

   ROOMING HOUSE. London, 1932. (New title).
   Stiff wraps — 75 100

Gresham, William Lindsay. NIGHTMARE ALLEY.
New York (1946)   —   50   125

Gressent, Professor. *See* David Garnett

Grey, Romer. THE CRUISE OF THE "FISHERMAN."
New York, 1929   —   —   300

Grey, (P.) Zane. BETTY ZANE. New York (1903). (Issued
without dustwrapper)   250   400   2,000

Gribble, Leonard R. THE CASE OF THE MARSDEN RUBIES.
Garden City, 1930   —   —   40

Grieve, C(hristopher) M(urray). ANNALS OF FIVE SENSES.
Montrose (Scotland), 1923   125   350   500

Griffin, Howard. CRY CADENCE. New York, 1947   —   30   100

Griffin, John H(oward). THE DEVIL RIDES OUTSIDE.
Fort Worth, 1952   —   75   100
London, 1953   —   60   75

Griffin, Jonathan. THE HIDDEN KING. London, 1955   —   75   75

Griffith, D. W. THE RISE AND FALL OF FREE SPEECH IN
AMERICA. Los Angeles, 1916   —   350   350

Griffith, (Jones) George. THE ANGEL OF THE REVOLUTION.
London, 1893   —   150   200

Grigson, Geoffrey. SEVERAL OBSERVATIONS . . .
London (1939)   20   75   100

Grile, Dod (Ambrose Bierce). THE FIEND'S DELIGHT.
London [no-date, 1873?]   125   600   1,250

New York, 1873. Brown or purple-brown cloth.
Without publisher's advertisements   50   400   750

Grimes, Martha. THE MAN WITH A LOAD OF MISCHIEF.
Boston (1981)   —   75   250

Grimke, A(ngelina) E(mily). APPEAL TO THE CHRISTIAN
WOMEN OF THE SOUTH (AN). (New York, 1836). Wraps   —   250   350

Grimm, M. M. GERMAN POPULAR STORIES. London, 1823
and 1826. 2 volumes. First in English. First issue:
without umlaut over "a" in "Märchen" on title page   —   —   5,000

Grinnell, George B. PAWNEE HERO . . . New York, 1889   —   150   450

Grisham, John. A TIME TO KILL. Tarrytown (1989).
Dustwrapper price, bar code on back, no mention of
The Firm on dustwrapper flap   —   —   1,750

Grogan, Emmett. RINGOLEVIO . . . London, 1972	—	—	60
New York (1978)	—	—	35
Groom, Winston. BETTER TIMES THAN THESE.			
New York (1978)	—	—	75
Gross, Milt. NIZE BABY. New York (1926)	—	—	125
Grossinger, Richard. THE STARMAKER. (Madison,			
Wisconsin, 1968). Wraps	15	40	40
Grossman, Alfred. ACROBAT ADMITS. New York, 1959	—	30	50
Grosz, Georg. TWELVE REPRODUCTIONS . . . Chicago,			
1921. Wraps. First American publication	—	150	600
Grubb, Davis. THE NIGHT OF THE HUNTER. (New York,			
1953). 1,000 signed copies	—	75	200
Trade edition	25	60	150
London (1954)	—	40	100
Gruber, Frank. PEACE MARSHALL. New York, 1939	—	—	150
THE FRENCH KEY. New York (1940)	—	100	125
Gruelle, Johnny (Barton). MR. TWEE DEEDLE.			
New York, 1913	—	—	250
Grumbach, Doris. THE SPOIL OF THE FLOWERS.			
Garden City, 1962	—	125	150
Guedalla, Philip. IGNIS FATUI . . . Oxford/London, 1911.			
Wraps	—	100	100
Guest, Barbara. THE LOCATION OF THINGS. New York,			
1960. Wraps. (300 copies)	35	90	100
Guest, Edgar Albert. HOME RHYMES. Detroit, 1909	50	50	50
Guest, Judith. ORDINARY PEOPLE. New York, 1976	—	25	50
Guiney, Louise Imogen. SONGS AT THE START. Boston,			
1884. BAL notes 5 bindings, priority unknown	35	100	125
(Preceded by two pamphlets and a broadside)			
Gunn, Thom(son William). (POEMS). Fantasy Press. Oxford,			
1953. Wraps	—	500	500
FIGHTING TERMS. (Oxford, 1954). Wraps. First issue:			
final "t" in "thought" omitted on first line of p. 38.			
Yellow cloth. Issued without dustwrapper	—	400	650
Second issue: Corrected	—	—	250

New York, 1958. Stiff wraps. First issue: without review
label attached — 20 · 50 · 150
Second issue: with review label attached — — · — · 100

FIGHTING TERMS: A SELECTION. Berkeley, 1983.
25 copies — — · — · 1,250

Gunther, John. THE RED PAVILION. New York, 1926 — 25 · 50 · 150
London, 1926 — — · — · 100

Gurganus, Allan. BREATHING LESSONS. Rocky Mount,
1981. Wraps — — · — · 250

OLDEST LIVING CONFEDERATE WIDOW TELLS ALL.
New York, 1989 — — · — · 60
London, 1989 — — · — · 50

Guthrie, A(lfred) B(ertram), Jr. MURDERS AT MOON DANCE.
New York, 1943 — 50 · 400 · 600

Guthrie, Ramon. TROBAR CLUS. Northampton,
Massachusetts, 1923. 250 signed copies — 75 · 75 · 75

Guthrie, Thomas Anstey. *See* F. Anstey

Guthrie, Woody. BOUND FOR GLORY. New York, 1945 — — · 150 · 300

Guy, Rosa. BIRD AT MY WINDOW. Philadelphia, 1966 — — · — · 125
(London, 1966) — — · — · 75

Gysin, Brion. TO MASTER, A LONG GOODNIGHT.
New York (1946) — 50 · 60 · 100

H

H. D. *See* D., H. (Hilda Doolittle)

H. H. (Helen Hunt Jackson). BETHMENDI: A PERSIAN TALE.
Boston, 1867. Translated by Doolittle — — · 200 · 300

VERSES. Boston, 1870 — 30 · 150 · 300

Habberton, John. HELEN'S BABIES. Boston, 1876. Wraps.
First issue: measures 1-3/16" — — · 150 · 300

Hacker, Marilyn. THE TERRIBLE CHILDREN. (No-place,
1967). Stapled wraps — — · — · 75

Hagedorn, Herman, Jr. THE SILVER BLADE. Berlin, 1907.
Wraps — — · 100 · 175

(Previous broadside and colaboration)

Haggard, H(enry) Rider. CETYWAYO . . . London, 1882.
(750 copies) — 200 · 500 · 1,500

Haig-Brown, Roderick. SILVER. London, 1931	—	—	500
Hailey, Arthur. FLIGHT INTO DANGER.			
London, 1958. (Written with John Castle)	—	75	150
Toronto, 1958. Published simultaneously	—	—	150
THE FINAL DIAGNOSIS. New York, 1959	—	50	60
Haines, John. WINTER NEWS. Middletown (1966)	15	30	50
Haines, William (William Heyen). WHAT HAPPENED IN FORT LAUDERDALE. New York (1958). Wraps. (Written with William Taggard)	—	50	75
Halberstam, David. THE NOBLEST ROMAN. Boston, 1961	—	35	60
Haldane, Charlotte. MAN'S WORLD. London, 1926	15	125	250
Haldane, J(ohn) B(urdon) S(anderson). MY FRIEND MR. LEAKEY. London, 1937	—	—	200
Haldeman, Charles. THE SUN'S ATTENDANT. London (1963)	—	25	75
Haldeman, Joe (W.). THE WAR YEAR. New York (1972)	—	30	100
Hale, Edward Everett. *See* MARGARET PERCIVAL IN AMERICA			
Hale, Kathleen. ORLANDO, THE MARMALADE CAT . . . London, 1938	—	—	300
Hale, Nancy. THE YOUNG DIE GOOD. New York, 1932	35	100	125
Hale, Sarah Josepha. *See* THE GENIUS OF OBLIVION			
Haley, Alex. ROOTS. Garden City (1974). 59-page excerpt from *Reader's Digest* in illustrated wraps	—	—	100
Garden City, 1976. 500 signed and numbered copies in slipcase	—	150	450
Trade	—	35	100
Also see Malcolm X.			
Haley, J. Evetts. THE XIT RANCH OF TEXAS. Chicago, 1929. Issued in tissue dustwrapper	200	500	500
Haliburton, Thomas Chandler. *See* THE CLOCKMAKER			
Hall, Adam. *See* Mansell Black			
Hall, Arthur Vine. TABLE MOUNTAIN . . . Capetown (1896)	—	175	200
Hall, Austin. PEOPLE OF THE COMET. (Los Angeles, 1948). First science fiction	—	25	35

CHICAGO SIDE-SHOW

BY

ALBERT HALPER

NUMBER 6

PAMPHLET SERIES ONE

DRIFT

A NOVEL
by
JAMES HANLEY

ERIC PARTRIDGE, LTD.
THIRTY, MUSEUM STREET, LONDON
1930

CETYWAYO

AND

HIS WHITE NEIGHBOURS:

OR,

REMARKS ON RECENT EVENTS IN ZULULAND,
NATAL, AND THE TRANSVAAL.

BY

H. RIDER HAGGARD.

LONDON:
TRÜBNER & CO., LUDGATE HILL.
1882.
[All rights reserved.]

Hall, Baynard Rush. RIGHTEOUSNESS THE SAFEGUARD . . .
(Indianapolis, 1827)   —   75   75

Hall, Donald (Andrew). (POEMS) FANTASY POETS # 4.
Oxford (1952). Wraps   30   200   250

    EXILE. Swinford (1952). Wraps   —   —   250

    (One book he edited precedes)

Hall, Henry. *See* THE TRIBUNE BOOK OF OPEN AIR SPORTS

Hall, J. C. THE SUMMER DANCE . . . London, 1951. (First
separate work)   —   60   75

Hall, James. LETTERS FROM THE WEST . . . London, 1828   —   400   350

    (Two previous pamphlets)

Hall, James B(yron). NOT BY THE DOOR.
New York (1954)   30   50   75

Hall, James Norman. KITCHENER'S MOB. Boston, 1916   25   50   75

Hall, James W. UNDER COVER BY DAYLIGHT.
New York, 1987   —   —   60

Hall, Marguerite Radclyffe. 'TWIXT EARTH AND STARS.
London, 1906   —   200   300

Hall, O(akley) M. MURDER CITY. New York (1949)   —   40   75
London, 1950   —   —   75

    SO MANY DOORS. New York (1950)   —   35   100

Halleck, Fitz-Greene. *See* CROAKER *and* FANNY . . .

Halliday, Brett (Davis Dresser). *See* Anthony Scott

Halper, Albert. CHICAGO SIDE-SHOW. New York, 1932.
(110 copies). Wraps   50   200   300

    UNION SQUARE. New York, 1933   —   75   75

Hamady, Walter. THE DISILLUSIONED SOLIPSIST. Mt. Horeb,
1954. (60 copies). (First Perishible Press book)   — 2,000 2,500

Hamburger, Michael. POEMS OF HÖLDERLIN. London, 1943.
(Translation and 97-page introduction)   —   75   75

    LATER HOGARTH. London, 1945   —   100   100

Hamill, Sam. HEROES OF THE TETON MYTHOS. Denver,
1973. Cloth. (10 copies)   —   —   200
Wraps   —   —   75

Hamilton, Alexander. *See* A FULL VINDICATION . . .

Hamilton, Clive (C. S. Lewis). SPIRITS IN BONDAGE.
    London, 1919   75   250   450

Hamilton, Edmond. THE METAL GIANTS. Washborn
    [no-date: 1932]. Mimeographed pamphlet   —   —   275

    THE HORROR ON THE ASTEROID. London, 1936   —   600   600

Hamilton, Gail (Mary Abigail Dodge). COUNTRY LIVING
    AND COUNTRY THINKING. Boston, 1862   —   150   150

Hamilton, George R. THE SEARCH FOR LOVELINESS . . .
    London, 1910   —   60   60

Hamilton, Gerald. *See* Patrick Weston

Hammett, (Samuel) Dashiell. RED HARVEST. New York,
    1929. First issue: no review on back panel of dustwrapper   350 2,000 8,500

Hamner, Earl, Jr. FIFTY ROADS TO TOWN. New York (1953)   —   35   60

Hamsun, Knut. HUNGER. London, 1899   —   —   350

Handke, Peter. KASPAR . . . New York, 1969. First English
    translation   —   —   40

Handy, W. C. BLUES: AN ANTHOLOGY. New York, 1926.
    Edited by Handy   —   300   500

Hanley, James. DRIFT. London, 1930. (10 signed copies)   15 1,000 1,000
    Trade edition. (490 copies)   —   150   200

Hannah, Barry. GERONIMO REX. New York (1972)   —   100   125

Hanrahan, Barbara. THE SCENT OF EUCALYPTUS.
    London, 1973   —   —   50

Hansberry, Lorraine. A RAISIN IN THE SUN. New York,
    (1959). Wraps   —   50   75
    New York (1959)   —   —   300

Hansen, Joseph. *See* James Colton

    FADEOUT. New York,
    1970. (First mystery)   —   —   150

Hansen, Ron. DESPERADOES. New York, 1979   —   —   75

Hanson, Pauline. THE FOREVER YOUNG . . . Denver (1948).
    Wraps. (300 copies)   —   35   40

Hardwick, Elizabeth. THE GHOSTLY LOVER.
    New York (1945)   35   125   200

Hardy, Thomas. *See* DESPERATE REMEDIES

Hare, Cyril (Alfred Alexander Gordon Clark). TENANT FOR DEATH. London, 1937	—	60	750
Hare, David. SLAG. London (1971). Wraps	—	40	40
Harington, Donald. THE CHERRY PIT. New York, 1965	—	—	75
Harland, Henry. *See* Sidney Luska			
Harland, Marion (Mary Hawes Terhune). ALONE. Richmond, 1854	—	350	350
Harman, William. TREASURY HOLIDAY. Middletown (1970)	—	—	35
Harper, Frances E(llen) W(atkins). MISCELLANEOUS POEMS. Philadelphia, 1854	—	—	1,500
IOLA LEROY, OR SHADOWS UPLIFTED. Philadelphia, 1892. (Later printings had Boston imprinted)	—	300	1,250
Harrigan, Stephen. ARANSAS. New York, 1980	—	25	30
Harrington, Alan. THE REVELATIONS OF DR. MODESTO. New York, 1955	25	40	50
(London, 1957). Len Deighton dustwrapper	—	50	75
Harrington, William. WHICH THE JUSTICE . . . London (1963)	—	35	50
Harris, Bertha. CATCHING SARADOVE. New York (1969)	—	40	75
Harris, Frank. ELDER CONKLIN . . . New York, 1894	25	75	75
London, 1895	20	50	50
Harris, Joel Chandler. UNCLE REMUS: HIS SONGS AND SAYINGS. New York, 1881. First state/printing: "presumptive" for "presumptuous" last line p. 9 and no mention of this book in advertisements at back. (Very fine copies have brought up to $4,000 at auction)	300	350	1,500
New York, 1881, second state/printing	—	—	450
UNCLE REMUS AND HIS LEGENDS OF THE OLD PLANTATION. London, 1881. (New title)	200	250	750
UNCLE REMUS: HIS SONGS AND SAYINGS. New York, 1895. 250 signed and numbered copies	—	—	2,000
Harris, M. Virginia. WEDDIN' TRIMMIN'S. New York (1949)	—	—	200
Harris, Mark. TRUMPET THE WORLD. New York (1946)	25	50	100
Harris, Thomas. BLACK SUNDAY. New York (1975)	—	—	175
London, 1975	—	—	75

Harris, Timothy. KRONSKI/MCSMASH.

London, 1969	—	—	75
New York, 1969	—	35	60

Harris, William J. HEY FELLA WOULD YOU MIND . . .

Ithaca (1974)	—	—	40

Harris, Wilson. PALACE OF THE PEACOCK. London (1960)	—	60	125

Harrison, Jim (James Thomas). PLAIN SONG. New York

(1965). Cloth	20	125	400
Wraps	—	—	75

Harrison, Michael. WEEP FOR LYCIDAS. London, 1934	—	—	125

Harrison, T(ony). EARTHWORKS. Leeds, 1964. Wraps	—	—	125

Harrison, Tom. LETTER TO OXFORD. (1933). Wraps	25	40	75

Harrison, William. THE THEOLOGIAN. New York (1965)	—	40	40

Harriss, Will. THE BAY PSALM BOOK MURDER.

New York, 1983	—	—	100

Hart, Joseph C. *See* MIRIAM COFFIN

Hart, Josephine. DAMAGE. London (1991)

Hart, Josephine. DAMAGE. London (1991)	—	—	75
New York, 1991	—	—	25

Hart, William S. and Mary. PINTO BEN . . .

New York (1919)	40	25	30

Harte, (Francis) Bret. *See* OUTCROPPINGS

CONDENSED NOVELS . . . New York, 1867. First book	60	250	500
THE LOST GALLEON. San Francisco, 1867. First verse	100	300	600

Hartley, L(eslie) P(oles). NIGHT FEARS . . . London, 1924	75	200	400

Hartley, Marsden. ADVENTURE IN THE ARTS.

New York (1921)	—	—	1,250
TWENTY-FIVE. (Paris, 1923). Wraps	—	400	750

Hartwell, Mary. A WOMAN IN ARMOUR. New York, 1875	—	—	275

Harwood, Lee. TITLE ILLEGIBLE. London, 1965.

Mimeographed stapled sheets	—	75	100

Hasford, Gustav. THE SHORT TIMERS. New York (1979)	—	50	125

THE HASHEESH EATER. (Fitz-Hugh Ludlow).

New York, 1857	—	200	500

Hass, Robert. FIELD GUIDE. New Haven, 1973	—	35	40

Hassall, Christopher. POEMS OF TWO YEARS. London, 1935.
Wraps   —   —   75

Hassler, Jon. FOUR MILES TO PINECONE. New York, 1977   —   —   150

     STAGGERFORD. New York, 1977. (First novel)   —   40   125

Hathaway, Katharine. THE LITTLE LOCKSMITH.
New York, 1943   —   —   40

Hauser, Marianne. DARK DOMINION. New York (1947)   25   40   40

Hautman, Pete. *See* Peter Murray

     DRAWING DEAD. New York 1993.
(First mystery)   —   —   50

     (34 children's books, 1992–94)

Hawkes, J(ohn) C(lendinnin) B(urne). FIASCO HALL.
Cambridge (Mass.), 1943. Wraps. (100 copies—
60 destroyed)   225   750   1,500

     THE CANNIBAL. Norfolk (1949). Gray cloth   —   —   250

Hawley, Cameron. EXECUTIVE SUITE. Boston (1952)   —   —   75

Hawthorne, Julian. BRESSANT. New York, 1873   25   100   150

Hawthorne, Nathaniel. *See* FANSHAWE

     TWICE-TOLD TALES . . . Boston, 1837   —   1,500   5,000

Hay, Helen. SOME VERSES. Chicago, 1898   —   —   75

Hay, John. JIM BLUDSO OF THE PRAIRIE BELLE. Boston,
1871. Orange wraps   60   100   150

     (Previous pamphlets)

Hayakawa, S. J. LANGUAGE IN THOUGHT AND ACTION.
Madison, 1939. Wraps   —   150   250

Hayes, Joseph. AND CAME THE SPRING. New York (1942).
Wraps. (Written with M. Hayes)   —   50   125

Hayne, Paul H(amilton). POEMS. 1855   —   —   350

Hays, H. R. STRANGE CITY. Boston (1929)   —   —   100

Haywarde, Richard (Frederick Swarthout Cozzens).
PRISMATICS. New York, 1853   125   150   250

Haywood, Gar Anthony. FEAR OF THE DARK.
New York, 1988   —   —   75

Hazel, Robert. POEMS 1951–1961. Morehead (1961)   —   30   50

Hazlitt, W. Carew. THE HISTORY OF THE ORIGIN AND RISE
    OF THE REPUBLIC OF VENICE. London, 1858. 2 volumes   75   100   150

Hazo, Samuel. DISCOVERY . . . New York (1959). Wraps   —   25   40

Hazzard, Shirley. CLIFFS OF FALL . . . London, 1963   —   60   200
    New York, 1963   — —   125

Healy, Dermot. BANISHED MISFORTUNE . . . London, 1982   — —   50

Healy, Jeremiah. BLUNT DARTS. New York, 1984   — —   250

Heaney, Seamus. ELEVEN POEMS. Belfast (1965). First issue:
    cream wraps, cover device in purple   —   600   1,750
    Second issue: wove paper, cover device in black purple   —   300   750
    Third issue: gray paper in stiff green wraps   —   150   350

    DEATH OF A NATURALIST. London (1966)   —   350   400
    New York, 1966. (U.K. sheets)   —   250   300

Hearn, Lafcadio. ONE OF CLEOPATRA'S NIGHTS. By T.
    Gautier. New York, 1882. Translated by Hearn. First
    issue: publisher's name in capitals on spine   75   200   1,000

    STRAY LEAVES FROM STRANGE LITERATURE. Boston,
    1884. First issue: has J.R. & O. on spine   150   250   650

Hearne, John. VOICES UNDER THE WINDOW.
    London (1955)   — —   100

Hearon, Shelby. AT HOME AFTER 1840 . . . Austin, 1966.
    100 signed and numbered copies. (Text by Hearon,
    drawings by Peggy Goldstein)   —   125   200
    Regular edition. (1,000 copies)   —   60   60

Heath-Stubbs, John. WOUNDED THAMMUZ. London, 1942.
    Wraps in dustwrapper   — —   60

Heat-Moon, William Least (William Trogdon). BLUE
    HIGHWAYS . . . Boston (1982)   —   40   90

Hecht, Anthony (Evan). A SUMMONING OF STONES.
    New York (1954)   25   100   150

Hecht, Ben. *See* Maxwell Bodenheim

THE HERO OF SANTA MARIA. New York (1920).
    Wraps. (Written with Frank Shay)   —   200   200

    ERIK DORN. New York, 1921. First issue: yellow
    lettering on cover   40   125   300

Hedge, Frederic Henry. A SERMON PREACHED . . . Boston, 1834. Wraps	—	100	150
Hedley, Leslie Woolf. THE EDGE OF INSANITY. Los Angeles, 1949. Wraps	30	60	100
Hegen, Alice Caldwell. MRS. WIGGS OF THE CABBAGE PATCH. New York, 1901. Gold sky on front cover	—	40	125
Heggen, Thomas. MISTER ROBERTS. Boston, 1946	20	50	100
London, 1948	—	50	75
Heinemann, Larry. CLOSE QUARTERS. New York (1977)	—	25	100
Heinlein, Robert (Anson). THE DISCOVERY OF THE FUTURE. Novacious Press. New York, 1941. (200 copies). Wraps	—	—	2,000
ROCKET SHIP GALILEO. New York (1947)	50	300	1,000
Heller, Joseph. CATCH-22. New York, 1961. (Dustwrapper price $5.95)	75	350	1,250
London (1962). First issue: dustwrapper with blurb about book on back	—	100	200
Second issue: dustwrapper with blurbs by other authors	—	—	150
Hellman, Lillian. THE CHILDREN'S HOUR. New York, 1934	50	250	650
London (1962). Wraps and dustwrapper	—	75	200
Helprin, Mark. A DOVE OF THE EAST . . . New York, 1975	—	40	100
London, 1976	—	—	75
Helps, Sir Arthur. *See* THOUGHTS IN THE CLOISTER			
Hemans, Felicia Dorothea. POEMS. London, 1808	—	200	250
Hemingway, Ernest. THREE STORIES AND TEN POEMS. (Paris, 1923). (300 copies). Wraps	3,000	5,000	20,000
IN OUR TIME. Paris, 1924. (170 copies)	2,000	4,000	17,500
New York, 1925	500	1,000	3,500
London, 1926	300	500	1,500
New York, 1930	—	300	500
Hemingway, Leicester. THE SOUND OF THE TRUMPET. New York (1953)	—	35	60
Hemley, Cecil. SEAS AND SEASONS. New York (1951). Wraps	—	—	100
Hempel, Amy. REASONS TO LIVE. New York (1985)	—	—	50
Henderson, David. FELIX OF THE SILENT FOREST. New York, 1967	—	—	75

Henderson, Elliot Blaine. PLANTATION ECHOES.
    Columbia, 1904   75   125   200

Henderson, George Wylie. OLLIE MISS. New York, 1935   30   75   150

Henderson, William McCranor. STARK RAVING ELVIS.
    New York (1984)   —   —   35

Henderson, Zenna. PILGRIMAGE. Garden City, 1961   —   —   350

Henley, Beth. AM I BLUE. (New York, 1982). Wraps   —   40   75

Henley, William Ernest. A BOOK OF VERSES. London, 1888.
    75 large paper copies in white tissue dustwrapper   25   600   600
    Trade edition. Stiff wraps   —   100   200

Henri, Adrian. TONIGHT AT NOON. London (1968).
    26 signed and lettered copies   —   60   60
    100 signed and numbered copies   —   30   30

Henry, Arthur. NICHOLAS BLOOD, CANDIDATE.
    New York (1890)   40   75   100

Henry, Sue. MURDER ON THE IDITAROD TRAIL.
    New York, 1992   —   —   75

Henry, Will (Henry Wilson Allen). NO SURVIVORS.
    New York, 1950   —   —   200

Henty, G(eorge) A(lfred). A SEARCH FOR A SECRET.
    London, 1867. 3 volumes   — 3,000 4,500

Herbert, Sir A(lfred) P(atrick). POOR POEMS AND ROTTEN
    RHYMES. Winchester, England, 1910. Wraps   25   175   300

Herbert, Frank (Patrick). SURVIVAL AND THE ATOM. (Santa
    Rosa, 1950). Wraps. An offprint   —   400   500

    THE DRAGON IN THE SEA. Garden City, 1956   —   —   350

Herbert, Henry William. See THE BROTHERS . . .

Herbert, James. THE RATS. London, 1974   —   —   450

Herbst, Josephine. NOTHING IS SACRED. New York, 1928   30   125   150

Herford, Oliver. ARTFUL ANTICKS. New York, 1888   —   125   150

Hergesheimer, Joseph. THE LAY ANTHONY. New York, 1914   50   75   100

Herlihy, James Leo. BLUE DENIM. New York, 1958.
    (Written with Wm. Noble)   20   40   75

    THE SLEEP OF BABY FILBERTSON. New York, 1959   25   50   75
    London, 1959   —   30   40

Herr, Michael. DISPATCHES. New York, 1977	—	75	100
London (1978). Wraps	—	—	35
Herriot, James. ALL CREATURES GREAT AND SMALL. New York (1972)	—	30	75
Herrmann, John. WHAT HAPPENS. (Paris, 1926). Wraps	—	150	200
Herron, Stella Wynne. BOWERY PARADE . . . New York (1936). Glassine dustwrapper	—	50	60
Hersey, John (Richard). MEN ON BATAAN. New York, 1942	15	125	200
Hertzog, Carl. *See* Owen P. White			
Hess, Joan. STRANGLED PROSE. New York, 1986	—	—	75
Hesse, Hermann. DEMIAN. New York, 1923. (First English translation)	—	300	500
Hewitt, John. NO REBEL WORD. London, 1948	—	—	250
Hewlett, Maurice. EARTHWORK OUT OF TUSCANY. London, 1895. (500 copies)	50	125	125
Heyen, William. *See* William Haines			
DEPTH OF FIELD. Baton Rouge, 1970	—	25	35
Heyer, Georgette (Mrs. George Ronald Rougier). THE BLACK MOTH. Boston, 1921	—	100	200
Heyward, DuBose. CAROLINA CHANSONS. New York, 1922. (Written with H. Allen)	20	100	175
SKYLINES AND HORIZONS. New York, 1924	25	100	150
Heyward, Jane Screven. WILD ROSES . . . New York/Washington, 1905	—	—	150
Hiaasen, Carl. *See* Neil Schulman			
POWDER BURN. New York, 1981. (Written with Wm. D. Montalbano)	—	—	250
TOURIST SEASON. New York, 1986. (First solely authored title)	—	—	125
(Two ghost-written books precede)			
Hickmott, Allerton Cushman. FABRIC OF DREAMS. (Hartford, 1925). 11 copies on Kelmscott	—	200	200
100 copies	—	100	100
Higgins, Brian. THE ONLY NEED. London, 1980	—	—	50
Higgins, Colin. HAROLD AND MAUDE. Philadelphia (1971)	—	30	60

Higgins, Dick. WHAT ARE LEGENDS? (Calais, Maine, 1960).
Wraps   — 25   75

Higgins, F. R. SALT AIR. Dublin, 1923   — —   100

Higgins, George V(incent). THE FRIENDS OF EDDIE COYLE.
New York, 1972. First issue: green cloth (priority
assumed)   15 35   60
Second issue: blue cloth   — 25   40
London (1972)   — 35   40

Highsmith, (Mary) Patricia (Ploughman). STRANGERS ON A
TRAIN. New York, 1950   — 350   750
London, 1950   — 300   600

Highwater, Jamake. See J. Marks

Hijuelos, Oscar. OUR HOUSE IN THE LAST WORLD.
New York (1983)   — —   100

Hildreth, Richard. See THE SLAVE

Hill, Geoffrey. (POEMS) FANTASY POETS #11.
Swinford, 1952. Wraps   — —   500

FOR THE UNFALLEN. London, 1959   — —   300

Hill, Headon (Francis Edward Grainger). CLUES FROM A
DETECTIVE'S CAMERA. London, 1893   — 50   125

Hill, Reginald. A CLUBABLE WOMAN. London, 1970   — —   200

Hill, Susan. THE ENCLOSURE. London, 1961   — 50   75

Hillerman, Tony. THE BLESSING WAY. New York (1970)   — — 1,250
(London, 1970)   — —   500
New York, 1989. 26 signed and lettered copies   — —   300
100 signed and numbered copies   — —   150

Hillyer, Robert S(illman). SONNETS . . . Cambridge, 1917 25 50   125

Hilton, James. CATHERINE HERSELF. London (1920)   — 400 1,000

Himes, Chester (Bomar). IF HE HOLLERS LET HIM GO.
Garden City, 1945   35 150   400
(London, 1947)   — —   200

HIND AND THE PANTHER . . . , THE. (Matthew Prior
and Charles Montagu). London, 1687   — —   400

Hine, Daryl. FIVE POEMS. Toronto (1955). Wraps   — 150   450

Hinton, S. E. THE OUTSIDERS. New York (1967)   — 75   200
Binding without dustwrapper   — —   100

Hirsch, Edward. FOR THE SLEEPWALKER. New York, 1981   — — 75

Hirsch, Sidney. THE FIRE REGAINED. New York, 1913.
Considered the first "Fugitive Book"   — 150 150

Hirschman, Jack. FRAGMENTS. (New York, 1952). (Privately
published). Wraps   50 250 250

A CORRESPONDENCE OF AMERICANS. Bloomington,
1960. Issued with glassine dustwrapper   25 60 75

HISTORY OF A SIX WEEK TOUR THROUGH A PART OF
FRANCE . . . (Mary W. and Percy B. Shelley).
London, 1817   — 1,500 2,000

Hjortsberg, William. ALP. New York (1969)   — 50 75
London (1970)   — 35 60

Hoag, Jonathan E. THE POETICAL WORKS OF . . . New
York, 1923. Anonymously edited by H. P. Lovecraft,
who also contributed the preface and six poems   — — 300

Hoagland, Edward. CAT MAN. Boston, 1956   20 60 100

Hoagland, Kathleen. FIDDLER IN THE SKY. New York (1944)   — 35 60

Hoban, Russell (Conwell). WHAT DOES IT DO . . .
New York, 1959   — — 175

HOBOMOK . . . (Lydia Marie Child). Boston, 1824   — 400 750

Hobson, Laura Z. DRY GULCH ADAMS. New York, 1934.
(Written with T. Hobson)   — 250 300

A DOG OF HIS OWN. New York, 1941   — 150 200

Hochman, Sandra. VOYAGE HOME. (Paris, 1960). Wraps   20 50 75

Hocking, Mary. THE WINTER CITY. London, 1961   —   —   60

Hodges, George W. SWAMP ANGEL. New York, 1958   —   —   75

Hodgson, Ralph. THE LAST BLACKBIRD . . . London, 1907.
  First issue: top edges gilt, edges uncut   50   75   100
  New York, 1907   —   50   50

Hodgson, William Hope. THE BOATS OF THE
  "GLEN CARRIG." London, 1907   —   500   850

  THE HOUSE ON THE BORDERLAND. London, 1908   —   450   1,250
  Sauk City, 1946   —   250   400

Hoff, H(arry) S(ummerfield). TRINA. London, 1934   40   75   75

Hoffenstein, Samuel. LIFE SINGS A SONG. New York, 1916   —   —   125

Hoffer, Eric. THE TRUE BELIEVER. New York (1951)   —   20   50

Hoffman, Abbie. *See* FUCK THE SYSTEM

Hoffman, Alice. PROPERTY OF. New York (1977)   —   —   100
  London, 1978   —   —   50

Hoffman, Charles Fenno. *See* A WINTER IN THE WEST

Hoffman, Daniel (Gerard). PAUL BUNYAN . . .
  Philadelphia, 1952   —   40   75

  AN ARMADA OF THIRTY WHALES. New York, 1954   25   35   75

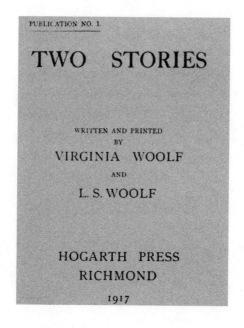

Hogarth Press. TWO STORIES. By V. and L. Woolf. Richmond (England), 1917. Wraps. (150 copies)	750	5,000	7,500
Hogg, James. SCOTTISH PASTORALS . . . Edinburgh, 1801	—	500	750
Holcombe, W(illiam) H(enry). A MYSTERY OF NEW ORLEANS. Philadelphia, 1890	—	60	200
Holdstock, Robert. EYE AMONG THE BLIND. London, 1976	—	—	50
Hollander, John. A CRACKLING OF THORNS. New Haven, 1958. (Foreword by Auden)	25	50	75
Hollinghurst, Alan. CONFIDENTIAL CHATS WITH BOYS. Oxford, 1982. Wraps	—	—	125
Hollo, Anselm (Paul Alexis). SATEIDEN VALILLA. Helsinki, 1956	—	100	150
ST. TEXT AND FINN POEMS. Birmingham (England), 1961	—	125	75
Holme, Constance. CRUMP FOLK GOING HOME. London, 1913	—	—	50
Holmes, John A. ALONG THE ROW . . . (Medford) 1929. Wraps. 500 copies	—	—	150
Holmes, John Clellon. GO. New York, 1952	100	300	750
THE BEAT BOYS. London (1959). Wraps	—	—	75
Holmes, Mary J(ane). TEMPEST AND SUNSHINE . . . New York, 1854. First issue: advertisement for "new copyright works . . . "	—	50	250
Holmes, Oliver Wendell. POEMS. Boston, 1836. (With Boston imprint only). No priority	50	250	400
London, 1846	—	—	250
Holmes, Justice Oliver Wendell. THE COMMON LAW. Boston, 1881. First issue: green cloth. Reading "John Wilson . . . "	150	300	1,750
Second issue: russet cloth. Reading "University Press"	—	—	1,500
Third issue: russet cloth. Reading "S. J. Park Hill & Co."	—	—	1,500
Holst, Spencer. 25 STORIES. (No-place, no-date). Wraps.	—	—	200
THIRTEEN ESSAYS. New York (1960). Wraps	—	60	60
Holt, Tom. POEMS. London, 1973	—	—	100
Holtby, Winifred. ANDERBY WOLD. London, 1923	35	75	125
HOME LIFE IN RUSSIA. (Nikolai Gogol). London, 1854. 2 volumes	400	750	1,250

Honig, Edwin. GARCIA LORCA. Norfolk (1944)   15   40   50
    London (1945)   —   35   40

Hood, Mary. HOW FAR SHE WENT. Athens, Georgia (1984)   —   —   50

Hook, James. *See* PEN OWEN

Hook, Sidney. THE METAPHYSICS OF PRAGMATISM.
    London, 1927   —   —   300

Hooker, Richard (H. Richard Hornberger). M*A*S*H.
    New York, 1968   —   60   350

Hoover, Herbert C. THE KAIPING COAL MINES AND COAL
    FIELD, CHIHLE PROVINCE, NORTH CHINA.
    (No-publisher, no-place, no-date). Stapled offprint(?).
    9 pages of text and 7 unnumbered color plates   —   —   1,000

    PRINCIPLES OF MINING. New York, 1909. (Written
    with Lou Henry Hoover)   150   150   350

Hope, Bob. THEY GOT ME COVERED. Hollywood, 1941.
    Wraps   —   35   40

Hopkins, Gerard Manley. POEMS. London (1918)   200   400   2,000

Horan, Robert. A BEGINNING. New Hampshire, 1948.
    (1,014 copies)   15   50   75

Horgan, Paul. VILLANELLE OF EVENING. (No-place) 1926.
    Wraps. (200 copies)   —   1,000   1,250

    LAMB OF GOD. Roswell, 1927. Wraps. (60 copies)   —   1,500   1,500

    MEN OF ARMS. Philadelphia (1931). (Juvenile).
    (500 copies). Boards   —   600   1,000

    THE FAULT OF ANGELS. New York (1933)   25   125   150

Hornung, E(rnest) W(illiam). UNDER TWO SKIES.
    London, 1892   —   50   75

Horwood, William. DUNCTON WOOD. London, 1980   —   —   75

Hoskins, Katherine. A PENETENTIAL PRIMER. Cummington,
    1945. (350 copies). Wraps   —   60   60

Hospital, Janette Turner. THE IVORY SWING. Toronto (1982)   —   —   100

Houdini, Harry (Ehrich Weiss). THE RIGHT WAY TO DO
    WRONG. Boston, 1906. Wraps   35   150   350

Hough, Emerson. THE SINGING MOUSE STORIES. New
    York, 1895. (Cover by Will Bradley)   40   150   200

Hough, Lindy. THE VIBRATING SERPENT. Madison (1968)	15	30	40
Houghton, Claude (C. H. Oldfield). THE PHANTOM HOST . . . London, 1917. Wraps	30	50	50
Hoult, Norah. POOR WOMEN! London, 1928. 960 copies for sale	—	60	60
Hours Press. PERONNIK THE FOOL. Written by George Moore. Chapelle-Reanville, 1928. (200 signed copies)	50	200	250
(2 previous pamphlets published for the authors)			
Household, Geoffrey (Edward West). THE TERROR OF VILLE-DONGA. London (1936)	—	150	300
THE SPANISH CAVE. Boston, 1936. (New title)	—	—	200
THE THIRD HOUR. London, 1937	30	75	150
Boston, 1938	—	60	125
Housman, A. E. A SHROPSHIRE LAD. London, 1896. (350 copies). "Shropshire" on label 33 millimeters wide	1,750	1,500	1,500
New York, 1897. (150 copies)	900	750	1,000
Housman, Clemence. THE WERE-WOLF. London/Chicago, 1896	—	125	200
Housman, Laurence. A FARM IN FAIRYLAND. London, 1894	40	200	1,000
Houston, James. THE WHITE DAWN. New York, 1971	—	—	40
Houston, Pam. COWBOYS ARE MY WEAKNESS. New York, 1991	—	—	125
Hovenden, Robert M. EPHEMERIDES . . . London, 1844	25	100	125
Hovey, Richard. POEMS. Washington, D.C., 1880. Cloth	—	500	1,000
Wraps	250	250	750
Howard, Brian. GOD SAVE THE KING. Hours Press. Paris (1930). (150 copies)	—	250	400
Howard, Elizabeth Jane. THE BEAUTIFUL VISIT. London (1950)	—	75	100
Howard, H. R. (editor). THE HISTORY OF VIRGIL A. STEWART. New York, 1836	250	250	300
Howard, (James) H. W. BOND AND FREE. Harrisburg, 1886. Portrait of author as frontis. Omitted from later editions	150	300	750
Howard, Maureen. NOT A WORD ABOUT NIGHTINGALES. London, 1960	—	—	125
New York (1962)	—	35	60

Howard, Richard. THE VOYEUR. Written by A. Robbe-
Grillet. New York, 1958. Translated by Howard. Wraps — 25 50

QUANTITIES. Middletown (1962). Wraps — 25 35

(6 previous translations)

Howard, Robert E. A GENT FROM BEAR CREEK. London
(1937). (Most destroyed) — 3,500 6,000
West Kingston, 1965. (732 copies) — — 150

SKULL FACE AND OTHERS. Sauk City, 1946 — — 600

Howe, E(dgar) W(atson). THE STORY OF A COUNTRY TOW.
Atchison, Kansas, 1882. First issue: no lettering on spine
base and "D. Caldwell, manufacturer, Atchison Kan"
rubber-stamped inside cover 60 100 150

Howe, Irving. THE U.A.W. AND WALTER REUTHER. New
York (1949). Written with B. J. Widick — — 60

SHERWOOD ANDERSON. (New York, 1951) — 35 40

Howe, Julia Ward. See PASSION FLOWERS

Howe, Mark A(nthony) DeWolfe. RARI NANTES . . . Boston,
1893. (80 copies). Wraps 50 150 150

Howells, William Dean. See POEMS OF TWO FRIENDS

LIVES AND SPEECHES OF ABRAHAM LINCOLN AND
HANNIBAL HAMLIN. Columbus, 1860. (Written with J. L.
Hayes) Wraps. First issue: pp. [95–96] blank — 300 400
Second issue: p. [96] has engraving — — 200

VENETIAN LIFE . . . London (1866) — 500 500
New York, 1866. (English sheets) — 400 400
Cambridge, 1892. 2 volumes in vellum. (250 copies) — — 250
Boston, 1842. 2 volumes — — 100
Cambridge, 1907. 2 volumes. 550 signed and numbered
copies — — 350

Howes, Barbara. THE UNDERSEA FARMER. Banyon Press.
Pawlet, 1948. (250 copies) 75 100 150

Hoyem, Andrew. THE WAKE. San Francisco, 1963.
35 deluxe copies — 100 250
Wraps. (750 copies) — 30 40

Hoyningen-Huene, George. AFRICAN MIRAGE.
New York, 1938 — 150 200

Hoyt, Richard. DECOYS. New York (1980)	—	—	30
Hubbard, L(afayette) Ron. BUCKSKIN BRIGADES. New York, 1937	—	1,500	2,500
Hudson, W. H. THE PURPLE LAND THAT ENGLAND LOST. London, 1885. 2 volumes. First issue: October advertisements in second volume	500	1,500	1,000
Hueffer, Ford Madox (Ford). THE BROWN OWL. London, 1892 (actually 1891)	300	600	750
Hughart, Barry. BRIDGE OF BIRDS . . . New York, 1984	—	—	35
Hughes, Daniel. WAKING IN A TREE. New York (1963)	—	25	30
Hughes, Dorothy B(elle Flannagan). DARK CERTAINTY. New Haven, 1931	—	—	200
THE SO BLUE MARBLE. New York (1940). (First mystery)	—	175	350
Hughes, Glenn. SOULS . . . San Francisco, 1917	—	60	60
Hughes, Glyn. THE STANEDGE BULL . . . London, 1966	—	—	60
Hughes, Hatcher. HELL-BENT FOR HEAVEN. New York, 1924. (Pulitzer Prize winner)	—	75	175
Hughes, Langston. THE WEARY BLUES. New York, 1926. First issue: dustwrapper without blurb on *Fine Clothes to the Jew*	150	600	3,500
Second issue: dustwrapper with blurb on *Fine Clothes to the Jew*	—	—	1,500
Hughes, Richard (Arthur Warren). GIPSY-NIGHT . . . Berkshire (1922). (750 copies)	40	150	200
Chicago, 1922. 63 signed copies	75	150	300
Hughes, Rupert. THE LAKERIM ATHLETIC CLUB. New York, 1898	75	75	600
Hughes, Ted. HAWK IN THE RAIN. London, (1957). (Preceded New York edition by five days)	35	150	200
New York (1957)	35	150	200
Hughes, Thomas. *See* TOM BROWN'S SCHOOL DAYS			
Hugo, Richard F. POEMS. (Portland, 1959). Wraps	—	100	450
A RUN OF JACKS. Minnesota (1961)	—	75	250
Hugo, Victor. HANS OF ICELAND. London, 1825	—	—	500
Huie, William Bradford. MUD ON THE STARS. New York (1942)	15	50	100

Hulme, Kathryn. HOW'S THE ROAD. Philadelphia, 1928.
30 copies — 100 100

ARAB INTERLUDE. Philadelphia, 1930 — 60 60

Hulme, Keri. THE BONE PEOPLE. Baton Rouge (1985).
(2,500 copies) — 30 60

Hulme, T. E. AN INTRODUCTION TO METAPHYSICS.
New York (1912) — — 300
London, 1913. Translation and introduction by Hulme
of Henri Bergson's work — 100 250

Hume, Cyril. WIFE OF THE CENTAUR. New York (1923) — 125 175

Hume, David. See A TREATISE OF HUMAN NATURE

Hume, Fergus. THE MYSTERY OF THE HANSOM CAB.
Melbourne, 1886. (4 known copies) 500 1,000 3,000
London (1887). Wraps 100 500 750

Humphrey, William. THE LAST HUSBAND . . .
New York, 1953 30 150 150
London, 1953 — 100 100

Humphries, Rolfe. A LITTLE ANTHOLOGY OF VERY SHORT
POEMS . . . (Chicago, 1922). Edited by Humphries 25 50 100

EUROPA . . . New York, 1928. (350 copies) 40 75 150

Huncke, Herbert. HUNCKE'S JOURNAL. New York, 1965.
Wraps — 30 60

Huneker, James G(ibbons). MEZZOTINTS IN MODERN
MUSIC. New York, 1899 50 100 150

Hunt, E. Howard. EAST OF FAREWELL. New York, 1942.
Signed tipped-in page — 75 125
Regular edition — 40 60

Hunt, Gill (John Brunner). GALACTIC STORM. London,
(1952). Wraps — 100 125

Hunt, (Leigh) J. H. JUVENILIA: OR, COLLECTION OF POEMS.
London, 1801 — 750 750

Hunt, Violet. THE MAIDEN'S PROGRESS . . . London, 1894 75 250 300
New York, 1894 50 200 250

Hunter, Dard. See RIP VAN WINKLE

OLD PAPERMAKING (Chillicothe) 1923.
200 signed copies — — 3,000

Hunter, Evan. FIND THE FEATHERED SERPENT.			
Philadelphia (1952)	30	50	150
Hunter, Kristen. GOD BLESS THE CHILD. New York (1964)	—	75	100
Hunter, Stephen. THE MASTER SNIPER. New York, 1980	—	—	40
Huntley, Lydia (Lydia Huntley Sigourney). MORAL			
PIECES . . . Hartford, 1815	—	150	200
Hurston, Zora Neale. JONAH'S GOURD VINE.			
Philadelphia, 1934	50	400	3,500
Hutchins, Maude (Phelps). DIAGRAMMATICS. New York (1932). (Written with M. J. Adler). First issue: 7 1/8" x 9 3/16". October 1932. (250 copies)	—	100	100
Second issue: 9 1/4" x 12 1/4". December 1932. (250 copies). Boxed	—	75	75
GEORGIANA (New York, 1948)	25	35	35
Hutton, Laurence. PLAYS AND PLAYERS. New York, 1875	—	75	100
Huxley, Aldous. THE BURNING WHEEL. Oxford, 1916.			
Wraps	400	750	1,000
Huxley, Elspeth. MURDER AT GOVERNMENT HOUSE.			
London, 1937	—	75	250
New York, 1937	—	—	175
Huxley, Julian. HOLYROOD: THE NEWDIGATE POEM.			
Oxford, 1908	—	—	150
THE INDIVIDUAL IN THE ANIMAL KINGDOM.			
Cambridge (Eng.), 1912	25	75	200
Hvass, Hans. ILLUSTRATED BOOK ABOUT REPTILES . . . Grosset & Dunlap. New York (1960). (Robert Bly translation)	—	—	250
Hyman, Mac. NO TIME FOR SERGEANTS. New York (1954)	—	35	60
Hyman, Stanley Edgar. THE ARMED VISION.			
New York, 1948	—	40	125

I

Ignatow, David. POEMS. Prairie City, Illinois (1948).			
Wraps	100	300	500
Imbs, Bravig. EDEN: EXIT THIS WAY . . . Paris, 1926. Wraps	—	150	200
INCIDENTAL NUMBERS. (Elinor Wylie). London, 1912.			
(65 copies)	3,500	5,000	5,000

INEZ: A TALE OF THE ALAMO. (Written by Augusta Jane
　　Evans Wilson). New York, 1855 　　　　　　　　　—　　150　　350

Infante, G. Cabrera. THREE TRAPPED TIGERS.
　　New York (1971)　　　　　　　　　　　　　　—　　—　　100

Ingalls, Rachel. THEFT. London, 1970　　　　　　　—　　—　　150

　　THEFT and THE MAN WHO WAS LEFT BEHIND.
　　New York, 1970　　　　　　　　　　　　　　—　　—　　100

Inge, William. COME BACK, LITTLE SHEBA.
　　New York (1950)　　　　　　　　　　　　　—　　60　　200

Ingersoll, Robert G. AN ORATION DELIVERED . . . AT
　　ROUSE'S HALL, PEORIA, ILL . . . Peoria, 1869. Wraps.
　　(First published work)　　　　　　　　　　—　　100　　150

Ingraham, Joseph Holt. See THE SOUTHWEST

Inman, Col. Henry. STORIES OF THE OLD SANTE FE TRAIL.
　　Kansas City, 1881　　　　　　　　　　　　—　　150　　250

Innes, Michael (John Innes MacIntosh Stewart). DEATH AT
　　THE PRESIDENT' LODGING. London, 1936　　—　　400　1,000

　　SEVEN SUSPECTS. New York, 1936. New title　—　　150　　350

INSUBORDINATION . . . (Written by T. S. Arthur).
　　New York, 1841　　　　　　　　　200　　300　　300

Invincible, Ned (Edward Smyth Jones). THE ROSE THAT
　　BLOOMETH IN MY HEART. (Louisville(?), 1908)　—　　200　　300

Iremonger, Valentin. RESERVATIONS. London, 1950.
　　(750 copies)　　　　　　　　　　　　　　—　　—　　75

Iris, Scharmel. LYRICS OF A LAD. Chicago, 1914　　—　　75　　75

Iron, Ralph (Olive Schreiner). THE STORY OF AN AFRICAN
　　FARM. London, 1883. 2 volumes　　　　　　—　　750　1,000

Irving, John. SETTING FREE THE BEARS. New York (1968)　—　　250　　750

Irving, Washington. See F. Depons Launcelot Langstaff and
　　Diedrich Knickerbocker

Irwin, Russell (Peter Russell). PICNIC TO THE MOON.
　　London (1944)　　　　　　　　　　　　　—　　100　　100

Irwin, Wallace. THE LOVE SONNETS OF A HOODLUM.
　　Paul Elder. San Francisco, 1901. Wraps　　　—　　20　　50
　　Second edition. Elder & Shepard. San Francisco, 1902　—　　—　　50

Isaacs, Susan. COMPROMISING POSITIONS. New York, 1978　—　　—　　40

Isherwood, Christopher. ALL THE CONSPIRATORS.

London, 1928	100	1,000	1,750
London, 1957. (New introduction)	—	—	75

Ishiguro, Kazuo. A PALE VIEW OF THE HILLS.

(London, 1982)	—	—	1,000
New York (1982)	—	—	200

ITALIAN SKETCH BOOK, THE. By an American (Henry T. Tuckerman). Philadelphia, 1835	—	125	200

Ives, Charles. ESSAYS BEFORE A SONATA. New York, 1920. Issued without dustwrapper?	—	300	1,250

Izzi, Eugene. THE TAKE. New York, 1987	—	—	40

J

Jackson, Charles. THE LOST WEEKEND. New York (1944)	15	60	150
London, 1945	—	—	100

Jackson, Daniel, Jr. *See* Isaac Mitchell

Jackson, Jon. THE DIEHARD. New York (1977)	—	—	200

Jackson, Shirley. THE ROAD THROUGH THE WALL. New York, 1948	50	125	350

Jacobi, Carl. REVELATIONS IN BLACK. Sauk City, 1947	—	60	125

Jacobs, W. W. MANY CARGOES. London, 1896	—	125	150

Jacobsen, Josephine. LET EACH MAN REMEMBER. Dallas (1940)	15	100	500

Jacobson, Dan. THE TRAP. New York (1955)	20	25	35

Jaeger, Doris U. (Doris Ullman). FACULTY OF THE COLLEGE OF PHYSICIANS & SURGEONS. New York, 1919	—	—	500

Jaffe, Rona. THE BEST OF EVERYTHING. New York (1958)	—	—	60

Jaffe, Sherril. YOUNG LUST & OTHERS. Santa Barbara, 1973.

Wraps	—	15	25

SCARS MAKE YOUR BODY MORE INTERESTING.
Santa Barbara, 1974. 26 signed and numbered copies in

acetate dustwrapper	—	60	100
200 signed and numbered copies in acetate dustwrapper	—	25	40

Jahnn, Hans Henry. THE SHIP. New York, 1961.

(First English translation)	—	—	40

Jakes, John (William). THE TEXANS RIDE NORTH . . .

Philadelphia (1952)	—	30	175

James, C(yril) L(ionel) R(obert). THE LIFE OF CAPTAIN
    CIPRIANI. Nelson (England), 1932. Wraps   —   175   175

James, Henry, Jr. A PASSIONATE PILGRIM . . . Boston, 1875.
    First issue: J. R. Osgood & Co. on spine   100   850 2,000
    Second issue: Houghton Osgood & Co.   —   400   750
    Third issue: Houghton, Mifflin & Co.   —   300   400

James, M(ontague) R(hodes). GHOST STORIES OF AN
    ANTIQUARY. London, 1904   —   200 1,750

James, Norah C. SLEEVELESS ERRAND. Paris, 1929. First
    book published by J. Kahane. 50 signed copies   —   400   400
    450 unsigned copies   —   100   125

James, P(hyllis) D(orothy). COVER HER FACE. London, 1962   —   300 1,250
    New York (1966)   —   75   450

James, Will(iam Roderick). COWBOYS NORTH AND SOUTH.
    New York, 1924   25   150   600

James, William. THE LITERARY REMAINS OF THE LATE
    HENRY JAMES. Boston, 1885. (Edited and introduction
    by WJ)   —   —   350

    PRINCIPLES OF PSYCHOLOGY. New York, 1890.
    Two volumes   —   750   750

Jameson, (M.) Storm. THE POT BOILS. London, 1919   —   75   100

Janeway, Elizabeth. THE WALSH GIRLS. Garden City, 1943   —   30   60

Janowitz, Tama. AMERICAN DAD. New York (1981)   —   —   50

Janvier, Thomas Allbone. COLOR STUDIES.
    New York, 1885. (1,000 copies)   —   125   150

Jarrell, Randall. BLOOD FOR A STRANGER. New York (1942) 125   350   500

    Also see FIVE YOUNG AMERICAN POETS

Jeffers, (John) Robinson. FLAGONS & APPLES. Los Angeles,
    1912. (500 copies)   500   750 1,500

    CALIFORNIANS. New York, 1916. First commercial book 125   175   300

Jefferson, Beatrice. SMALL TOWN MURDER.
    New York, 1941   —   —   35

Jefferson, Thomas. NOTES ON THE STATE OF VIRGINIA.
    London, 1787   — 2,500 7,500
    Philadelphia, 1788   —   — 3,000

    [Preceded by 1782 (actually 1785) Paris edition]

Jen, Gish. TYPICAL AMERICAN. Boston, 1991	—	—	40
Jenkins, Dan. SPORTS ILLUSTRATED'S BEST 18 GOLF HOLES IN AMERICA. New York, 1966	—	—	75
Jenkins, John Edward. *See* GINX'S BABY.			
Jennings, Elizabeth. (POEMS) FANTASY POETS #1. (Swinford, 1953). Wraps	25	75	150
A WAY OF LOOKING. London, 1955	—	50	50
Jennings, Humphrey. POEMS. New York, 1951. 100 numbered copies. Wraps	—	—	150
Jepson, Edgar (Alfred). THE DICTATOR'S DAUGHTER. London, 1902	—	75	75
Jerome, Jerome K. ON STAGE AND OFF. London, 1885	50	200	300
IDLE THOUGHTS OF AN IDLE FELLOW. London, 1886	—	150	200
Jerrold, Douglas William. MEN OF CHARACTER. London, 1838	—	—	350
Jessup, Richard. THE CUNNING AND THE HAUNTED. New York (1954). Wraps	—	—	40
THE CINCINNATI KID. Boston (1963)	—	30	60
Jewett, Sarah Orne. DEEPHAVEN. Boston, 1877. First issue: "was" vs "so" p. 65:16	50	200	500
Second issue: "so" vs "was"	—	75	250
Cambridge (Mass.), 1894. 250 large paper copies	—	—	250
Jhabvala, R(uth) Prawer. TO WHOM SHE WILL. London (1955)	—	125	250
AMRITA. New York, 1956. (New title)	—	—	125
Johns, Orrick. ASPHALT . . . New York, 1917	—	60	100
Johns, W(illiam) E(arle). THE CAMELS ARE COMING. London, 1932	—	—	200
Johnson, B. S. TRAVELLING PEOPLE. (London, 1963)	—	150	250
Johnson, Benj. F. (James Whitcomb Riley). THE OLD SWIMMING HOLE . . . Indianapolis, 1883. Wraps	250	600	600
Facsimile in 1909 lacks "W" in "Williams" on p. 41	10	25	50
Johnson, Charles R(ichard). BLACK HUMOR. Chicago, 1970. Wraps	—	—	200

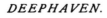

DEEPHAVEN.

BY

SARAH O. JEWETT.

BOSTON:
JAMES R. OSGOOD AND COMPANY,
Late Ticknor & Fields, and Fields, Osgood, & Co.
1877.

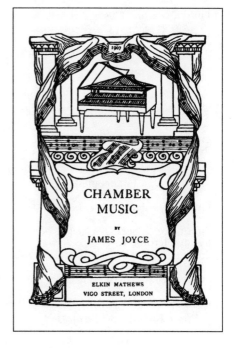

CHAMBER
MUSIC

BY

JAMES JOYCE

ELKIN MATHEWS
VIGO STREET, LONDON

FAITH AND THE GOOD THING. New York (1974). First novel	—	—	150
Johnson, Denis. THE MAN AMONG THE SEALS. Iowa City (1969). Issued without dustwrapper	—	—	350
Johnson, Diane. FAIR GAME. New York, 1965	—	60	75
Johnson, Dorothy M. MISS BUNNY INTERVENES. London, 1948	—	—	50
Johnson, E. Pauline. WHITE WAMPUM. London, 1895	—	—	350
Johnson, James Weldon. *See* AUTOBIOGRAPHY . . .			
Johnson, Josephine (Winslow). NOW IN NOVEMBER. New York, 1934	20	40	60
Johnson, Lionel. SIR WALTER RALEIGH IN THE TOWER. (Chester) 1885. Wraps	—	—	6,000
THE ART OF THOMAS HARDY. London, 1894. (150 copies)	100	500	650
Trade edition	25	150	200
POEMS. London/Boston, 1895. 25 signed and numbered copies	—	1,000	6,000
Trade edition. (750 copies)	—	750	350

Johnson, Martin. THROUGH THE SOUTH SEAS.
New York, 1913 — — 250

Johnson, Merle (DeVore). A BIBLIOGRAPHY OF MARK
TWAIN. New York, 1910. (500 copies) — 150 200

Johnson, Pamela Hansford. SYMPHONY FOR FULL
ORCHESTRA. London, 1934. Cloth — — 250
Wraps — 125 125

Johnson, Ronald. A LINE OF POETRY, A ROW OF TREES.
Highlands, 1964. 50 signed and numbered copies — 200 350
Stiff wraps. (500 copies) — 75 75

Johnson, Samuel. *See* Mr. Le Grande

Johnson, Uwe. SPECULATIONS. New York (1963) — 25 35

Johnston, Jill. MARMALADE ME. New York, 1971 — — 40

Johnston, Mary. PRISONER OF HOPE. Boston, 1898 20 50 75

Jolas, Eugene. RHYTHM'S Volume II. Peoria, 1924. Wraps.
Entire issue devoted to Jolas — — 125

CINEMA: POEMS. New York, 1926 50 200 300

Jolly, Andrew. LIE DOWN IN ME. New York (1970) — 50 50

Jones, Brian. POEMS. London, 1966. Wraps — — 40

Jones, D. G. FROST ON THE SUN. Toronto, 1957. Wraps in
dustwrapper — — 150

Jones, David (Michael). IN PARENTHESIS. London (1937) 125 500 850
London (1961). 70 signed and numbered copies.
(Jones and Eliot) — 900 2,500
New York (1961). First issue: Eliot introduction not
listed on contents page — 75 100
Second issue: Eliot introduction listed — 35 60

Jones, Douglas C. THE TREATY OF MEDICINE LODGE.
Norman, Oklahoma, 1966 — — 75

Jones, Edith Newbold (Edith Wharton). VERSES.
Newport, Rhode Island, 1878. Wraps 5,000 25,000 50,000

Jones, Edward Smyth. *See* Ned Invincible

THE SYLVAN CABIN . . . Boston, 1911 — 50 75
San Francisco, 1915. Wraps. (First separate edition) — 150 75

Jones, Gayl. CORREGIDORA. New York (1975) — 40 75

Jones, Glyn. THE BLUE BED . . . London (1937) 15 50 75

Jones, Gwyn. RICHARD SAVAGE. London, 1935 — 60 75

Jones, Howard Mumford. A LITTLE BOOK OF LOCAL VERSE.
   La Crosse, 1915. Wraps 30 60 75

Jones, James. FROM HERE TO ETERNITY. New York, 1951.
   Presentation edition with signed and numbered tipped–in
   page. (About 1,500 copies) — 225 300
   Unsigned 50 125 175
   London, 1952 — 75 100

Jones, James Athearn. *See* Matthew Murgatroyd

Jones, Joshua Henry. BY SANCTION OF LAW. Boston, 1924 — 75 75

Jones, (Everett) Leroi (Imamu Amiri Baraka). CUBA LIBRE.
   New York, 1961. Wraps 75 200 250

   PREFACE TO A TWENTY VOLUME SUICIDE NOTE.
   New York (1961). Wraps. First issue: ads in bold caps 25 35 100
   Second issue: ads not in bold caps 15 25 40

   (3 intervening broadsides)

Jones, Madison Percy. THE INNOCENT. New York (1957) — 60 75

Jones, Nettie. FISH TALES. New York (1983) — — 25

Jones, Thom. PUGILIST AT REST. Boston, 1993 — — 50

Jong, Erica. FRUITS AND VEGETABLES. New York (1971).
Cloth	25	35	75
Wraps	15	15	25

Jonson, Ben(jamin). EVERY MAN OUT OF HIS HUMOUR.
London, 1600 — 2,500 5,000

Jordan, Neil. NIGHT IN TUNISIA. Dublin (1976). Wraps — — 250
London, 1979 — — 100
New York, 1980 — — 60

Jordon, June. WHO LOOK AT ME. New York, 1969 — 30 40

Joseph, Clifton. METROPOLITAN BLUES. (Toronto, 1983).
500 copies — — 40

Joseph, Jenny. THE UNLOOKED FOR SEASON. London, 1960 — — 75

Josephson, Matthew. GALIMATHIAS. New York (1923).
Stiff wraps. (250 numbered copies) 35 125 200

Joss, John. SIERRA. (Los Altos, 1977) — — 100

JOURNAL OF A FEW MONTHS' RESIDENCE IN
PORTUGAL . . . (Dorothy Wordsworth Quillinan).
London, 1847. Two volumes — — 750

Joyce, James. TWO ESSAYS. Dublin (1901). Wraps. (Written
with F. J. C. Skellington). (Contains "Day of the
Rabblement") 3,500 5,000 10,000

THE HOLY OFFICE. (Pola, 1904 or 1905). Broadside 2,500 8,000 12,500

CHAMBER MUSIC. London, 1907. First issue: thick laid
endpapers with horizontal chain lines. Poems in
signature C are well centered 2,000 6,000 7,500
Second issue: thick wove endpapers, signature C is
poorly centered 1,000 1,250 2,500
Third issue: thin wove transparent endpapers, signature
C is poorly centered 750 1,250 2,500
London, 1918. Wraps. "Second Edition" — 250 400
Boston (1918). Unauthorized edition. Issued in tissue
dustwrapper 75 200 250
New York, 1918. (No dustwrapper?) 100 200 200
Egoist Press. London, 1923. (107 copies) — 200 600
Jonathan Cape (1927). (393 copies) — 100 450

Judah, Samuel B(enjamin) H(erbert). THE MOUNTAIN
TORRENT . . . New York, 1820 — 200 350

Just, Ward. TO WHAT END. Boston, 1968 — 30 60

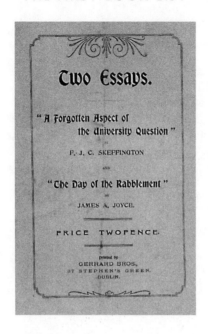

Justice, Donald. THE OLD BACHELOR . . . Miami, 1951.
Wraps. (240 copies)   —   250   600

THE SUMMER ANNIVERSARIES. Middletown, Conn.
(1960). Cloth   25   50   100
Wraps   —   20   30

K

K., R. A. (Ronald Knox). SIGNA SEVERA. Eton College,
1906. Wraps   50   250   350

Kael, Pauline. I LOST IT AT THE MOVIES. Boston (1965)   —   40   60
London (1966)   —   —   50

Kafka, Franz. THE CASTLE. London, 1930. (First English
translation)   75   250   1,250
New York, 1930   —   150   500

Kahane, Jack. TWO PLAYS. Manchester (England), 1912.
Wraps   50   150   300

Kahn, E. J., Jr. THE ARMY LIFE. New York, 1942   —   —   75

Kahn, Roger. INSIDE BIG LEAGUE BASEBALL. New York,
1962. Issued without dustwrapper   —   —   150

Kaler, James Otis. *See* James Otis

Kallman, Chester. ELEGY. New York (1951). Wraps.
(500 copies)   —   50   75

Kaltenborn, H. V. KALTENBORN EDITS THE NEWS. New
York (1937). (Ghostwritten by Mary McCarthy). Cloth
in dustwrapper   75   125   200
Wraps in dustwrapper   —   50   100

Kaminsky, Stuart M. DON SIEGEL: DIRECTOR. New York
(1974). Wraps   —   —   40

BULLET FOR A STAR. New York, 1977   —   —   150

Kandel, Lenore. A PASSING DRAGON. (Studio City, Calif.,
1959). Wraps   —   30   75

Kanin, Garson. BORN YESTERDAY. New York, 1946   —   50   150

Kantor, McKinley. DIVERSAY. New York, 1928. First
book by Coward-McCann. First issue: no reviews on
dustwrapper   35   125   200

Karp, David. THE BIG FEELING. New York (1952). Wraps   25   35   35

ONE. New York (1953). (First hardback—sixth book)   —   35   50

Karp, Ivan. DOOBIE DOO. Garden City (1965). Warhol and
Lichtenstein dustwrapper   —   30   100

Katz, Steven. THE LESTRIAD. Leece, 1962. (300 copies).
Wraps   —   100   125

Kaufman, George S. DULCY. New York (1921). Written
with Marc Connelly   —   200   600

Kavan, Anna. *See* Helen Ferguson

Kavanagh, Dan (Julian Barnes). DUFFY. London (1980).
Second book. (First mystery)   —   40   200

Kavanagh, Patrick. D'OLIER MUSIC CO'S FAMOUS SONGS.
Dublin, 1930. Wraps   —   —   750

PLOUGHMAN . . . London, 1936. Wraps   —   75   1,000

Kaye, Philip B. TAFFY. New York, 1950   —   75   100

Kaye-Smith, Sheila. THE TRAMPING METHODIST.
London, 1908   45   125   150

Kazan, Elia. AMERICA AMERICA. New York (1962)   —   30   40

Kazantzakis, Nikos. ZORBA THE GREEK. London (1952).
(First English translation)   —   150   250

Kazin, Alfred. ON NATIVE GROUND. New York (1942)   15   75   125
    London (1943)   —   50   75

Keating, H. R. F. DEATH AND THE VISITING FIREMAN.
    London, 1959   —   40   125
    New York, 1973   —   —   30

Keats, John. POEMS. London, 1817   5,000 8,000 10,000

Keene, Carolyn. THE SECRET OF THE OLD CLOCK. New
    York, 1930. First issue: dustwrapper with Nancy Drews
    1 through 3 advertised; book has ad for first 8
    Hardy Boys   —   —   1,250
    Second issue: dustwrapper advertises first 4 Nancy Drews
    and book advertises 9 hardbacks   —   —   600

KEEP COOL. (John Neal). Baltimore, 1817. Two volumes   —   300   500

Kees, Weldon. THE LAST MAN. San Francisco, 1943. Boards
    without dustwrapper. (300 copies)   75   200   600

Keillor, Garrison. G. K. THE DJ. New York, 1977. Stapled
    wraps   —   —   125

    HAPPY TO BE HERE. New York, 1982.   —   30   75

Keller, David H(enry). THE THOUGHT PROJECTOR. New
    York (1929). Wraps   —   60   150

Keller, Helen. OUR DUTIES TO THE BLIND. Boston, 1904.
    Wraps   —   125   125

Kellerman, Faye. THE RITUAL BATH. New York, 1986   —   —   40

Kellerman, Jonathan. WHEN THE BOUGH BREAKS.
    New York, 1985   —   —   150

    (Two nonfiction titles precede)

Kelley, Edith Summers. WEEDS. New York (1923)   100   125   250
    London, 1924   75   100   200

Kelley, Emma Dunham. MEGDA. Boston, 1891   —   —   600

Kelley, William Melvin. A DIFFERENT DRUMMER.
    Garden City, 1962   50   75   150

Kellogg, Marjorie. TELL ME THAT YOU LOVE ME, JUNIE
    MOON. New York, 1968   —   30   30

Kelly, Robert. ARMED DESCENT. (New York, 1961).
    Stiff wraps   40   50   75

Kelly, Susan. THE GEMINI MAN. New York, 1985   —   —   75

Kelly, Walt. POGO. New York (1961). Wraps. Five variants,
priority unknown — 50 60

Kelty, Mary Ann. *See* THE FAVOURITE OF NATURE

Kemble, Frances Anne. FRANCIS THE FIRST. London, 1832.
Wraps — — 200

Kemelman, Harry. FRIDAY THE RABBI SLEPT LATE. New
York (1964). Price of $3.95 and bulking one-inch thick — 35 75

Kemp, Arnold. EAT OF ME, I AM THE SAVIOR.
New York, 1972 — — 40

Kenan, Randall. A VISITATION OF SPIRITS.
New York (1989) — — 60

Keneally, Thomas. THE PLACE AT WHITTON. London (1964) — 100 350

Kennan, George. TENT LIFE IN SIBERIA. New York, 1870 — 100 125

Kennan, George F. AMERICAN DIPLOMACY 1900–1950.
Chicago (1951) — 40 50

Kennedy, Edward. THE FRUITFUL BOUGH. Privately printed,
1965. (Tribute to father collected by EMK) — 100 250

DECISIONS FOR A DECADE. New York, 1968 20 40 50

Kennedy, John F(itzgerald). WHY ENGLAND SLEPT.
New York, 1940 200 400 750
London (1940) 100 150 200

Kennedy, John Pendleton. *See* SWALLOW BARN

Kennedy, Mark. THE PECKING ORDER. New York (1953) 15 30 75

Kennedy, Raymond. MY FATHER'S ORCHARD. Boston, 1963 — 30 40

Kennedy, Robert. THE ENEMY WITHIN. New York (1960) — 40 100

Kennedy, Thomas. POEMS. Washington, D.C., 1816 — 100 150

Kennedy, William. THE INK TRUCK. New York, 1969 — 175 450

Kennedy, X. J. (Joseph Charles Kennedy). NUDE
DESCENDING A STAIRCASE. Garden City (1961) 25 50 60

Kenner, Hugh. PARADOX IN CHESTERTON.
New York, 1947 — — 125
London, 1948 — 125 100

Kenny, Maurice. DEAD LETTERS SENT . . .
San Francisco (1958). Wraps in dustwrapper — — 50

Kent, Rockwell. *See* ARCHITEC-TONICS

THE SEVEN AGES OF MAN. New York, 1918. First
collected illustrations | 150 | 150 | 250

WILDERNESS . . . New York, 1920. First issue: cover in
gray | 125 | 250 | 400
Second issue: cover in tan | 75 | 150 | 300
Los Angeles (1970). 1,500 signed copies in slipcase | — | — | 150

Kernahan, (John) Coulson. A BOOK OF STRANGE SINS.
London, 1893 | — | 40 | 50

Kerouac, John (Jack) (Jean-Louis). THE TOWN AND THE
CITY. New York (1950) | 100 | 300 | 600
London, 1951 | 75 | 200 | 250

Kerr, Jean. OUR HEARTS WERE YOUNG AND GAY.
Chicago (1946) | — | — | 75

Kerr, Philip. MARCH VIOLETS. London, 1989 | — | — | 100

Kerrigan, Anthony. LEAR IN THE TROPIC OF PARIS.
Barcelona, 1953. Wraps. (100 copies) | 30 | 60 | 75

Kersh, Gerald. JEWS WITHOUT JEHOVAH. London, 1934 | — | 125 | 200

Kesey, Ken (Elton). ONE FLEW OVER THE CUCKOO'S NEST.
New York, 1962 | 100 | 300 | 1,500
London, 1962. (Some revisions) | — | 75 | 300

Keyes, Frances Parkinson. THE OLD GRAY HOMESTEAD.
New York, 1919 | — | — | 60

Keyes, Sidney. THE IRON LAUREL. London, 1942.
Stiff wraps and dustwrapper | 20 | 40 | 75

Kidder, Tracy. THE ROAD TO YUBA CITY.
Garden City, 1974 | — | — | 150

Kiefer, Warren. THE LINGALA CODE. New York, 1972 | — | — | 60

Kiely, Benedict. COUNTIES OF CONTENTION. Cork, 1945 | — | 75 | 100

Kienzle, William. ROSARY MURDERS. New York, 1979 | — | — | 50

Kijewski, Karen. KATWALK. New York, 1989 | — | — | 175

Killens, John O. YOUNGBLOOD. New York, 1954 | 30 | 75 | 150

Kilmer, Aline. CANDLES THAT BURN. New York (1919) | — | 30 | 50

Kilmer, (Alfred) Joyce. SUMMER OF LOVE. New York, 1911.
Baker & Taylor at foot of spine. Issued in glassine
dustwrapper | 150 | 250 | 350

Kincaid, Jamaica. AT THE BOTTOM OF THE RIVER.
New York (1983) | — | 35 | 100

King, Alan. ANYBODY WHO OWNS HIS OWN HOME
DESERVES IT. New York, 1962 — — 40

King, Alexander. MINE ENEMY GROWS OLDER. New York
(1958). In two dustwrappers — — 75

King, Florence. SOUTHERN LADIES AND GENTLEMEN.
New York (1975) — — 75

King, Francis. TO THE DARK TOWER. (London) 1946 — 100 150

King, Grace (Elizabeth). MONSIEUR MOTTE.
New York, 1888 — 75 125

King, John. LECTURES UPON IONAS. Oxford, 1597 — — 600

King, Kennedy (George Douglas Brown). LOVE AND A
SWORD. London, 1899 — — 100

King, Larry L. THE ONE-EYED MAN. New York (1966) — 50 75

King, Martin Luther, Jr. STRIDE TOWARD FREEDOM.
New York, 1958 — 100 250
London, 1959 — 50 150

King, Rufus (Frederick). NORTH STAR, DOG OF THE
NORTHWEST. New York, 1925 — — 125

MYSTERY DELUXE. New York (1927) — 35 75

King, Stephen. CARRIE. Garden City, 1974 — 175 750
London, 1974 — — 600

Kingsley, Charles. THE SAINT'S TRAGEDY. . . London, 1848 — 200 600

Kingsley, Henry. THE RECOLLECTIONS OF GEOFFREY
HAMLYN. Cambridge (Eng.), 1859. Three volumes 150 300 300

Kingsmill, Hugh. *See* Hugh Lunn

Kingsolver, Barbara. THE BEAN TREES. New York (1988) — — 175

Kingston, Maxine Hong. THE WOMAN WARRIOR.
New York, 1976 — 50 100
London, 1977 — — 75

Kinnell, Galway. BITTER VICTORY. (Written by Rene
Hardy, translated by GK). Garden City, 1956 25 125 200

WHAT A KINGDOM IT WAS. Boston, 1960 50 125 150

Kinsella, Thomas. THE STARLIT EYE. Dublin, 1952 — 100 250

Kinsella, W(illiam) P(atrick). DANCE ME OUTSIDE.
Ottawa, 1977. Cloth — 250 1,250

Wraps. (No differentiation among a number of printings)	—	40	50
Boston, 1986	—	—	75

Kipling, Rudyard. SCHOOLBOY LYRICS. Lahore, 1881.

Wraps. (50 copies). White presumed to precede brown	1,000	12,000	17,500

DEPARTMENTAL DITTIES . . . Lahore, 1886. Wraps	—	—	2,000

Kirkup, James (Falconer). INDICATIONS. London, 1942.

Written with J. Ormond and J. Bayliss	—	125	150

COSMIC SHAPE. London (1946). 500 numbered copies. (Written with Ross Nichols)	—	75	100

THE DROWNED SAILOR . . . London, 1947	30	60	100

Kirkwood, Jim (James). THERE MUST BE A PONY.

Boston (1960)	15	40	50

Kirsch, Robert R. IN THE WRONG RAIN. Boston (1959)	—	40	40

Kirst, Hans Helmut. THE REVOLT OF GUNNAR ASHE.

Boston (1955)	15	40	75

Kirstein, Lincoln. FLESH IS HEIR. New York, 1932	25	75	150

Kissinger, Henry A. A WORLD RESTORED . . . Boston, 1957	—	75	100

Kitchin, C(lifford) H(enry) B(enn). CURTAINS.

Oxford, 1919. Wraps	—	75	300

Kittredge, William. THE VAN GOGH FIELD . . . Columbia,

Missouri, 1978. Issued without dustwrapper	—	—	300

Kizer, Carolyn. POEMS. Portland (1959). Wraps	—	100	300

THE UNGRATEFUL GARDEN. Bloomington (1961). Cloth	35	75	125
Wraps	—	20	30

Kjelgaard, Jim. FOREST PATROL. New York, 1948	—	—	75

Klane, Robert. THE HORSE IS DEAD. New York, 1968. First

edition stated	—	50	100

Klein, A. M. HATH NOT A JEW. New York, 1940. Issued

without dustwrapper	—	—	500

Klein, Ted. THE CEREMONIES. New York, 1984	—	—	40

Klein, William. NEW YORK. LIFE IS GOOD . . .
London (1956). Including small guide book attached

with ribbon	—	—	1,250

Kneale, Nigel. TOMATO CAIN . . . London, 1949	—	40	40

Knickerbocker, Diedrich (Washington Irving). A HISTORY
OF NEW YORK FROM THE BEGINNING OF THE
WORLD . . . New York, 1809. 2 volumes with 268
pages in volume 1   500   1,000   1,250

Knight, Clifford (Reynolds). *See* Reynolds Knight

    THE AFFAIR OF THE SCARLET CLUB. New York, 1937.
    (Second book, first mystery)   —   —   250

Knight, Eric. LASSIE COME HOME. Philadelphia (1940)   —   —   350
    London (1941)   —   —   200

Knight, Reynolds. TOMMY OF THE VOICES. Chicago, 1913   —   —   75

    Also see Clifford Knight

Knowles, John. A SEPARATE PEACE. London, 1959   50   400   750
    New York, 1960. First issue: pictorial dustwrapper   25   150   500
    Second issue: printed dustwrapper   —   75   150

Knowlton, Charles. ELEMENTS OF MODERN
MATERIALISM . . . Adams, Mass., 1829   —   750   600

Knox, Ronald A(rbuthnott). *See* R. A. K.

Kober, Arthur. THUNDER OVER THE BRONX.
New York, 1935   —   35   50

Koch, Kenneth. POEMS. (With Nell Blaine's *Prints*). New
York, 1953. Stiff wraps. (300 copies)   150   400   1,000

Koestler, Arthur. *See* A. Costler

    SPANISH TESTAMENT. London, 1937.
    Cloth   35   250   300
    Wraps. (Left Book Club)   —   75   75

Kohler, Wolfgang. THE MENTALITY OF APES.
New York, 1925   —   100   150

Koontz, Dean R(ay). STAR QUEST. New York (1968).
Wraps   —   —   75

    Also see K. R. Dwyer

Korda, Michael. MALE CHAUVINISM! HOW IT WORKS.
New York (1973)   —   40   50

Kornbluth, C. M. NOT THIS AUGUST. Garden City, 1955   —   —   150

Kosinski, Jerzy (Nikodem). *See* Joseph Novak

    THE PAINTED BIRD. Boston, 1965. (Third book—first
    under his name). First issue: extraneous line top of p. 270   35   200   300

Kotzwinkle, William. THE FIREMAN. New York, 1969.
    (Juvenile) — 75 250

Kovacs, Ernie. ZOOMAR. New York, 1957 — 35 60

Kovic, Ron. BORN ON THE FOURTH OF JULY.
    New York, 1976 — — 75

Kramer, Jane. OFF WASHINGTON SQUARE.
    New York (1963) — — 40

Kramm, Joseph. THE SHRIKE. New York (1952) — — 75

Kreymborg, Alfred. LOVE AND LIFE . . . New York (1908).
    (500 copies) 50 75 100

Krim, Seymour. VIEWS OF A NEARSIGHTED CANNONEER.
    New York (1961). Wraps — 20 30

Kroll, Harry Harrison. THE CABIN IN THE COTTON.
    New York, 1931 20 35 75

Kromer, Tom. WAITING FOR NOTHING. New York, 1935 — 125 250

Kronenberger, Louis. THE GRAND MANNER.
    New York, 1929 15 40 100

Krutch, Joseph Wood. COMEDY AND CONSCIENCE . . .
    New York, 1924. Wraps 35 100 200

Kuhn, Thomas S. THE COPERNICAN REVOLUTION.
    Cambridge, 1957 — — 100

Kumin, Maxine W. SEBASTIAN AND THE DRAGON. New
    York, 1960. (Juvenile) — 50 100

    HALFWAY. New York (1961) 15 50 60

Kundera, Milan. THE JOKE. London, 1969 — — 150
    New York, 1969 — 100 125

Kunitz, Stanley (Jasspon). INTELLECTUAL THINGS.
    Garden City, 1930 50 125 150

Kupferberg, Tuli. SELECTED FRUITS AND NUTS.
    New York (1959). Wraps — — 100

Kurz, Ron. LETHAL GAS. New York, 1974 — — 50

Kuttner, Henry. *See* Will Garth *and* Lewis Padgett

Kyd, Thomas (Alfred Bennett Harbage). BLOOD IS A
    BEGGAR. Philadelphia/New York (1946) — 35 50

Kyger, Joanne. THE TAPESTRY AND THE WEB.
    San Francisco, 1965. 27 signed and numbered copies   —   125   125
    Trade. Cloth   —   50   50
    Wraps   —   15   15

L

L., E. V. (Edward Verrall Lucas). SPARKS FROM A FLINT.
    London, 1890   25   60   100

L., W. EPISODES AND EPISTLES. New York, 1925   35   125   200

LaFarge, Christopher. HOXIE SELLS HIS ACRES.
    New York, 1934   20   25   100

LaFarge, Oliver (Hazard Perry). LAUGHING BOY.
    Boston, 1929   —   75   250

    (Previous collaboration)

Lafferty, R. A. PAST MASTER. New York (1968). Wraps   —   —   40
    London, 1968   —   —   125

Laing, Alexander. FOOL'S ERRAND. New York, 1928   —   —   100

Laing, Oilys. ANOTHER ENGLAND. New York, 1941   —   —   35

Lamantia, Philip. EROTIC POEMS. (Berkeley) 1946   35   200   300

Lamar, Mirabeu B. VERSE MEMORIALS. New York, 1857   —   1,500   2,000

Lamb, Charles. POEMS. London, 1797. (Published with
    Poems by S. T. Coleridge. Second edition)   —   —   1,000

    A TALE OF ROSAMUND GRAY . . . London, 1798. (First
    separate book. Also two known copies with
    "Birminham" on title page)   —   —   2,500

Lambert, Gavin. THE SLIDE AREA. London, 1959   —   —   75

Lamkin, Speed. TIGER IN THE GARDEN. Boston, 1950   25   40   40

Lamming, George (Eric). IN THE CASTLE OF MY SKIN.
    London (1953)   —   50   100
    New York, 1953   —   —   75

L'Amour, Louis. SMOKE FROM THIS ALTAR. Oklahoma City
    (1939). First issue: Orange cloth   —   150   750
    Second issue: Green cloth   —   —   600

LAMPLIGHTER, THE. (Maria S. Cummins). Boston, 1854.
    (Noted in black BAL, green or blue cloth)   —   —   1,000

Lampman, Archibald. AMONG THE MILLET . . . Ottawa,
1888. First issue: double rule above & below title on
spine. In rose cloth   —   175   250

Lampson, M. Robbins (Robin). ON REACHING
SIXTEEN . . . Geyserville, 1916. String-tied wraps   —   —   100

Lamson, David. WE WHO ARE ABOUT TO DIE.
New York, 1936   —   50   50

Landor, Walter Savage. GEBIR: A POEM. London, 1798   —   —   3,000

Lane, Margaret. FAITH, HOPE, NO CHARITY. London, 1935   —   50   75

Lane, Pinkie Gordon. WIND THOUGHTS. Fort Smith (1972).
Wraps   —   —   50

Lang, Andrew. BALLADS AND LYRICS OF OLD FRANCE . . .
London, 1872   40   60   300

Lang, V. R. THE PITCH. New York, 1962. (Edw. Gorey
illustrations). Wraps   —   60   100

Lange, Dorothea. AN AMERICAN EXODUS . . . New York,
1939. Written with Paul S. Taylor   —   —   300

Lange, John (Michael Crichton). ODDS ON.
New York, 1966. Wraps   —   30   125

Langer, Susanne K. PHILOSOPHY IN A NEW KEY.
Cambridge (Mass.), 1942   —   —   250

Langstaff, Launcelot (Washington Irving, Wm. Irving, and
J. K. Paulding). SALMAGUNDI . . . New York, 1807/8.
20 parts. Bound without wraps. (complex, check BAL)   —   2,500 2,500

Langston, Jane. THE TRANSCENDENTAL MURDER.
New York, 1964   —   —   250

Lanham, Edwin. SAILORS DON'T CARE. Paris, 1929.
10 signed and numbered copies   —   —   650
Wraps. (500 copies)   —   400   400
New York, 1930   —   125   150

Lanier, Sidney. TIGER-LILIES. New York, 1867. First issue:
title page on stub   50   100   500

Larcom, Lucy. SIMILITUDES. Boston, 1854   20   75   125

Lardner, Ring(old Wilmer). ZANZIBAR. Niles, Michigan
(1903). Wraps   200   —   6,000

MARCH SIXTH THE HOMECOMING. (Chicago, 1914). First edition not stated. Issued without dustwrapper	—	—	5,000
BIB BALLADS. Chicago (1915). (500 copies). (More if in orignal box)	100	125	350
Lardner, Ring, Jr. THE YOUNG IMMIGRUNTS. Indianapolis (1920). With a preface by the father	—	150	350
JUNE MOON. New York, 1930. Written with Geo. S. Kaufman	—	150	250
Larkin, Philip. THE NORTH SHIP. London (1945).			
Black cloth	75	600	2,500
Second edition: dark red buckram [1965]	—	—	200
Third edition. Faber. London (1966)	—	—	100
Larner, Jeremy. DRIVE, HE SAID. New York (1964).			
First issue: wraps	20	15	15
Second issue: hardback	—	25	25
LaSpina, Greye. INVADERS FROM THE DARK. Sauk City, 1960	—	—	100
Lathen, Emma (Mary Jane Latsis and Martha Henissart). BANKING ON DEATH. New York, 1961	—	200	400
Latimer, Jonathan (Wyatt). MURDER IN THE MADHOUSE. Garden City, 1935	—	200	400
Latimer, Margery. WE ARE INCREDIBLE. New York (1928)	—	175	250
Lattimore, Richard (Alexander). HANOVER POEMS. New York, 1927. Written with A. K. Laing	40	60	75
Laughlin, Clarence John. NEW ORLEANS AND ITS LIVING PAST. Boston, 1941. Text by David L. Cohen. 1,030 signed copies (in glassine dustwrapper) in slipcase	—	—	600
Laughlin, James. THE RIVER. Norfolk, 1938. Wraps	—	150	150
SOME NATURAL THINGS. Norfolk, 1945	—	75	100
Laurence, Margaret. A TREE FOR POVERTY. Nairobi, 1954. (Somali anthology edited by Laurence). Wraps	—	150	1,250
THIS SIDE OF JORDAN. Toronto, 1960	—	150	300
New York, 1960	—	35	100
Laurents, Arthur. HOME OF THE BRAVE. New York (1946)	20	75	125
Laver, James. CERVANTES . . . Oxford (1921). Wraps	—	50	125

Lavin, Mary. TALES FROM BECTIVE BRIDGE. Boston, 1942.

(999 copies)	—	125	350
London, 1943	—	125	250

Lawrence, D(avid) H(erbert). THE WHITE PEACOCK. New

York, 1911. (Copyright 1910)	2,500	7,000	7,500
New York, 1911. (Copyright 1911). (Precedes English edition by one day)	1,000	2,500	2,000
London, 1911. First issue: publisher's windmill device on back cover; pp. 227–230 tipped in	500	750	1,250
Second issue: pp. 227–230 integral	—	400	500

Lawrence, Hilda. BLOOD UPON THE SNOW.

New York, 1944	—	—	50

Lawrence, T(homas) E(dward) (T. E. Shaw). CARCHEMISH.

London, 1914. (Written with C. L. Woolley)	200	500	850

THE WILDERNESS OF ZIN. (London, 1915). (Written with C. L. Woolley)	150	300	500

SEVEN PILLARS OF WISDOM. (London) 1926. Inscribed "complete" and signed "T. E. S." (170 of 211 copies)	5,000	12,000	40,000
London (1935). (750 copies)	—	750	1,500
New York, 1935. (750 copies)	—	600	1,500

Lawson, Henry. SHORT STORIES IN VERSE AND PROSE.

Sydney, 1894. Wraps	—	—	850

Lax, Robert. THE CIRCUS OF THE SUN. (New York, 1960).

Cloth. 500 signed and numbered copies	—	—	150
Wraps	—	—	50

Layton, Irving. HERE AND NOW. Montreal, 1945. Wraps	—	500	1,500

LAYTON COURT MYSTERY (THE) by "?" (Anthony Berkeley, pseudonym of A. B. Cox). London, 1925	—	400	1,250

Lazarus, Emma. POEMS AND TRANSLATIONS.

New York, 1866	—	150	300

Lea, Homer. THE VERMILLION PENCIL. New York, 1908	25	60	75

Lea, Tom. RANDADO. (El Paso, Texas, 1941). Stiff wraps.

100 signed copies. Wraps	100	3,500	3,500
Cloth (bound later)	—	—	2,250

Leacock, Stephen (Butler). ELEMENTS OF POLITICAL

SCIENCE. Boston, 1906	50	100	150

LITERARY LAPSES . . . Montreal, 1910	100	150	200

Lear, Edward. VIEWS IN ROME AND ITS ENVIRONS.
London, 1841. Folio　　　　　　　　　　　　　— 2,000 4,000

　A BOOK OF NONSENSE. (London) 1846. 2 volumes　　— — 12,500

　Also see DERRY, DERRY DOWN

LEATHER STOCKING AND SILK. (John Esten Cooke).
New York, 1854　　　　　　　　　　　100 200 300

LEAVES OF GRASS. (Walt Whitman). Brooklyn, 1855. First
issue: marbled endpapers, frontis on plain paper, no press
notices　　　　　　　　　　　　　　　— 7,500 35,000
Second issue: yellow endpapers, frontis on plain India
paper, 8 pages of notices　　　　　　　　— 2,500 15,000

Leavis, F. R. MASS CIVILIZATION AND MINORITY CULTURE.
Cambridge, 1930. Wraps　　　　　　　　— 50 75

Leavitt, David. FAMILY DANCING. New York, 1984　— 60 75
　London, 1985　　　　　　　　　　　　— — 75

LeBlanc, Maurice (Marie Emile). THE EXPLOITS OF ARSENE
LUPIN. New York, 1907　　　　　　　　— 50 250

LeCain, Errol. KING ARTHUR'S SWORD. London, 1968　— — 50

Le Carré, John (David John Moore Cornwell). CALL FOR
THE DEAD. London, 1960　　　　　　　25 1,250 3,500
New York, 1962　　　　　　　　　　　— 200 1,000

Le Clezio, M. M. G. THE INTERROGATION. London, 1964　— 25 35

Le Doux, Louis Vernon. SONGS FROM THE SILENT LAND　— — 75

Lee, Andrea. RUSSIAN JOURNAL. New York (1981)　— — 50

Lee, Andrew (Louis Auchincloss). THE INDIFFERENT
CHILDREN. New York (1947)　　　　　40 150 400

Lee, Dennis. THE KINGDOM OF ABSENCE. Toronto (1967).
300 numbered copies. Wraps　　　　　　— 125 200

Lee, George W. BEALE STREET: WHERE THE BLUES BEGAN.
New York, 1934　　　　　　　　　　　— — 300

Lee, Gus. CHINA BOY. New York (1991)　　　　— — 40

Lee, Gypsy Rose (Rose Louise Hovick). THE G-STRING
MURDERS. New York, 1941　　　　　　— 125 175

Lee, Harper. TO KILL A MOCKINGBIRD. Philadelphia (1960).
First issue: dustwrapper photo of author by Truman
Capote. "First Edition" stated　　　　　50 250 2,500
London, 1960　　　　　　　　　　　　30 75 300

Lee, Laurie. THE SUN MY MONUMENT. London, 1944	25	75	75
Garden City, 1947	—	25	40

Lee, Manfred Bennington. *See* Ellery Queen

Lee, Spike. SHE'S GOTTA HAVE IT. New York, 1987. Wraps	—	—	35

Lee, William (William Burroughs). JUNKIE.			
New York (1953). (Ace Double-book). Wraps	35	175	450
London (1957). Wraps	—	—	150
London (1973). First hardback	—	—	150

Le Fanu, Joseph Sheridan. THE COCK AND ANCHOR. Dublin, 1845. 3 volumes	150	350	2,000

Leffland, Ella. MRS. MUNCK. Boston, 1970	—	—	75

Le Gallienne, Richard. MY LADIES' SONNETS.			
(Liverpool, England) 1887. (250 signed copies)	150	300	500
Trade edition	—	100	250
VOLUMES IN FOLIO. London, 1889. (Also first book published by Elkin Mathews). 53 large paper copies	—	250	300
250 regular copies	—	100	150

(Three privately printed books or leaflets preceded)

Legman, G(ershon). ORALGENITALISM. New York, 1940	—	—	400
LOVE & DEATH. (New York) 1949.			
Red cloth	—	150	250
Wraps	—	50	75

Le Grande, Mr. A VOYAGE TO ABYSSINIA BY FATHER JEROME LOBO. London, 1735. (Translated by Samuel Johnson)	—	1,500	1,500

Le Guin, Ursula. ROCANNON'S WORLD. New York (1966). Wraps. Bound dos-a-dos with a novel by A. Davidson	—	60	50
New York, 1975. First hardback. Issued without dustwrapper	—	—	75

Lehmann, John. A GARDEN REVISITED . . . London, 1931. (400 copies)	60	125	175

(1928 broadsheets preceded)

Lehmann, Rosamond (Nina). DUSTY ANSWER. London, 1927	—	125	125

Lehrer, Warren. VERSATIONS . . . Mattapoinset, 1980. 150 signed and numbered copies	—	—	200

Leiber, Fritz (Reuter), Jr. NIGHT'S BLACK AGENTS.			
Sauk City, 1947	50	125	250
London, 1975	—	—	75
Leigh-Fermor, Patrick. THE TRAVELLER'S TREE.			
London, 1950	—	50	125
Leland, Charles (Godfrey). MEISTER KARL'S SKETCH BOOK.			
Philadelphia, 1855	—	100	300
Leland, Jeremy. A RIVER DECREES. London, 1969	—	—	50
LeMay, Alan. PAINTED PONIES. New York (1927)	—	100	200
Lengel, Frances (Alexander Trocchi). THE CARNAL DAYS			
OF HELEN SEFERIS. Paris, 1954. Wraps	35	175	175
L'Engle, Madeleine. THE SMALL RAIN. New York (1945)	—	—	150
Lennon, John. IN HIS OWN WRITE. London, 1964. Issued			
without dustwrapper	—	60	75
Leonard, Elmore. THE BOUNTY HUNTERS. Houghton-			
Mifflin. Boston, 1954	—	300	1,750
Ballantine. New York, 1954. Wraps	—	75	150
Leonard, George. SHOULDER THE SKY. New York (1959)	—	30	30
Leonard, John. THE NAKED MARTINI. New York (1964)	—	35	60
Leonard, William Ellery. BYRON AND BYRONISM IN			
AMERICA. Boston, 1905. Wraps	—	—	150
SONNETS AND POEMS. Boston, 1906	50	75	75
Leopold, Aldo. A SAND COUNTY ALMANAC.			
New York, 1949	—	—	500
Lerman, Rhoda. CALL ME ISHTAR. Garden City, 1973	—	—	30
Leroux, Gaston. THE MYSTERY OF THE YELLOW ROOM.			
London, 1908	—	50	100
Lesley, Craig. WINTER KILL. Boston, 1984	—	—	75
Leslie, David Stuart. THE DEVIL BOAT. London, 1956	—	—	50
Leslie, (Sir John Randolph) Shane. SONGS OF ARIEL.			
Dublin, 1908	30	100	200
Lessing, Doris (May). THE GRASS IS SINGING. London (1950)	50	150	300
New York, 1950	35	75	200
Lester, Julius. TO BE A SLAVE. New York, 1968	—	35	100

THE
DOUBLE
IMAGE

by

DENISE LEVERTOFF

THE CRESSET PRESS
LONDON

THE SON OF THE WOLF

𝕿𝖆𝖑𝖊𝖘 𝖔𝖋 𝖙𝖍𝖊 𝖋𝖆𝖗 𝕹𝖔𝖗𝖙𝖍

BY

JACK LONDON

BOSTON AND NEW YORK
HOUGHTON, MIFFLIN AND COMPANY
𝕿𝖍𝖊 𝕽𝖎𝖛𝖊𝖗𝖘𝖎𝖉𝖊 𝕻𝖗𝖊𝖘𝖘, 𝕮𝖆𝖒𝖇𝖗𝖎𝖉𝖌𝖊
1900

LETTERS FROM AN AMERICAN FARMER. (Michel Crevecoeur). Dublin, 1782. (Two folding maps) — — 2,500
London, 1782. Wraps. (Two folding maps) — 1,000 2,000

Lever, Charles. *See* THE CONFESSIONS OF HARRY LORREQUER

Levertoff, Denise (Levertov). THE DOUBLE IMAGE. London, 1946 125 175 200

Levi, Peter (Chad Tiger). EARTHLY PARADISE. (Privately printed, 1958) — 100 200

THE GRAVEL PONDS. London, 1960 — 75 75

Levi, Primo. IF THIS IS A MAN. New York, 1959. (First English translation) — — 200

Levin, Bernard. THE PENDULUM YEARS. London, 1970 — — 35

Levin, Harry. THE BROKEN COLUMN . . . Cambridge (Mass.), 1931 — 75 75

Levin, Ira. A KISS BEFORE DYING. New York (1953). Issued without endpapers 25 35 125

Levin, Meyer. REPORTER. New York (1929). (Withdrawn by publisher)	40	75	100
Levine, Norman. MYSSIUM. Toronto, 1948	—	—	300
THE ANGLED ROAD. Toronto, 1952. (First novel)	—	—	150
Levine, Paul. TO SPEAK FOR THE DEAD. New York, 1990	—	—	35
Levine, Philip. ON THE EDGE. Iowa City (1961). 220 numbered copies. Issued without dustwrapper	—	250	750
Lewin, Michael Z. HOW TO BEAT COLLEGE TEXTS. New York, 1970	—	—	40
ASK THE RIGHT QUESTIONS. New York, 1971	—	—	75
Lewis, Alfred Henry. WOLFVILLE. New York (1897). First issue: "Moore" in perfect type p. 19:18	60	100	150
Lewis, Aluin. RAIDERS' DAWN . . . London, 1942	—	—	100
Lewis, C. S. See Clive Hamilton			
Lewis, David. END AND BEGINNING. Johannesburg, 1945. Wraps. 50 signed and numbered copies	—	75	125
450 unsigned	—	25	40
Lewis, Ethelreda. THE HARP. New York (1925)	—	75	75
Lewis, Grace Hegger. HALF A LOAF. New York (1931). (Sinclair's wife)	20	60	75
Lewis, Janet. THE INDIANS IN THE WOODS. (Bonn, Germany, 1922). Wraps	40	400	500
Lewis, Matthew Gregory. THE MONK. London, 1796. 3 volumes	—	750	3,500
Lewis, Norman. SEA AND SAND. London, 1938	—	—	200
Lewis, (Harry) Sinclair. See Tom Graham			
OUR MR. WRENN. New York, 1914. First under own name	75	75	200
Lewis, Wyndham. TIMON OF ATHENS. (London, 1913). 16 plates in large portfolio	—	2,000	6,000
THE IDEAL GIANT. London (1917). (200 copies in folder)	250	600	2,000
TARR. New York, 1918. Red cloth	—	250	500
Blue cloth	—	150	300
London, 1918	200	100	300
Lezama Lima, Jose. PARADISO. New York, 1974	—	—	75

Lhomond, M. *See* Henry Wadsworth Longfellow

Lieber, Joel. HOW THE FISHES LIVE. New York, 1967 — 30 30

Lieberman, M. M. MAGGOT AND WORM.
West Branch, 1968 — 40 75

Liebling, A. J. THEY ALL SANG . . . New York, 1934 50 125 350

BACK WHERE I CAME FROM . . . New York (1938) 30 200 500

LIFE OF SCHILLER (THE). (Thomas Carlyle). London, 1825 60 850 250

Lifshin, Lyn (Diane). WHY IS THE HOUSE DISSOLVING? San
Francisco, 1968. Wraps — 40 40

Lightman, Alan. EINSTEIN'S DREAM. New York, 1992 — — 40

Lima, Frank INVENTORY. (New York, 1964). Wraps — 40 40

Lin, Frank (Gertrude Franklin Atherton). WHAT DREAMS
MAY COME. Chicago (1888). Wraps — 300 750
Cloth 50 150 350
London, 1889 50 100 250

Lincoln, Joseph (Crosby). CAPE COD BALLADS.
Trenton, New Jersey, 1902 75 125 150

Lindbergh, Anne Morrow. NORTH TO THE ORIENT.
New York, 1935 — 35 75

Lindbergh, Charles A. WE . . . New York, 1927. 1,100
signed and numbered copies, boxed. 100 for presentation.
Numbered M1–M100? — — 3,000
1,000 numbered copies. numbered 1–1,000 — 800 2,000
Trade. First issue: red buckram with top
edges gilt 15 100 400
Second issue: blue cloth (priority assumed) — — 250

Lindsay, David. A VOYAGE TO ARCTURUS. London (1920).
Red cloth. 8-page catalog at rear 75 1,000 2,000

Lindsay, Jack. FAUNS AND LADIES. Sydney, 1923 — 500 750

Lindsay, Norman. NORMAN LINDSAY'S BOOK NUMBER ONE.
Sydney, 1912. Wraps — — 250
With *Book Number Two*. Sydney, 1915 — — 500

Lindsay, (Nicholas) Vachel. THE TREE OF LAUGHING BELLS.
(New York, 1905). Wraps — 2,000 2,500

A MEMORIAL OF LINCOLN . . . (Springfield, Illinois,
1908/1909) — 500 750

THE TRAMP'S EXCUSE . . . (Springfield, Illinois, 1909).
Wraps   400   1,500   1,500

GENERAL WM BOOTH ENTERS INTO HEAVEN . . .
New York, 1913   35   75   100

Linebarger, Paul (Myron Anthony). GOSPEL OF CHUNG SHAN.
  Paris, 1932. Edited with introduction and
  comments by Linebarger.   —   —   250

THE POLITICAL DOCRINE OF SUN YAT-SEN.
Baltimore, 1937   —   —   150

Also see Felix C. Forrest. (Best known as Cordwainer
Smith)

LINES ON LEAVING THE BEDFORD STREET SCHOOLHOUSE.
  (George Santayana). (Boston, 1880). 4 pages.
  Wraps   750   750   750

Lion & Unicorn Press. PREFACE TO THE MANUALE
  TIPOGRAFICO OF 1818. London (1953). 60 copies   —   100   150

Lippard, George. ADRIAN, THE NEOPHYTE . . .
  Philadelphia, 1843. Wraps   —   75   75

Lippmann, Walter. A PREFACE TO POLITICS. New York,
  1913   25   50   75

(Previous translations)

Litvinoff, Emanuel. CONSCRIPTS. London, 1941.
  Wraps   —   75   75

Lively, Penelope. ASTERCOTE. London, 1970   —   —   150

Livesay, Dorothy. GREEN PITCHER. Toronto, 1928.
  (200 copies)   —   —   750

Livingstone, David. *See* A NARRATIVE . . .

Llewellyn, Richard (Richard David Vivian Llewellyn Lloyd).
  HOW GREEN WAS MY VALLEY. London (1939).
  200 signed and numbered copies in slipcase   —   250   400
  Trade edition   —   100   125
  New York, 1940   —   75   75

Lobo, Father Jerome. *See* Mr. Le Grande

Locke, David Ross. *See* PETROLEUM V. NASBY

Locker, Frederick. LONDON LYRICS. London, 1857	—	250	300
Lockridge, Richard. MR. AND MRS. NORTH. New York, 1936	—	75	350
Lockridge, Richard and Frances. THE NORTHS MEET MURDER. New York, 1940	—	150	450
Lockridge, Ross. RAINTREE COUNTY. Boston, 1948	—	75	125
London (1949)	50	50	100
Lodge, David. THE PICTUREGOERS. London, 1960	—	275	350
Lodge, George Cabot. THE SONG OF THE WAVE. New York, 1898	—	50	75
Loeb, Harold (Albert). DOODAB. New York, 1925	—	125	125
Loewinsohn, Ron(ald William). WATERMELONS. New York, 1959. Wraps. (1,000 copies)	15	35	40
Lofting, Hugh. THE STORY OF DOCTOR DOOLITTLE. New York, 1920	50	200	1,250
Lofts, Norah. I MET A GYPSY. New York, 1936. (250 numbered copies in dustwrapper and slipcase)	—	40	75
Logan, John. CYCLE FOR MOTHER CABRINI. New York (1955). 30 signed and numbered copies with signed wood block	—	200	250
250 signed and numbered copies	35	125	125
Hardcover copy of trade edition for review	—	—	75
Trade edition. Wraps	—	30	40
Logue, Christopher. WAND AND QUADRANT. Paris, 1953. Wraps. 300 numbered copies	30	125	150
300 unnumbered	25	75	75
London, Jack (John Griffith). THE SON OF THE WOLF. Boston, 1909. Belt stamped in silver on cover. First issue: 8 preliminary unnumbered pages (i–viii)	150	500	1,500
Second issue: 6 preliminary unnumbered pages (i–vi)	—	400	1,000
Long, Frank Belnap. A MAN FROM GENOA . . . Athol, 1926	—	750	850
Long, Haniel. POEMS. New York, 1920	15	500	500
Longfellow, Henry Wadsworth. ELEMENTS OF FRENCH GRAMMAR. By M. Lhomond. Portland, 1830. (HWL translated anonymously)	—	250	250
FRENCH EXERCISES. By M. Lhomond. Portland, 1830. (HWL translated)	—	250	250

EXERCISES AND ELEMENTS . . . Bound as one volume in 1830. (Represents first book to bear HWL's name)	—	350	350

Also see OUTRE-MER

Longfellow, Samuel. THE WORD PREACHED . . . New York, 1853. Wraps	—	75	75
Longstreet, Augustus Baldwin. AN ORATION . . . (Augusta, 1831). Wraps	750	3,500	3,500
Re-bound	—	—	2,000

Also see GEORGIA SCENES . . .

Loos, Anita. HOW TO WRITE PHOTOPLAYS. New York, 1920. Written with W. J. Emerson	—	200	400
BREAKING INTO THE MOVIES. New York (1921). Written with W. J. Emerson	—	200	350
GENTLEMEN PREFER BLONDES. New York, 1925. First issue: incorrect spelling on contents page; chapter 4 "Divine" for "Devine"	35	175	350
Lopez, Barry. DESERT NOTES. Kansas City (1976)	—	—	250
Lorde, Audre. THE FIRST CITIES. New York (1968). Wraps	—	20	100

Lothrop, Harriet (Mulford Stone). *See* Margaret Sidney

Lovecraft, H. P. *See* Jonathan E. Hoag

THE SHUNNED HOUSE. Athol, Mass., 1928. (Bound by Paul Cook, about 8 copies)	2,500	3,500	10,000
Unbound folded signatures. (Derleth sold about 50 sets. The rest were used on Arkham House edition)	—	1,500	2,500
Various bindings of sheets between 1928-1963	2,000	1,500	2,500
Arkham House. Sauk City, Wisc., 1963. (100 copies) in plain brown dustwrapper	500	1,250	4,500

(At least four pamphlets/offprints precede)

LOVE EPISTLES OF ARISTAENETUS, THE. (Richard Sheridan, co-translator). London, 1771	—	600	1,250

Lovell, Robert. *See* Robert Southey

Lovesey, Peter. WOBBLE TO DEATH. London, 1970	—	40	200
New York (1970)	—	—	100

Lowell, Amy. *See* DREAM DROPS . . . BY A DREAMER

A DOME OF MANY-COLORED GLASS. Boston, 1912	40	300	400

Lowell, James Russell. *See* CLASS POEM

    A YEAR'S LIFE. Boston, 1841. (With or without errata)   150   225   300

Lowell, Robert. THE LAND OF UNLIKENESS. (Cunningham,
    Mass.) 1944. 26 signed and numbered copies   2,500 7,500 7,500
    224 copies   2,000 3,000 3,000

    LORD WEARY'S CASTLE. New York (1946)   —   300   300

Lowenfels, Walter. *See* W. L.

Lowndes, Marie Belloc. THE PHILOSOPHY OF THE
    MARQUISE. London, 1899   —   75   75

Lowry, Beverly. COME BACK, LOLLY RAY.
    Garden City, 1977   —   —   100

Lowry, Malcolm. ULTRAMARINE. London, 1933   1,000 5,000 6,500
    Revised edition. Philadelphia, 1962   —   75   150
    London (1963)   —   50   100
    Toronto (1963)   —   50   100

Lowry, Robert. MURDER PIE. Cincinnati, 1939. Wraps   —   —   150

    TRIP TO BLOOMIN' MOON. Cincinnati, 1939. Wraps.   —   —   150

    (Priority uncertain)

Lowther, Pat. THIS DIFFICULT FLOWERING.
    Vancouver, 1968. Wraps   —   —   40

Loy, Mina. SONGS TO JOANNES. New York, 1917. Wraps.
    (April issue of *Others* magazine)   125   300   300

    LUNAR BAEDECKER. (Paris, 1923). Wraps   100   750   750

Lubschez, Ben Judah. MANHATTAN . . . New York, 1927   —   —   400

Lucas, E. V. *See* E. V. L.

Lucie-Smith, (John) Edward (McKenzie). (POEMS). Fantasy
    Press. Oxford, 1954. Wraps   —   125   125

Ludlow, Fitz-Hugh. *See* THE HASHEESH EATER

Ludlum, Robert. THE SCARLATTI INHERITANCE. New York
    (1971). Printed acetate dustwrapper   —   75   250
    London (1971)   —   60   125
    New York, 1990. 26 signed and lettered copies   —   —   150
    100 signed and numbered copies   —   —   75

Luhan, Mabel Dodge. LORENZO IN TAOS. New York, 1932   —   200   300

Lumley, Brian. THE CALLER OF THE BLACK. 　　Sauk City, 1971	—	—	50
Lumpkin, Grace. TO MAKE MY BREAD. New York (1932)	35	75	75
Lunn, Hugh (Hugh Kingsmill). THE WILL TO LOVE. 　　London, 1919	50	50	75
Lurie, Alison. V. R. LANG. Munich (1959). (300 copies). 　　Wraps. (Edw. Gorey cover)	—	175	250
Luska, Sidney (Henry Harland). AS IT IS WRITTEN. 　　New York (1885)	—	150	150
Lustgarten, Edgar (Marcus). A CASE TO ANSWER. 　　London, 1947	—	35	75
ONE MORE UNFORTUNATE. New York, 1947. 　　(New title)	—	25	50
Lyall, Gavin. THE WRONG SIDE OF THE SKY. 　　New York, 1961	—	35	50
Lyon, Harris Merton. SARDONICS: SIXTEEN SKETCHES. 　　New York, 1909	—	125	150
Lyons, Arthur. THE SECOND COMING: SATANISM IN 　　AMERICA. New York (1970)	—	50	200
THE DEAD ARE DISCREET. New York (1974)	—	—	300
Lytle, Andrew (Nelson). BEDFORD FORREST AND HIS 　　CRITTER COMPANY. Minton Balch. New York, 1931 　　Putnam. New York (1931).	75 —	350 125	600 200
Lytton, David. THE GODDAM WHITE MAN. London, 1960	—	30	40

M

M., E. H. W. (E. H. W. Meyerstein). THE DOOR. 　　Oxford/London, 1911. Wraps	—	40	40
Maas, Willard. FIRE TESTAMENT. New York, 1935. Wraps. 　　135 signed and numbered copies	50	75	100
Mabie, Hamilton Wright. NORSE STORIES RETOLD . . . 　　Boston, 1882	—	75	125
McAlmon, Robert. EXPLORATIONS. London, 1921. Issued 　　without dustwrapper	200	750	1,000
MacArthur, Charles G. (Private). A BUG'S-EYE VIEW OF THE 　　WAR. (No-place) 1919	—	—	125

MacArthur, Douglas. MILITARY DEMOLITIONS. (Fort Leavenworth, 1909)	—	—	600
Macauley, Robie. THE DISGUISES OF LOVE. New York (1952)	—	—	75
Macaulay, Rose. ABBOTS VERNEY. London, 1906	—	100	100
Macaulay, Thomas Babington. POMPEII, A POEM . . . (Cambridge, 1819)	—	250	350
MacBeth, George. A FORM OF WORDS. Oxford, 1954. (150 copies)	—	125	150
McCaffrey, Anne. RESTOREE. New York (1967). Wraps	—	—	35
London (1968)	—	—	150
MacCaig, Norman. FAR CRY. London, 1943. Wraps	—	—	100
McCammon, Robert R. BAAL. New York (1978). Wraps	—	—	50
Bath, 1985	—	—	400
McCarry, Charles. CITIZEN NADER. New York, 1972	—	40	100
THE MIERNICK DOSSIER. New York (1973)	—	50	100
McCarthy, Cormac. THE ORCHARD KEEPER. New York (1965)	15	75	2,000
(London, 1966)	—	50	1,000
MacCarthy, Desmond. THE COURT THEATRE 1904–1907. London, 1907	40	100	150
McCarthy, Mary (Therese). *See* H. V. Kaltenborn			
THE COMPANY SHE KEEPS. (New York) 1942	50	125	150
London, 1943	—	75	75
McClanahan, Ed. THE NATURAL MAN. New York, 1983	—	20	30
McClure, James. THE STEAM PIG. London, 1971	—	30	150
New York (1971)	—	25	75
McClure, Michael. PASSAGE. Big Sur, 1956. Stiff wraps. (200 copies)	75	450	500
McCluskey, John. LOOK WHAT THEY DONE TO MY SONG. New York, 1974	—	—	75
McCord, David (Thompson Watson). ODDLY ENOUGH. Cambridge (Eng.), 1926	25	40	75
McCord, Howard. PRECISE FRAGMENTS. Dublin, 1963. Wraps. (250 copies)	—	40	75

McCorkle, Jill. THE CHEER LEADER. (Chapel Hill, 1984) — — 150

JULY 7TH. (Chapel Hill, 1984). (Published simultaneously) — — 150

McCourt, James. MAWRDEW CZGOWCHWZ.
New York (1975) — — 50

McCoy, Horace. THEY SHOOT HORSES, DON'T THEY.
New York, 1935 50 300 450

McCrum, Robert. IN THE SECRET STATE. London, 1980 — — 50

McCrum, Sharyn. SICK OF SHADOWS. New York (1984).
Wraps — — 40

McCullers, (Lula) Carson. THE HEART IS A LONELY
HUNTER. Boston, 1940 75 350 750
London, 1943 35 200 250

McCullough, Colleen. TIM. New York (1974) — 50 125

McCutcheon, George Barr. GRAUSTARK. Chicago, 1901.
First issue: "Noble" for "Lorry" p. 150:6 35 75 100

McDermott, Alice. A BIGAMIST'S DAUGHTER.
New York (1982) — — 75

MacDiarmid, Hugh. SANGSCHAW. Edinburgh, 1925 — — 350

MacDonagh, Donagh. TWENTY POEMS. Dublin, 1934.
Wraps. (Written with Niall Sheridan) — — 200

VETERANS . . . Cuala Press. Dublin, 1941. (270 copies) 75 250 250

MacDonald, George. WITHIN AND WITHOUT . . .
London, 1855	30	300	3,500
New York, 1872	—	—	350

Mcdonald, Gregory. RUNNING SCARED. New York (1964)   —   —   60

McDonald, John D(ann). THE BRASS CUPCAKE.
New York, 1950. Wraps	—	50	75
London, 1974. First hardback edition	—	—	100

WINE OF THE DREAMER. New York (1951). First U.S.
hardback   —   100   200

MacDonald, Philip. *See* Oliver Fleming

MacDonald, Ross. *See* Kenneth Millar

McElroy, Joseph. A SMUGGLER'S BIBLE. New York (1966)	—	150	250
London (1968)	—	—	150

MacEwan, Gwendolyn. SELAH. Toronto, 1961   —   —   1,200

McEwan, Ian. FIRST LOVE, LAST RITES. London (1975)	—	75	350
New York (1975)	—	25	75

McFadden, Roy. SWORDS AND PLOUGHSHARES.
London (1943)   —   —   100

MacFall, Haldane. THE WOOINGS OF JEZEBEL PETTYFER.
London, 1898. First issue: picture of Jezebel front cover   100   150   300

THE HOUSE OF THE SORCERER. Boston, 1900.
(New title)   75   100   175

McFarland, Dennis. THE MUSIC ROOM. Boston, 1990   —   —   60

McFee, William (Morley Dunshon). LETTERS FROM AN
OCEAN TRAMP. London, 1908. First issue: "Cassell &
Co." on spine   100   125   200

McGahern, John. THE BARRACKS. London, 1963	—	—	500
New York, 1964	—	—	100

McGinley, Patrick. BOGMAIL. London, 1978   —   40   75
New York, 1981. First issue: Priced $9.95. Joan Kahn
comment on back   —   —   50
Second issue: Priced $10.95. Review on back   —   —   35

McGinley, Phyllis. ON THE CONTRARY. New York, 1934   25   100   150

McGivern, William P(eter). BUT DEATH RUNS FASTER.
New York, 1948   —   35   75

McGovan, James (William C. Honeyman). BROUGHT TO
BAY. Edinburgh, 1878   —   100   200

MacGrath, Harold. ARMS AND THE WOMAN.
New York, 1899   —   40   40

    THE PUPPET CROWN. Indianapolis, 1901   —   —   30

McGrath, Patrick. BLOOD AND WATER AND OTHER TALES.
New York, 1988   —   —   50

McGreevy, Thomas. INTRODUCTION TO . . . DA VINCI.
London, 1929. 875 numbered copies. McGreevy's
translation of Valéry's work   —   75   100

    THOMAS STEARNS ELIOT. London, 1931   —   60   75

McGuane, Thomas. THE SPORTING CLUB. New York (1968)   20   75   200
(London, 1969)   —   60   100

McHale, Tom. PRINCIPATO. New York (1970)   —   25   40

MacHarg, William (Briggs). THE ACHIEVEMENTS OF
LUTHER TRANT. Boston (1910). (Written with
E. Balmer)   —   100   150

Machen, Arthur. ELEUSINIA. Hereford, 1881. Wraps. (One
known copy)   3,000   10,000   15,000

    Also see Leolinus Siluriensis

McIlvanney, William. REMEDY IS NONE. London (1966)   —   —   150

McInerney, Jay. BRIGHT LIGHTS, BIG CITY. New York
(1984). Wraps   —   35   50
London, 1985. First hardback   —   50   100

MacInnes, Colin. TO THE VICTOR THE SPOILS.
London (1950)   —   100   175

MacInnes, Helen. ABOVE SUSPICION. Boston, 1941   —   50   75

    (Two previous translations)

McKay, Claude. SONGS OF JAMAICA. Kingston, Jamaica,
1912. Stiff wraps   600   1,500   3,000

    SPRING IN NEW HAMPSHIRE . . . London (1920).
Wraps. (Third book)   200   400   1,500

MacKay, Sheena. TODDLER ON THE RUN . . .
London, 1964   —   —   125

MacKaye, Percy (Wallace). JOHNNY CRIMSON. Boston, 1895.
Wraps. (50 copies)   100   300   350
Trade edition   —   —   150

MacKaye Brown, George. THE STORM . . . (No-place) 1954. Wraps	—	—	500
McKenna, Richard. THE SAND PEBBLES. New York (1962)	—	25	125
McKenna, Stephen. THE RELUCTANT LOVER. London, 1913	—	100	200
MacKenzie, (Montague) Compton. POEMS. Oxford, 1907. Wraps	50	150	250
McKinley, Georgia. THE MIGHTY DISTANCE. Boston, 1965	—	40	40
McKuen, Rod. AND AUTUMN CAME. New York (1954)	50	90	150
MacLaine, Christopher. THE CRAZY BIRD. (San Francisco) 1951. Boards. 100 numbered copies	—	75	75
MacLane, Mary. THE STORY OF MARY MACLANE BY HERSELF. Chicago, 1902	—	50	100
MacLaren, Ross J. THE STUFF TO GIVE THE TROOPS. London, 1944	—	75	75
MacLaverty, Bernard. SECRETS . . . Belfast, 1977	—	—	100
McLaverty, Michael. LOST FIELDS. London, 1942	—	35	60
MacLean, Alistair. H. M. S. ULYSSES. London, 1955	—	40	75
Garden City, 1956	—	—	50
MacLean, Norman. A RIVER RUNS THROUGH IT. Chicago (1976)	—	75	1,250
Chicago (1983). 500 signed and numbered copies	—	—	750
West Hatfield (1989). 200 signed and numbered copies. Issued without dustwrapper	—	—	750
London, 1990	—	—	50
MacLeish, Archibald. CLASS POEM. (New Hampshire) 1915. (4-page leaflet)	2,500	2,500	2,500
SONGS FOR A SUMMER DAY. (New Hampshire) 1915. Wraps	500	500	500
TOWER OF IVORY. New Hampshire, 1917. (750 copies)	—	150	150
MacLennan, Hugh. OXYRHYNEHUS: AN ECONOMIC & SOCIAL STUDY. Princeton University Press. Princeton, 1935. First book under this name	—	—	1,200
MacLeod, Charlotte. REST YOU MERRY. Bath, New Brunswick, 1978	—	—	300
MacLeod, Fiona (William Sharp). PHARAIS. Derby, 1894. (75 signed and numbered copies)	—	200	200

MacLeod, Joseph (Todd Gordon). BEAUTY AND THE BEAST. London, 1927	—	75	75
THE ECLIPTIC. London, 1930. Wraps	—	50	50
MacLeod, Norman. HORIZONS OF DEATH. New York, 1934. Wraps. 100 signed and numbered copies	—	125	250
263 numbered copies	—	50	150
MacLow, Jackson. THE PRONOUNS. (Bronx, 1964). Stapled mimeographed sheets	—	—	60
McLuhan, (Herbert) Marshall. FOOTPRINTS IN THE SAND OF CRIME. 1946. *Sewanee Review* offprint. Stapled wraps?	—	—	1,000
THE MECHANICAL BRIDE. New York (1951). Reprinted in "Limited Edition" (1973) according to dustwrapper but book itself does not indicate. (Differences between first edition and "Limited Edition": $4.50 vs $12.50; white endpaper vs yellow; and white cover lettering vs gold)	60	75	175
London, 1967	—	—	50
McMahon, Thomas. PRINCIPLES OF AMERICAN NUCLEAR CHEMISTRY: A NOVEL. Boston (1970)	—	—	60
McManus, Kay. RAVEN . . . Leeds (1966)	—	25	60
LISTEN AND I'LL TALK. (London, 1969)	—	25	40
McMillan, Terry. MAMA. Boston, 1987	—	—	300
McMurtrie, Douglas C(rawford). THE DISABLED SOLDIER. New York, 1919	—	40	300
(Previous pamphlets)			
McMurtry, Larry (Jeff). HORSEMAN, PASS BY. New York (1961)	150	500	1,750
MacNamara, Brinsley. THE VALLEY OF THE SQUINTING WINDOWS. Dublin, 1918	25	75	125
MacNeice, (Frederick) Louis. BLIND FIREWORKS. London, 1929. First issue: light gray cloth	150	400	1,000
McNeile, H(erman) C(yril) (Sapper). THE LIEUTENANT AND OTHERS. London, 1915	—	100	150
McNichols, Charles L. CRAZY WEATHER. New York, 1943	—	—	150
McNight, Reginald. 'MOUSTAPHA'S ECLIPSE.' Pittsburgh, 1988	—	—	50
McNulty, John. THIRD AVENUE, NEW YORK. Boston, 1946	—	—	75

McPhee, John. A SENSE OF WHERE YOU ARE.
New York (1965) — 150 500

McPherson, James A. HUE AND CRY. Boston (1969) — 40 250
(London, 1969) — — 125

MacPherson, Jay. NINETEEN POEMS. Mallorca, 1952. Wraps — — 650

McPherson, Sandra. ELEGIES FOR THE HOT SEASON.
Bloomington (1970) — — 75

McPherson, William. TESTING THE CURRENT. New York
(1984) — 25 35

MacSweeney, Barry. THE BOY FROM THE GREEN
CABARET . . . Sussex, 1967. (100 copies) — 40 60

McTaggart, John. STUDIES IN THE HEGELIAN DIALECTIC.
Cambridge, 1896 — — 150

Madden, David. THE BEAUTIFUL GREED. New York (1961) — 50 75

Madge, Charles. THE DISAPPEARING CASTLE. London (1937) 25 40 40

Magee, David. JAM TOMORROW. Boston, 1941 — 60 100

Magowan, Robin. IN THE WASH. Mallorca, 1958. Wraps — 35 75

Mahan, A. T. THE NAVY IN THE CIVIL WAR.
New York, 1883 75 125 350

Mahon, Derek. TWELVE POEMS. Belfast (no-date[1965]).
Wraps — — 600

Mailer, Norman. THE NAKED AND THE DEAD.
New York (1948) 75 250 750
London (1949). (240 copies) 125 400 600
London, 1949. Trade edition 35 150 150

(Preceded by *The Foundation.* Privately printed
mimeographed sheets)

Mainwaring, Daniel (Geoffrey Homes). ONE AGAINST THE
EARTH. New York, 1933 — — 300

Maitland, Margaret (Margaret Oliphant). PASSAGES IN THE
LIFE OF . . . London, 1849. 3 volumes — 350 450

Major, Charles. *See* Edwin Caskoden

Malamud, Bernard. THE NATURAL. New York (1952). Red,
blue, or gray cloth. (Priority uncertain, although 2 review
copies been seen in gray. Author's copy was blue) 75 250 1,250
London, 1963. (Glossary added) — 75 300

THE WOOINGS OF
JEZEBEL PETTYFER

Being the personal history of Jehu
Sennacherib Dyle, commonly called
Masheen Dyle ; together with an
account of certain things that chanced
in the House of the Sorcerer ;
here set down

by
HALDANE MACFALL

LONDON
GRANT RICHARDS
9 HENRIETTA STREET, COVENT GARDEN, W.C.
1898

LIZA
OF LAMBETH

BY

William Somerset Maugham

LONDON
T. FISHER UNWIN
Paternoster Square
1897

Malanga, Gerard. 3 POEMS FOR BENEDETTA BARZINI. (New York, 1967). Wraps. (500 copies)	—	75	75
Malcolm X. THE AUTOBIOGRAPHY OF MALCOLM X. New York (1965). (Written with Alex Haley)	35	75	850
Mallea, Eduardo. THE BAY OF SILENCE. New York, 1944. First book in English	—	—	75
Malone, Michael. PAINTING THE ROSES RED. New York, 1974	—	—	125
Malouf, David. BICYCLE AND OTHER POEMS. St. Lucia (1970). Wraps	—	—	300
THE YEAR OF THE FOX . . . New York, 1979. (New title)	—	—	75
Malraux, André. THE CONQUERORS. London, 1929	—	75	300
Maltz, Albert. PEACE ON EARTH. French. New York, 1934. Wraps. Written with George Sklar	—	—	125
BLACK PIT. New York, 1935. (First solely authored book)	—	100	175

Mamet, David. AMERICAN BUFFALO. New York (1977).
Wraps	—	40	75
New York (1978). Cloth	—	50	150
San Francisco, 1992. 400 signed and numbered copies	—	—	350

Manchester, William. DISTURBER OF THE PEACE.
New York (1951).	—	40	75
THE SAGE OF BALTIMORE. London (1952). (New title)	—	35	60

Mandel, Eli Fuseli. POEMS. Toronto (1960). 250 copies.
Wraps	—	—	300

Manfred, Frederick (Feikema). *See* Feike Feikema

Manhood, H. A. NIGHTSEED. London, 1928	—	50	60
Mann, Horace. LECTURES ON EDUCATION. Boston, 1845	—	300	300

(Preceded by a number of pamphlets)

Mann, Thomas. ROYAL HIGHNESS. New York, 1916. (First
English translation)	—	75	200
Mannes, Myra. MESSAGE FROM A STRANGER. London, 1948	—	25	25
Manning, Frederic. THE VIGIL OF BRUNHILD. London, 1907	50	75	125
Manning, Olivia. THE WIND CHANGES. London, 1937	—	—	150
Mano, D. Keith. BISHOP'S PROGRESS. Boston, 1968	40	40	60

Mansfield, Katherine. IN A GERMAN PENSION. London
(1911). (500 copies)	250	500	1,500

March, Joseph Moncure. THE SET-UP. New York, 1928.
(275 copies)	20	60	75

March, William (Wm. Edw. March Campbell). COMPANY K.
New York, 1933. Issued in clear dustwrapper with
printed paper flaps	30	300	300

Marcus, Frank. THE KILLING OF SISTER GEORGE.
London, 1965	—	60	60

MARGARET PERCIVAL IN AMERICA. (Edw. Everett Hale).
Boston, 1850	—	100	175
Marius, Richard. THE COMING OF RAIN. New York, 1969	—	—	60

Marjoram, J. (Ralph H. Mottram). REPOSE . . .
London, 1907. Wraps	50	125	125

Markfield, Wallace (Arthur). TO AN EARLY GRAVE.
New York, 1964	15	40	50

Markham, Beryl. WEST WITH THE NIGHT. Boston, 1942   —   —   500
    London (1943)   —   —   350

Markham, (Charles) Edwin. THE MAN WITH THE HOE . . .
    Appeared as supplement to *San Francisco Examiner.*
    4 pages   150   250   350
    San Francisco, 1899. Wraps   100   125   250
    New York, 1899. Second edition. First issue: "fruitless"
    p. 35:5   50   75   75

Marks, J. (Jamake Highwater). ROCK & OTHER FOUR
    LETTER WORDS. New York, 1968. Wraps   —   —   60

Markson, David. EPITAPH FOR A TRAMP. (New York, 1959).
    Wraps   15   20   35

    (Edited two books previously as Mark Merrill)

Markus, Julia. LA MORA. Washington (1976). Wraps.
    (1,000 copies)   —   25   30

Marlowe, Derek. A DANDY IN ASPIC. London, 1966   —   —   75
    New York (1966)   —   25   40

Marquand, John Philips. *See* Charles E. Clark

    THE UNSPEAKABLE GENTLEMEN. New York, 1922. First
    issue: Scribner's seal on copyright page   40   150   300
    Second issue: Scribner's seal on copyright page. Note to
    ABA members signed by Marquand tipped in. Gray
    buckram spine and dark gray boards with ABA label on
    front   —   —   75

Marquis, Don(ald Robert Perry). DANNY'S OWN STORY.
    Garden City, 1912   40   75   75

Marryat, Frederick. A CODE OF SIGNALS FOR USE OF
    VESSELS . . . London, 1818   —   250   250

    THE NAVAL OFFICER . . . London, 1829. 3 volumes   —   300   350

Marsh, (Dame Edith) Ngaio. A MAN LAY DEAD.
    London, 1934   —   250   500

Marsh, Patrick. BREAKDOWN. New York, 1953   —   25   25

Marsh, Willard. WEEK WITH NO FRIDAY.
    New York (1965)   —   40   40

Marshall, Paule. BROWN GIRL, BROWNSTONES.
    New York, 1959   40   150   600

Mars-Jones, Adam. LANTERN LECTURE . . . London, 1981	—	—	50
Marston, Philip. SONG TIDE . . . London, 1871	60	100	250
Martin, George V(ictor). FOR OUR VINES HAVE TENDER GRAPES. New York (1940)	—	—	50
Martin, Peter. THE LANDSMAN. Boston (1952)	—	—	50
Martin, Steve. CRUEL SHOES. Los Angeles, 1977. Issued without dustwrapper. 750 numbered copies	—	40	50
Marvel, Ik. (Donald Grant Mitchell). FRESH GLEANINGS . . . New York, 1847. 2 volumes. Wraps	—	100	125
1 volume. Cloth	—	50	75
Marx, Groucho. BEDS. New York, 1930. (Has publisher's colophon on copyright page)	—	125	650
Marx, Harpo. HARPO SPEAKS. New York, 1961	—	—	100
Marx, Karl. CAPITAL: A CRITICAL ANALYSIS . . . London, 1887. 2 volumes	—	—	3,000
New York, 1889	—	—	2,000
MARY BARTON: A TALE OF MANCHESTER LIFE. (Elizabeth C. Gaskell). London, 1848. 2 volumes	250	500	1,250
Masefield, John. SALT WATER BALLADS. London, 1902. First issue: "Grant Richards" on title page	300	500	600
Second issue: "Elkin Mathews" on title page	—	350	350
Mason, A(lfred) E(dward) W(oodley). BLANCHE DE MALETROIT. London, 1894. (Adapted from Robert Louis Stevenson's work)	—	40	100
A ROMANCE OF THE WASTE-LAND. London (1895)	50	75	150
Mason, Bobbie Ann. NABOKOV'S GARDEN. Ann Arbor (1974). (Precedes *The Girl Sleuth* although dust-wrapper implies otherwise). Cloth	—	100	250
Wraps	—	—	75
Mason, (Francis) Van Wyck. SEEDS OF MURDER. New York, 1930	—	—	300
Massey, T. Gerald. VOICE OF FREEDOM AND LYRICS OF LOVE. London, 1851	35	125	250
Massie, Alan. CHANGE AND DECAY IN ALL AROUND I SEE. London, 1978	—	—	60

Masson, David I. THE CALTRAPS OF TIME. London (1968)	—	—	150
Masters, Anthony. A POCKETFUL OF RYE. London, 1964	—	35	40
Masters, Edgar Lee. A BOOK OF VERSES. Chicago, 1898	125	200	750
Masters, Hilary. THE COMMON PASTURE. New York (1967)	—	35	35
Masters, John. COMPLEAT INDIAN ANGLER. London, 1938	—	100	200
NIGHTRUNNERS OF BENGAL. New York, 1951	—	50	75
Mather, Increase. THE MYSTERY OF ISRAEL'S SALVATION. (London) 1669	—	3,000	6,000
Matheson, Richard. SOMEONE IS BLEEDING. New York (1953). Wraps	—	100	150
BORN OF MAN AND WOMAN. Philadelphia, 1954. (First hardback, third book)	30	150	400
Mathews, Elkin, Publisher. *See* Richard Le Gallienne			
Mathews, Jack (John Harold). BITTER KNOWLEDGE. New York (1964)	—	35	40
Matthews, Harry. THE CONVERSIONS. New York (1962)	—	60	75
Matthews, T. S. TO THE GALLOWS I MUST GO. New York, 1931	—	—	100
Matthiessen, Peter. RACE ROCK. New York (1954)	—	100	300
London, 1954	—	100	175
Maugham, Robin. THE 1946 MS. London, 1943	—	125	150
Maugham, W(illiam) Somerset. LIZA OF LAMBETH. London, 1897. First issue: Brackets around "All Rights Reserved" on copyright page. (2,000 copies)	300	600	1,250
Second issue	—	—	750
London, 1947. 1,000 signed and numbered copies	—	—	300
Mauldin, Bill (William Henry). STAR SPANGLED BANTER. San Antonio, Texas, 1941. Wraps	35	125	200
Maurois, André. THE SILENCE OF COLONEL BRAMBLE. London, 1919	—	40	60
New York, 1920	—	150	150
Maxwell, Gavin. HARPOON AT A VENTURE. London, 1952	—	60	60
Maxwell, Gilbert. LOOK TO THE LIGHTNING. New York, 1933	—	50	75
Maxwell, William. BRIGHT CENTER OF HEAVEN. New York, 1934	—	250	750

May, Elaine. A MATTER OF POSITION. New York, 1962.
Mimeographed sheets in folder   —   —   175

     NOT ENOUGH ROPE. New York (1964). Wraps   —   —   75

Mayer, Tom. BUBBLE GUM AND KIPLING. New York, 1964   —   35   75

Mayfield, Julian. THE HIT. New York (1957)   15   40   75

Mayhall, Jane. COUSIN TO HUMAN. New York (1960)   —   —   60

Mayne, William. FOLLOW THE FOOTPRINTS. London, 1953   —   —   150

Mayo, E(dward) L(eslie). THE DIVER. Minneapolis (1947)   —   50   50

Meacham, Ellis K. THE EAST INDIAMAN. Boston (1968)   —   —   50

Mead, Harold. THE BRIGHT PHOENIX. (New York, 1956).
Cloth   —   75   75
Wraps   —   15   15

Mead, Margaret. COMING OF AGE IN SAMOA. London, 1929   —   —   250

Meagher, Maude. WHITE JADE. Boston, 1930   —   50   75

Mehta, Ved. FACE TO FACE. Boston (1957)   —   —   50

Melanter (R. D. Blackmore). POEMS. London, 1854   —   600   750

Meltzer, David. POEMS. (San Francisco, 1957). (Written with
D. Schenker). 25 signed copies. Cloth   50   150   250
5 signed copies. Cloth. Bloodstained copies   100   250   400
Wraps. (470 copies)   20   75   75

     RAGAS. San Francisco, 1959. Wraps. (1,500 copies)   —   30   50

Melville, Herman. NARRATIVE OF A FOUR MONTH . . .
London, 1846. First issue: "Pomarea" on p. 19:1.
2 volumes in original wraps   2,000   5,000   15,000
1 volume. In original red cloth   2,000   2,000   3,000
Second issue: "Pomare" on p. 19.1   —   1,000   1,500

     TYPEE: A PEEP AT POLYNESIAN LIFE. New York, 1846.
2 volumes in wraps   1,000   3,000   8,500
1 volume: blue or brown cloth   1,000   1,500   2,500

Mencken, H(enry) L(ouis). VENTURES INTO VERSE.
Baltimore, 1903. Two issues, bound in boards   2,500   4,000   7,500
Wraps. (100 copies in total)   2,500   4,000   5,000

     GEORGE BERNARD SHAW. Boston, 1903. (noted at 7 3/4"
tall and 7 7/8"; priority unknown)   —   175   350

Menen, (Salvator) Aubrey. THE PREVALENCE OF WITCHES.
London, 1947   —   50   50

NARRATIVE

OF A

FOUR MONTHS' RESIDENCE

AMONG THE NATIVES OF A VALLEY OF

THE MARQUESAS ISLANDS;

OR,

A PEEP AT POLYNESIAN LIFE.

By HERMAN MELVILLE.

LONDON:
JOHN MURRAY, ALBEMARLE STREET.
1846.

P O E M S
BY MARIANNE MOORE

LONDON
THE EGOIST PRESS
2 Robert Street, Adelphi, W.C.
1921

Meredith, George. POEMS. London (1851). Half-title and			
errata at end. Purple cloth	250	750	1,500
Green cloth	—	400	1,000
Meredith, William (Morris). LOVE LETTERS FROM AN			
IMPOSSIBLE LAND. New Hampshire, 1944	—	125	150
Merriam, Eve. FAMILY CIRCLE. New Haven, 1946	—	25	50
Merril, Judith. SHADOW ON THE HEARTH.			
Garden City, 1950	—	25	60
Merrill, James (Ingram). JIM'S BOOK. Privately printed.			
New York, 1942	—	3,500	4,000
THE BLACK SWAN . . . Athens, 1946. Wraps.			
(100 copies)	—	1,500	3,000
FIRST POEMS. New York, 1951. (990 copies). (First			
regularly published book)	75	175	200
Merritt, A(braham). THE MOON POOL. New York (1919).			
Cloth. First issue: no ad on p. (434). Sheets bulk 3.2 cm	—	75	250
Merton, Thomas. THIRTY POEMS. Norfolk (1944). Boards	50	150	350
Wraps	35	60	125

Merwin, W(illiam) S(tanley). A MASK FOR JANUS.
New Hampshire, 1952   75   300   350

Metalious, Grace. PEYTON PLACE. New York, 1956   —   —   125

Metcalf, John. THE SMOKING LEG. London, 1925   —   100   250

Metcalf, John. THE LADY WHO SOLD FURNITURE.
Toronto, 1970   —   —   75

Metcalf, Paul. WILL WEST. Asheville, 1956.
Wraps. (500 copies)   —   75   125

Mew, Charlotte. THE FARMER'S BRIDE. London, 1916.
Wraps   75   125   150
London, 1921   —   —   50

Mewshaw, Michael. MAN IN MOTION. New York (1970)   —   30   50

Meyer, Nicholas. TARGET PRACTICE. New York (1974)   —   —   60

Meyer, Thomas. THE BANG BOOK. Jargon. (No-place) 1971.
Cloth in acetate dustwrapper   —   60   75
Wraps in acetate dustwrapper   —   30   35

Meyerstein, Edward Henry W. *See* E. H. W. M.

Meynell, Alice. *See* A. C. Thompson

Mezey, Robert. THE WANDERING JEW. Mt. Vernon, 1960.
Wraps. 350 copies   —   60   125

(Previous collected appearance in 1957)

Michaels, Barbara (Barbara Louise Gross Mertz). THE
MASTER OF BLACK TOWER. New York, 1966   —   —   200
London, 1967   —   —   100

Michaels, Leonard. GOING PLACES. New York (1969)   15   —   40

Micheaux, Oscar (or Micheaud). *See* THE CONQUEST

Micheline, Jack. RIVER OF RED WINE . . .
New York (1958). Wraps   —   40   75

Michener, James A(lbert). THE UNIT IN THE SOCIAL STUDIES.
Cambridge (Mass., 1940). Wraps. (Non-fiction
collaboration. Written with Harold M. Long)   —   500   600

TALES OF THE SOUTH PACIFIC. New York, 1947   40   225   1,250
New York, 1950. 1,500 signed copies. Special ABA
edition without dustwrapper   —   100   350
London, 1951   —   —   350

THE MIDDLE PARTS OF FORTUNE. (Frederick Manning).
   London, 1929. (520 copies)   —   —   400

Middleton, Arthur (Edward J. O'Brien). FORGOTTEN
   THRESHOLD. New York (1914)   —   75   75

Middleton, Christopher. POEMS. London (1944)   —   75   100

Middleton, Richard. THE GHOST SHIP . . . London, 1912   —   100   100

Middleton, Stanley. A SHORT ANSWER. London, 1958   —   60   60

Midwood, Barton. BODKIN. New York (1967)   —   25   40

Milburn, George. OKLAHOMA TOWN. New York (1931)   —   —   125

Miles, Josephine. LINES AT THE INTERSECTION.
   New York, 1939   15   50   100

Millar, Kenneth (Ross MacDonald). DARK TUNNEL.
   New York, 1944   40   2,000   4,000

Millar, Margaret (Mrs. Kenneth Millar). THE INVISIBLE
   WORM. Garden City, 1941   —   250   300

Millay, Edna St. Vincent. RENASCENCE . . . New York, 1917.
   15 signed copies on Japanese vellum   5,500   4,000   7,500
   First edition: Glaslan watermark paper. (2 blank leaves
   precede half-title   —   125   250
   Third edition: not on Glaslan watermark paper.
   (No blank leaves)   —   50   100

   (Previous Vassar material)

Millen, Gilmore. SWEET MAN. New York, 1930   —   100   250

Miller, Alice. See Alice Duer

Miller, Arthur. SITUATION NORMAL . . . New York (1944)   50   150   250

Miller, Caroline. LAMB IN HIS BOSOM. New York, 1933.
   (Only book—Pulitzer Prize winner)   —   100   150

Miller, Geoffrey. THE BLACK GLOVE. New York, 1981   —   —   35

Miller, Heather Ross. THE EDGE OF THE WOODS.
   New York, 1964   —   50   75

Miller, Henry (Valentine). TROPIC OF CANCER. Paris (1934).
   Decorated wraps. First issue: has "First published
   September 1934" on copyright page and a wrap-around
   band   2,000   3,000   7,500
   Second issue: without notice   500   750   1,500

THE COSMOLOGICAL EYE. Norfolk, 1939. (First U.S. publication). First issue: eye on cover, dustwrapper price $2.50 — 125 250

Miller, Jason. NOBODY HEARS A BROKEN DRUM. New York (1971). Wraps 15 25 40

Miller, Joaquin (Cincinnatus Hiner Miller). *See* SPECIMENS

Miller, Max. I COVER THE WATERFRONT. New York (1932) — — 150

Miller, Merle. ISLAND 49. New York (1945) — 35 40

Miller, Patrick. THE NATURAL MAN. London, 1924 25 100 125

Miller, Sue. THE GOOD MOTHER. New York (1986) — — 40

Miller, Vassar. ADAM'S FOOTPRINT. New Orleans, 1956. Wraps — 60 75

Miller, Walter (M., Jr.). A CANTICLE FOR LEIBOWITZ. Philadelphia/New York (1960) — 400 1,000
London (1960) — 150 350

Miller, Warren. THE SLEEP OF REASON. London, 1956 35 100 100
New York, 1960. Wraps. (New introduction) — — 40

Also see Amanda Vail

Millhauser, Steven. EDWIN MULLHOUSE. New York, 1972 — — 60

Mills, James. PANIC IN NEEDLE PARK. New York (1966) — 35 50

Milne, A(lan) A(lexander). LOVERS IN LONDON. London, 1905	50	100	500
Milosz, Czeslaw. THE CAPTIVE MIND. New York, 1953	—	—	60
Milton, Ernest. TO KILL A CROCODILE. New York, 1928	20	50	125
Mingus, Charlie. BENEATH THE UNDERDOG. New York, 1977	—	—	75
Minot, Stephen. CHILL OF DUCK. Garden City, 1964	—	35	75
Minot, Susan. MONKEYS. New York (1986)	—	—	50
MIRIAM COFFIN: OR, THE WHALE FISHERMAN. (Joseph C. Hart). New York/Philadelphia, 1834. 2 volumes	200	250	400
Mishima, Yukio (Hiraoka Kimitake). THE SOUND OF WAVES. New York, 1956. (First English translation)	—	50	75
MR. DOOLEY IN PEACE AND WAR. (Finley Peter Dunne). Boston, 1898	25	50	75
Mistry, Robinton. TALES FROM FIOZSHA BRAG. Toronto, 1981	—	—	100
Mitchell, Adrian. (POEMS) FANTASY POETS #24. London, 1954. Wraps	—	40	40
Mitchell, Donald G(rant). THE DIGNITY OF LEARNING. New York, 1841. Wraps bound in	—	200	250
Also see Ik Marvel			
Mitchell, Gladys. SPEED DEATH. New York, 1929	—	—	200
Mitchell, Isaac. THE ASYLUM: OR, ALONSO AND MELISSA. Poughkeepsie, 1811. 2 volumes. (Many later editions credited to Daniel Jackson, Jr.)	250	500	1,000
Mitchell, Joseph. MY EARS ARE BENT. New York (1938)	—	40	150
Mitchell, Julian. IMAGINARY TOYS. London, 1961	—	40	40
Mitchell, Margaret. GONE WITH THE WIND. New York, 1936. "May 1936" on copyright page	300	850	4,000
New York, 1939. 2 volumes in slipcase	—	—	1,000
Mitchell, S(ilas) Weir. *See* E. W. S.			
THE WONDERFUL STORIES OF . . . Philadelphia, 1867. (170 large paper copies)	50	750	1,000
Trade edition	35	200	300

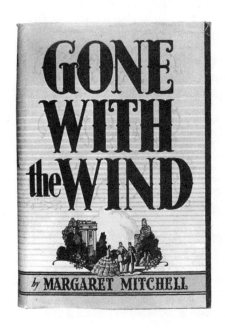

(A number of biological and natural science pamphlets preceded)

Mitchell, Stewart. POEMS. New York, 1921	—	75	150
Mitchell, W. O. WHO HAS SEEN THE WIND.			
Toronto, 1947	—	—	500
Boston, 1947	—	40	60
Mitford, Mary Russell. POEMS. London, 1810. First issue:			
leaf of "alterations"	250	400	1,000
Mitford, Nancy. HIGHLAND FLING. London, 1931	—	125	175
Mittelholzer, Edgar (Austin). CREOLE CHIPS.			
British Guiana, 1937	50	125	250
CORENTYNE THUNDER. London, 1941	—	100	200
Mo, Timothy. THE MONKEY KING. (London, 1978)	—	35	250
MODERN PAINTERS . . . (John Ruskin). London, 1843	—	—	1,750
Moffett, Cleveland (Langston). THROUGH THE WALL.			
New York, 1909	—	100	125
Molloy, Robert. PRIDE'S WAY. New York, 1945	—	40	40

Momaday, N(atachee) Scott. THE COMPLETE POEMS OF
FREDERICK GODDARD TUCKERMAN. New York, 1965.
(Edited by Momaday) — 50 125

OWL IN THE CEDAR TREE. (No-place, 1965). Issued
without dustwrapper — — 200

THE JOURNEY OF TAI-ME. Santa Barbara (1968). (100
copies). Boxed 150 500 2,000

Monahan, James. FAR FROM THE LAND . . . London, 1944 — — 150

Monk, Maria. AWFUL DISCLOSURES . . . New York, 1836.
In original cloth — 400 250

Monro, Harold. POEMS. London, 1906. Wraps — — 100

Monroe, Harriet. VALERIA . . . Chicago, 1891. Subscribers
edition. (300 copies) 75 200 200
Chicago, 1892. Regular edition 35 75 75

Montagu, Charles. *See* THE HIND AND THE PANTHER . . .

Montague, C(harles) E(dward). A HIND LET LOOSE. London
(1910). (150 copies) 60 150 350
Trade edition 35 75 150

Montague, John. FORMS OF EXILE. Oxford (1958). Wraps — 75 150

(Preceded by *Poems* on mimeographed sheets, about 1955)

Montecino, Marcel. CROSS KILLER. New York, 1988 — — 100

Montgomery, L(ucy) M(aud). ANNE OF GREEN GABLES.
Boston, 1908 — 175 5,000

Montgomery, Marion. THE WANDERING OF DESIRE.
New York, 1962 — 40 60

Moody, William Vaughn. THE MASQUE OF JUDGEMENT.
Boston, 1900. Boards. (150 copies) 40 150 100
Trade edition — 50 50

Mooney, Ted. EASY TRAVEL TO OTHER PLANETS. New
York (1981) — — 25

Moorcock, Michael. *See* Desmond Reid

THE STEALER OF SOULS. London (1963). First issue:
orange boards 40 75 150
Second issue: green boards — 60 100

Moore, Brian. WREATH FOR A REDHEAD. Winnipeg, 1951.
Wraps — 200 300

SAILOR'S LEAVE. New York (1953). New title. Wraps	—	—	250
JUDITH HEARNE. London (1955). (First hardback)	40	125	300
THE LONELY PASSION OF JUDITH HEARNE. Boston, 1955. (First U.S. hardback)	20	100	150
Moore, Catherine Lucile. *See* Lewis Padgett			
Moore, Clement C(larke). *See* OBSERVATIONS UPON CERTAIN PASSAGES . . . *and* A NEW TRANSLATION . . .			
Moore, Edward (Edwin Muir). WE MODERNS . . . London (1918)	—	200	200
Moore, George. FLOWERS OF PASSION. London, 1878	—	250	500
Moore, Julia A. THE SENTIMENTAL SONG BOOK. (Grand Rapids, 1876). Wraps	—	—	500
Moore, Marianne. POEMS. London, 1921. Wraps	300	500	750
Moore, Merrill. THE NOISE THAT TIME MAKES . . . New York (1929)	30	125	125
Moore, Susanna. MY OLD SWEETHEART. Boston, 1982	—	—	35
Moore, T(homas) Sturge. TWO POEMS. London, 1893	—	—	250
THE VINEDRESSER . . . London, 1899	90	100	150
(Previous privately printed pamphlet)			
Moore, Thomas. ODES OF ANACREON. London, 1800. (Translation and notes)	125	250	400
Moraes, Dom. GREEN IS THE GRASS. London, 1951	—	—	200
Morand, Paul. OPEN ALL NIGHT. New York, 1923. (First English translation)	15	40	75
Moravia, Alberto (Alberto Pincherle). THE INDIFFERENT ONES. New York (1932)	30	75	150
Morecamp, Arthur (Thomas Pilgrim). THE LIVE BOYS . . . Boston (1878)	150	200	300
Morgan, Berry. PURSUIT. Boston, 1966	—	—	75
London, 1967	—	—	50
Morgan, Charles (Langbridge). THE GUNROOM. London, 1919. Blue-grained or blue-ribbed cloth— priority uncertain	—	75	150
Morgan, Seth. HOMEBOY. New York, 1992	—	—	75

Morgan, Thomas Hunt. THE DEVELOPMENT OF THE FROG'S
EGG. New York, 1897 — — 400

(Student pamphlet preceded)

Morison, Samuel Eliot. HARRISON GRAY OTIS. Boston, 1913 — 150 250

Morley, Christopher (Darlington). THE EIGHTH SIN.
Oxford/London, 1912. Wraps. (250 copies) 500 1,000 1,500

PARNASSUS ON WHEELS. Garden City, 1917. First issue:
space between "y" and "e" p. 4:8 — 150 150

Morley, John David. PICTURES FROM THE WATER TRADE.
London (1985) — — 60

Morrell, David. FIRST BLOOD. New York (1972) — 40 125
London (1972) — 35 75

Morris, James (later Jan). COAST TO COAST. London, 1956 — — 175

AS I SAW THE U.S.A. (New York, 1956). (New title) — — 125

Morris, Julian (Morris West). MOON IN MY POCKET.
Sidney (1948) — 100 150

Morris, William. THE DEFENSE OF GUENEVERE . . .
London, 1858. 10 copies on vellum — — 10,000
Trade edition. (250 copies sold) — 600 600

Morris, Willie. NORTH TOWARD HOME. Boston, 1967 — 50 60

Morris, Wright. MY UNCLE DUDLEY. New York (1942) 125 1,000 1,000

Morrison, Arthur. THE SHADOWS AROUND US . . .
London, 1891 — 250 250

MARTIN HEWITT, INVESTIGATOR. London, 1894. (Third
book, first mystery) — 1,000 1,000

Morrison, James Douglas (Jim). THE LORDS.
Los Angeles, 1969. 100 copies — 100 850

THE NEW CREATURES. Los Angeles, 1969. 100 copies — — 750

THE LORDS AND THE NEW CREATURES.
New York (1970) — — 175

Morrison, Theodore. THE SERPENT IN THE CLOUD.
Boston, 1931 15 40 60

Morrison, Toni. THE BLUEST EYE. New York (1970) 25 300 1,750
London, 1979 — 40 200

Morse, L. A. THE FLESH EATERS. New York, 1979 — — 75

Morse, Samuel French. THE YELLOW LILIES. Hanover, 1935.
85 signed and numbered copies   — — 250

    TIME OF YEAR. (Cummington) 1943. (275 copies)   — 75 100

Mortimer, John. CHARADE. London (1947)   — — 250

Morton, David. SHIPS IN HARBOR. New York, 1921   — 60 75

Morton, J. B. *See* GORGEOUS POETRY

Morton, Sarah Wentworth. OUABI: OR THE VIRTUES OF
NATURE. Boston, 1790   — 100 500

MORTON OF MORTON'S HOPE . . . (John Lothrop Motley).
London, 1839. 3 volumes   — 300 400

MORTON'S HOPE . . . (John Lothrop Motley). New York,
1839. 2 volumes   — 250 350

Mosel, Tad. JINXED. French. [No-date: circa 1949]. Wraps   — — 75

    OTHER PEOPLE'S HOUSES. New York, 1956   — — 75

Moses, Robert. THE CIVIL SERVICE OF GREAT BRITAIN.
New York, 1914. Wraps   — 50 100

Mosley, Walter. DEVIL IN A BLUE DRESS. New York, 1990   — — 75

Moss, Howard. THE WOUND AND THE WEATHER. New
York (1946)   60 75 100

Moss, Stanley. THE WRONG ANGEL. New York (1966)   — — 30

Motion, Andrew. GOODNESTONE. (London, 1972). Wraps   — — 75

Motley, John Lothrop. *See* MORTON OF . . .
and MORTON'S HOPE

Motley, Willard. KNOCK ON ANY DOOR. New York (1947)   25 50 100

Mottram, Ralph Hale. *See* J. Marjoram

MOUNSEER NONTONGPAW: A NEW VERSION. (Mary W.
Shelley). London, 1808. Original wraps   — 5,000 7,500
Re-bound   — — 2,500

Mowat, Farley. PEOPLE OF THE DEER. Boston, 1952   — 75 125

Mowry, Jess. RATS IN THE TREES. Santa Barbara, 1990.
Wraps   — — 50

Moyes, Patricia. DEAD MEN DON'T SKI. London, 1959   — — 75

Moynahan, Julian. SISTERS AND BROTHERS.
New York (1960)   — 25 35

Muir, Edwin. *See* Edward Moore

WE MODERNS. New York, 1920. Includes Mencken introduction	50	150	250

Muir, Emily. SMALL POTATOES. New York, 1940   —   35   50

Muir, John. THE MOUNTAINS OF CALIFORNIA. New York, 1894. (Page "1" so numbered)	150	250	750
Second issue	—	—	600
London, 1894	—	—	500

(Previous offprints and edited books)

Mukherjee, Bharati. THE TIGER'S DAUGHTER. Boston, 1972   —   —   75

Mulford, Clarence Edward. BAR-20. (HOPALONG CASSIDY). New York, 1907. First issue: "Blazing Star" in list of illustrations	—	125	350
Second issue: without "Blazing Star" in list	—	60	250

Muller, Marcia. EDWIN OF THE IRON SHOES.
New York (1977)   —   —   125

Mumey, Nolie. A STUDY OF RARE BOOKS. Denver, 1930.
(1,000 signed copies)   100   150   175

Mumford, Lewis. THE STORY OF UTOPIAS.
New York (1922)   25   200   400

Mundy, Talbot (William Lancaster Gribbon). RUNG HO!
New York, 1914   60   100   250

Munro, Alice. DANCE OF THE HAPPY SHADES. (Toronto, 1968). (Award sticker applied later)	—	125	300
(New York, 1973)	—	—	150

Munro, H(ector) H(ugh) (Saki). THE RISE OF THE RUSSIAN
EMPIRE. London, 1900   100   200   300

Also see Saki

Munro, Neil. THE LOST PIBROCK . . . Edinburgh, 1896   50   75   125

Munroe, Kirk. WAKULLA . . . New York, 1886   40   50   60

Munson, Douglas Anne. EL NIÑO. New York, 1990   —   —   40

Munson, Gorham. WALDO FRANK: A STUDY.
New York (1923). (Stieglitz frontis photo). 500
numbered copies, issued without dustwrapper   —   300   500

Murdoch, (Jean) Iris. SARTRE: ROMANTIC RATIONALIST.
    Cambridge (Eng., 1953) — 25 150 300
    New York, 1953 — 25 — 200

Murgatroyd, Captain Matthew (James Athearn Jones).
    THE REFUGEE. New York, 1823. 2 volumes — 300 400 400

Murphy, Audie. TO HELL AND BACK. New York (1949) — — 60 75

Murphy, Dennis. THE SERGEANT. New York, 1958 — — — 35

Murphy, Dervla. FULL TILT. London, 1965 — — — 50

Murphy, Richard. THE ARCHAEOLOGY OF LOVE.
    Dublin, 1955 — — — 125

Murray, Albert. THE OMNI-AMERICANS . . .
    New York (1970) — — 40 75

Murray, M(argaret) A. EGYPTIAN POEMS. London (1920) — — 75 75

Murray, Pauli. PROUD SHOES. New York (1956) — 30 60 150

Murray, Peter. YOU CAN JUGGLE. (Plymouth, Mass.). Issued
    without dustwrapper — — — 35

Murray, William. THE FUGITIVE ROMANS. New York (1955) — — — 100

Murry, John Middleton. FYODOR DOSTOEVSKY.
    London, 1916 — — — 100

Musgrave, Susan. SONGS OF THE SEA-WITCH.
    Vancouver, 1970 — — — 150

Myers, John Myers. THE HARP AND THE BLADE.
    New York, 1941 — — — 150

Myles, Simon (Ken Follett). THE BIG BLACK. London, 1974 — — 75 150

Myrer, Anton. EVIL UNDER THE SUN. New York, 1951 — — 35 60

N

Nabokoff (Nabokov), Vladimir. LAUGHTER IN THE DARK.
    Indianapolis (1938). (First U.S. edition. Revised version
    of *Camera Obscura*). Green cloth is said to be first
    issue, also in red and brown cloths — 100 400 1,250

    Also see Vladimir Nabokoff-Sirin

Nabokoff-Sirin (Nabokov), Vladimir. CAMERA OBSCURA.
    London (1936). (First book translated into English) — 1,000 1,500 15,000

Nabokov, Vladimir. *See* Vladimir Nabokoff *and*
    Vladimir Nabokoff-Sirin

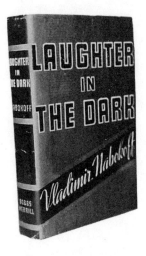 

Naipaul, Shiva. FIREFLIES. London, 1970. Cloth	—	75	150
Wraps	—	—	50
New York, 1971	—	35	75
Naipaul, V(idiadhar) S. THE MYSTIC MASSEUR. London, 1957	—	250	400
New York (1959)	—	75	200
Narayan, R. J. SWAMI AND FRIENDS. London, 1935.	—	—	150
Narayan, R. K. THE FINANCIAL EXPERT. (No-place) 1953	—	—	100
Nardi, Marci. POEMS. Denver (1956)	—	50	50
NARRATIVE OF DR. LIVINGSTON'S DISCOVERIES IN CENTRAL AFRICA. (David Livingstone). London, 1857	—	400	750
Nasby, Petroleum V. (David Ross Locke). THE NASBY PAPERS. Indianapolis, 1864. Wraps. First issue:			
"Indianapolic" front cover	100	150	350
Second issue: spelled correctly	50	100	250
Nash, Ogden. THE CRICKET OF CAVADOR. Garden City, 1925. (Written with J. Alger)	50	250	600
HARD LINES. New York, 1931	60	250	250
(London, 1932)	—	150	150

Nast, Thomas. *See* THE FIGHT AT DAME EUROPA'S SCHOOL

Nathan, George Jean. THE ETERNAL MYSTERY.
New York, 1913   25   60   75

Nathan, Robert (Gruntal). PETER KINDRED.
New York, 1919   25   60   150

Native, A (Thomas Jefferson). A SUMMARY VIEW OF THE
RIGHTS OF BRITISH AMERICA . . . Williamsburg (1774)   —   25,000 250,000
Philadelphia, 1774   —   10,000 30,000

NATURE. (Ralph Waldo Emerson). Boston, 1836. First issue:
p. 94 numbered 92. In original cloth   —   750   2,500
Second issue: p. 94 correctly numbered. In original cloth —   350   1,250

Naylor, Gloria. THE WOMEN OF BREWSTER PLACE.
New York, 1982   —   50   400
London, 1983

Neagoe, Peter. STORM. Paris, 1932. Published by New
Review. Wraps. (1 copy noted in cloth. Preceded
Obelisk edition)   60   150   200

Neal, John. See KEEP COOL

Neely, Barbara. BLANCHE ON THE LAM. New York, 1992   —   —   125

Negro Pioneer, A. See THE CONQUEST

Neihardt, John G(neisenau). THE DIVINE
ENCHANTMENT . . . New York, 1900. (Supposedly he
burned most copies)   250   650   750

Neilson, Francis. MANABOZO. London, 1899   —   —   100

Neilson, (J.) Shaw. HEART OF SPRING. Sydney, 1919   —   —   60

(Two previous pamphlets)

Nemerov, Howard. THE IMAGE AND THE LAW. (New York,
1947)   75   100   100

Nesbit, E(dith). LAYS AND LEGENDS. London, 1886   —   200   300

(Preceded by edited anthology: *Spring Songs and
Sketches*)

Neugeboren, Jay. BIG MAN. Boston, 1966   —   35   50

NEW BATH GUIDE, OR, MEMOIRS . . . , THE. (Christopher
Anstey). London, 1766   —   100   300

Newbolt, Sir Henry. See A FAIR DEATH

Newby, Eric. THE LAST GRAIN RACE. London, 1956   —   50   100

Newby, P(ercy) H(oward). A JOURNEY TO THE INTERIOR.
London, 1945 — 60 75

New Directions. PIANOS OF SYMPATHY. Norfolk, 1936.
Wraps. Written by Montagu O'Reilly. First book of
the press. First issue: blue wraps 75 300 300
Second issue: red wraps — — 200

NEW DIRECTIONS IN PROSE AND POETRY. Norfolk, 1936.
(First in series). Yellow boards. Issued without
dustwrapper 35 200 300
Wraps 35 100 150

Newell, Peter. *See* TOPSYS AND TURVEYS

Newhouse, Edward. YOU CAN'T SLEEP HERE. New York
(1934) — 100 250

Newlove, John. GRAVE SIRS. Vancouver, 1962. Stiff wraps — 200 250

Newman, Frances. THE SHORT STORY'S MUTATIONS.
New York, 1924. (Noted in pink or gray dustwrapper) — 250 350

Newton, A(lfred) Edward. THE AMENITIES OF BOOK
COLLECTING. Boston, 1918. First issue: without index;
p. 268:3 has "Piccadilly" 60 60 125
Second issue: has index 15 25 75

NEW TRANSLATION WITH NOTES OF THE THIRD SATIRE OF
JUVENAL. (Clement Moore and John Duer).
New York, 1806. First issue: "additional errata" leaf 100 250 500

Ng, Fae Myene. BONE. New York, 1993 — — 35

Nichols, Beverley. PRELUDE. London, 1929 — — 300

Nichols, John. THE STERILE CUCKOO. New York (1965) — 50 125

Nichols, Robert. INVOCATION . . . London, 1915.
First issue: blue wraps 40 75 150
Second issue: green wraps — — 100
Third issue: white cloth with black lettering — — 75

Nicholson, Meredith. SHORT FLIGHTS. Indianapolis, 1891 — 125 125

Nicholson, Norman. FIVE RIVERS. (London, 1944) — 60 75

Nicolson, Harold. PAUL VERLAINE. London (1921) — 250 350

SWEET WATERS. London, 1921 — — 350

Niedecker, Lorine. NEW GOOSE. Prairie City (1946) — 800 1,250

A N A Ï S   N I N

D. H. LAWRENCE

An unprofessional Study

*With two facsimile manuscript pages out of
Lady Chatterley's Lover*

Paris 1932

EDWARD W. TITUS
at the sign of the black manikin
4, RUE DELAMBRE, MONTPARNASSE

THE STORY OF THE IRISH CITIZEN ARMY

By P. O CATHASAIGH

The first account that has been given of the
formation of the Irish Citizen Army during the
Dublin strike of 1913-14, and the part played
by it in the subsequent history of Ireland. The
author, who was himself a leading figure in the
movement, writes with vigour and conviction
upon the role of labour in Ireland, and ex-
pressing a very definite opinion as to the relations
of the workers to the National movement. The
book contains original character sketches of
Larkin, Connolly, Captain White, and Madame
Markiewicz, and some facts bearing on the
relations between the Citizen Army and the
Volunteers now emerge for the first time.

MAUNSEL & CO., LTD.

ONE SHILLING NET

Nightingale, Florence. NOTES ON NURSING.
New York, 1860 — — 250

NILE NOTES OF A HOWADJI. (George William Curtis).
New York, 1851. Wraps 100 200 200
Cloth 100 100 100

NIMPORT. (Edwin Lasseter Bynner). Boston, 1877 — — 175

Nims, John Frederick. THE IRON PASTORAL.
New York (1947) 25 35 60

Nin, Anaïs. D. H. LAWRENCE: AN UNPROFESSIONAL STUDY.
Paris, 1932. 550 numbered copies 125 250 450
London, 1961 20 — 50

Nissenson, Hugh. A PILE OF STONES. New York (1965) — 60 75

Niven, Larry (Laurence Vancott). WORLD OF PTAVVS.
New York (1966) — — 35
(London, 1968) — — 200

Nixon, Richard. THE CHALLENGES WE FACE.
New York (1960) — 75 125

Noah, Mordecai Manuel. *See* THE FORTRESS . . .

Noguchi, Yone. SEEN & UNSEEN. San Francisco, 1896 — 75 300

Nonesuch Press. GENESIS. London, 1924. Twelve woodcuts by Paul Nash. First Nonesuch book. 375 copies in orange dustwrapper	—	—	1,250
Nordhoff, Charles Bernard. THE FLEDGLING. Boston, 1919	20	—	75
Nordhoff, Charles B., and James N. Hall. THE LAFAYETTE FLYING CORPS. Boston, 1920. 2 volumes	300	600	1,250
Norman, Charles. TRAGIC BEACHES. New York, 1925. 100 signed copies	—	100	125
Norman, Howard. THE OWL SCATTERER. Boston (1986)	—	—	125
(Previous translation)			
Norman, Marc. BIKE RIDING IN LOS ANGELES. New York, 1972	—	20	50
Normyx (Norman Douglas). UNPROFESSIONAL TALES. London, 1901. (750 copies printed. 8 were sold by author; about 600 copies pulped)	300	650	1,000
(Preceded by a number of pamphlets)			
Norris, (Benjamin) Frank(lin). YVERNELLE . . . Philadelphia, 1892 (actually 1891)	600	1,000	2,000
Norris, Gloria. LOOKING FOR BOBBY. New York, 1985	—	—	35
Norris, Hoke. ALL THE KINGDOMS OF EARTH. New York (1956)	—	—	35
Norris, Kathleen. MOTHER, A STORY. New York, 1911	—	60	150
Norse, Harold. THE UNDERSEA MOUNTAIN. Denver, 1953	25	40	75
North, Sterling. THE PEDRO GORINO. Boston, 1929. (Written with Capt. Harry Dean)	20	125	150
TIGER. Chicago, 1933	—	—	125
PLOWING ON SUNDAY. New York, 1934	20	75	75
Norton, Andre (Alice Mary Norton). THE PRINCE COMMANDS . . . New York, 1934	—	600	750
Norton, Charles Eliot. See CONSIDERATIONS . . .			
Norton, Mary. THE MAGIC BED-KNOB . . . New York, 1943	—	—	250
Nott, Kathleen. MILE END. Hogarth. London, 1938	—	75	150
Nourse, Alan Edward. TROUBLE ON TITAN. Philadelphia (1954)	—	40	150

Nova, Craig. TURKEY HASH. New York (1972)	—	35	60
Novak, Joseph (Jerzy Kosinski). THE FUTURE IS OURS, COMRADE. Garden City, 1960	50	250	250
Noyes, Alfred. THE LOOM OF YEARS. London, 1902	35	50	50
Noyes, John H(umphrey). THE BEREAN . . . Putney, 1847	—	200	300
Nunn, Kem. TAPPING THE SOURCE. New York, 1984	—	—	40
Nutt, Howard. SPECIAL LAUGHTER . . . Prairie City (1940)	—	125	125
Nye, Edgar Wilson. A HOWL IN ROME. Chicago (1880). Wraps	—	100	150
BILL NYE AND BOOMERANG . . . Chicago, 1881	—	75	125
Nye, Hermes. FORTUNE IS A WOMAN. (New York, 1958). Wraps	—	30	30
Nye, Nelson. PISTOLS FOR HIRE. New York (1941)	—	—	125
Nye, Robert. JUVENILIA 1. (Northwood, Middlesex, 1961). 25 signed and numbered copies	—	75	100

O

Oakes, Philip. UNLUCKY JONAH. Reading, 1954	—	—	75
Oates, Joyce Carol. BY THE NORTH GATE. New York (1963)	40	100	300
Obelisk Press. SLEEVELESS ERRAND. Paris, 1930. (Written by Norah C. James. First book of press)	—	100	100
OBITER DICTA. (Augustine Birrell). London, 1884	40	50	75
O'Brian, Patrick. THE LAST POOL. London, 1950	—	—	600
O'Brien, Dan. EMINENT DOMAIN. Towacity (1987)	—	—	50
O'Brien, Edna. THE COUNTRY GIRLS. London, 1960	—	50	150
O'Brien, Edward J. THE FLOWING OF THE TIDE. New York, 1910	30	50	100
O'Brien, Fitzjames. A GENTLEMAN FROM IRELAND. New York (no-date [1858]). Wraps	—	—	350
O'Brien, Flann (Brian O'Nolan). AT SWIM-TWO-BIRDS. London (1939). First issue: black cloth	50	2,000	4,500
Second issue: gray-green cloth. (Issued in 1941 or 1942)	—	800	3,500
New York, 1939 (actually 1951)	—	100	175
O'Brien, Kate. DISTINGUISHED VILLA. London, 1926	—	125	250

O'Brien, Tim. IF I DIE IN A COMBAT ZONE.			
New York (1973)	—	250	1,000
London (1973)	—	50	200
OBSERVATION UPON CERTAIN PASSAGES in Mr. Jefferson's "Notes on Virginia." (Clement C. Moore possible author). New York, 1804. Wraps	100	300	500
O'Casey, Sean. *See* P. O'Cathasaigh			
O'Cathasaigh, P. (Sean O'Casey). THE STORY OF THE IRISH ARMY. Dublin, 1919. Wraps. First issue: gray wraps	100	100	300
Second issue: tan wraps	75	75	150
(Preceded by previous pamphlets)			
O'Connor, Edwin. THE ORACLE. New York (1951)	—	25	60
O'Connor, (Mary) Flannery. WISE BLOOD.			
New York (1952)	100	650	1,750
London (1955)	—	250	350
O'Connor, Frank (Michael O'Donovan). GUESTS OF THE NATION. London, 1931	75	250	750
O'Connor, Jack. CONQUEST. New York, 1930	—	125	200
O'Connor, Philip F. OLD MORALS, SMALL CONTINENTS . . . Iowa City (1971)	—	25	60
Odets, Clifford. THREE PLAYS. Covici-Friede.			
New York (1935)	—	60	250
Second issue: Random House	—	—	125
O'Donnell, Peter. MODESTY BLAISE. (London, 1965)	—	75	75
New York, 1965	—	35	40
O'Duffy, Eimhar. A LAY OF THE LIFFEY . . . Dublin, 1918. Wraps	—	60	100
O'Faolain, Julia. WE MIGHT *SEE* SIGHTS. London (1968)	—	60	75
O'Faolain, Sean. MIDSUMMER NIGHT MADNESS . . .			
London (1932)	75	250	300
New York, 1932	—	125	150
Offord, Carl Ruthaven. THE WHITE FACE. New York (1943)	20	100	150
O'Flaherty, Liam. THY NEIGHBOR'S WIFE. London (1923)	100	175	250
Ogawa, Florence. *See* Ai			
OGILVIES, THE. (Dinah Craik). London, 1849. 3 volumes	—	300	500

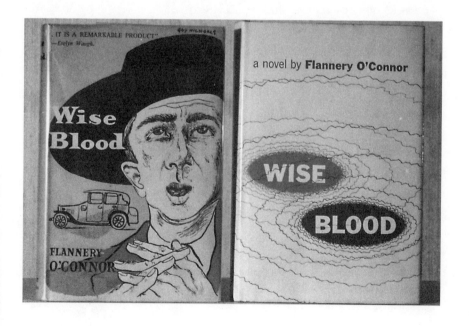

O'Gorman, Ned (Edward Charles). THE NIGHT OF THE HAMMER. New York, 1959	—	20	40
O'Hara, Frank (Francis Russell). A CITY WINTER . . . New York, 1951. (Larry Rivers illustrations). 20 signed copies. Cloth	900	1,500	7,500
130 numbered copies. Wraps	450	500	1,000
O'Hara, John. APPOINTMENT IN SAMARRA. New York (1934). First issue: back panel of dustwrapper has ads for "Recent Fiction"	150	600	3,500
London (1935)	125	250	500

(Preceded by *Reminiscences: From "Kungsholm,"* written anonymously for Swedish American Line)

O. Henry (Wm. Sidney [later Sydney] Porter). CABBAGES AND KINGS. New York, 1904. First issue: McClure, Phillips & Co. on spine	100	150	350
OLD LIBRARIAN'S ALMANACK, THE. (Edmund L. Pearson). Woodstock, Vermont, 1909	—	75	100

Oliphant, Margaret. *See* Margaret Maitland

Oliver, Chad. MISTS OF DAWN. Philadelphia (1952)	—	30	60
Oliver, Mary. NO VOYAGE . . . London (1963)	—	—	300
Boston, 1965. Wraps	—	60	100
Ollivant, Alfred. BOB, SON OF BATTLE. New York, 1898	—	75	300
Olsen, Tillie. TELL ME A RIDDLE. Philadelphia, 1961. Cloth	60	150	400
London, 1964. Wraps	30	30	50
New York, 1978. 100 signed and numbered copies. Issued without dustwrapper in slipcase	—	—	200

Olson, Charles. *See* SPANISH SPEAKING . . .

CALL ME ISHMAEL. New York (1947)	100	250	350
New York (1958). 100 numbered copies	—	—	200
London, 1962. Wraps	35	50	75
Olson, Elder. THING OF SORROW. New York, 1934	—	25	60
Olympia Press. AMOROUS EXPLOITS OF A YOUNG RAKEHELL. Paris, 1953. (R. Seaver's translation of *Apollonaire*). (First book of press). Wraps	—	50	125
Ondaatje, Michael. THE DAINTY MONSTERS. Toronto, 1967. 500 numbered copies	—	200	1,500
O'Neill, Eugene G(ladstone). THIRST . . . Boston (1914). (1,000 copies)	—	250	400

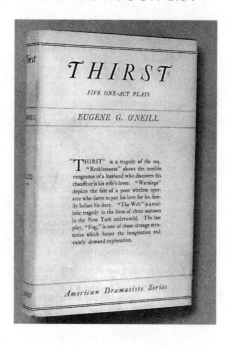

O'Neill, Rose Cecil. THE LOVES OF EDWY. Boston (1904)   20   40   100

Onetti, Juan Carlos. THE SHIPYARD. New York, 1968. First
    English translation   —   —   100

Onions, Oliver. THE COMPLEAT BACHELOR. London, 1900   50   60   75

Oppen, George. DISCRETE SERIES . . . New York, 1934   —   300   500

Oppenheim, E(dward) Phillips. EXPIATION. London, 1887   —   50   200

Oppenheimer, Joel (Lester). FOUR POEMS TO SPRING.
    (Black Mountain, 1951). Wraps   —   250   750

    THE DANCER. Highlands, North Carolina, 1952.
    (Jargon 2)   75   500   1,500

Optic, Oliver. *See* William Taylor Adams

Orage, A. R. FRIEDRICH NIETZSCHE . . . London, 1906   —   50   100
    Chicago, 1911. (U.K. sheets)   —   —   75

Orcutt, William Dana. ROBERT CAVALIER. Chicago, 1904   35   60   125

Orczy, Baroness (Emmuska). THE EMPEROR'S
    CANDLESTICKS. London, 1899   —   150   250

O'Reilly, Montagu. *See* New Directions

Origo, Iris. *See* GIANNI JUNE 23RD . . .

Orlovitz, Gil. CONCERNING MAN. Banyan Press.
New York, 1947. 350 numbered copies. (Also first of
press) — 75 100

O'Rourke, P. J. PARLIAMENT OF WHORES.
New York (1991) — — 40

Ortega y Gassett, José. THE REVOLT OF THE MASSES.
London (1932) — 125 300
New York (1932) — 75 150

Orton, Joe. ENTERTAINING MR. SLOANE. London (1964) — 75 125

Orwell, George (Eric Arthur Blair). DOWN AND OUT IN
PARIS AND LONDON. London, 1933 200 3,000 4,000
New York, 1933 150 850 1,750

Osborn, John Jay, Jr. THE PAPER CHASE. Boston, 1971 — 35 125

Osborn, Laughton. See SIXTY YEARS . . .

Osborn, Paul. THE VINEGAR TREE. New York (1931) — — 75

Osborne, John. LOOK BACK IN ANGER. London, 1957.
Wraps. (Evans Bros edition preceded Faber edition) 30 100 200
New York, 1957 — 40 60

O'Shaughnessy, Arthur W. E. AN EPIC OF WOMEN . . .
London, 1870. First issue: pictorial title precedes title 125 200 200

O'Sheel, Shaemus. THE BLOSSOMY BOUGH.
New York, 1911 25 35 100

Ostenso, Maria. A FAR LAND. New York, 1924. 25 signed
and lettered copies — — 250
125 signed and numbered copies — 50 100

Ostroff, Anthony. IMPERATIVES. New York (1962) — 25 50

O'Sullivan, Seumas (James Sullivan Starkey). THE TWILIGHT
PEOPLE. Dublin, 1905. Wraps — 125 200

Otis, James (Otis Kaler). TOBY TYLER OR TEN WEEKS
WITH A CIRCUS. New York, 1881. First issue: title and
illustration on spine centered 100 150 350

OUR NIG; OR, SKETCHES FROM THE LIFE OF A FREE
BLACK . . . (Harriet E. Wilson). Boston, 1859 — — 10,000

Oursler, Fulton. BEHOLD THE DREAMER! New York (1924) — — 125

Also see Anthony Abbott

OUTCROPPINGS . . . (Edited anonymously by Bret Harte).
San Francisco, 1866 150 250 350

OUTRE-MER: A PILGRIMAGE BEYOND THE SEA. NO. I . . .
  (Henry Wadsworth Longfellow). Boston, 1833–4.
  Volume I: wraps. Binding A: five-line quotation; imprint
  in two lines; no publisher's name. (Blanck notes that
  there are a number of variant wrappered and cloth
  bindings). Volume II: printed blue wraps. (Blanck notes
  a number of variant bindings with variant binding A
  being in brown paper boards with brown muslin spine
  lettered in gold) — 1,000 1,500 1,500
  New York, 1835. 2 volumes in original cloth — — 750

  (Five Spanish translations between French grammars
  and this)

Overbrook Press. MODERN LOVE. By George Meredith.
  Stamford, 1934. 150 copies in slipcase. First book of
  press — — 125

Owen, Howard. LITTLE JOHN. Sag Harbor (1992). Cloth — — 200
  Wraps — — 50

Owen, Mary Alicia (Editor). VOODOO TALES AS TOLD
  AMONG THE NEGROES . . . New York, 1893 — — 350

Owen, Robert. A NEW VIEW OF HUMAN SOCIETY . . .
  London, 1813/14. (Four parts in one). (£14,000 at auction
  in 1991) — 1,200 7,500

Owen, Robert Dale. MORAL PHYSIOLOGY . . . New York,
  1831 — 750 1,000

Owen, Wilfred. POEMS. London, 1920 200 600 1,250
  New York (1921) — 350 750

Owens, Rochelle. NOT BE ESSENCE THAT CANNOT BE.
  New York (1961). Wraps 25 50 50

OWL CREEK LETTERS, THE. (Wm. C. Prime). New York,
  1848 — 125 250

Oxenham, Elsie J(eanette) (Dunkerley). GOBLIN ISLAND.
  London, 1907 — — 350

Ozick, Cynthia. TRUST. New York (1966) — 100 250
  (London, 1966) — 75 100

P

Padgett, Lewis (H. Kuttner and C. L. Moore). THE BRASS
  RING. New York, 1946. (Moore's first book) — 100 250

Padgett, Ron. IN ADVANCE OF THE BROKEN ARM. New
  York, 1964. Wraps. 200 numbered copies — 50 150

Page, Dorothy Myra. GATHERING STORM. London, 1932	—	—	125
Page, Stanton (Henry Blake Fuller). THE CHEVALIER OF PENSIERI-VANI. Boston, 1890. Wraps	30	200	350
Cloth	30	75	200
Page, Thomas Nelson. IN OLE VIRGINIA . . . New York, 1887. First issue: has ads headed "Popular Books . . . Old Creole Days . . . "	35	60	150
Paine, Albert Bigelow. GABRIEL: A POEM. (Fort Scott, 1889). Wraps	—	—	30
RHYMES BY TWO FRIENDS. Fort Scott (1893). (Written with W. A. White). (500 copies)	40	75	450
Painter, Charlotte. THE FORTUNES OF LAURIE BREAUX. Boston, 1961	—	40	40
Pakenham, Antonia (Antonia Fraser). KING ARTHUR AND THE KNIGHTS OF THE ROUND TABLE. London, 1954	—	—	100
Paley, Grace. THE LITTLE DISTURBANCES OF MAN. Garden City, 1959	25	75	200
London, 1960	—	35	100
Palmer, (Charles) Stuart. THE ACE OF JADES. New York, 1931	—	300	600
THE PENGUIN POOL MURDERS. New York, 1931	—	250	500
Pancake, Breece D'J. THE STORIES OF BREECE . . . Boston (1983)	—	30	35
Pangborn, Edgar. WEST OF THE SUN. New York, 1953	—	—	125
Paretsky, Sara. INDEMNITY ONLY. New York (1982)	—	—	1,250
London, 1982	—	—	350
Pargeter, Edith (Ellis Peters). HORTENSIUS . . . New York, 1937	—	—	450
Parini, Jay. SINGING IN TIME. St. Andrews (Scotland, 1972). Wraps	—	—	60
Parker, Dorothy. MEN I'M NOT MARRIED TO. Garden City, 1922. (Dos-a-dos)	75	200	450
(Previous collaborations)			
Parker, Robert B(rown). THE GODWULF MANUSCRIPT. Boston, 1974	—	150	350
Parker, T. Jefferson. LAGUNA HEAT. New York, 1985	—	—	30

Parker, Theodore. THE PREVIOUS QUESTION . . . Boston, 1840. Wraps	—	100	200
Parkinson, C. Northcote. EDWARD PELLEW . . . London (1934)	—	125	200
Parkman, Francis, Jr. THE CALIFORNIA AND OREGON TRAIL. New York, 1849. 2 volumes in wraps	—	8,500	8,500
1 volume. Cloth. First issue: terminal catalog inserted	—	1,000	1,500
Parks, Gordon. FLASH PHOTOGRAPHY. Grosset & Dunlap. New York (1947). Wraps	—	—	150
THE LEARNING TREE. New York (1963)	—	35	100
Parks, Tim. TONGUES OF FLAME. New York (1985)	—	—	35
Parley, Peter (S. G. Goodrich). THE TALES OF PETER PARLEY ABOUT AMERICA. Boston, 1827	2,000	3,500	7,500
Parrish, Anne. A POCKETFUL OF POSES. New York (1923)	—	75	175
Parrish, Maxfield. *See* L. Frank Baum			
Parsons, Louella. HOW TO WRITE FOR THE MOVIES. Chicago, 1915	—	75	100
Parton, James. THE LIFE OF HORACE GREELEY . . . New York, 1855	—	75	100
PASSAGES FROM THE DIARY OF A LATE PHYSICIAN. (Samuel Warren). New York, 1831. (Pirated)	—	350	350
London, 1832. 2 volumes	—	150	150
PASSION FLOWERS. (Julia Ward Howe). Boston, 1854	—	125	350
Pastan, Linda. A PERFECT CIRCLE OF SUN. Chicago (1971)	—	40	60
Patchen, Kenneth. BEFORE THE BRAVE. New York (1936)	100	250	300
Pater, Walter. STUDIES IN THE HISTORY OF THE RENAISSANCE. London, 1873	60	75	200
Patmore, Coventry. POEMS. London, 1844	50	750	600
Paton, Alan (Stewart). MEDITATION FOR A YOUNG BOY CONFIRMED. London, 1944	—	200	750
CRY THE BELOVED COUNTRY. London, 1948	15	100	300
New York, 1948	—	50	250
Patrick, Q. (Richard Wilson Webb et al.). COTTAGE SINISTER. London, 1931	—	100	500
Patrick, Vincent. THE POPE OF GREENWICH VILLAGE. New York, 1979	—	—	25

Patterson, Harry. SAD WIND FROM THE SEA. London, 1959	—	—	100
Patterson, Richard North. THE LASKO TANGENT. New York, 1979	—	—	50
Pauker, John. YOKED BY VIOLENCE. Denver, 1949	—	75	75
Paul, Eliot. INDELIBLE, A STORY OF LOVE . . . Boston, 1922	30	200	600
Paul, Louis. THE PUMPKIN COACH. New York, 1935	—	25	40
Paulding, J(ames) K(irke). *See* Hector Bull-us *and* Launcelot Langstaff			
PAULINE: A FRAGMENT OF A CONFESSION. (Robert Browning). London, 1833	25,000	25,000	40,000
Also see Robert Browning			
Pavey, L. A. MR. LINE. London, 1931	—	40	75
Payne, David. CONFESSIONS OF A TAOIST ON WALL STREET. Boston, 1984	—	—	60
Payton, Lew. DID ADAM SIN? Los Angeles (1937). Wraps	35	50	100
Peabody, Elizabeth Palmer. *See* FIRST LESSONS . . .			
Peake, Mervyn. CAPTAIN SLAUGHTERBOARD DROPS ANCHOR. London, 1939	250	2,000	2,500
London, 1945	—	250	300
SHAPES AND SOUNDS. London, 1941	35	—	350
Pearce, Donn. COOL HAND LUKE. New York (1965)	—	50	100
London, 1965	—	—	60
Pears, Iain. THE RAPHAEL AFFAIR. London, 1990	—	—	60
Pearson, Edmund L. *See* THE OLD LIBRARIAN'S ALMANACK			
Pearson, T. R. A SHORT HISTORY OF A SMALL PLACE. New York, 1985	—	—	75
Peattie, Donald Culross. BLOWN LEAVES. (Chicago) 1916. Wraps	—	1,000	1,000
Peck, George (Wilbur). ADVENTURES OF ONE TERRENCE MCGRANT . . . New York, 1871	75	150	300
PECK'S BAD BOY AND HIS PA. Chicago, 1883. Cloth	40	250	400
Wraps	—	—	300
Pelican Books. THE INTELLIGENT WOMAN'S GUIDE TO SOCIALISM. By G. B. Shaw. London, 1937. 2 volumes. Wraps in dustwrapper. (First book of this imprint)	—	50	150

Pelieu, Claude. AUTOMATIC PILOT. New York/San Francisco (1964). Wraps	15	35	60
Pemberton, Sir Max. DIARY OF A SCOUNDREL. London, 1891	—	50	300
JEWEL MYSTERIES I HAVE KNOWN . . . London, 1894	—	100	250
Pendleton, Tom. THE IRON ORCHARD. New York (1966)	—	40	40
Penguin Books. ARIEL. By André Maurois. London, 1935. Wraps in dustwrapper	—	—	300
Penn, Irving. MOMENTS PRESERVED. New York, 1960. Issued in dustwrapper and slipcase	—	—	500
Pennington, Patience (Elizabeth Pringle). A WOMAN RICE PLANTER. New York, 1913	—	60	100
PEN OWEN. (James Hook). Edinburgh, 1822. 3 volumes	—	—	350
Pentecost, Hugh (Judson Pentecost Philips). CANCELLED IN RED. New York, 1939	—	40	150
PENTLAND RISING, THE. (Robert Louis Stevenson). Edinburgh, 1866. Wraps	400	1,750	3,000
Perchik, Simon. THE BOMBER MOON. (New York, 1950). Wraps	—	50	75
Percy, Walker. SYMBOL AS NEED. Fordham University. New York (1954). An offprint in stapled wraps	—	500	1,000
THE MOVIEGOER. New York, 1961	50	600	2,000
London, 1963	—	200	600
Percy, William Alexander. SAPPHO IN LEVKAS . . . New York, 1915	—	75	150
Perelman, S(idney) J(oseph). DAWN GINSBURG'S REVENGE. New York (1929). First issue: apple green binding	125	600	1,250
Second issue: silver binding	50	250	750
Perishable Press. *See* Walter Hamady			
Perkins, Charlotte. IN THIS OUR WORLD . . . London, 1893	—	—	3,000
San Francisco, 1895. Wraps	—	—	1,000
Second edition: add'l 46 poems			
Perkoff, Stuart Z. THE SUICIDE ROOM. Karlsruhe, 1956. Wraps. (200 copies)	—	50	175
Perles, Alfred. SENTIMENTS LIMITROPHES. Paris, 1935. Wraps	—	125	150

SYMBOL AS NEED

WALKER PERCY

Reprinted from
THOUGHT
FORDHAM UNIVERSITY QUARTERLY
Vol. XXIX, No. 114, Autumn, 1954

Perry, Charles. PORTRAIT OF A YOUNG MAN DROWNING.
New York, 1962 — 40 50

Perry, George S. WALLS RISE UP. New York, 1939 — 60 60

Perry, Thomas. THE BUTCHER'S BOY. New York, 1982 — 100 150

Perse, St. J(ohn) (Alexis St. Leger). ANABASIS. London,
1930. (Translated by T. S. Eliot). 350 copies signed by
Eliot. Slipcase 200 500 600
Trade edition. Top edge green. White dustwrapper — 150 200

PESSIMUS: A RHAPSODY . . . (Frederick William Orde
Ward). London, 1865 — — 200

Peterkin, Julia. GREEN THURSDAY. New York, 1924.
2,000 numbered copies 40 125 200

Peters, Curtis Arnoux. See Peter Arno

Peters, Elizabeth (Barbara Louise Gross Mertz). THE JACKEL'S
HEAD. New York (1968). (First under this name) — — 200

Also see Barbara Michaels

Peters, Ellis. DEATH MASK. London, 1959. (First under this
name) — — 500

Also see Edith Pargeter

Peters, Lenrie. POEMS. Ibadan (1964). Wraps — — 100

Petievich, Gerald. MONEY MEN AND ONE-SHOT DEAL.
New York, 1981 — — 75

Petrakis, Harry Mark. LION AT MY HEART. Boston, 1959 — 60 75
London, 1959 — 40 60

Petry, Ann (Lane). THE STREET. Boston, 1946 25 75 350

Pharr, Robert Dean. THE BOOK OF NUMBERS. Garden City,
1969 — 50 75

Phillips, David Graham. See John Graham

Phillips, Jayne Anne. SWEETHEARTS. Carrboro, 1976.
10 copies in boards. Signed — — 750
Wraps. (400 copies) — 125 200
St. Paul, 1978. Wraps. (600 copies) — 30 75

(Preceded by two related broadsides)

Phillips, Mike. BLOOD RIGHTS. London, 1989 — — 50

Phillips, Stephen. ORESTES . . . London, 1884. Wraps — 150 150

Phillpotts, Eden. *See* THE GHOST IN THE BANK OF ENGLAND

MY ADVENTURES IN THE FLYING SCOTSMAN. London, 1888. Stiff wraps. First issue:			
rainbow-colored cloth	100	1,000	1,500
Wraps	—	—	1,750

Phoutrides, Aristides. LIGHTS AT DAWN. Boston, 1917	—	30	50

Piatt, John J. *See* POEMS OF TWO FRIENDS

Pickard, Tom. HIGH ON THE WALLS. London, 1967.			
50 signed copies	15	60	100
Trade edition	—	20	40

Picthall, Marmaduke. SAID THE FISHERMAN. London, 1903	50	75	100

Piercy, Marge. BREAKING CAMP. Middletown (1968). Cloth	—	50	125
Wraps	—	15	35

Pierpont, John. THE PORTRAIT. Boston, 1812	30	35	75

PIGS IS PIGS. (Ellis Parker Butler). Chicago, 1905. (Author's name on first page of text)	—	200	400

Pike, Albert. PROSE SKETCHES AND POEMS . . . Boston, 1834	—	1,250	2,000

Pilgrim, Thomas. *See* Arthur Morecamp

Pillin, William. POEMS. Prairie City, 1939. Wraps	15	40	100

Pim, Herbert Moore. THE PESSIMIST. Dublin, 1914	—	—	125
SELECTED POEMS. Dublin, 1917. Wraps	25	60	60

Pinchot, Gifford. BILTMORE FOREST. Chicago, 1893	—	75	75

Pinckney, Darryl. HIGH COTTON. New York (1992)	—	—	75

Pinckney, Josephine. SEA-DRINKING CITIES. New York, 1927. 225 signed and numbered copies	—	—	300
Trade edition. 250 copies	—	125	150

Pinkerton, Allan. TESTS ON PASSENGER CONDUCTORS. Chicago, 1867. Wraps	150	200	250

Pinter, Harold. THE BIRTHDAY PARTY. London, 1959. (Encore Publications). Wraps	40	175	250

Pirsig, Robert M. ZEN AND THE ART OF MOTORCYCLE MAINTENANCE. New York (1974)	—	50	250
London (1974)	—	40	75
New York, 1984. 1,000 signed and numbered copies	—	—	250

Pitter, Ruth. FIRST POEMS. London, 1920. Stiff wraps 50 75 175

Pitt-Kethley, Fiona. LONDON. London, 1984. Wraps — — 50

Plaidy, Jean. BEYOND THE BLUE MOUNTAINS.
New York (1947) — 50 60

Plante, David. THE GHOST OF HENRY JAMES. London,
1970. With or without errata — 100 200
Boston, 1970 — 50 125

Plath, Sylvia. SCULPTOR. Greencourt Review. (No-place, 1959).
Wraps. Offprint. (Reportedly 25 copies) — — 1,500

THE COLOSSUS . . . London (1960) 75 850 850
New York (1962) 50 125 200

Also see A WINTER SHIP

Player, Robert. THE INGENIOUS MR. STONE . . .
London, 1945 — — 100

Plimpton, George. LETTERS IN TRAINING. (No-place) 1946 — — 300

THE RABBIT'S UMBRELLA. New York, 1955 30 50 150

Plomer, William (Charles Franklyn). TURBOTT WOLFE.
London, 1925 40 200 400

Plowman, Max. FIRST POEMS. London, 1913 — 50 75

Plunket, Robert. MY SEARCH FOR WARREN HARDING.
New York, 1983 — — 35

Plunkett, James. THE EAGLES AND THE TRUMPETS.
Dublin, 1954 — — 150

THE TRUSTING AND THE MAIMED . . . London, 1959.
(New title) — 35 100

Plunkett, Joseph Mary. THE CIRCLE AND THE SWORD.
Dublin, 1911. Wraps 125 200 200

Poe, Edgar Allan. *See* TAMERLANE

TAMERLANE . . . London, 1884. Vellum. (100 copies) 100 1,250 2,500
San Francisco, 1923. 125 numbered copies. 2 volumes.
Issued in slipcase — — 1,000
(No-place, no-date [London, 1931]). 295 numbered
copies. Wraps — — 350

POEM AND VALEDICTORY ORATION . . . (Edw. R. Sill).
New York, 1861. Wraps — 150 150

POEM ON THE RISING GLORY OF AMERICA. (Hugh Henry
    Brackenridge and Philip Freneau). Philadelphia, 1772   —   200   2,500

POEMS. (Anna Laetitia Alkin). London, 1773   —   —   300

POEMS. (Siegfried Sassoon). (London, 1906). Wraps.
    (50 copies)   150   2,500   5,000

    Also see KAIN

POEMS BY TWO BROTHERS. (Charles Alfred and Frederick
    Tennyson). London (1827). Boards. Large paper copies.
    (Alfred's first book)   400   1,500   7,500
    Re-bound   —   —   3,000
    Wraps. Small paper copies   —   750   3,500
    Re-bound   —   —   1,000

POEMS OF TWO FRIENDS. (William Dean Howells and John
    J. Piatt). Columbus, Ohio, 1860   250   800   750

Pohl, Frederik. THE SPACE MERCHANTS. New York (1953).
    (Written with C. M. Kornbluth). Cloth   —   100   300
    Wraps   —   15   40

    ALTERNATING CURRENTS. New York, 1956. Cloth   —   500   500
    Wraps   —   25   35

    (Previous edited anthologies)

Polite, Carlene Hatcher. THE FLAGELLANTS. New York
    (1967)   —   25   60

    (French edition in 1966 preceded)

Politi, Leo. LITTLE PANCHO. New York, 1938   —   75   75

Pollini, Francis. NIGHT. Paris (1960). Wraps and
    dustwrapper   —   50   100

Pollock, Channing. BEHOLD THE MAN. Washington, 1901   25   75   100

Ponicsan, Darryl. THE LAST DETAIL. New York, 1970   —   35   75

Pool, Marie Louise. A VACATION IN A BUGGY. New
    York, 1887   —   50   50

Poole, Ernest. KATHERINE BRESHOVSKY . . . Chicago, 1905.
    Pictorial wraps   75   100   300

Porter, Alan. THE SIGNATURE OF PAIN . . .
    New York, 1931   30   50   75
    London, 1930   —   —   60

Porter, Eleanor H(odgman). CROSS CURRENTS. Boston,
    1907   —   —   150

Porter, Gene Stratton. THE SONG OF THE CARDINAL. Indianapolis (1903)	60	125	250
Porter, Katherine Anne. See M. T. F.			
OUTLINE OF MEXICAN POPULAR ARTS AND CRAFTS. (Los Angeles) 1922. Wraps	150	500	2,000
Porter, Katherine Anne Herwig Shaw. See Kathleen Winsor			
Porter, Peter. ONCE BITTEN, TWICE BITTEN. London, 1961	—	—	75
Porter, William Sidney. See O. Henry			
Porterfield, Nolan. A WAY OF KNOWING. New York (1971)	—	40	50
Portis, Charles. NORWOOD. New York (1966)	15	40	125
Posner, David. AND TOUCH. Trenton, 1940	—	—	150
THE DOUBLE VISION. Paris, 1948. Wraps	—	75	100
Post, Melville Davisson. THE STRANGE SCHEMES OF RANDOLPH MASON. New York, 1896. Wraps	—	350	500
Cloth	—	300	400
Postgate, Raymond (William). VERDICT OF TWELVE. London (1940)	—	100	200
New York, 1940	—	40	100
Potok, Chaim. THE CHOSEN. New York, 1967	—	—	75
Potter, Beatrix. THE TALE OF PETER RABBIT. London (1901). (Privately printed). December, 1901. (250 copies)	2,000	3,000	85,000
February, 1902. (200 copies)	1,250	2,000	15,000
October, 1902. First trade edition. Boards and cloth. First issue: holly leaf end papers; "wept" for "shed" p. 51	750	750	1,500
Potter, Dennis. THE GLITTERING COFFIN. London, 1960	—	35	100
Pottle, Frederick A. SHELLY AND BROWNING. Chicago, 1923. (125 numbered copies)	—	—	200
Pound, Ezra (Loomis). A LUME SPENTO. (Venice, Italy) 1908. Wraps. (150 copies)	10,000	20,000	40,000
Powell, Adam Clayton, Jr. MARCHING BLACKS. New York, 1945	—	40	75
Powell, Anthony (Dymoke). BARNARD LETTERS. London, 1928. (Edited)	—	—	1,000
AFTERNOON MEN. London, 1931	150	750	1,750
New York (1932)	—	350	1,000

Powell, Enoch. FIRST POEMS. Oxford, 1937. Wraps	—	—	40
Powell, Lawrence Clark. AN INTRODUCTION TO ROBINSON JEFFERS. Dijon, 1932. Wraps. (225 copies—85 for presentation)	50	300	500
ROBINSON JEFFERS: THE MAN AND HIS WORKS. Los Angeles, 1934. (750 copies)	35	200	350
Powell, Padgett. EDISTO. New York (1984)	—	20	50
Powers, J(ames) E(arl). PRINCE OF DARKNESS. Garden City, 1947	35	75	150
London, 1948	—	60	75
Powers, Richard. THREE FARMERS ON THEIR WAY TO A DANCE. New York (1985).	—	—	175
London (1988)	—	—	75
Pownall, David. THE RAINING TREE WAR. London, 1974	—	—	50
Powys, John Cowper. CORINTH. (Oxford, 1891). Wraps. Cover states "English Verse." Powys's name appears at the end of the text	—	750	750
ODES . . . London, 1896	—	600	600
Powys, Laurence. AT THE HARLOT'S BURIAL. London, 1930. Wraps	—	—	50
Powys, Llewelyn. CONFESSIONS OF TWO BROTHERS. Rochester, 1916. (Written with J. C. Powys)	—	50	75
THIRTEEN WORTHIES. London, 1923	35	125	150
Powys, Philippa. DRIFTWOOD. London, 1930	—	125	150
Powys, T(heodore) F(rancis). AN INTERPRETATION OF GENESIS. London, 1907. (100 copies)	500	400	500
THE SOLILOQUY OF A HERMIT. New York, 1916	—	60	300
SOLILOQUIES OF A HERMIT. London, 1918. First issue: light blue boards	—	40	75
Second issue: dark blue boards	—	35	50
Prager, Emily. A VISIT FROM THE FOOTBINDER. New York (1982)	—	—	35
Prather, Richard S(cott). CASE OF THE VANISHING BEAUTY. New York (1950). Wraps	—	20	40
Pratt, E. J. See RACHEL: A SEA-STORY OF NEWFOUNDLAND			

Pratt, Fletcher. THE HEROIC YEARS . . . 1801–1815.
New York, 1934 — 60 75

PRECAUTION: A NOVEL. (James Fenimore Cooper). New
York, 1820. 2 volumes. First issue: errata slip.
In original boards 300 2,000 4,500
Re-bound — — 1,500
London, 1821. 3 volumes — — 1,500

Prewett, Frank. POEMS. Richmond (England, 1921). Wraps 40 60 75

Price, Emerson. INN OF THAT JOURNEY.
Caldwell (Iowa), 1939 — 40 50

Price, (Edward) Reynolds. ONE SUNDAY IN LATE JULY.
London, 1960. Wraps. (Offprint from *Encounter*
Magazine). Wraps 100 2,500 2,500

A LONG AND HAPPY LIFE. New York, 1962. First issue:
names on dustwrapper blurbs printed in pale
yellowish-green 25 100 150
London, 1962 15 75 100

Price, Richard. THE WANDERERS. Boston, 1974 — 35 75
London, 1975 — 35 50

Priest, Christopher. INDOCTRINAIRE . . . London, 1970 — — 125

Priestly, J(ohn) B(oynton). THE CHAPMAN OF RHYMES.
London, 1918. Wraps 35 400 600

Prime, William Cowper. *See* THE OWL CREEK LETTERS . . .

PRIMULA . . . (Richard Garnett). London, 1858 — 200 300

Prince, F(rank) T(empleton). POEMS. London (1938) — 75 75
(Norfolk, 1941). Wraps in dustwrapper — 60 60

Pringle, Elizabeth Waties Allston. *See* Patience Pennington

Prior, Matthew. *See* THE HIND AND THE PANTHER . . .

Pritchett, V(ictor) S(awdon). MARCHING SPAIN. London,
1928. Cloth 25 250 350
Wraps. (Left Book Club) — 75 75

Probyn, May. POEMS. London, 1881 — — 100

Proffitt, Nicholas. GARDENS OF STONE. New York, 1983 — — 35

Prokosch, Frederick. THREE MYSTERIES. New Hampshire,
1932 — 250 250

THE ASIATICS. New York, 1935. (First novel, tenth book)	30	75	100
London, 1935	—	75	75
Pronzini, Bill. THE STALKER. New York (1971)	—	—	100
Prose, Francine. JUDAH THE PIOUS. New York, 1973	—	30	60
London (1973)	—	—	40
Proteus (Wilfred Scawen Blunt). SONNETS AND SONGS. London, 1875	200	200	200
Proulx, E. Annie. THE COMPLETE DAIRY FOODS COOKBOOK. Emmaus, Penna. (1982). Written with Lew Nichols. Pictorial boards. Perhaps issued both with and without dustwrapper	—	—	125
HEART SONG . . . New York, 1988. (First fiction)	—	—	300
Pryce-Jones, David. OWLS AND SATYRS. London, 1961	—	—	50
Prynne, J. H. NEWS OF THE WARRING CLANS. London, 1977. Wraps	—	—	75
Pudney, John. SPRING ENCOUNTER. London, 1933	—	50	60
Puig, Manuel. BETRAYED BY RITA HAYWORTH. New York, 1971	—	—	175
Purdy, Al. THE ENCHANTED ECHO. Vancouver, 1944	—	600	600
Purdy, James. DON'T CALL ME BY MY RIGHT NAME . . . New York, 1956. Wraps (noted in both gray and white variants)	50	125	250
Putnam, Howard Phelps. TRINC. New York (1927)	—	75	75
Putnam, Samuel. EVAPORATION . . . Winchester, 1923. (Written with Mark Turbyfill)	—	100	200
FRANÇOIS RABELAIS . . . New York (1929)	—	50	125
Puzo, Mario. THE DARK ARENA. New York (1955)	25	60	100
Pyle, Ernie. ERNIE PYLE IN ENGLAND. New York (1941)	—	—	75
Pyle, Howard. YANKEE DOODLE. New York, 1881. First illustrated book	75	500	750
THE MERRY ADVENTURES OF ROBIN HOOD. New York, 1883. Leather	150	—	1,000
Cloth	—	400	600
London, 1883	75	300	500
Pym, Barbara. SOME TAME GAZELLE. London, 1950	—	125	300

Don't Call Me By My Right Name

AND OTHER STORIES

by James Purdy

WITH ILLUSTRATIONS BY THE AUTHOR

 THE WILLIAM-FREDERICK PRESS

NEW YORK   1956

Pynchon, Thomas. V. Philadelphia (1963)	125	350	850
London (1963)	75	200	250

Q

Q. (Sir Arthur Quiller-Couch). DEAD MAN'S ROCK.
London, 1887	—	250	400

Queen, Ellery (Frederic Dannay and Manfred B. Lee).
ROMAN HAT MYSTERY. New York, 1929	100	1,000	3,500
New York (1974). 250 signed and numbered copies in dustwrapper	—	—	200

Quennell, Peter. MASQUES AND POEMS. Berkshire (1922)	40	125	200

Quiller-Couch, Sir Arthur. *See* Q.

Quillinan, Dorothy Wordsworth. *See* JOURNAL OF A FEW
MONTHS' RESIDENCE IN PORTUGAL . . .

Quine, W. V. O. A SYSTEM OF LOGISTIC. Cambridge, 1934	—	—	150

Quinn, Arthur Hobson. PENNSYLVANIA STORIES.
Philadelphia, 1899	35	75	100

Quinn, Seabury (Grandin). ROADS. (New York, 1938).
Wraps. (Reprinted from *Weird Tales*)	—	150	2,500
Sauk City, 1948	—	75	150

R
R.,C. G. (Christina G. Rossetti). VERSES. London, 1847	—	4,000	6,000
R. E. (W. W. E. Ross). LACONICS. Ottawa, 1930	—	—	1,750

Raban, Jonathan. THE TECHNIQUE OF MODERN FICTION.
London, 1968. Wraps	—	—	40

Rabe, David. THE BASIC TRAINING OF PAVLO HUMMEL and
STICKS AND BONES. New York (1973). Cloth	—	—	60
Wraps	—	—	20

RACHEL: A SEA-STORY OF NEWFOUNDLAND. (E. J. Pratt).
New York, 1917. Wraps	—	—	3,000

Radcliffe, Ann (Ward). THE MYSTERIES OF UDOLPHO.
London, 1794. 4 volumes	—	500	1,500

Radiguet, Raymond. THE COUNT'S BALL. New York (1929)	—	—	200

Rago, Henry. THE PHILOSOPHY OF ESTHETIC
INDIVIDUALISM. Notre Dame, 1941. Wraps	—	75	100

Raine, Kathleen (Jessie). STONE AND FLOWER.
(London, 1943)	25	90	125

Raine, William MacLeod. A DAUGHTER OF RAASAY.
   New York (1902)   —   150   150

Rakosi, Carl. SELECTED POEMS. (New York, 1941). Wraps   —   —   150

Ramal, Walter (Walter De La Mare). SONGS OF
     CHILDHOOD. London, 1902   500   400   600
     London, 1923. 310 signed copies   —   —   150

Rand, Ayn. WE THE LIVING. London (1936)   —   1,000   2,500
   New York, 1936   60   750   2,500

   NIGHT OF JANUARY 16TH. New York (1936). Wraps   50   250   750

Randall, Julia. THE SOLSTICE TREE. Baltimore, 1952   35   50   60

Randall, Robert (Randall Garrett and Robert Silverberg).
   THE SHROUDED PLANET. New York, 1957   —   35   50

Random House. CANDIDE. New York, 1928. 1,470 copies
   signed by Rockwell Kent   75   150   300

Ransom, John Crowe. POEMS ABOUT GOD. New
   York, 1919   —   500   600

Ransome, Arthur. THE SOULS OF THE STREET . . .
   London, 1904   —   60   600

Ransom Press. OPEN SHUTTERS. By Oliver Jenkins.
   Chicago, 1922. (245 copies)   50   150   125

Raphael, Frederic. OBBLIGATO. London, 1956   —   50   60

Raphaelson, Samson. THE JAZZ SINGER. New York, 1925   —   —   200

Rathbone, Julian. DIAMONDS BID. London, 1967   —   —   40

Rattigan, Terrence (Mervyn). FRENCH WITHOUT TEARS.
   London, 1936. Cloth   —   75   200
   Wraps   —   —   75
   New York, 1938   —   —   150

Raven, Simon. THE FEATHERS OF DEATH. London, 1959   —   50   150

Rawlings, Marjorie Kinnan. SOUTH MOON UNDER. New
   York, 1933. (Scribner's "A" on copyright page)   —   150   750

Raworth, Tom. THE RELATION SHIP. (London, 1966).
   50 signed and numbered copies. Wraps   —   50   125
   450 copies. Wraps   —   30   60

Rawson, Clayton. DEATH FROM A TOP HAT. New
   York, 1938   —   250   350

Reach, Angus B(ethune). CLEMENT LORIMER . . . London,
   1849. With frontis and 11 plates   —   400   500

Read, Herbert. SONGS OF CHAOS. London (1915)	—	200	450
NAKED WARRIORS. London, 1919. (First commercially published book)	25	100	300
Read, Piers Paul. GAME IN HEAVEN WITH TUSSY MARX. London, 1966	—	50	50
New York, 1966	—	25	25
Read, Thomas Buchanan. PAUL REDDING . . . Boston, 1845	—	125	150
Reade, Charles. PEG WOFFINGTON. London, 1853	—	100	200
Reading, Peter. WATER AND WASTE. Walton-on-Thames, 1970. Wraps	—	—	150
Reamy, Tom. BLIND VOICES. New York, 1978	—	—	40
Reaney, James. THE RED HEART. Toronto, 1949	—	300	350
Reavey, George. FAUST'S METAMORPHOSES . . . Seine (1932). Wraps	—	100	250
Rechy, John. CITY OF THE NIGHT. New York (1963)	—	30	75
London, 1964	—	—	50
Redding, J(ay) Saunders. TO MAKE A POET BLACK. Chapel Hill, 1939	30	50	350
Redgrove, Peter (William). THE COLLECTOR . . . London, 1960	15	40	100
Redman, Ben Ray. MASQUERADE. New York, 1923	—	25	35
Reed, Henry. A MAP OF VERONA . . . London (1946)	—	75	75
Reed, Ishmael. THE FREELANCE PALLBEARERS. Garden City, 1967	20	60	150
Reed, Jeremy. TARGET: PRELIMINARY POEMS. LaHaule, Jersey, 1972. 100 signed and numbered copies. Wraps	—	—	75
Reed, John Silas. DIANA'S DEBUT. Harvard (Cambridge, 1910). Lyrics by Reed. Wraps	—	—	1,750
SANGAR, TO LINCOLN STEFFENS. Riverside, Conn., 1913. Wraps. 500 copies. Boxed	100	100	300
THE DAY IN BOHEMIA. New York, 1913. Stiff wraps. 500 copies. In slipcase. (Priority uncertain)	100	100	300
Reed, Kit. MOTHER ISN'T DEAD, SHE'S ONLY SLEEPING. New York, 1961	—	35	50
Reese, Lizette Woodworth. A BRANCH OF MAY. Baltimore, 1887	100	250	300

Reeve, Arthur B(enjamin). THE SILENT BULLET. New York, 1912	—	100	125
THE BLACK HAND. London, 1912	—	100	100
Reeves, James. THE NATURAL NEED. Oeya/London (1935)	—	125	125
Reid, Alastair. TO LIGHTEN MY HOUSE. Scarsdale (1953)	—	40	60
(Previous privately printed pamphlet)			
Reid, Desmond (Michael Moorcock and Jim Cawthorn). CARIBBEAN CRISIS. London (1962). Wraps	—	75	175
Reid, Forrest. THE KINGDOM OF TWILIGHT. London, 1904	50	125	350
Reid, (Thomas) Mayne. THE WHITE CHIEF . . . London, 1855. 3 volumes	—	500	600
Reid, Victor S. NEW DAY. New York, 1949	—	75	75
London, 1950	—	—	50
Reiser, Anton. ALBERT EINSTEIN: A BIOGRAPHICAL PORTRAIT. New York, 1931. (Translated anonymously by Louis Zukofsky)	—	600	750
London (1931)`	—	400	500
Remarque, Erich Maria. ALL QUIET ON THE WESTERN FRONT. London (1929)	40	125	250
Boston, 1929	30	75	150
Remington, Frederic (Sackrider). PONY TRACKS. New York, 1895. Suede	150	1,000	1,000
Cloth	—	250	450
Renault, Mary (Mary Challans). PURPOSES OF LOVE. London, 1939	25	125	300
PROMISE OF LOVE. New York, 1940. (New title)	15	75	175
Rendell, Ruth. FROM DOON WITH DEATH. London (1964)	—	125	1,250
Garden City, 1965	—	—	600
Renek, Morris. THE BIG HELLO. New York, 1961	—	30	30
Repplier, Agnes. BOOKS AND MEN. Boston, 1888	25	50	75
Rexroth, Kenneth. IN WHAT HOUR. New York, 1940	50	200	250
Reynolds, Tim. POEMS 1962-4. (No-place) 1964. 25 signed and numbered copies. Wraps. (8" x 11" stapled sheets)	—	—	150
RYOANJI. New York, 1964	15	35	40
(Preceded by a self-published item)			

PONY TRACKS

WRITTEN AND
ILLUSTRATED BY
FREDERIC REMINGTON

NEW YORK
HARPER & BROTHERS PUBLISHERS
FRANKLIN SQUARE
1895

GOODBYE, COLUMBUS

AND FIVE SHORT STORIES

BY PHILIP ROTH

1959

HOUGHTON MIFFLIN COMPANY BOSTON

The Riverside Press Cambridge

Two hundred copies of this
book have been printed, of
which this is No. 198...

Karl Jay Shapiro

Poems

Karl Jay Shapiro

Baltimore, Maryland
1935

Reznikoff, Charles. RHYTHMS. Brooklyn (Privately printed, 1918). Wraps	400	1,000	1,750
Rhode, John (Major Cecil John Charles Street). A. S. F. THE STORY OF A GREAT CONSPIRACY. London (1924)	—	150	300
THE WHITE MENACE. New York (1926). New title	—	100	200
Rhodes, Eugene Manlove. GOOD MEN AND TRUE. New York, 1910	100	100	200
Rhodes, W(illiam) H(enry). CAXTON'S BOOK. San Francisco, 1876	30	250	250
RHYMES OF IRONQUILL. (By Eugene Fitch Ware). Topeka, 1885	—	75	75
Rhys, Ernest. A LONDON ROSE . . . London, 1894	—	75	125
Rhys, Jean. LEFT BANK . . . New York (1927) 500Ricci, Nina. LIVES OF THE SAINTS. Toronto, 1990	100 —	400 —	75
Rice, Alice (Caldwell) Hegen. See Alice Hegen			
Rice, Anne. INTERVIEW WITH THE VAMPIRE. New York, 1976	—	50	750
London, 1976	—	—	350
New York, 1992. 1,000 signed copies	—	—	250
Rice, Craig (Georgiana Ann Randolph). 8 FACES AT 3. New York, 1939	—	150	250
Rich, Adrienne Cecile. ARIADNE: A PLAY IN THREE ACTS. (Baltimore) 1939. Wraps	1,500	2,000	1,500
NOT I, BUT DEATH. Baltimore, 1941. Wraps	—	1,500	1,500
A CHANGE OF WORLD. New York, 1951	40	350	450
Richard, Mark. THE ICE AT THE BOTTOM OF THE WORLD. New York, 1989	—	—	40
Richards, David Adams. SMALL HEROICS. Fredericton, 1972	—	—	125
COMING OF WINTER. Ottawa, 1974. (First novel)	—	—	300
Richards, I. A. THE FOUNDATIONS OF AESTHETICS. London (1922). Written with C. K. Ogden and James Wood	—	100	150
THE MEANING OF MEANING. New York, 1923. Written with C. K. Ogden	—	100	150
PRINCIPLES OF LITERARY CRITICISM. New York, 1924	—	100	125
London, 1925	—	75	100

Richardson, Dorothy. THE QUAKERS PAST AND PRESENT. London, 1914	—	—	250
GLEANINGS FROM THE WORK OF GEORGE FOX. London, 1914	—	—	200
POINTED ROOFS. London, 1915	—	150	150
New York, 1916	—	125	125
Richardson, O(wen) W(illians). THE ELECTRON THEORY OF MATTER. Cambridge (Eng.), 1914	—	—	200
Richler, Mordecai. THE ACROBATS. (London, 1954)	—	200	450
New York, 1954. (Less than 1,000 copies)	—	100	300
Richter, Conrad. BROTHERS OF NO KIN . . . New York (1924). White dustwrapper	100	500	600
Orange dustwrapper	—	300	400
Rickword, Edgell. BEHIND THE EYES. London, 1921	—	30	30
Ridge, Lola. THE GHETTO . . . New York, 1918	—	40	75
Riding, Laura. *See* Laura Riding Gottschalk			
Ridler, Anne (Barbara). SHAKESPEARE CRITICISM, 1919–1935. (By Ridler). London, 1936	—	60	125
POEMS. London, 1939. (Most destroyed in Blitz)	40	100	125
Riley, James Whitcomb. *See* Benj. F. Johnson			
Rilke, Rainer Maria. POEMS. New York, 1918. 500 copies. (First English publication)	—	125	300
Rinehart, Mary Roberts. THE CIRCULAR STAIRCASE. Indianapolis (1908). (September copyright)	50	75	125
RIP VAN WINKLE. (By Washington Irving). Roycrofters'. (East Aurora, 1905). Initials and title page by Dard Hunter (his first book contribution)	—	100	200
Rives, Amelia. A BROTHER TO DRAGONS. New York, 1888	—	75	75
Rives, Richard. EMERGENCY. London, 1966	—	—	50
Roark, Garland. WAKE OF THE RED WITCH. Boston, 1946	—	30	50
Robbins, Harold (Harold Ruben). NEVER LOVE A STRANGER. New York, 1948	—	30	75
Robbins, Tom. GUY ANDERSON. Seattle, 1965. Wraps	—	—	750
ANOTHER ROADSIDE ATTRACTION. Garden City, 1971	—	150	500
London, 1973	—	—	200

Roberson, Ed. WHEN THE KING IS A BOY. Pittsburgh
(1970). Cloth — — 50
Wraps — — 20

Roberts, B(righam) H(enry). THE LIFE OF JOHN TAYLOR.
Salt Lake, 1892 — 150 175

Roberts, Elizabeth Madox. IN THE GREAT STEEP'S GARDEN.
(Colorado Springs, 1915). Wraps 40 3,500 4,000

UNDER THE TREE. New York, 1922 — 150 350

Roberts, Keith. THE FURIES. (London, 1966) — — 125

Roberts, Kenneth L(ewis). PANATELA . . . (Ithaca) 1907.
Wraps. (Songbook written with R. Berry) — 300 600

EUROPE'S MORNING AFTER. New York (1921) 30 200 500

Roberts, Morley. THE WESTERN AVERNUS . . . London,
1887 — 150 250

Roberts, Robert. THE HOUSE SERVANT'S DIRECTORY . . .
Boston/New York, 1827 — — 6,500

Robertson, Ben. TRAVELERS' REST. Clemson, South
Carolina (1938) — — 500

Robertson, E. (Earle Birney). CONVERSATIONS WITH
TROTSKY. London, 1936 — 1,500 2,500

Robeson, Paul. HERE I STAND. New York (1958). Cloth — 100 300
Wraps — — 150
London (1958) — — 150

Robinson, Edwin Arlington. THE TORRENT AND THE
NIGHT BEFORE. Cambridge (Mass.), 1896. Wraps 400 2,000 2,500

THE CHILDREN OF THE NIGHT. Boston, 1897.
50 copies. Vellum — 1,500 2,000
500 copies. Laid paper 300 400 750

Robinson, Linda S. MURDER IN THE PLACE OF ANUBIS.
New York, 1994 — — 50

Robinson, Marilynne. HOUSEKEEPING. New York, 1980 — 20 60

Robinson, Peter. WITH EQUAL EYE. Toronto, 1979. Wraps — — 250

GALLOWS VIEW. Markham (Canada), 1987 — — 200
New York, 1990 — — 40

Robinson, Rowland Evans. *See* Awahsoose the Bear

UNCLE 'LISHA'S SHOP.
New York, 1887 — 50 300

Robison, Mary. DAYS. New York, 1979	—	25	75
Rodd, (James) Rennell. SONGS TO THE SOUTH. London, 1881	75	125	1,000
Philadelphia, 1882	—	—	350
(Previous 1880 Newdigate prize poem)			
Rodgers, W. R. AWAKE . . . London, 1941	15	40	40
Roditi, Edouard (Herbert). POEMS FOR F. Paris (1935). Wraps	75	175	500
Rodker, John. POEMS. London (1914). Boards. 50 signed and numbered copies	—	600	750
Wraps	35	150	250
Rodman, Seldon. MORTAL TRIUMPH . . . New York (1932)	15	60	125
Roe, Edward Payson. BARRIERS BURNED AWAY. New York, 1872	50	50	50
Roethke, Theodore. OPEN HOUSE. New York, 1941. (1,000 copies)	200	600	750
Rogers, Will(iam Penn Adair). THE COWBOY PHILOSOPHER ON PROHIBITION. New York (1919)	25	50	150
Rogin, Gilbert. THE FENCING MASTER . . . New York, 1965	—	25	40
Rohmer, Sax (Arthur Henry Sarsfield Ward). PAUSE! London, 1910	—	200	600
DR. FU-MANCHU. London (1913)	—	250	500
THE INSIDIOUS DR. FU-MANCHU. New York, 1913. (New title)	—	75	150
Rolfe, Frederick William. See Baron Corvo			
Rolvaag, O. E. GIANTS IN THE EARTH. New York, 1927	—	100	175
Romanof, Panteleimon. THREE PAIRS OF SILK STOCKINGS. New York, 1931. (First English translation)	—	—	100
Romilly, Gilles and Edmond. OUT OF BOUNDS. London, 1935	—	—	175
Rook, Alan. SONGS FROM A CHERRY TREE. Oxford, 1938. Wraps	—	50	75
Rooke, Leon. LAST ONE HOME SLEEPS IN THE YELLOW BED. Baton Rouge (1968)	—	25	40

ROOKWOOD. (By William Harrison Ainsworth). London, 1834. 3 volumes — — 600

Rooney, Andy. AIR GUNNER. New York (1944). Written with Bud Hutton — 40 60

Roosevelt, Eleanor. IT'S UP TO THE WOMEN. New York, 1933 — 75 200

Roosevelt, Franklin D. WHITHER BOUND? Boston, 1926 50 200 600

Roosevelt, Theodore. THE SUMMER BIRDS OF THE ADIRONDACKS. (Salem, 1877). Wraps. (Written with H. D. Minot) 50 400 1,750

THE NAVAL WAR OF 1812 . . . New York, 1882 35 200 750

Root, E. Merrill. LOST EDEN. New York, 1927 — 50 50

Rorem, Ned. THE PARIS DIARY OF NED ROREM. New York (1966) — — 40

Ros, Amanda M'Kittrick. IRENE IDDESLEIGH. Belfast, 1897 — 75 250
Second issue in scarlet cloth — — 150

Rosen, R. D. STRIKE THREE YOU'RE DEAD. New York, 1984 — — 125

Rosenbach, A. S. W. SAMUEL JOHNSON'S PROLOGUE . . . New York, 1902. (100 copies) — 350 500
30 copies on Japan vellum — — 1,000

THE UNPUBLISHABLE MEMOIRS. New York, 1917. (First regularly published) — 35 125

Rosenberg, Harold. TRANCE ABOVE THE STREETS. New York (1942). 80 signed and numbered copies. Issued without dustwrapper — — 300

Rosenberg, Isaac. NIGHT AND DAY. (London, 1912). Wraps — 6,000 7,500

YOUTH. London, 1915. Wraps 75 600 750

Rosenfeld, Isaac. PASSAGE FROM HOME. New York (1946) — 60 60

Roskolenko, Harry. SEQUENCE ON VIOLENCE. New York (1938) — — 150

Ross, Alan. THE DERELICT DAY. London, 1947 — 60 75

Ross, Maggie. THE GASTERO POD. London, 1968 — — 50

Ross, W. W. E. See E. R.

Rossetti, Christina. *See* C. G. R.

GOBLIN MARKET . . . London, 1862. (16-page catalog at rear)	—	400	500
London, 1893. 160 copies. Illustrated by Laurence Housman	—	—	750

Rossetti, Dante Gabriel. SIR HUGO THE HERON. London, 1843. Wraps — 1,500 2,500

Rossetti, William Michael. THE COMEDY OF DANTE ALIGHIERI PART 1. London, 1865. (Translated by Rossetti) — — 350

SWINBURNE'S POEMS & BALLADS. London, 1886 40 75 250

Rossner, Judith. WHAT KIND OF FEET DOES A BEAR HAVE? Indianapolis, 1963 — 75 200

TO THE PRECIPICE. New York (1966) — 50 75

Rosten, Leo C. THE WASHINGTON CORRESPONDENTS. New York (1937) — — 100

Rosten, Norman. RETURN AGAIN, TRAVELLER. New Haven, 1940 — 40 125

Roth, Henry. CALL IT SLEEP. New York, 1934	60	1,500	2,500
London, 1963	—	50	100
Paterson, New Jersey, 1960	—	—	150

Roth, Philip (Milton). GOODBYE, COLUMBUS . . . Boston, 1959	60	175	600
London, 1959. (Title story only)	—	100	150

Roth, Samuel. FIRST OFFERING. New York, 1917. (500 copies) 15 50 75

Rothenberg, Jerome. *See* David Antin

NEW YOUNG GERMAN POETS. San Francisco, 1959. Wraps. (Edited and translated) — 35 75

WHITE SUN BLACK SUN. (New York, 1960). Wraps 15 60 100

Rowan, Carl T. SOUTH OF FREEDOM. New York, 1952 — 40 75

Royall, Anne (Newport). *See* SKETCHES OF HISTORY . . .

Royce, Josiah. THE RELIGIOUS ASPECT OF PHILOSOPHY. Boston, 1885 — — 250

Royde-Smith, Naomi. UNA AND THE RED CROSS . . . London, 1905 — 60 100

Ruark, Robert. GRENADINE ETCHING. New York, 1947	15	60	100
Rubens, Bernice. SET ON EDGE. London, 1960	—	40	60
Rukeyser, Muriel. THEORY OF FLIGHT. New York, 1935	75	250	300
Rule, Jane. THE DESERT OF THE HEART. Toronto, 1964	—	60	60
London, 1964	—	—	40
Rumaker, Michael. EXIT 3 . . . New York, 1958	—	40	75
Runyon, Damon. THE TENTS OF TROUBLE. New York (1911). Flex cover	40	75	250
Rush, Norman. WHITES. London, 1986	—	—	125
New York, 1986	—	—	100
Rushdie, Salman. GRIMUS. London, 1975	—	100	300
New York (1979)	—	35	100
Ruskin, John. SALSETTE AND ELEPHANTA . . . Oxford, 1839. In original wraps	—	600	1,500
Also see MODERN PAINTERS			
Russ, Joanna. PICNIC ON PARADISE. New York (1968). Wraps	—	—	25
London (1969)	—	—	100
Russell, Bertrand. GERMAN SOCIAL DEMOCRACY. London, 1896	—	1,500	2,500
Russell, Charles (Marion). STUDIES OF WESTERN LIFE. Cascade, Montana (1890)	—	4,500	6,000
New York, 1890. First issue: no text on "War"	—	2,000	2,000
Second issue: text on "War"	—	1,750	1,750
Russell, Eric Frank. SINISTER BARRIER. Surrey (1943)	—	200	450
Reading, 1948. 500 signed and numbered copies	—	125	200
Trade edition	—	50	100
Russell, George. *See* A. E.			
Russell, Peter. *See* Russell Irwin			
Russell, Sanders. POEMS. Woodstock, 1941	—	75	75
THE CHEMICAL IMAGE. (San Francisco, 1947). Wraps	—	50	50
Russell, William. *See* Waters			
Russell, William Clark. FRA ANGELO. London, 1865. Wraps	—	2,500	2,500
THE HUNCHBACK'S CHARGE. London, 1867. 3 volumes	—	2,000	2,500
Russo, Richard. MOHAWK. New York, 1986. Wraps	—	—	40
London, 1987	—	—	75

Rutherford, Ernest. RADIO-ACTIVITY. Cambridge, 1904	—	—	600
Rutledge, Archibald. UNDER THE PINES . . . (No-place) 1906	40	75	100
Ryan, Abram Joseph. FATHER RYAN'S POEMS.			
Mobile, 1879	75	125	200
Baltimore, 1880	—	75	125
Ryan, Don. ANGEL'S FLIGHT. New York, 1927	—	75	75
Ryan, Richard. LEDGES. (Oxford, 1970). Wraps	—	30	30
Ryga, George. SONGS OF MY HANDS . . . Edmonton, Alberta, 1956. Wraps	—	—	200

S

S., E. W., and S. W. M. (E. W. Sherman and S. Weir Mitchell). THE CHILDREN'S HOUR. Philadelphia, 1864	75	300	600
S., I. (Isidor Schneider). DOCTOR TRANSIT. New York, 1925	40	125	175
S., P. B. (Percy Bysshe Shelley). ZASTROZZI. London, 1810	—	—	15,000
S., S. H. (Stephen Spender). NINE EXPERIMENTS. Oxford, 1928	2,000	6,000	25,000
Sabatini, Rafael. THE SUITORS OF YVONNE. New York, 1902	—	—	350
THE TAVERN KNIGHT. London, 1914	25	60	250
Sábato, Ernesto. THE OUTSIDER. New York, 1950.	—	—	250
Sackler, Howard. WANT MY SHEPHERD: POEMS. New York, 1954	—	40	125
THE GREAT WHITE HOPE. New York, 1968	—	40	75
Sackville-West, Edward. PIANO QUINTET. London, 1925	—	75	250
New York, 1925. (U.K. sheets)	—	—	150
Sackville-West, V(ictoria Mary). CHATTERTON. Seven Oaks, 1909. Boards	—	—	7,500
Wraps	—	3,500	5,000
CONSTANTINOPLE. London, 1915. Wraps	—	450	500
Sadler, Barry. I'M A LUCKY ONE. New York, 1967	—	—	100
Sadler, Michael (Thomas Harvey). HYSSOP. London (1915)	—	60	75
Sagan, Françoise (pseudonym). BONJOUR TRISTESSE. New York, 1955	—	35	60
London, 1955	—	—	50

Saint-Aubin de Teran, Lisa. THE STREAK. London, 1980.
50 signed and numbered copies. Wraps   —   —   300

    KEEPERS OF THE HOUSE. London (1982)   —   75   150

Saint-Exupéry, Antoine de. NIGHT FLIGHT. Paris, 1932.
Wraps   —   75   300
London (1932)   —   —   250
New York (1932)   —   50   150

Saki (Hector H. Munro). *See* H. H. Munro

THE WESTMINSTER ALICE.
London, 1902. Wraps. First issue: pale green wraps   50   75   350
Second issue: darker matte green wraps   —   —   300
Pictorial cloth   —   200   300

Salamanca, J. R. THE LOST COUNTRY. New York, 1958   25   50   100

Salas, Floyd. TATTOO THE WICKED CROSS. New York
(1967)   —   20   25

Salinger, J(erome) D(avid). THE CATCHER IN THE RYE.
New York (1951). "First Edition" stated   100   500   3,000
London 1951   —   200   450

SALMAGUNDI . . . *See* Launcelot Langstaff

Salt, Sydney. THIRTY PIECES. Majorca, 1934. 500 numbered
copies. First issue: back panel of dustwrapper without
reviews   —   75   75

Salter, James. THE HUNTERS. New York (1956)   —   50   350

Saltus, Edgar Evertson. BALZAC. Boston, 1884   25   50   100

Salzman, Mark. IRON & SILK. New York (1986)   —   —   125
(London, 1987)   —   —   75

Sams, Ferrol. RUN WITH THE HORSEMAN. (Atlanta, 1982)   —   —   40

Sanborn, Franklin Benjamin. EMANCIPATION IN THE WEST
INDIES. Concord, 1862. Wraps   —   150   400

(Two previous broadsides)

Sanborn, Pitts. VIE DE BORDEAUX. Philadelphia, 1916.
Boards   25   40   60

Sanchez, Thomas. RABBIT BOSS. New York, 1973   —   25   60

Sandburg, Carl (Charles August). IN RECKLESS ECSTASY.
Galesburg, 1904   1,250   6,000   7,500

    INCIDENTALS. Galesburg (1907). Wraps   —   2,500   3,500

Modern Masterpieces in English

Night-Flight

by

Antoine de Saint-Exupéry

Translated by Stuart Gilbert

Crosby Continental Editions

Paris

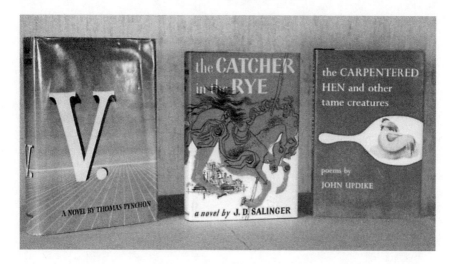

CHICAGO POEMS. New York, 1916. First issue: ads
dated 3/16   75   150   250
Second issue: ads undated   —   60   100

Sanders, Dori. CLOVER. Chapel Hill, 1990   —   —   60

Sanders, Ed. POEM FROM JAIL. (San Francisco, 1963). Wraps   —   50   60

Sanders, Lawrence. THE ANDERSON TAPES. New York
(1970)   —   40   60

Sandlin, Tim. SEX AND SUNSETS. New York, 1987   —   —   40

Sandoz, Mari. OLD JULES. Boston, 1935   15   60   75

Sandoz, Paul. LEGEND. Geneva, 1925. Wraps   —   50   75

Sandy, Stephen. CAROMS. Groton, Mass., 1960. Wraps.
(70 copies)   35   60   125

Sanford, John. *See* Julian L. Shapiro

THE OLD MAN'S PLACE. New York, 1935.
25 signed and numbered copies   —   125   150
Unsigned   —   75   75

Sansom, Clive. THE UNFAILING SPRING. London, 1943.
Stiff wraps   —   35   75

Sansom, William. *See* FIRE OVER LONDON

FIREMAN FLOWER. London, 1944   35   125   200
New York (no-date [1944])   —   —   75

(Previous collaboration)

Santayana, George. *See* LINES ON LEAVING . . .

SONNETS AND OTHER VERSES. Cambridge/Chicago, 1894. 60 numbered, large paper copies	—	400	750
Trade edition. (450 copies)	30	100	200

Santee, Ross. MEN AND HORSES. New York (1926)   —   150   250

Saperstein, Alan. MOM KILLS KIDS AND SELF. New York, 1979   —   —   35

Saroyan, Aram. POEMS. New York, 1963. (Written with J. Caldwell and R. Kolmer)	—	25	50
IN. Eugene, Oregon, 1964	—	25	50

Saroyan, William. THE DARING YOUNG MAN . . . New York, 1934	50	150	350
(Covela, 1984). (220 copies). Issued in slipcase	—	—	250

Sarraute, Nathalie. PORTRAIT OF A MAN UNKNOWN. New York, 1958   —   —   50

Sarton, May. ENCOUNTER IN APRIL. Boston, 1937   50   200   450

Sartre, Jean-Paul. NO EXIT and THE FLIES. London, 1946   —   —   200

Sassoon, Siegfried. *See* POEMS

Satterthwait, Walter. WALL OF GLASS. New York, 1987   —   —   150

Savage, Thomas. THE PASS. Garden City, 1944   25   40   75

Savoy, Willard. ALIEN LAND. New York, 1944   —   50   75

Saxe, John Godfrey. PROGRESS: A SATIRICAL POEM. New York, 1846. Boards   35   100   150

Sayers, Dorothy. OP. 1. Oxford, 1916. Wraps. (350 copies)   150   500   750

WHOSE BODY? New York (1923). First issue: without "Inc." after Boni & Liveright on title	—	1,500	2,500
London (1923)	—	1,000	2,000

Sayles, John. PRIDE OF THE BIMBOS. Boston, 1975   —   50   125

Scarborough, Elizabeth Ann. THE HEALER'S WAR. New York (1988)   —   —   40

Scarfe, Francis. INSCAPES. London (1940)   —   40   60

Schaefer, Jack. SHANE. Boston, 1949	—	250	1,500
London, 1963	—	40	450

Schaeffer, Susan Fromberg. THE WITCH AND THE WEATHER REPORT. New York, 1972. Wraps   —   —   75

Schevill, James. TENSIONS. (Berkeley, 1947)   25   60   75

Schiff, Sydney. CONCESSIONS. London, 1913   —   50   125

Schlesinger, Arthur M., Jr. ORESTES A. BROWNSON.
    Boston, 1939   40   40   75

Schlick, Moritz. SPACE AND TIME IN CONTEMPORARY
    PHYSICS. New York, 1920   —   —   250

Schmidt, Arno. EVENING EDGED IN GOLD. New York, 1980 —   —   200

Schneck, Stephen. THE NIGHT CLERK. New York, 1965   —   —   75

Schneider, Isidor. *See* I. S.

Schoolcraft, Henry Rowe. A VIEW OF THE LEAD MINES . . .
    New York, 1819   —   400   750

Schoonover, Lawrence. THE BURNISHED BLADE. New
    York, 1948   —   35   75

Schorer, Mark. A HOUSE TOO OLD. New York (1935)   25   75   75

Schreiner, Olive. *See* Ralph Iron

Schulberg, Budd. WHAT MAKES SAMMY RUN? New York
    (1941)   30   200   750

Schulman, Neil. FINALLY . . . I'M A DOCTOR. New York
    (1976). Ghostwritten by Carl Hiaasen   —   —   200

Schuyler, James (Marcus). SHOPPING AND WAITING.
    New York, 1953. 6 stapled mimeographed sheets   —   —   750

    ALFRED AND GUINEVERE. New York, 1958   —   50   250

    SALUTE. New York (1960). Folio. (Prints by Grace
    Hartigan). 225 signed and numbered copies. Glassine
    dustwrapper   —   400   750

Schwartz, Delmore. IN DREAMS BEGIN RESPONSIBILITIES.
    Norfolk (1938)   75   200   600

Schwartz, Lynne Sharon. ROUGH STRIFE. New York, 1980 —   20   40

Schwerner, Armand. THE LIGHT FALL. (New York, 1963).
    Wraps   —   —   40

Scott, Alexander. THE LATEST IN ELEGIES. Glasgow, 1949.
    300 numbered copies   —   60   75

Scott, Anthony (Davis Dresser). MARDI GRAS MADNESS.
    New York, 1934   —   —   300

Scott, Duncan Campbell. THE MAGIC HOUSE . . . London,
    1893   —   125   150

Scott, Evelyn. PRECIPITATIONS. New York, 1920. First issue: blue-green cloth	20	100	250
Second issue: red cloth (priority assumed)	—	—	200

Scott, John. *See* FOUR ELEGIES

Scott, Michael. *See* TOM CRINGLE'S LOG

Scott, Paul. "I GERONTIUS." London (1941). Wraps	—	—	750
JOHNNIE SAHIB. London, 1952	—	200	300

Scott, Winfield Townley. ELEGY FOR ROBINSON. New York (1936). (100 copies). Wraps	50	175	200

Screen, Robert Martin. WE CAN'T RUN AWAY FROM HERE. New York (1958)	15	25	25

Scully, James. THE MARCHES. New York, 1967	—	25	60

(Edited two previous books 1965/66)

Scupham, Peter. THE SMALL CONTAINERS. London, 1972	—	—	75

Seabrook, William. *See* DIARY OF SECTION . . .

Seale, Bobby. SEIZE THE TIME. New York (1970)	—	30	60

Searle, Ronald. COOPERATION IN A UNIVERSITY TOWN. London (1939). Searle's first illustrated book. Text by W. Henry Brown	—	100	200
FORTY DRAWINGS. Cambridge (Eng.), 1946	—	200	300

Seaver, Edwin. THE COMPANY. New York, 1930	—	40	40

See, Carolyn. THE REST IS DONE WITH MIRRORS. Boston, 1970	—	—	75

Seeger, Alan. POEMS. New York, 1916	40	60	75
London, 1917	—	40	50

Segal, Erich. THE BRAGGART SOLDIER . . . New York (1963). Wraps. (Translation of play by Plautus)	—	30	75
ROMAN LAUGHTER. Cambridge (Mass.), 1968	—	50	75

Segal, Lore. OTHER PEOPLE'S HOUSES. New York (1964)	—	—	75
London, 1965	—	—	50

Seitz, Don C(arlin). SURFACE JAPAN. London, 1911	—	60	100
ELBA AND ELSEWHERE. London, 1910	—	—	75

(Two previous books)

Seizen Press. LOVE AS LOVE, DEATH AS DEATH. By Laura
    Riding. London, 1928   60   400   500

Selby, Hubert. LAST EXIT TO BROOKLYN. New York (1964)   —   35   125
    London, 1966   —   60   75

SELF-CONTROL. (Mary Brunton). London, 1810. 3 volumes   —   —   750

Seltzer, Charles Alden. THE COUNCIL OF THREE.
    New York, 1900   50   60   75

Selvon, Samuel. A BRIGHTER SUN. London, 1952   —   —   50

Sendak, Maurice (Bernard). ATOMICS FOR THE MILLIONS.
    New York (1947). Text by Eidinoff & Ruchlis. (First
    book illustrationed by MS). (Statement on paper quality
    on copyright page, omitted in later printings)   100   250 1,000

    KENNY'S WINDOW. New York, 1956   —   —   750

SENSE AND SENSIBILITY. (Jane Austen). London, 1811.
    3 volumes. First issue: ruled lines on half title in volume
    1 4/5"   5,500 12,000 12,000
    Second issue: lines 1-1/7"   — 3,000 3,500

Serling, Rod. PATTERNS. New York, 1957   —   40   75

Service, Robert. SONG OF A SOURDOUGH. Toronto, 1907.
    "Author's Edition" on title page. 100 copies according
    to Service   —   600 2,500
    Trade edition without "Author's Edition"   —   —   250

Serviss, Garrett P(utnam). THE MOON METAL.
    New York, 1900   —   75   150

Seth, Vikram. MAPPINGS. (Saratoga, California, 1980).
    150 signed copies in wraps   —   —   450

    FROM HEAVEN LAKE: TRAVELS THROUGH SINK-IANG
    AND TIBET London (1983)   —   —   250

Seton, Anya. MY THEODOSIA. Boston, 1941   —   50   75

Seton, Ernest Thompson. A LIST OF THE MAMMALS OF
    MANITOBA. Toronto (1886). Wraps   — 1,500 2,000

    STUDIES IN THE ART OF ANATOMY OF ANIMALS.
    London, 1896   —   300   850

Settle, Mary Lee. THE LOVE EATERS. London (1954)   25   200   300
    New York (1954). (First not stated)   —   100   200

Sewell, A(nna). BLACK BEAUTY . . . London (1877). Wraps.
First issue: red, green or blue pictorial cloth, horse's head
in gilt looking right. (See Carter's *More Binding*
Variants for more detail) — 1,200 4,000
Boston (1890). Wraps — 300 750

Sexton, Anne. TO BEDLAM AND PART WAY BACK.
Boston, 1960 75 100 250

Shaara, Michael. THE BROKEN PLACE. New York (1968) — 60 150

Shacochis, Bob. EASY IN THE ISLANDS. New York (1985) — — 50

Shaffer, Peter. *See* Peter Anthony

Shakespear, O(livia). LOVE ON A MORTAL LEASE. London,
1894 — — 125

Shange, Ntozake. FOR COLORED GIRLS WHO HAVE
CONSIDERED SUICIDE . . . (San Lorenzo, 1976). Wraps.
First issue: name spelled Ntosake; $.95 cover price — 125 250
New York (1977) — 35 60

Shanks, Edward. SONGS. London, 1915. Wraps — 100 125

Shannon, Dell (Barbara Elizabeth Livington). CASE
PENDING. New York, 1960 — 50 125

Shapiro, David. JANUARY. New York (1965). First regularly
published book 15 35 60

(Preceded by three privately printed books)

Shapiro, Harvey. THE EYE. Denver (1953) 20 35 40

Shapiro, Julian L. (John Sanford). THE WATER WHEEL.
Ithaca (1933) — 350 1,000

Shapiro, Karl (Jay). POEMS. Baltimore, 1935. 200 signed and
numbered copies 500 900 750

PERSON PLACE AND THING. (New York, 1942) 50 75 75

Sharp, Luke (Robert Barr). FROM WHOSE BOURNE?
London, 1893 — 75 100

Sharp, William. THE HUMAN INHERITANCE, THE NEW
HOPE, MOTHERHOOD . . . London, 1882 — — 250

Also see Fiona MacLeod

Sharpe, Tom. RIOTOUS ASSEMBLY. London (1971) — 200 250
New York, 1973 — — 100

Shattuck, Roger. THE BANQUET YEARS . . . New York
(1958) — 40 40

Shaw, George Bernard. CASHEL BYRON'S PROFESSION.
    (London) 1886. Wraps. First issue: 24.8 x 15.4 cm   150   500   1,500
    Second issue: varied from 22.9 x 14 cm to
    23.6 x 14.9 cm   —   —   1,250
    New York (1886). Seaside Library, white wraps lettered
    in blue. (Unauthorized)   —   —   450

    (Two previous pamphlets)

Shaw, Irwin. BURY THE DEAD. New York (1936)   40   100   175

Shaw, Robert. THE HIDING PLACE. London (1959)   —   50   60
    Cleveland/New York (1959)   —   35   40

Sheckley, Robert E. UNTOUCHED BY HUMAN HANDS.
    New York (1954). Cloth   —   75   150
    Wraps   —   15   25

Sheed, Wilfred. JOSEPH. New York (1958)   15   60   75

Sheldon, Sidney. THE NAKED FACE. New York (1970)   —   —   75

Shelley, Mary Wollstonecraft. *See* HISTORY OF A SIX . . . and
    FRANKENSTEIN

Shelly, Percy Bysshe. *See* P. B. S.

Shepard, Odell. A LONELY FLUTE. Boston, 1917. Boards   40   50   75

Shepard, Sam. FIVE PLAYS. Indianapolis (1967)   —   90   250
    London (1969)   —   60   100

Shepherd, Jean. IN GOD WE TRUST, ALL OTHERS PAY CASH.
    Garden City, 1966   —   —   40

Sheppard, Elizabeth Sara. *See* CHARLES AUCHESTER

Sheridan, Richard Brinsley. *See* THE LOVE EPISTLES . . .

Sherwin, Judith Johnson. URANIUM POEMS. New Haven,
    1969   —   20   25

Sherwood, Robert E(mmet). BARNUM WAS RIGHT.
    Cambridge, 1920. Stiff wraps   —   —   250

    THE ROAD TO ROME. New York, 1927   20   50   75

Shiel, M. P. PRINCE ZALESKI. London, 1895. (16-page
    catalog at rear)   —   200   850
    Boston, 1895   —   —   275

Shields, Carol. OTHERS. Ottawa, 1972   —   —   125

    SMALL CEREMONIES. Toronto, 1976. (First edition)   —   —   250

Shippey, Lee. THE TESTING GROUND. Boston, 1926	—	—	100
WHERE NOTHING EVER HAPPENS. Boston, 1935	—	—	75
Shivers, Louise. HERE TO GET MY BABY OUT OF JAIL. New York, 1983	—	—	75
Shockley, Ann Allen. LOVING HER. Indianapolis (1974)	—	40	75
Sholokhov, Mikhail. AND QUIET FLOWS THE DON. London (1934). (First English translation)	—	—	150
Shorthouse, J. Henry. JOHN INGLESANT. Birmingham (England), 1880. 100 copies	—	300	750
Shove, Fredegond. DREAMS AND JOURNEY. Oxford, 1918. Wraps	—	—	50
Shulman, Irving. THE AMBOY DUKES. New York, 1947	25	50	125
Shute, Nevil (Norway). MARAZAN. London, 1926	40	300	500
Shuttle, Penelope. NOSTALGIA NEUROSIS . . . London, 1968. 26 signed and lettered copies. Issued in plain dustwrapper	—	—	150
Trade edition in wraps	—	—	50
ALL THE USUAL HOURS OF SLEEPING. London, 1969	—	—	50
Siddons, Anne River. JOAN CHANCELLOR MAKES ME CRY. New York, 1974	—	—	100
Sidney, Margaret (Harriet Mulford Stone Lothrop). FIVE LITTLE PEPPERS AND HOW THEY GREW. Boston (1880). First issue: caption p. 231 reads "said Polly"	150	350	450
Sidney, Philip. A WOORKE CONCERNING THE TREWNESSE OF THE CHRISTIAN RELIGION . . . London, 1587. Translation of Philippe Mornay	—	—	1,250
Sienkiewicz, Henryk. IN VAIN. Boston, 1899	—	—	100
Sigal, Clancy. WEEKEND IN DINLOCK. London, 1960	—	40	40
Boston, 1960	—	35	35
Sigerson, Dora. VERSES. London, 1893	—	—	125
Sigourney, Lydia Huntley. See Lydia Huntley			
Silber, Joan. HOUSEHOLD WORDS. New York (1980)	—	—	40
Silkin, Jon. THE PORTRAIT . . . Ilfracombe (1950). Wraps	—	150	250
THE PEACEABLE KINGDOM. London, 1954	—	60	125

Silko, Leslie Maron. LAGUNA WOMAN. Greenfield Center, New York (1974). Wraps	—	—	500
CEREMONY. New York (1977)	—	—	350
Sill, Edward Rowland. *See* POEM AND VALEDICTORY ORATION . . .			
THE HERITAGE . . . New York, 1868	—	125	125
Sillitoe, Alan. CHOPIN'S WINTER IN MAJORCA 1838–1839. Mallorca, 1955. Translated by Sillitoe	—	—	300
WITHOUT BEER OR BREAD. Dulwich Village, 1957. Wraps	50	350	450
SATURDAY NIGHT AND SUNDAY MORNING. London, 1958	—	100	250
Silone, Ignazio. FONTAMARA. New York, 1934	—	—	50
Siluriensis, Leolinus (Arthur Machen). THE ANATOMY OF TOBACCO. London (1884). Second book	150	200	400
Silverberg, Robert. REVOLT ON ALPHA C. New York (1955)	—	60	200
Silverstein, Shel. TAKE TEN. (Tokyo) 1955. Issued without dustwrapper	—	60	100
Simak, Clifford. THE CREATOR. (Los Angeles, 1946). Wraps	—	50	100
Simenon, Georges. THE DEATH OF MONSIEUR GALLET. New York, 1932. (First English translation)	—	100	750
Simic, Charles. WHAT THE GRASS SAYS. Santa Cruz (1967). Wraps. (1,000 copies)	—	60	75
Simmons, Charles. PLOTS THAT SELL TO TOP-PAY MAGAZINES. New York (1952)	—	—	150
POWDERED EGGS. New York, 1964	—	25	50
Simmons, Dan. SONG OF KALI. (New York, 1985)	—	—	200
Simmons, Herbert A. CORNER BOY. Boston, 1957	20	25	60
Simms, William Gilmore. LYRICAL . . . Charlestown, 1827	300	500	850
Simon, (Marvin) Neil. HEIDI. New York, 1959. Wraps. Written with Wm. Friedburg	—	75	125
COME BLOW YOUR HORN. New York, 1963. ("First Printing" not stated)	—	60	150
Simon, Roger L. THE BIG FIX. San Francisco, 1973. Wraps	—	—	25

Simon, Roger Lichtenberg. HEIR. New York (1968)	—	25	30
Simpson, Harriette. MOUNTAIN PATH. New York (1936)	—	600	750
Also see Harriette Arnow			
Simpson, Helen. LIGHTNING SKETCHES. Boston, 1918. Wraps	25	50	50
Simpson, Louis (Aston Marantz). THE ARRIVISTES. New York (1949). Wraps. (500 copies)	125	200	250
Paris (1950)	100	175	200
Simpson, Mona. ANYWHERE BUT HERE. New York, 1987	—	—	50
Sims, George R(obert). THE TERRIBLE DOOR.			
London (1964)	—	75	75
New York, 1964	—	—	35
Sinclair, Andrew. THE BREAKING OF BUMBO.			
New York, 1959	—	40	50
London, 1959	—	35	40
Sinclair, April. COFFEE WILL MAKE YOU BLACK.			
New York, 1994	—	—	40
Sinclair, Clive. BIBLIOSEXUALITY. London, 1973	—	35	40
Sinclair, Upton. SAVED BY THE ENEMY. New York, 1898	75	150	300
Singer, Burns (James Hyman). THE GENTLE ENGINEER. Rome, 1952	—	40	40
Singer, I. J. THE SINNER. New York (1933). (First translation in English)	—	125	125
Singer, Isaac Bashevis. THE FAMILY MUSKAT. New York, 1950. (First translation in English)	—	100	250
Singer, Mark. FUNNY MONEY. New York, 1985	—	—	25
Sinjohn, John (John Galsworthy). FROM THE FOUR WINDS. London (1897). (500 copies)	450	500	750
SIR JOHN CHIVERTON. (Wm. H. Ainsworth and John P. Aston). London, 1826	—	250	300
Siringo, Charles Angelo. A TEXAS COWBOY . . .			
Chicago, 1885. Cloth	—	7,500	12,500
Chicago/New York, 1886. Cloth or Wraps	—	—	850
Sissman, L. E. DYING: AN INTRODUCTION. Boston (1967)	—	25	25
Sisson, C(harles) H(ubert). AN ASIATIC ROMANCE. London, 1953	20	40	50

Sitwell, Constance. FLOWERS AND ELEPHANTS.
London, 1927 — — 50

Sitwell, Edith. THE MOTHER . . . Oxford, 1915. (500 copies, 200 pulped). Wraps — 300 500 600

Sitwell, Osbert. TWENTIETH CENTURY HARLEQUINADE . . . Oxford, 1916. Written with Edith Sitwell. (500 copies). Wraps — 75 200 250

THE WINSTONBURG LINE. London, 1919. Pictorial wraps — 75 150 200

Sitwell, Sacheverell. THE PEOPLE'S PALACE. Oxford, 1918. Wraps. (400 copies) — 75 150 500

SIX TO ONE: A NANTUCKET IDYL. (Edward Bellamy). New York, 1878. Cloth — 50 300 400
Wraps — — 200 300

SIXTY YEARS OF THE LIFE OF JEREMY LEVIS. (Laughton Osborn). New York, 1831 — — 100 125

Sjoewall, Maj, and Per Wahloo. ROSEANNA. New York, 1967 — — — 125

SKETCHES BY "BOZ." (Charles Dickens). London, 1836/7. 3 volumes. (2 volumes—1836, 1 volume—1837).
In original cloth — 500 3,500 10,000
London, 1837–39. 20 parts in original wraps — — 10,000 30,000

SKETCHES OF HISTORY, LIFE AND MANNERS . . . (Anne Royall). New Haven, 1826 — — 400 750

Skinner, M. L. BLACK SWAN. London, 1925 — 20 60 75

(Previous book with D. H. Lawrence)

Slade, Michael. HEADHUNTER. New York, 1985 — — — 150

Slaughter, Carolyn. THE STORY OF THE WEASEL. London, 1976 — — — 50

SLAVE (THE); OR, THE MEMOIRS OF ARCHY MOORE. (Richard Hildreth). Boston, 1836. 2 volumes — 150 300 500

Slesar, Henry. THE GRAY FLANNEL SHROUD. New York, 1959 — — — 40

Slesinger, Tess. THE UNPOSSESSED. New York, 1934 — 35 50 75

Slick, Jonathan (Ann Sophia Stephens). HIGH LIFE IN NEW YORK. (New York, 1843). Wraps — — 150 750

Smart, Elizabeth. BY GRAND CENTRAL STATION . . . London, 1945	—	—	350
Smiley, Jane. BARN BLIND. New York (1980)	—	—	350
Smith, A. J. M. POETRY OF ROBERT BRIDGES. Montreal (no-date [early 1930s]). Wraps	—	1,200	1,500
NEWS OF THE PHOENIX . . . Toronto, 1943	—	100	150
Smith, Adam. THE THEORY OF MORAL SENTIMENTS. London, 1759	550	1,000	8,500
Philadelphia, 1817. 2 volumes	—	—	750
Smith, Alexander. POEMS. London, 1853. First issue: ads dated November 1852	35	60	125
Smith, C. W. THIN MEN OF HADDAM. New York, 1973	—	—	60
Smith, Charlie. CANAAN. New York (1984)	—	—	125
London, 1985	—	—	50
Smith, Clark Ashton. THE STARTREADERS . . . San Francisco, 1912	—	125	125
Smith, Cordwainer. *See* Felix Forrest *and* Paul Linebarger			
Smith, Dave. BULL ISLAND. Poquoson, Virginia (1970). Wraps	—	—	600
Smith, Dodie (Dorothy Gladys). THE HUNDRED AND ONE DALMATIONS. London, 1956	—	—	250
New York, 1957	—	—	150
Also see C. L. Anthony			
Smith, E. Boyd. MY VILLAGE. New York, 1896	—	—	125
Smith, Edward E. THE SKYLARK OF SPACE. (Buffalo Book Co. Providence, 1946). (Written with Mrs. Lee Hawkins Garby). (500 copies)	25	175	350
Hadley Co. Providence (1947)	—	50	75
Smith, F(rancis) Hopkinson. OLD LINES IN NEW BLACK. Boston, 1885	30	60	150
Smith, George O. VENUS EQUILATERAL. Philadelphia, 1947	—	60	75
Smith, J. Thorne. BILTMORE OSWALD. New York (1918)	—	50	75
Smith, Johnston (Stephen Crane). MAGGIE: A GIRL OF THE STREETS. (New York, 1893). Wraps	5,000	7,500	17,500
Smith, Joseph, Jr. THE BOOK OF MORMON. Palmyra, New York, 1830. Contemporary leather	2,000	5,000	10,000

Second edition. Kirtland, Ohio, 1837	—	—	6,000
Third edition. Nauvoo, Illinois, 1840. Original sheep	—	—	3,500
Liverpool, 1841. Original calf	—	—	2,500
Smith, Julie. DEATH TURNS A TRICK. New York (1982)	—	—	150
Smith, Kate Douglas (Wiggin). THE STORY OF PATSY . . . San Francisco, 1883. Wraps	200	500	1,000
Smith, Ken. ELEVEN POEMS. Leeds, 1964. Wraps	—	—	100
Smith, Lee. THE LAST DAY THE DOGBUSHES BLOOMED. New York, 1968	—	100	250
Smith, Lillian. THESE ARE THINGS TO DO. Clayton, Georgia, 1943	—	—	150
STRANGE FRUIT. New York, 1944	—	35	100
London, 1945	—	25	75
Smith, Logan Pearsall. THE YOUTH OF PARNASSUS . . . London, 1895. Blue or red cloth, priority unknown	50	125	200
Smith, Mark. TOYLAND. Boston (1965)	—	40	40
Smith, Martin (Cruz). THE INDIANS WON. New York (1970). Wraps	—	—	125
GYPSY IN AMBER. New York (1971)	—	35	200
Smith, Pauline. THE LITTLE KAROO. London, 1925	—	—	100
Smith, Robert Paul. SO IT DOESN'T WHISTLE. New York (1941)	—	40	50
Smith, Stevie (Florence Margaret Smith). NOVEL ON YELLOW PAPER. London (1936)	40	300	350
New York, 1937. First issue: blue cloth. Dustwrapper priced $2.50	25	150	200
Second issue: patterned cloth. Dustwrapper clipped stamped $2.00. (Priority assumed)	—	—	150
Smith, T. Dudley (Elleston Trevor). OVER THE WALL. London, 1943	—	150	200
INTO THE HAPPY GLADE. London, 1943. (Priority unknown)	—	150	200
Smith, Wilbur. WHEN THE LION FEEDS. London (1964)	—	60	100
New York (1964)	—	—	75
Smith, William Gardner. LAST OF THE CONQUERERS. New York, 1948	35	75	100

Smith, William Jay. POEMS. Banyon Press. Pawlett, Vermont, 1947. 500 numbered copies	30	75	125
Smollett, Tobias. *See* THE ADVENTURES OF RODERICK			
Snelling, William J. *See* TALES OF THE NORTHWEST . . .			
Snider, Denton Jacques. CLARENCE. St. Louis, 1872. Wraps	75	125	125
Snodgrass, W(illiam) D(ewitt). HEART'S NEEDLE. New York, 1959. (1,500 copies)	75	150	200
Hessle (England), 1960	50	100	175
Snow, C(harles) P(ercy). DEATH UNDER SAIL. London (1932)	75	300	750
Garden City (1932)	—	125	200
Snow, Charles Wilbert. SONGS OF THE NEUKLUK. Council, Alaska, 1912. Written with Ewen MacLennan	300	250	350
Snyder, Gary (Sherman). RIPRAP. (Ashland, Mass.) 1959. Wraps. (500 copies)	200	300	400
Solano, Solita. THE UNCERTAIN FEAST. New York, 1924	—	40	40
Solomon, Carl. MISHAPS PERHAPS. (San Francisco, 1966). Wraps	—	20	40
Solzhenitsyn, Alexander. ONE DAY IN THE LIFE OF IVAN DENISOVICH. Praeger. New York (1963). (First English translation)	25	50	150
Dutton. New York, 1963. Cloth	—	50	100
Wraps	—	10	25
Pall Mall, London, 1963. (Never seen)	—	—	100
Gollancz. London, 1963	—	—	100
SOMEBODY. *See* John Neal			
Sommerfield, John. THEY DIE YOUNG. London, 1930	—	50	50
Somner, Scott. NEARING'S GRACE. New York, 1979	—	25	40
Sontag, Susan. THE BENEFACTOR. New York (1963)	15	35	45
Sorrentino, Gilbert. THE DARKNESS SURROUNDS US. Highlands, North Carolina, 1960. Wraps	—	40	75
Soto, Gary. THE ELEMENTS OF SAN JOAQUIN. (Pittsburgh, 1977). 50 signed and numbered copies in unprinted dustwrapper	—	50	75
Souster, (Holmes) Raymond. WHEN WE ARE YOUNG. Montreal, 1946. Wraps	—	500	750

Southern, Terry. FLASH & FILIGREE. (London, 1958)   15   100   150
New York (1958). Dustwrapper priced $3.50 and no
mention of *Dr. Strangelove* in blurbs. Full cloth   15   50   100

Southey, Robert. POEMS . . . Written with Robert Lovell.
Bath, 1795   —   300   1,500
Boston, 1799   —   150   750

SOUTH-WEST, THE. (Joseph Holt Ingraham). New York,
1835. 2 volumes. In original cloth   —   400   500

Southworth, Emma Dorothy. RETRIBUTION . . . New
York, 1849   —   100   300

Spackman, W. M. HEYDAY. New York (1953). Cloth   —   75   125
Wraps   —   20   35

Spade, Mark (Nigel Balchin). HOW TO RUN A BASSOON
FACTORY. London, 1934   —   50   50

SPANISH SPEAKING AMERICANS IN THE WAR. (Charles
Olson). Washington (D.C., 1944). Wraps   —   —   1,500

Spark, Muriel (Sarah). *See* Muriel Camberg

REASSESSMENT. London (1948).
Written with W. Howard Sergeant. Folded leaf   —   —   200

TRIBUTE TO WORDSWORTH. London (1950). Edited
with Derek Stanford   —   75   150
200 numbered copies   —   —   250

CHILD OF LIGHT. Essex (1951)   —   150   175

SPECIMENS. (Joaquin Miller). (Canyon City, Oregon, 1868).
Wraps. (Preface signed C. H. Miller)   1,000   3,000   4,500

Speicher, John. LOOKING FOR BABY PARADISE. New York
(1967)   —   40   40

Spencer, Bernard. AEGEAN ISLAND . . . London (1946)   —   30   60

Spencer, Claire. GALLOW'S ORCHARD. London (1930)   —   35   75
New York (1930)   —   35   50

Spencer, Elizabeth. FIRE IN THE MORNING. New York,
1948   20   200   500

Spencer, Herbert. THE PROPER SPHERE OF GOVERNMENT.
London, 1843   —   —   250

SOCIAL STATISTICS . . . London, 1851   40   150   200

Spencer, Scott. LAST NIGHT AT THE BRAIN THIEVES BALL.
Boston, 1973   —   40   100

Spencer, Theodore. STUDIES IN METAPHYSICAL POETRY. New York, 1939. Written with Mark Van Doren	—	60	100
THE PARADOX IN THE CIRCLE. Norfolk (1941). Wraps	15	40	75
Spender, Stephen (Harold). *See* S. H. S.			
TWENTY POEMS. Oxford (1930).			
75 signed copies	—	750	1,000
60 unsigned copies	200	400	750
POEMS. London (1933)	50	175	250
New York, 1934	—	100	175
Speyer, Leonora. HOLY NIGHT. (By Hans Travsil). New York, 1919. Paraphrased into English by LS. (500 copies). (Cover by Eric Gill)	30	75	125
A CANOPIC JAR. New York (1921)	—	75	100
Spicer, Jack. CORRELATION METHODS OF COMPARING IDOLECTS . . . Offprint of *Language* 1952. Wraps. Written with David W. Reed. (Less than 100 copies)	—	400	1,250
AFTER LORCA. (San Francisco, 1957). Wraps. 26 signed copies	125	300	400
(474 copies)	75	125	175
Spillane, Mickey (Frank Morrison Spillane). I, THE JURY. New York, 1947	—	200	750
Springarn, J(oel) E(lias). A HISTORY OF LITERARY CRITICISM . . . New York, 1899	—	—	200
Springs, Elliott White. NOCTURNE MILITAIRE. New York (1927)	—	200	300
Square, A. (Edward Abbott Abbott). FLATLAND . . . Boston, 1885	—	—	150
Squire, Ephraim G. *See* WAIKNA			
Squire, Jack Collings. SOCIALISM AND ART. London (1907)	—	150	175
Squires, James. RADCLIFFE CORNAR. Philadelphia (1940). Issued with printed tissue dustwrapper	—	50	50
Stacton, David. AN UNFAMILIAR COUNTRY. (Swinford, 1953). Wraps	—	225	300
Stafford, Jean. BOSTON ADVENTURE. Boston (1944)	15	50	100
Stafford, William E(dgar). DOWN IN MY HEART. Elgin, Illinois (1947)	—	850	850

WEST OF YOUR CITY. Los Gatos, l960. Cloth and boards. Issued with plain white dustwrapper with price on rear flap	—	500	750
Wraps. Issued with plain white dustwrapper with price on rear flap	—	300	300
Standish, Robert. THE THREE BAMBOOS. London, 1942	—	50	50
Stanford, Ann. IN NARROW BOUND. Denver (1943). Wraps	15	125	125
Stanford, Donald E. NEW ENGLAND EARTH . . . San Francisco (1941). Wraps	—	125	125
Stanford, Theodore Anthony. DARK HARVEST. Philadelphia (1936). Issued without dustwrapper	25	35	35
Stanley, Arthur Penrhyn. THE GYPSIES . . . Oxford, 1837	—	—	150
Stanley, Edward. ELMIRA . . . Norwich, 1790	—	—	400
Stapledon, W(illiam) Olaf. LATTER-DAY PSALMS. London, 1914	75	150	200
Starbuck, George. BONE THOUGHTS. New Haven, 1960	15	25	40
Stark, Freya. BAGHDAD SKETCHES. Baghdad, 1932	—	150	250
Starrett, (Charles) Vincent (Emerson). ARTHUR MACHEN. Chicago, 1918. 250 signed and numbered copies	150	200	300
Stavis, Barrie. THE CHAIN OF COMMAND. New York (1945)	—	—	50
Stead, Christina (Ellen). THE SALZBURG TALES. London (1934)	100	150	250
New York, 1934	—	100	175
Steadman, Ralph. STILL LIFE WITH RASPBERRY . . . London, 1969. 50 signed and numbered copies with original drawings	—	200	1,000
(First book illustrations were in Daisy Ashford's *Love & Marriage*. London, 1965)			
Stearns, Harold. LIBERALISM IN AMERICA. New York (1919)	—	—	50
Stedman, Edmund Clarence. POEMS, LYRICAL AND IDYLLIC. New York, 1860	—	100	100
Steed, Neville. TIN PLATE. London, 1986	—	—	35
Steele, Max. DEBBY. New York, 1950	—	—	30
Stefansson, Vilhjalmur. MY LIFE WITH THE ESKIMO. New York, 1913	—	175	200
London, 1913. (U.S. sheets)	—	125	150

Steffens, (Joseph) Lincoln. THE SHAME OF THE CITIES. New York, 1904	25	150	200
Stegner, Page. ESCAPE INTO AESTHETICS . . . New York, 1966	—	25	50
Stegner, Wallace (Earle). CLARENCE EDWARD DUTTON: AN APPRAISAL. Salt Lake City (1935?). Wraps	—	—	600
London (1937)	—	—	500
REMEMBERING LAUGHTER. Boston, 1937	30	125	350
Steig, Henry. SEND ME DOWN. New York, 1941	—	35	40
Steig, William. MAN ABOUT TOWN. New York, 1932	—	40	100
Stein, Aaron Marc. SPIRALS. New York, 1930	—	—	300
Stein, Gertrude. THREE LIVES. New York, 1909. (700 copies). Issued without dustwrapper	500	900	1,500
London, 1915. (300 copies from U.S. sheets)	150	200	1,000
Steinbeck, John (Ernst). CUP OF GOLD. McBride. New York, 1929. First issue: top edge stained (although price same for unstained)	750	3,500	7,500

Second issue: Covici-Friede. New York (1936).

Remainder sheets. Maroon cloth	—	400	750
Blue cloth	—	125	300
London (1937)	—	1,200	1,250

Steinem, Gloria. THE BEACH BOOK. New York, 1963	—	40	60

Steiner, F(rancis) George. (POEMS) FANTASY POETS #8. Swinford, 1952. Wraps	—	100	150

Stepanchev, Stephen. THREE PRIESTS IN APRIL. Baltimore, 1956	—	50	75

Stephens, Ann Sophie. *See* Jonathan Slick

Stephens, James. INSURRECTIONS. Dublin, 1909	50	75	100

Sterling, George. THE TESTIMONY OF THE SUNS . . . San Francisco, 1903. 650 copies	50	100	125
San Francisco, 1927. 300 numbered copies with comments by Ambrose Bierce	—	—	300

Stern, James. THE HEARTLESS LAND. London, 1932. (First regularly published)	—	200	200

Stern, Richard G(ustave). GOLK. New York (1960)	—	25	25
London, 1960	—	—	25

Stevens, Shane. GO DOWN DEAD. New York, 1966	—	25	75

Stevens, Wallace. HARMONIUM. New York, 1923.

First issue: checkered boards. (500 copies)	200	1,000	3,000
Second issue: striped boards. (215 copies)	150	500	1,750
Blue cloth. (715 copies)	100	400	1,250
New York, 1931. Drops 3 poems that were in the first edition and adds 14 new poems. Various bindings	—	—	500

Stevenson, Adlai E. MAJOR CAMPAIGN SPEECHES . . . New York, 1953	—	75	100

Stevenson, Robert Louis. *See* THE PENTLAND RISING

AN INLAND VOYAGE.			
London, 1878	100	400	1,000
Boston, 1883	—	—	350

Stewart, Donald Ogden. A PARODY OUTLINE OF HISTORY. New York, 1921	—	35	60

Stewart, Fred Mustard. THE MEPHISTO WALTZ. New York (1960)	—	35	35

Stewart, George R., Jr. MODERN METRICAL TECHNIQUE. New York, 1922. Wraps	—	—	150

THREE LIVES

STORIES OF THE GOOD
ANNA, MELANCTHA AND
THE GENTLE LENA

BY
GERTRUDE STEIN

THE GRAFTON PRESS
NEW YORK   MCMIX

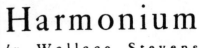

Harmonium
by Wallace Stevens

New York Alfred · A · Knopf Mcmxxiii

Stewart, John. THE PLEASURES OF LOVE. London, 1806	—	—	175
Stewart, Mary. MADAM, WILL YOU TALK? London, 1955	—	60	200
Still, James. HOUNDS ON THE MOUNTAIN. New York, 1937. 50 numbered copies (not for sale)	—	—	350
(750 copies)	15	150	200
Stockton, Frank R(ichard). TING-A-LING. New York, 1870	150	250	750
(Previous pamphlet)			
Stoddard, Charles Warren. POEMS. San Francisco, 1867. (750 copies)	—	100	125
SOUTH-SEA IDYLS. Boston, 1875	—	75	100
Stoddard, Richard Henry. FOOTPRINTS. New York, 1849. Wraps	—	1,500	1,500
Stoker, Bram. ADDRESS . . . DINING HALL . . . TRINITY COLLEGE . . . Dublin, 1872. Wraps	—	500	1,500
THE DUTIES OF CLERKS . . . Dublin, 1879. Wraps	—	400	1,000
UNDER THE SUNSET. London, 1882	—	200	450
Stone, A. R. A BOOK OF LETTERING. London, 1935	40	60	150

Stone, Chuck. KING STRUT. Indianapolis (1970) — — 40

Stone, I. F. (Isidor Feinstein). THE COURT DISPOSES. New
York (1937) — 75 150

Stone, Irving. PAGEANT OF YOUTH. New York, 1933 15 75 175

Stone, Robert. A HALL OF MIRRORS. Boston, 1967. The
author is holding a cup of coffee on the first issue
dustwrapper 15 150 500
London (1968) — 75 250

Stopes, Marie C(harlotte). THE STUDY OF PLANT LIFE FOR
YOUNG PEOPLE. London, 1906 50 100 100

Stoppard, Tom. LORD MALQUIST AND MR. MOON.
(London, 1966) 20 125 200
New York, 1968 — 40 75

Storey, David (Malcolm). THIS SPORTING LIFE. (London,
1960) 50 125 300
New York, 1960 — — 100

Storm, Hans Otto. FULL MEASURE. New York, 1929 20 50 75

Story, Joseph. THE POWER OF SOLITUDE. Boston (1800) — 200 300

Stout, Rex (Todhunter). HOW LIKE A GOD. New York,
1929 75 350 1,500
London, 1931 — — 750

FER-DE-LANCE. New York, 1934. (First mystery) — — 5,000

Stow, Randolph. A HAUNTED LAND. London, 1956 — 75 75

Stowe, Harriet (Elizabeth) Beecher. *See* Harriet Beecher

Strachey, G. L(ytton). LANDMARKS IN FRENCH
LITERATURE. London (1912). First issue: top edge
stained green. 8 pages of ads 65 150 200

Strachey, Mrs. Richard. NURSERY LYRICS. London, 1893 — 200 350
(Reissued with new title page and binding—"Lady
Strachey") — 100 100

Straley, John. THE WOMAN WHO MARRIED A BEAR. New
York (1992) — — 35

Strand, Mark. SLEEPING WITH ONE EYE OPEN. Iowa City,
1963. (225 copies) — 300 750

Strand, Paul. PHOTOGRAPHS 1915–1945. New York (1945).
Cloth — — 100
Wraps — — 50

(Previous issues of *Camera Work* were devoted to his work)

Strange, Michael. MISCELLANEOUS POEMS. New York, 1916	—	—	40
STRATFORD-BY-THE-SEA. (Alice Brown). New York, 1844	—	75	100
Straub, Peter. ISHMAEL. (London, 1972). Wraps. 100 signed and numbered copies. Issued in dustwrapper	—	200	200
Strauss, David Friedrich. THE LIFE OF JESUS. London, 1846. 3 volumes. Translated by Mary Ann Evans (George Eliot)	400	750	5,000
Strauss, Theodore. NIGHT AT HOGWALLOW. Boston, 1937	—	35	30
Strawberry Hill Press. ODES. (Thomas Gray). London, 1757. With "Ilissus" on p. 8 and no comma after "swarm" on p. 16	—	600	1,000
Streatfeild, (Mary) Noel. THE WHICHARTS. London, 1931	—	—	75
BALLET SHOES. London, 1936	—	—	200
Street, Cecil John Charles. *See* John Rhode			
Street, George Edmund. BRICK AND MARBLE IN THE MIDDLE AGES. London, 1855	75	400	600
Street, James H. LOOK AWAY. New York, 1936	—	50	75
Street, Julian (Leonard). MY ENEMY THE MOTOR. New York, 1908	25	40	75
Streeter, Edward. DERE MABLE: LOVE LETTERS OF A ROOKIE. New York (1918). Pictorial boards	25	25	25
Stribling, T(homas) S(igismund). CRUISE OF THE DRY DOCK. Chicago (1917). (250 copies published per author)	40	75	150
Strong, Jonathan. TIKE . . . Boston, 1969	—	25	50
Strong, L. A. G. DALLINGTON RHYMES. (200 copies privately printed, 1919)	150	300	400
DUBLIN DAYS. Oxford, 1921. Wraps	50	75	100
Strong, Phil. STATE FAIR. New York, 1932. First issue: copyrighted by publisher	—	—	150
Second issue: copyright by author (handstamped)	—	—	125
Third issue: cancelled title/copyright page (copyright by author)	—	—	75
Stroud, Robert (Birdman of Alcatraz). DISEASES OF CANARIES. Kansas City, 1933	—	125	150

Struther, Jan (Joyce Maxtone Graham). BETSINDA
    DANCES . . . Oxford/London, 1931. Wraps — 75 75

Stuart, Dabney. THE DIVING BELL. New York, 1966 — — 50

Stuart, H. (Francis Stuart). WE HAVE KEPT THE FAITH.
    Dublin, 1923 — 350 350

Stuart, Jesse (Hilton). HARVEST OF YOUTH. Howe,
    Oklahoma (1930). (20 copies per author) 600 2,000 3,000

    MAN WITH A BULL TONGUE PLOW. (New York, 1934) 150 400 600

Sturgeon, Theodore. IT. Philadelphia, 1948. 29-page
    excerpt from *Without Sorcery* 150 500 1,500

    WITHOUT SORCERY. Philadelphia, 1948. 80 signed
    copies. Red buckram. Issued in slipcase 75 300 1,750
    Trade edition 50 125 250

Styron, William. LIE DOWN IN DARKNESS. Indianapolis
    (1951) 35 150 300
    London, 1952 — — 150

Suckow, Ruth. COUNTRY PEOPLE. New York, 1924.
    (600 copies) 15 100 125
    Trade edition — 50 75

Sullivan, Frank. THE LIFE AND TIMES OF MARTHA
    HEPPLETWAITE. New York, 1926 — 50 125

Summers, Hollis (Spurgeon). CITY LIMIT. Boston, 1948 — 50 75

Summers, Montague. ANTINOUS . . . London [1907] — — 450

Suthren, Victor. THE BLACK COCKADE. Toronto, 1977 — — 50

Swados, Harvey. JEWISH POPULATION STUDIES IN THE
    U.S. New York, 1949. Wraps. Written with Ben B.
    Seligman — — 150

    OUT WENT THE CANDLE. New York, 1955 50 50 50

Swallow, Alan. THE PRACTICE OF POETRY. Albuquerque,
    1942. Wraps — — 125

    XI POEMS. Prairie Press. Muscatine, 1943. 300 numbered
    copies. Wraps — 60 100

SWALLOW BARN. (Joseph Pendleton Kennedy). Philadelphia,
    1832. 2 volumes 125 400 600

    (Previous collaboration)

Swanwick, Michael. IN THE DRIFT. London, 1989. (First
    hardback) — — 50

Sward, Robert. ADVERTISEMENTS. Chicago, 1958. (368 copies). Wraps	15	30	40
Swarthout, Glendon. WILLOW RUN. New York, 1943	—	—	100
Swenson, May. ANOTHER ANIMAL. New York, 1954	—	—	75
Swift, Graham. THE SWEET-SHOP OWNER. (London, 1980)	—	75	350
Swinburne, Algernon Charles. THE QUEEN-MOTHER and ROSAMOND. London, 1860. First issue: "A. G. Swinburne" on spine	200	600	2,500
Second issue: B. M. Pickering imprint	—	400	2,000
Third issue: J. C. Hotten title page	—	300	500
Swingler, Randall. DIFFICULT MORNING. London (1933)	—	60	60
Sykes, Gerald. THE NICE AMERICANS. New York, 1951	—	35	60
Symonds, J(ohn) A(ddington). THE ESCORIAL. Oxford, 1860. Wraps	200	200	400
Symons, A. J. A. EMIN. London, 1928. 300 numbered copies. Issued without dustwrapper	50	100	150
Symons, Arthur. AN INTRODUCTION TO THE STUDY OF ROBERT BROWNING. London, 1886. Ads dated January 1887. Green cloth (later decorated brown cloth)	50	100	125
DAYS AND NIGHTS. London, 1889	—	1,000	1,500
Symons, Julian (Gustave). CONFUSIONS ABOUT X. London (1939)	—	250	250
Synge, John M(illington). IN THE SHADOW OF THE GLEN. New York, 1904. Wraps. (50 copies)	300	1,000	2,000
THE SHADOW OF THE GLEN . . . London, 1905. Wraps	100	225	500
T			
Tabb, John Banister. POEMS. (Baltimore, 1882)	300	400	400
Taggard, Genevieve. WHAT OTHERS HAVE SAID . . . Berkeley (1919). Wraps	—	150	150
FOR EAGER LOVERS. New York, 1922	75	100	100
Taine, John (Eric Temple Bell). THE PURPLE SAPPHIRE. New York (1924)	—	150	450
Talbot, William Henry Fox. THE PENCIL IN NATURE. London, 1844–46. In 6 installments in printed wraps. (First commercially published book to use photographic illustrations)	—	—	250,000

Talese, Gay. NEW YORK: A SERENDIPITER'S JOURNEY.
New York (1961) — 35 50

TALES OF THE NORTHWEST . . . (William J. Snelling).
Boston, 1830 — — 350

Tallent, Elizabeth. IN CONSTANT FLIGHT. New York, 1983 — — 35

TAMERLANE. By a Bostonian. (Edgar Allan Poe). Boston,
1827. Wraps 150,000 250,000 250,000

Also see Edgar Allan Poe

Tan, Amy. THE JOY LUCK CLUB. New York (1989) — — 300
London (1989) — — 100

Tappley, William G. DEATH AT CHARITY'S POINT. New
York (1984) — — 150

TARCISSUS, THE BOY MARTYR OF ROME . . . (Baron Corvo
Frederick Wm. Rolfe). (Essex, England, 1880). Wraps 2,000 3,000 3,500

Tarkington, (Newton) Booth. THE GENTLEMAN FROM
INDIANA. New York, 1899. First issue: p. 245:12 last
word "eye" and p. 245:16 reads "so pretty" 60 75 150
Second issue: p. 245:12 as in first issue; p. 245:16 reads
"her heart" — — 100
Third issue: p. 245:12 last word "glance" — — 75

Tarn, Nathaniel. OLD SAVAGE/YOUNG CITY. London (1964) — 50 60

Tartt, Donna. THE SECRET HISTORY. New York, 1992 — — 40

Tate, Allen (John Orley). THE GOLDEN MEAN . . .
(Nashville, 1923). (Written with R. Wills).
200 numbered copies — 3,500 3,500

STONEWALL JACKSON. New York, 1928 50 400 500

MR. POPE . . . New York, 1928 150 450 750
London, 1930. (U.S. sheets) — — 450

Tate, James (Vincent). CAGES. Iowa City, 1966.
45 numbered copies. Wraps — 250 300

THE LOST PILOT. New Haven, 1967 — 100 150

Tauber, Peter. THE SUNSHINE SOLDIERS. New York (1971) — 25 40

Tavel, Ronald. STREET OF STAIRS. New York (1968) — — 50

Taylor, (James) Bayard. XIMENA . . . Philadelphia, 1844 — 250 1,000

Taylor, Eleanor Ross. WILDERNESS OF LADIES. New
York (1960) — 50 75

Taylor, Elizabeth. AT MRS. LIPPINCOTE'S. London, 1945	—	125	200
New York (1946)	—	75	100
Taylor, Frederick Winslow. THE PRINCIPLES OF SCIENTIFIC MANAGEMENT . . . New York, 1911. Green cloth	—	—	1,250
Red cloth	—	—	750
Taylor, Margaret. JASPER THE DRUMMIN' BOY. New York, 1947	—	—	75
Taylor, Peter (Hillsman). A LONG FOURTH . . . New York (1948)	40	150	350
London (1948)	—	150	150
Taylor, Philip Meadows. CONFESSIONS OF A THUG. London, 1839. 3 volumes. Original boards or half-cloth and boards	250	200	850
Taylor, Phoebe Atwood. THE CAPE COD MYSTERY. Indianapolis (1931)	—	250	750
Taylor, Robert Lewis. ADRIFT IN A BONEYARD. Garden City, 1947	—	60	100
Teasdale, Sara. SONNETS TO DUSE . . . Boston, 1907	150	200	750
Tenn, William (Philip J. Klass). OF ALL POSSIBLE WORLDS. New York, 1955	—	—	200
London (1956). (Adds 3 stories not in U.S. edition)	—	—	75
Tennant, Emma. *See* Catherine Aydy			
THE TIME OF THE CRACK. London, 1973	—	40	100
Tennyson, Alfred, Lord. *See* POEMS BY TWO BROTHERS			
TIMBUCTOO. (Cambridge, 1829). (Winner of Cambridge Prize). Wraps	—	1,250	2,000
Re-bound	—	—	1,250
POEMS, CHIEFLY LYRICAL. London, 1830. In original drab or pink paper boards. First issue: p. 91 misnumbered "19"	300	1,000	1,500
Second issue: p. 91 correctly numbered	—	—	1,000
Tennyson, Frederick. DAYS AND HOURS. London, 1854	—	100	100
TENTH MUSE, LATELY SPRUNG UP IN AMERICA, THE. (Anne Bradstreet). London, 1650	—	5,000	10,000
Boston, 1678	—	—	30,000
Terhune, Albert Payson. SYRIA FROM THE SADDLE. New York, 1896	75	150	200
Terkel, Studs. GIANTS OF JAZZ. New York (1957)	—	75	150

Terry, Rose. POEMS. Boston, 1861   —   —   75

Tevis, Walter. THE HUSTLER. (New York, 1959)   25   75   350
    London (1960)   —   40   125

Tey, Josephine. *See* Gordon Daviot

Thackeray, William Makepeace. *See* Theophile Wagstaff

    THE YELLOW PLUSH CORRESPONDENCE.
    Philadelphia, 1838   —   1,500   1,500

Thaxter, Celia. POEMS. New York, 1872   60   100   250

Thayer, Ernest L. CASEY AT THE BAT. Amsterdam Book
    Co. New York (1901). Wraps   —   —   6,000

Thayer, Lee. THE MYSTERY OF THE THIRTEENTH FLOOR.
    New York, 1919   —   25   50

    (Two juveniles preceded)

Theroux, Alexander. THREE WOGS. Boston, 1972. First issue
    dustwrapper has sepia-toned photograph and back flap
    text including "Trappist Monastery in Kentucky"   —   60   200

Theroux, Paul. WALDO. Boston, 1967   25   150   200
    London, 1968   —   125   150

Thom, Robert. VIATICUM. Columbus, 1949. 200 numbered
    copies. Wraps   —   30   35

Thoma, Richard. GREEN CHAOS. Seine (1931). Wraps.
    100 signed and numbered copies   —   150   150

Thomas, Audrey. TEN GREEN BOTTLES. Indianapolis, 1967   —   —   150

Thomas, D(onald) M(ichael). PERSONAL AND POSSESSIVE.
    London, 1964   —   350   750

    TWO VOICES. London, 1968. Cloth. Issued in glassine
    dustwrapper. 50 signed and numbered copies   —   250   250
    Wraps in glassine dustwrapper   —   75   75
    New York, 1968. Wraps in glassine dustwrapper   —   50   50

Thomas, Dylan (Marlais). 18 POEMS. Sunday Referee &
    Parton Bookshop. London (1934). First issue: flat spine,
    leaf between half-title and title pages, front page roughly
    trimmed. (250 copies)   600   2,000   3,000
    Second issue: rounded spine. (1936). (250 copies)   —   750   1,000

Thomas, Edward. WOODLAND LIFE. London, 1897   300   400   600

Thomas, Gwyn. WHERE DID I PUT MY PITY? London, 1946.
    Stiff wraps and dustwrapper   —   60   75

Thomas, Hugh. THE WORLD'S GAME. London, 1957	—	60	60
Thomas, Jerry. THE BARTENDER'S GUIDE. New York, 1862	—	125	175
Thomas, John. DRY MARTINI . . . New York (1926)	—	—	100
Thomas, Joyce Carol. BITTERSWEET. San Jose (1973)	—	—	60
Thomas, Leslie. THIS TIME NEXT WEEK. London, 1964	—	40	50
Thomas, Lowell. TALL STORIES. New York, 1931	—	—	50
Thomas, Norman. THE CONSCIENTIOUS OBJECTOR IN AMERICA. New York, 1923	25	100	150
Thomas, Piri. DOWN THESE MEAN STREETS. New York, 1967	—	35	60
Thomas, R(onald) S(tuart). THE STONES OF THE FIELD. Carmarthen, 1946	—	300	500
Thomas, Robert Bailey. THE FARMER'S ALMANAC . . . FOR . . . 1793. Belknap & Hall. Boston (1793)	—	—	3,000
Thomas, Ross. THE COLD WAR SWAP. New York, 1965	—	200	750
Thomas, Will. GOD IS FOR WHITE FOLKS. New York (1947)	35	60	125
Thomason, John W. FIX BAYONETS. New York, 1926	—	150	200
Thomes, William Henry. *See* THE GOLD-HUNTER'S . . .			
Thompson, A. C. (Alice Meynell). PRELUDES. London, 1875. First issue: brown endpapers	60	75	150
Thompson, Daniel Pierce. *See* THE ADVENTURES OF TIMOTHY PEACOCK . . .			
THE LAWS OF VERMONT. Montpelier, 1835	50	250	350
Thompson, Dorothy. THE DEPTHS OF PROSPERITY. New York (1925). Written with P. Bottome	—	150	250
Thompson, Dunstan. THE SONG OF TIME. Cambridge (Mass., 1941). (50 copies). Wraps	—	100	150
Thompson, Earl. A GARDEN OF SAND. New York (1970) London, 1971	—	40	40
	—	40	40
Thompson, Flora. BOG MYRTLE AND PEAT. London, 1922. Wraps	—	—	250
Thompson, Francis. THE LIFE AND LABORS OF BLESSED JOHN BAPTIST . . . London (1891). Green wraps	—	—	1,500

POEMS. London, 1893. 12 signed copies   75 1,000 4,500
(500 copies). First issue: ads dated October   —   300   350

Thompson, Hunter S. HELL'S ANGELS. New York (1967)   —   90   400

Thompson, Jim (James Myers). NOW AND ON EARTH.
New York, 1942   —   — 3,500

Thompson, Lawrence. THE NAVY HUNTS THE CGR.
Garden City, 1944   —   40   60

Thompson, (James) Maurice. HOOSIER MOSAICS. New
York, 1875   40   75   125

Thompson, Ruth Plumly. THE PRINCESS OF COZY TOWN.
Chicago, 1922. Issued in box   —   —   600

Thomson, James. THE CITY OF DREADFUL NIGHT . . .
London, 1880. (40 large paper copies)   —   500   750
Regular edition   —   125   250

Thomson, June. NOT ONE OF US. London, 1972   —   —   60

Thomson, Virgil. THE STATE OF MUSIC. New York, 1939   20   60   100

Thoreau, Henry David. A WEEK ON THE CONCORD AND
MERRIMACK RIVERS. Boston, 1849. (405 copies)   1,000 1,250 10,000
Boston, 1862. First edition sheets with new title page —   — 1,250
Boston, 1868. (Includes all Thoreau's changes)   —   —   300

Thorp, Roderick. INTO THE FOREST. New York (1961)   —   —   50

Thorpe, T(homas) B(angs). THE MYSTERIES OF THE
BACKWOODS. Philadelphia, 1846   —   —   500

THOUGHTS IN THE CLOISTER AND THE CROWD. (Sir
Arthur Helps). London, 1835. In original cloth   —   150   250

Thubron, Colin. MIRROR TO DAMASCUS. London, 1967   —   —   75

Thurber, James. IS SEX NECESSARY? Written with E. B.
White. New York, 1929   75   350 1,000
London (1930)   —   200   500

THE OWL IN THE ATTIC. New York, 1931   50   250   750

(Also 6 musical scores between 1922 and 1924, all for
Ohio State's Scarlet Mark Club)

Thurman, Wallace. NEGRO LIFE IN NEW YORK'S HARLEM.
Little Blue Book #494. Girard, Kansas (no-date).
Wraps   —   150   150

THE BLACKER THE BERRY. New York, 1929   —   300 1,000

Thwaite, Anthony. (POEMS) FANTASY POETS #17. Eynsham
   (England), 1952. Wraps — 50 150

   HOME TRUTHS. London, 1957 — — 60

Thwaites, Reuben Gold. HISTORIC WATERWAYS . . .
   Chicago, 1888 25 100 175

Tidyman, Ernest. FLOWER POWER. New York (1968).
   Wraps — — 75

Tietjens, Eunice. PROFILES FROM CHINA. Chicago, 1917 — 125 175

Tilghman, Christopher. IN A FATHER'S PLACE. New York
   (1990) — — 40

Timlin, William M. THE SHIP THAT SAILED TO MARS.
   London (1923). Half vellum. 48 colored plates. (In
   dustwrapper) — 1,500 2,500
   New York (1923) — 1,250 1,750

Timrod, Henry. POEMS. Boston, 1860 — 150 150

Tinker, Chauncey Brewster. DR. JOHNSON AND FANNY
   BURNEY . . . New York, 1911 — 60 125

Todd, Mabel (Loomis). FOOTPRINTS. Amherst, 1883.
   Wraps — 200 300

Todd, Ruthven. OVER THE MOUNTAIN. London (1939)   40   100   150

    LAUGHING MULATTO . . . London (1939 or 1940?).
    (May have preceded)   —   —   150

Tolkien, J(ohn) R(onald) R(euel). A MIDDLE
ENGLISH VOCABULARY. Oxford, 1922. Wraps. First
issue: ads dated October 1921. 186 ornaments in cover
design   150   850   850
Second issue: ads undated; "Printed in England" at
bottom of title page, 184 ornaments   —   400   400

Tolkin, Michael. THE PLAYER. New York (1988)   —   —   75

Toller, Ernest. MASSES AND MEN. London, 1923. (First
    English translation)   50   125   150

Tolson, Melvin B. RENDEZVOUS WITH AMERICA. New
    York, 1944   30   60   100

Tolstoy, Leo. CHILDHOOD AND YOUTH. London, 1862.
    (First English translation)   —   500   750

TOM BROWN'S SCHOOL DAYS. (Thomas Hughes).
    Cambridge, 1857. First issue: "nottable" for "notable"
    p. 24:15   —   350   750

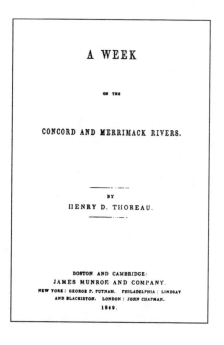

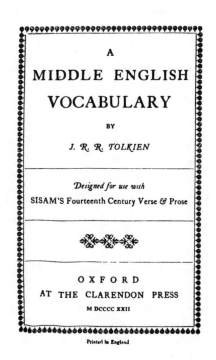

TOM CRINGLE'S LOG. (Michael Scott). Edinburgh, 1833.
    2 volumes. In original cloth   —   200   450
    Boston, 1833. 2 volumes   —   —   200

Tomkins, Calvin. INTERMISSION. New York, 1951   —   35   35

Tomlinson, Charles. RELATIONS AND CONTRARIES.
    Aldington [England] (1951). Wraps   60   75   75

Tomlinson, H(enry) M(ajor). THE SEA AND THE JUNGLE.
    London (1912)   250   100   200
    New York, 1913   —   60   100

Tooker, Richard. THE DAY OF THE BROWN HORDE.
    Payson & Clarke. New York, 1929   25   75   125
    Brewer & Warren. New York, 1929   —   50   100

Toole, John Kennedy. A CONFEDERACY OF DUNCES. Baton
    Rouge, 1980. (2,500 copies)   —   175   750
    (London, 1981). (1,500 copies)   —   75   350

Toomer, Jean. CANE. New York, 1923   —   2,000   5,000

TOPSYS & TURVEYS. (Peter Newell). New York, 1893.
    Pictorial boards   50   250   500

Torrey, Bradford. BIRDS IN THE BUSH. Boston, 1885   —   50   50

Tourgee, Albion W. BOOK OF FORMS. (Raleigh, 1868).
    Wraps   —   200   250

    Also see Henry Churton

Tourtel, Mary. A HORSE BOOK. London, 1901   —   —   250

Towle, Tony. AFTER DINNER WE TAKE A DRIVE INTO
    THE NIGHT. New York, 1968. Wraps. 20 signed and
    numbered copies   —   —   175
    250 numbered copies   —   —   50

Toynbee, Arnold J. GREEK POLICY SINCE 1882. London,
    1914. Wraps   —   100   125

Tracy, Honor. KAKEMANO . . . London, 1950   —   —   100

Train, Arthur (Chesney). MCALLILSTER AND HIS DOUBLE.
    New York, 1905   25   50   75

Traven, B. THE DEATH SHIP. London, 1934. (First English
    translation by Eric Sutton)   50   450   750
    New York, 1934. (English translation by Traven, revised)   25   350   750

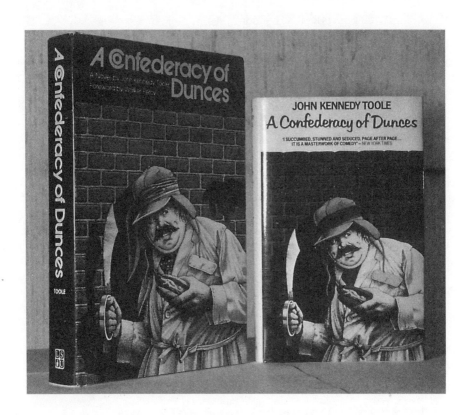

Traver, Robert. (John Donaldson Voelker).
    TROUBLE-SHOOTER. New York, 1943   —   125   150

Travers, P(amela) L(yndon). MARY POPPINS. (London, 1934)   —   350   500
    New York (1934)   —   250   400

TREATISE OF HUMAN NATURE, A. (David Hume). London,
    1739–40. 3 volumes   2,250 9,000 20,000

Tree, Iris. POEMS. Nassau, 1917. Wraps   —   75   400

Treece, Henry. 38 POEMS. London (1940)   —   100   125

Trelawny, Edward John. *See* ADVENTURES OF A YOUNGER
    SON

Tremayne, Sydney. FOR WHOM THERE IS NO SPRING.
    London, 1946. Wraps   15   50   50

Trevanian (Rodney Whitaker). THE EIGER SANCTION.
    New York (1972)   —   40   75

Trevelyan, R. C. POLYPHEMUS. London, 1901	—	—	175
Trevor, William (William Trevor Cox). A STANDARD OF BEHAVIOR. London (1958)	—	350	750
THE OLD BOYS. London (1964)	—	150	300
New York, 1964	—	—	150
TRIBUNE BOOK OF OPEN AIR SPORTS, (THE). (Henry Hall). New York, 1887. (Hall edited this book—believed to be the first printed from machine set type)	—	250	250
Trillin, Calvin. AN EDUCATION IN GEORGIA . . . New York (1964)	—	35	75
Trilling, Diana. CLAREMONT ESSAY. New York (1964)	—	25	60
Trilling, Lionel. MATTHEW ARNOLD. New York (1939)	20	75	75
Trocchi, Alexander. *See* Frances Lengel			
Trollope, Anthony. THE MACDERMOTS OF BALLYCLORAN. London, 1847. 3 volumes	2,000	4,000	12,500
Trollope, T(homas) Adophus. A SUMMER IN BRITTANY . . . London, 1840. 2 volumes	—	250	450
Trotsky, Lev Davydovich. FROM THE WORKERS MOVEMENT . . . Geneva, 1900	200	350	750
Trowbridge, John Townsend. *See* Paul Creyton			
Trudeau, Garry. BULL TALES. (New Hampshire, 1969). Wraps	—	—	125
Trumbo, Dalton. ECLIPSE. London (1935)	—	1,000	2,500
WASHINGTON JITTERS. New York, 1936. (Noted in both blue and yellow cloth—priority unknown)	—	100	250
Tryon, Thomas. THE OTHER. New York, 1971	—	25	75
Tucker, Barbara. *See* Barbara Wertheim			
Tucker, Wilson. THE CHINESE DOLL. New York, 1946	—	—	100
Tully, Jim. EMMETT LAWLER. New York (1922)	—	150	250
Turbyfill, Mark. THE LIVING FRIEZE. Evanston (1921). 350 numbered copies	—	100	150
Also see Samuel Putnam			
Turner, Frederick Jackson. THE CHARACTER AND INFLUENCE OF THE FUR TRADE . . . (Madison, 1889). Wraps	300	500	500

Turow, Scott. ONE L. New York, 1977   —   —   175

Turpin, Waters Edward. THESE LOW GROUNDS. New
   York, 1937   —   —   350

Tuten, Frederic. THE ADVENTURES OF MAO ON THE LONG
   MARCH. (New York, 1971)   —   —   50

Tutuola, Amos. THE PALM-WINE DRINKARD . . .
   London, 1952   —   50   75
   New York, 1953   —   40   60

Twain, Mark (Samuel Langhorne Clemens). THE
   CELEBRATED JUMPING FROG OF CALAVERAS COUNTY.
   New York, 1867. First issue: ad before title page; p. 66
   last line "life" unbroken; p. 198, last line "this" unbroken   2,000 4,000 17,500
   Second issue: lacks ads and type noted above either
   broken or worn   —   —   3,000
   London, 1867. Wraps   —   1,500   3,500

TWO PHILOSOPHERS, THE. (John Jay Chapman). Boston
   (1892). Wraps   150   200   200

TWO YEARS BEFORE THE MAST. (Richard Henry Dana).
   New York, 1840. Presumed first issue: perfect "i" in the
   word "in," first line of copyright   1,000 2,000 5,000
   Second issue: un-dotted "i." BAL notes two bindings:
   black cloth and muslin, no priority. (Also noted in
   brown cloth). Three states of the muslin. Ads in back
   for Harpers' Family Library. First state lists nos. 1–105;
   second state lists nos. 1–121; and third state lists nos.
   1–129   —   —   1,750
   Boston, 1869. Revised. Add'l chapter   —   —   200

Tyler, Anne. IF MORNING EVER COMES. New York (1964)   —   400   1,500

Tyler, Parker. *See* Charles Ford

Tynan, Katherine (K. T. Hinkson). LOUIS DE LA
   VALLIERE . . . London, 1885   20   90   150

Tynan, Kenneth. HE THAT PLAYS THE KING. London, 1950   —   50   75

U
Ullman, Doris. *See* Doris V. Jaeger

Ullman, James Ramsey. MAD SHELLEY. Princeton, 1930.
   Wraps   —   30   100

Underhill, Evelyn. A BAR-LAMB'S BALLAD BOOK. London,
   1902   —   —   100

Unger, Douglas. LEAVING THE LAND. New York (1984)	—	—	100
Unsworth, Barry. THE PARTNERSHIP. London, 1966	—	—	150
Untermeyer, Louis. FIRST LOVE. Boston, 1911	40	50	75
Updike, D. B. (printer). VEXILLA REGIS QUOTIOE. Boston, 1893. 100 copies	—	150	350
Updike, John (Hoyer). THE CARPENTERED HEN. New York (1958)	150	350	750
HOPING FOR A HOOPEE. London, 1959. (New title)	35	75	100
Upfield, Arthur W(illiam). THE HOUSE OF CAIN. London, 1928	—	600	4,500
New York, 1928	—	200	1,500
Upson, William Hazlett. THE PIANO MOVERS. St. Charles, Illinois, 1927	15	60	75
Upward, Allen. SONGS IN ZIKLAG. London, 1888	—	200	150
Upward, Edward. JOURNEY TO THE BORDER. Hogarth Press. London, 1938	—	150	300
(Previous verse work in 1924)			
Urdang, Constance. CHARADES AND CELEBRATIONS. New York, 1965. Wraps	—	30	40
Uris, Leon. BATTLE CRY. New York (1953)	30	100	350
London, 1953	—	50	150
Urquart, Jane. WHIRLPOOL. Toronto, 1990	—	—	125
Ustinov, Peter (Alexander). HOUSE OF REGRETS. London (1943)	—	50	100
Uttley, Alison (Alice Jane). THE SQUIRREL, THE HARE AND THE LITTLE GREY RABBIT. London, 1929	—	—	350
V			
Vachss, Andrew H. FLOOD. New York (1985)	—	—	60
Vail, Amanda (Warren Miller). LOVE ME LITTLE. New York (1957). (Second book)	25	25	30
Also see Warren Miller			
Valentino, Rudolph. DAY DREAMS. New York, 1923. Assumed issued without dustwrapper	—	—	300
Valin, Jonathan. THE LIME PIT. New York, 1980	—	35	75
Van, Melvin (Peebles). THE BIG HEART. San Francisco, 1957	25	40	75

Vance, Jack (John Holbrook). THE DYING EARTH.
New York (1950). Wraps — 150 250
San Francisco/Columbia, 1976. (First hardcover) — — 150

Van Der Post, Lawrence. IN A PROVINCE. London, 1934.
(1,250 copies) — 150 200
New York (no-date) — 100 125

Van Dine, S. S. (Willard Huntington Wright). THE BENSON
MURDER CASE. New York, 1926. (First under this
name) — 400 4,500

Van Dore, Wade. FAR LAKE. New York, 1930 — 50 50

Van Doren, Carl. THE LIFE OF THOMAS LOVE PEACOCK.
Boston, 1911 50 150 100
London, 1911 — 100 75

Van Doren, Mark. HENRY DAVID THOREAU. Boston, 1916 50 150 100

Van Dyke, Henry. LADIES OF THE RACHMANINOFF EYES.
New York (1965) 15 40 75

Van Gieson, Judith. NORTH OF THE BORDER. New York
(1988) — — 350

Van Gulik, Robert (Hans). AN ENGLISH-BLACKFOOT
VOCABULARY BASED ON MATERIAL FROM THE
SOUTHERN PEIGANS. Leiden, 1930. Written with C. C.
Uhlenbeck — — 600

DEE GOONG AN. Tokyo, 1949. 1,200 signed and
numbered copies. Issued without dustwrapper — 750 1,000

THE CHINESE MAZE MURDERS. The Hague, 1956 — 400 400
London, 1957 — 300 300

Van Loon, Hendrik Willem. THE FALL OF THE DUTCH
REPUBLIC. Boston, 1913 40 100 150

Van Lustbader, Eric. THE SUNSET WARRIOR. Garden City,
1977 — — 100

Van Peebles, Melvin. *See* Melvin Van

Van Vechten, Carl. MUSIC AFTER THE GREAT WAR. New
York, 1915 35 75 100

(Previous musical score and promotional pamphlet)

Van Vogt, A. E. SLAN. Sauk City, 1946 — 150 250

Vargas Llosa, Mario. THE TIME OF THE HERO. New York,
1966. First English translation — 40 75
London (1967) — — 100

Varley, John. THE OPHIUCHI HOTLINE. New York, 1977	—	—	40
Veblen, Thorstein. THE THEORY OF THE LEISURE CLASS. London, 1899	75	400	600
New York, 1899	75	250	500
Velikovsky, Immanuel. WORLDS IN COLLISION. New York, 1950	—	50	150
Verne, Jules. FIVE WEEKS IN A BALLOON. New York, 1869. (First English)	—	200	500
VERSES BY TWO UNDERGRADUATES. (Van Wyck Brooks and John Hall Wheelock). (Cambridge, Mass., 1905). Wraps	200	500	500
Very, Jones. ESSAYS AND POEMS. Boston, 1839	—	—	300
Vesey, Paul (Samuel Allen). ELFENBEIN ZÄHNE/IVORY TUSKS. Heidelberg (1956). English/German text	—	300	300
Vestal, Stanley. FANDANGO . . . Boston, 1927	—	150	175
Vidal, Gore. WILLIWAW. New York, 1946	50	175	400
Vidocq, François Eugène. MEMOIRS OF VIDOCQ . . . London, 1828–30. 4 volumes	—	600	1,500
London, 1929	—	—	750
Viereck, Georg Sylvester. GEDICHTE. New York, 1904. Wraps. 300 numbered copies	—	—	300
Viertel, Peter. THE CANYON. New York, 1940	—	—	150
Villa, José García. FOOTNOTE TO YOUTH. New York, 1933	35	75	125
Vinal, Harold. WHITE APRIL. New Haven, 1922. Stiff wraps	—	40	75
Virginian, A. (William Alexander Caruthers). THE KENTUCKIAN IN NEW YORK. New York, 1834. 2 vols.	200	300	450
Visiak, E. H. BUCCANEER BALLADS. London, 1910. Introduction by John Masefield	—	40	75
Visscher, William Lightfoot. BLACK MAMMY . . . Cheyenne, 1885	50	250	350
Vliet, Russ. A MANUAL OF WOODSLORE SURVIVAL. (Cimarron, 1949). Wraps	—	—	200
Vollmann, William T. YOU BRIGHT AND RISEN ANGELS. (London, 1987)	—	—	250
New York, 1987	—	—	150
Vonnegut, Kurt, Jr. PLAYER PIANO. New York, 1952. First issue: "A" and seal on copyright page	75	300	1,000
London, 1953	25	200	500

Voynich, E. L. THE GADFLY. London, 1897   30   30   50

W

W., E. B. (E. B. White). THE LADY IS COLD. New York,
1929. First issue: Plaza Hotel statue on cover, spine
lettered in gold   75   300   400
Second issue: city skyline on cover, spine lettered
in green   —   250   350

Waddell, Helen. THE SPOILED BUDDHA. Dublin, 1919.
Wraps   —   35   100

Waddington, Miriam. GREEN WORLD. Montreal, 1945. Stiff
wraps and dustwrapper   —   250   250

Wade, Henry (Henry Lancelot Aubrey-Fletcher). THE
VERDICT OF YOU ALL. London, 1926   —   100   175

Wagoner, David. DRY SUN, DRY WIND. Bloomington, 1953   —   75   125

Wagstaff, Theophile (Wm. Makepeace Thackeray). FLORE
ET ZEPHYR. London, 1836. (Wrapper folio with nine
unnumbered plates by Thackeray)   300 1,500 3,000

Wahlöö, Per. THE ASSIGNMENT. New York, 1966   —   —   100

WAIKNA . . . (Ephraim G. Squier). New York, 1955   —   —   150

Wain, John (Barrington). MIXED FEELINGS: NINETEEN
POEMS. University of Reading for Subscribers. 1951.
Wraps. 120 numbered copies   35   250   400

HURRY ON DOWN. London, 1953   20   100   100

BORN IN CAPTIVITY. New York, 1954. (New title)   15   50   50

Wainwright, John. DEATH IN A SLEEPING CITY.
London, 1965   —   —   50

Waite, A. E. A LYRIC OF THE FAIRY LAND . . .
London, 1879   —   —   500

Wakefield, Dan. ISLAND IN THE CITY. Boston, 1959   —   30   40

Wakefield, H(erbert) R(ussell). GALLIMAUFRY.
London (1928)   —   150   250

THEY RETURN AT EVENING. New York, 1928.
(First fantasy)   —   125   250

Wakeman, Frederic. SHORE LEAVE. New York (1944)   —   —   50

Wakoski, Diane. JUSTICE IS REASON ENOUGH. (Berkeley
[privately printed]) 1959. (50 mimeographed copies)   150 1,500   500

COINS AND COFFINS. (New York, 1962). Wraps	50	100	150
Walcott, Derek. IN A GREEN NIGHT. London, 1962. (First outside Caribbean)	—	200	300
SELECTED POEMS. New York, 1964. (First U.S. publication)	—	—	150
Waldman, Anne. ON THE WING. New York, 1967. Wraps.			
25 signed and numbered copies	—	75	150
475 numbered copies	—	35	50
GIANT NIGHT. (New York, 1968). Stapled wraps. (100 copies)	—	35	100
New York, 1970	—	15	25
Waley, Arthur. *See* CHINESE POEMS			
Walker, Alice. ONCE: POEMS. New York (1968)	20	200	850
Walker, Margaret (Abigail). FOR MY PEOPLE.			
New York, 1942	40	150	350
Walker, Ted. THESE OTHER GROWTH. Leeds, 1964. Wraps	—	—	50
Wallace, Alfred Russel. PALM TREES OF THE AMAZON. London, 1853. (250 copies)	—	—	1,500
Wallace, David Foster. THE BROOM OF THE SYSTEM. New York, 1987. Cloth	—	—	75
Wraps	—	—	20
Wallace, (Richard Horatio) Edgar. THE MISSION THAT FAILED. Cape Town, 1898. Wraps	75	500	600
Wallace, Irving. THE FABULOUS ORIGINALS.			
New York, 1955	—	50	50
London, 1956	—	40	40
Wallace, Lew(is). THE FAIR GOD. Boston, 1873. First issue: sheets bulk 1" scant, signature mark "k" on p. 161	25	100	125
Second issue: sheets bulk 15/16", signature mark "k" on p. 161 lacking	—	—	40
Wallant, Edward Lewis. THE HUMAN SEASON.			
New York (1960)	35	75	75
Waller, Mary Ella. THE ROSE BUSH OF HILDESHEIM.			
Boston (1889)	—	100	100
Waller, Robert James. JUST BEYOND THE FIRELIGHT.			
Ames, Iowa, 1988	—	—	150

Wallop, Douglas. THE YEAR THE YANKEES LOST THE
PENNANT. New York (1954) — — 125

Walpole, Sir Hugh Seymour. THE WOODEN HORSE.
London, 1909. With the original Smith Elder binding
and title page 35 50 150

Walrond, Eric. TROPIC DEATH. New York, 1926 40 150 150

Walsh, Chad. THE FACTUAL DARK. Prairie City (1949) — 75 75

Walsh, Ernest. POEMS AND SONNETS. New York (1934) 75 150 250

Walters, Minette. THE ICE HOUSE. London, 1992 — — 900
New York (1992) — — 300

Walton, Izaak. THE COMPLEAT ANGLER . . . London, 1653 — 7,500 30,000
London/Edinburgh/Philadelphia, 1837. 2 volumes — — 1,000
New York, 1847. States "First American Edition" — — 600

Walton, Todd. INSIDE MOVES. Garden City, 1978 — 25 35

Wambaugh, Joseph. THE NEW CENTURIONS. Boston (1970) — 25 50
London, 1971 — 25 30

Wandrei, Donald. ECSTASY. Athol, 1928 50 400 400

Waniek, Marilyn Nelson. FOR THE BODY.
Baton Rouge, 1978 — — 40

Ward, Anthony. THE TENT OF GOD. London, 1963 — — 35

Ward, Frederick William Orde. See PESSIMUS

Ward, Gregory. CARPET KING. Toronto, 1991 — — 100

Ward, Lynd. GOD'S MAN. New York (1929). 409 signed
copies. Issued in slipcase 150 400 500
Trade edition 75 150 200

Ward, Mary Jane. THE TREE HAS ROOTS. New York (1937) — — 100

Ware, Eugene Fitch. See RHYMES OF IRONQUILL

Warhol, Andy. LOVE IS A PINK CAKE CORKIE & ANDY.
[New York, 1953]. 23 leaves in folder. 4to spiral bound — 250 600

Waring, Robert Lewis. AS WE SEE IT. Washington, 1910 60 75 75

Warner, Charles Dudley. THE BOOK OF ELOQUENCE.
Cazenovia. New York, 1852 — — 150

MY SUMMER IN A GARDEN. Boston, 1871 25 75 100

Warner, Rex (Ernest). THE KITE. Oxford, 1936 35 125 150

Warner, Susan. *See* Elizabeth Wetherell

Warner, Sylvia Townsend. THE ESPALIER. London, 1925   —   175   250

Warren, Charles Marquis. ONLY THE VALIANT.
New York, 1943   —   —   50

Warren, Robert Penn. JOHN BROWN . . . New York, 1929   150   750   1,250

Warren, Samuel. *See* PASSAGES FROM THE DIARY . . .

Washington, Booker T(aliaferro). DAILY RESOLVE.
London/New York, 1896. "Booker T. Washington"
on title page   —   400   2,500

   BLACK BELT DIAMONDS. New York, 1898   —   400   1,250

   THE FUTURE OF THE AMERICAN NEGRO.
   Boston, 1899   50   250   600

Washington, Doris V. YULAN. New York (1964)   —   —   40

Wasserstein, Wendy. BACHELOR GIRLS. New York, 1990   —   —   25

Waterhouse, Keith. THE CAFE ROYAL . . . London, 1955.
(Written with Guy Deghy)   —   75   100

   THERE IS A HAPPY LAND. London, 1957   15   50   75

Waterman, Andrew. LIVING ROOM. London, 1974. Wraps   —   —   40

Waters, Frank. FEVER PITCH. New York (1930)   —   400   750

Waters, (William Russell). RECOLLECTIONS OF A
POLICEMAN. New York, 1852   —   —   300

   RECOLLECTIONS OF A DETECTIVE POLICE OFFICER.
   London, 1856   —   —   750

Watkins, Paul. NIGHT OVER DAY OVER NIGHT.
London, 1988   —   —   100

Watkins, Vernon (Phillips). BALLAD OF THE MARI LWYD . . .
London (1941)   30   75   100

Watson, Colin. COFFIN SCARCELY USED. London, 1958   —   —   150
New York, 1967   —   —   75

Watson, Ian. JAPAN: A CAT'S-EYE VIEW. (No-place) 1969.
Wraps   —   —   150

   THE EMBEDDING. London, 1973   —   —   250

Watson, Lawrence. IN A DARK TIME. New York (1980)   —   —   100

Watson, Sheila. THE DOUBLE HOOK. Toronto, 1959   —   —   350

Watson, Wilfred. FRIDAY'S CHILD. London (1955)	15	35	35
Watson, William. THE PRINCE'S QUEST. London, 1880	50	75	75
Watts, Alan W. AN OUTLINE OF ZEN BUDDHISM. London (1932). Wraps	25	125	150
BUDDHISM IN THE MODERN WORLD. London (no-date [1933]). Wraps	—	50	75
Watts-Dunton, Theodore. JUBILEE GREETING AT SPITHEAD . . . London, 1897. Wraps	—	—	150
Waugh, Alec. THE LOOM OF YOUTH. London, 1917	—	100	150
New York (1917)	—	60	100
Waugh, Auberon. THE FOXGLOVE SAGA. London, 1960	—	35	40
New York, 1961	—	25	30
Waugh, Evelyn (Arthur St. John). THE WORLD TO COME. (Privately printed) 1916	—	7,500	10,000
P. R. B. AN ESSAY ON THE PRE-RAPHAELITE BROTHERHOOD. (Privately printed) 1926	—	2,500	4,000
ROSSETTI: HIS LIFE AND WORKS. London, 1928	125	1,000	2,000
New York, 1928	—	600	1,250
DECLINE AND FALL. London, 1928	200	600	3,000
Waugh, Frederic J. THE CLAN OF MUNES. New York, 1916	—	400	400
WAVERLEY . . . (By Sir Walter Scott). Edinburgh, 1814. 3 volumes. First issue: "our" vs "your" in first line of volume 2, p. 136	—	—	3,000
New York, 1815. 3 volumes	—	—	1,000
Weaver, John V. IN AMERICA—POEMS. New York, 1921	—	50	50
Webb, Charles. THE GRADUATE. (New York, 1963)	—	40	125
Webb, Francis. A DRUM FOR BEN BOYD. Sydney, 1948	—	—	125
Webb, James. FIELDS OF FIRE. Englewood Cliffs (1978)	—	35	60
Webb, Mary. THE GOLDEN ARROW. London, 1916	125	125	200
Weber, Max. CUBIST POEMS. London, 1914. Cloth and boards. 100 numbered copies	100	250	450
Blue pictorial cloth	—	200	250
Wraps	—	100	200
Webster, John White. A DESCRIPTION OF THE ISLAND OF ST. MICHAEL. Boston, 1821	—	200	200

Weedon, Howard. SHADOWS ON THE WALL.
New York, 1898 — 50 350

Weegee (Arthur Fellig). NAKED CITY. New York (1945).
First issue: rough and heavy gray/green buckram 60 125 250
Second issue: smooth tan cloth — — 200

Weidman, Jerome. I CAN GET IT FOR YOU WHOLESALE.
New York, 1937 25 250 350

Weinbaum, Stanley G(rauman). DAWN OF FLAME. (Jamaica,
New York, 1936). Issued without dustwrapper. First
issue: introduction by Palmer. (7 copies) — 1,750 2,500
Second issue: introduction by Keating. (250 copies) — 1,000 1,500

Weir, Hich C. MISS MADELYN MACK, DETECTIVE.
Boston, 1914 — — 200

Weiss, Ehrich. See Harry Houdini

Weissmuller, Johnny. SWIMMING THE AMERICAN CRAWL.
Boston, 1930 — 125 150

Weissner, Carl. MANIFESTO FOR THE GREY GENERATION.
(No-place)1966. (Written with D. Georgakas and
Poessnecker) 15 35 40

Welch, Denton. MAIDEN VOYAGE. London, 1943 — 200 250
New York, 1945 — 60 100

Welch, James. RIDING THE EARTHBOY FORTY. World.
New York/Cleveland (1971). Reportedly not distributed — 40 250
Harper. New York (1976). Revised — 20 125

Welch, Lew. WOBBLY ROCK. (San Francisco) 1960. Wraps.
(500 copies) 25 60 75

Weldon, Fay. THE FAT WOMAN'S JOKE. London, 1967 — 30 100

. . . AND THE WIFE RAN AWAY. New York, 1968 — — 60

Welles, Orson. EVERYBODY'S SHAKESPEARE: THREE PLAYS.
(Written with Roger Hill). Woodstock, Illinois (1934) — — 250

Welles, Winifred. THE HESITANT HEART, New York, 1919 — 40 40

Wellesley, M. A. (Dorothy). EARLY POEMS. London, 1913 — — 60

Wellman, Manly Wade. THE INVADING ASTEROID. New
York (1932). Wraps 40 100 125

Wells, Carolyn (Mrs. Hadwin Houghton). THE STORY OF
BETTY. New York, 1899 — 125 175

Wells, H(erbert) G(eorge). TEXT BOOK OF BIOLOGY.
London (1893). 2 volumes — 100 · 600 · 1,000

SELECT CONVERSATIONS WITH AN UNCLE.
London, 1895 — 35 · 350 · 450
New York, 1895 — — · 250 · 350

(Previous doctoral dissertation)

Welty, Eudora. THE KEY. (Garden City, 1941). Wraps — — · 2,000 · 2,500

A CURTAIN OF GREEN. Garden City, 1941 — 75 · 750 · 1,000

Wertheim, Barbara (Barbara Tuchman). THE LOST BRITISH
POLICY. London, 1938. Stiff wraps — — · — · 300

WERTHER'S YOUNGER BROTHER . . . (Michael Fraenkel).
New York/Paris (1931). Stiff wraps — 75 · 100 · 175

Wescott, Glenway. THE BITTERNS. Evanston (1920). Wraps.
(200 copies) — 250 · 500 · 600

West, Anthony. GLOUCESTERSHIRE. London, 1939 — — · — · 150

ON A DARK NIGHT. London (1949) — — · — · 75

THE VINTAGE. Boston, 1950 — — · 30 · 35

West, Dorothy. LIVING IS EASY. Boston, 1948 — — · 200 · 600

West, Jessamyn. THE FRIENDLY PERSUASION.
New York (1945) — — · — · 100

West, Mae. BABE GORDON. New York, 1930 — — · 75 · 200

West, Morris. *See* Julian Morris

West, Nathanael (Nathanael W. Weinstein). THE DREAM
LIFE OF BALSO SNELL. Paris (1931). (500 copies).
15 copies in cloth — 600 · 1,750 · 7,500
485 copies in wraps — 400 · 1,000 · 1,500

West, Paul. (POEMS) FANTASY POETS #7. Eynsham, 1952.
Wraps — — · — · 75

West, Rebecca (Cicily Isabel Fairfield Andrews). HENRY
JAMES. London, 1916 — — · 60 · 150
New York, 1916 — — · 40 · 125

THE RETURN OF THE SOLDIER. New York, 1918 — — · 60 · 75
London, 1918. First issue: blue cloth stamped in green
and gilt — — · 50 · 60

Westcott, Edward Noyes. DAVID HARUM. New York, 1898.
First issue: perfect "J" in "Julius" penultimate line p. 40 — 60 · 60 · 100

Westlake, Donald E(dwin). THE MERCENARIES.
New York (1960)   30   125   250
London, 1961   —   75   150

Weston, Edward. EDWARD WESTON. New York, 1932.
550 signed and numbered copies. Issued
without dustwrapper   —   1,250 2,000

(Exhibition brochure preceded)

Weston, Patrick (Gerald Hamilton). DESERT DREAMERS.
London (1914). (250 copies)   —   125   125

Westwood, Thomas. POEMS. London, 1840   20   60   150

Wetherell, Elizabeth (Susan Warner). THE WIDE, WIDE
WORLD. New York, 1851. 2 volumes. First issue: p. 157
in volume 1 and p. 34 in volume 2 have numbers
misplaced   —   —   750

Weyman, Stanley. THE HOUSE OF THE WOLF. London, 1890 60   75   100

Whalen, Philip. THREE SATIRES. (Portland, Oregon, 1951).
Wraps   50   400   450

SELF-PORTRAIT FROM ANOTHER DIRECTION.
(San Francisco) 1959. Wraps   —   35   50

Whaler, James. HALE'S POND . . . New York, 1927   25   35   40

Wharton, Edith Newbold Jones. See Edith Newbold Jones

THE DECORATION OF HOUSES. (Written with O.
Codman). New York, 1897   —   350   600
London, 1898   —   250   500

THE GREATER INCLINATION. New York, 1899   50   125   300

Wharton, Will. GRAPHITI FROM ELSINORE.
Prairie City (1949)   —   75   75

Wharton, William. BIRDY. New York, 1979   —   35   75
London, 1979   —   35   50

Wheatley, Dennis (Yates). THE FORBIDDEN TERRITORY.
London (1933)   —   75   300
New York (1933)   —   —   150

Wheatley, Phillis. POEMS ON VARIOUS SUBJECTS,
RELIGIOUS AND MORAL. London, 1773   —   2,000 6,000
Philadelphia, 1786   —   1,000 3,500

Wheeler, Ella (Wilcox). DROPS OF WATER.
New York, 1872   —   50   75

Wheelock, John Hall. *See* VERSES BY TWO UNDERGRADUATES

    THE HUMAN FANTASY. Boston, 1911   —   75   150

Wheelwright, John Brooks. NORTH ATLANTIC PASSAGE.
    (Florence, Italy, 1924)   100   750   1,000

Whichler, George F(risbie). ON THE TIBER ROAD.
    Princeton, 1911   —   50   50

Whigham, Peter. CLEAR LAKE COMES FROM ENJOYMENT.
    London (1959). Written with Denis Goacher   —   —   75

Whistler, James Abbott McNeill. WHISTLER V. RUSKIN.
    Chelsea, 1878. Wraps. First edition: 12mo   75   350   600
    Second edition: 4to   —   200   300

White, Antonia. FROST IN MAY. London (1933)   —   200   250

White, E(lwyn) B(rooks). *See* Sterling Finney, James
    Thurber, *and* E. B. W.

White, Edmund. FORGETTING ELENA. New York (1973)   —   40   100

White, Edward Lucas. NARRATIVE LYRICS. New York and
    London, 1908   15   30   30

White, Eric Walter. THE ROOM . . . London, 1927. Issued
    without dustwrapper   —   —   50

White, Grace Miller. A CHILD OF THE SLUMS. Ogilvie, 1904.
    Wraps   —   200   250

White, Owen P. JUST ME . . . El Paso, 1924. Stiff wraps.
    (Carl Hertzog's first typography). 275 numbered copies   —   —   350

White, Patrick (Victor Martindale). THE PLOUGHMAN . . .
    Sydney, 1935   —   1,000   2,500

    HAPPY VALLEY. London, 1939   —   600   1,500
    New York, 1940   —   300   850

White, Stewart Edward. THE BIRDS OF MACKINAC ISLAND.
    New York, 1893. Wraps   —   400   750

    THE CLAIM JUMPERS. New York, 1901. Pictorial cloth   —   75   200
    (Town & Country Library). Wraps   —   60   150

White, T(erence) H(anbury). THE GREEN BAY TREE.
    (Cambridge, Eng., 1929). Wraps   —   350   400

    LOVED HELEN . . . London (1929)   75   300   500

White, T(heodore) H. THUNDER OUT OF CHINA. New
    York, 1946. Written with Annalee Jacoby   —   25   40

White, W(illiam) L(indsay). WHAT PEOPLE SAID. New York, 1936	—	35	35
White, Walter F(rancis). THE FIRE IN THE FLINT. New York, 1924	60	150	200
White, William Allen. RHYMES BY TWO FRIENDS. Fort Scott (1893). (Written with A. B. Paine). (500 copies)	40	75	150
THE REAL ISSUE. Chicago, 1896	—	40	50
Whitehead, E. A. THE FOURSOME. London, 1972. Wraps	—	30	30
Whitehead, Henry S(t. Clair). JUMBEE . . . (Sauk City) 1944	—	175	300
White Rabbit Press. LAMENT FOR THE MAKERS. (By Jack Spicer). Oakland, 1962. Wraps. (First book of the press)	—	300	300
Whitlock, Brand. THE 13TH DISTRICT . . . Indianapolis (1902)	15	25	30
Whitman, Sarah Helen (Power). POEMS. (Providence, 1847). Wraps	—	50	150
HOURS OF LIFE . . . Providence, 1853	—	—	150
Whitman, Walt(er). FRANKLIN EVANS: OR, THE ENEBRIATE. (New York, 1842). Wraps. First issue: 12 1/2 cent price	—	5,000	8,500
Second issue: 6 1/2 cent price	—	4,000	5,000
New York, 1929. 700 copies	—	—	150
Also see LEAVES OF GRASS			
Whittemore, Edward. QUIN'S SHANGHAI CIRCUS. New York, 1974	—	35	75
Whittemore, (Edward) Reed. HEROS AND HEROINES. New York (1946)	—	50	75
Whittier, John Greenleaf. LEGENDS OF NEW ENGLAND. Hartford, 1831. First issue: last line, p. 98 "The go" for "They go." In original cloth	150	250	750
Whyte-Melville, George John. DIGBY GRAND. London, 1853. 2 volumes	75	200	300
Wideman, John Edgar. A GLANCE AWAY. New York (1967)	20	75	200
Wiebe, Rudy. PEACE SHALL DESTROY MANY. Toronto, 1962	—	—	60
WIELAND . . . (Charles Brockden Brown). New York, 1798	—	—	1,500
Wiener, Norbert. CYBERNETICS . . . New York (1948)	—	125	350

Wieners, John (Joseph). THE HOTEL WENTLY POEMS. (San
   Francisco) 1958. Wraps. First issue: censored   40   50 100
   Second issue: unexpurgated (press listed at "1334 Franklin
   Street")   20   30   40

Wiesel, Elie. NIGHT. Paris, 1958   —   75 200
   New York (1960)   —   — 150

Wiggin, Kate Douglas. *See* Kate Douglas Smith

Wilbur, Richard (Purdy). THE BEAUTIFUL CHANGES . . .
   New York (1947). (750 copies)   75 250 350

Wilde, Oscar (Fingal O'Flahertie Wills). RAVENNA. Oxford,
   1878. Wraps. First issue: Oxford University arms on title
   and cover   250 600 1,000

Wilder, Amos N(iven). BATTLE-RETROSPECT . . . New
   York, 1923   — 150 200

Wilder, Isabel. MOTHER AND FOUR. New York, 1933   —   — 100

Wilder, Laura Ingalls. LITTLE HOUSE IN THE BIG WOODS.
   New York, 1932   —   — 400

Wilder, Thornton. THE CABALA. New York, 1926. First
   issue: "conversation" for "conversion" on p. 196:13,
   "explaininn" for "explaining" p. 202:12. Blue patterned
   cloth reportedly scarcer than red   100 250 350
   London, 1926   —   75 150

Wilhelm, Kate. MORE BITTER THAN DEATH.
   New York, 1963   —   50   75

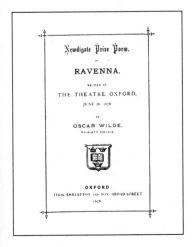

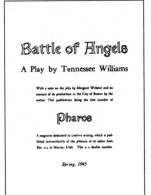

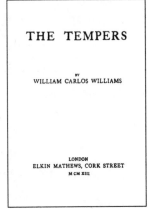

Wilkins, Mary E. (Mary E. W. Freeman). DECORATIVE PLAQUES. Boston (1883). (Written with George F. Barnes)	—	600	2,000
Wilkinson, Sylvia. MOSS ON THE NORTH SIDE. Boston, 1967	—	60	60
Will, George. THE PURSUIT OF HAPPINESS . . . New York, 1979	—	35	75
Willeford, Charles. PROLETARIAN LAUGHTER. Yonkers, 1948. Wraps. 1,000 copies	—	125	150
Williams, Alfred. SONGS IN WILTSHIRE. London, 1909. (500 copies)	25	40	40
Williams, Ben Ames. ALL THE BROTHERS WERE VALIANT. New York, 1919. In N. C. Wyeth dustwrapper	—	50	400
Williams, C(harles) K(enneth). A DAY FOR ANNE FRANK. Philadelphia (1968)	—	40	75
LIES. Boston, 1969	—	—	75
Williams, Charles (Walter). THE SILVER STAIR. London, 1912	—	300	300
Williams, Heathcote. THE SPEAKERS. London, 1964	—	35	35
Williams, Joan. THE MORNING AND THE EVENING. New York, 1961	—	25	50
London, 1962	—	25	40
Williams, John. THE BROKEN LANDSCAPE. Denver, 1949. (500 copies)	—	50	75
Williams, John A(lfred). THE ANGRY ONES . . . New York (1960). Wraps	40	50	75
Williams, Jonathan (Chamberlain). PAINTING & GRAPHICS. Highlands, 1950. (Exhibition folder)	—	500	500
(Previous pamphlet may exist)			
Williams, Joy. STATE OF GRACE. Garden City, 1973	—	25	100
Williams, Margery. THE LATE RETURNING. London, 1902	—	—	100
THE VELVETEEN RABBIT . . . London, 1922. First children's book	—	—	350
New York (1922)	—	—	200

Also see Margery Bianco

Williams, Oscar. THE GOLDEN DARKNESS. New Haven,
1921. Wraps over boards — 60 125

Williams, Sherley Anne. GIVE BIRTH TO BRIGHTNESS.
New York, 1972 — — 125

Williams, Tennessee (Thomas Lanier). BATTLE OF ANGELS.
Murray, Utah, 1945. Published as Pharos Nos. 1 and 2.
Wraps 200 350 750

Williams, Terry Tempest. PIECES OF WHITE SHELL.
New York (1984) — — 75

Williams, Thomas. CEREMONY OF LOVE. Indianapolis (1955) — 40 75

Williams, William Carlos. POEMS. (Rutherford, New Jersey)
1909. Wraps. (100 copies). First issue: 2 known copies. Line
5 of first poem reads "of youth himself, all rosey-clad" 15,000 15,000 30,000
Second issue: fewer than 15 known copies. Line 5 of
first poem reads "of youth himself all rosey clad" — — 17,500

THE POEMS. London, 1913 — 800 1,500

Williamson, Henry. THE BEAUTIFUL YEARS. London, 1921.
(750 copies) 125 300 750

Williamson, Jack. THE GIRL FROM MARS. New York (1929).
Wraps. (Written with Dr. M. Breuer) — 75 100

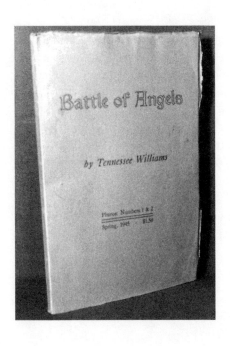

THE LEGION OF SPACE. Reading, 1947. 500 signed and numbered copies	—	90	150
Trade edition	—	35	75
Willingham, Calder (Bayard). END AS A MAN. New York (1947). First issue: no text on back panel of dustwrapper	25	75	150
Second issue: text on back panel of dustwrapper	—	—	75
Willington, James (Oliver Goldsmith). MEMOIRS OF A PROTESTANT. London, 1758	—	2,000	3,000
Willis, George. TANGLEWEED. Garden City, 1943	—	35	50
Willis, N(athaniel) P(arker). SKETCHES. Boston, 1827	40	100	200
Wills, Garry. CHESTERTON. New York (1961)	—	50	75
Willson, Meredith. AND THERE I STOOD WITH MY PICCOLO. New York, 1948	—	50	60
Wilson, A(ndrew) N(orman). THE SWEETS OF PIMLICO. London (1977)	—	—	350
Wilson, Adrian. PRINTING FOR THE THEATRE. San Francisco, 1957. (250 copies)	—	—	1,250
Wilson, Angus (Frank Johnstone). THE WRONG SET . . . London, 1949	30	60	75
Wilson, Augusta Jane Evans. See INEZ . . .			
Wilson, Carroll Atwood. VERDENT GREEN. (No-place) 1933. Wraps	15	40	75
Wilson, Colin (Henry). THE OUTSIDER. London, 1956. First issue: date on title page. At least 3 different binding variants without dates, but stating "First American Edition" on copyright page have been seen	—	75	200
Boston, 1956	20	40	100
Wilson, Edmund. THE UNDERTAKER'S GARLAND. New York, 1922. (Written with J. P. Bishop). 50 copies for "Bookseller Friends." Issued without dustwrapper	—	250	250
Trade edition in dustwrapper	50	350	350
DISCORDANT ENCOUNTERS. New York (1927)	25	350	500
Wilson, Harry Leon. ZIG ZAG TALES FROM EAST TO WEST. New York, 1894. Wraps	75	100	200
Cloth	40	75	125
Wilson, Lanford. BALM IN GILEAD . . . New York, 1965. Wraps	—	35	75

Wilson, William S. BIRTHPLACE. San Francisco, 1982   — — 30

Wilson, (Thomas) Woodrow. CONGRESSIONAL
GOVERNMENT. Boston, 1885. First issue: publisher's
monogram on spine   35 100 250

Wiltz, Chris. THE KILLING CIRCLE. New York, 1981   — — 60

Windham, Donald. YOU TOUCHED ME. New York (1947).
(Written with Tennessee Williams). 506 hardcover in
white pictorial dustwrapper   — — 400
Cream-colored wraps with preliminary price of $.75   — — 200
Gray wraps printed in black with 85 cent price. (All
subsequent printings in bright orange)   — 75 150

THE HITCHHIKER. (Florence, 1950). 250 signed and
numbered copies. Wraps   — 125 125

Wingfield, Sheila. POEMS. London (1938)   — — 75

Winogrand, Garry. THE ANIMALS. New York, 1969. Wraps   — — 75

Winslow, Don. A COOL BREEZE ON THE UNDERGROUND.
New York (1991)   — — 50

Winsor, Justin. A HISTORY OF THE TOWN OF DUXBURY . . .
Boston, 1849   — 150 250

Winsor, Kathleen (Herwig Shaw Porter). FOREVER AMBER.
New York, 1944   25 60 75

Winter, William. POEMS. Boston, 1855   — 150 200

WINTER IN THE WEST, A. By a New Yorker. (Charles
Fenno Hoffman). New York, 1835. 2 volumes. In
original cloth   — 150 650

Winters, Ivor. DIADEMS AND FAGOTS. Sante Fe (1920).
(Translation by Winters of Olavo Bilac's book).
(50 copies)   250 500 600

WINTER SHIP, A. (By Sylvia Plath). Edinburgh, 1960. Wraps   150 1,000 1,000

THE IMMOBILE WIND. Evanston (1921). Wraps   300 450 500

Winterson, Jeanette. ORANGES ARE NOT THE ONLY FRUIT.
London (1985). Wraps   — — 200
New York (1987)   — — 75

Wister, Owen. THE LADY OF THE LAKE.
(Cambridge, Mass.) 1881. (Chorus book)   — 200 300

THE NEW SWISS FAMILY ROBINSON.
(Cambridge, Mass., 1882)   25 250 500

Witwer, Harry Charles. FROM BASEBALL TO BOCHES.			
Boston (1918)	25	40	40
Wodehouse, P(elham) G(renville). THE POTHUNTERS.			
London, 1902. First issue: silver cup on front	200	1,750	3,500
Second issue: finish line on front	—	—	750
Woiwode, Larry. WHAT I'M GOING TO DO . . .			
New York (1969)	—	40	50
London, 1970	—	40	40
Wolfe, Bernard. REALLY THE BLUES. New York (1946).			
Written with Milton Mezzrow	—	75	75
LIMBO. New York (1952)	—	75	75
Wolfe, Gene. OPERATION ARES. New York (1970)	—	—	40
London, 1977. First hardcover	—	—	50
Wolfe, Humbert. THE OLD MAN OF KOENIGSBERG . . .			
Holy Well, 1907	—	—	300
THE COUNT OF SALDEYNE. London, 1915	25	50	100
Wolfe, Susan. THE LAST BILLABLE HOUR. New York, 1989	—	—	175
Wolfe, Thomas (Clayton). THE CRISIS IN INDUSTRY.			
Chapel Hill, 1919. Wraps	2,500	6,000	7,500

LOOK HOMEWARD, ANGEL. New York, 1929.

First issue: dustwrapper has author's picture on back	450	1,500	2,500
Second issue: author's picture not on back of dustwrapper	350	750	1,250
London, 1930. (Few textual changes)	—	650	750

Wolfe, Tom. THE KANDY KOLORED . . . New York (1965)	—	60	175
Wolfert, Ira. TUCKER'S PEOPLE. New York, 1943	—	—	75
BATTLE FOR THE SOLOMONS. Boston, 1943	—	—	75
Wolff, Geoffrey. BAD DEBTS. New York, 1969	—	20	35
Wolff, Maritta M. WHISTLE STOP. New York (1941)	20	40	40
Wolff, Tobias. UGLY RUMOURS. London (1975)	—	—	500

IN THE GARDEN OF THE NORTH AMERICAN MARTYRS. New York (1981). Cloth	—	40	100
Wraps	—	—	35

Wolheim, Donald A(llen). THE SECRET OF SATURN'S RINGS. Philadelphia (1954)	—	35	125

(Previous edited anthologies)

Wood, Charles Erskine Scott. IMPERIALISM VS. DEMOCRACY. New York, 1899. (Offprint from "Pacific Monthly")	—	100	150
A MASQUE OF LOVE. Chicago, 1904	25	60	75
Wood, Clement. GLAD OF EARTH. New York, 1917	—	40	60
Wood, Ted. DEAD IN THE WATER. Toronto, 1983	—	—	200
New York, 1983	—	—	35

Woodberry, George Edward. THE RELATIONS OF PALLAS ATHENE TO ATHENS. (Privately printed, 1877?). Wraps	—	—	300
HISTORY OF WOOD-ENGRAVING. New York, 1883	—	125	150
THE NORTH SHORE WATCH. New York, 1883. 200 copies	—	—	150
THE NORTH SHORE WATCH . . . Boston, 1890	—	—	75

Woodcock, George. 6 POEMS. London, 1938	—	—	750

Woodford, Jack. EVANGELICAL COCKROACH. New York, 1929	—	60	75

Woods, Sara. BLOODY INSTRUCTIONS. London, 1962	—	—	100
New York, 1963	—	—	40

Woods, Stuart. CHIEFS. New York, 1981	—	—	125

Woodward, C(omer) Vann. TOM WATSON: AGRARIAN REBEL. New York, 1938	—	—	200
Woodward, W(illiam) E. BUNK. New York, 1923	25	60	75
Woolf, Douglas. THE HYPOCRITIC DAYS. Divers Press, 1955. Wraps	15	50	75
Woolf, L(eonard) S. THE VILLAGE IN THE JUNGLE. London (1913)	—	250	350
Woolf, Virginia. THE VOYAGE OUT. London, 1915.			
Green cloth	—	500	1,500
Red cloth (trial binding?)	—	400	1,500
New York (1920). Text revised by Woolf. In dustwrapper	—	—	2,000
Woollcott, Alexander. MRS. FISKE . . . New York, 1915. First issue: author's name misspelled on title page	15	50	50
Woolly Whale, Press of. LE CHAPEAU IMMORTEL. (New York, 1928). 350 copies. (First publication of press a broadside by Earl H. Emmons)	—	75	75
Woolner, Thomas. MY BEAUTIFUL LADY. London, 1863	—	—	250
Woolrich, Cornell. COVER CHARGE. New York, 1926	50	750	2,000
Wordsworth, William. AN EVENING WALK. London, 1793	—	5,000	5,000
Wouk, Herman. THE MAN IN THE TRENCH COAT. New York (1941). Wraps	50	750	1,250
AURORA DAWN. New York, 1947	15	100	175
London, 1947	—	75	100
Wright, Austin Tappan. ISLANDIA. New York (1942). With *Introduction to Islandia,* by Basil Davenport. 2 volumes	—	300	400
Wright, Charles. THE DREAM ANIMAL. Toronto, 1968.			
Issued without dustwrapper	—	—	200
Wraps	—	—	35
THE GRAVE OF THE RIGHT HAND. Middletown (1970).			
Cloth	—	35	75
Wraps	—	—	30
Wright, Charles (Stevenson). THE MESSENGER. New York (1963)	—	40	75
Wright, Eric. THE NIGHT THE GODS SMILED. London, 1983	—	—	150

Wright, Frank Lloyd. THE JAPANESE PRINT. Chicago, 1912.
50 copies. Pictorial boards and handmade endpapers — 600 3,000
   Trade edition — — 2,000
New York, 1967. Issued in slipcase — — 300

Wright, Harold Bell. THAT PRINTER OF UDELL'S.
Chicago, 1903 25 40 60

Wright, James (Arlington). THE GREEN WALL.
New Haven, 1957 — 250 350

Wright, Jay. DEATH AS HISTORY. Milbrook (1967). Wraps.
(200 copies) — — 150

Wright, Judith. THE MOVING IMAGE. Melbourne (1946) 75 100 125

Wright, L. R. THE SUSPECT. Toronto, 1985 — — 100

Wright, Richard (Nathaniel). UNCLE TOM'S CHILDREN.
New York, 1938 150 600 1,250
New York (1938). Enlarged edition — — 600

Wright, Richard B. ANDREW TOLLIVER. Toronto, 1965 — — 125

   THE WEEKEND MAN. Toronto, 1970 — — 75
New York (1970) — 30 40

Wright, S(ydney) Fowler. THE AMPHIBIANS. London (1925) — 100 350

Wright, Sarah E. GIVE ME THIS CHILD. (Written with Lucy
Smith). Philadelphia (1955). Wraps — 50 200

   THIS CHILD'S GONNA LIVE. (New York, 1969) — 35 75
London, 1969 — — 60

Wright, Stephen. MEDITATIONS IN GREEN. New York, 1983 — — 50

Wright, Willard Huntington. SONGS OF YOUTH.
New York, 1913 — 60 500

Also see S. S. Van Dine

Wurlitzer, Rudolph. NOG. New York (1968) — 35 50

   THE OCTOPUS. London, 1969. (New title) — 30 30

Wylie, Elinor (Hoyt). *See* INCIDENTAL NUMBERS

   NETS TO CATCH THE WIND. New York, 1921.
First issue: unwatermarked paper 75 300 300
London, 1928 — — 150

Wylie, Philip (Gordon). HEAVY LADEN. New York, 1928 40 150 250

Wyndham, Francis. OUT OF THE WAR. London, 1974	—	—	50

Wyndham, John (John Beynon Harris). *See* John Beynon

THE DAY OF THE TRIFFIDS. Garden City, 1951. (First novel)	20	150	300
London (1951). (Contains textual revisions)	—	200	400

Y

Yarbro, Chelsea Quinn. TIME OF THE FOURTH HORSEMAN. Garden City, 1976	—	—	30
Yates, Edmund Hodgson. MY HAUNTS AND THEIR FREQUENTERS. London, 1854. Wraps	50	125	150
Yates, Elizabeth. QUEST IN THE NORTH-LAND. New York, 1940	—	35	50
Yates, Richard. REVOLUTIONARY ROAD. Boston (1961)	20	60	150
(London, 1962)	—	50	75
Yeats, Jack B(utler). JAMES FLAUNTY. London (1901). Wraps	50	200	350
Yeats, W(illiam) B(utler). MOSADA. Dublin, 1886. (100 copies)	3,000	35,000	75,000
THE WANDERINGS OF OISIN . . . London, 1889. (500 copies)	500	1,000	3,000
Yellen, Samuel. IN THE HOUSE AND OUT . . . Bloomington, 1952	—	—	40
Yerby, Frank (Garvin). THE FOXES OF HARROW. New York, 1946	—	60	100
Yevtushenko, Yevgeny. SELECTED POEMS. New York, 1962. (First English translation)	—	—	75
Yglesias, Jose. A WAKE IN YBOR CITY. New York (1963)	—	30	40

(Previous translations)

Yorke, Henry Vincent. *See* Henry Green

Young, Al. DANCING. New York (1969). Wraps. 50 signed and numbered copies	—	150	200
Unsigned edition	—	30	50
Young, Andrew. SONG OF NIGHT. London [1910]	—	200	200

Young, Art. *See* R. Palasco Drant

Young, Marguerite. PRISMATIC GROUND. New York, 1937	30	50	50
Young, Stark. THE BLIND MAN AT THE WINDOW . . . New York, 1906	—	100	200

MOSADA.

A Dramatic Poem.

BY

W. B. YEATS.

WITH A

Frontispiece Portrait of the Author

By J. B. YEATS.

Reprinted from the DUBLIN UNIVERSITY REVIEW.

DUBLIN:

PRINTED BY SEALY, BRYERS, AND WALKER,

94, 95 AND 96 MIDDLE ABBEY STREET.

1886.

Young Lady, A. *See* AGNES DE CASTRO

Yount, John. WOLF AT THE DOOR. New York, 1967	—	40	75
Yurick, Sol. THE WARRIORS. New York (1965)	—	40	60

Z

Zagat, Arthur Lee. SEVEN OUT OF TIME. Reading, 1949	—	25	35
Zangwill, I. THE BACHELOR'S CLUB. London, 1891	—	150	300
Zanuck, Darryl F. HABIT . . . London, 1923	—	—	150
Zaroulis, N(ancy) L. THE POE PAPERS. New York (1977)	—	—	75
Zaturenska, Marya. THRESHOLD AND HEARTH. New York, 1934	—	—	150
Zeitlin, Jake. FOR WHISPERS AND CHANTS. San Francisco, 1927. (500 copies)	40	200	175
Zindel, Paul. THE PIGMAN. New York (1968)	—	35	50
Zindell, David. NEVERNESS. New York, 1988	—	—	35
Zugsmith, Leane. ALL VICTORIES ARE ALIKE. New York, 1929	—	100	100

Zukofsky, Louis. *See* Anton Reiser

LE STYLE APOLLINAIRE. Paris, 1934. Wraps	—	4,000	4,000
FIRST HALF OF 'A'—9. New York, 1940. 55 mimeographed signed copies	—	1,500	2,000

APPENDIX A

PSEUDONYMS

The following is a list of authors and their pseudonyms. The sources include practically all the reference works listed in the Selected Bibliography, plus individual bibliographies.

The list has been arbitrarily limited to pseudonyms used by the authors when publishing books and does not include pseudonyms used in magazine appearances.

The names are listed alphabetically. The names in **Bold Face** type are the real names of the authors.

A.	**Matthew Arnold**
A., T. B.	**Thomas Bailey Aldrich**
Abbott, Anthony	**Fulton Oursler**
Acre, Stephen	**Frank Gruber**
Adams, William Taylor	Warren T. Ashton; Oliver Optic
Ai	**Florence Anthony**
Akers, Floyd	**L. Frank Baum**
Aldrich, Thomas Bailey	T. B. A.
Alger, Horatio	Arthur Lee Putnam; Julian Starr
Allen, Grace	Allen Weston (with **Alice Mary Norton**)
Allen, Hervey	Hardly Alum
Allen, Steve	William Allen Stevens; William Christopher Stevens
Allingham, Margery	Maxwell March
Alum, Hardly	**Hervey Allen**
Ambler, Eric	Eliot Reed (with **Charles Rodda**)
Amis, Kingsley	Robert Markham; William Tanner
Anderson, Maxwell	John Nairne Michaelson
Anderson, Poul	A. A. Craig; Michael Karageorge; Winston P. Sanders

Andrezel, Pierre	**Karen Blixen**
Anstey, F.	**Thomas Anstey Guthrie**
Anthony, C .L.	**Dodie Smith**
Anthony, Florence	Ai
Anthony, Peter	**Peter** and **Anthony Shaffer**
Antoninus, Brother (Dominican lay brother, 1951–1969)	**William Everson**
Ard, Willam	Ben Kerr; Mike Moran; Jonas Ward; Thomas Wills
Arden, William	**Dennis Lynds**
Armstrong, Terence Fytton	**John Gawsworth**
Arno, Peter	**Curtis Arnoux Peters**
Arnold, Matthew	A.
Arnow, Harriette	**Harriett Simpson**
Ashdown, Clifford	**R. Austin Freeman** and **John James Pitcairn**
Ashe, Gordon	**John Creasey**
Ashton, Warren T.	**William Taylor Adams**
Asimov, Isaac	George E. Dale; Paul French
Aston, James	**T. H. White**
Atherton, Gertrude	Frank Lin
Aubrey-Fletcher, Henry Lancelot	Henry Wade
Auchincloss, Louis	Andrew Lee
August, John	**Bernard De Voto**
Auster, Paul	Paul Benjamin
Austin, Mary H.	Gordon Stairs
Axton, David	**Dean R. Koontz**
B., E. C.	**Edmund Blunden**
B., J. K.	**John Kendrick Bangs**
Bachman, Richard	**Stephen King**
Bagby, George	**Aaron Marc Stein**
Baker, Asa	**Davis Dresser**
Bancroft, Laura	**L. Frank Baum**
Bangs, John Kendrick	J. K. B.
Banshuck, Grego	**Hugo Gernsback**
Baraka, Imamu Amiri (legal name change)	**Leroi Jones**
Barbellion, W. N. P.	**Bruce Frederick Cummings**
Barbette, Jay	Bart Spicer (with **Betty Spicer**)
Barclay, Bill	**Michael Moorcock**
Barnes, Julian	Dan Kavanagh
Barnsley, Alan	Gabriel Fielding
Barr, Robert	Luke Sharp
Baum, L. Frank	Floyd Akers; Laura Bancroft; John Estes Cook; Edith Van Dyne
Bax, Roger	**Paul Winterton**
Baxter, George Owen	**Frederick Faust**

Baxter, John	**Howard Hunt**
Beaton, George	**Gerald Brenan**
Beaumont, Charles	**Charles Nutt**
Beecher, Harriet	**Harriet Beecher Stowe** (married name)
Bell, Acton	**Ann Brontë**
Bell, Currer	**Charlotte Brontë**
Bell, Ellis	**Emily Brontë**
Bell, Eric Temple	John Taine
Benjamin, Paul	**Paul Auster**
Benson, A. C.	Christopher Carr
Bentley, E. C.	E. Clerihew
Berkeley, Anthony	Francis Iles
Berne, Victoria	**M. F. K. Fisher and Dillwyn Parrish**
Betjeman, John	Richard M. Farren
Beynon, John	**John Wyndham P. L. B. Harris**
Bierce, Ambrose	Dod Grile; William Herman
Bigby, Cantell A.	**George W. Peck**
Birdwell, Cleo	**Don DeLillo**
Birney, Earle	E. Robertson
Black, Mansell	**Elleston Trevor**
Blair, Eric Arthur	George Orwell
Blaisdell, Anne	**(Barbara) Elizabeth Linington**
Blake, Nicholas	**C. Day Lewis**
Bland, E.	**E. Nesbit**
Bland, Fabian	**E. Nesbit**
Bleeck, Oliver	**Ross Thomas**
Bliss, Reginald	**H. G. Wells**
Blixen, Karen	Pierre Andrezel; Isak Dinesen; Osceola
Block, Lawrence	Chip Harrison
Blood, Matthew	**Davis Dresser** (with **Ryerson Johnson**)
Blunden, Edmund	E. C. B.
Boston, Charles K.	**Frank Gruber**
Boucher, Anthony	**William Anthony Parker White**
Bowen, Marjorie	George R. Preedy; Joseph Shearing
Box, Edgar	**Gore Vidal**
Boyd, Nancy	**Edna St. Vincent Millay**
Boyle, Kay	Mrs. Laurence Vail
Boz	**Charles Dickens**
Bradbury, E. P.	**Michael Moorcock**
Bramah, Ernest	**Ernest Bramah Smith**
Brand, Christianna	**Mary Christianna Lewis**
Brand, Max	**Frederick Faust**
Brawner, Helen	Geoffrey Coffin (with **F. Van Wyck Mason**)
Brenan, Gerald	George Beaton
Bright, Mary Chavelita Dunne	**Mary Chevalita Dunne** (maiden name); George Egerton
Brock, Rose	**Joseph Hansen**
Brontë, Ann	Acton Bell

Brontë, Charlotte	Currer Bell
Brontë, Emily	Ellis Bell
Brown, Frederic	Felix Graham
Brown, Zenith Jones	Leslie Ford; David Frome
Bruce, Leo	**Rupert Croft-Cooke**
Brunner, John	Gill Hunt
Buchanan, Eileen-Marie Duell	Clare Curzon; Rhona Petrie
Buck, Pearl S.	John Sedges
Burgess, Anthony	**John Anthony Burgess Wilson**
Burgess, Trevor	**Elleston Trevor**
Burke, Leda	**David Garnett**
Burn, Tex	**Louis L'Amour**
Burnett, W. R.	James Updyke; John Monahan
Burroughs, William	William Lee
Burton, Miles	**Cecil John Charles Street**
Butler, Gwendoline	Jennie Melville
Butler, Walter C.	**Frederick Faust**
Butler, William Vivian	J. J. Marric (continuation of series originally written by **John Creasey)**
Bynner, Witter	Emanuel Morgan
Cain, Paul	**George Sims**
Campbell, R. T.	**Ruthven Todd**
Campbell, William Edward March	William March
Canning, Victor	Alan Gould
Cannon, Curt	**Evan Hunter**
Carco, Francis	**Jean Rhys**
Carr, Christopher	**A. C. Benson**
Carr, John Dickson	Carr Dickson; Carter Dickson; Roger Fairbairn; Torquemada
Carroll, Lewis	**Charles Lutwidge Dodgson**
Carter, Nick	**Dennis Lynds; Martin Cruz Smith**
Cary, Arthur	Joyce Cary
Cary, Joyce	**Arthur Cary**
Cauldwell, Frank	**Francis King**
Cawthorn, Jim	Desmond Reid (with **Michael Moorcock)**
Challis, George	**Frederick Faust**
Charles, Will	**Charles Willeford**
Charteris, Leslie	**Leslie C. B. Lin**
Chaucer, Daniel	**Ford Madox Ford**
Chester, Miss Di	**Dorothy Sayers**
Christie, Agatha	Mary Westmacott
Clark, Alfred A. G.	Cyril Hare
Clark, Curt	**Donald Westlake**
Claude	**Claude Durrell**
Clemens, Samuel Langhorne	Mark Twain
Clement, Hal	**Harry Clement Stubbs**
Clerihew, E.	**E. C. Bentley**
Clerk, N. W.	**C. S. Lewis**

Coe, Tucker	**Donald Westlake**
Coffey, Brian	**Dean R. Koontz**
Coffin, Geoffrey	**F. Van Wyck Mason** (with **Helen Brawner**)
Coffin, Peter	**Jonathan Latimer**
Coleman, Emmett	**Ishmael Reed**
Coles, Cyril H.	Manning Coles (with **Adelaide Manning**); Francis Gaite
Coles, Manning	**Adelaide Manning** and **Cyril H. Coles**
Collins, Hunt	**Evan Hunter**
Collins, Michael	**Dennis Lynds**
Colton, James	**Joseph Hansen**
Colvin, James	**Michael Moorcock**
Conrad, Joseph	**Teodor Jósef Konrad Korzeniowski**
Cook, John Estes	**L. Frank Baum**
Cooper, James Fenimore	Jane Morgan
Cooper, William	H. S. Hoff
Cornwell, David J. M.	John Le Carré
Corvo, Baron	**Frederick William Rolfe**
Costler, A.	**Arthur Koestler**
Coward, Noel	Hernia Whittlebot
Cox, William Trevor	William Trevor
Cozzens, Frederick S.	Richard Haywarde
Craig, A. A.	**Poul Anderson**
Crane, Stephen	Johnston Smith
Crayon, Geoffrey	**Washington Irving**
Creasey, John	Gordon Ashe; Norman Deane; Robert Caine Frazer; Michael Halliday; Kyle Hunt; Peter Manton; J. J. Marric; Richard Martin; Anthony Morton; Ken Ranger; William K. Reilley; Tex Riley; Jeremy York
Crews, Judson	Mason Jordon Mason
Creyton, Paul	**John T. Trowbridge**
Crichton, Michael	Jeffrey Hudson; John Lange
Crispin, Edmund	**Robert Bruce Montgomery**
Croft-Cooke, Rupert	Leo Bruce
Cross, Amanda	**Carolyn Gold Heilbrun**
Crowe, John	**Dennis Lynds**
Crowfield, Christopher	**Harriet Beecher Stowe**
Crowley, Aleister	Leo Vincey
Culver, Kathryn	**Davis Dresser**
Culver, Timothy J.	**Donald Westlake**
Cummings, Bruce Frederick	W. N. P. Barbellion
Cunningham, E. V.	**Howard Fast**
Curzon, Clare	**Eileen-Marie Duell Buchanan**
D., H.	**Hilda Doolittle**

Dale, George E.	**Isaac Asimov**
Dannay, Frederic	Ellery Queen; Barnaby Ross
	(both with **Manfred B. Lee**);
	Daniel Nathan
Davidson, Lawrence H.	**D. H. Lawrence**
Daviot, Gordon	**Elizabeth Mackintosh**
Davis, Don	**Davis Dresser**
Davis, Gordon	**Howard Hunt**
Deane, Norman	**John Creasey**
Debrett, Hal	**Davis Dresser**
Deghy, Guy	Herald Froy; Lee Gibb (both
	with **Keith Waterhouse**)

Delacorta	**Daniel Odier**
de la Mare, Walter	Walter Ramal
DeLillo, Don	Cleo Birdwell
Derleth, August	Stephen Grendon; Eldon Heath; Tally Mason
De Voto, Bernard	John August
Dickens, Charles	Boz
Dickson, Carr	**John Dickson Carr**
Dickson, Carter	**John Dickson Carr**
Dietrich, Robert	**Howard Hunt**
Dinesen, Isak	**Karen Blixen**
Dr. Seuss	**Theodor Seuss Geisel**
Dodge, Mary Abigail	Gail Hamilton
Dodgson, Charles Lutwidge	Lewis Carroll
Dominic, R. B.	**M. Latsis and M. Henissart**
Donovan, Dick	**Joyce E. P. Muddock**
Dooley, Mr.	**Finley Peter Dunne**
Doolittle, Hilda	H. D.; John Helforth
Douglas, Ellen	Josephine Haxton
Douglas, Norman	Normyx
Downes, Quentin	**Michael Harrison**
Doyle, John	**Robert Graves**
Dresser, Davis	Asa Baker; Matthew Blood (with **Ryerson Johnson**); Kathryn Culver; Don Davis; Hal Debrett; Brett Halliday; Anthony Scott; Anderson Wayne
Drinan, Adam	**Joseph MacLeod**
Dudley-Smith, T.	**Elleston Trevor**
Duke, Will	**Wm. Campbell Gault**
Dunne, Finley Peter	Mr. Dooley
Dunne, Mary Chavelita (married name **Bright**)	George Egerton
Dunsany, Lord (title)	**Edward John M. Drax Plunkett**
Durrell, Claude	Claude
Durrell, Lawrence	Charles Norden
Dwyer, Deanna	**Dean R. Koontz**
Dwyer, K. R.	**Dean R. Koontz**
E., A.	**George Russell**
Earle, William	**W. E. John**
Early, Jon	**W. E. John**
Eddy, Mary Baker	**Mary Baker Glover** (first marriage)
Egerton, George	**Mary Chavelita Dunne** (married name **Bright**)
Ellison, Harlan	Paul Merchant
Engelhardt, Frederick	**L. Ron Hubbard**
Epernay, Mary	**Kenneth Galbraith**
Ericson, Walter	**Howard Fast**

Esse, James	**James Stephens**
Evans, Evan	**Frederick Faust**
Evans, Margiad	Peggy Whistler
Everson, William	**Brother Antoninus** (Dominican lay brother, 1951–1969)
Ewing, Frederick R.	**Theodore Sturgeon**
F, Inspector	**William Russell**
F., M. T.	**Katherine Anne Porter**
Fair, A. A.	**Erle Stanley Gardner**
Fairbairn, Roger	**John Dickson Carr**
Farjeon, Eleanor	Tom Fool
Farmer, Philip José	Kilgore Trout
Farrell, James T.	Jonathan Titulesco Fogarty
Farren, Richard M.	**John Betjeman**
Fast, Howard	E. V. Cunningham; Walter Ericson
Faulkner, William	Ernest V. Trueblood
Faust, Frederick	George Owen Baxter; Max Brand; Walter C. Butler; George Challis; Evan Evans; John Frederick; Frederick Frost; David Manning; Peter Henry Morland
Feikema, Feike	**Frederick Manfred**
Feinstein, Isidor	I. F. Stone
Ferguson, Helen	**Helen Woods**
Field, Gans T.	**Manly Wade Wellman**
Fielding, Gabriel	**Alan Barnsley**
Finney, Jack	**Walter B. Finney**
Finney, Walter B.	Jack Finney
Fips, Mohammed Ulysses Socrates	**Hugo Gernsback**
Fish, Robert L.	Robert L. Pike
Fisher, M. F. K.	Victoria Berne (with **Dillwyn Parrish**)
Flapdoodle, Phineas	**Henry Miller**
Fleming, Oliver	**Philip MacDonald**
Fogarty, Jonathan Titulesco	**James T. Farrell**
Follett, Ken	Simon Myles; Zachary Stone
Fool, Tom	**Eleanor Farjeon**
Ford, Ford Madox (legal name change)	**Ford Madox Hueffer;** Daniel Chaucer; Fenil Haig
Ford, Leslie	**Zenith Jones Brown**
Forester, Frank	**Henry William Herbert**
Forrest, Felix C.	**Paul Linebarger**
Frazer, Robert Caine	**John Creasey**
Frederick, John	**Frederick Faust**
Freedgood, Morton	John Godey; Stanley Morton
Freeman, R. Austin	Clifford Ashdown (with **John James Pitcairn**)
French, Paul	**Isaac Asimov**

Frome, David	**Zenith Jones Brown**
Frost, Frederick	**Frederick Faust**
Froy, Herald	**Keith Waterhouse** (with **Guy Deghy**)
Fuller, Henry Blake	Stanton Page
Gaite, Francis	**Cyril H. Coles**
Galbraith, Kenneth	Mark Epernay
Galsworthy, John	John Sinjohn
Galt, Walter	**Talbot Mundy**
Gardner, Erle Stanley	A. A. Fair; Carleton Kendrake
Garnett, David	Leda Burke
Garrett, Randall	Robert Randall (with **Robert Silverberg**)
Garth, Will	**Henry Kuttner**
Garve, Andrew	**Paul Winterton**
Gash, Jonathan	Graham Gaunt
Gashbuck, Greno	**Hugo Gernsback**
Gault, Wm. Campbell	Will Duke
Gaunt, Graham	**Jonathan Gash**
Gawsworth, John	**Terence Fytton Armstrong**
Geisel, Theodor Seuss	Dr. Seuss
Gernsback, Hugo	Grego Barshuck; Mohammed U. S. Fips; Greno Gashbuck; Gus N. Habergock
Gibb, Lee	**Keith Waterhouse** (with **Guy Deghy**)
Gibson, Walter	Maxwell Grant
Gibson, Walter B.	Maxwell Grant
Glover, Mary Baker (first marriage)	**Mary Baker Eddy**
Godey, John	**Morton Freedgood**
Goldman, William	S. Morgenstern; Harry Longbaugh
Goldsmith, Oliver	James Willington
Goodrich, S. G.	Peter Parley
Gopaleen, Myles Na	**Brian O'Nolan**
Gorey, Edward	Ogdred Weary
Gottschalk, Laura (first married name; later **Laura Jackson**)	**Laura Riding**
Gould, Alan	**Victor Canning**
Graham, Felix	**Frederic Brown**
Graham, John	**David Graham Phillips**
Graham, Tom	**Sinclair Lewis**
Grainger, Francis Edward	Headon Hill
Grant, Maxwell	**Dennis B. Lynds**
Grant, Maxwell	**Walter B. Gibson**
Grantland, Keith	**Charles Nutt**
Graves, Robert	John Doyle; (ghostwriter for **Frank Richards;** Barbara Rich (with **Laura Riding**)
Green, Hannah	**Joanne Greenburg**
Green, Henry	**Henry Vincent Yorke**

Greenburg, Joanne	Hannah Green
Gregory, J. Dennis	**John A. Williams**
Grendon, Stephen	**August Derleth**
Gribben, William L.	**Talbot Mundy**
Grieve, C. M.	Hugh Mac(or Mc or M')Diarmid
Grile, Dod	**Ambrose Bierce**
Gruber, Frank	Stephen Acre; Charles K. Boston; John K. Vedder
Guthrie, Thomas Anstey	F. Anstey
H., H.	**Helen Hunt Jackson**
Habergock, Gus N.	**Hugo Gernsback**
Haig, Fenil	**Ford Madox Ford**
Haines, William	**William Heyen**
Hale, Edward Everett	Frederic Ingham
Hall, Adam	**Elleston Trevor**
Halliday, Brett	**Davis Dresser**
Halliday, Michael	**John Creasey**
Hamilton, Clive	**C. S. Lewis**
Hamilton, Gail	**Mary Abigail Dodge**
Hannon, Ezra	**Evan Hunter**
Hansen, Joseph	Rose Brock; James Colton
Harbage, Alfred B.	Thomas Kyd
Hare, Cyril	**Alfred A. G. Clark**
Harris, John Wyndham Parkes Lucas Beynon	John Beynon; Johnson Harris; Lucas Parkes; John Wyndham
Harris, Johnson	**John Wyndham P. L. B. Harris**
Harrison, Chip	**Lawrence Block**
Harrison, Michael	Quentin Downes
Haxton, Josephine	**Ellen Douglas**
Haywarde, Richard	**Frederick S. Cozzens**
Heath, Eldon	**August Derleth**
Heilbrun, Carolyn Gold	Amanda Cross
Heinlein, Robert A.	Simon York
Helforth, John	**Hilda Doolittle**
Henissart, Martha	R. B. Dominic; Emma Lathen (with **M. Latsis**)
Henry, Edgar	**Albion W. Tourgée**
Herbert, Henry William	Frank Forester
Herman, William	**Ambrose Bierce**
Hext, Harrington	**Eden Phillpotts**
Heyen, William	William Haines
Heyer, Georgette	**Mrs. George R. Rougier**
Hibbert, Elizabeth Alice	Jean Plaidy
Highsmith, Patricia	Claire Morgan
Hill, Headon	**Francis Edward Grainger**
Hill, John	**Dean R. Koontz**

Hill, Reginald	Patrick Ruell
Hilton, James	Glen Trevor
Hirschfield, Magnus	**Arthur Koestler**
Hoff, H. S.	**William Cooper**
Holmes, H. H.	**William Anthony Parker White**
Holmes, Raymond	**Raymond Souster**
Holt, Samuel	**Donald Westlake**
Honeyman, William C.	James McGovan
Hooker, Richard	**Dr. H. Richard Hornberger**
Hopley, George	**Cornell Woolrich**
Hornberger, Dr. H. Richard	Richard Hooker
Houdini, Harry	**Ehrich Weiss**
Houghton, Claude	**Claude Houghton Oldfield**
Howard, Robert E.	Sam Walser
Hubbard, L. Ron	Frederick Engelhardt; Rene Lafayette
Hudson, Jeffrey	**Michael Crichton**
Hudson, Stephen	**Sydney Schiff**
Hueffer, Ford Madox	**Ford Madox Ford** (legal name change)
Hunt, Gill	**John Brunner**
Hunt, Howard	John Baxter; Gordon Davis; Robert Dietrich; David St. John
Hunt, Kyle	**John Creasey**
Hunter, Evan (born Salvatore Lombino)	Curt Cannon; Hunt Collins; Ezra Hannon; Richard Marsten; Ed McBain
Huntley, Lydia	**Lydia Sigourney**
Iles, Francis	**Anthony Berkeley**
Ingham, Frederic	**Edward Everett Hale**
Innes, Michael	**John Innes M. Stewart**
Inspector F	**William Russell**
Irish, William	**Cornell Woolrich**
Iron, Ralph	**Olive Schreiner**
Irving, Washington	Geoffrey Crayon; Diedrich Knickerbocker; Launcelot Langstaff
Jackson, Helen Hunt	H. H.
Jackson, Laura (second marriage)	**Laura Riding** (maiden name); **Laura Gottschalk** (first marriage)
Jakes, John	Alan Payne; Jay Scotland
John, W. E.	William Earle; Jon Early
Johnson, Benj. F.	**James Whitcomb Riley**
Johnson, Ryerson	Matthew Blood (with **Davis Dresser**)
Jones, Edith Newbold (maiden name)	**Edith Wharton**
Jones, James Athearn	Matthew Murgatroyd
Jones, Leroi	**Imamu Amiri Baraka** (legal name change)

K., R. A	**Ronald Knox**
Kain, Saul	**Siegfried Sassoon**
Kaler, Otis J.	James Otis
Karageorge, Michael	**Poul Anderson**
Kavan, Anna	**Helen Woods**
Kavanagh, Dan	**Julian Barnes**
Kell, Joseph	**John Anthony Burgess Wilson**
Kelley, Martha	Q. Patrick (with **Richard W. Webb**)
Kendrake, Carleton	**Erle Stanley Gardner**
Kerr, Ben	**William Ard**
King, Francis	Frank Cauldwell
King, Stephen	Richard Bachman
Kingsmill, Hugh	Hugh Lunn
Knickerbocker, Diedrich	**Washington Irving**
Knight, Clifford	Reynolds Knight
Knight, Reynolds	**Clifford Knight**
Knox, Ronald	R. A. K.
Koestler, Arthur	A. Costler; Magnus Hirschfield
Koontz, Dean R.	David Axton; Brian Coffey; Deanna Dwyer; K. R. Dwyer; John Hill; Leigh Nichols; Anthony North; Richard Paige; Owen West; Aaron Wolfe
Korzeniowski, Jósef Teodor Konrad	Joseph Conrad
Kosinski, Jerzy	Joseph Novak
Kurnitz, Harry	Marco Page
Kuttner, Henry	Will Garth; Lewis Padgett (and many others with **C. L. Moore**)
Kyd, Thomas	**Alfred B. Harbage**
Kyle, Robert	**Robert Terrall**
Lafayette, Rene	**L. Ron Hubbard**
L'Amour, Louis	Tex Burn
Lange, John	**Michael Crichton**
Langstaff, Launcelot	**Washington Irving**
Lathen, Emma	**M. Latsis** and **M. Henissart**
Latimer, Jonathan	Peter Coffin
Latsis, Mary J.	R. B. Dominic; Emma Lathen (both with **M. Henissart**)
Lawless, Anthony	**Philip MacDonald**
Lawrence, D. H.	Lawrence H. Davidson
Lawrence, T. E.	J. H. Ross; L. H. Ross; T. E. Shaw
Lear, Peter	**Peter Lovesey**
Le Carré, John	**David J. M. Cornwell**
Lee, Andrew	**Louis Auchincloss**
Lee, Manfred B.	Ellery Queen; Barnaby Ross (both with **Frederic Dannay**)
Lee, William	**William Burroughs**
Léger, Aléxis St.	St. John Perse

Lemke, Henry E.
Lessing, Doris
Lewis, C. S.
Lewis, Cecil Day
Lewis, Mary Christianna
Lewis, Sinclair
Lin, Frank
Lin, Leslie C. B.
Linebarger, Paul
Linington, (Barbara) Elizabeth
Locke, David Ross
Logan, Jake
Longbaugh, Harry
Lord, Sheldon
Lothrup, Harriet Mulford Stone
Lovecraft, H. P.
Lovesey, Peter
Lucas, Victoria
Ludlum, Robert
Lunn, Hugh
Lynds, Dennis

Lyre, Pynchbeck

M., S. W.
McBain, Ed
Mac(or Mc or M')Diarmid, Hugh
Macdonald, John (and John Ross).
MacDonald, Phillip

Macdonald, Ross
McGivern, William Peter
McGovan, James
Machen, Arthur
Mackin, Edward
McInerny, Ralph
Mackintosh, Elizabeth
MacLeod, Fiona
MacLeod, Joseph
McNeile, Herman C.
Madge, Kathleen
Manfred, Frederick
Manning, Adelaide
Manning, David
Manton, Peter
Mara, Bernard
March, Maxwell
March, William

Richard Tooker
Jane Somers
N. W. Clerk; Clive Hamilton
Nicholas Blake
Christianna Brand
Tom Graham
Gertrude Atherton
Leslie Charteris
Felix C. Forrest; Cordwainer Smith
Anne Blaisdell; Dell Shannon
Petroleum V. Nasby
Martin Cruz Smith
William Goldman
Donald Westlake
Margaret Sidney
Lewis Thoebold, Jr.
Peter Lear
Sylvia Plath
Jonathan Ryder; Michael Shepherd
Hugh Kingsmill
William Arden; Nick Carter;
    Michael Collins; John Crowe;
    Maxwell Grant; Mark Sadler
Siegfried Sassoon

S. Weir Mitchell
Evan Hunter
C. M. Grieve
Kenneth Millar
Oliver Fleming; Anthony
    Lawless; Martin Porlock
Kenneth Millar
Bill Peters
William C. Honeyman
Leolinus Siluriensis
Ralph McInerny
Edward Mackin, Monica Quill
Gordon Daviot; Josephine Tey
William Sharp
Adam Drinan
Sapper
Kathleen Raine
Feike Feikema
Manning Coles (with **Cyril H. Coles**)
Frederick Faust
John Creasey
Brian Moore
Margery Allingham
William Edward March Campbell

Markham, Robert	**Kingsley Amis**
Marric, J. J.	**John Creasey** (series later written by **William Vivian Butler**)
Marsten, Richard	**Evan Hunter**
Martin, Richard	**John Creasey**
Marvil, Ik	**Donald Grant Mitchell**
Mason, F. Van Wyck	Geoffrey Coffin (with **Helen Brawner**); Frank W. Mason; Ward Weaver
Mason, Frank W.	**F. Van Wyck Mason**
Mason, Mason Jordon	**Judson Crews**
Mason, Tally	**August Derleth**
Matheson, Richard	Logan Swanson
Melville, Jennie	**Gwendoline Butler**
Merchant, Paul	**Harlan Ellison**
Mertz, Barbara G.	Barbara Michaels; Elizabeth Peters
Meynell, Alice	A. C. Thompson
Michaels, Barbara	**Barbara G. Mertz**
Michaelson, John Nairne	**Maxwell Anderson**
Middleton, Arthur	**Edward J. O'Brien**
Millar, Kenneth	John, John Ross, and Ross Macdonald
Millay, Edna St. Vincent	Nancy Boyd
Miller, Henry	Phineas Flapdoodle
Miller, Warren	Amanda Vail
Mitchell, Donald Grant	Ik Marvel
Mitchell, S. Weir	S. W. M.
Monahan, John	**W. R. Burnett**
Montgomery, Robert Bruce	Edmund Crispin
Moorcock, Michael	Bill Barclay; E. P. Bradbury; James Colvin; Desmond Reid (with **Jim Cawthorn**)
Moore, Brian	Bernard Mara
Moore, Catherine Lucille	Lewis Padgett (with **Henry Kuttner**)
Moore, Edward	**Edwin Muir**
Moran, Mike	**William Ard**
Morecamp, Arthur	**Thomas Pilgrim**
Morgan, Claire	**Patricia Highsmith**
Morgan, Emanuel	**Witter Bynner**
Morgan, Jane	**James Fenimore Cooper**
Morgenstern, S.	**William Goldman**
Morland, Peter Henry	**Frederick Faust**
Morris, Julian	**Morris West**
Morton, Anthony	**John Creasey**
Morton, Stanley	**Morton Freedgood**
Muddock, Joyce E. P.	Dick Donovan
Muir, Edwin	Edward Moore
Mundy, Talbot	Walter Galt; William L. Gribben
Munro, Hector Hugh	Saki
Murgatroyd, Matthew	**James Athearn Jones**
Myles, Simon	**Ken Follett**

Nabokoff-Sirin, V. — **Vladimir Nabokov**
Nabokov, Vladimir — V. Nabokoff-Sirin; V. Sirin
Nasby, Petroleum V. — **David Ross Locke**
Nathan, Daniel — **Frederic Dannay**
Nesbit, E. — E. Bland; Fabian Bland
Nichols, Leigh — **Dean R. Koontz**
Norden, Charles — **Lawrence Durrell**
Normyx — **Norman Douglas**
North, Andrew — **Alice Mary Norton**
North, Anthony — **Dean R. Koontz**
Norton, Alice Mary — Andrew North; Andre Norton; Allen Weston (with **Grace Allen**)

Norton, Andre — **Alice Mary Norton**
Norway, Nevil Shute — Nevil Shute
Novak, Joseph — **Jerzy Kosinski**
Nutt, Charles — Charles Beaumont; Keith Grantland

Oates, Joyce Carol — Rosamond Smith
O'Brien, Edward J. — Arthur Middleton
O'Brien, Flann — **Brian O'Nolan**
O'Casey, Sean — P. O'Cathasaigh
O'Cathasaigh, P. — **Sean O'Casey**
O'Connor, Frank — **Michael O'Donovan**
Odier, Daniel — Delacorta
O'Donovan, Michael — Frank O'Connor
O. Henry — **William Sydney Porter**
Oldfield, Claude Houghton — Claude Houghton
Oliver, George — Oliver Onions
Onions, Oliver — **George Oliver**
O'Nolan, Brian — Myles Na Gopaleen; Flann O'Brien
Oppenheim, E. Phillips — Anthony Partridge
Optic, Oliver — **William Taylor Adams**
Orwell, George — **Eric Arthur Blair**
Osceola — **Karen Blixen**
Otis, James — **Otis J. Kaler**
Oursler, Fulton — Anthony Abbott

Padgett, Lewis — **C. L. Moore** and **Henry Kuttner**
Page, Marco — **Harry Kurnitz**
Page, Stanton — **Henry Blake Fuller**
Paige, Richard — **Dean R. Koontz**
Palmer, Stuart — Jay Stewart
Pargeter, Edith — Ellis Peters
Parkes, Lucas — **John Wyndham P. L. B. Harris**
Parley, Peter — **S. G. Goodrich**
Parrish, Dillwyn — Victoria Berne (with **M. F. K. Fisher**)
Partridge, Anthony — **E. Phillips Oppenheim**
Patrick, Q. — **Richard W. Webb** (alone and with **Martha Kelley**)

Payne, Alan	**John Jakes**
Peck, George W.	Cantell A. Bigby
Pennington, Patience	**Elizabeth Pringle**
Pentecost, Hugh	**Judson Phillips**
Percy, Charles Henry	**Dodie Smith**
Perse, St. John	**Aléxis St. Léger**
Peters, Bill	**William Peter McGivern**
Peters, Curtis Arnoux	Peter Arno
Peters, Elizabeth	**Barbara G. Mertz**
Peters, Ellis	**Edith Pargeter**
Petrie, Rhona	**Eileen-Marie Duell Buchanan**
Phillips, David Graham	John Graham
Phillips, Judson	Hugh Pentecost
Phillpotts, Eden	Harrington Hext
Pike, Robert L.	**Robert L. Fish**
Pilgrim, Thomas	Arthur Morecamp
Pitcairn, John James	Clifford Ashdown (with **R. Austin Freeman**)
Plaidy, Jean	**Elizabeth Alice Hibbert**
Plath, Sylvia	Victoria Lucas
Plunkett, Edward J. M. D.	**Lord Dunsany** (title)
Porlock, Martin	**Philip MacDonald**
Porter, Eleanor H.	Eleanor Stuart
Porter, Katherine Anne	M. T. F.
Porter, William Sydney	O. Henry
Preedy, George R.	**Marjorie Bowen**
Pringle, Elizabeth W. A.	Patience Pennington
Putnam, Arthur Lee	**Horatio Alger**
Q	**Arthur Quiller-Couch**
Queen, Ellery	**Frederic Dannay** and **Manfred B. Lee**
Quentin, Patrick	**Richard W. Webb** and **Hugh C. Wheeler**
Quill, Monica	**Ralph McInerny**
Quiller-Couch, Arthur	Q
Quinn, Martin (and Simon)	**Martin Cruz Smith**
R., C. G.	**Christine G. Rossetti**
Raine, Kathleen	Kathleen Madge
Ramal, Walter	**Walter de la Mare**
Rampling, Anne	**Anne Rice**
Randall, Robert	**Randall Garrett** and **Robert Silverberg**
Randolph, Georgiana Ann	Craig Rice; Daphne Sanders; Michael Venning
Ranger, Ken	**John Creasey**
Rattray, Simon	**Elleston Trevor**
Reed, Eliot	**Eric Ambler** and **Charles Rodda**
Reed, Ishmael	Emmett Coleman
Reid, Desmond	**Michael Moorcock** (with **Jim Cawthorn**)

Reilly, William K.	**John Creasey**
Rendell, Ruth	Barbara Vine
Rhode, John	**Cecil John Charles Street**
Rhys, Jean	Francis Carco
Rice, Anne	Anne Rampling; A. N. Roquelaure
Rice, Craig	**Georgiana Ann Randolph**
Rich, Barbara	**Laura Riding** and **Robert Graves**
Richards, Frank	**Robert Graves** (ghostwriter)
Riding, Laura	**Laura Gottschalk** (first married name; later **Laura Jackson**)
Riley, James Whitcomb	Benj. F. Johnson
Riley, Tex	**John Creasey**
Robertson, E.	**Earle Birney**
Rodda, Charles	Eliot Reed (with **Eric Ambler**)
Rohmer, Sax	**Arthur Henry S. Ward**
Rolfe, Frederick William	Baron Corvo
Roquelaure, A. N.	**Anne Rice**
Ross, Barnaby	**Frederic Dannay** and **Manfred B. Lee**
Ross, J. H. and L. H.	**T. E. Lawrence**
Rossetti, Christine G.	C. G. R.
Rougier, Mrs. George R.	Georgette Heyer
Ruell, Patrick	**Reginald Hill**
Ruric, Peter	**George Sims**
Russell, George	A. E.
Russell, William	Inspector F; Waters
Ryder, Jonathan	**Robert Ludlum**
S., E. W.	**E. W. Sherman**
S., S. H.	**Siegfried Sassoon**
Sadler, Mark	**Dennis Lynds**
St. John, David	**Howard Hunt**
Saki	**Hector Hugh Munro**
Sanders, Daphne	**Georgiana Ann Randolph**
Sanders, Winston P.	**Poul Anderson**
Sanford, John	Julian L. Shapiro
Sapper	**Herman C. McNeile**
Sassoon, Siegfried	Saul Kain; Pynchbeck Lyre; S. H. S.
Sayers, Dorothy	Miss Di Chester
Scarlett, Susan	**Noel Streatfield**
Schiff, Sydney	Stephen Hudson
Schreiner, Olive	Ralph Iron
Scotland, Jay	**John Jakes**
Scott, Anthony	**Davis Dresser**
Scott, Evelyn	Ernest Souza
Scott, Warwick	**Elleston Trevor**
Sedges, John	**Pearl S. Buck**
Shaffer, Anthony	Peter Anthony (with **Peter Shaffer**)
Shaffer, Peter	Peter Anthony (with **Anthony Shaffer**)
Shannon, Dell	**(Barbara) Elizabeth Linington**

Shapiro, Julian L.	**John Sanford**
Sharp, Luke	**Robert Barr**
Sharp, William	Fiona MacLeod
Shaw, T. E.	**T. E. Lawrence**
Shearing, Joseph	**Marjorie Bowen**
Shepherd, Michael	**Robert Ludlum**
Sherman, E. W.	E. W. S.
Shute, Nevil	**Nevil Shute Norway**
Sidney, Margaret	**Harriet Mulford Stone Lothrup**
Sigourney, Lydia	Lydia Huntley
Siluriensis, Leolinus	**Arthur Machen**
Silverberg, Robert	Robert Randall (with **Randall Garrett**)
Sim, Georges	Georges Simenon
Simenon, Georges	**Georges Sim**
Simpson, Harriet	Harriette Arnow
Sims, George	Paul Cain; Peter Ruric
Sinjohn, John	**John Galsworthy**
Sirin, V.	**Vladimir Nabokov**
Smith, Cordwainer	**Paul Linebarger**
Smith, Dodie	C. L. Anthony; Charles Henry Percy
Smith, Ernest Bramah	Ernest Bramah
Smith, Johnston	**Stephen Crane**
Smith, Kate Douglas	Kate Douglas Wiggin
Smith, Martin Cruz	Nick Carter; Jake Logan; Martin Quinn; Simon Quinn
Smith, Rosamond	**Joyce Carol Oates**
Somers, Jane	**Doris Lessing**
Somers, Paul	**Paul Winterton**
Souster, Raymond	Raymond Holmes
Souza, Ernest	**Evelyn Scott**
Spicer, Bart	**Betty Spicer** and **Jay Barbette**
Spicer, Betty	Bart Spicer (with **Jay Barbette**)
Stagge, Jonathan	**Richard W. Webb** and **Hugh Wheeler**
Stairs, Gordon	**Mary H. Austin**
Stark, Richard	**Donald Westlake**
Starr, Julian	**Horatio Alger**
Stein, Aaron Marc	George Bagby; Hampton Stone
Stephens, James`	James Esse
Stevens, William Allen (and William Chrisopher)	**Steve Allen**
Stewart, Jay	**Stuart Palmer**
Stewart, John Innes M.	Michael Innes
Stone, Hampton	**Aaron Marc Stein**
Stone, I. F.	**Isidor Feinstein**
Stone, Zachary	**Ken Follett**
Stowe, Harriet Beecher	**Harriet Beecher** (maiden name); Christopher Crowfield
Streatfield, Noel	Susan Scarlett

Street, Cecil John Charles — Miles Burton; John Rhode
Stuart, Eleanor — **Eleanor H. Porter**
Stubbs, Harry Clement — Hal Clement
Sturgeon, Theodore — Frederick R. Ewing
Swanson, Logan — **Richard Matheson**

Taine, John — **Eric Temple Bell**
Tanner, William — **Kingsley Amis**
Taylor, Phoebe Atwood — Alice Tilton
Terrall, Robert — Robert Kyle
Tey, Josephine — **Elizabeth Mackintosh**
Thackeray, William Makepeace — M. A. Titmarsh; Theophile Wagstaff
Theobold, Lewis, Jr. — **H. P. Lovecraft**
Thomas, Ross — Oliver Bleeck
Thompson, A. C. — **Alice Meynell**
Tilton, Alice — **Phoebe Atwood Taylor**
Titmarsh, M. A. — **William Makepeace Thackeray**
Todd, Ruthven — R. T. Campbell
Tooker, Richard — Harry E. Lemke
Torquemada — **John Dickson Carr**
Torsvan, Berick Traven — B. Traven
Tourgée, Albion W. — Edgar Henry
Traven, B. — **Berick Traven Torsvan**
Traver, Robert — **John Donaldson Voelker**
Trevanian — **Rodney Whitaker**
Trevor, Elleston — Mansell Black; Trevor Burgess;
    T. Dudley-Smith; Adam Hall;
    Simon Rattray; Warwick Scott
Trevor, Glen — **James Hilton**
Trevor, William — **William Trevor Cox**
Trout, Kilgore — **Philip José Farmer**
Trowbridge, John T. — Paul Creyton
Trueblood, Ernest V. — **William Faulkner**
Twain, Mark — **Samuel Langhorne Clemens**

Updyke, James — **W. R. Burnett**

Vail, Amanda — **Warren Miller**
Vail, Mrs. Laurence — **Kay Boyle**
Van, Melvin — **Melvin Van Peebles**
Van Dine, S. S. — **Willard Huntington Wright**
Van Dyne, Edith — **L. Frank Baum**
Van Peebles, Melvin — Melvin Van
Vedder, John K. — **Frank Gruber**
Venning, Michael — **Georgiana Ann Randolph**
Vidal, Gore — Edgar Box
Vincey, Leo — **Aleister Crowley**
Vine, Barbara — **Ruth Rendell**
Voelker, John Donaldson — Robert Traver

W., E. B.	**E. B. White**
Wade, Henry	**Henry Lancelot Aubrey-Fletcher**
Wagstaff, Theophile	**William Makepeace Thackeray**
Walser, Sam	**Robert E. Howard**
Ward, Arthur Henry S.	Sax Rohmer
Ward, Jonas	**William Ard**
Waterhouse, Keith	Herald Froy; Lee Gibb (both with **Guy Deghy**)
Waters	**William Russell**
Wayne, Anderson	**Davis Dresser**
Weary, Ogdred	**Edward Gorey**
Weaver, Ward	**F. Van Wyck Mason**
Webb, Richard W.	Q. Patrick (alone and with **Martha Kelley**) and others; Patrick Quentin and Jonathan Stagge (with **Hugh Wheeler**)
Weiss, Ehrich	Harry Houdini
Wellman, Manly Wade	Gans T. Field
Wells, Carolyn	Roland Wright
Wells, H. G.	Reginald Bliss
West, Morris	Julian Morris
West, Owen	**Dean R. Koontz**
Westlake, Donald	Curt Clark; Tucker Coe; Timothy J. Culver; Samuel Holt; Sheldon Lord; Richard Stark
Westmacott, Mary	**Agatha Christie**
Weston, Allen	**Grace Allen and Alice Mary Norton**
Wharton, Edith	**Edith Newbold Jones** (maiden name)
Wharton, William	(Undisclosed)**?**
Wheeler, Hugh Callingham	Patrick Quentin; Jonathan Stagge (both with **Richard W. Webb**)
Whistler, Peggy	**Margiad Evans**
Whitaker, Rodney	Trevanian
White, E. B.	E. B. W.
White, T. H.	James Aston
White, William Anthony Parker	Anthony Boucher; H. H. Holmes
Whittlebot, Hernia	**Noel Coward**
Wiggin, Kate Douglas	**Kate Douglas Smith**
Wilde, Oscar	Fingal O'Flahertie Wills
Willeford, Charles	Will Charles
Williams, John A.	J. Dennis Gregory
Willington, James	**Oliver Goldsmith**
Wills, Fingal O'Flahertie	**Oscar Wilde**
Wills, Thomas	**William Ard**
Wilson, John Anthony Burgess	Anthony Burgess; Joseph Kell
Winterton, Paul	Roger Bax; Andrew Garve; Paul Somers
Wolfe, Aaron	**Dean R. Koontz**
Woods, Helen	Helen Ferguson; Anna Kavan
Woolrich, Cornell	George Hopley; William Irish

Wright, Roland
Wright, Willard Huntington
Wyndham, John

York, Jeremy
York, Simon
Yorke, Henry Vincent

Carolyn Wells
S. S. Van Dine
John Wyndham P. L. B. Harris

John Creasey
Robert A. Heinlein
Henry Green

APPENDIX B

BOOK DEALERS

The following is a list of book dealers who issue catalogs, primarily of literary (fiction, poetry, drama, detective, science fiction, etc.) first editions. Also included, when they sent us their catalogs, are those dealers who issue catalogs in other areas of collecting interest. It is certainly not complete, but represents the dealers who keep our name on their mailing lists. The asterisk (★) denotes dealers that are members of the International League of Antiquarian Booksellers (ILAB) through their countries' organizations; the Antiquarian Booksellers' Association of America (ABAA), in the United States.

About Books, 83 Harbord Street, Toronto, Ontario M5S-1G4, Canada★
Adjala Bookshop, 252 Cottingham Street, Toronto, Ontario M4V-1C6, Canada
Charles Agvent, RD 2, Box 377A, Mertztown, PA 19539★
Allen and Patricia Ahearn, see Quill & Brush★
Alder Books, 13743 Lakeside Drive, Clarksville, MD 21029
Aldredge Book Shop, 2909 #1A Maple Ave., Dallas, TX 75201
Alphabet Bookshop, 145 Main Street West, Port Colborne, Ontario L3K-3V3, Canada★
American Dust Co., 47 Park Ct., Staten Island, NY 10301
The Americanist, 1525 Shenkel Rd., Pottstown, PA 19464★
Am Here Books, P.O. Box 574, Philo, CA 95466
Ampersand Books, P.O. 674 Cooper Station, New York, NY 10276
Anacapa Books, 3090 Claremont Ave., Berkeley, CA 94705
Anchor & Dolphin, 30 Franklin St., Newport, RI 02840★
Annex Books, 1083 Bathurst Street, Toronto, Ontario M5R-3G8, Canada★
Hugh Anson-Cartwright, 229 College St., Toronto, Ontario M5T-1R4, Canada★
Antic Hay Rare Books, P.O. Box 2185, Asbury Park, NJ 07712★
Antipodean Books Maps & Prints, P.O. Box 189, Cold Spring, NY 10516★
Any Amount of Books, 62 Charing Cross Road, London WC2H-0BB, United Kingdom
Archer's Used and Rare Books, 104 South Lincoln St., Kent, OH 44240
Argosy Book Store, 116 East 59th St., New York, NY 10022★

Artis Books, P.O. Box 822, 410 North Second Ave., Alpena, MI 49707

The Arundel Press, 8380 Beverly Blvd., Los Angeles, CA 90048

Ash Rare Books, 25 Royal Exchange, Threadneedle Street, London EC3V-3LP, United Kingdom

The Associates, P.O. Box 4747, Falls Church, VA 22044★

Attic Books, P.O. Box 611136, Port Huron, MI 48061

Authors of the West, 191 Dogwood Dr., Dundee, OR 97115

Bert Babcock, 9 East Derry Rd., P.O. Box 1140, Derry, NH 03038★

The Backlist, P.O. Box 791, Doylestown, PA 18901

Bartleby's Books, P.O. Box 15400, Chevy Chase, MD 20825

Bay Side Books, P.O. Box 57, Soquel, CA 95073

Derrick Josua Beard, P.O. Box 25318, Washington, DC 20007

Beasley Books, 1533 West Oakdale, Chicago, IL 60657★

Gordon Beckhorn, 23 Ashford Ave., Dobbs Ferry, NY 10522

Bell, Book & Radmall, 4 Cecil Court, London WC2N-4HE, United Kingdom★

Messrs Berkelouw, 830 N. Highland Ave., Los Angeles, CA 90038★

Steven C. Bernard, 15011 Plainfield La., Darnestown, MD 20874★

Between the Covers, 132 Kings Highway East, Haddonfield, NJ 08033★

Biblioctopus, P.O. Box 309, Idyllwild, CA 92549★

Biodata, 97 Violet Lane, Croydon, Surrey CR0-4HL, United Kingdom

Bishop of Books, 328 Market St., P.O. Box 579, Steubenville, OH 43952

Black-Bird Books, 24 Grampton Gardens, London NW2-1JG, United Kingdom

Black Sun Books, 157 East 57th St., New York, NY 10022★

Black Voices, 5 Caledonian Road, London N1-9DX United Kingdom

Blackwell's Rare Books, 38 Holywell Street, Oxford OX1-3SW, United Kingdom★

Adam Blakeney, 4/10 Charles Street, London W1X-7BH, United Kingdom

Marjorie Block, P.O. Box 773, Kentfield, CA 94914

Bolerium Books, 2141 Mission #300, San Francisco, CA 94110★

Nelson Bond, 4724 Easthill Dr., Sugarloaf Farms, Roanoak, VA★

Book Barn, 41 West Main St., Niantic, CT 06357

The Book Block, 8 Loughlin Ave., Cos Cob, CT 06807★

Bookdales, 406 West 65th St., Richfield, MN 55423

Book Finders International, 216 Ringwood La., Route 2, Elgin, SC 20945

Book Harbor, 201 N. Harbor Blvd., Fullerton, CA 92632

Bookpress, Box KP, Williamsburg, VA 23187★

The Book Shelf, 1308 Sussex La., Newport Beach, CA 92660

The Bookshop, 400 West Franklin St., Chapel Hill, NC 27516

Books & Autographs, 287 Goodwin Rd., Eliot, ME 03903★

Books West Southwest, 2452 North Campbell Ave., Tucson, AZ 85719

The Book Symposium, 1745 Kenneth Rd., Glendale, CA 91201

The Book Treasury, P.O. Box 20033, Long Beach, CA 90801★

Boston Book Company & Book Annex, 705 Centre Ave., Jamaica Plain, MA 02130★

Bowie & Company, 314 First Ave. South, Seattle, WN 98104★

Marilyn Braiterman, 20 Whitfield Rd., Baltimore, MD 21210★

The Brick Row Bookshop, 278 Post St. #303, San Francisco, CA 94108★

Bromer Booksellers, 607 Boylston St., Boston, MA 02116★

Buckingham Books, 8058 Stone Bridge Rd., Greencastle, PA 17225

Brian & Margaret Buckley, 11 Convent Close, Kenilworth CV8-2FQ, United Kingdom

Buddenbrooks, 31 Newbury St., Boston, MA 02116★

Burke's Book Store, 1719 Poplar Ave., Memphis, TN 38104

Nicholas and Helen Burrows, 136 Engadine Street, London SW18-5DT, United Kingdom

Harold M. Burstein & Company, 36 Riverside Dr., Waltham, MA 02154★

John R. Butterworth, 742 West 11th St., Claremont, CA 91711

By the Way Books, P.O. Box 23359, Columbia, SC 29224

Andrew Cahan, 3000 Blueberry La., Chapel Hill, NC 27516★

Caliban Book Shop, 416 South Craig St., Pittsburgh, PA 15213★

Caney Booksellers, 1 Cherry Hill Rd., Suite 220, Cherry Hill, NJ 08002★

The Captain's Book Shelf, P.O. Box 2258, Asheville, NC 28802-2258★

Cardinal Books, 25718 Arden Park Dr., Farmington Hills, MN 48018

Nicholas Certo, P.O. Box 322, Circleville, NY 10919

Bev Chaney, Jr., 73 Croton Ave., Ossining, NY 10562

Chapel Hill Rare Books, P.O. Box 456, Carrboro, NC 27510★

Chloe's Books, P.O. Box 2249, Loomis, CA 95650

Clearwater Books, 19 Matlock Road, Ferndown, Wimborne, Dorset BH22-8QT, United Kingdom★

Clover Hill Books, P.O. Box 6278, Charlottesville, VA 22906

Cobbydale Books, 13 Aireville Drive, Silsden, Yorkshire BD20 0H4, United Kingdom

Considine Books, 41 South Main St., Marlbourough, CT 06447

Conundrum, 1309 Laurel St. #2, Menlo Park, CA 94025

Cornstalk Bookshop, P.O. 336, Glebe, New South Wales 2037, Australia

Country Lane Books, P.O. Box 47, Collinsville, CT 06022★

N. A. Cournoyer Books, 1194 Bank Street, Ottawa, Ontario K1S-3Y1, Canada

William Cowan Books, 29/3 West Nicolson Street, Edinburgh EH8-9DB, United Kingdom

Robert Cramer, 5332 Janisann Ave., Culver City, CA 90230

Cultured Oyster Books, P.O. Box 404 Planararium Station, New York, NY 10024-0404

James Cummins, 699 Madison Ave., New York, NY 10021★

L. W. Currey, P.O. Box 187 (Water St.), Elizabethtown, NY 12932★

G. Curwen Books, 1 West 67th St. #710, New York, NY 10023

Barbara Cutts, 2206 North East 40th Ave., Portland, OR 97212

D & D Galleries, P.O. Box 8413, Somerville, NJ 08876★

Robert Dagg, P.O. Box 4758, Santa Barbara, CA 93140★

William & Victoria Dailey, 8216 Melrose Ave., P.O. Box 69160, Los Angeles, CA 90069★

Dalian Books, 81 Albion Drive, London Fields, London E8-4LT, United Kingdom

Tom Davidson, 37-3 Avenue L, Brooklyn, NY 11210

Decline and Fall, P.O. Box 659, Stevens Point, WI 54481

Joseph A. Dermont, 13 Arthur St., P.O. Box 654, Onset, MA 02558

Derozier & Derozier, P.O. Box 8836, Green Bay, WI 54308-8836

Detering Book Gallery, 2311 Bissonnet, Houston, TX 77005★

Dinkytown Antiquarian Bookstore, 1316 SE 4th St., Minneapolis, MN 55414★

John Dinsmore & Associates, 1037 Castleton Way South, Lexington, KY 40517

Thomas Dorn, P.O. Box 2585, Decatur, GA 30031-2585

James M. Dourgarian, 1595-A Third Ave., Walnut Creek, CA 94596

Duga's Books, 610 Aldama Ct., Ocoee, FL 32761

Dunn and Powell, The Hideaway, Bar Harbor, ME 04609-1714

I. D. Edrich, 17 Selsdon Road, Wanstead, London E11-2QF, United Kingdom

Francis Edwards, The Old Cinema, Castle Street, Hay-on-Wye, via Herford HR2-5DF, United Kingdom

Else Fine Books, P.O. Box 43, Dearborn, MI 48121★

William English, 48 Galway House, Radnor St., London EC1V-3SL, United Kingdom

Ergo Books, 46 Lisburne Road, London NW3-2NR, United Kingdom

Estates of Mind, 85 Bayview Ave., Great Neck, NY 11021★

Euclid Books, 227 Euclid St., Santa Monica, CA 90402

Exemplum, P.O. Box 1313, North Riverside, IL 60546

Ferret Fantasy, 27 Beechcroft Road, Upper Tooting, London SW19-7BX, United Kingdom

The Fine Books Co., 781 E. Snell Rd., Rochester, MI 48306★

First Editions, 11004 Summitview Ext., Yakima, WN 98908

First Editions Books, 1405 Nottoway Ave., Richmond, VA 23227

First Folio, 1206 Brentwood, Paris, TX 38242-3804★

First Impressions, P.O. Box 889, Orland Park, IL 60462

Forest Books, Knipton, Grantham, Lincs. NG32-IRF, United Kingdom

Fuller & Saunders, 3238 P St., NW, Washington, DC 20007

Robert Gavora, 4514 East Burnside St., Portland, OR 97215★

R. A. Gekoski, 15a Bloomsbury Square, London WC1A-2LP, United Kingdom★

Michael Ginsberg, Box 402, Sharon, MA 02067★

Thomas A. Goldwasser, 126 Post St., Suite 407, San Francisco, CA 94108-4704★

William A. Graf, 717 Clark St., Iowa City, IA 52240-5640

Grant's Bookshop, 12 Toorak Rd., Victoria 3141, Australia

Gravesend Books, P.O. Box 235, Pocono Pines, PA 18350

Great Northwest Bookstore, 1234 SW Stark St., Portland, OR 97205

Paulette Greene, 7152 Via Palomar, Boca Raton, FL 33433★

Hawthorn Books, 7 College Park Drive, Westbury-on-Trym, Bristol BS10 -7AN, United Kingdom★

Heirloom Bookstore, 4100 Atlanta Hwy., Bogart, GA 30622

Susan Heller, Box 2200-E, Cleveland, OH 44122★

Heritage Bookshop, 8540 Melrose Ave., Los Angeles, CA 90069★

The Hermitage Bookshop, 290 Filmore St., Denver, CO 80206-5020★

Willis E. Herr, 7004 Camino Pachero, San Diego, CA 92111

Historicana, 1200 Edgehill Dr., Burlingame, CA 94010★

Richard L. Hoffman, 420 12th St., Apt. F3R, Brooklyn, NY 11215

David Holloway, 7430 Grace St., Springfield, VA 22150

Holloway's Books, P.O. Box 8294, Dallas, TX 75205

David J. Holmes, 230 South Broad St., 3rd Floor, Philadelphia, PA 19102★

Glenn Horowitz, 141 East 44th St., Suite 712, New York, NY 10017

George Houle, 7260 Beverly Blvd., Los Angeles, CA 90036★

John Hudak, 184 Columbia Heights #1D, Brooklyn, NY 11201

In Our Time, P.O. Box 390386, Cambridge, MA 02139

Island Books, P.O. Box 19, Old Westbury, NY 11568

It Came From Mt. Shasta, P.O. Box 11120, Mt. Shasta, CA 96067

James S. Jaffe, 367 West Lancaster Ave., Haverford, PA 19041

Janus Books, P.O. Box 40787, Tucson, AZ 85717

Jarndyce Antiquarian Books, 46 Great Russell Street, London WC1B-3PA, United Kingdom

Joseph the Provider Books, 10 West Micheltorena, Santa Barbara, CA 93101★

The Jumping Frog, 585 Prospect Ave., W. Hartford, CT 06105
Priscilla Juvelis, 1166 Massachusetts Ave., Cambridge, MA 02138★
K Books, Allerthorpe, Walpington Hall, York, United Kingdom
Kenneth Karmiole, P.O. Box 464, Santa Monica, CA 90406★
Katie Books, 461 East Main St., Suite C, Ventura, CA 93001
Katonah Book Scout, 75 Meadow La., Katonah, NY 10536
Keane-Egan Books, P.O. Box 529, State College, PA 16804
Key West Island Bookstore, 513 Fleming St., Key West, FL 33040
The Kid Newsletter, P.O. Box 848, New York, NY 10024
Gerry Kleier, 322 Manhattan Dr., Vallejo, CA 94591
John W. Knott, Jr., 8453 Early Bud Way, Laurel, MD 20707
Ralph Kristiansen, P.O. Box 524, Kenmore Station, Boston, MA 02215★
Kugleman & Bent, P.O. Box 18292, Denver, CO 80218
Lame Duck Books, 90 Moraine St., Jamaica Plain, MA 02130★
Larsen Books, 6 Goodhope St., Paddington 2021, Sydney, Australia
James & Mary Laurie, 251 South Snelling Ave., St. Paul, MN 55105★
Leaves of Grass, 2433 Whitmore Lake Rd., Ann Arbor, MI 48103★
John Le Bow, 117 Langford Rd., P.O. Box 737, Candia, NH 03034
Barry R. Levin, 2265 Westwood Blvd., #669, Los Angeles, CA 90069★
Limestone Hills Book Shop, P.O. Box 1125, Glen Rose, TX 76043★
Ken Lopez, 51 Huntington Rd., Hadley, MA 01035★
Robert Loren, Link, Booksellers, P.O. Box 511, Las Cruces, NM 88004★
Lost Horizon Bookstore, 703 Anacapa St., Santa Barbara, CA 93101★
Stephen Lupack, 449 Hanover Ave., S. Meriden, CT 06451
McClintock Books, P.O. Box 1949, 1454 Sheridan Ave. NE, Warren, OH 44483
MacDonnell Rare Books, 9307 Glendale Dr., Austin, TX 78730
McGowan Book Company, P.O. Box 16325, Chapel Hill, NC 27516
Ian McKelvie, 45 Hertford Road, London N2-9BX, United Kingdom
R. McLaughlin, 1613 Monterey Dr., Livermore, CA 94550
George S. Macmanus Co., 1317 Irving St., Philadelphia, PA 19017★
Robert A. Madle, 4406 Bestor Dr., Rockville, MD 20853
Maggs Brothers Ltd, 50 Berkeley Square, London W1X-6EL, United Kingdom★
Magic Lantern Books, 107 Broyles Dr., Johnson City, TN 37601
Magnum Opus, P.O. Box 1301, Charlottesville, VA 22902
Main Street Fine Books & Manuscripts, 301 S. Main St., Galena, IL 61036
David Mason, 342 Queen Street West, 2nd floor, Toronto M5V 2A2, Canada★
Bryan Matthews, 742 North Cherokee Ave., Hollywood, CA 90038
David Mayou, 87 Old Brompton Road, London SW7-3LD, United Kingdom★
Ming Books, 110 Gloucester Avenue, London NW1-8JA, United Kingdom
George Robert Minkoff, 26 Rowe Rd., Alford, MA 01230★
Monroe Books, 359 E. Shaw Ave, Suite 102, Fresno, CA 93710★
Hartley Moorhouse Books, 17 Hampstead Lane, Highgate, London N6-4RT, United
   Kingdom
Mordida Books, P.O. Box 79322, Houston, TX 77279
S. M. Mossberg, 50 Talcott Rd., Rye Brook, NY 10573
Howard S. Mott, 170 South Main St., P.O. Box 309, Sheffield, MA 01257★
Mountain Mysteries, P.O. Box 870966, Stone Mountain, GA 30087
J. B. Muns, 1162 Shattuck Avenue, Berkeley, CA 94707★
Mysterious Bookshop, 129 W. 56th St., New York, NY 10019

Mystery & Imagination Bookshop, 515 1/2 E. Broadway, Glendale, CA 91205

New England Antiquarian Booksellers Guild, Rt. 101, The Castles, Brentwood, NH 03833

Stuart Ng, 8810 1/2 Belford Ave., Los Angeles, CA 90045

Nineteenth Century Shop, 1047 Hollins St., Baltimore, MD 21223

Nouveau, P.O. Box 12471, 5005 Meadow Oaks Park Dr., Jackson, MS 39211

Oak Knoll Books, 414 Delaware St., New Castle, DE 19720★

October Farm, 2609 Branch Rd., Raleigh , NC 27610

OK Books, 2 N. Last Chance Gulch, Helena, MT 59601

Old New York Book Shop, 1069 Juniper St. NE, Atlanta, GA 30309★

The Old Paperphiles, P.O. Box 135, Tiverton, RI 02878

John Oliveri, 104 Goldenwood Ct., Cary, NC 27513

David L. O'Neal, 234 Clarenden St., Boston, MA 02116★

James F. O'Neil, 160 Commonwealth Ave., #521, Boston, MA 02116

Orpheus Books, 11522 NE 20th St., Bellevue, WN 98004

Palace Collectibles, 15222 Stradbrook, Houston, TX 77062

Pepper & Stern, 1980 Cliff Dr., Suite 224, Santa Barbara, CA 93109★

R. & A. Petrilla, P.O. Box 306, Roosevelt, NJ 08555

Pettler & Lieberman, 8033 Sunset Blvd., #977, Los Angeles, CA 90046

Pharos Books, P.O. Box 17, Fair Haven Sta., New Haven, CT 06513

Phoenix Bookshop South, P.O. Box 1018, St. Michaels, MD 21663

James M. Pickard, Pendragon, 21 Grenfell Road, Leicester LE2-2PA, United Kingdom

Philip J. Pirages, P.O. Box 504, 2205 Nut Tree La., McMinnville, OR 97128★

Polyanthos Books, 600 Park Ave., P.O. Box 343, Huntington, NY 11743

Nicholas Pounder's Bookshop, P.O. Box 451, Kings Cross, New South Wales, 2011 Australia★

Providence Bookstore Cafe, 500 Angell St., Providence, RI 02906

John William Pye, 79 Hollis St., Brocton, MA 02402

Bernard Quaritch, Ltd, 5-8 Lower John Street, Golden Square, London W1R-4AU, United Kingdom★

Quill & Brush, P.O. Box 5365, Rockville, MD 20848★

Randall House, 835 Laguna St., Santa Barbara, CA 93101★

Paul Rassam, Flat 5, 18 East Heath Road, London NW3-1AJ, United Kingdom★

The Reading Lamp, 24032 79th Place W., Edmonds, WA 98026

David Rees, 18A Prentis Road, London SW16-1QD, United Kingdom

William Reese Co., 409 Temple St., New Haven, CT 06511★

Jo Ann Reisler, Ltd., 360 Glyndon St. N.E., Vienna, VA 22180★

L. & T. Respess Books, P.O. Box 1604, Charlottesville, VA 22902★

Revere Books, P.O. Box 420, Revere, PA 18953

Alice Robbins, 3002 Roundhill Rd., Greensboro, NC 27408

Robert Frost Books, P.O. Box 719, Rensselear, NY 12144

Charlotte Robinson, 4 Morgan House, 127 Longacre, London WC2E-9AA, United Kingdom

B&L Rootenberg, P.O. Box 5049, Sherman Oaks, CA 91403★

Bertram Rota, 31 Long Acre, Covent Garden, London WC2E 9LT, United Kingdom★

P. & B. Rowan, Carlton House, 92 Marlowe Road, Belfast BT9-5HP, Northern Ireland

The Rue Morgue, P.O. Box 4119, 946 Pearl St., Boulder, CO 80306

Rykken and Scull, P.O. Box 1979, Guerneville, CA 95446★

Sablestar, 872 Mesa View, Upland, CA 91786

Rod Samonte, 1025 N. Catalina St., Burbank, CA 91505
Sandpiper Books, P.O. Box 1273, Long Beach, CA 98631
Schoyer's Books, 1404 S. Negley Ave., Pittsburgh, PA 15217★
Bud Schweska, P.O. Box 754010, Parkside Station, Forrest Hills, NY 11375
Andrew Sclanders, 11 Albany Road, Stroud Green, London N4-4RR, United Kingdom
Seattle Book Center, 2231 Second Ave, Seattle, WA 98121
Second Life Books, P.O. Box 242, 55 Quarry Rd., Lanesborough, MA 01237★
Second Story Books, 12160 Parklawn Drive, Rockville, MD 20852★
Anthony Sellem, 9 Tackleway, Old Town, Hastings, East Sussex TN34-3DE, United Kingdom
Peter Selley, Ground Floor Flat, 29 Miranda Road, London N19, United Kingdom
Serendipity Books, 1201 University Ave., Berkeley, CA 94702★
Sherlock & Co., 695 35th Ave., San Francisco, CA 94121
Sherwood Fine Books, 5911 East Spring St., Suite 402, Long Beach, CA 90808
Skyline Books, P.O. Box T, Forest Knolls, CA 94933★
Monroe Stahr Books, 4420 Ventura Canyon Ave., #2, Sherman Oaks, CA 91423
Christopher P. Stephens, 12 Washington Ave., P.O. Box 303, Hastings-on-Hudson, NY 10706
Joan Stevens, "Rosslyn House," High Street, Yoxford, Suffolk IP17-3EP, United Kingdom
Strand Book Store, 828 Broadway, New York, NY 10003★
Stratford Books, 3230 E. Fleming Rd., Las Vegas, NV 89121
Sturford Books, Sturford Mead, Corsley, Warminster, Wiltshire BA12-7QT, United Kingdom
Summer & Stillman, P.O. Box 973, Yarmouth, ME 04096★
Raymond M. Sutton, Jr., 430 Main St., P.O. Box 30, Williamsburg, KY 40769
Sylvester & Orphanos, 2484 Cheremoya Ave., P.O. Box 2567, Los Angeles, CA 90078-2567
Tall Stories, 2141 Mission St., Suite 301, San Francisco, CA 94110
Tall Tales, 1551 San Pablo Ave., Oakland, CA 94612
Tamerlane Books, P.O. Box C, Havertown, PA 19083★
Tappin Book Mine, 705 Atlantic Blvd., Atlantic Beach, FL 32233-3914
Taugher Books, 2550 Somerset Dr., Belmont, CA 94002-2926
Robert Temple, 65 Midway Road, London N1-4PU, United Kingdom
Steven Temple Books, 489 Queen Street West, Toronto, Ontario M5V-2B4, Canada★
Michael Thompson, 311 W. Cordova St., Vancouver, British Columbia V6B-1E5, Canada★
Michael R. Thompson, 8312 West Third St., Los Angeles, CA 90048★
Thorn Books, 624 Moorpark Ave., P.O. Box 1244, Moorpark, CA 93020★
TLC Books, 9 N. College Ave., Salem, VA 34153
Henry E. Turlington, P.O. Box 190, Carrboro, NC 27510★
The Turret Bookshop, 36 Great Queen Street, London WC2B-5AA, United Kingdom
Turtle Island Booksellers, 2067 Center St., Berkeley, CA 94704★
Tuttle Antiquarian Books, Inc., 26 S. Main St., P.O. Box 541, Rutland, VT 05702★
Ulysses Bookshop, 31 & 40 Museum Street, London WC1A-1LH, United Kingdom★
Len Unger Rare Books, P.O. Box 5858, Sherman Oaks, CA 91413★
Vagabond Books, 2076 Westwood Blvd., Los Angeles, CA 90025★
The Veatchs, 20 Veronica Ct., Smithtown, NY 11787
Fernando E. Vega, 5817 Haymeadow Ct., 3B, Peoria, IL 61615

Versetility Books, P.O. Box 1366, Burlington, VT, 06013

Virgo Books, "Little Court," South Wraxall, Bradford-on-Avon, Wilts., BA15 2SE United Kingdom

Wahrenbrock's Book House, 726 Broadway, San Diego, CA 92101★

Waiting for Godot Books, P.O. Box 331, Hadley, MA 01035

Rob Warren, 13 W. 18th St., New York, NY 10011

Watermark West, 149 N. Broadway, Wichita, KS 67202

Water Row Books, P.O. Box 438, Sudbury, MA 01776

Waverly Books, 948 9th St., Santa Monica, CA 90403

Wessel & Lieberman, 121 First Avenue South, Seattle, WA 98104

E. Wharton & Co., 3232 History Dr., Oakton, VA 22124

Wheldon & Wesley, Ltd., Lytton Lodge, Codicote, Hitchin, Herts., SG4-8TE United Kingdom

Jett W. Whitehead, 1412 Center Ave., Bay City, MI 48708

Edna Whiteson, 66 Belmont Avenue, Cockfosters, Herts. EN4-9LA, United Kingdom

Wilder Books, P.O. Box 762, Elmhurst, IL 60126

Nigel Williams, 7 Waldeck Grove, London SE27-0BE, United Kingdom

Richard Williams, 15 High Street, Dragonby, Scunthorpe, South Humberside DN15-0BE, United Kingdom

John Windle, 1226 Johnson St., Menlo Park, CA 94025★

J. Howard Woolmer, 577 Marienstein Road, Revere, PA 18953★

Words Etcetera, Hinton Lodge, Crown Road, Marnhull, Dorset DT10-1DE, United Kingdom★

Robert Wright Books, 1083 Bathurst St., Toronto, Ontario M5R-3G8, Canada

Wrigley-Cross Books, 8001 A SE Powell, Portland, OR 97206

Herb Yellin, 10973 Los Alamos St., Northridge, CA 91326

Yesterday's Books, 25625 Southfield Rd., Suite # 104, Southfield, MI 48075

Yesteryear Book Shop, 3201 Maple Dr., NE, Atlanta, GA 30305★

Zeno's, 1955 34th Ave., San Francisco, CA 94116

APPENDIX C

AUCTION HOUSES

Baltimore Book Auction, 2112 North Charles Street, Baltimore, MD 21201

Christie's, 502 Park Avenue, New York, NY 10022

Christie's East, 219 East 67th Street, New York, NY 10021

Samuel T. Freeman and Co., 1808 Chestnut Street, Philadelphia, PA 19103

Kane Antiquarian Auction, 1525 Shenkel Road, Pottstown, PA 19464

Richard E. Oinonen Book Auctions, Box 470, Sunderland, MA 01375

Pacific Book Auction Galleries, 139 Townsend Street, Ste. 305, San Francisco, CA 94107

Phillips, Sons & Neale, Inc., 406 East 79th Street, New York, NY 10021

Plandome Book Auctions, Box 395, Glen Head, NY 11545

Sotheby Parke Bernet, Inc., 1334 York Avenue, New York, NY 10021

Superior Galleries, 9478 W. Olympic Boulevard, Beverly Hills, CA 90212

Swann Galleries, 104 East 25th Street, New York, NY 10010

Waverly Auctions, 4931 Cordell Avenue, Suite AA, Bethesda, MD 20814

Samuel Yudkin & Associates, 3636 16th Street, NW, Washington, D.C. 20010

APPENDIX D

SELECTED BIBLIOGRAPHY OF
WORKS CONSULTED

General Bibliographies Consulted

(AMERICANA) Howes, Wright. *U.S.Iana (1650–1950)*. New York: Bowker, 1962.

(CHILDREN'S BOOKS) Blanck, Jacob. *Peter Parley to Penrod*. Waltham, Mass.: Mark Press, 1974.

(CHILDREN'S BOOKS) Kirkpatrick, D. L., ed. *Twentieth-Century Children's Writers*. 2d ed. New York: St. Martin's Press (1983).

(GENERAL) Kunitz, Stanley J., and Haycraft, Howard, eds. *Twentieth Century Authors: A Biographical Dictionary of Modern Literature*. New York: The H. W. Wilson Co., 1942.

(GENERAL) Kunitz, Stanely J., ed. *Twentieth Century Authors First Supplement: A Biographical Dictionary of Modern Literature*. New York: The H. W. Wilson Co, 1945.

(GENERAL) Schwartz, Dr. Jacob. *1100 Obscure Points*. Bristol (England): Chatford House Press (1931).

(GENERAL) Zemple, Edward N. and Linda A. *First Editions: A Guide to Identification*. 2d ed. (Peoria): Spoon River Press (1989).

(GOLF) Donovan, Richard E., and Murdoch, Joseph S. F. *The Game of Golf and the Printed Word 1566-1985: A Bibliography of Golf Literature in the English Language*. Endicott, N.Y.: Castalio Press, 1988.

(LITERATURE) Blanck, Jacob. *Bibliography of American Literature*. New Haven: Yale University, 1953–73. (7 volumes). (BAL)

(LITERATURE) Bruccoli, Matthew; Clark, Jr., C. E. Frazer; Layman, Richard; and Franklin, Benjamin V. (eds). *First Printings of American Authors*. 5 vols. Detroit: Gale Research, 1977–89.

(LITERATURE) Cutler, B. D., and Stiles, Villa. *Modern British Authors*. New York: Greenberg Publisher (1930).

(LITERATURE) Johnson, Merle. *American First Editions*. Revised and Enlarged by Jacob Blanck. Waltham, Mass.: Mark Press, 1969.

(LITERATURE) Kirkpatrick, D. L., and Vinson, James, eds. *Contemporary Novelists*. 4th ed. New York: St. Martin's Press (1986).

(LITERATURE) Lepper, Gary M. *A Bibliographical Introduction to Seventy-Five Modern American Authors*. Berkeley: Serendipity Books, 1976.

(LITERATURE, WESTERN) Adams, Ramon F. *The Rampaging Herd*. Cleveland: (Zubal, 1982).

(LITERATURE, WESTERN) Adams, Ramon F. *Six-Guns and Saddle Leather*. (Cleveland): Zubal (1982).

(LITERATURE, WESTERN) Dykes, Jeff. *Western High Spots*. No-place: Northland Press (1977).

(MORMON) Flake, Chad J. *A Mormon Bibliography, 1830–1930*. Salt Lake City: University of Utah Press, 1978.

(MYSTERIES) Reilly, John M., ed. *Twentieth-Century Crime and Mystery Writers*. 2d ed. New York: St. Martin's Press (1985).

(POETRY) Vinson, James, and Kirkpatrick, D. L., eds. *Contemporary Poets*. 4th ed. New York: St. Martin's Press (1985).

(PRICE GUIDES) Ahearn, Allen and Patricia. *Collected Books: The Guide to Values*. New York: G. P. Putnam's Sons (1991).

(PRICE GUIDES) Ahearn, Allen and Patricia. *Author Price Guides*. Rockville, Md.: 1987-93.

(PRICE GUIDES) *American Book Prices Current*. New York: Bancroft-Parkman, 1981-89.

(PRICE GUIDES) McGrath, Daniel, ed. *Bookman's Price Index*. (Vols. 36–48) Detroit: Gale Research (1987-1990).

(PRICE GUIDES) Bradley, Van Allen. *The Book Collector's Handbook of Values, 1982-83*. New York: G. P. Putnam's Sons, 1982 (VAB).

(SCIENCE FICTION) Bleiler, E. F. *The Checklist of Science-Fiction and Supernatural Fiction*. Glen Rock, N.J.: Firebell Books (1978).

(SCIENCE FICTION) Currey, L. W. *Science Fiction and Fantasy Authors: A Bibliography of First Printings...* Boston: G. K. Hall (1979).

(SCIENCE FICTION) Smith, Curtis C., ed. *Twentieth-Century Science-Fiction Writers*. New York: St. Martin's Press (1981).

(SPORTING BOOKS) Phillips, John C. *A Bibliography of American Sporting Books: Sport-Natural History-Hunting-Dogs-Trapping-Shooting-Early American. . .* New York: James Cummins Bookseller, 1991.

(WESTERN AMERICANA) Streeter, Thomas W. *Bibliography of Texas 1795–1845*. Cambridge: Harvard University Press, 1960.

(WESTERN AMERICANA) Wagner, Henry R., and Camp, Charles L. *The Plains & the Rockies*. San Francisco: John Howell-Books, 1982.

INDIVIDUAL BIBLIOGRAPHIES CONSULTED

(ABBEY) Maxwell, Spencer. *Collecting Abbey: A Checklist of the First Editions of Edward Abbey*. Sante Fe, New Mexico: Vinegar Tom Press (1991).

(ABERCROMBIE) Cooper, Jeffrey. *A Bibliography and Notes on the Works of Lascelles Abercrombie*. (London): Archon Books, 1969. See also *Gawsworth*

(ACTON) Ritchie, Neil. *A Bibliography of Harold Acton*. Florence: no-publisher, 1934.

(ADAMIC) Christian, Henry A. *Louis Adamic: A Checklist*. No-place: Kent State University Press (1971).

(ADE) Russo, Dorothy Ritter. *A Bibliography of George Ade, 1866–1944*. Indianapolis: Indiana Historical Society, 1947.

(AIKEN) Bonnell, F. W. and F. C. *Conrad Aiken: A Bibliography, (1902-1978)*. San Marino: Huntington Library, 1982.

(ALCOTT) Gulliver, Lucille. *Louisa May Alcott: A Bibliography*. Boston: Little Brown, 1932.

(ALDINGTON) See *Casanova*

(ALGER) Gardner, Ralph D. *Road to Success: A Bibliography of the Works of Horatio Alger.* Mendota, Ill.: Wayside Press, 1971.

(ALGREN) Bruccoli, Matthew J. *Nelson Algren: A Descriptive Bibliography.* (Pittsburgh): University of Pittsburgh Press, 1985.

(AMIS, K.) Gohn, Jack Benoit. *Kingsley Amis: A Checklist.* No-place: Kent State University Press (1976).

(AMIS, M.) See *Rees*

(ANDERSON) Sheehy, Eugene P., and Lohf, Kenneth A. *Sherwood Anderson: A Bibliography.* Los Gatos: Talisman Press, 1960.

(ANDREWS) Webber, William Hallam. *William Loring Andrews: A Study and Bibliography.* Rockville, Md.: no-publ.,1980.

(ARMSTRONG) See *Casanova*

(ARNOLD) Smart, Thomas Burnett. *The Bibliography of Matthew Arnold.* Reprinted. New York: Burt Franklin (1968).

(ASHBERY) Kermani, David K. *John Ashbery: A Comprehensive Bibliography.* New York: Garland Publishing, 1976.

(ASHENDENE PRESS) See *Franklin, C.*

(ASIMOV) Miller, Marjorie M. *Isaac Asimov: A Checklist of Works Published in the United States, March 1939–May 1972.* No-place: Kent State University Press (1972).

(ATWOOD) Horne, Alan J. *A Preliminary Checklist of Writings By and About Margaret Atwood.* In the *Malahat Review* No. 41. Victoria, British Columbia, Canada: University of Victoria, 1977.

(AUDEN) Bloomfield, B. C., and Mendelson, Edward. *W. H. Auden: A Bibliography, 1924–1969.* Charlottesville: University of Virginia (1972).

(AUSTEN) Keynes, Geoffrey. *Jane Austen: A Bibliography.* London: Nonesuch Press, 1929.

(BALLANTINE BOOKS) Aronovitz, David. *Ballantine Books: the First Decade.* Rochester, Michigan: Bailiwick Books (1987).

(BALLANTYNE) Quayle, Eric. *R. M. Ballantyne: A Bibliography of First Editions.* London: Dawsons of Pall Mall, 1968.

(BARING) Chaundy, Leslie. *A Bibliography of the First Editions of the Works of Maurice Baring.* London: Dulau & Co., 1925.

(BARNES, D.) Messeri, Douglas. *Djuna Barnes: A Bibliography.* (New York): David Lewis, 1975.

(BARNES, J.) See *Rees*

(BARRIE) Cutler, B. D. *Sir James M. Barrie: A Bibliography.* New York, 1931.

(BARRIE) Garland, Herbert. *A Bibliography of the Writings of Sir James Matthew Barrie.* London: Bookman's Journal, 1928.

(BARTH) Weixlmann, Joseph. *John Barth: A Descriptive . . . Bibliography.* New York: Garland, 1976.

(BARTHELME) Klinkowitz, Jerome; Pieratt, Asa; and Davis, Robert Murray. *Donald Barthelme: A Comprehensive Bibliography.* (Hamden, Ct.): Archon Books, 1977.

(BASKIN, L.) See *Gehenna Press*

(BAUM) See *Oz*

(BECKETT) Lake, Carlton, et al. *No Symbols Where None Intended.* (Samuel Beckett). Austin: Humanities Research Center, University of Texas (1984).

(BEEBE) Berra, Tim. *William Beebe: An Annotated Bibliography.* (Hamden, Ct.): Archon Books, 1977.

(BEERBOHM) Gallatin, A. E., and Oliver, L. M. *A Bibliography of the Works of Max Beerbohm.* London: Rupert Hart-Davis, 1952.

(BELLOC) Cahill, Patrick. *The English First Editions of Hilaire Belloc.* London: (Privately published) 1953.

(BENSON, Mildred Wirt) See *Drew, Nancy*

(BERRYMAN) Stefanik, Ernest C., Jr. *John Berryman: A Descriptive Bibliography*. No-place [Pittsburgh]: University of Pittsburgh, 1974.

(BETJEMAN) Stapleton, Margaret L. *Sir John Betjeman: A Bibliography of Writings By and About Him*. Metuchen, N.J.: Scarecrow Press, 1974.

(BIERCE) Starrett, Vincent. *Ambrose Bierce: A Bibliography*. Philadelphia: The Centaur Book Shop, 1929.

(BISHOP) MacMahon, Candace. *Elizabeth Bishop: A Bibliography, 1927–1979*. Charlottesville: University of Virginia (1980).

(BLACK SUN PRESS) Minkoff, George Robert. *A Bibliography of the Black Sun Press*. Great Neck: G. R. Minkoff, 1970.

(BLOCH) Larson, Randall D. *The Complete Robert Bloch*. Sunnyvale, Calif.: Fandom Unlimited, 1986.

(BLUNDEN) Kirkpatrick, Brownlee. *A Bibliography of Edmund Blunden*. Oxford: Clarendon Press, 1979.

(BLY) Roberson, William H. *Robert Bly: A Primary and Secondary Bibliography*. Metuchen, N.J., and London: The Scarecrow Press, 1986.

(BORROW) Collie, Michael, and Fraser, Angus. *George Borrow: A Bibliographical Study*. Hampshire: St. Paul's Bibliographies, 1984.

(BOWLES) Miller, Jeffrey. *Paul Bowles: A Descriptive Bibliography*. Santa Barbara: Black Sparrow, 1986.

(BRADBURY) Nolan, William F. *The Ray Bradbury Companion*. Detroit: Bruccoli Clark/Gale Research, 1975.

(BRAND) Richardson, Darrell C. *Max Brand (Frederick Faust): The Man and His Work*. Los Angeles: Fantasy Publishing (1952).

(BRAUTIGAN) Barber, John F. *Richard Brautigan: An Annotated Bibliography*. Jefferson, North Carolina and London: McFarland & Co. (1990).

(BRONTË) Wise, Thomas J. *A Bibliography of the Writings . . . of the Brontë Family*. London: Dawsons of Pall Mall (1917).

(BROOKE) Keynes, Geoffrey. *A Bibliography of the Works of Rupert Brooke*. London: Rupert Hart-Davis, 1964.

(BROWN) Baird, Newton. *A Key To Frederic Brown's Wonderland*. Georgetown, Calif.: Talisman Literary Research, 1981.

(BROWNING) Barnes, Warner. *A Bibliography of Elizabeth Barrett Browning*. (Austin): University of Texas . . . (1967).

(BROWNING) Wise, Thomas J. *A Bibliography of the Writings . . . of Robert Browning*. London: Dawsons of Pall Mall, 1971.

(BUCHAN) Blanchard, Robert G. *The First Editions of John Buchan*. (Hamden, Conn.): Archon Books, 1981.

(BUKOWSKI) Dorbin, Sanford. *A Bibliography of Charles Bukowski*. Los Angeles: Black Sparrow, 1969.

(BUKOWSKI) Fogel, Al. *Charles Bukowski: A Comprehensive Checklist*. (Miami: Sole Proprietor Press, 1982).

(BUKOWSKI) Fogel, Al. *Under the Influence: A Collection of Works by Charles Bukowski, Illustrated with Original Drawings by the Author*. (Sudbury, Mass.: Jeffrey H. Weinberg Books, 1984).

(BUNTING) Guedalla, Roger. *Basil Bunting: A Bibliography of Works and Criticism*. Norwood, Pa.: Norwood Editions, 1973.

(BURGESS, A.) Brewer, Jeutonne. *Anthony Burgess: A Bibliography*. Metuchen, N.J. & London: The Scarecrow Press, 1980.

(BURGESS, T.) Dowhan, Michael W., Jr. *Thornton W. Burgess, Harrison Cady: A Book, Magazine and Newspaper Bibliography*. New York: Carlton Press (1990).

(BURGESS, T.) Wright, Wayne W. *Thornton W. Burgess: A Descriptive Book Bibliography*. Sandwich, Mass.: Burgess Society, 1979.

(BURKE) Todd, William B. *A Bibliography of Edmund Burke*. (Surrey, England): St. Paul's Bibliographies, 1982.

(BURNS) (Gibson, James). *The Bibliography of Robert Burns* . . . Reprinted. New York: Kraus Reprint Co., 1969.

(BURROUGHS, E. R.) Heins, Henry Hardy. *A Golden Anniversary Bibliography of Edgar Rice Burroughs*. (Revised). West Kingston, R.I.: Donald Grant, 1964.

(BURROUGHS, W.) Maynard, Joe, and Miles, Barry. *William S. Burroughs: A Bibliography, 1953-73*. Charlottesville: University of Virginia Press (1978).

(BURTON) Penzer, Norman M. *An Annotated Bibliography of Sir Richard Francis Burton*. New York: Burt Franklin (1970).

(BUTLER) Harkness, Stanley B. *The Career of Samuel Butler (1835–1902): A Bibliography*. London: The Bodley Head (1955).

(BUTLER) Hoppe, A. J. *A Bibliography of the Writings of Samuel Butler*. New York: Burt Franklin (1968).

(BYRNE) Wetherbee, Winthrop, Jr. *Donn Byrne: A Bibliography*. New York: New York Public Library, 1949.

(BYRON) Wise, Thomas J. *A Bibliography of the Writings in Verse and Prose of George Gordon Noel, Lord Byron*. 2 vols. London: Dawsons of Pall Mall, 1972.

(CABELL) Brussel I. R. *James Branch Cabell: A Revised Bibliography*. Philadelphia: Centaur Book Shop, 1932.

(CALDWELL) See *Casanova*

(CARADOC PRESS) See *Franklin, C.*

(CARLYLE) Dyer, Isaac Watson. *A Bibliography of Thomas Carlyle's Writings* . . . New York: Burt Franklin (1968).

(CARLYLE) Tarr, Rodger L. *Thomas Carlyle: A Descriptive Bibliography*. (Pittsburgh): University of Pittsburgh Press, 1989.

(CARROLL) Williams, Sidney Herbert. *A Bibliography of the Writings of Lewis Carroll*. (Charles Lutwidge Dodgson). London: *Bookman's Journal*, 1924.

CASANOVA Booksellers' Checklists of Twentieth Century Authors. Second Series, Milwaukee: 1933 (Richard Aldington, Martin Armstrong, Aldous Huxley, James Joyce and Christopher Morley); Third Series, Milwaukee: 1935 (Erskine Caldwell, Frank Harris, Robert Nathan, A. Edward Newton and Gertrude Stein).

(CASTLEMON) Blanck, Jacob. *Harry Castlemon Boy's Own Author*. Waltham, Mass.: Mark Press, 1969.

(CATHER) Crane, Joan. *Willa Cather: A Bibliography*. Lincoln: University of Nebraska Press (1982).

(CERVANTES) Grismer, Raymond L. *Cervantes: A Bibliography*. Reprinted. New York: Kraus, 1970.

(CHANDLER) Bruccoli, Matthew. *Raymond Chandler: A Descriptive Bibliography*. (Pittsburgh): University of Pittsburgh Press, 1979.

(CHATWIN) See *Rees*

(CHEKHOV) Meister, Charles W. *Chekhov Bibliography: Works in English by and about Anton Chekhov; American, British and Canadian Performances*. Jefferson, N.C., and London: McFarland & Co. (1985).

(CHESTERTON) Sullivan, John. *G. K. Chesterton: A Bibliography*. Warwick Square, London: University of London Press (1958).

(CHURCHILL) Woods, Frederick. *A Bibliography of the Works of Sir Winston Churchill.* (London): St. Paul's Bibliographies (1975).

(CITY LIGHTS) Cook, Ralph T. *The City Lights Pocket Poets Series: A Descriptive Bibliography.* La Jolla, Calif.: Laurence McGilvery/Atticus Books, 1982.

(CIVIL WAR) Menendez, Albert. *Civil War Novels: An Annotated Bibliography.* New York, and London: Garland Publishing, 1986.

(COLERIDGE) Haney, John Louis. *A Bibliography of Samuel Taylor Coleridge.* Philadelphia: Privately printed, 1903.

(COLLINS, W.) Beetz, Kirk H. *Wilkie Collins: An Annotated Bibliography, 1889-1976.* Metuchen, N.J. & London: The Scarecrow Press, 1978.

(COLLINS CRIME CLUB) Foord, Peter, and Williams, Richard. *Collins Crime Club: A Checklist of the First Editions.* South Humberside (England): Dragonby Press, 1987.

(CONRAD) Cagle, William. *A Bibliography of Joseph Conrad.* (Unpublished).

(CONRAD) Wise, Thomas J. *A Bibliography of the Writings of Joseph Conrad, (1895–1921).* (London): Dawsons of Pall Mall, 1972.

(COOPER) Spiller, Robert E., and Blackburn, Philip C. *A Descriptive Bibliography of the Writings of James Fenimore Cooper.* New York: R. R. Bowker Company, 1934.

(COPPARD) Fabes, Gilbert H. *The First Editions of A. E. Coppard, A. P. Herbert and Charles Morgan.* London: Myers & Co. (1933).

(COPPARD) Schwartz, Jacob. *The Writings of Alfred Edgar Coppard.* London: The Ulysses Bookshop, 1931.

(CORSO) Wilson, Robert. *A Bibliography of Works by Gregory Corso, 1954–1965.* New York: The Phoenix Book Shop, Inc., 1966.

(CORVO) Woolf, Cecil. *A Bibliography of Frederick Rolfe Baron Corvo.* London: Rupert Hart-Davis, Soho Square, 1957.

(COWLEY) Perkin, M. R. *Abraham Cowley: A Bibliography.* (Kent, England): Dawson, (1977).

(COZZENS) Bruccoli, Matthew. *James Gould Cozzens: A Descriptive Bibliography.* (Pittsburgh): University of Pittsburgh Press, 1981.

(CRANE, H.) Schwartz, Joseph, and Schweik, Robert C. *Hart Crane: A Descriptive Bibliography.* No-place (Pittsburgh): University of Pittsburgh Press (1972).

(CRANE, S.) Stallman, R. W. *Stephen Crane: A Critical Bibliography.* Ames: Iowa State University Press, 1972.

(CRANE, S.) Williams, Ames W., and Starrett, Vincent. *Stephen Crane: A Bibliography.* Glendale, Calif.: John Valentine, Publisher, 1948.

(CREASEY) *John Creasey: Master of Mystery.* (London: Hodder & Stoughton, no-date).

(CREASEY) (Creasey, John) *John Creasey in Print.* (New York, and London: Walker and Company, and Hodder & Stoughton, 1969).

(CREELEY) Novik, Mary. *Robert Creeley: An Inventory, 1945–1970.* No-place: Kent State University Press (1973).

(CREWS) Hargraves, Michael. *Harry Crews: A Bibliography.* (Westport, Ct.): Meckler Publishing Corporation (1986).

(CUMMINGS) Firmage, George J. *E. E. Cummings: A Bibliography.* (Middletown, Ct.): Wesleyan University Press (1960).

(CUNNINGHAM) Gullans, Charles. *A Bibliography of the Published Works of J. V. Cunningham.* Los Angeles: University of California Library, 1973.

(DAHLBERG) Billings, Harold. *A Bibliography of Edward Dahlberg.* Austin: University of Texas Press (1971).

(DANIEL PRESS) See *Franklin, C.*

(DARWIN) Freeman, R. B. *The Works of Charles Darwin: An Annotated Bibliographical Handlist*. (Hamden, Ct.): Dawson-Archon Books (1977).

(DAVIES, Rhys) See *Gawsworth*

(DAVIES, Robertson) Ryrie, John. *Robertson Davies: An Annotated Bibliography*. (Downsview, Ontario: Stong College, York University, 1981).

(DAVIES, W. H.) Harlow, Sylvia *W. H. Davies: A Bibliography*. Winchester, and New Castle, Delaware: St. Paul's Bibliographies, and Oak Knoll Books (1993).

(DAVIS) Quinby, Henry Cole, A. M. *Richard Harding Davis: A Bibliography*. New York: E. P. Dutton & Company (1924).

(DAY-LEWIS) Handley-Taylor, Geoffrey, and Timothy d'Arch Smith. *C. Day-Lewis the Poet Laureate: A Bibliography*. Chicago and London: St. James Press, 1968.

(DE CAMP) Laughlin, Charlotte, and Levack, Daniel J. H. *An L. Sprague De Camp Bibliography*. San Francisco, Calif./Columbia, Pa.: Underwood/Miller, 1983.

(DEIGHTON) Milward-Oliver, Edward. *Len Deighton: An Annotated Bibliography, 1954–1985*. (Kent, England): The Sammler Press (1985).

(DERLETH) (Derleth, August). *100 Books by August Derleth*. Sauk City: Arkham House, 1962.

(DERLETH) Wilson, Alison M. *August Derleth: A Bibliography*. Metuchen, N.J., & London: Scarecrow Press, 1983.

(DERRYDALE PRESS) Frazier, Don, and Koch, Jo. *Derrydale Press Books*. Calderwoods Books, Catalogue K-4, circa 1984. Long Valley, N.J.: Calderwoods Books, no-date.

(DE VRIES) Bowden, Edwin T. *Peter De Vries: A Bibliography, 1934–1977*. Austin: University of Texas (1978).

(DIBDIN) O'Dwyer, E. J. *Thomas Frognall Dibdin: Bibliographer & Bibliomaniac Extraordinary 1776–1847*. Pinner (Middlesex, England): Private Libraries Association (1967).

(DICK) Levack, Daniel J. H. *PKD: A Philip K. Dick Bibliography*. San Francisco, Calif./Columbia, Pa.: Underwood/Miller, 1981.

(DICKENS) Eckel, John C. *The First Editions of the Writings of Charles Dickens and Their Values: A Bibliography*. London: Chapman & Hall, Ltd., 1913.

(DICKENS) Smith, Walter E. *Charles Dickens in the Original Cloth: A Bibliographical Catalogue. Part I: The Novels with Sketches by Boz*. Los Angeles: Heritage Book Shop, 1982.

(DICKENS) Smith, Walter E. *Charles Dickens in the Original Cloth: A Bibliographical Catalogue. Part II: The Christmas Book and Selected Secondary Novels*. Los Angeles: Heritage Book Shop, 1982.

(DICKEY) Bruccoli, Matthew J., and Baughman, Judith S. *James Dickey: A Descriptive Bibliography*. (Pittsburgh): University of Pittsburgh Press, 1990.

(DICKINSON) Myerson, Joel. *Emily Dickinson: A Descriptive Bibliography*. (Pittsburgh): University of Pittsburgh Press, 1984.

(DINESEN) Henriksen, Liselotte. *Isak Dinesen: A Bibliography*. (Viborg, Denmark): Gyldendal (1977).

(DISCH) Stephens, Christopher. *A Checklist of Thomas M. Disch*. (Hastings-on-Hudson, N.Y.): Ultramarine, 1991.

(DOBIE) McVicker, Mary Louise. *The Writings of J. Frank Dobie: A Bibliography*. Lawton (Okla.): Museum of the Great Plains (1968).

(DORN) Streeter, David. *A Bibliography of Ed Dorn*. New York: The Phoenix Bookshop, 1973.

(DOS PASSOS) Sanders, Harvey. *John Dos Passos: A Comprehensive Bibliography*. New York and London: Garland Publishing, Inc., 1987.

(DOUGLAS) McDonald, Edward D. *A Bibliography of the Writings of Norman Douglas*. Philadelphia: The Centaur Book Shop, 1927.

(DOVES PRESS) See *Franklin, C.*

(DOYLE) Green, Richard Lancelyn, and Gibson, John Michael. *A Bibliography of A. Conan Doyle.* Oxford: Clarendon Press (1983).

(DREISER) McDonald, Edward D. *A Bibliography of the Writings of Theodore Dreiser.* New York: Burt Franklin (1968).

(DREW) Farah, David. *Farah's Price Guide to Nancy Drew Books and Collectibles.* Seventh printing. No-place: Farah's Books (1990).

(DUNCAN) Bertholf, Robert J. *Robert Duncan: A Descriptive Bibliography.* Santa Rosa, Calif.: Black Sparrow Press, 1986.

(DURRELL) Fraser, G. S., and Thomas, Alan G. *Lawrence Durrell: A Study.* London: Faber and Faber (1968).

(E., A.) Denson, Alan. *Printed Writings by George W. Russell (A. E.) A Bibliography.* Evanston: Northwestern University Press, 1961.

(EGERTON, George) See *Gawsworth*

(EIGNER) Wyatt, Andrea. *A Bibliography of Works by Larry Eigner.* Berkeley: Oyez, 1970.

(ELIOT, G.) Lake, Brian, and Nassau, Janet. *George Eliot in Original Cloth: A Bibliographical Catalogue.* (Bloomsbury): Jarndyce Antiquarian Books (1988).

(ELIOT, T. S.) Gallup, Donald. *T. S. Eliot: A Bibliography.* London: Faber & Faber (1970).

(EMERSON) Myerson, Joel. *Ralph Waldo Emerson: A Descriptive Bibliography.* (Pittsburgh): University of Pittsburgh Press, 1982.

(ERAGNY PRESS) See *Franklin, C.*

(ESSEX HOUSE) See *Franklin, C.*

(EVERSON) Sipper, Ralph. *William Everson, A Collection of Books & Manuscripts.* Santa Barbara: Joseph the Provider (1987).

(FARRELL) Branch, Edgar. *A Bibliography of James T. Farrell's Writings 1921–1957.* Philadelphia: University of Pennsylvania Press (1959).

(FAULKNER) Massey, Linton R. *"Man Working," 1919-1962 William Faulkner.* Charlottesville, Va.: Bibliographical Society of the University of Virginia (1968).

(FAULKNER) Petersen, Carl. *Each in Its Ordered Place: A Faulkner Collector's Notebook.* Ann Arbor: Ardis (1975).

(FIRBANK) Benkovitz, Miriam J. *A Bibliography of Ronald Firbank.* London: Rupert Hart-Davis, 1963.

(FIRBANK) Benkovitz, Miriam J. *Supplement to a Bibliography of Ronald Firbank.* London: Enitharmon Press, 1980.

(FITZGERALD, E.) Prideaux, Colonel W. F. *Notes for a Bibliography of Edward FitzGerald.* New York: Burt Franklin (1968).

(FITZGERALD, F. S.) Bruccoli, Matthew J. *F. Scott Fitzgerald: A Descriptive Bibliography.* (Pittsburgh): University of Pittsburgh Press, 1987.

(FLEMING) Campbell, Iain. *Ian Fleming: A Catalogue of a Collection.* Liverpool: Iain Campbell (1978).

(FLETCHER) Morton, Bruce. *John Gould Fletcher: A Bibliography.* (Kent): Kent State University Press (1979).

(FORD) Harvey, David Dow. *Ford Madox Ford 1873-1939.* New York: Gordian Press, 1972.

(FORESTER, F.) See *Herbert, H. W.*

(FORSTER) Kirkpatrick, B. J. *A Bibliography of E. M. Forster.* Oxford: Clarendon Press, 1985.

(FRANKLIN, B.) Ford, Paul Leicester. *A List of Books Written By, or Relating to Benjamin Franklin.* Reprinted. New York: Burt Franklin (1968).

FRANKLIN, Colin. *The Private Presses.* (Chester Springs, Penn.): Dufour (1969).

(FROST) Crane, Joan St. C. *Robert Frost: A Descriptive Catalogue of Books and Manuscripts in the Clifton Waller Barrett Library*. Charlottesville: University Press of Virginia (1974).

(FULLER) Myerson, Joel. *Margaret Fuller: A Descriptive Bibliography*. (Pittsburgh): University of Pittsburgh Press, 1978.

(GALSWORTHY) Fabes, Gilbert H. *John Galsworthy His First Editions: Points and Values*. London: W. and G. Foyle (1932).

(GARDNER) Howell, John M. *John Gardner: A Bibliographical Profile*. Carbondale and Edwardsville: Southern Illinois University Press (1980).

(GARRETT) Wright, Stuart. *George Garrett: A Bibliography, 1947–1988*. (Huntsville, Tx.): Texas Review Press, Sam Houston State University, 1989.

(GASCOYNE) Benford, Colin T. *David Gascoyne: A Bibliography of His Works (1929–1985)*. Isle of Wight: Heritage Books (no-date).

GAWSWORTH, John. *Ten Contemporaries: Notes Toward Their Definitive Bibliography*. London: Ernest Benn Ltd. (1932).

(GEHENNA PRESS) Franklin, Colin; Baskin, Hosea; and Baskin, Leonard. *The Gehenna Press: The Work of Fifty Years, 1942–1992*. No-place: The Birdwell Library, and The Gehenna Press (1992).

(GIBBINGS) Kirkus, A. Mary. *Robert Gibbings: A Bibliography*. London: J. M. Dent (1962).

(GIBSON, Wilfrid) See *Gawsworth*

(GILL) Gill, Evan R. *Bibliography of Eric Gill*. Folkeston & London: Rowman and Littlefield, Dawsons of Pall Mall, 1973.

(GINSBERG) Dowden, George. *A Bibliography of Works by Allen Ginsberg*. (San Francisco): City Lights Books (1971).

(GISSING) Collie, Michael. *George Gissing: A Bibliography*. (Toronto and Buffalo): Dawson (1975).

(GLASGOW) Kelly, William W. *Ellen Glasgow: A Bibliography*. Charlottesville: The Bibliographical Society of the University of Virginia (1964).

(GOLDEN COCKEREL PRESS) See *Franklin, C.*

(GOYEN) Wright, Stuart. *William Goyen: A Descriptive Bibliography, 1938-1985*. (Westport, Ct.): Meckler Publishing (1986).

(GRAVES) Higginson, F. H., and Williams, William P. *Robert Graves: A Bibliography*. (Hampshire, England): St. Paul's Bibliographies, 1987.

(GRAY, Alasdair) See *Rees*

(GREEN) Wilson, Robert A. *Ben K. Green: A Descriptive Bibliography of Writings By and About Him*. Flagstaff: Northland Press (1977).

(GREENAWAY) Engen, Rodney. *Kate Greenaway: A Biography*. New York: Schocken Books, 1981.

(GREENAWAY) Kiger, Robert, ed. *Kate Greenaway: Catalogue of an Exhibition of Original Artworks and Related Materials . . .* Pittsburgh: Hunt Institute for Botanical Documentation, Carnegie-Mellon University, 1980.

(GREENE) Wobbe, R. A. *Graham Greene: A Bibliography and Guide to Research*. New York and London: Garland Publishing, Inc., 1979.

(GREGYNOG PRESS) See *Franklin, C.*

(GREY) Myers, Edward and Judith. *A Bibliographical Check List of the Writings of Zane Grey*. Collinsville, Ct.: Country Lane Books, 1986.

(GUNN) Hagstrom, Jack W. C., and Bixby, George. *Thom Gunn: A Bibliography 1940–78*. London: Bertram Rota (1979).

(HAGGARD) McKay, George L. *A Bibliography of the Writings of Sir Rider Haggard*. London: *The Bookman's Journal*, 1930.

(HAGGARD) Scott, J. E. *Sir Henry Rider Haggard 1856-1925*. Takeley (England): Elkin Mathews Ltd., 1947.

(HAMMETT) Layman, Richard. *Dashiell Hammett: A Descriptive Bibliography*. (Pittsburgh): University of Pittsburgh Press, 1979.

(HANLEY) Gibbs, Linnea. *James Hanley: A Bibliography*. Vancouver: William Hoffer, 1980.

(HARDY) Purdy, Richard Little. *Thomas Hardy: A Bibliographical Study*. Reprinted. Oxford: Clarendon Press (1978).

(HARDY) Webb, A. P. *A Bibliography of the Works of Thomas Hardy 1865–1915*. New York: Burt Franklin (1968).

(HARRIS) See *Casanova*

(HASSLER) Powers, Michael. *An Interview with Jon Hassler*. With a bibliography by Larry Dingman. Minneapolis: Dinkytown Antiquarian Bookstore, 1990.

(HAWTHORNE) Clark, C. E. Frazer, Jr. *Nathaniel Hawthorne: A Descriptive Bibliography*. (Pittsburgh): University of Pittsburgh Press, 1978.

(HEARN) Perkins, P. D. and Ione. *Lafcadio Hearn: A Bibliography of His Writings*. Boston and New York: Houghton Mifflin Company, 1934.

(HEINLEIN) Owings, Mark. *Robert A. Heinlein: A Bibliography*. Baltimore: Croatan House (1973).

(HEMINGWAY) Hanneman, Andre. *Ernest Hemingway: A Comprehensive Bibliography*. Princeton, N.J.: Princeton University Press, 1967.

(HEMINGWAY) Hanneman, Andre. *Supplement to Ernest Hemingway: A Comprehensive Bibliography*. Princeton, N.J.: Princeton University Press, 1975.

(HENRY, O.) See *Porter, W. S.*

(HENTY) Dartt, Robert L. *G. A. Henty: A Bibliography*. Cedar Grove (N.J.), and Altricham: Dar-Web, Inc., and John Sherratt (1971).

(HERBERT, A. P.) See *Coppard*

(HERBERT, F.) Levack, Daniel J. H. *Dune Master: A Frank Herbert Bibliography*. (Westport, Ct.): Meckler (1988).

(HERBERT, H. W.) Van Winkle, William Mitchell. *Henry William Herbert (Frank Forester): A Bibliography of His Writings 1832–1858*. Portland, Ore.: Southworth-Anthoesen Press, 1936.

(HERGESHEIMER) Swire, H. L. R. *A Bibliography of the Works of Joseph Hergesheimer*. Philadelphia: Centaur Book Shop, 1922.

(HILLERMAN) Heib, Louis A. *Tony Hillerman: A Bibliography*. Tucson: Press of the Gigantic Hound, 1990.

(HILLERMAN) Heib, Louis A. *Collecting Tony Hillerman: A Checklist of the First Editions of Tony Hillerman*. Sante Fe, N. M.: Vinegar Tom Press (1992).

(HODGSON) Sweetser, Wesley D. *Ralph Hodgson A Bibliography*. New York & London: Garland Publishing, Inc., 1980.

(HOGARTH PRESS) Woolmer, J. Howard. *A Checklist of The Hogarth Press 1917–1946*. Revere, Mass.: Woolmer/Brotherson Ltd., 1986.

(HOLMES, J. C.) Ardinger, Richard K. *An Annotated Bibliography of Works by John Clellon Holmes*. Pocatello, Id.: Idaho State University Press, 1979.

(HOLMES, O. W.) Currier, Thomas Franklin. *A Bibliography of Oliver Wendell Holmes*. Washington Square, N.Y., and London: New York University Press, and Oxford University Press, 1953.

(HOPKINS) Dunne, Tom. *Gerard Manley Hopkins: A Comprehensive Bibliography*. Oxford: Clarendon Press (1978).

(HORGAN) Horgan, Paul. *Approaches to Writing*. Farrar, Straus and Giroux, New York (1973).

(HOUSMAN) Carter, John, and Sparrow, John. *A. E. Housman: A Bibliography*. 2d ed., rev. William White. (Suffolk): St. Paul's Bibliographies, 1982.

(HOUSMAN) Ehrsam, Theodore G. *A Bibliography of Alfred Edward Housman*. Boston: F. W. Faxon Company, 1941.

(HOWARD) Lord, Glenn. *The Last Celt: A Bio-Bibliography of Robert Ervin Howard*. West Kingston (R.I.): Donald M. Grant, 1976.

(HOWELLS) Gibson, William M., and Arms, George. *A Bibliography of William Dean Howells*. New York: New York Public Library (1971).

(HUDSON) Payne, John R. *W. H. Hudson: A Bibliography*. (Hamden, Ct.): Archon Books (1977).

(HUGHES, L.) Dickinson, Donald C. *A Bio-Bibliography of Langston Hughes 1902–1967*. (Hamden, Ct.): Archon Books, 1972.

(HUGHES, T.) Sagar, Keith, and Tabor, Stephen. *Ted Hughes: A Bibliography 1946–1980*. (London): Mansell Publishing Ltd (1983).

(HUXLEY) Eschelbach, Claire John, and Shober, Joyce Lee. *Aldous Huxley: A Bibliography 1916-1959*. Berkeley: University of California Press, 1961. See also *Casanova*

(INGERSOLL) Stein, Gordon. *Robert G. Ingersoll: A Checklist*. No-place: Kent State University Press (1969).

(IRVING) Langfeld, William R. *Washington Irving: A Bibliography*. New York: New York Public Library, 1933.

(IRVING) Williams, Stanley T., and Edge, Mary Allen. *A Bibliography of the Writings of Washington Irving: A Check List*. Reprinted. New York: Burt Franklin (1970).

(ISHERWOOD) Westby, Selmer, and Brown, Clayton M. *Christopher Isherwood: A Bibliography*. Los Angeles: California State College at Los Angeles Foundation, 1968.

(JACOBS) Lamerton, Chris. *W. W. Jacobs: A Bibliography*. (Margate, Kent): Greystone Press (1988).

(JAMES) Edel, Leon, and Laurence, Dan H. *A Bibliography of Henry James*. Oxford: Clarendon Press, 1982.

(JAMES) Philips, LeRoy. *A Bibliography of the Writings of Henry James*. New York: Coward McCann, 1930.

(JARRELL) Wright, Stuart. *Randall Jarrell: A Descriptive Bibliography 1929–1983*. Charlottesville: University Press of Virginia (1986).

(JEFFERS) Alberts, S. S. *A Bibliography of the Works of Robinson Jeffers*. Rye, N.Y.: Cultural History Research, 1961.

(JOHNSON) Courtney, William Prideaux, and Smith, David Nichol. *A Bibliography of Samuel Johnson*. With *Johnsonian Bibliography: A Supplement to Courtney* by R. W. Chapman and Allen Hazen. (New Castle, Del.): Oak Knoll Books and Gerald M. Goldberg, 1984.

(JONES, J.) Hopkins, John R. *James Jones: A Checklist*. Detroit: Gale Research Co., 1974.

(JONES, L.) Dace, Letitia. *LeRoi Jones (Imamu Amiri Baraka): A Checklist of Works By and About Him*. London: Nether Press, 1971.

(JOYCE) Slocum, John J., and Cahoon, Herbert. *A Bibliography of James Joyce*. Westport, Ct.: Greenwood Press (1953). See also *Casanova*

(KAFKA) Flores, Angel. *A Kafka Bibliography 1908–1976*. New York: Gordian Press, 1976.

(KEATS) MacGillivray, J. R. *Keats: A Bibliography and Reference Guide with an Essay on Keats' Reputation*. Canada: University of Toronto Press (1949).

(KELMSCOTT PRESS) Peterson, William S. *A Bibliography of the Kelmscott Press*. Reprinted with corrections. Oxford: Clarendon Press, 1985. See also *Franklin, C.*

(KEROUAC) Charters, Ann. *A Bibliography of Works by Jack Kerouac*. New York: Phoenix Bookshop, 1975.

(KIPLING) Livingston, Flora V. *Bibliography of the Works of Rudyard Kipling*. New York: Burt Franklin (1968).

(KIPLING) Livingston, Flora V. *Supplement to a Bibliography of the Works of Rudyard Kipling*. New York: Burt Franklin (1968).

(KOESTLER) Merrill, Reed, and Frazier, Thomas. *Arthur Koestler: An International Bibliography*. Ann Arbor: Ardis (1979).

(KOONTZ) Stephens, Christopher P. *A Checklist of Dean R. Koontz*. Hastings-on-Hudson, N.Y.: Ultramarine Publishing Co., 1987.

(LAMB) Livingston, Luther S., Thomson, J. C., and Roff, Renée (compiler). *A Bibliography of the Writings of Charles and Mary Lamb*. Bronxville, New York: Nicholas T. Smith (1979).

(LARDNER) Bruccoli, Matthew J., and Richard Layman. *Ring W. Lardner: A Descriptive Bibliography*. (Pittsburgh): University of Pittsburgh Press (1976).

(LARKIN) Bloomfield, B. C. *Philip Larkin: A Bibliography 1933–1976*. London/Boston: Faber and Faber (1979).

(LAWRENCE, D. H.) Roberts, Warren. *A Bibliography of D. H. Lawrence*. 2d ed. Cambridge: Cambridge University Press (1982).

(LAWRENCE, T. E.) O'Brien, Philip M. *T. E. Lawrence: A Bibliography*. Boston: G. K. Hall (1988).

(LEACOCK) Lomer, Gerhard R. *Stephen Leacock: A Check-list and Index of His Writings*. Ottawa: National Library of Canada, 1954.

(LEAVIS) McKenzie, D. F., and Allum, M-P. *F. R. Leavis: A Check-list 1924–1964*. London: Chatto & Windus, 1966.

(LEIBER) Morgan, Chris. *Fritz Leiber: A Bibliography 1934–1979*. Selly Oak, Birmingham, England: Morgenstern, 1979.

(LE GUIN) Cogell, Elizabeth Cummins. *Ursula K. Le Guin A Primary and Secondary Bibliography*. Boston: G. K. Hall (1983).

(LESSING) Brueck, Eric T. *Doris Lessing: A Bibliography of Her First Editions*. (London): Metropolis (Antiquarian Books) Ltd, 1984.

(LEVERTOV) Wilson, Robert. *A Bibliography of Denise Levertov*. New York: Phoenix Bookshop, 1972.

(LEWIS, C. S.) Christopher, Joe R., and Ostling, Joan K. *C. S. Lewis: An Annotated Checklist of Writings About Him and His Works*. (Rochester): Kent State University Press (no-date).

(LEWIS, W.) Morrow, Bradford, and Lafourcade, Bernard. *A Bibliography of the Writings of Wyndham Lewis*. Santa Barbara: Black Sparrow Press, 1978.

(LINCOLN) Smith, William H., Jr. *A Priced Lincoln Bibliography*. New York: Privately published, 1906.

(LONDON) Sisson, James E., III, and Robert W. Martens. *Jack London First Editions*. Oakland: Star Rover House, 1979.

(LONDON) Walker, Dale L., and Sisson, James E., III. *The Fiction of Jack London: A Chronological Bibliography*. El Paso: Texas Western Press, 1972.

(LONDON) Woodbridge, Hensley C.; London, John; and Tweney, George H. *Jack London: A Bibliography*. Georgetown: Talisman Press, 1966.

(LONGFELLOW) Livingston, Luther S. *A Bibliography of the First Editions . . . of Henry Wadsworth Longfellow*. New York: Burt Franklin (1968).

(LOVECRAFT) Owings, Mark, with Chalker, Jack L. *The Revised H. P. Lovecraft Bibliography*. Baltimore: Mirage Press, 1973.

(LOWELL) Chamberlain, Jacob Chester, and Livingston, Luther S. *A Bibliography of the First Editions in Book Form of the Writings of James Russell Lowell*. New York: Privately printed, 1914.

(LOWRY) Woolmer, J. Howard. *Malcolm Lowry: A Bibliography*. Revere, Mass.: Woolmer/Brotherson Ltd., 1983.

(LYTLE) Wright, Stuart. *Andrew Nelson Lytle: A Bibliography 1920–1982*. Sewanee (Tenn.): University of the South, 1982.

(MACDONALD, J. D.) Shine, Walter and Jean. *A Bibliography of the Published Works of John D. MacDonald*. Gainesville: University of Florida, 1980.

(MACDONALD, J. D.) Shine, Walter and Jean. *A MacDonald Potpourri:—Being a Miscellany of Post-perusal Pleasures of the John D. MacDonald Books. . . .* Gainesville, Fla.: University of Florida Libraries, 1988.

(MACDONALD, R.) Bruccoli, Matthew J. *Ross Macdonald/Kenneth Millar: A Descriptive Bibliography*. (Pittsburgh): University of Pittsburgh Press, 1983.

(MACHEN) Goldstone, Adrian, and Sweetser, Wesley. *A Bibliography of Arthur Machen*. New York: Haskell House, 1973.

(MACLEISH) Mullaly, Edward J. *Archibald MacLeish: A Checklist*. Kent State University Press (1973).

(MACNEICE) Brown, Terence, and Reid, Alec. *Time Was Away: The World of Louis MacNeice*. (Dublin): Dolmen Press (1974).

(MALAMUD) Kosofsky, Rita Nathalie. *Bernard Malamud: An Annotated Checklist*. Kent State University Press (1969).

(MANSFIELD) Kirkpatrick, J. *A Bibliography of Katherine Mansfield*. Oxford: Clarendon Press, 1989.

(MARSH) Gibbs, Rowan, and Williams, Richard. *Ngaio Marsh: A Bibliography of English Language Publications in Hardback and Paperback*. South Humberside, England: Dragonby Press, 1990.

(MASEFIELD) Handley-Taylor, Geoffrey. *John Masefield, O.M. The Queen's Poet Laureate*. London: Cranbrook Tower Press (1960).

(MATTHIESSEN) Nicholas, D. *Peter Matthiessen: A Bibliography 1951–1979*. Canoga Press, Calif.: Orirana Press (1979).

(MAUGHAM) Stott, Raymond Toole. *A Bibliography of the Works of W. Somerset Maugham*. Edmonton: University of Alberta Press, 1973.

(MCCARTHY) Goldman, Sherli Evens. *Mary McCarthy: A Bibliography*. New York: Harcourt, Brace & World (1968).

(MCCLURE) Clements, Marshall. *A Catalog of Works by Michael McClure 1956–1965*. New York: Phoenix Bookshop (1965).

(MCCULLERS) Shapiro, Adrian M.; Bryer, Jackson R.; and Field, Kathleen. *Carson McCullers: A Descriptive Listing and Annotated Bibliography of Criticism*. New York and London: Garland Publishing Inc., 1980.

(MCEWAN) See *Rees*

(MCFEE) Babb, James T. *A Bibliography of the Writings of William McFee*. Garden City: Doubleday, Doran & Co., 1931.

(MCGAHERN) See *Rees*

(MCMURTRIE) Bruntjen, Scott, and Young, Melissa L. *Douglas C. McMurtrie: Bibliographer and Historian of Printing*. Metuchen, N.J. & London: Scarecrow Press, 1979.

(MELTZER) Kherdian, David. *David Meltzer: A Sketch from Memory and Descriptive Checklist*. Berkeley: Oyez, 1965.

(MENCKEN) Adler, Betty, and Wilhelm, Jane. *H. L. M. The Mencken Bibliography.* Baltimore: Enoch Pratt Free Library (1961).

(MENCKEN) Frey, Carroll. *A Bibliography of the Writings of H. L. Mencken.* Philadelphia: The Centaur Book Shop, 1924.

(MEREDITH) Collie, Michael. *George Meredith: A Bibliography.* (Toronto and Buffalo): University of Toronto Press (1974).

(MEREDITH) Forman, Maurice Buxton. *A Bibliography of the Writings in Prose and Verse of George Meredith.* New York: Haskell House, 1971.

(MEREDITH) Forman, Maurice Buxton. *Meredithiana, Being a Supplement to the Bibliography of Meredith.* New York: Haskell House, 1971.

(MERTON) Breit, Marquita E. *Thomas Merton: A Comprehensive Bibliography.* New ed. New York and London: Garland Publishing, Inc., 1986.

(MILLAY) Yost, Karl. *A Bibliography of the Works of Edna St. Vincent Millay.* New York and London: Harper & Brothers, 1937.

(MILLER, A.) Jensen, George H. *Arthur Miller: A Bibliographical Checklist.* (Columbia, S.C.): J. Faust & Co. (1976).

(MILLER, H.) Moore, Thomas H. *Bibliography of Henry Miller.* (Minneapolis): Henry Miller Literary Society, 1961.

(MILLER, H.) Porter, Bern. *Henry Miller: A Chronology and Bibliography.* (Baltimore: Waverly Press, 1945).

(MILLER, H.) Shifreen, Lawrence J., and Jackson, Roger. *Henry Miller: A Bibliography of Primary Sources.* (Ann Arbor, Mich., and Glen Arm, Md.: Roger Jackson, and Lawrence J. Shifreen) 1993.

(MOORE, B.) See *Rees*

(MOORE, G.) Gilcher, Edwin. *A Bibliography of George Moore.* Dekalb: Northern Illinois University Press (1970).

(MOORE, M.) Abbott, Craig S. *Marianne Moore: A Descriptive Bibliography.* (Pittsburgh): University of Pittsburgh Press, 1977.

(MORGAN, Chas.) See *Coppard*

(MORLEY) Lee, Alfred P. *A Bibliography of Christopher Morley.* Garden City: Doubleday, Doran & Company, 1935. See also *Casanova*

(MORLEY) Lyle, Guy R., and Brown, H. Tatnall, Jr. *A Bibliography of Christopher Morley.* Washington, D.C.: The Scarecrow Press, 1952.

(MORRIS) Pye, John William. *A Bibliography of the American Editions of William Morris Published by Roberts Brothers, Boston, 1867–1898.* Brockton, Mass.: John William Pye Rare Books, 1993.

(MUIR, E.) Mellown, Elgin W. *Bibliography of the Writings of Edwin Muir.* University, Ala.: University of Alabama Press (1964)

(MUIR, J.) Kimes, William F. and Maymie B. *John Muir: A Reading Bibliography.* Fresno: Panorama West Books, 1986.

(MUIR, P. H.) *P. H. Muir: A Check List of His Published Work.* (No author listed). Blakeney (Norfolk, England): Elkin Mathews, 1983.

(MUMFORD) Newman, Elmer S. Lewis. *Lewis Mumford: A Bibliography 1914-1970.* New York: Harcourt Brace Jovanovich, Inc. (1971).

(MUNDY) Grant, Donald M. *Talbot Mundy: Messenger of Destiny.* West Kingston, (R.I.): Donald M. Grant, 1983.

(MURDOCH) Tominaga, Thomas T., and Schneidermeyer, Wilma. *Iris Murdoch and Muriel Spark: A Bibliography.* Metuchen, N.J.: Scarecrow Press, 1976.

(NABOKOV) Juliar, Michael. *Vladimir Nabokov: A Descriptive Bibliography.* New York and London: Garland Publishing, Inc., 1986.

(NATHAN) Laurence, Dan H. *Robert Nathan: A Bibliography*. New Haven: Yale University Library, 1960. See also *Casanova*

(NEWTON) (Fleck, Robert). *A. Edward Newton: A Collection of His Work*. (New Castle, Del.): Oak Knoll Books, 1986. See also *Casanova*

(NICHOLS, Robert) See *Gawsworth*

(NIN) Franklin, Benjamin, V. *Anaïs Nin: A Bibliography*. Kent State University Press (1973).

(NORRIS) Lohf, Kenneth A., and Sheehy, Eugene P. *Frank Norris: A Bibliography*. Los Gatos (Calif.): The Talisman Press, 1959.

(OATES) Lercangee, Francine. *Joyce Carol Oates: An Annotated Bibliography*. New York and London: Garland Publishing, Inc., 1986.

(O'CASEY) Ayling, Ronald, and Durkan, Michael J. *Sean O'Casey: A Bibliography*. Seattle: University of Washington Press (1978).

(O'CONNOR, Flannery) Farmer, David. *Flannery O'Connor: A Descriptive Bibliography*. New York and London: Garland Publishing Inc., 1981.

(O'CONNOR, Frank) Sheehy, Maurice. *Michael/Frank: Studies on Frank O'Connor*. Dublin: Gill & Macmillan (1969).

(O'FLAHERTY) Doyle, Paul A. *Liam O'Flaherty: An Annotated Bibliography*. Troy, N.Y.: Whitston Publishing Co., 1972.

(O'HARA, F.) Smith, Alexander, Jr. *Frank O'Hara: A Comprehensive Bibliography*. New York and London: Garland Publishing Inc., 1979.

(O'HARA, J.) Bruccoli, Matthew J. *John O'Hara: A Descriptive Bibliography*. (Pittsburgh): University of Pittsburgh Press, 1978.

(OLSON) Butterick, George F., and Glover, Albert. *A Bibliography of Works by Charles Olson*. New York: Phoenix Bookshop, 1967.

(OLYMPIA PRESS) Kearney, Patrick J. *The Paris Olympia Press*. London: Black Spring Press (1987).

(O'NEILL) Atkinson, Jennifer McCabe. *Eugene O'Neill: A Descriptive Bibliography*. (Pittsburgh): University of Pittsburgh Press, 1974.

(OSLER) Golden, Richard L., M.D., and Roland, Charles G., M.D. *Sir William Osler: An Annotated Bibliography with Illustrations*. San Francisco: Norman Publishing, 1988.

(OZ) Martin, Dick; Greene, David L.; and. Haff, James E. *Bibliographia Oziana: A Concise Bibliographical Checklist of the Oz Books by L. Frank Baum and His Successors*. (No-place): International Wizard of Oz Club (1976).

(PASTERNAK) Holtzman, Irwin T. *A Check List of Boris Leonidovich Pasternak (1890-1960) Books in English*. (Southfield, Mich.: Irwin T. Holtzman, 1990).

(PATCHEN) Morgan, Richard G. *Kenneth Patchen*. Mamaroneck, N.Y.: Paul P. Appel (1978).

(PEARSON) Webber, Hallum. *Edmund Lester Pearson*. Not published.

(PERCY) Hobson, Linda Whitney. *Walker Percy: A Comprehensive Descriptive Bibliography*. New Orleans: Faust Publishing Co., 1988.

(PERCY) Wright, Stuart. *Walker Percy: A Bibliography: 1930–1984*. (Westport, Ct.): Meckler Publishing (1986).

(POE) Robertson, John W., M.D. *Bibliography of the Writings of Edgar A. Poe*. New York: Kraus Reprint Co., 1969.

(POETRY BOOKSHOP) Woolmer, J. Howard. *The Poetry Bookshop 1912–1935: A Bibliography*. Revere, Penn., and Winchester (England): Woolmer/Brotherson Ltd., and St. Paul's Bibliographies, 1988.

(PORTER, G. S.) MacLean, David G. *Gene Stratton-Porter*. Decatur: (Americana Books) 1987.

(PORTER, K. A.) Waldrip, Louise, and Bauer, Shirley Ann. *A Bibliography of the Works of Katherine Anne Porter* and *A Bibliography of the Criticism of the Works of Katherine Anne Porter*. Metuchen, N.J.: Scarecrow Press, 1969.

(PORTER, W. S.) Clarkson, Paul S. *A Bibliography of William Sydney Porter (O. Henry)*. Caldwell (Idaho): Caxton Printers, 1938.

(POTTER) Linder, Leslie. *A History of the Writings of Beatrix Potter*. London/New York: Frederick Warne (1971).

(POUND) Gallup, Donald. *Ezra Pound: A Bibliography*. Charlottesville: University Press of Virginia (1983).

(POWELL) Lilley, George. *Anthony Powell: A Bibliography*. Winchester, and New Castle, Del.: St. Paul's Bibliographies, and Oak Knoll Books, 1993.

(POWYS) Thomas, Dante. *A Bibliography of the Writings of John Cowper Powys: 1872–1963*. Mamaroneck, N.Y.: Paul P. Appel, 1975.

(PRICE) Wright, Stuart, and West, James L. W., III. *Reynolds Price: A Bibliography 1949–1984*. Charlottesville: University Press of Virginia (1986).

(PYNCHON) Mead, Clifford. *Thomas Pynchon: A Bibliography of Primary and Secondary Materials*. (Elmwood Park, Ill.): Dalkey Archive Press (1989).

(QUILLER-COUCH) Brittain, F. *Arthur Quiller-Couch: A Biographical Study of Q*. Cambridge and New York: University Press/Macmillan, 1948.

(RACKHAM) Latimore, Sarah Briggs, and Haskell, Grace Clark. *Arthur Rackham: A Bibliography*. Jacksonville, Fla.: San Marco Bookstore (1936)

(RAND) Perinn, Vincent L. *Ayn Rand: First Descriptive Bibliography*. (Rockville, Md.): Q & B (Quill & Brush), 1990.

(RANSOM) Young, Thomas Daniel. *John Crowe Ransom: Critical Essays and a Bibliography*. Baton Rouge: Louisiana State University Press (1968).

REES, David. *Brian Moore, Alasdair Gray, John McGahern: A Bibliography of Their First Editions*. (London): Colophon Press (1991).

REES, David. *Bruce Chatwin, Martin Amis, Julian Barnes: A Bibliography of Their First Editions*. (London): Colophon Press (1992).

REES, David. *Muriel Spark, William Trevor, Ian McEwan: A Bibliography of Their First Editions*. (London): Colophon Press (1992).

(REXROTH) Hartzell, James, and Zumwinkle, Richard. *Kenneth Rexroth: A Checklist of His Published Writings*. Los Angeles: Friends of the UCLA Library, 1967.

(RICKETTS) Barclay, Michael Richard. *Catalogue of the Works of Charles Ricketts R.A. (from The Collection of Gordon Bottomley)*. Stroud Glos: Catalpa Press Ltd., 1985.

(RIDING) Wexler, Joyce Piell. *Laura Riding: A Bibliography*. New York and London: Garland Publishing, Inc., 1981.

(RIIS) Fried, Lewis, and Fierst, John. *Jacob A. Riis: A Reference Guide*. Boston, Mass.: G. K. Hall & Co. (1977).

(RILEY) Russo, Anthony J. and Dorothy R. *A Bibliography of James Whitcomb Riley*. Indianapolis: Indiana Historical Society, 1944.

(ROBERTS) Murphy, P. *Kenneth Lewis Roberts: A Bibliography*. Privately printed (1975).

(ROBINSON) Hogan, Charles Beecher. *A Bibliography of Edwin Arlington Robinson*. New Haven, and London: Yale University, and Oxford University Press, 1936.

(ROETHKE) McLeod, James Richard. *Theodore Roethke: A Bibliography*. Kent State University Press, 1973.

(ROOSEVELT) Wheelock, John Hall. *A Bibliography of Theodore Roosevelt*. New York: Charles Scribner's Sons, 1920.

(RUSKIN) *The Bibliography . . . Arranged in Chronological Order of the Published Writings in Prose and Verse of John Ruskin, M.A. (From 1834 to 1881)*. Paternoster Row, London: Eliot Stock, no-date.

(RUSKIN) Wise, Thomas J., and Smart, James P. *A Complete Bibliography of the Writings in Prose and Verse of John Ruskin, LL.D.* Reprinted. 2 vols. Folkestone and London: Dawsons of Pall Mall, 1974.

(RUSSELL) Yost, Karl, and Renner, Frederic G. *A Bibliography of the Published Works of Charles M. Russell.* Lincoln: University of Nebraska Press (1971).

(SALINGER) Starosciak, Kenneth. *J. D. Salinger: A Thirty-Year Bibliography, 1938–1968.* (No-place: no-publ, no-date).

(SAROYAN) Kherdian, David. *A Bibliography of William Saroyan 1934–64.* San Francisco: Roger Beacham (1965).

(SARTRE) Belkind, Allen. *Jean-Paul Sartre: Sartre and Existentialism in English, A Bibliographical Guide.* Kent State University Press (1970).

(SASSOON) Farmer, David. *Siegfried Sassoon: A Memorial Exhibition.* Austin: Humanities Research Center, University of Texas, 1969.

(SAYERS) Gilbert, Colleen B. *A Bibliography of the Works of Dorothy L. Sayers.* Hamden, Ct.: Archon Books, 1978.

(SHAKESPEARE HEAD PRESS) See *Franklin, C.*

(SHIEL) Morse, A. Reynolds. *The Works of M. P. Shiel.* Los Angeles: Fantasy Publishing Co., Inc., 1948. See also *Gawsworth*

(SILLITOE) Gerard, David. *Alan Sillitoe: A Bibliography.* (London): Mansell Publishing Limited, 1988.

(SIMENON) Foord, Peter; Williams, Richard; and Swan, Sally. *Georges Simenon: A Bibliography of the British First Editions . . . and of the Principal French and American Editions.* South Humberside, England: Dragonby Press, 1988.

(SITWELL) Fifoot, Richard. *A Bibliography of Edith, Osbert and Sacheverell Sitwell.* London: Rupert Hart-Davis, 1963. See also *Gawsworth*

(SMITH) Sidney-Fryer, Donald, and Hands, Divers. *Emperor of Dreams, A Clark Ashton Smith Bibliography.* West Kingston, Rhode Island: Donald M. Grant, Publisher, 1978.

(SNYDER) Kherdian, David. *Gary Snyder: A Biographical Sketch and Descriptive Checklist.* Berkeley: Oyez, 1965.

(SNYDER) McNeil, Katherine. *Gary Snyder: A Bibliography.* New York: The Phoenix Bookshop, 1983.

(SOLZHENITSYN) Fiene, Donald M. *Alexander Solzhenitsyn: An International Bibliography of Writings By and About Him.* Ann Arbor: Ardis (1973).

(SPARK) See *Murdoch; Rees*

(SPENDER) Kulkarni, H. B. *Stephen Spender Works and Criticism: An Annotated Bibliography.* New York and London: Garland Publishing, 1976.

(STEGNER) Colberg, Nancy. *Wallace Stegner: A Descriptive Bibliography.* Lewiston, Idaho: Confluence Press, Inc. (1990).

(STEIN) Wilson, Robert A. *Gertrude Stein: A Bibliography.* Rockville, Md.: Quill & Brush, 1994. See also *Casanova*

(STEINBECK) Goldstone, Adrian H., and Payne, John R. *John Steinbeck: A Biographical Catalogue of the Adrian H. Goldstone Collection.* Austin: The University of Texas Press (1974).

(STEVENS) Edelstein, J. M. *Wallace Stevens: A Descriptive Bibliography.* (Pittsburgh): University of Pittsburgh Press, 1973.

(STEVENSON) Prideaux, Colonel W. F. *A Bibliography of the Works of Robert Louis Stevenson.* New York: Burt Franklin (1968).

(STONE) Lopez, Ken, and Chaney, Bev. *Robert Stone: A Bibliography, 1960–1992.* Hadley, Mass.: Numinous Press, 1992.

(STOUT) Townsend, Guy M. *Rex Stout: An Annotated Primary and Secondary Bibliography.* New York and London: Garland Publishing, Inc., 1980.

(STOWE) Hildreth, Margaret Holbrook. *Harriet Beecher Stowe: A Bibliography*. (Hamden, Ct.): Archon Books, 1976.

(STRATTON-PORTER) See *Porter, G. S.*

(SWIFT) Teerink, H. *A Bibliography of the Writings of Jonathan Swift*. 2d ed., revised and corrected. Philadelphia: University of Pennsylvania Press (1963).

(SWINBURNE) Wise, Thomas J. *A Bibliography of the Writings in Prose and Verse of Algernon Charles Swinburne*. Vols. 1 & 2. London: Dawsons of Pall Mall, 1966.

(SYMONDS) Babington, Percy L. *Bibliography of the Writings of John Addington Symonds*. New York: Burt Franklin (1968).

(TARKINGTON) Currie, Barton. *Booth Tarkington: A Bibliography*. Garden City, N.Y.: Doubleday, Doran & Company, Inc., 1932.

(TARKINGTON) Russo, Dorothy Ritter, and Sullivan, Thelma L. *A Bibliography of Booth Tarkington, 1869–1946*. Indianapolis: Indiana Historical Society, 1949.

(TATE) Falwell, Marshall Jr. *Allen Tate: A Bibliography*. New York: David Lewis, 1969.

(TAYLOR, E.) Gefvert, Constance J. *Edward Taylor: An Annotated Bibliography, 1668–1970*. Kent State University Press (1971).

(TAYLOR, P.) Wright, Stuart. *Peter Taylor: A Descriptive Bibliography, 1934–87*. Charlottesville: University Press of Virginia (1988).

(TENNYSON) Shepherd, Richard Herne. *The Bibliography of Tennyson*. New York: Haskell House Publishers Ltd., 1970.

(TENNYSON) Tennyson, Charles, and Fall, Christine. *Alfred Tennyson: An Annotated Bibliography*. Athens: University of Georgia Press (1967).

(THACKERAY) Van Duzer, Henry Sayre. *A Thackeray Library*. New York: Burt Franklin (1971).

(THOMAS) Maud, Ralph. *Dylan Thomas in Print: A Bibliographical History*. London: J. M. Dent (1970).

(THOMAS) Rolph, J. Alexander. *Dylan Thomas: A Bibliography*. New York: New Directions (1956).

(THOMPSON) Stephens, Christopher P. *A Checklist of Jim Thompson*. (Hastings-on-Hudson, N.Y.): Ultramarine, 1991.

(THOREAU) Borst, Raymond R. *Henry David Thoreau: A Descriptive Bibliography*. (Pittsburgh): University of Pittsburgh Press, 1982.

(THURBER) Bowden, Edwin T. *James Thurber: A Bibliography*. Columbus: Ohio State University Press (1968).

(TOLKIEN) Hammond, Wayne G., and Anderson, Douglas A. *J. R .R. Tolkien: A Descriptive Bibliography*. Winchester (England), and New Castle, Del.: St. Paul's Bibliographies, and Oak Knoll Books, 1993.

(TOYNBEE) Morton, S. Fiona. *A Bibliography of Arnold J. Toynbee*. Oxford: Oxford University Press, 1980.

(TREVOR, William) See *Rees*

(TROLLOPE) Sadleir, Michael. *Trollope: A Bibliography*. (Kent, England): Dawson, 1977.

(TWAIN) Johnson, Merle. *A Bibliography of the Work of Mark Twain*. New York and London: Harper & Brothers Publishers, 1910.

(TWAIN) McBride, William M. *Mark Twain: A Bibliography of the Collections of the Mark Twain Memorial and the Stowe-Day Foundation*. Hartford, Ct.: McBride/Publisher (1984).

(VALE PRESS) See *Franklin, C.*

(VAN VECHTEN) Kellner, Bruce. *A Bibliography of the Work of Carl Van Vechten*. Westport, Ct., and London, England: Greenwood Press (1980).

(VERNE) Gallagher, Edward J.; Mistichelli, Judith A.; and Van Eerde, John A. *Jules Verne: A Primary and Secondary Bibliography*. Boston, Mass.: G. K. Hall & Co. (1980).

(VERNE) Myers, Edward and Judith. *Jules Verne: A Bibliography*. New Hartford, Ct.: Country Lane Books, 1989.

(VLIET) Freedman, Russell. *A Bibliography of the Writings of R. G. Vliet*. In *At Paisano* by R. G. Vliet. Lanesborough, Mass.: Second Life Books, 1989.

(VONNEGUT) Pieratt, Asa B., Jr.; Huffman-Klinkowitz, Julie; and Klinkowitz, Jerome. *Kurt Vonnegut: A Comprehensive Bibliography*. (Hamden, Ct.): Archon Books, 1987.

(WALLACE) Kiddle, Charles. *A Guide to the First Editions of Edgar Wallace*. Motcombe, Dorset (England): The Ivory Head Press (1981).

(WALLACE) Lofts, W. O. G., and Adley, Derek. *The British Bibliography of Edgar Wallace*. London: Howard Baker (1969).

(WALPOLE) Hazen, A. T. *A Bibliography of Horace Walpole*. Folkestone, England: Dawsons of Pall Mall, 1973.

(WARREN) Grimshaw, James A., Jr. *Robert Penn Warren: A Descriptive Bibliography, 1922-79*. Charlottesville: University Press of Virginia (1981).

(WATERS) Tanner, Terence A. *Frank Waters: A Bibliography*. Glenwood, Ill.: Meyerbooks (1983).

(WAUGH) Davis, Robert Murray; Doyle, Paul A.; Gallagher, Donat; Linck, Charles E.; and Bogaards, Winifred M. *A Bibliography of Evelyn Waugh*. Troy, N.Y.: The Whitston Publishing Company, 1986.

(WELLS) Chappell, Fred A. *Bibliography of H. G. Wells*. Chicago: Covici-McGee Co., 1924.

(WELLS) *H. G. Wells: A Comprehensive Bibliography*. 2d. edition, revised. London: H. G. Wells Society (1968).

(WELLS) Wells, Geoffrey H. *A Bibliography of the Works of H. G. Wells 1893–1925 (With Some Notes and Comments)*. Reprinted. New York: Burt Franklin (1968).

(WEST) White, William. *Nathanael West: A Comprehensive Bibliography*. Kent State University Press (1975).

(WHARTON) Davis, Lavinia. *A Bibliography of the Writings of Edith Wharton*. Portland, Maine: The Southworth Press, 1933.

(WHARTON) Garrison, Stephen. *Edith Wharton: A Descriptive Bibliography*. (Pittsburgh): University of Pittsburgh Press, 1990.

(WHARTON) Melish, Lawson McClung. *A Bibliography of the Collected Writings of Edith Wharton*. New York: The Brick Row Book Shop, Inc., 1927.

(WHIGHAM) Sipper, Ralph B. *A Checklist of the Works of Peter Whigham: With a Memoir of the Poet*. Santa Barbara, Calif.: Joseph the Provider, no-date.

(WHITE, E. B.) Hall, Katherine Romans. *E. B. White: A Bibliographical Catalogue of Printed Materials in the Department of Rare Books, Cornell University Library*. New York and London: Garland Publishing, 1979.

(WHITE, P.) Lawson, Alan. *Patrick White*. London and Melbourne: Oxford University Press (1974).

(WHITE, T. H.) Gallix, Francois. *T. H. White: An Annotated Bibliography*. New York and London: Garland Publishing, Inc., 1986.

(WHITMAN) Shay, Frank. *The Bibliography of Walt Whitman*. New York: Friedmans', 1920.

(WHITMAN) Wells, Carolyn, and Goldsmith, Alfred F. *A Concise Bibliography of the Works of Walt Whitman*. New York: Burt Franklin (1968).

(WILDE) Mason, Stuart. *Bibliography of Oscar Wilde*. London: T. Werner Laurie Ltd. (1914).

(WILLIAMS, C.) Glenn, Lois. *Charles W. S. Williams: A Checklist*. Kent State University Press (1975).

(WILLIAMS, J.) Jaffe, James S. *Jonathan Williams: A Bibliographical Checklist of His Writings, 1950–1988*. Haverford, Penn.: no-publ., 1989.

(WILLIAMS, T.) Gunn, Drewey Wayne. *Tennessee Williams: A Bibliography*. Metuchen, N.J., and London: The Scarecrow Press, Inc., 1980.

(WILLIAMS, W.) Wallace, Emily Mitchell. *A Bibliography of William Carlos Williams*. Middletown, Ct.: Wesleyan University Press (1968).

(WILSON) Stanley, Colin. *The Work of Colin Wilson: An Annotated Bibliography & Guide*. San Bernardino: The Borgo Press, 1989.

(WODEHOUSE) Jasen, David A. *A Bibliography and Reader's Guide to the First Editions of P. G. Wodehouse*. (London): Greenhill Books (1970).

(WODEHOUSE) McIlvaine, Eileen; Sherby, Louise S.; and Heineman, James H. *P. G. Wodehouse: A Comprehensive Bibliography and Checklist*. New York, and Detroit, Mich.: James H. Heineman, and Omnigraphics (1990).

(WOLFE) Johnston, Carol. *Thomas Wolfe: A Descriptive Bibliography*. (Pittsburgh): University of Pittsburgh Press, 1989.

(WOLLSTONECRAFT) Todd, Janet M. *Mary Wollstonecraft: An Annotated Bibliography*. New York and London: Garland Publishing, Inc., 1976.

(WOLLSTONECRAFT) Windle, J. R. *Mary Wollstonecraft (Godwin): A Bibliography of Her Writings*. Los Angeles: (John Windle) 1988.

(WOOLF, L.) Luedeking, Leila, and Edmonds, Michael. *Leonard Woolf: A Bibliography*. Winchester (England), and New Castle, Del.: St. Paul's Bibliographies, and Oak Knoll Books, 1992.

(WOOLF, V.) Kirkpatrick, B. J. *A Bibliography of Virginia Woolf*. Oxford: Clarendon Press, 1980.

(WORDSWORTH) Wise, Thomas J. *A Bibliography of the Writings in Prose and Verse of William Wordsworth*. London: Printed for private circulation, 1916.

(YEATS) Wade, Allan. *A Bibliography of the Writings of W. B. Yeats*. London: Rupert Hart-Davis, 1958.

(ZUKOFSKY) Zukofsky, Celia. *A Bibliography of Louis Zukofsky*. Los Angeles: Black Sparrow Press, 1969.